Work and Disability
Issues and Strategies in Career Development and Job Placement

Second Edition

Edited by

Edna Mora Szymanski

Randall M. Parker

8700 Shoal Creek Boulevard
Austin, Texas 78757-6897
800/897-3202 Fax 800/397-7633
www.proedinc.com

© 2003 by PRO-ED, Inc.
8700 Shoal Creek Boulevard
Austin, Texas 78757-6897
800/897-3202 Fax 800/397-7633
www.proedinc.com

Library of Congress Cataloging-in-Publication Data

Work and disability : issues and strategies in career development and job placement/edited by Edna Mora Szymanski, Randall M. Parker.—2nd ed

p. cm.

ISBN-13: 978-089079910-9

ISBN-10: 0-89079-910-5

1. Handicapped—Employment—United States. 2. Handicapped—Counseling of—United States. 3. Insurance, Disability—United States 4. Workers' compensation—United States. 5. Vocational rehabilitation—Law and legislation—United States. I. Szymanski, Edna. II. Parker, Randall M., 1940–

HD7256.U5 W67 2003

331.5′9′0973—dc21 2002068054

This book is designed in Utopia and Goudy.

Printed in the United States of America

3 4 5 6 7 8 9 10 07

Contents

Contributors

Kimberly K. Asner-Self
Assistant Professor
Counselor Education
Educational Psychology and Special Education
Southern Illinois University
MC 4618
Carbondale, IL 62901-4618

Martin Brodwin
Professor and Coordinator
Rehabilitation Counselor Education Program
Division of Administration and Counseling
California State University, Los Angeles
Los Angeles, CA 90032

Jennifer A. Brown
School of Industrial and Labor Relations—Extension Division
Cornell University
Ithaca, NY 14853-3901

Susanne M. Bruyère
Director
Program on Employment and Disability
School of Industrial and Labor Relations—Extension Division
Cornell University
Ithaca, NY 14853-3901

Richard V. Burkhauser
Sarah Gibson Blanding Professor and Chair
Department of Policy Analysis and Management
Cornell University
Ithaca, NY 14853-4401

Denise DeLaGarza
Project Director
Center for Disability Studies
University of Texas at Austin
Austin, TX 78712

Mary S. Enright
Adjunct Faculty
Capella University
222 S. 9th Street
Minneapolis, MN 55402

Judith M. Ettinger
Senior Outreach Specialist
Center for Education and Work
University of Wisconsin–Madison
1025 W. Johnson Street
Madison, WI 53706

Ellen Fabian
Associate Professor
Department of Counseling and Personnel Services
3214 Benjamin Building
College of Education
University of Maryland
College Park, MD 20742

Dennis Gilbride
Associate Professor
Department of Counseling and Human Services
Syracuse University
257 Huntington Hall
Syracuse, NY 13244-2340

David Hagner
Rehabilitation Projects Director
Institute on Disability
7 Leavitt Lane
University of New Hampshire
Durham, NH 03824

Cheryl Hanley-Maxwell
Professor
Department of Rehabilitation Psychology and Special Education
University of Wisconsin–Madison
432 N. Murray
Madison, WI 53706

David B. Hershenson
Professor
Department of Counseling and Personnel Services
College of Education
3214 Benjamin Building
University of Maryland
College Park, MD 20742

Andrew J. Houtenville
Senior Research Associate
Program on Employment and Disability
School of Industrial and Labor Relations
Cornell University
Room 106, Extension Building
Ithaca, NY 14853-3901

Sarah Johnston-Rodriguez
Assistant Professor
Department of Educational Studies
University of Wisconsin–La Crosse
340A Morris Hall
La Crosse, WI 54601

James J. Liesener
Doctoral Candidate
Department of Counseling and Personnel Services
College of Education
3214 Benjamin Building
University of Maryland
College Park, MD 20742

Donald Linkowski
Professor of Counseling
Rehabilitation Counseling
The George Washington University
Counseling, Human, and Organizational Studies
2134 G Street, NW 3rd Floor
Washington, DC 20052

Mary Ann Merz
Assistant Professor
Rehabilitation Counseling Program
School of Health Professions
Maryville University
13550 Conway Road
St. Louis, MO 63141

David J. Miller
Information Liaison
Louisiana Business Leadership Network
857 Wilson Drive
New Orleans, LA 70119

Michael J. Millington
Executive Director
Louisiana Business Leadership Network
857 Wilson Drive
New Orleans, LA 70119

Laura Owens-Johnson
Assistant Professor
Department of Exceptional Education
University of Wisconsin–Milwaukee
P.O. Box 413
Milwaukee, WI 53201

Randall M. Parker
Melissa Elizabeth Stuart Centennial Professor in Education
Rehabilitation Counseling Program
Department of Special Education
University of Texas at Austin
Austin, TX 78712

Jeanne Boland Patterson
Professor
Department of Health Science
University of North Florida
4567 St. Johns Bluff Road South
Jacksonville, FL 32224-2645

Carole Ryan
Rehabilitation Specialist
Aurora Health Care
945 N. 12th Street
Milwaukee, WI 53201

James L. Schaller
Associate Professor
Rehabilitation Counseling Program
Department of Special Education
University of Texas at Austin
Austin, TX 78712

Robert Stensrud
Director
Rehabilitation Institute
Drake University
3206 University Avenue
Des Moines, IA 50311-4505

Edna Mora Szymanski
Professor and Dean
College of Education
3119 Benjamin Building
University of Maryland
College Park, MD 20742

Beatriz Treviño-Espinoza
Dean of Educational Partnerships
North Lake College
5001 N. MacArthur Boulevard
Irving, TX 75038

Conservation Note. Most publishers include what is known as a *half title page* in their books. This page immediately precedes the title page and contains nothing other than the book's title. Including a half title page generally has been PRO-ED's practice as well. In this book, however, we have chosen to eliminate this page. By so doing, PRO-ED has saved the following:

- 100 pounds of paper
- 2.35 pounds of caustic soda, sulfuric acid and other chemicals
- 14 pounds of coal
- 7.5 gallons of water

Work and Disability: Basic Constructs

Edna Mora Szymanski, Randall M. Parker, Carole Ryan, Mary Ann Merz, Beatriz Treviño-Espinoza, and Sarah Johnston-Rodriguez

Work is a central aspect of human life. Not only is work a means by which individuals define themselves in society, but it is also part of the very fabric of societies. The relationship of people to work is interactive and complex. Specifically, work affects and is affected by individual, economic, social, cultural, and other factors.

Recent work trends pose significant challenges for workers and counselors (Szymanski, 1999). Layoffs, downsizing, and restructring have become common, and employment stability has become rarer (Burke & Nelson, 1998). Hall and Mirvis (1996) have suggested that "the company's commitment to the employee extends only to the current need for that person's skills and performance" (p. 17).

Disability complicates the interrelationships between people and work. It may affect work productivity and relationships with coworkers. Rehabilitation professionals who work with people with disabilities must therefore understand the complex nature of work to assist individuals in not only attaining and maintaining work but also interacting with workplace colleagues. This chapter addresses these and related issues through a discussion of (a) work and society; (b) psychological aspects of work; (c) disability, gender, race, culture, and work; and (d) summary and implications.

WORK AND SOCIETY

What is work? At first blush, this is a trivial question. However, work has many meanings that vary over time and across cultures (Herr &

Cramer, 1992; Neff, 1985). Indeed, work is a complex cultural transaction (Neff, 1985) that has economic, social, and economic purposes (Herr & Cramer, 1992). In this section, we will describe (a) definitions of work, (b) the meaning of work, (c) occupational structures and cultures, and (d) power, prestige, and professions.

Definitions of Work

Work is a multidimensional term that often overlaps with such terms as *job*, *position*, and *occupation*. In fact, *Webster's II New Riverside Dictionary* (1984) even listed *job* and *occupation* as synonyms of *work*. Work and work-related terms are defined in this section to form a common base for future discussion.

The most general definition of *work* is that it is an "activity performed to produce goods or services of value to others" (Rothman, 1987, p. 5). Work has also been defined as "physical or mental effort directed toward a goal" (*Webster's II*, 1984). Thus, in the broadest sense, work is goal-directed activity.

Another broad term is *career*, which has been defined both as an individual's lifelong work pattern and as the sum of all life experiences (Isaacson & Brown, 2000). A comprehensive definition for this word uses Super's (1990, 1994) concept of a *life career rainbow* to emphasize that a career combines work, family, and other life roles that vary in relative prominence over time and across individuals.

Position, in contrast, is a specific term denoting "a group of tasks performed by one person" (Herr & Cramer, 1992, p. 29; Super, 1976). A *job* is "a group of similar, paid positions requiring some similar attributes in a single organization" (Herr & Cramer, 1992, p. 29; Super, 1976). In other words, a job is "a specific set of technical and social activities located within a specific context" (Rothman, 1987, p. 5). An *occupation* is a group of similar jobs found in different organizations or industries (Herr & Cramer, 1992, p. 29; Super, 1976).

Tasks, on the other hand, are specific elements of jobs (Ettinger, 1991). Tasks form the building blocks for job functions, which have become a critical concern since the passage of the Americans with Disabilities Act of 1990. The *essential functions* of the job are those "basic job duties that an employee must be able to perform, with or without reasonable accommodation" (U.S. Equal Employment Opportunity Commission, 1991, p. 3).

Jobs cannot be taken out of the context of *industries*, which are "groups of firms that produce similar goods and services" (Ettinger, 1991, pp. 2–9). There are two major types of industries: goods producing (e.g., agriculture, mining, contract construction, manufacturing) and service (e.g., transportation, communication, and public utilities; trade; finance, insurance, and real estate; services; government).

The definitions presented in this section provide some common ground for discussion. Despite these definitions, evidence suggests that the meaning of work varies across individuals and nations (Quintanilla, 1990).

The Meaning of Work

Work is central to our lives (Moos, 1986). Although work was regarded with disdain by some early societies, many religions have ascribed spiritual value to work (e.g., work is good for the soul; Neff, 1985). In fact, some religious groups define work as a calling from God (Isaacson & Brown, 2000). Regardless of the definition used, the complex interaction of work, individuals, and societies provides fertile ground for differences in how work is perceived, that is, what work means to individuals.

The meaning of work is one variable that has been used to examine social construction of work across individuals, groups, societies, and nations. Work meanings affect the valence of job outcomes, influence expectancies, affect goal setting and acceptance, and mediate responses to feedback (Quintanilla, 1991). The work goals aspect of work meaning varies across occupations (Quintanilla, 1990), and the work meanings aspect tends to change over time with societal trends (Quintanilla, 1991). Not surprisingly, differences in the relative importance of work goals exist across nations and over time (Silverthorne, 1992).

Quintanilla (1991) studied the meaning-of-work construct in a research project that spanned eight countries and included intensive, structured interviews with more than 14,000 individuals. He operationalized meaning of work as consisting of four measures: work centrality, work goals, societal norms about working, and work definitions (Quintanilla, 1991).

Work Centrality

Work centrality was defined as "the degree of general importance that working has in the life of an individual at any given point in time" (Quintanilla, 1991, p. 85). Work centrality varies within and across nations, with Japanese workers having higher centrality than U.S. workers, who, in turn, reported more centrality than did German workers (Quintanilla, 1990). In the United States, work centrality decreased from 1982 to 1989. Interestingly, there was a concomitant decrease in leisure centrality and an increase in family importance (England, 1991).

Work Goals

The work goals facet of the meaning-of-work construct was operationalized through comparisons of the relative importance of 11 work goals. These work goals, which are listed in order of their importance (England, 1991), are (a) good pay, (b) interesting work, (c) good job security, (d) opportunity to learn, (e) good interpersonal relations, (f) a lot of variety, (g) a good match between the worker and the job, (h) good opportunity for upgrading or promotion, (i) job autonomy, (j) convenient work hours, and (k) good physical working conditions. International comparisons demonstrated that the U.S. and German workforces were relatively similar and quite different from the Japanese workforce in their rankings of these work goals. Although interesting work was rated in the top three in importance in all three nations, Japanese workers also ranked a good worker–job match and autonomy as more important, whereas U.S. and German workers accorded more importance to economic goals (e.g., pay, security; Quintanilla, 1990).

Societal Norms About Working

The meaning-of-work studies (Quintanilla, 1990, 1991) used 10 normative statements and factor analysis to operationalize social norms along two dimensions: entitlement and obligations. "While the entitlement norm represents the underlying rights of individual and the work-related responsibilities of society and organizations toward all individuals, the obligation norm represents the underlying duties of all individuals to organizations and to society with respect to working" (Quintanilla, 1991, p. 85). In the United States, there was little substantive change and no major shift toward an entitlement-oriented workforce from 1982 to 1989 (England, 1991). Interestingly, 1987 data showed the U.S. workforce to be less entitlement oriented and more obligation oriented than the Japanese and German workforces (Quintanilla, 1990).

Work Definitions

For the purpose of the meaning-of-work study, Quintanilla (1990) operationalized work definitions across the following three dimensions: reasons for working, personal outcomes resulting from working, and constraints related to working. Between 1982 and 1989, the U.S. work-force shifted "from collective to personal rationales, . . . [moving] toward defining work more in terms of constraints and controls, and from affective to physical state outcomes of working" (England, 1991, p. 123).

In summary, the meaning-of-work studies have provided concrete evidence that work meanings vary across individuals and countries as well as over time. So, too, have studies on role salience and work values in counseling (Super & Nevill, 1986a, 1986b). These findings reinforce the complexity of the construct of work in relation to other aspects of life.

The meaning-of-work construct operationalizes some aspects of how individuals relate to work. Organizations, the topic of the following section, represent another unit of analysis in understanding the complex social nature of work.

Occupational Structures and Cultures

Because work is a social endeavor, it has inherent organizations and cultures. Two types of organizations are those determined by the type of work that is done (i.e., work roles) and those determined by the situation or location in which the work is done (i.e., organizational culture).

Social Organization of Work Roles

There are a variety of ways to organize work roles. Two frameworks common in counseling are (a) field and level of complexity and (b) interest (Herr & Cramer, 1992). Another framework, which is more common outside of counseling, classifies work into the following types: self-regulating professions, the administrative hierarchy, administrative support work, the blue-collar hierarchy, direct-service work, family farm work, unpaid work, and deviant work (Rothman, 1987).

Professions are groups of occupations in which members are accorded respect and self-regulation due to their expert knowledge and specialized training. They have some level of autonomy over their affairs and monopoly over certain tasks and services (Abbott, 1988; Rothman, 1987). Accreditation and licensure are means by which professions exercise their autonomy over education, admission to the profession, and scope of practice. Professionals comprise approximately 13% of the workforce (McGaghie, 1993).

The administrative hierarchy includes executives, managers, and first-line supervisors. Workers in this category are responsible for managing, directing, and supervising the work of others. They comprise between 10% and 15% of the workforce. Supporting the administrative hierarchy is the administrative support hierarchy, which includes clerical workers and technicians (Rothman, 1987).

Blue-collar occupations are those that "involve technical operations performed on, or with, tangible physical products and machines, rather than people or information" (Rothman, 1987, p. 14). Included in this category are craft work and unskilled labor. Whereas blue-collar occupations are concerned with products, direct-service work is concerned with people. This category of jobs includes salespersons, personal service workers, domestic workers, and some protective occupations (Rothman, 1987).

Other categories of work are family farm work, unpaid work, and deviant work. Family farm work is unique in that it requires a multiperson work unit (e.g., husband, wife, and children). Unpaid work includes the occupation of homemaker and volunteer work. Deviant work, an often overlooked reality in occupational classification, includes criminal activity and other occupations that, although sometimes legal, operate on the fringe of society (Rothman, 1987).

Organizational Culture

People who work together develop distinct subcultures that typically include socialization of initiates (Neff, 1985; Rothman, 1987). In studies of organizational behavior, these concepts have been termed *organizational culture* and *organizational socialization*.

Organizational culture refers to "the shared beliefs, expectations, and values held by members of a given organization, and to which newcomers must adjust" (Baron & Greenberg, 1990, p. 296). It is affected by an organization's founders, its external environment, the nature of its business, and its employees. Organizational culture is a potent force that affects the processes of an organization and the behavior of its employees (Baron & Greenberg, 1990). Evidence of organizational culture can often be seen in language or jargon, artifacts (e.g., tools, uniforms), beliefs, values, norms, and rituals (e.g., rites of passage for promotion; Rothman, 1987).

Organizational socialization is a cultural process that is of particular importance to people with disabilities and those who desire to assist them in obtaining and maintaining employment. It is "the process through which individuals are transformed from outsiders to participating, effective members of organizations" (Baron & Greenberg, 1990, p. 302). Socialization differs according to the goals of the organization (Baron & Greenberg, 1990).

Power, Prestige, and Professions

Another dimension along which work can be studied relates to power. "Individuals and occupational groups act self-consciously to enhance their own interests and rewards" (Rothman, 1987, p. 23). Power and prestige are products of the social enterprise of work, and professions are often considered a special category of power relationships in work.

Power

Power is a regular part of the workplace. It is "the capacity to change the behavior or attitudes of another in a desired manner" (Baron & Greenberg, 1990, p. 411). Individuals derive power from the following bases: expertise (i.e., recognized special skills or professional status), referents (i.e., power based on previous, positive relationships), legitimate authority (i.e., recognized organizational position of authority), coercion (i.e., control over punishment), and rewards (i.e., control over rewards). Organizational or occupational groups derive power from controlling resources or encouraging dependence (i.e., making themselves indispensable; Baron & Greenberg, 1990). Power is a part of daily work life, and failure to understand and use it wisely can have deleterious consequences for individuals and organizations.

Prestige

Who receives the most respect, a garbage collector or a college professor? Not surprisingly, college professors are near the high end of the occupational prestige ladder, and garbage collectors are near the bottom. In the United States, the highest prestige is accorded to executives and members of self-regulating professions, and lowest prestige is accorded to unskilled workers and those who do work that society regards as dirty (e.g., janitors, garbage collectors). Occupational prestige ratings are relatively consistent across nations and affect personal prestige (Rothman, 1987). Thus, the job one does affects the relative respect one commands in many nonwork interactions. Setting also may be related to prestige, with some settings (e.g., hospitals, college campuses) potentially more prestigious than others (e.g., food processing plants).

Professions

Professions are distinguished from most occupational groups by the fact that they self-regulate through autonomy and monopoly. Expert knowledge has been considered the basis of the power of professions and the autonomy accorded to them by society. Professions exert their power through accreditation and licensure, which control who enters their ranks, how newcomers are educationally prepared, and how they will practice. Professional groups are often involved in power relations with each other, and the current work role of particular professions is thought to reflect the sum effect of these interactions (Rothman, 1987).

Professional power is weakening due to recent changes in society, including increased education and knowledge of client populations, more employment of professionals in organizations (e.g., health maintenance organizations, large law practices), and increased consumerism (McGuire, 1993). Although this trend may be regarded with disdain by professional groups, it is important to note that some authors have blamed professional power for many of society's current problems (see, e.g., Illich, 1977; McKnight, 1977). Professional power has been seen as a particularly complex problem for occupations serving people with disabilities (see, e.g., Amado, 1988; Rubenfeld, 1988; Salifos-Rothschild, 1976; Skrtic, 1991; Stubbins, 1988; Szymanski & Trueba, 1994).

In summary, power and prestige are often overlooked parts of working that should be considered in career counseling with people with disabilities. Not only must counselors assist their clients in understanding the power dynamics of the workplace and the prestige implications of specific career choices, but counselors must also be aware of possible problems with the power status accorded to them as professionals.

Although prestige of jobs and settings may be important to individuals, work trends may make this consideration less important. As stable jobs become rarer, people may be less opposed to working in low-prestige positions or settings.

PSYCHOLOGICAL ASPECTS OF WORK

Work and personality are reciprocally interactive, each mutually affecting the other (Kohn, 1990). Work may ease, cause, or exacerbate psychological or physical problems (Neff, 1985; Quick, Murphy, & Hurrell, 1992). Conversely, individual personality traits may affect the work environment (Kohn, 1990).

The potential effect of work trends has prompted more attention to how the design of organizations and jobs affects individuals. Service sector jobs, which are on the rise, tend to be associated with higher than average levels of stress for reasons that are not yet clear (Landy, 1992). Employers with foresight are recognizing the necessity of attending to human resource needs to maximize the potential contribution of advancing technology in the workplace (Turnage, 1990). Principles of "psychological ergonomics" have been developed as well as psychological job analysis techniques (Greiner & Leitner, 1989; Singleton, 1989).

Volumes have been devoted to psychological aspects of work (see, e.g., International Labor Office, 1992; Johnson & Johansson, 1991; Karasek & Theorell, 1990; Keita & Sauter, 1992; Muchinsky, 1997; Warr, 1987). For this chapter, however, we will provide only a brief overview of some of the more salient issues—specifically, (a) work motivation, (b) work and personality, (c) work stress, and (d) job satisfaction.

Work Motivation

"People think, and . . . how and what they think will affect how they behave" (Landy, 1985, p. 366). Applying this concept to work, the study of work motivation is the constant quest to find out why people work and what will make them more productive. Work motivation is "a broad construct pertaining to the conditions and processes that account for the arousal, direction, magnitude, and maintenance of effort in a person's job" (Katzell & Thompson, 1990, p. 144). The study of work motivation appears to be the psychological counterpart to the more sociologically oriented meaning-of-work studies presented earlier.

Work motivation is a multifaceted construct that influences job performance in complex ways (Baron & Greenberg, 1990). Types of work motivation theories abound and include a focus on the following constructs: direction of behavior, intensity of action, and persistence of behavior (Muchinsky, 1997). Motivational studies remain important to organizations both for purposes of improving performance and job satisfaction and for finding ways to decrease job stress.

Work and Personality

The connection of work and personality is relatively complex (Kohn, 1990). Some career development theories, which are discussed in Chapter 4, are based on the connection of personality and work (e.g., Hershenson's, Holland's, Super's, and the Minnesota work adjustment theories). These theories tend to focus on the effect of personality on occupational choice and work adjustment. In addition, it is thought that personality may have a mediating effect on the impact of various occupational stressors (Quick, Quick, Nelson, & Hurrell, 1997).

Another focus of study has been the ways in which work affects personality. Types of work conditions that affect personality are "a worker's place in the organizational structure, opportunities for occupational self-direction, the principal job pressures to which the worker is subject, and the principal extrinsic risks and rewards associated with the job" (Kohn, 1990, p. 41). Workers who have passive jobs (i.e., low-level demands and low levels of control) have also been found to be passive in their leisure and political activities, unless their work becomes more active, at which time their leisure and political involvement also becomes more active (Karasek & Theorell, 1990). Thus, work–personality linkage should be considered both an important antecedent and consequence to be considered in career counseling.

Work Stress

Work can provide a sense of well-being and belonging. It can also cause psychological and physical problems. The National Institute for Occupational Safety and Health (NIOSH) has recognized psychological disorders as one of the 10 leading work-related diseases and injuries and has presented a strategy for prevention (Sauter, Murphy, & Hurrell, 1990). "Gradual mental stress" accounts for 11% of all claims, according to a study by the National Council on Compensation Insurance (Hatfield, 1990).

Work stress has been a topic of recent concern both in psychology and business (see, e.g., Baron & Greenberg, 1990; Kahn & Byosiere, 1990; Quick et al., 1992; Quick et al., 1997). Broadly defined, stress is "a pattern of emotional states and physiological reactions occurring in situations where individuals perceive threats to their important goals which they may be unable to meet" (Baron & Greenberg, 1990, p. 226). Prolonged stress may lead to "strain," which implies physical and emotional consequences such as cardiovascular disease, decreased job performance, or marriage and family problems (Landy, 1992).

Researchers with interdisciplinary perspectives (e.g., medicine, sociology, social epidemiology, biobehaviorism, industrial engineering and ergonomics, social psychology, cognitive science, applied physiology, organizational and clinical psychology) have furthered our understanding of work stress. Theoretical models of the relationship between work and mental health incorporate multiple factors of the person and the environment (see, e.g., Kahn & Byosiere, 1990; Karasek & Theorell, 1990; Quick et al., 1997; Sauter & Murphy, 1995; Warr, 1987).

In the past, more focus had been on the individual than on the environment. This emphasis is gradually shifting to a more balanced perspective. Accumulating empirical evidence has shown that certain psychosocial factors of the environment override the power of personal coping techniques (Johnson & Johansson, 1991; Landsbergis & Cahill, 1994). The combination of this research and the difficulty of effecting lasting individual behavioral change suggest that it may be more efficient to change aspects of the environment than the person. Thus, the following five psychosocial factors of the work environment have received the greatest amount of attention from researchers: (a) amount of control over one's work (e.g., schedule, pace, use of skills); (b) the nature of job demands (e.g., monotony vs. variety, high vs. low level), especially as it interacts with the level of control; (c) social support, both inside and outside the workplace, which acts as a mediator of stress; (d) conflicts between task demands (especially when time pressures do not permit optimum performance), between work roles (e.g., serving client needs vs. employer interests), and between work and family responsibilities; and (e) degree of uncertainty (e.g., job security, performance evaluation criteria; Landy, 1992; Quick et al. 1997; Sauter & Murphy, 1995).

The relationships of individuals, jobs, and stress are complex, and much research is needed. For example, although the nature of a job is known to affect stress (Landy, 1992; Sauter & Murphy, 1995), it also appears that the effects of job stressors and the mediating effect of social support vary with career stage (Murphy, Hurrell, & Quick, 1992). In addition, there is a cognitive appraisal aspect to the stress experience (Quick et al., 1997), which means that what is experienced by some individuals as stressful may be experienced by others as exhilarating. Nonetheless, at this time, it is known that work stress can be costly to individuals as well as to business (Quick et al., 1992). Disability may further complicate individual stress reactions. Thus stress is an important consideration in career planning with people with disabilities (Szymanski, 1999).

Issues relating to work stress are particularly important to counselors and educators who work with people with disabilities in supported employment. Service sector jobs, which are particularly susceptible to job stress, are often sites for supported employment placements. Unfortunately, some individuals with severe disabilities in supported employment may have difficulty in communicating about their job stress. In addition, they might lack the social support that can mediate the effect of job stress. Research on job stress of supported employees is certainly needed. However, at this time, counselors and educators can be aware of the possibilities and consider them in planning with people with disabilities (Szymanski, 1999).

Job Satisfaction

Job satisfaction is a construct that addresses individual attitudes toward a job. It is defined as "affect — or feeling and emotion — resulting from one's evaluation of the situation" (Dawis, 1994, p. 35). The construct can be positive (i.e., job satisfaction) or negative (i.e., job dissatisfaction). As with many other work-related constructs, links between job satisfaction and productivity are complex (Baron & Greenberg, 1990). For example, although job redesign seems to improve job satisfaction, its effect on performance is less clear (Kelly, 1992).

Job satisfaction is often considered in terms of intrinsic and extrinsic factors, as proposed by Herzberg's theory (Baron & Greenberg, 1990). Intrinsic factors (e.g., opportunities for advancement and growth, recognition, responsibility, achievement) promote job satisfaction, whereas extrinsic factors (e.g., supervision, pay, policies, working conditions, interpersonal relations, security) prevent job dissatisfaction (Baron & Greenberg, 1990).

Again, consideration of job satisfaction is an important dimension of career counseling.

Clearly, individual interaction with work is complex and reciprocal. Work can have a substantial psychological impact and is also affected by psychological characteristics of workers. In addition to psychological characteristics, work is affected by gender, race, culture, and disability.

DISABILITY, GENDER, RACE, CULTURE, AND WORK

Our nation continues to diversify. Reports from the 2000 U.S. Census indicate that the nation's population is 13% Latino. Racially, the population is reported as 75% White, 12% African American, 1% American Indian or Alaskan Native, 4% Asian, 0.1% Native Hawaiian or other Pacific Islander, 5.5% some other race, and 2.4% two or more races. Note that the "some other race" category is 97% Latino, and Latinos are also represented in the White and African American race totals (Grieco & Cassidy, 2001).

The participation of individuals in the labor market is often influenced by personal characteristics other than interests and abilities (Cox, 1993). The purpose of this section is to describe the interaction of these individual factors with labor market participation and vocational behavior through the following topics: (a) factors underlying differential labor market access, (b) disability, (c) gender, (d) race and ethnicity, and (e) culture.

Factors Underlying Differential Labor Market Access

Differential labor market access for minorities appears to relate both to societal factors and to education. The results are, nonetheless, far-reaching. When minority workers, including people with disabilities, are discriminated against in the labor market, they are denied full use of their productive abilities. Their incomes are depressed, and they are overrepresented in the ranks of the poor. Hence, discrimination against racial and ethnic minority groups, women, and people with disabilities in the labor market tends to undermine human capital and society as a whole (Schiller, 1989).

Discrimination relates to social beliefs and structures. People tend to have very firm ideas about what causes some people to be "dirt poor" and others to be "filthy rich." Societies' explanations for inequalities are summed up in three contrasting arguments: flawed character, restricted opportunity, and Big Brother (Schiller, 1989).

From the flawed character perspective, poverty is regarded as the natural result of individual defects in aspirations or abilities. That is, anyone who wants to move up in the income distribution can do so because of the abundant opportunities for material advancement. In terms of the flawed character perspective, ethnic minorities bring little human capital to the labor market and are rewarded accordingly. The restricted opportunity argument, on the other hand, attributes inequalities to differential access to good schools, jobs, government protection, subsidies, or services. The underlying argument is that only equitable opportunities in education and the labor market can ensure less poverty. In contrast to the flawed character argument, the Big Brother argument blames the government for destroying incentives for stable families and economic self-sufficiency. High taxes, welfare benefits, racial quotas, and other public policies are intended to help but actually destroy work incentives (Schiller, 1989) and create a "blight of dependency" (Gilder, 1981, p. 12).

Education contributes to labor market access. Educational discrimination is still practiced (see, e.g., Kozol, 1991), even though it violates commonly accepted standards of social justice. Nearly four decades after the *Brown v. Board of Education* (1954) ruling, "schools in lower-income areas are notoriously ill equipped to transmit interest, enjoyment, or ability" (Schiller, 1989, p. 108). The following points made in a discussion of nationwide educational data illustrate current educational inequities.

> By the time they reach grade 12, if they do so at all, minority students are about four years behind other young people. Indeed, 17-year-old African American and Latino students have skills in English, mathematics, and science similar to those of 13-year old Whites. Unfortunately, these gaps continue into and through college. . . . African Americans and Latinos obtain college degrees at only half the rate of White students. And well-to-do students are nearly seven times as likely as those from poor families to earn a bachelor's degree. (Haycock, Jerald, & Huang, 2001, p. 3)

Disability

Definitions of disability abound, making this construct difficult to specify or discuss in general terms (Oi, 1991; also see Chapters 3 and 6, this volume, for a discussion of disability definitions and statistics). Clearly, disability cannot really be considered a static variable because definitions differ across time and cultures (Zola, 1993). Significantly, people with disabilities constitute the largest, single minority in the United States (Kaye, 1998).

Data from the 1994 National Health Interview Survey (NHIS) reported by Kaye (1998) showed that 39.1 million people (15%) in the noninstitutionalized U.S. population reported limitation in activity due to a chronic health condition. Interestingly, disability rates differ across ethnic and racial groups. Data from the 1992 NHIS revealed that Native Americans had a 17.6% rate of activity limitation, compared to 15.9% of African Americans and 15.3% of Whites. The lowest rate was 7.2% for Asians and Pacific Islanders (Kaye, 1998).

Disability is often related to both unemployment and poverty. A 1994 Harris Poll indicated that two thirds of Americans with disabilities between the ages of 16 and 64 were not working, although 79% of these individuals reported that they want to work (Taylor, 1994). The study also reported that, in contrast to 37% of adults without disabilities, 59% of adults with disabilities lived in households earning less than $25,000. In contrast, only 37% of employed adults with disabilities lived in such households (Taylor, 1994). The situation had not changed appreciably by the 1998 poll, when only 29% of adults with disabilities reported employment (Taylor, 1998). Not surprisingly, employment is thus an important part of the connection between disability and poverty.

The relationship of disability to labor market participation is also complicated by disability support programs (Yelin, 1991). Although the growth in the Social Security Disability Insurance (SSDI) program was accompanied by a decrease in labor market participation of people with disabilities, the mass elimination of individuals from the SSDI rolls in the early 1980s was also accompanied by a similar type of decrease (Yelin, 1991). On the individual side of this phenomenon, it is interesting to note that approximately 60% of unemployed adults with disabilities reported fear of losing income or health care benefits if they join the workforce (Taylor, 1994).

Yelin (1991) has suggested the structure of work and employment as a major culprit in limiting the labor market participation of people with disabilities. According to Yelin,

> The rise in work disability rates is concentrated among workers in industries undergoing contraction and has occurred because firms in these industries fail to make the accommodations necessary for persons with impairments to continue working and because the firms and their employees can call upon the disability compensation system to buffer unemployment. (p. 13)

Workers with flexible jobs or discretion over their work schedules are less likely to leave work due to disability.

Yelin (1991) also suggested that the essential functions clause of the Americans with Disabilities Act may hinder rather than facilitate the employment of people with disabilities "because it models work in a way more consistent with a more primitive form of industrialism" (p. 159). In other words, it is not consistent with some of the modern management strategies (e.g., matrix management) that increase the number of tasks within each job.

The Americans with Disabilities Act of 1990 (ADA; see Chapter 2, this volume) was designed to facilitate participation in the labor market and other aspects of society by people with disabilities. There is considerable debate over whether it will accomplish these aims or perhaps have unintended negative consequences. On one hand, some have argued that because the act primarily relies on controls rather than incentives, it may actually create additional barriers (see, e.g., Arokiasamy & Millington, 1994; Rosen, 1991; Weaver, 1991). On the other hand, it has been argued that controls are needed to address very real prejudices that limit opportunities for people with disabilities (Kemp, 1991).

In summary, labor market participation of people with disabilities is a complex phenomenon. It is influenced by trends in the labor market and the structure of work as well as by transfer payments (e.g., SSDI) and rights-related legislation (e.g., ADA) and regulations. Nonetheless, it is also a serious social problem. "Displaced from employment opportunities a little more each year, and with progressively less access to transfer payments, the well-being of persons with disabilities is gradually being eroded" (Yelin, 1991, p. 138).

General levels of the economy and unemployment have strong influences on workers of color and workers with disabilities. The difficult economic period from 1970 to 1987 was marked by decreased labor market participation by men and by older workers. Women, including those with disabilities, made some gains, but race and age mitigated against gains. Race and disability appeared to compound negative trends. Thus, people of color and people with disabilities, who already had lower labor market participation rates, lost more ground during the period (Yelin, 1991).

Although some people of color, women, and people with disabilities have made gains, they still remain at disadvantage in many facets of the labor market. Education and work experience are associated with wage growth both for individuals and for the economy. Thus, counselors should pay particular attention to educational and training outcomes for minorities, women, and people with disabilities.

Gender

Gender has significant impact on the benefits derived from work. Although 60.2% of women participate in the labor force, the median earnings of full-time working women older than age 25 are 73% of that of their male counterparts (Spraggins, 2000).

Inequities in women's wages disadvantage future generations. "In 1998, the median income for families maintained by a woman with no husband present ($22,163) was lower than for families maintained by a man with no wife present ($35,681), and substantially lower than for married-couple families ($54,180)" (Spraggins, 2000, p. 2).

Employers in the United States are more likely to consider workers' gender than any other personal characteristic in assigning them to jobs (Reskin & Padvic, 1994), a process reflected in the term *gendered work*. In fact, twice as much segregation is based on gender as on race. Gendered work includes the following forms: (a) job-level segregation (i.e., within an organization) and occupational-level segregation, (b) gender differences in promotion, (c) gender differences in authority, and (d) gender differences in earnings (Reskin & Padavic, 1994). The results of gendered work are potent.

Around the world, men outearn women. "Women's average wages are consistently lower than men's average wages in all countries, even after adjustments for differences in working hours" (Rubery, 1989, p. 282). Although job segregation is a primary cause of pay inequity (Reskin & Padvic, 1994), occupational segregation also plays a role. Within the same occupation, women earn only 70% to 85% of what men earn (Reskin & Padvic, 1994). The key issue in gender inequity is not so much that men and women do different work but that this work is differently valued (Sapiro, 1994).

Social scientists have postulated a variety of reasons for the apparent systemic inequalities in the workplace. These reasons include (a) cultural beliefs about gender and work, which are created by both workers and employers and by men and women, such as assuming that women are better suited to nurturing jobs such as nursing and teaching; (b) men's efforts to preserve their advantage in the workplace; (c) employer's actions, intentional and unintentional, which often result in few, if any, women being hired for certain kinds of jobs; and (d) workers' own preferences and abilities as individuals or as group members (Reskin & Padvic, 1994). Whatever the causes, it is clear that gender-based inequities pose potent workplace barriers for all women, including those with disabilities.

Race and Ethnicity

Race and ethnicity are additional sources of workplace inequities. Within each gender, people of color and Hispanics, regardless of color, tend to work in less desirable occupations than Whites and non-Hispanics (Reskin & Padvic, 1994). Race further complicates the disadvantage of gender, with African American women college graduates earning less than White male high school dropouts (Women's Action Coalition, 1993). In fact, "it is often possible to rehearse the history of discrimination against racial, religious, or ethnic minorities by tracing their allocation into the least desirable forms of labor" (Rothman, 1987, p. 5).

Trueba (1993) suggested castification as an explanation for workplace segregation of racial and ethnic minorities:

> Castification is fundamentally an institutionalized way of exploiting one social group (ethnic, racial, low-income, or other minority group), thus reducing this group to the status of a lower caste that cannot enjoy the same rights and obligations possessed by the other groups. (p. 30)

The effects of castification are evident in patterns of labor market participation. Occupations with the greatest concentrations of men and women of color pay the lowest average earnings (Reskin & Padvic, 1994). The consequences of workplace segregation are serious. Women and minorities have been overrepresented in the contingent workforce (i.e., part-timers, temporaries, freelancers, consultants). "They generally work without health care and pension benefits and are excluded from a whole battery of labor and civil rights laws, covering everything from minimum-wage legislation to age, gender, and racial discrimination; from occupational health and safety to sexual harassment" (Judd & Pope, 1994, p. 87).

Occupational attainment and education are closely related. Current and future jobs are increasingly requiring more education (Hall & Mirvis, 1996; Wegman, Chapman, & Johnson, 1989). Although a recent analysis of the Current Population Surveys (a federally conducted monthly survey of households) revealed continued discrepancies in salary level based on race, it also revealed that degree attainment was related with higher salary levels ("Attaining a Degree," 1994). This is particularly troubling considering the differential degree attainment noted earlier in this chapter.

Culture

Culture is a system of concepts that provides a lens through which individuals interpret events and behavior (Trueba, Rodriguez, Zou, & Cintron, 1993). However, culture cannot be considered to be the major determinant of differential labor market participation of ethnic minorities. Research has suggested structural factors such as racial discrimination and socioeconomic status to be more potent (Arbona, 1990; Cotton, 1993). Nonetheless, some cultural factors may influence the ways in which minorities participate in the workforce.

Advocating cultural diversity in the workplace, Cox (1993) has suggested that the following factors be considered as possibly influencing intergroup relations: "(1) time and space orientation, (2) leadership style orientations, (3) individualism versus collectivism, (4) competitive versus cooperative behavior, (5) locus of control, and (6) communication styles" (p. 108). Similarly, Sue and Sue (1990) have called for consideration of language, socioeconomic class, and culture in career counseling.

Knowledge of individuals' cultural background does not automatically convey an understanding of belief structures. Members of cultural minority groups living in a majority society may have adopted varying degrees of the majority group culture. The processes associated with biculturalism are complex (LaFromboise, Coleman, & Gerton, 1993). Nonetheless, levels of cultural identity may relate to job choice and job satisfaction (Cox, 1993; Helms & Piper, 1994).

Although there is an obvious need to understand the ways in which race and culture affect career development, most theories do not consider these variables (Fitzgerald & Betz, 1994). In fact, until quite recently, very little research attention has been given to these variables (Tinsley, 1994). Nonetheless, there is little disagreement that "individuals from different cultural backgrounds can be expected to differ in the expectations, aspirations, and values they bring to the career development process" (Tinsley, 1994, p. 115). There is also little doubt that vocational assessment, which is dependent on worldview, can unintentionally perpetuate negative stereotypes about minority individuals when the results are used in culturally insensitive ways (Fuoad, 1993). Counselors are thus advised to study and practice cultural sensitivity in counseling (see, e.g., Lee & Richardson, 1991; Pederson, 1994; Sue & Sue, 1990).

SUMMARY AND IMPLICATIONS

Work is a complex phenomenon. It affects social interactions, psychological well-being, and lifestyle. Interestingly, work also is affected by social interactions and individual characteristics (e.g., race, gender, disability). The changing nature of the labor market further complicates the study of work.

The U.S. labor market has undergone considerable change during the past century. Manual workers succeeded farm workers as the largest occupational group in the United States. Currently, blue-collar preeminence has given way to knowledge workers with symbolic interaction skills requiring advanced education with continued learning and offering good pay with greater autonomy. Workers are working more and earning less, with little time for leisure activities and an actual decline in spendable income. Many available jobs are part-time or of short duration, offering no security, no opportunities for career advancement, and no benefits or worker protections.

A range of employment opportunities will continue, but the best jobs will be for those persons who are literate, can adapt to change, and will continue to learn new skills. In addition, there will be an increased emphasis on the development of human resources—improving the quality of the labor force to maintain a workforce that is qualified to meet the ever-changing needs of the world economy.

Current work trends portend increasing challenges for workers, including those with disabilities, and for professionals who assist them. A rapidly changing economy will continue to contribute to organizational and structural downsizing and restructuring, offering most workers little job security regardless of skill level. Therefore, all workers must expect to change jobs with increasing frequency and to learn to compete fiercely for available jobs. In addition, people who are unemployed must be able to identify and access alternative employment options efficiently and quickly, making job-seeking skills a necessary survival tool for all workers.

In conclusion, it is likely that work will continue to be a major part of most people's lives, but there will be fewer choices for those who are ill-prepared to meet the demands of the changing workplace. These workers are likely to earn less money and experience an even greater decline in standard of living.

The complexity of work and of individuals precludes easy answers. Nonetheless, our study of work has suggested the following considerations for counselors and educators assisting people with disabilities in career counseling and job placement.

1. Work may mean different things to different people. Counselors and educators cannot assume that their views of work are shared by clients and students. At a bare minimum, it is important to ask people about (a) why they work (e.g., which benefits are most and least important), (b) how important or central work is in their lives, and (c) what they believe about their responsibilities to their employers and their employers' responsibilities to them.

2. Work is a social endeavor. Competence in navigating the social structure of the workplace may be at least as important as competent task performance. It is important to include consideration of workplace socialization, organizational culture, occupational prestige, and power in career counseling and job preparation.

3. Work is changing. Clients and students should be encouraged to develop long-term plans to ensure continued employment and

advancement. These plans should include continuing education to preclude skill obsolescence in a rapidly changing work world.

4. Work has psychological and physical effects on individuals. It may ease, cause, or exacerbate psychological or physical problems. For some individuals, placement in a job in which there is little opportunity for control may cause job-related stress. Thus, counselors and educators should discuss job stress issues with their clients and students before placement and during the first months of employment if possible.

5. Minorities, women, and people with disabilities face structural impediments in the workplace. Education has been shown to be a potent force in improving labor market participation. Thus, education should be a major consideration in assisting people with disabilities in entering and retaining value in the labor force.

REFERENCES

Abbott, A. (1988). *The system of professions: An essay on the division of expert labor*. Chicago: University of Chicago Press.

Amado, A. R. N. (1988). A perspective on the present and notes for new directions. In L. W. Heal, J. I. Haney, & A. R. Novak Amado (Eds.), *Integration of developmentally disabled individuals into the community* (2nd ed., pp. 299–305). Baltimore: Brookes.

Americans with Disabilities Act of 1990, 42 U.S.C. §12101 *et seq*.

Arbona, C. (1990). Career counseling research and Hispanics: A review of the literature. *The Counseling Psychologist, 18*, 300–323.

Arokiasamy, C., & Millington, M. (1994). ADA and the goose that lays golden eggs. *Rehabilitation Education, 8*, 93–95.

Attaining a degree increases earning potential. (1994, July). *Higher Education & National Affairs, 43*(14), 4.

Baron, R. A., & Greenberg, J. (1990). *Behavior in organizations: Understanding and managing the human side of work* (3rd ed.). Boston: Allyn & Bacon.

Brown v. Board of Education, 347 U.S. 483 (1954).

Burke, R. J., & Nelson, D. (1998). Mergers and acquisitions, downsizing, and privatization: A North American perspective. In M. K. Gowing, J. D. Kraft, & J. C. Quick (Eds.), *The new organizational reality: Downsizing, restructuring, and revitalization* (pp. 21–54). Washington, DC: American Psychological Association.

Cotton, J. (1993). Color or culture? Wage differences among non-Hispanic Black males, Hispanic Black males, and Hispanic White males. *Review of Black Political Economy, 21*(4), 53–67.

Cox, T. (1993). *Cultural diversity in organizations: Theory, research, and practice*. San Francisco: Berrett-Koehler.

Dawis, R. V. (1994). The theory of work adjustment as convergent theory. In M. L. Savickas & R. W. Lent (Eds.), *Convergence in career development theories: Implications for science and practice* (pp. 33–43). Palo Alto, CA: Consulting Psychologists Press.

England, G. W. (1991). The meaning of work in the USA: Recent changes. *European Work and Organizational Psychologist, 1*, 111–124.

Ettinger, J. M. (Ed.). (1991). *Improved career decision making in a changing world*. Garret Park, MD: Garret Park.

Fitzgerald, L. F., & Betz, N. E. (1994). Career development in cultural context: The role of gender, race, class, and sexual orientation. In M. L. Savickas & R. W. Lent (Eds.), *Convergence in career development theories: Implications for science and practice* (pp. 103–117). Palo Alto, CA: Consulting Psychologists Press.

Fuoad, N. A. (1993). Cross-cultural vocational assessment. *Career Development Quarterly, 42*, 4–13.

Gilder, G. (1981). *Wealth and poverty*. New York: Basic Books.

Greiner, B., & Leitner, K. (1989). Assessment of job stress: The RHIA instrument. In K. Landau & W. Rohmert (Eds.), *Recent developments in job analysis* (pp. 53–66). London: Taylor & Francis.

Grieco, E. M., & Cassidy, R. C. (2001). *Overview of race and Hispanic origin* (Census 2000 Brief No. C2KBR/01-1). Washington, DC: U.S. Department of Commerce, Economics and Statistics Administration, U.S. Census Bureau.

Hall, D. T., & Mirvis, P. H. (1996). The new protean career: Psychological success and the path with a heart. In D. T. Hall & Associates (Eds.), *The career is dead: Long live the career* (pp. 15–45). San Francisco: Jossey-Bass.

Hatfield, M. O. (1990). Stress and the American worker. *American Psychologist, 45*, 1162–1164.

Haycock, K., Jerald, C., & Huang, S. (2001). Closing the gap: Done in a decade. *Thinking K–16, 5*(2), 3–22.

Helms, J. E., & Piper, R. E. (1994). Implications of racial identity theory for vocational psychology. *Journal of Vocational Behavior, 44*, 124–138.

Herr, E. L., & Cramer, S. H. (1992). *Career guidance and counseling through the lifespan: Systematic approaches* (4th ed.). New York: HarperCollins.

Illich, I. (1977). Disabling professions. In I. Illich, I. K. Zola, J. McKnight, J. Caplan, & H. Shaiken (Eds.), *Disabling professions* (pp. 11–39). London: Marion Boyars.

International Labor Office. (1992). *Conditions of work digest: Preventing stress at work*. Geneva: Author.

Isaacson, L., & Brown, D. (2000). *Career information, career counseling, and career development* (7th ed.). Boston: Allyn & Bacon.

Johnson, J. V., & Johansson, G. (1991). *The psychological work environment: Work organization, democratization and health. Essays in memory of Bertil Gardell*. New York: Baywood.

Judd, K., & Pope, S. (1994, May/June). The new job squeeze: Women pushed into part-time work. *Ms.*, *4*(6), 86–91.

Kahn, R. L., & Byosiere, P. (1990). Stress in organizations. In M. Dunnette (Ed.), *Handbook of industrial and organizational psychology* (Vol. 3, 2nd ed., pp. 571–650). Chicago: Rand-McNally.

Karasek, R., & Theorell, T. (1990). *Healthy work: Stress, productivity, and the reconstruction of working life*. New York: Basic Books.

Katzell, R. A., & Thompson, D. E. (1990). Work motivation: Theory and practice. *American Psychologist*, *45*, 144–153.

Kaye, S. (1998). *Disability watch: The status of people with disabilities in the United States*. San Francisco: Disability Statistics Center.

Keita, G. P., & Sauter, S. L. (Eds.). (1992). *Work and well being: An agenda for the 1990s*. Washington, DC: American Psychological Association.

Kelly, J. (1992). Does job re-design theory explain job re-design outcomes? *Human Relations*, *45*, 753–774.

Kemp, E. J. (1991). Disability in our society. In C. L. Weaver (Ed.), *Disability and work: Incentives, rights, and opportunities* (pp. 56–58). Washington, DC: American Enterprise Institute.

Kohn, M. L. (1990). Unresolved issues in the relationship between work and personality. In K. Erickson & S. P. Vallas (Eds.), *The nature of work: Sociological perspectives* (pp. 36–68). New Haven, CT: Yale University Press.

Kozol, J. (1991). *Savage inequalities: Children in America's schools*. New York: Crown.

LaFromboise, T., Coleman, H. L. K., & Gerton, J. (1993). Psychological impact of biculturalism: Evidence and theory. *Psychological Bulletin*, *114*, 395–412.

Landsbergis, P. A., & Cahill, J. (1994). Labor union programs to reduce or prevent occupational stress in the United States. *International Journal of Health Services*, *24*(1), 105–129.

Landy, F. J. (1985). *Psychology of work behavior* (3rd ed.). Homewood, IL: Dorsey.

Landy, F. J. (1992). Work design and stress. In G. P. Keita & S. L. Sauter (Eds.), *Work and well being: An agenda for the 1990s* (pp. 119–158). Washington, DC: American Psychological Association.

Lee, C. C., & Richardson, B. R. (Eds.). (1991). *Multicultural issues in counseling: New approaches to diversity*. Alexandria, VA: American Counseling Association.

McGaghie, W. C. (1993). Evaluating competence for professional practice. In L. Curry & J. F. Wergin (Eds.), *Educating professionals: Responding to new expectations for competence and accountability* (pp. 229–261). San Francisco: Jossey-Bass.

McGuire, C. H. (1993). Sociocultural changes affecting professions and professionals. In L. Curry & J. F. Wergin (Eds.), *Educating professional: Responding to new expectations for competence and accountability* (pp. 3–16). San Francisco: Jossey-Bass.

McKnight, J. (1977). Professionalized service and disabling help. In I. Illich, I. K. Zola, J. McKnight, J. Caplan, & H. Shaiken (Eds.), *Disabling professions* (pp. 69–91). London: Marion Boyars.

Moos, R. H. (1986). Work as a human context. In M. S. Pallak & R. Perloff (Eds.), *Psychology and work: Productivity, change, and employment* (pp. 9–52). Washington, DC: American Psychological Association.

Muchinsky, P. M. (1997). *Psychology applied to work* (5th ed.). Pacific Grove, CA: Brooks/Cole.

Murphy, L. R., Hurrell, J. J., Jr., & Quick, J. C. (1992). Work and well being: Where do we go from here? In J. C. Quick, L. R. Murphy, & J. J. Hurrell, Jr. (Eds.), *Stress and well-being at work: Assessments and interventions for occupational mental health* (pp. 331–347). Washington, DC: American Psychological Association.

Neff, W. S. (1985). *Work and human behavior*. New York: Aldine.

Oi, W. Y. (1991). Disability and a workfare–welfare dilemma. In C. L. Weaver (Ed.), *Disability and work: Incentives, rights, and opportunities* (pp. 31–45). Washington, DC: American Enterprise Institute.

Pederson, P. (1994). *A handbook for developing multicultural awareness* (2nd ed.). Alexandria, VA: American Counseling Association Press.

Quick, J. C., Murphy, L. R., & Hurrell, J. J., Jr. (Eds.). (1992). *Stress and well-being at work: Assessments and interventions for occupational mental health*. Washington, DC: American Psychological Association.

Quick, J. C., Quick, J. D., Nelson, D. L., & Hurrell, J. J., Jr. (1997). *Preventative stress management in organizations*. Washington, DC: American Psychological Association.

Quintanilla, S. A. R. (1990). Major work meaning patterns toward a holistic picture. In U. Kleinbeck, H. Quast, H. Thiery, & H. Hacker (Eds.), *Work motivation* (pp. 257–272). Hillsdale, NJ: Erlbaum.

Quintanilla, S. A. R. (1991). Introduction: The meaning of work. *European Work and Organizational Psychologist, 1*, 81–89.

Reskin, B., & Padvic, I. (1994). *Women and men at work*. Thousand Oaks, CA: Pine Forge.

Rosen, S. (1991). Disability accommodation and the labor market. In C. L. Weaver (Ed.), *Disability and work: Incentives, rights, and opportunities* (pp. 18–30). Washington, DC: American Enterprise Institute.

Rothman, R. A. (1987). *Working: Sociological perspectives*. Englewood Cliffs, NJ: Prentice Hall.

Rubenfeld, P. (1988). The rehabilitation counselor and the disabled client: Is a partnership of equals possible? In S. E. Rubin & N. M. Rubin (Eds.), *Contemporary challenges to the rehabilitation counseling profession* (pp. 31–44). Baltimore: Brookes.

Rubery, J. (1989). Women's wages. In J. Eatwell, M. Milgate, & P. Newman (Eds.), *Social economics* (pp. 282–288). New York: Norton.

Salifos-Rothschild, C. (1976). Disabled persons' self-definitions and their implications for rehabilitation. In G. L. Albrecht (Ed.), *The sociology of physical disability and rehabilitation* (pp. 39–56). Pittsburgh, PA: University of Pittsburgh Press.

Sapiro, V. (1994). *Women in American society: An introduction to women's studies* (3rd ed.). Mountain View, CA: Mayfield.

Sauter, S. L., & Murphy, L. R. (Eds.). (1995). *Organizational risk factors for job stress*. Washington, DC: American Psychological Association.

Sauter, S. L., Murphy, L. R., & Hurrell, J. J. (1990). Prevention of work-related psychological disorders: A national strategy proposed by the National Institute for Occupational Safety and Health (NIOSH). *American Psychologist, 45*, 1146–1158.

Schiller, B. R. (1989). *The economics of poverty and discrimination* (5th ed.). Englewood Cliffs, NJ: Prentice Hall.

Silverthorne, C. P. (1992). Work motivation in the United States, Russia, and the Republic of China (Taiwan): A comparison. *Journal of Applied Social Psychology, 22*, 1631–1639.

Singleton, W. T. (1989). *The mind at work: Psychological ergonomics*. Cambridge, MA: Cambridge University Press.

Skrtic, T. M. (1991). *Behind special education: A critical analysis of professional culture and school organization*. Denver, CO: Love.

Spraggins, R. E. (2000). *Women in the United States: A profile* (Census 2000 Brief No. CENBR/00-1). Washington, DC: U.S. Department of Commerce, Economics and Statistics Administration, U.S. Census Bureau.

Stubbins, J. (1988). The politics of disability. In H. E. Yuker (Ed.), *Attitudes toward persons with disabilities* (pp. 22–32). New York: Springer.

Sue, D. W., & Sue, D. (1990). *Counseling the culturally different: Theory and practice*. New York: Wiley.

Super, D. E. (1976). *Career education and the meaning of work*. Washington, DC: Government Printing Office.

Super, D. E. (1990). A life-span, life-space approach to career development. In D. Brown & L. Brooks (Eds.), *Career choice and development: Applying contemporary theories to practice* (2nd ed., pp. 197–261). San Francisco: Jossey-Bass.

Super, D. E. (1994). A life span, life space perspective on convergence. In M. L. Savickas & R. W. Lent (Eds.), *Convergence in career development theories: Implications for science and practice* (pp. 63–74). Palo Alto, CA: Consulting Psychologists Press.

Super, D. E., & Nevill, D. D. (1986a). *The Salience Inventory*. Palo Alto, CA: Consulting Psychologists Press.

Super, D. E., & Nevill, D. D. (1986b). *The Values Scale*. Palo Alto, CA: Consulting Psychologists Press.

Szymanski, E. M. (1999). Disability, job stress, the changing nature of careers, and the career resilience portfolio. *Rehabilitation Counseling Bulletin, 42*, 279–289.

Szymanski, E. M., & Trueba, H. T. (1994). Castification of people with disabilities: Potential disempowering aspects of classification in disability services. *Journal of Rehabilitation, 60*(3), 12–20.

Taylor, H. (1994, May). N.O.D. Survey of Americans with disabilities: Employment related highlights [Special advertising section]. *Business Week*.

Taylor, H. (1998, October 14). Americans with disabilities still pervasively disadvantaged on a broad range of key indicators (Harris Poll 56). Retrieved October 2, 2002 from http://www.harrisinteractive.com/harris_poll/index.asp?pid=152

Tinsley, H. E. A. (1994). Racial identity and vocational behavior [Editorial]. *Journal of Vocational Behavior, 44*, 115–117.

Trueba, H. T. (1993). Castification in multicultural America. In H. T. Trueba, C. Rodriguez, Y. Zou, & J. Cintron (Eds.), *Healing multicultural America: Mexican immigrants rise to power in rural California* (pp. 29–51). Philadelphia: Falmer Press.

Trueba, H. T., Rodriguez, C., Zou, Y., & Cintron, J. (1993). *Healing multicultural America: Mexican immigrants rise to power in rural California*. Philadelphia: Falmer Press.

Turnage, J. J. (1990). The challenge of new workplace technology for psychology. *American Psychologist, 45*, 171–178.

U.S. Equal Employment Opportunity Commission. (1991). *The Americans with Disabilities Act: Your responsibilities as an employer*. Washington, DC: Government Printing Office.

Warr, P. (1987). *Work, unemployment, and mental health*. Oxford, United Kingdom: Clarendon.

Weaver, C. L. (1991). Incentives versus controls in federal disability policy. In C. L. Weaver (Ed.), *Disability and work: Incentives, rights, and opportunities* (pp. 3–17). Washington, DC: American Enterprise Institute.

Webster's II new Riverside dictionary. (1984). Springfield, MA: Merriam-Webster.

Wegman, R., Chapman, R., & Johnson, M. (1989). *Work in the new economy*. Alexandria, VA: American Association for Counseling and Development.

Women's Action Coalition. (1993). *The facts about women*. New York: New York Press.

Yelin, E. H. (1991). *Disability and the displaced worker*. Brunswick, NJ: Rutgers University Press.

Zola, I. K. (1993). Disability statistics, what we count and what it tells us: A personal and political analysis. *Journal of Disability Policy Studies, 4*(2), 9–39.

Legislation Affecting Employment for Persons with Disabilities

Susanne M. Bruyère and Jennifer A. Brown

A focus on successful employment outcomes is at the heart of vocational rehabilitation services. Success in this process is markedly heightened when the practitioner has an understanding of the legislation that governs and supports employment of people with disabilities (Bruyère, 2000a). An understanding of the regulatory environment that governs the employment process is also crucial to effective job placement and the retention of persons with disabilities (Bruyère, 1999). The purpose of this chapter is to provide an overview of selected laws that support the employment of persons with disabilities, as well as legislation that affects policies and practices in human resources and the workplace.

A decade or more after civil rights legislation protecting the rights of women and ethnic and racial minorities was passed in the 1960s, people with disabilities began to see their civil rights protected—first in the provisions of the Rehabilitation Act of 1973 and later by the Americans with Disabilities Act (ADA) of 1990. More recently, legislation such as the Workforce Investment Act of 1998 from the U.S. Department of

Preparation of this chapter was funded in part by a grant to Cornell University from the U.S. Department of Education, National Institute on Disability and Rehabilitation Research, for a research and demonstration project entitled "Improving Employer Practices Covered by Title I of the Americans with Disabilities Act" (Grant No. H133A70005). The authors would like to acknowledge the assistance in the preparation of this manuscript of Sara VanLooy, research/administrative assistant in the Cornell University Program on Employment and Disability; Josh Ferrentino, student at the Cornell University School of Industrial and Labor Relations; and Thomas Golden, director of the Work Incentives Project, Program on Employment and Disability at Cornell University.

Labor and the Ticket to Work and Work Incentives Improvement Act of 1999 from the Social Security Administration have created state-specific structures that can expand the employment services and training available to individuals, as well as increase incentives for Social Security beneficiaries and recipients to seek employment.

It is imperative that rehabilitation professionals understand the protections and opportunities that these laws provide and how the regulations unfold at the state and local levels for implementation. Ethical rehabilitation practice and provision of services demand that counselors equip themselves as best as possible to maximize potential opportunities for the persons with disabilities served. Part of this responsibility is becoming aware of the legal environment that governs service delivery, in-kind benefits to individuals with disabilities, and workplace requirements that influence the function of workplace agents such as human resource professionals, health and safety specialists, and benefits officers.

LEGISLATION OVERVIEW AND PRACTICE IMPLICATIONS

This chapter provides an overview of key pieces of legislation that govern the delivery of rehabilitation and other employment services, as well as equal opportunity and affirmative action, for people who have disabilities in the workplace and in accessing other goods and services. The laws that are discussed include the Rehabilitation Act of 1973 as amended, the Americans with Disabilities Act of 1990, the Ticket to Work and Work Incentives Improvement (TWWIIA) Act of 1999, veterans rehabilitation legislation, and the Workforce Investment Act of 1998. An overview is also provided of laws that affect and govern workplace practices, such as the Family and Medical Leave Act of 1993, short-term disability laws, state workers' compensation laws, the Occupational Safety and Health Act of 1970, and the National Labor Relations Act. These laws are summarized in Table 2.1.

This overview is designed to provide a basic understanding of the purpose of these laws and their significance to the rehabilitation practitioner, as they govern or affect the provision of employment services and the employment and retention of persons with disabilities. Information is provided about the purpose of each law, its basic requirements, the agency that enforces it, and where further information can be obtained. Discussion of the impact on rehabilitation practice is presented within the discussion of each of the laws and is also summarized in the Conclusions and Implications section of this chapter.

(*text continues on p. 33*)

TABLE 2.1. Laws Affecting the Employment of People with Disabilities

	Purpose	Applicable Populations	Covered Entities	Responsible Agencies	Web Sites for Further Information
Rehabilitation Act of 1973, Title V (as amended)	Prevent/prohibit discrimination in employment by federal agencies, programs receiving federal financial assistance, and federal contractors.	The standards for determining employment discrimination under the Rehabilitation Act are the same as those used in Title I of the Americans with Disabilities Act of 1990.	Federal agencies (Section 501)	Individual federal agencies have their own Equal Employment Opportunity offices, which are charged with ensuring nondiscriminatory employment practices under Section 501.	http://www.usdoj.gov/crt/ada/cguide.htm
			Federal contractors and subcontractors with contracts of more than $10,000 (Section 503)	The Office of Federal Contract Compliance Programs of the U.S. Department of Labor	http://www.dol.gov/esa/ofcp_org.htm
			Programs receiving federal financial assistance (Section 504)	Each federal agency has its own set of regulations that apply to its own programs	http://usdoj.gov/crt/ada/adahom1.htm
	Ensure that federal electronic and information technology be accessible to people with disabilities, including employees and members of the public.		Federal agencies (Section 508)	Center for IT Accommodation (CITA) of the U.S. General Services Administration (GSA)	http://www.itpolicy.gsa.gov/cita

(continues)

TABLE 2.1 *Continued.*

	Purpose	Applicable Populations	Covered Entities	Responsible Agencies	Web Sites for Further Information
Americans with Disabilities Act of 1990, Title I	Title I of the ADA prohibits discrimination on the basis of disability in employment. Title II prohibits discrimination by state and local governments in several areas, including employment.	To be protected by the ADA, one must have a disability or have a relationship or association with an individual with a disability. An individual with a disability is defined by the ADA as a person who has a physical or mental impairment that substantially limits one or more major life activities, a person who has a history or record of such an impairment, or a person who is perceived by others as having such an impairment.	Employers with 15 or more employees	Equal Employment Opportunity Commission (EEOC), an independent federal agency	http://www.eeoc.gov
			State and local governments	Disability Rights Section, Civil Rights Division, U.S. Department of Justice	http://www.usdoj.gov/crt/ada/adahom1.htm
Ticket to Work and Work Incentives Improvement Act of 1999	Lower the barriers to employment for individuals who receive Supplemental Security Income (SSI) and Social Security Disability Insurance (SSDI) and encourage beneficiaries and recipients to access vocational services to assist their return to work. Designed to provide more vocational options for Social Security Administration beneficiaries.	The Ticket to Work Self-Sufficiency Program (Title I) applies to Social Security and Supplemental Security Income (SSI) disability beneficiaries.		Social Security Administration (SSA), Office of Employment Support Programs	http://www.ssa.gov/work
		The Expansion of Health Care portion (Title II) expands Medicaid and Medicare coverage to more people with disabilities who work.		U.S. Department of Health and Human Services, through the Health Care Financing Administration (HCFA)	http://cms.hhs.gov/twwiia
Veterans rehabilitation legislation	Grant rehabilitation services and preferential hiring status to disabled veterans of the U.S. Armed Forces.	Entitlement is afforded to veterans with disabilities rated at 20% or more.	Preferential hiring measures apply to U.S. government agencies and contractors.	U.S. Department of Veterans Affairs	http://www.va.gov/index.htm

Workforce Investment Act (WIA) of 1998	Consolidate, coordinate, and improve employment, training, literacy, and vocational rehabilitation programs in the United States.	Mandates that "core employment services" be eligible to all Americans. Core services include determinations of eligibility for assistance, intake and initial reassessment services, job search, placement and career counseling, and provision of vocational rehabilitation services. Recipients of SSDI or SSI are automatically eligible under the WIA for vocational rehabilitation services.	Provides assistance to state and local government entities in coordinating rehabilitation and other services for people with disabilities.	Employment and Training Administration (ETA) of the U.S. Department of Labor	http://www.doleta.gov/usworkforce/
Family Medical Leave Act (FMLA) of 1993	Require employers to provide unpaid leave (up to 12 weeks a year) for employees to care for newborn children, foster/adopted children, a relative with a serious medical condition, or the employee's own serious medical condition.	To be eligible for FMLA leave, an employee must be employed by a covered employer and work at a work site within 75 miles of where that employer employs at least 50 employees; must have worked at least 12 months (which do not have to be consecutive) for the employer; and must have worked at least 1,250 hours during the 12 months immediately preceding the date of commencement of FMLA leave.	Private-sector entities that employ 50 or more people for at least 20 weeks in the current or preceding calendar year. All public employers, including state and local governments and public school districts, are covered, regardless of size.	Wage and Hour Division of the U.S. Department of Labor's Employment Standards Administration	http://www.dol.gov/elaws/fmla.htm

(*continues*)

TABLE 2.1 *Continued.*

	Purpose	Applicable Populations	Covered Entities	Responsible Agencies	Web Sites for Further Information
State short-term disability laws	Pay covered workers with disabilities or medical conditions benefits for a relatively short period of time—typically 26 weeks.	Varies from state to state.	Varies from state to state.	Varies from state to state. Only California, Hawaii, New Jersey, New York, Puerto Rico, and Rhode Island have laws requiring such benefits.	
State workers' compensation laws	Designed to insure workers against the possibility of lost income due to injuries on the job.	Varies from state to state.	Varies from state to state.	All 50 states, the District of Columbia, Guam, Puerto Rico, and the Virgin Islands have workers' compensation programs, but there is no uniform nationwide administrative body. Each state or territory has its own governing agency.	http://www.ssa.gov/statistics/sspus/workcomp.pdf
Occupational Safety and Health Act of 1970	Ensure safe and healthful working conditions for working people.	All persons employed in the United States.	All employers in the United States, regardless of size.	Occupational Safety and Health Administration (OSHA) of the U.S. Department of Labor	http://www.osha.gov/
National Labor Relations Act (NLRA)	Protect the rights of employees to form, join, or assist a labor organization and to bargain collectively through representatives of their own choosing or to refrain from such activities.	Nonsupervisory employees engaged in "concerted activity" are protected.	All private, nonagricultural entities engaged in interstate commerce.	National Labor Relations Board, an independent federal agency	http://www.nlrb.gov/

Rehabilitation Act of 1973 As Amended

The congressional intent for the Rehabilitation Act of 1973 (P.L. 93-112) was to develop and implement—through research, training, services, and the guarantee of equal opportunity—comprehensive and coordinated programs of vocational rehabilitation and independent living for individuals with disabilities to maximize their employability, independence, and integration into the workplace and the community. The Rehabilitation Act, as amended, prohibits discrimination on the basis of disability in programs conducted by federal agencies, in programs receiving federal financial assistance, in federal employment, and in the employment practices of federal contractors. Entities that receive federal funding and the federal government must continually review their programs and activities to ensure that they are effectively serving people with disabilities. The standards for determining employment discrimination under the Rehabilitation Act are the same as those used in Title I of the Americans with Disabilities Act. Title V of the Rehabilitation Act is the section that governs employment nondiscrimination and affirmative action, and so it will be the focus here.[1] For purposes of this discussion, we will briefly mention Sections 501 and 503 and discuss more fully Sections 504 and 508.

Section 501 of the Rehabilitation Act requires affirmative action and nondiscrimination in employment by federal agencies of the executive branch.[2] Section 503 requires affirmative action and prohibits employment discrimination by federal government contractors and subcontractors with contracts of more than $10,000.[3] Section 504 of the Rehabilitation Act prohibits discrimination on the basis of disability in programs and activities, public and private, that receive federal financial assistance or under any program or activity conducted by any executive agency or by the United States Postal Service.[4] Section 508 requires federal electronic and information technology to be accessible to people with disabilities, including employees and members of the public.

Each federal agency has its own set of Section 504 regulations that apply to its own programs. Agencies that provide federal financial assistance also have Section 504 regulations covering entities that receive federal aid. Requirements common to these regulations include reasonable accommodation for employees with disabilities, program accessibility (i.e.,

---

[1] See http://www.usdoj.gov/crt/ada/cguide.htm for a further resource from the U.S. Department of Justice, titled *A Guide to Disability Rights Laws*, May 2000.

[2] 29 U.S.C. § 791: http://www4.law.cornell.edu/uscode/29/791.html

[3] 29 U.S.C. § 794: http://www4.law.cornell.edu/uscode/29/793.html

[4] 29 U.S.C. § 794: http://www4.law.cornell.edu/uscode/29/794.html

making sure that programs and activities do not exclude persons because of their disabilities), effective communication with people who have hearing or vision disabilities (e.g., documents in alternative formats or sign language interpreters), and accessible new construction and alterations. Each agency is responsible for enforcing its own regulations. Section 504 may also be enforced through private lawsuits. It is not necessary to file a complaint with a federal agency or to receive a "right-to-sue" letter before going to court.

The definition of *disability* under Section 504 was the basis for the definition of disability under the ADA. It includes any person who (a) has a physical or mental impairment that substantially limits one or more major life activities, (b) has a record of such an impairment, or (c) is regarded as having such an impairment. Major life activities include walking, seeing, hearing, speaking, breathing, learning, working, caring for oneself, and performing manual tasks.

On June 25, 2001, accessibility requirements for federal electronic and information technology (EIT) took effect under Section 508 of the Rehabilitation Act. This law requires that such technology be accessible according to standards developed by the Architectural and Transportation Barriers Compliance Board (the Access Board), which are now part of the federal government's procurement regulations.[5]

Section 508 of the Rehabilitation Act applies to all federal agencies when they develop, procure, maintain, or use electronic and information technology. The law covers all types of electronic and information technology in the federal sector and is not limited to assistive technologies used by people with disabilities. The Access Board's standards cover products that store, process, transmit, convert, duplicate, and receive electronic information, including computer hardware and software, Web sites, information kiosks, phone systems, fax machines, copiers, and similar technologies. Federal agencies must ensure that technology is accessible to employees and members of the public with disabilities to the extent that this does not pose an "undue burden." Retrofitting of existing technology is not required.

An accessible information technology system is one that can be operated in a variety of ways and does not rely on a single sense or ability of the user. An agency's obligation to provide comparable access under Section 508 is satisfied by acquiring EIT that meets the applicable technical provisions set forth in the Access Board's standards. The Access Board's standards also provide that agencies may accept EIT offered by vendors that uses designs or technologies that do not meet the applicable techni-

---

[5] See the Access Board Web site at http://www.access-board.gov/news/508.htm for information about these standards.

cal provisions but provide substantially equivalent or greater access to and use of a product for people with disabilities. This is referred to as *equivalent facilitation*, which is based on the recognition that technologies may be either developed or used in ways not currently envisioned in the future.

Americans with Disabilities Act of 1990

Title I of the Americans with Disabilities Act of 1990 extended the prohibitions against discrimination in employment on the basis of race, sex, religion, and national origin to persons with disabilities.[6] The goal of the ADA employment provisions is to provide equal rights to people with disabilities, thus increasing their labor market opportunities. Title I regulations apply to private employers with at least 15 employees, but where state laws are more inclusive, they may cover employers with fewer employees. The ADA employment provisions prohibit job-related discrimination against people with disabilities and require that employers provide reasonable accommodations. Therefore, those involved in vocational counseling and job development and placement for persons with disabilities must have an understanding of who is covered by the law and the principles of reasonable accommodation.

The ADA protects qualified individuals with disabilities from employment discrimination. In determining whether the employment provisions of the ADA cover an individual, it must first be determined whether the ADA's very specific definitions of *disability* and *qualified individual with a disability* are met. This is always a case-by-case determination. Under the ADA, an individual with a disability has a physical or mental impairment that substantially limits one or more major life activities, has a record of such an impairment, or is regarded as having such an impairment. Major life activities are activities that the average person can perform with little or no difficulty, including walking, speaking, breathing, performing manual tasks, seeing, hearing, learning, caring for oneself, and working. Mitigating measures such as medication or a hearing aid must be considered in determining whether an individual has a disability. A qualified individual with a disability satisfies the requisite skill, experience, education, and other job-related requirements of the employment position that such an individual holds or desires and can perform the essential functions of such position with or without reasonable accommodation.

---

[6] See the U.S. Equal Employment Opportunity Comission Web site at http://www.eeoc.gov/laws/ada.html for more information.

Providing a necessary reasonable accommodation for an individual with a disability is considered a form of nondiscrimination under the ADA. Reasonable accommodation is a modification or adjustment to a job, the work environment, or the way things usually are done that enables a qualified individual with a disability to enjoy an equal employment opportunity. The ADA requires reasonable accommodation in three aspects of employment: the application process, the performance of the essential functions of the job, and the benefits and privileges of employment. Examples of reasonable accommodations include making facilities accessible; restructuring a job by reallocating or redistributing marginal job functions; altering when or how an essential job function is performed; creating part-time or modified work schedules; obtaining or modifying work schedules; modifying exams, training materials, or policies; providing qualified readers or interpreters; or reassigning someone to a vacant position.

An employer is not required to provide a reasonable accommodation that would impose an undue hardship on the operation of the business. The concept of undue hardship includes any action that is unduly costly or disruptive. Factors to be considered in making the case-by-case determination of whether a reasonable accommodation would impose an undue hardship include the nature and net cost of the accommodation, the financial resources and number of employees of both the particular facility and the larger covered entity, and the covered entity's type of operations, including the structure and functions of its workforce and its relationship with the facility making the accommodation.

The ADA employment provisions (Title I) are enforced by the Equal Employment Opportunity Commission (EEOC). The EEOC provides continuing regulatory and policy guidance on implementing the ADA employment provisions, which is available on its Web site.[7]

According to EEOC statistics, 52% of the 108,939 charges filed from July 26, 1992, through September 30, 1998, related to alleged unlawful discharge. Thus, it appears that employers need assistance in navigating the requirements for workplace nondiscrimination at several points in the employment process. Employers are experiencing disability discrimination claims not just in the recruitment and application processes but throughout the employment process for incumbents as well. By helping to clarify the protections against disability nondiscrimination throughout the employment process, rehabilitation professionals can provide a valu-

[7] See http://www.eeoc.gov/policy/guidance.html for EEOC guidance documents.

able service to both employers and individuals with disabilities in the workplace.

Ticket to Work and Work Incentives Improvement Act of 1999

The Ticket to Work and Work Incentives Improvement Act, signed into law on December 17, 1999, was passed to provide beneficiaries and recipients of either Supplemental Security Income (SSI), Social Security Disability Insurance (SSDI), or both the incentives and supports needed to either prepare for, attach to, or advance in work.[8] The goals of the Work Incentives Improvement Act are to reduce and remove certain barriers to employment for individuals who receive SSI and SSDI and to encourage beneficiaries and recipients to access the services and supports needed to assist them in their pursuit of employment. At the heart of the act was a desire by Congress to increase options available to beneficiaries of the Social Security Administration's (SSA) disability programs by expanding on the existing network of service providers available and creating a more comprehensive set of supports for people with disabilities considering work.

The Work Incentives Improvement Act includes three important titles: Ticket to Work and Self-Sufficiency, Expansion of Health Care, and Demonstration Projects/Studies. As our focus here is on implications for rehabilitation practice, we will concentrate on the first two titles. Title I expands vocational services options for persons with disabilities. The Ticket to Work and Self-Sufficiency Program is an important provision of Title I. This new program replaces SSA's existing vocational rehabilitation program with an outcomes-based and market-driven program.

On a phase-in basis, everyone age 18 and older receiving SSI and/or SSDI will receive a "ticket" for vocational services. If an individual receiving SSI and/or SSDI seeks vocational services, he or she can give the ticket to any registered employment network. SSA is phasing in the ticket program nationally over a 3-year period that began January 1, 2001. Currently the program is active in the following states: Arizona, Colorado, Delaware, Florida, Illinois, Iowa, Massachusetts, New York, Oklahoma, Oregon, South Carolina, Vermont, and Wisconsin. Second phase states to be rolled out 2002 include Connecticut, New Hampshire, New Jersey,

[8]See the SSA Web site at http://www.ssa.gov/work/Ticket/ticket.html for more information on the Work Incentives Improvement Act.

Washington DC, Virginia, Georgia, Kentucky, Mississippi, Tennessee, Indiana, Michigan, Louisiana, New Mexico, Kansas, Missouri, Montana, North Dakota, South Dakota, Nevada, and Arkansas. The remaining states will roll out in 2003 and include Maine, Rhode Island, Maryland, Pennsylvania, West Virginia, Alabama, North Carolina, Minnesota, Ohio, Texas, Nebraska, Utah, Wyoming, Idaho, Washington, Puerto Rico, Virgin Islands, American Samoa, California, Guam, Hawaii, and the Northern Mariana Islands. As a state rolls out the program, tickets will be mailed to eligible beneficiaries within specific states over a period of 4 months with 10% the first month, 20% the second month, 30% the third month, and the remaining tickets in the fourth month. The Social Security Administration administers the provisions of Title I.[9]

The ticket program permits the individual beneficiary or recipient to choose from an array of service providers (called employment networks), placing control over provider selection in the hands of the consumer. The ticket program is purely voluntary, and beneficiaries and recipients can choose whether to use their ticket, decide who to deposit their ticket with, and decide at any point to retract their ticket from a provider if they feel the services they are receiving are inadequate. Under the old program, beneficiaries and recipients were referred to their designated state vocational rehabilitation (VR) agency and were either selected to participate by the agency or referred by SSA to select alternative providers who were willing to serve their geographic location and disability type. Although under the ticket program, beneficiaries and recipients can still choose to go to the state VR agency, SSA is now also recruiting other qualified service providers.

An approved service provider under the ticket program, the employment network (EN), can be a private organization or public agency that agrees to work with SSA to provide vocational rehabilitation, employment, and/or other support services to assist a SSA beneficiary or recipient to prepare for, attach to, and remain at work. Under the ticket program, a service provider can elect to become an EN, become a service provider under another EN, or both. A state VR agency can be a part of multiple employment networks across a given state, but each EN must have agreement with VR before initiating a referral to the designated state VR agency. An employment network that agrees to provide services can decide to receive either outcome payments for months in which a beneficiary does not receive benefits due to work activity (up to 60 months) or reduced outcome

---

[9] Further information about the ticket program is available through the SSA Web site at http://www.ssa.gov/work or on its toll-free number at 800/772-1213.

payments in addition to payments for assisting the beneficiary to achieve milestones connected with employment. In addition, state VR agencies can also select to receive payment as they have in the past under the "cost reimbursement option." This special status is in recognition of the fact that under the Rehabilitation Act of 1973, as amended, state VR agencies cannot deny services and supports to a consumer who is eligible. State VR agencies differ from other ENs in that the other ENs can make a decision to not accept someone's ticket.

Title II of the Ticket to Work and Work Incentives Improvement Act governs the provision of health care services to workers with disabilities. This section of the law attempts to reduce the disincentives to employment for people with disabilities posed by the threat of loss of health care benefits. Under this part of the act, states are encouraged to improve access to health care coverage available under Medicare and Medicaid. Under this provision, new optional eligibility groups are established, creating two new eligibility categories; in addition, the period of premium-free Medicare Part A eligibility is extended, and certain individuals with Medigap are protected. The Department of Health and Human Services, through the Centers for Medicare and Medicaid Services (CMS), administers the health care provisions.[10]

Veterans Rehabilitation Legislation

Various pieces of legislation have incrementally afforded rehabilitation services and preferential hiring status to U.S. veterans. The following discussion provides a brief overview of some of these laws, which may be relevant to rehabilitation services providers working with veterans who have disabilities. Modern-day efforts to address the needs of veterans date back to the post–World War I era and the Smith-Sears Act of 1918 (P.L. 65-178). Returning World War II veterans' interests and eligibility for rehabilitation services were addressed in the Disabled Veterans Rehabilitation Act of 1943 (P.L. 78-16; Wright, 1980). These provisions have been expanded several times: In 1950, benefits were extended to Korean War veterans disabled as a result of military action after June 27, 1950, and in 1962, rehabilitation benefits were authorized for veterans of peacetime as well as war periods. The Vietnam Era Veterans' Readjustment Assistance Act of 1974, as amended, requires government contractors to provide equal

[10]See http://cms.hhs.gov/twwiia/ for further information about the Medicaid buy-in program.

opportunity and affirmative action in employment to Vietnam-era veterans, special disabled veterans, and certain active-duty veterans who served during a war or campaign (P.L. 93-508). The Rehabilitation Act amendments of 1976 (P.L. 94-502) completely eliminated eligibility termination dates for seriously disabled vets.

The Vocational Rehabilitation and Employment program, administered by the Veterans Administration (VA),[11] helps veterans with service-connected disabilities who have a demonstrated employment handicap in two ways: Veterans who are feasible for employment are provided assistance in preparing for, obtaining, and maintaining suitable employment, and veterans who cannot work because of the severity of their disabilities may be provided assistance to improve their ability to live as independently as possible.

The services provided in this program that are needed to enable a veteran to achieve maximum independence in daily living include counseling, diagnostic, medical, social, psychological, and educational services, determined by the Department of Veterans Affairs to be necessary,[12] and a monthly authorized allowance[13] for such a veteran.

A veteran is considered to have an "employment handicap" if there is "an impairment of the individual veteran's ability to prepare for, obtain, or retain employment consistent with his or her abilities, aptitudes, and interests, and the impairment results in substantial part from a service-connected disability. For veterans rated as 20 percent or more, a finding of emploment handicap results in a finding of 'entitled.'" A veteran having basic entitlement may be provided a program of rehabilitative services during the 12-year period following discharge. The beginning date of the 12-year period is the day of the veteran's discharge or release from his or her last period of active military, naval, or air service, and the ending date is 12 years from the discharge or release date, unless the beginning date is deferred or the ending date is deferred or extended.

The Vocational Rehabilitation and Employment program's goals include assistance in finding and maintaining suitable employment; an evaluation of veterans' abilities, skills, interests, and needs; vocational counseling and planning; if needed, training such as on-the-job and nonpaid work experiences; if needed, educational training such as certificate or 2- or 4-year college programs; and supportive rehabilitation services and additional counseling.

---

[11] See the VA's Web site at http://www.vba.va.gov/bln/vre/index.htm for more information.
[12] Refer to the Department of Veterans Affairs Web site at http://www.va.gov for more information.
[13] Authorized by 38 U.S.C. Chapter 31.

Workforce Investment Act (WIA) of 1998

The Workforce Investment Act of 1998 was enacted "to consolidate, coordinate, and improve employment, training, literacy, and vocational rehabilitation programs in the United States" (quoted from P.L. 105-220). The Employment and Training Administration of the U.S. Department of Labor coordinates the Workforce Investment Act.[14] The act provides assistance to states interested in establishing statewide and local workforce investment systems to increase levels of employment, retention, and earnings of participants. The law authorizes development of a statewide system of employment services and a strategy of accountability to ensure that customer needs are met. Provisions of the WIA require states to compose workforce development plans describing how the state plans to meet the needs of its constituents, including persons with disabilities, and demonstrate how the plans will ensure nondiscrimination and equal opportunity.

Title I authorizes the Workforce Investment System. State workforce investment boards are to be established and states are to develop 5-year strategic plans. Governors are made responsible for designating local "workforce investment areas" and overseeing local workforce investment boards. The concept behind this approach is that customers of employment and training services will benefit from a "one-stop" delivery system, with career centers in their neighborhoods where they can access core employment services and be referred directly to job training, education, or other services. It is hoped that this approach will make it easier for individuals to identify the needed services and quickly move through the employment services systems, rather than having to go to a myriad of providers, as is now the case in most states.

Of particular importance for people with disabilities, the WIA mandates that the core services of "one-stop" systems be accessible to all Americans. Core services include determinations of eligibility for assistance, intake and initial assessment services, job search, placement and career counseling, and provision of vocational rehabilitation services. Core services are provided for youth and adults who meet certain state criteria for employment, income, and/or disability. All individuals who receive SSDI or SSI are automatically eligible under the WIA for vocational rehabilitation services. The one-stop service mandates 19 partners, including the state vocational rehabilitation agency.[15]

---

[14] See http://www.doleta.gov/usworkforce for further information on the Workforce Investment Act.

[15] An easy-reading resource on WIA can be found in the Institute for Community Inclusion newsletter, volume 8, number 2, March 2000, titled "People with Disabilities: Having a Voice in the

The Family and Medical Leave Act (FMLA) of 1993

The Family and Medical Leave Act of 1993 provides job-protected unpaid leave entitlement for eligible employees for up to 12 workweeks. An employer must grant an eligible employee up to a total of 12 workweeks of unpaid leave during any 12-month period for the birth of a child and care of that child, the placement of a child for adoption or foster care, the care of an immediate family member with a serious health condition, and an employee's own serious health condition.

A *serious health condition* is defined as an "illness, injury, impairment, or physical or medical condition involving: any period of incapacity or treatment connected with inpatient care in a hospital, hospice or residential medical care facility."[16] The definition also includes continuing treatment by or under the supervision of a health care provider that involves a period of incapacity of more than 3 consecutive calendar days, a period of incapacity due to pregnancy or for prenatal care, or a period of incapacity for a chronic serious health condition. Absences that occur as a result of receiving and recovering from multiple treatments, or due to a permanent or long-term condition for which treatment may not be effective, are also covered.

The law provides an assurance of employment for the individual upon return to work from such an absence. Upon return from leave, an employee must be restored to the position of employment held before leave began or to an equivalent job with equal pay, benefits, and other terms and conditions of employment. In addition, FMLA leave cannot result in the loss of any benefit of employment the employee earned or was entitled to before using FMLA leave. Group health insurance coverage must be continued by the employer while the employee is on FMLA leave, but an employee taking unpaid leave may have to pay his or her share of the premium.

The FMLA is applicable to any private-sector employers engaged in commerce, or in any industry or activity affecting commerce, that employs 50 or more employees in 20 or more workweeks in the current or preceding calendar year. Public agencies, as well as public and private secondary

---

Creation of the New Workforce Investment System," by David Hoff. For more information, contact David Hoff at the Institute for Community Inclusion, Children's Hospital, 200 Longwood Avenue, Boston, MA 02115, hoff_d@a1.tch.harvard.edu, 617/355-7486, 617/355-6956 (TTY).

[16]The definition of *serious health condition* comes from P.L. 103-3, Title I, Sec 101(11). See http://www.dol.gov/esa/regs/statutes/whd/fmla.htm. See http://www.dol.gov/dol/allcfr/ESA/Title_29/Part_825/29CFR825.800.htm for a restatement of the definition in the CFR regulations in the FMLA 29 CFR 825.800.

and elementary schools, are also covered without regard to the number of employees.

To be eligible for FMLA leave, an employee must be employed by a covered employer and work at a work site within 75 miles of where that employer employs at least 50 employees, must have worked at least 12 months (which do not have to be consecutive) for the employer, and must have worked at least 1,250 hours during the 12 months immediately preceding the date of commencement of FMLA leave.

The Wage and Hour Division of the U.S. Department of Labor's Employment Standards Administration enforces the FMLA.[17] This agency investigates complaints of violations. If complaints cannot be satisfactorily resolved, the department may bring action in court to compel compliance. An eligible employee may bring a private civil action against an employer for violations. An employee is not required to file a complaint with the Wage and Hour Division prior to bringing such action.

Knowledge of the FMLA is important for rehabilitation professionals who are assisting workplace incumbents who need to take a leave to deal with a chronic health condition. Moreover, employers often find it confusing to wind their way between the FMLA, short-term disability and workers' compensation requirements, and disability nondiscrimination laws (Bell, 1995; Scott, 1996). Rehabilitation professionals who understand the complexities of these laws can be of significant consultative assistance to employers.

Short-Term Disability Laws

The field of vocational rehabilitation focuses on facilitating the acquisition and maintenance of employment for persons whose disabilities are likely long term and severe in nature. Therefore, the idea of being familiar with short-term disability benefits may at first not appear directly applicable. However, both employer-provided short-term disability and sickness leave benefits may be of great assistance in helping an individual with a chronic health condition or exacerbated health issue for a particular disability to stay afloat financially through a critical period. Therefore, understanding the state laws and specific benefits available may help to guide the individual through what is sometimes a maze of requirements to determine eligibility for such benefits.

[17] See the U.S. Department of Labor's Web site at http://www.dol.gov for more information.

Short-term disability insurance is a cost-sharing program administered by state governments that has a provision to pay covered disabled workers benefits for a relatively short period of time—typically 26 weeks.[18] Short-term disability is also known as sickness and accident insurance, as it provides insurance against the risk of lost earnings. The benefit received is known as an income replacement rate and is equal to a percentage of a worker's weekly earnings (usually one half to two thirds). This is a form of cost sharing between employer and employee because the income replacement acts as coinsurance to the employee. Before benefits start, a waiting period is usually required; this is commonly less than 1 week. This acts as a deductible and the employee has to wait until benefits start, reducing what is known as "moral hazard," or the risk of abuse of the insurance program.

Some states and territories (e.g., California, Hawaii, New Jersey, New York, Puerto Rico, and Rhode Island) require that employers have such nonoccupational temporary (short-term) disability programs.[19] Across the United States in medium and large private businesses, approximately 55% of workers are covered by these benefits (Bureau of Labor Statistics, 1997).

In addition to short-term disability, which may be state mandated, employers often build a sickness absence or paid time-off opportunity into their employee benefits package. Paid sick leave is provided at the discretion of the employer and is available to about 56% of full-time employees in medium- to large-size private companies (and most public companies; Bureau of Labor Statistics, 1997). Sickness leave and paid time-off benefits are typically available to employees after a predetermined time in employment; this often is a 6- to 12-month waiting period.

Those providing employment services to people with disabilities may find that assisting individuals in clarifying eligibility for short-term disability and sickness benefits can be of invaluable help during a time of severe health setback or a need for a critical disability-related treatment. Salary replacement or paid time-off support can ensure that individuals get the needed time off without a loss of critical financial resources for themselves and their families. Employers are also increasingly looking to integrate disability resource teams within their own structure to more effectively manage their own health and injury-related benefits services (Murphy & Wille, 1999).

---

[18] For an overview of short-term disability laws (also known as state temporary disability benefits laws), see the *Compensation and Benefits Guide* (Bureau of National Affairs, 1997).

[19] For a detailed comparison of state laws, see the *Compensation and Benefits Guide* (Bureau of National Affairs, 1997).

State Workers' Compensation Laws

Workers' compensation is a social insurance program that is a collection of state systems designed to insure workers against the possibility of lost income due to injuries on the job.[20] Although all 50 states have some sort of workers' compensation laws, there is no single nationwide standard.[21] Typically, workers' compensation premiums vary based on the employer's industry, size, and past losses ("experience rating"). Workers' compensation benefits are a form of no-fault insurance in which employers agree to pay specified benefits to workers injured on the job in return for limited liability (Ehrenberg, 1988).

There are several areas worthy of attention for rehabilitation professionals in the workers' compensation area. Indeed, private-sector rehabilitation service providers often are either singularly or largely focused on these types of disability-related issues. However, all practitioners, whether in the private or public sector, can benefit greatly from understanding this system and using this knowledge to support clients with work-related injuries, as well as to provide guidance to employers who are sometimes confused about the interplay between disability nondiscrimination legislation and the state laws governing work-related injury (Bruyère, 2000b).

Five types of benefits are paid under the workers' compensation system. First, medical benefits are provided to injured workers. Second, temporary total disability benefits are paid to injured workers who temporarily cannot work at all but for whom recovery is expected. There typically is a waiting period, which varies across states, before benefits commence, and the benefits are specified as a fraction of preinjury earnings. This fraction, the income replacement rate, commonly is set at two thirds; however, each state specifies a minimum and maximum benefit level (the latter is often tied to average weekly earnings in the state; Ehrenberg, 1988). Compensation is usually calculated as a percentage of weekly earnings. This replacement rate acts as coinsurance, and the cost of the injury is shared between employer and employee.

Third, permanent total disability benefits are paid when an individual is permanently prevented from working at all. The structure of benefits is similar to temporary total disability benefits; in some cases, there is also a

---

[20] See http://www.ssa.gov/statistics/sspus/workcomp.pdf for more information about workers' compensation.

[21] See http://www.comp.state.nc.us/ncic/pages/all50.htm for links to individual state workers' compensation programs. See http://www.wcrinet.org/ for public policy information and research involving workers' compensation.

maximum duration of time in which benefits can be received. Fourth, permanent partial disability benefits are paid for injuries that are expected, even after the healing period, to result in permanent physical impairments and/or limitations on earning capacity and/or reductions in actual earnings. Finally, burial and survival benefits are paid on death claims, which are a small share of claims. Temporary total disability claims are by far the most frequent type of claims (Ehrenberg, 1988).

An additional point for rehabilitation practitioners to be aware of is that the interplay between workers' compensation legislation and disability nondiscrimination legislation, such as the Americans with Disabilities Act (ADA), is often a source of confusion for employers (Bell, 1994). Rehabilitation counselors can play a consultative role in clarifying for individuals with disabilities and their employers some of the significant aspects of workers' compensation legislation as it relates to the protections of the ADA. These include such issues as whether the injured worker is a protected person under the ADA, queries by an employer about a worker's or applicant's prior claims for workers' compensation, the hiring of persons with a prior history of occupational injuries and the application of the direct threat standard, reasonable accommodation for persons with disability-related occupational injuries, light duty issues, and exclusive remedy provisions in workers' compensation laws (Bruyère & DeMarinis, 1999). In response to the need for clarification of these issues, the EEOC issued an enforcement guidance concerning the interaction between Title I of the ADA and state workers' compensation laws that can be of great assistance to rehabilitation professionals responding to many of these employer questions[22] (U.S. Equal Opportunity Commission, 1996; Welch, 1996).

Occupational Safety and Health Act of 1970

The Occupational Safety and Health Act of 1970 has at its core the recognition that every worker has a right to a workplace that is free from recognized hazards.[23] When a potential hazard is identified, the Occupational Safety and Health Administration (OSHA), a part of the Labor Department, develops a standard against which workplace practices or conditions should be measured. Unlike some other employment regulations, OSHA requirements are applied universally to all employers, regardless

---

[22] See http://www.eeoc.gov/docs/workcomp.html for this enforcement guidance.

[23] Please refer to the Occupational Safety and Health Administration Web site at http://www.osha.gov for more information.

of the volume of business they conduct or the number of people in their employ (Rothstein, 1990). Three procedures exist— one for interim standards, one for permanent standards, and one for emergency temporary standards. Investigation and evaluation of a standard-warranting situation begin when OSHA becomes aware of pertinent information about that situation. With the exception of emergency hazards that require immediate precautionary treatment, a committee of no more than 15 members will be assigned to determine an appropriate standard within a 260-day period from the committee's assignment. The committee's recommendations are submitted and reviewed by all affected parties, comments are taken from interested persons, and a public hearing is held. OSHA then decides to accept the committee's recommended standard or to deny it based on stated reasons (Bureau of National Affairs, 1997).

After the implementation of a standard, the Labor Department can determine which workplaces will be inspected—either by the request of an employee in the particular workplace or at OSHA's discretion. Inspections are conducted with the permission of the employer and according to OSHA guidelines. Violations of a standard are punishable by government-ordered abatement and monetary fines, set according to the size of the business, the seriousness of the violation, the good faith of the employer, and the record of prior violations. Violations that result in the death of an employee are punishable under criminal law (Bureau of National Affairs, 1997).[24]

Some of the issues surrounding implementation of OSHA in the workplace that may affect employees with disabilities, and therefore the functioning of rehabilitation professionals, are the interplay of OSHA requirements with prohibitions against employment screening, medical confidentiality of records, and accommodations required under disability employment nondiscrimination laws (Bruyère & DeMarinis, 1999). For example, the ADA requires strict confidentiality of medical records. OSHA, on the other hand, requires employers to keep records of workplace injuries and illnesses and grants OSHA personnel access to such records in the interest of exposing potential hazards and their causes.

The ADA also places a limitation on employee testing, requiring that screening by the employer must be proven to be job related and consistent with business necessity. The ADA places significant restrictions on an employer's right to require preemployment physicals, make medical inquiries

[24]See the U.S. Department of Justice, *Criminal Resource Manual* (1997), available at the DOJ Web site at http://www.usdoj.gov/usao/eousa/foia_reading_room/usam/title9/crm02012.htm, for further information.

of employees and applicants, and require that employees submit to physical examinations. The ADA restricts access to such information in an effort to prevent potential discrimination. The Occupational Safety and Health Act, in contrast, requires employers to conduct testing in a variety of situations to ensure safety. For example, employees exposed to high noise levels are required to be included within an audiometric testing program, which includes, among other things, annual hearing tests (Taylor, 1995). The ADA's limits on employee and applicant testing may conflict with OSHA's need for testing in the furtherance of workplace safety goals and the employer's responsibility for the safety of all workers (Blais, 1999; Greenwald, 2000; "Fifth circuit," 2000).

Again, the confusion about how to navigate between these two laws is an area in which rehabilitation professionals can play a consultative role, helping the employer work through how to meet OSHA standards without needlessly screening out or discriminating against applicants or employees with disabilities. As case law around these issues continues to evolve, rehabilitation professionals and employment specialists can assist in helping businesses to address the questions that surface regarding decisions about workplace safety and the rights of employees with disabilities.

The National Labor Relations Act (NLRA)

The National Labor Relations Act, also called the Wagner Act, stands as the prevailing framework for labor relations in the United States, covering union–management relations in virtually every private firm in operation. The law, enacted in 1935, protects workers from the effects of unfair labor practices by employers and requires employers to recognize and bargain collectively with a union that the workers elect to represent them (Gold, 1998).

The NLRA guarantees employees "the right to self-organization, to form, join, or assist labor organizations, to bargain collectively through representatives of their own choosing, and to engage in concerted activities for the purpose of collective bargaining or other mutual aid and protection."[25] The NLRA is administered by the National Labor Relations Board (NLRB), which has the authority to prevent employers from engaging in unfair labor practices specified in the act.[26] The NLRB also ad-

[25] See http://www.nlrb.gov/rr.html for 29 U.S.C. §. 151–169.

[26] See the NLRB's Web site at http://www.nlrb.gov/ for more information on the National Labor Relations Act (NLRA) and the National Labor Relations Board (NLRB).

ministers union elections. Examples of unfair labor practices include acts of interference, restraint, or coercion on employees with respect to their right to organize and bargain collectively; domination of or interference with the formation or administration of any labor organization, or the contribution of financial or other support thereto; discrimination in regard to hiring or dismissing employees or to any term or condition of employment, in order to encourage or discourage membership in any labor organization; discrimination against any employee for filing charges or giving testimony under the provisions of the act; and refusal to bargain collectively with the representative chosen by a majority of employees in a bargaining unit deemed appropriate by the NLRB.

Seniority rights gained through collective bargaining are also among the most valued benefits of having a unionized workplace (Gold, 1998). Seniority rights are often exercised when a more senior employee uses this right to request an available alternate position or a change in responsibilities when the opportunity arises by a new position opening. Thus, an older or more senior union member may seek a less strenuous or more desirable position than more junior coworkers and fellow union members.

Reasonable accommodations for individuals with disabilities may present a problematic situation for employers and unions. Both parties are required by law to operate in a nondiscriminatory manner: The employer must accommodate a worker so that his or her essential job functions may be performed regardless of disability and must provide terms and conditions of employment that are free of discriminatory intent. The union must represent its constituency equally and consistently while allowing accommodations for people with disabilities to be implemented without unreasonable opposition.

These areas may result in conflict when applicants or union members with disabilities already employed seek to invoke protection under disability nondiscrimination laws such as the ADA or the Rehabilitation Act. The laws designed to protect the rights of persons with disabilities rely on making exceptions to or changes in terms and conditions of employment on an individual basis, whereas the nature of collective bargaining agreements puts the emphasis on the collective rights of employees.

Compliance with these laws may include dealings with the employer that fall outside the scope of the union's normal interactions, the implementation of an accommodation for an employee without union agreement, the appointment of a junior employee to a position traditionally filled under the seniority system, and the closing of medical records that the union may feel it has the right to access under the NLRA (Evans, 1992). Here, again, the rehabilitation professional can serve a consultative role between the applicant or union member who is an individual with a disability, the union, and the employer and assist in bridging the interests of all three, thereby minimizing conflict and maximizing union support in the accommodation process.

CONCLUSIONS AND IMPLICATIONS FOR REHABILITATION PRACTICE

The purpose of this chapter has been to provide an overview and preliminary understanding of the legislative and regulatory context that governs the rights of individuals with disabilities and the responsibilities of employers, including disability nondiscrimination legislation such as the ADA and the Rehabilitation Act, veterans rehabilitation legislation, and new laws such as the Workforce Investment Act and the Ticket to Work and Work Incentives Improvement Act. In addition, we have provided information on employment laws at the state and national levels that may affect the ability of an individual with a disability to access sick leave when needed to address a chronic health condition or disability resulting from an accident, get income maintenance or replacement during an absence from work due to an serious illness or disability-related condition, or win the support of his or her union in getting an accommodation.

Knowledge of these laws and their requirements can be of significant assistance to rehabilitation professionals who are helping individuals consider the benefits of moving from SSA benefits, seeking employment training, or trying to understand their rights on the job. In addition, equipped with such knowledge, rehabilitation professionals can serve a useful consultative role to employers who are trying to understand and fulfill their responsibilities under various employment and disability nondiscrimination laws that may sometimes conflict. This chapter is only the beginning of the process for professionals who wish to competently equip themselves in this area; additional resources are referenced in hopes of assisting the continuation of this process.

REFERENCES

Americans with Disabilities Act of 1990, 42 U.S.C. § 12101 *et seq*.

Bell, C. (1994). The Americans with Disabilities Act and injured workers: Implications for rehabilitation professionals and the workers' compensation system. In S. Bruyère & J. O'Keeffe (Eds.), *Implications of the Americans with Disabilities Act for psychology* (pp. 137–149). New York / Washington, DC: Springer/American Psychological Association.

Bell, C. (1995). Integrating ADA and FMLA into workers' compensation and STF policies and practices. *Employee Benefits Digest, 32*(5), 3–7, 12.

Blais, B. (1999). An eye on essential functions. *Occupational Health and Safety, 68*(9), 42–51.

Bruyère, S. (1999). *Working effectively with human resource professionals using the employment provisions of the Americans with Disabilities Act*. New York: Hatherleigh.

Bruyère, S. (2000a). The Americans with Disabilities Act: Where we stand ten years later. In *Directions in rehabilitation counseling* (Vol. 11, Lesson 3). New York: Hatherleigh.

Bruyère, S. (2000b). *Disability employment policies and practice in private and federal sector organizations*. Ithaca, NY: Cornell University, School of Industrial and Labor Relations Extension Division, Program on Employment and Disability.

Bruyère, S., & DeMarinis, R. (1999). Legislation and rehabilitation service delivery. In M. Eisenberg, R. Glueckauf, & H. Zaretsky (Eds.), *Medical aspects of disability: A handbook for the rehabilitation professional* (2nd ed., pp. 679–695). New York: Springer.

Bureau of Labor Statistics, U.S. Department of Labor. (1997). *Employee benefits in medium and large private establishments*. Retrieved September 8, 2002, from http://www.bls.gov/ncs/ebs/sp/ebnr0005.pdf

Bureau of National Affairs. (1997). *Compensation and benefits guide*. Washington, DC: Author.

Ehrenberg, R. G. (1988). Workers' compensation, wages, and the risk of injury. In J. Burton (Ed.), *New perspectives in workers' compensation* (pp. 171–196). Ithaca, NY: Cornell University, ILR Press.

Evans, B. (1992). Will employers and unions cooperate? *HR Magazine, 37*(11), 59–63.

Family and Medical Leave Act of 1993, 29 U.S.C. § 2601.

Fifth circuit disregards EEOC's ADA safety standard interpretations. (2000, July). *Supervision, 61*(7), 25–26.

Gold, M. (1998). *An introduction to labor law* (Rev. ed.). Ithaca, NY: Cornell University, ILR Press.

Greenwald, J. (2000). Ruling on safety issues. *Business Insurance, 34*(23), 23.

Murphy, S., & Wille, R. (1999). Disability resource teams aid cost effectiveness. *National Underwriter, 103*(46), 25–26.

National Labor Relations Act, 29 U.S.C. § 151.

Occupational Safety and Health Act of 1970, 29 U.S.C. § 651.

Rehabilitation Act of 1973, 29 U.S.C. § 701 *et seq.*

Rothstein, M. A. (1990). *Occupational safety and health law* (3rd. ed.). St. Paul, MN: West.

Scott, M. (1996). Compliance with ADA, FMLA, workers' compensation, and other laws requires road map. *Employee Benefits Plan Review, 50*(9), 20–22.

Taylor, R.W. (1995). Medical examinations under the ADA and OSH Act: A camarinan dilemma for employers. *Employment in the Mainstream, 20*(6), 23–25.

Ticket to Work and Work Incentives Improvement Act of 1999, 42 U.S.C. § 1320 *et seq*.

U.S. Equal Opportunity Commission. (1996). *EEOC enforcement guidance: Workers' compensation and the ADA*. Washington, DC: Author.

Vietnam Era Veterans' Readjustment Assistance Act of 1974, 38 U.S.C. § 4212 *et seq*.

Welch, E. (1996). The EEOC, the ADA, and WC. *Ed Welch on Workers' Compensation*, 6(9), 178–179.

Workforce Investment Act of 1998, 29 U.S.C. § 2801 *et seq*.

Wright, G. (1980). *Total rehabilitation*. Boston, MA: Little, Brown.

Employment Among Working-Age People with Disabilities: What Current Data Can Tell Us

Richard V. Burkhauser and Andrew J. Houtenville

To measure the employment of the working-age population with disabilities, it is first necessary to define that population. Unfortunately, unlike age, which is a relatively straightforward and easily measured demographic characteristic, disability has proven to be a far more controversial concept to define and measure.[1] In this chapter, we first discuss the conceptual issues related to defining the working-age population with disabilities and then, based on that discussion, use data from three major representative samples of the U.S. population—the Survey of Income and Program Participation (SIPP), the Current Population Survey (CPS), and the National Health Interview Survey (NHIS)—to profile the

This research is funded by the United States Department of Education, National Institute on Disability and Rehabilitation Research, Cooperative Agreement No. 13313980038. It does not necessarily reflect the view of the National Institute on Disability and Rehabilitation Research.

[1] Although there is little controversy over the objective standards for measuring age, the justification for using age as a standard for ability to work and for "age-based" welfare benefits is more controversial. For instance, the literature argues that categorical age is not a useful measure of ability to work (see Library of Congress, 1998). In addition, the Age Discrimination in Employment Act of 1997, which provides protection against age discrimination, parallels the Americans with Disabilities Act of 1990, which provides protection against discrimination based on disability. But if age is not a useful measure for determining ability to work, then should the Supplemental Security Income (SSI) program guarantee a minimum safety net on income to all those age 65 and older but not those younger persons in similar economic circumstances? The controversy surrounding these issues suggests that social concepts with respect to the rights and responsibilities of both older persons and persons with disabilities with respect to work have been undergoing major revisions over the past few decades (see Daly & Burkhauser, in press, for a fuller discussion of the underlying policy issues related to age or disability status as categorical standards for SSI eligibility).

employment experience of various subcomponents of the working-age population with disabilities. Finally, we discuss what this fuller picture of the work experience of people with disabilities implies for future policy.

CONCEPTUALIZING DISABILITY

There is no universal agreement on the most appropriate definition of the population with disabilities. Mashaw and Reno (1996) argue that the appropriateness of any definition of disability depends on the purpose for which it is used. They document more than 20 definitions of disability used for purposes of entitlement to public or private income transfers, government services, or statistical analysis. We begin with the definition of disability conceptualized by Nagi (1965, 1969, 1991). He distinguishes three components of disability. The first component, *pathology*, is the presence of a physical or mental condition that interrupts the physical or mental process of the human body. An example is deafness. This leads to the second component, *impairment*, which Nagi defines as a physiological, anatomical, or mental loss or abnormality that limits a person's capacity to function. For example, deafness limits the ability to interpret sound. The final component, *disability*, is an inability to perform or a limitation in performing roles and tasks that are socially expected. For example, a person with deafness is unable to use the telephone.

Nagi's definition is controversial because of the relative importance it places on socioeconomic environment in determining how pathology results in impairment that leads to disability. Less controversial is his recognition that disability is a dynamic process in which an individual's pathology interacts with the socioeconomic environment.

Using the Nagi concept, those with a pathology that causes a physical or mental impairment that subsequently limits one or more life activities—such as work—but who nevertheless work would not be considered to have a work disability. (This is the case whether work was possible through changes in the work environment, access to rehabilitation, or individual adaptability.) Hence the Nagi concept of disability is narrower than that of the Americans with Disabilities Act (ADA) of 1990, in which disability is defined as having a physical or mental impairment that substantially limits one or more major life activities, having a record of such an impairment, or being regarded as having such an impairment.

Alternatively, the Nagi definition is much broader than that used by the Social Security Administration (SSA) to determine eligibility for both Social Security Disability Income (SSDI) and Supplemental Security Income (SSI) benefits. In both programs, benefits are limited to those who are unable to perform "any substantial gainful activity" as the result of a specific set of medical listings (a combination of pathology and functional measures) or a combination of specific medical listings and vocational characteristics that predict little future work capacity. Clearly, the ADA definition is meant to ensure that a much larger group of people with disabilities are guaranteed access to work than are entitled to transfer income benefits by the SSA definition if they do not work (see Gordon & Groves, 2000, for a broader discussion of the definition of disability in the context of the ADA).

Here we use the Nagi three-part definition to categorize the questions used in three nationally representative data sets to gain information on impairments, work limitations, and eligibility for SSDI or SSI benefits into a consistent framework for measuring the work experience of different populations with disabilities. By doing so, we provide a more nuanced picture of various subpopulations with disabilities and their employment experiences.

EMPIRICAL MEASURES OF DISABILITY

Ideally, data collection efforts focused on capturing the employment experience of the working-age population with disabilities would have a purely random sample design and be sufficiently large to estimate relatively precise statistics for demographic subpopulations (by age, race, gender, etc.) in each year, in policy-relevant jurisdictions (states), and within and across key pathology or impairment groups. Because the consequences of the onset of a disability on work and economic well-being are profoundly different depending on when in the life course it occurs, it is important to have data over the entire transition—before and after the onset. Detailed information on health must be linked to detailed information on the social environment and important economic outcomes. In addition to self-reported health ratings, objective measures such as medical measures of health and function should be included. Information on possible pathologies, functional impairments, actual and desired assistive devices, actual and desired accommodations and social supports, environmental and social barriers, and actual and desired social roles should also be collected over time so that the timing of important events and their consequences can be evaluated. Employment, program participation, and income information should be collected. When survey participants make decisions, the survey should capture the full set of available options, including those not chosen.

No current data set provides sufficient information on the pathologies, impairments, functional limitations, environmental surroundings, and employment outcomes of a representative sample of the U.S. population to fully capture any of the definitions of the working-age population with disabilities discussed above. But major data collection efforts have been made to capture the employment experience of people with disabilities, and we will focus on three such attempts.

The U.S. Bureau of the Census collects data every 10 years in the constitutionally mandated census of every U.S. resident. The 1990 U.S. Census long form sample is a very large random sample of the population, but its information on disability is restricted to a single work limitation question:

> Does this person have a physical, mental or other health condition that has lasted for 6 or more months and which—Limits the kind or amount of work this person can do at a job? (yes/no) Prevents this person from working at a job? (yes/no)

This type of question is consistent with the Nagi framework of disability springing from a pathology that limits a social activity—work—but may systematically miss people with pathologies and impairments who are nevertheless working and do not consider themselves to be work limited.

The 2000 U.S. Census long form has an improved series of questions focusing on disability. They are as follows:

16. Does this person have any of the following long-lasting conditions:
    a. Blindness, deafness, or a severe vision or hearing impairment? (yes/no)
    b. A condition that substantially limits one or more basic physical activities such as walking, climbing stairs, reaching, lifting, or carrying? (yes/no)
17. Because of a physical, mental, or emotional condition lasting 6 months or more, does this person have any difficulty in doing any of the following activities:
    a. Learning, remembering, or concentrating? (yes/no)
    b. Dressing, bathing, or getting around inside the home? (yes/no)
    c. (Answer if this person is 16 YEARS OLD OR OVER.) Going outside the home alone to shop or visit a doctor's office? (yes/no)
    d. (Answer if this person is 16 YEARS OLD OR OVER.) Working at a job or business? (yes/no)

These data were not yet released at the time we performed our analysis.

Two other Census Bureau surveys are conducted much more frequently. The Current Population Survey (CPS) annually surveys approximately 50,000 U.S. households (about 150,000 noninstitutionalized civilians) and is the main source of official employment and income statistics in the United States. In 1981, the March Demographic Supplement of the CPS began to ask a question about work limitations: "Does anyone in this household have a health problem or disability which prevents them from working or which limits the kind or amount of work they can do? [If so,] who is that? (Anyone else?)" Like the decennial census work limitation questions, this question captures those who report pathology-based impairments to work, but it may miss those with such characteristics who are working and do not consider themselves to be work limited. The major advantage of the CPS is that its design and size allow for state-level estimates and that its work limitation question has been consistently asked since 1981.

The Census Bureau also conducts the Survey of Income and Program Participation (SIPP), a longitudinal survey of about approximately 14,000 to 36,700 households. The first easily usable panel began in 1988. The same people are followed every month over a period of about 2½ years. New samples begin every year or so thereafter. The SIPP allows for dynamic analysis of employment and program participation. The SIPP also contains information on limitations of daily activities, work limitation (similar to the CPS question), and a limited set of specific pathology and impairment categories. A few of the SIPP panels are linked to SSA administrative records that contain work, program participation, and earnings histories for many years before and after the SIPP survey.

Unlinked administrative records from the SSA and the Rehabilitation Services Administration are not random samples of the population with disabilities or even of the population eligible for these administrations' services. Such administrative records only contain people who apply for or use their services. Both those with pathologies and functional limitations who are integrated into the workforce and those who are not working but unable or unwilling to apply for services are missed in these nonrandom, choice-based samples.

The National Health Interview Survey (NHIS) is an annual cross-sectional survey of approximately 100,000 noninstitutionalized civilians conducted by the U.S. Centers for Disease Control and Prevention. The NHIS is used to monitor trends in illness, analyze access to health care and health insurance, and evaluate federal health programs. It contains detailed information on pathologies, impairments, and work limitations. Useful data are available beginning in 1983, but the NHIS was substantially changed in 1997. The major advantage of the NHIS is that it contains impairment-specific information. Furthermore, a subset of NHIS respondents is directly asked about pathologies (e.g., "deaf in both ears," "blind in both eyes") without first going through a work limitation screener question, which allows researchers to capture a random sample of the population with a given set of impairments, including those who report that they have no work limitations despite their impairment.

The National Health Interview Survey on Disability 1994 (NHIS-D), a special and separate study from the NHIS focusing on disability, represents a major effort by the federal government to capture the population with disabilities. The NHIS-D provides data on a set of pathologies, impairments, and activity limitations. A major advantage of the NHIS-D is that it contains extensive information on perceived barriers to work (e.g., lack of transportation) and work supports (e.g., accommodations). Loprest and Maag (2001) provide a useful analysis of barriers to work and work support in broadly defined populations with disabilities. However, small sample sizes within impairment subgroups limit the specificity of the pathology and impairment categories, and unlike the NHIS, which is fielded annually, multiple years of the NHIS-D cannot be pooled together to boost sample sizes. See Kirchner, Schmeidler, and Todorov (1999) for an excellent example of a pathology- and impairment-specific employment study using the NHIS-D. They perform a detailed analysis of the health and employment experience of those reporting serious visual impairments. See also the Web site of the Centers for Disease Control and Prevention at http://www.cdc.gov for more information on the NHIS-D.

In the next section, we combine results from the SIPP, CPS, and NHIS to provide a more nuanced picture of the employment experience of the various populations with disabilities than can be drawn from any one of these data sets alone.

CONCEPTUALIZING THREE DISABILITY POPULATIONS

Figure 3.1 illustrates how we conceptualize the interrelationships of the disability populations captured by our SIPP, CPS, and NHIS data. The square represents the entire working-age population. The largest circle within the square represents the largest subset of working-age people with disabilities captured in our data—those who report having a pathology or impairment. Each wedge represents people with a specific impairment. The NHIS data best capture this population. Although not represented in Figure 3.1, these wedges can overlap because people can have more than one impairment. The NHIS does not ask a global question on impairment, so we are not able to capture the entire population with impairments. We

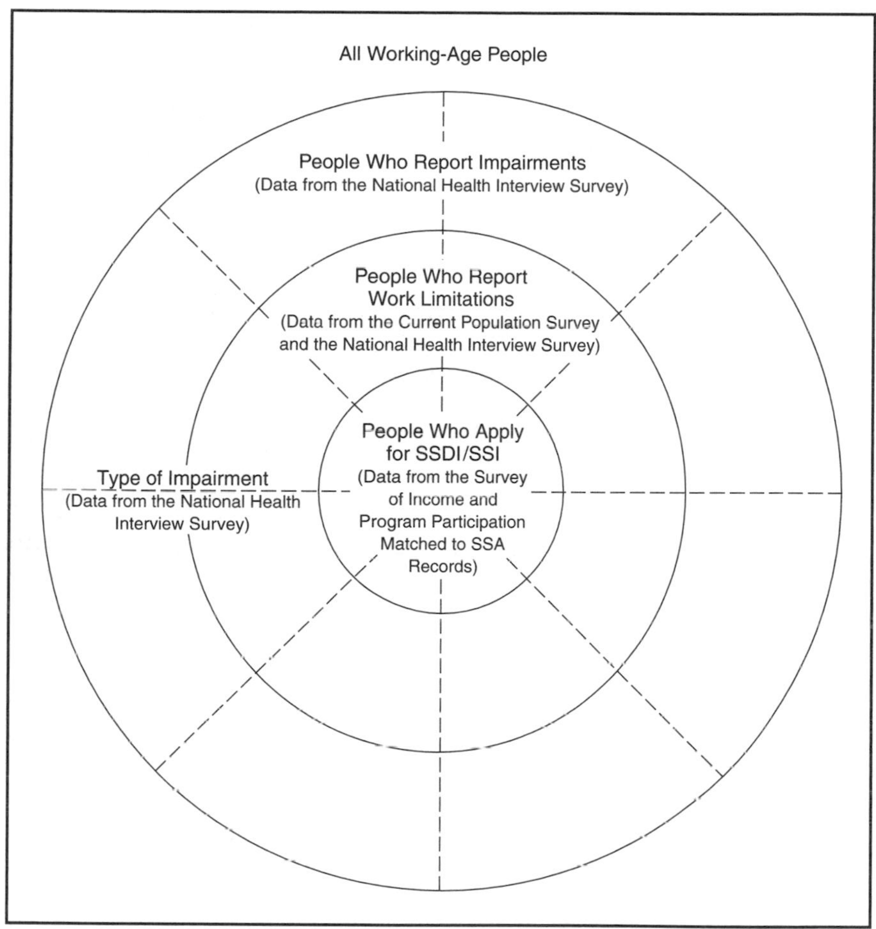

FIGURE 3.1. The relationship of operational disability concepts from the Current Population Survey, Survey of Income and Program Participation, and National Health Interview Survey.

are able to capture a subset of the impairment wedges pictured in Figure 3.1. This population is most closely representative of the ADA-eligible population, in that it includes both those who are working despite their impairments and may not even report a work limitation as well as those whose impairments and social environment lead them to report a work limitation.

The second largest circle represents people with impairments who report work limitations, also divided into impairment-specific wedges. This is the group captured by the general work limitation questions in the NHIS,

CPS, and SIPP data. It is most closely representative of the Nagi conceptualization of work disability.

The smallest circle represents persons with work limitations so severe that they apply for SSI or SSDI. This is only a small portion of the larger population with disabilities. The matched SIPP–SSA administrative records best capture the employment experience of this group. As before, impairment-specific wedges also separate this group.[2]

THE WORK EXPERIENCE OF THOSE WHO APPLY FOR SSDI AND SSI

Only those with the most severe pathologies and impairments, which substantially limit the kind and/or amount of work these individuals do, are likely to apply for SSDI or SSI benefits. Using SIPP data matched to SSA disability determination records, Bound, Burkhauser, and Nichols (in press) traced the monthly employment experience of those who applied for SSDI or SSI benefits in the 1980s and 1990s. Using multiperiod information, they estimated monthly employment rates from 36 months prior to application to 39 months following application for a random sample of SSDI and SSI applicants.[3] They disaggregated their sample by those who were awarded or denied benefits.

Figure 3.2, taken from Bound et al. (in press), shows that most who applied for SSDI benefits were employed 36 months prior to application. Their monthly employment rates decline thereafter and then fall precipitously about 12 months prior to application. Those awarded benefits have higher employment rates in the months prior to application, which then fall to a low of about 10% in the months just after application and remain at that low level over the rest of the period. Those denied SSDI benefits also reach an employment rate low of about 10% just after application, but 18 months after application, their employment rate slowly rises to about 35% and remains at about that level over the rest of the period.

Figure 3.3, also taken from Bound et al. (in press), presents a much different employment history for SSI applicants. The vast majority were not employed 36 months prior to their application for SSI benefits. Their

---

[2] Small sample sizes prevent us from comparing the employment experience of impairment-specific subpopulations in these data.

[3] They defined *employed* in a given month as having received positive earnings from work in that month. In Figures 3.2 and 3.3, they excluded dual applicants, those who apply for both programs. They used an unbalanced panel design so that employment rates are not based on data on the same population over the entire 7-year period. Rather, they reported averages of a different set of people each month.

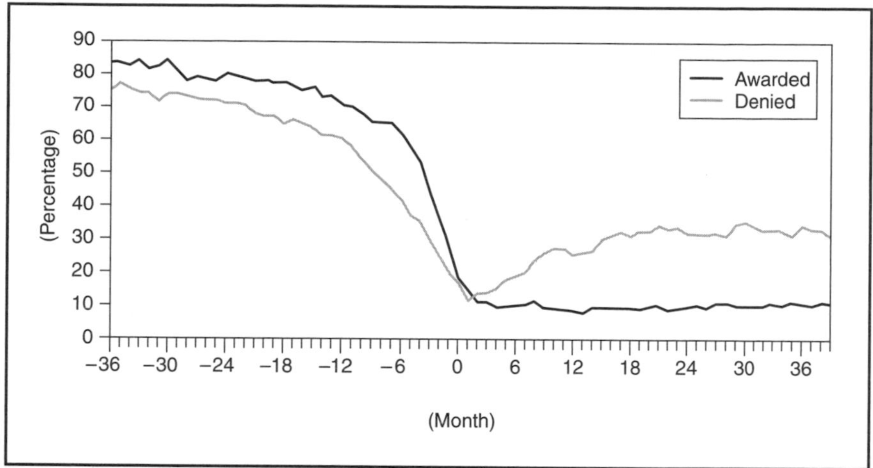

FIGURE 3.2. Monthly employment rates of awarded and denied SSDI applicants before and after application. From "Tracking the Household Income of SSDI and SSI Applicants," by J. Bound, R. Burkhauser, and A. Nichols, in *Research in Labor Economics*, by S. W. Polachek (Ed.), 2003, Oxford, England: Elsevier Science. Copyright 2003 by Elsevier Science. Reprinted with permission.

Any person reporting positive labor earnings in a given month is considered to be employed in that month.

Month 0 is the month of SSDI application.

These data are from matched Survey of Income Participation (SIPP) and Social Security Administration administrative records.

monthly employment rate remains low but relatively stable until about 6 months prior to application. Among those who were accepted onto the SSI rolls, monthly employment rates fall to a low of around 5% just after application and remain at approximately that level over the rest of the period. Among those who were denied benefits, monthly employment rates rise from a low of around 8% just after application to around 18% thereafter.

These findings suggest that even within the subpopulation with the most severe impairments—SSDI and SSI applicants—there are substantial differences in work experience. SSDI applicants are much more likely to be employed than SSI applicants both prior to and following application. Furthermore, those denied benefits (either SSDI or SSI) are more likely to become employed after application than are those accepted onto the program. Hence, even in this group, permanent exit from the workforce does not automatically follow the onset of a disability. Rather, policies that affect the work environment, access to rehabilitation, or the willingness and ability of individuals to make use of these links to the workforce may affect work outcomes. But they also suggest the limitations of such efforts.

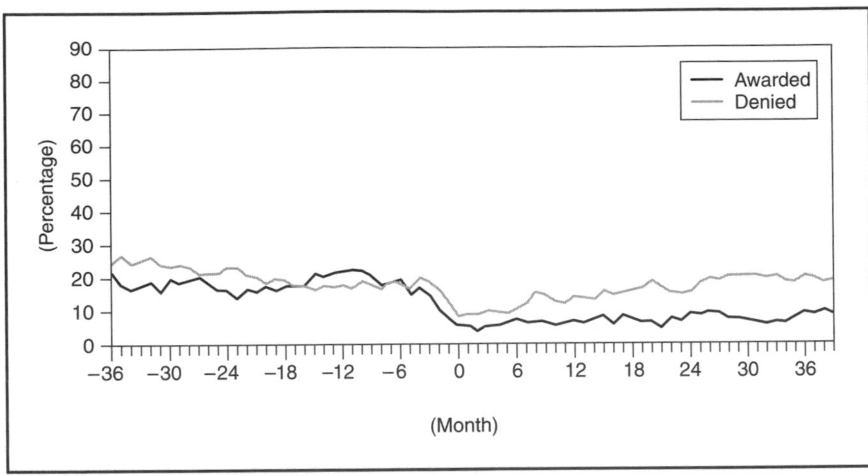

FIGURE 3.3. Monthly employment rates of awarded and denied SSI applicants before and after application. From "Tracking the Household Income of SSDI and SSI Applicants," by J. Bound, R. Burkhauser, and A. Nichols, in *Research in Labor Economics*, by S. W. Polachek (Ed.), 2003, Oxford, England: Elsevier Science. Copyright 2003 by Elsevier Science. Reprinted with permission.

Any person reporting positive labor earnings in a given month is considered to be employed in that month.

Month 0 is the month of SSI application.

These data are from matched Survey of Income Participation (SIPP) and Social Security Administration administrative records. Reprinted with permission.

Unless researchers identify and policymakers attend to the factors that prevent SSI applicants from working at a much higher rate than SSDI applicants prior to their applications, it is unlikely that medical-based rehabilitation interventions alone will move them into the labor force.

THE EMPLOYMENT EXPERIENCE OF THOSE WITH WORK LIMITATIONS IN THE 1980s AND 1990s

Here we report on the use of cross-sectional data to compare the employment trends of those with and without work limitations over the past two business cycles. Burkhauser, Daly, Houtenville, and Nigras (2002) traced the prevalence of work limitations and employment of working-age (ages 25–61) men and women with and without work limitations over the period of the 1980s and 1990s using data from the March CPS.

Although economic growth in the United States has been substantial over its long history, that growth has come through business cycles in which years of economic growth were followed by years of economic decline (recession years). The last two business cycles have roughly coincided with the decades of the 1980s and 1990s. The business cycle peak of 1979 was followed by declines in growth until the business cycle trough of 1982. This was followed by growth years until the peak year of 1989. Declines in economic growth followed until the trough year of 1992. The rest of the 1990s was continuous growth.

Table 3.1, from Burkhauser et al. (in press), shows the prevalence of work limitations among different demographic groups in the noninstitutionalized civilian working-age U.S. population over the survey years 1981 to 2000.[4] The prevalence of work limitations among all working-age people remained fairly stable at about 8% over these two decades, with no clearly discernable trend. However, the prevalence rate was generally higher among men, those ages 55 to 61, Blacks, and those with less than a high school degree.

Table 3.2, from Burkhauser et al. (in press), shows that movements in the employment rates of persons with and without work limitations were procyclical over the business cycle of the 1980s. Employment fell for both groups from the near business cycle peak year of 1980 to the business cycle trough year of 1982. Both groups' employment rate then rose over the next 7 years of economic growth. From 1989 to 1992, the 1990s business cycle trough year, the employment rates for both groups fell again as economic growth declined. From 1992 through 1999, the economy once again improved, and the employment rates of persons without work limitations once again increased. But unlike the 1980s, the employment rates of persons with work limitations continued to fall despite substantial economic growth in the economy as a whole. From the last business cycle peak year of 1989 to 1999, the employment rate of working-age men and women with work limitations declined 25.7% and 11.6%, respectively.

Table 3.3, which is a variation of a table in Burkhauser et al. (in press), shows that the decline in employment rates of men with work limitations leads to a shift away from their own labor earnings toward public disability transfers as a source of their household's income. The share of household income contributed by men with work limitations fell from 20.4% in 1980 to 15.4% in 1999, a decline of 23.5%. Over the same period, the share of household income coming from public disability transfers rose from 15.0% to 22.8%, an increase of more than 40%. Importantly, almost

(*text continues on p. 70*)

---

[4] Work limitation status is determined in March of the *survey* year, whereas employment and program participation is based on the previous calendar *work* year.

TABLE 3.1. Prevalence of Work Limitation Among Civilians Ages 25–61, by Various Demographic Categories, Survey Years 1981–2000[a]

		Gender		Age				Race/Ethnicity[c]			Education[d]			
Survey Year[b]	Total	Men	Women	25–34	35–44	45–54	55–61	White	Black	Hispanic	Less Than HS	High School	Some College	College or More
1981	7.88	8.15	7.64	4.02	5.93	10.27	16.84	7.28	13.65	6.96	16.33	6.57	5.26	2.92
1982	7.90	8.18	7.64	3.88	5.92	10.43	17.43	7.41	12.90	6.93	16.49	6.67	5.55	3.05
1983	7.48	7.81	7.17	3.82	5.65	9.67	16.73	7.05	11.73	7.21	16.18	6.18	5.43	3.02
1984	7.58	7.99	7.20	4.05	5.57	9.84	17.14	7.14	11.81	6.82	16.60	6.60	5.21	3.06
1985	7.83	8.23	7.45	4.09	6.03	10.23	17.54	7.16	13.16	8.07	17.29	7.02	5.57	2.92
1986	7.73	8.26	7.24	4.35	6.03	9.78	17.21	7.29	12.26	6.63	17.19	6.91	5.90	2.84
1987	7.67	8.19	7.18	4.41	6.21	9.48	17.03	7.18	12.37	7.06	17.72	7.04	5.27	2.81
1988	7.21	7.72	6.72	4.44	5.94	8.59	15.65	6.69	11.73	7.01	16.12	6.59	5.76	2.59
1989	7.23	7.64	6.84	3.97	6.25	8.96	15.99	6.85	11.08	6.24	16.89	6.66	5.50	2.59
1990	7.40	7.85	6.97	4.20	5.98	9.50	16.58	6.89	11.66	7.49	16.98	7.33	5.14	2.79
1991	7.45	7.70	7.22	4.40	6.28	9.37	15.80	6.90	11.92	7.30	16.80	7.35	5.61	2.95
1992	7.64	8.08	7.22	4.58	6.36	9.73	15.92	7.22	11.39	7.09	18.13	7.62	5.95	2.69

1993	7.78	8.39	7.19	4.83	6.53	9.71	15.57	7.45	10.77	7.72	18.24	8.01	6.46	2.63
1994	8.36	8.78	7.95	5.05	6.95	10.65	17.08	7.77	13.44	7.78	20.64	8.57	6.73	2.72
1995	8.33	8.51	8.16	4.67	7.32	10.62	16.65	7.74	13.36	7.83	19.33	9.07	6.85	3.03
1996	8.29	8.22	8.37	4.45	7.25	10.51	16.79	7.64	13.67	7.40	19.01	8.93	6.86	3.19
1997	8.30	8.25	8.34	4.31	7.13	10.57	16.92	7.81	13.34	7.00	18.68	8.92	7.25	3.18
1998	8.06	7.80	8.30	3.64	7.00	10.45	16.45	7.63	12.27	7.07	18.11	8.92	7.02	3.10
1999	7.92	7.97	7.86	3.81	6.70	9.95	16.16	7.35	12.88	7.22	17.28	9.01	7.10	3.13
2000	7.94	7.96	7.92	3.81	6.70	9.84	16.09	7.54	12.76	6.40	17.94	9.23	6.87	3.18

Note. These data are adapted from "Self-Reported Work Limitation Data: What They Can and Cannot Tell Us," by R. Burkhauser, M. Daly, A. Houtenville, and N. Nigras, 2002, *Demography*, *39*(3), p. 555, using the March Current Population Survey (CPS), survey years 1981–2000.

[a]Persons in the armed forces excluded. People are considered to have work limitations if they report having a health problem or disability that prevents them from working or limits the kind or amount of work they can do.

[b]In April of survey year 1984, sample weights based on the 1970 U.S. Census were replaced with sample weights based on the 1980 U.S. Census, and the sample design was changed to increase the accuracy of state estimates. In survey year 1994, there were several changes in the CPS, including moving fully to computer-assisted survey interviews. Sample weights based on the 1980 U.S. Census were replaced with sample weights based on the 1990 U.S. Census. The Monthly Basic Survey was revised, and three new disability questions were added. It is possible that these changes affected the measurement of the population with work limitations.

[c]White Hispanics and Black Hispanics are coded as Hispanic.

[d]Beginning in survey year 1992, educational attainment questions in the CPS were changed to reflect credentials and degrees rather than grades (years) complete.

TABLE 3.2. Employment Rates of Civilians Ages 25–61, by Gender and Work Limitation Status, Work Years 1980–1999[a]

Work Year	Employment Rate[b]			
	Men		Women	
	Without Work Limitations	With Work Limitations	Without Work Limitations	With Work Limitations
1980	96.7	42.6	69.2	28.5
1981	96.4	44.8	69.9	28.0
1982	95.0	41.7	69.2	29.3
1983	94.6	39.7	70.6	28.9
1984	95.7	40.3	72.5	30.2
1985	95.7	42.8	73.0	32.4
1986	96.0	43.7	74.4	32.0
1987	95.7	42.9	75.2	33.9
1988	95.7	42.9	76.6	36.1
1989	96.0	43.9	77.0	37.4
1990	95.9	42.0	77.5	34.9
1991	95.3	41.4	77.8	35.0
1992	94.7	41.6	77.6	34.2
1993	94.4	37.1	78.3	33.3
1994	94.8	37.9	79.1	36.0
1995	94.7	34.8	79.6	33.8
1996	94.9	38.2	80.0	33.9
1997	95.1	35.5	80.6	31.9
1998	95.1	34.4	80.7	29.5
1999	95.1	33.9	81.5	33.3
1980–1982	−1.8	−2.1	0.0	2.8
1982–1989	1.0	5.1	10.7	24.3
1980–1989	−0.7	3.0	10.7	27.0

(*continues*)

TABLE 3.2. *Continued.*

	Percentage Change[c]			
	Men		Women	
Work Year	Without Work Limitations	With Work Limitations	Without Work Limitations	With Work Limitations
1989–1992	−1.4	−5.4	0.8	−8.9
1992–1999	0.4	−20.4	4.9	−2.7
1989–1999	−0.9	−25.7	5.7	−11.6

Note. These data are from the March Current Population Survey (CPS), survey years 1981–2000. From *Relative Outcomes of Working-Age People with Disabilities Over the Business Cycle* (Cornell Rehabilitation Research and Training Center Working Paper) by R. Burkhauser, M. Daly, A. Houtenville, and N. Nigras, in press, Ithaca, NY: Research and Rehabilitation Training Center for Economic Research on Employment Policy for Persons with Disabilities, Cornell University.

[a]Persons in the armed forces are excluded. People are considered to have work limitations if they report having a health problem or disability that prevents them from working or limits the kind or amount of work they can do. Work limitation status determined in March of the *survey year*. The March CPS collects employment for the year prior to the survey, the *work year*. In April of survey year 1984, sample weights based on the 1970 U.S. Census were replaced with sample weights based on the 1980 U.S. Census, and the sample design was changed to increase the accuracy of state estimates. In survey year 1994, there were several changes in the CPS. It moved fully to computer-assisted survey interviews. Sample weights based on the 1980 U.S. Census were replaced with sample weights based on the 1990 U.S. Census. The Monthly Basic Survey was revised, and three new disability questions were added. It is possible that these changes affected the measurement of the population with work limitations.

[b]Individuals who report that they worked at least 52 hours annually in the previous calendar year, the work year, at civilian jobs or businesses, including temporary, part-time, or seasonal work, are considered to have been employed.

[c]When calculating percentage change, we use the average of the 2 years as the base.

TABLE 3.3. Share of Various Sources in Household Income of Civilians Ages 25–61 with Work Limitations, by Gender, Work Years 1980–1999[a]

	Men		Women	
Work Year	Own Labor Earnings	Public Disability Transfers[b]	Own Labor Earnings	Public Disability Transfers[b]
1980	20.4	15.0	9.6	13.7
1981	21.3	16.0	9.8	13.6
1982	18.9	14.7	9.9	13.8
1983	18.9	14.3	10.2	12.8
1984	19.6	15.7	11.2	12.7
1985	20.7	14.5	10.9	13.6
1986	20.3	15.2	11.7	13.0
1987	19.4	16.2	11.3	15.0
1988	18.9	17.0	13.4	15.9
1989	19.5	15.9	13.2	14.9
1990	17.5	16.7	12.6	16.3
1991	17.8	17.2	12.9	17.4
1992	16.7	18.6	11.9	17.8
1993	14.9	18.6	12.6	18.8
1994	16.5	20.1	13.0	17.6
1995	16.4	20.6	13.4	19.1
1996	17.3	20.6	12.6	20.5
1997	14.6	24.0	11.7	21.7
1998	15.1	23.2	11.7	22.8
1999	15.4	22.8	13.4	20.4

(*continues*)

Table 3.3. *Continued.*

Work Year	Percentage Change[c]			
	Men		Women	
	Own Labor Earnings	Public Disability Transfers[b]	Own Labor Earnings	Public Disability Transfers[b]
1980–1982	−7.6	−2.0	3.1	0.7
1982–1989	3.1	7.8	28.6	7.7
1980–1989	−4.5	5.8	31.6	8.4
1989–1992	−15.5	15.7	−10.4	17.7
1992–1999	−8.1	20.3	11.9	13.6
1989–1999	−23.5	35.7	1.5	31.2

Note. These data are from the March Current Population Survey (CPS), survey years 1981–2000. Adapted from *Relative Outcomes of Working-Age People with Disabilities Over the Business Cycle* (Cornell Rehabilitation Research and Training Center Working Paper), by R. Burkhauser, M. Daly, A. Houtenville, and N. Nigras, in press, Ithaca, NY: Research and Rehabilitation Training Center for Economic Research on Employment Policy for Persons with Disabilities, Cornell University.

[a]Persons in the armed forces are excluded. People are considered to have work limitations if they report having a health problem or disability that prevents them from working or limits the kind or amount of work they can do. Work limitation status determined in March of the *survey year*. The March CPS collects income for the year prior to the survey, the *work year*. In April of survey year 1984, sample weights based on the 1970 census were replaced with sample weights based on the 1980 census, and the sample design was changed to increase the accuracy of state estimates. In survey year 1994, there were several changes in the CPS. It moved fully to computer-assisted survey interviews. Sample weights based on the 1980 census were replaced with sample weights based on the 1990 census. The Monthly Basic Survey was revised, and three new disability questions were added. It is possible that these changes affected the measurement of the population with work limitations either in the sample weights or in the way respondents answered the work limitation question.

[b]Public disability transfers include Social Security Disability Income payments and Supplemental Security Income payments.

[c]When calculating percentage change, we use the average of the 2 years as the base.

all of the decline in labor earnings and the concurrent rise in public disability transfers occurred in the period from 1989 through 1999.

The pattern for women with work limitations is somewhat different. Women's own earnings as a share of their household's income rose dramatically in the 1980s, especially between 1982 and 1989. Their earnings fell substantially between 1989 and 1992 but returned to their 1989 level by 1999. Over the same period, the share of their household's income coming from public disability transfers grew, although like men, most of this growth occurred in the 1990s.

These three tables suggest that although the prevalence of work limitations did not dramatically change over the past two decades, the employment, labor earnings, and public disability transfers experienced by those reporting work limitations did. The decline in the employment of men and women with disabilities in the 1990s is both surprising and disconcerting for those committed to integrating working-age men and women with disabilities more fully into the workforce. As yet, the causes for this decline are not well understood, but the decline is real and too large to be ignored.[5]

The trends in prevalence and employment that Burkhauser et al. (2002) reported at the national level were documented by Houtenville (2000a, 2000b) at the state level. Houtenville (2000a, 2000b) pooled the March CPS from 1981 to 2001 to explore differences across states in the prevalence of work limitations and the employment rates of those with and without work limitations. Table 3.4, taken from Houtenville (2000a), shows that within the U.S. working-age population, there are geographic differences in the prevalence of work limitations. The average annual prevalence rate ranges from 12.2% in West Virginia to 5.7% in New Jersey. The five states with the highest prevalence of work limitations are West Virginia, Arkansas, Kentucky, Tennessee, and Mississippi, whereas the five states with the lowest prevalence are Hawaii, Utah, Nebraska, Connecticut, and New Jersey. Likewise, McCoy and Weems (1989) found that the highest rates of SSDI and SSI recipiency occurred in the "disability belt" of Appalachia and the lower Mississippi Valley. LaPlante (1993) reported similar findings using the 1980 and 1990 census.

Table 3.5, taken from Houtenville (2000b), shows that the employment

(text continues on p. 76)

[5] See Burkhauser et al. (2002) for a brief review of the literature on this topic and the validity of using CPS data to measure the employment rates of working-age people with disabilities. Burkhauser et al. (2002) found that the employment rates of those reporting work limitations in the NHIS are uniformly higher than the employment rates in the CPS over the years 1983–1996, but the trends in the employment rates of these two samples in the NHIS and CPS are not significantly different. See Burkhauser et al. (2002) for a fuller discussion.

TABLE 3.4. Prevalence of Work Limitations Among Noninstitutionalized Civilians Ages 25–61 in the United States and for Each State and the District of Columbia, Averaged Over Survey Years 1981–1999, and Corresponding State Rankings, by Gender[a]

	Total		Men		Women	
Location	Average	Rank[b]	Average	Rank[b]	Average	Rank[b]
United States	7.8	—	8.8	—	8.1	—
West Virginia	12.2	1	16.5	1	11.8	3
Arkansas	11.5	2	13.9	2	12.1	2
Kentucky	11.0	3	13.9	3	11.1	5
Tennessee	10.9	4	12.4	5	12.2	1
Mississippi	10.5	5	12.2	6	11.4	4
Louisiana	10.0	6	12.4	4	10.0	7
Alabama	9.5	7	11.0	9	10.1	6
Maine	9.4	8	11.5	8	9.4	11
Georgia	9.1	9	10.5	11	9.7	9
New Mexico	9.0	10	11.8	7	8.4	21
Michigan	9.0	11	10.0	15	9.9	8
South Carolina	8.8	12	10.0	14	9.3	12
Montana	8.7	13	10.9	10	8.3	24
Delaware	8.7	14	10.2	13	8.9	14
Oklahoma	8.7	15	10.5	12	8.6	17
Oregon	8.6	16	9.5	18	9.4	10
Rhode Island	8.5	17	9.4	20	9.1	13
North Carolina	8.5	18	9.7	17	8.8	15
Florida	8.3	19	9.9	16	8.3	22
Pennsylvania	8.3	20	9.4	19	8.6	18
Washington	8.2	21	9.3	23	8.7	16
Ohio	8.1	22	9.4	21	8.4	20
Idaho	8.1	23	9.3	22	8.4	19
Missouri	8.0	24	9.1	24	8.3	25
Vermont	7.9	25	9.0	25	8.3	23
Arizona	7.8	26	8.9	26	8.2	26
California	7.4	27	8.0	33	8.0	27
New York	7.3	28	8.1	32	7.8	29
Wyoming	7.3	29	8.5	28	7.4	30
Virginia	7.3	30	8.6	27	7.2	33
Indiana	7.1	31	7.4	40	7.9	28

(continues)

TABLE 3.4. *Continued.*

Location	Total		Men		Women	
	Average	Rank[b]	Average	Rank[b]	Average	Rank[b]
Massachusetts	7.1	32	8.1	31	7.2	32
New Hampshire	7.1	33	8.2	29	7.1	36
Texas	7.0	34	8.0	34	7.0	38
Minnesota	6.9	35	8.1	30	6.8	41
South Dakota	6.9	36	7.6	38	7.2	31
Colorado	6.8	37	7.5	39	7.2	34
DC	6.8	38	7.7	36	7.0	39
Wisconsin	6.8	39	7.7	35	6.8	40
Illinois	6.7	40	7.3	41	7.2	35
Nevada	6.4	41	6.7	47	7.1	37
Iowa	6.4	42	7.1	45	6.6	43
Maryland	6.3	43	7.2	42	6.3	44
Kansas	6.2	44	6.7	46	6.6	42
North Dakota	6.2	45	7.2	43	6.0	49
Alaska	6.1	46	7.2	44	6.0	48
Hawaii	6.1	47	7.6	37	5.6	51
Utah	5.9	48	6.4	49	6.1	47
Nebraska	5.8	49	6.5	48	5.9	50
Connecticut	5.8	50	6.1	50	6.2	45
New Jersey	5.7	51	6.0	51	6.1	46

Note. These data are from the March Current Population Survey (CPS), survey years 1981–1999. From *Economics of Disability Research Report #2: Estimates of Employment Rates for Persons with a Disability in the United States by State, 1980 through 1998* (pp. 24–25), by A. Houtenville, 2000, Ithaca, NY: Research and Rehabilitation Training Center for Economic Research on Employment Policy for Persons with Disabilities, Cornell University. Copyright 2000 by Cornell University. Reprinted with permission.

[a]Persons in the armed forces are excluded. People are considered to have work limitations if they report having a health problem or disability that prevents them from working or limits the kind or amount of work they can do. Work limitation status determined in March of the survey year. In April of survey year 1984, sample weights based on the 1970 U.S. Census were replaced with sample weights based on the 1980 U.S. Census, and the sample design was changed to increase the accuracy of state estimates. In survey year 1994, there were several changes in the CPS. It moved fully to computer-assisted survey interviews. Sample weights based on the 1980 U.S. Census were replaced with sample weights based on the 1990 U.S. Census. The Monthly Basic Survey was revised, and three new disability questions were added. It is possible that these changes affected the measurement of the population with work limitations either in the sample weights or in the way respondents answered the work limitation question.

[b]Looking at the employment rates, some states appear to be tied and thus should have the same rank. However, the rankings are based on prevalence rates to the third decimal place. There were no ties.

TABLE 3.5. Employment and Relative Employment Rates of Noninstitutionalized Civilians Ages 25–61 for the United States and for Each State and the District of Columbia, over the Period of Work Years 1980–1998, and Rankings, by Gender and Work Limitation Status[a]

	Men				Women			
	Employment Rate[b]				Employment Rate[b]			
Location	Without Work Limitations	With Work Limitations	Relative Employment[c]	Ranked by Relative Employment[d]	Without Work Limitations	With Work Limitations	Relative Employment[c]	Ranked by Relative Employment[d]
United States	95.4	40.5	42.4	—	75.8	32.6	43.1	—
Minnesota	97.5	62.5	64.1	1	84.1	57.0	67.7	1
Wyoming	97.3	61.4	63.0	2	79.2	46.9	59.2	5
Utah	97.4	59.5	61.1	3	73.8	44.5	60.3	2
North Dakota	97.6	57.3	58.8	4	80.3	47.8	59.6	4
Oregon	95.5	54.9	57.4	5	78.7	42.1	53.4	16
Connecticut	96.4	55.1	57.2	6	80.0	43.8	54.8	12
Alaska	95.5	54.1	56.7	7	78.9	46.5	58.9	6
Idaho	97.4	55.1	56.6	8	78.7	44.5	56.6	8
Colorado	96.8	54.5	56.3	9	80.4	44.2	55.0	11
South Dakota	97.1	54.3	56.0	10	83.4	49.8	59.7	3
Montana	96.4	53.1	55.1	11	80.2	43.9	54.8	13
Nebraska	97.9	53.6	54.7	12	81.5	44.3	54.4	14
Iowa	97.3	52.8	54.2	13	81.1	43.6	53.8	15
Nevada	95.9	51.7	53.9	14	79.4	44.7	56.3	9
Washington	96.0	51.7	53.9	15	77.0	38.3	49.8	20
Kansas	97.6	52.1	53.4	16	81.2	44.7	55.1	10

(continues)

TABLE 3.5 *Continued.*

Location	Men				Women			
	Employment Rate[b]				Employment Rate[b]			
	Without Work Limitations	With Work Limitations	Relative Employment[c]	Ranked by Relative Employment[d]	Without Work Limitations	With Work Limitations	Relative Employment[c]	Ranked by Relative Employment[d]
New Hampshire	97.6	51.4	52.7	17	81.7	41.9	51.3	19
Vermont	97.4	50.7	52.1	18	83.7	44.4	53.1	17
Wisconsin	97.1	50.4	51.9	19	82.7	47.2	57.1	7
Arizona	95.4	48.4	50.7	20	74.3	38.3	51.6	18
Maryland	95.5	45.4	47.6	21	80.1	32.3	40.3	35
Oklahoma	95.7	44.3	46.3	22	76.1	34.1	44.9	27
Texas	96.4	43.8	45.4	23	74.8	36.7	49.0	21
Delaware	96.6	43.6	45.1	24	79.5	35.9	45.1	26
Missouri	95.6	42.0	43.9	25	79.5	36.4	45.9	24
Michigan	94.2	41.0	43.5	26	73.8	29.7	40.3	34
Massachusetts	95.9	41.2	43.0	27	79.1	32.7	41.4	33
California	94.3	40.3	42.7	28	73.5	34.5	46.9	23
Indiana	95.9	40.8	42.5	29	78.0	32.3	41.4	32
Florida	95.1	40.1	42.1	30	76.3	33.4	43.8	29
Maine	96.2	40.1	41.7	31	79.7	36.0	45.2	25
Rhode Island	95.8	39.7	41.5	32	80.1	33.6	42.0	31
Hawaii	93.8	38.7	41.3	33	79.5	38.0	47.7	22
New Jersey	96.1	39.5	41.1	34	74.9	32.7	43.7	30
Illinois	95.1	39.1	41.1	35	75.3	29.5	39.2	37

Virginia	97.0	38.7	39.9	36	78.9	30.5	38.7	39
Georgia	96.6	38.6	39.9	37	78.3	29.9	38.2	41
North Carolina	96.3	37.8	39.2	38	80.9	30.7	37.9	43
Ohio	95.6	36.5	38.2	39	74.0	28.5	38.5	40
New Mexico	94.2	35.9	38.1	40	71.7	32.0	44.6	28
Pennsylvania	95.1	35.9	37.7	41	72.8	28.5	39.1	38
Tennessee	94.8	34.9	36.8	42	76.0	25.1	32.9	48
Arkansas	95.6	35.1	36.7	43	76.8	30.5	39.7	36
New York	93.7	33.7	36.0	44	70.6	26.5	37.5	44
Mississippi	94.9	33.3	35.1	45	74.7	22.3	29.8	51
Louisiana	94.6	33.0	34.9	46	69.2	23.7	34.2	46
DC	89.9	30.8	34.3	47	83.3	28.6	34.3	45
Kentucky	95.5	31.2	32.6	48	72.7	24.3	33.5	47
South Carolina	95.4	30.2	31.6	49	77.1	29.3	38.1	42
Alabama	95.1	27.5	28.9	50	73.1	23.0	31.5	49
West Virginia	92.3	26.1	28.3	51	63.4	19.9	31.3	50

Note. These data are from the March Current Population Survey (CPS), survey years 1981–1999. From *Economics of Disability Research Report #2: Estimates of Employment Rates for Persons with a Disability in the United States by State, 1980 through 1998* (pp. 20–21), by A. Houtenville, 2000, Ithaca, NY: Research and Rehabilitation Training Center for Economic Research on Employment Policy for Persons with Disabilities, Cornell University. Copyright 2000 by Cornell University. Reprinted with permission.

[a]Persons in the armed forces are excluded. Persons are considered to have a work limitation if they report having a health problem or disability that prevents them from working or limits the kind or amount of work they can do. Work limitation status determined in March of the survey year.

[b]Individuals who report that they worked at least 52 hours annually in the previous calendar year, the work year, at civilian jobs or businesses, including temporary, part-time, or seasonal work, are considered to have been employed.

[c]Relative employment is defined as the employment of those with work limitations as a percentage of the employment of those without work limitations.

[d]Looking at the employment rates, some states appear to be tied and thus should have the same rank. However, the rankings are based on employment rates to the third decimal place. There were no ties.

rates of men and women with work limitations vary greatly across the states. State annual employment rates are averaged for the period 1980 through 1998.[6] To control for variations in the economic conditions in the states, employment rates of men with work limitations are also shown relative to those of men without work limitations in each state. Minnesota has the highest relative employment rate for men with work limitations (64.1%) and West Virginia has the lowest (28.3%). For women with work limitations, relative employment rates range from 67.7% in Minnesota to 29.8% in Mississippi.

It is not surprising that the prevalence of work limitations varies substantially across states. But the dramatic difference in the relative employment rates of those with work limitations is quite surprising. Clearly, the gap between the 64.1% ratio in Minnesota and the 28.3% ratio in West Virginia cannot be accounted for solely by differences in the severity of the underlying pathologies and impairments of the work limitations for men in these two states. Nor can it be fully be accounted for by differences in demographic characteristics (e.g., age, race) relative to men without work limitations. It is much more likely to be related to the work environment, access to rehabilitation, and the incentive structure for work found in each state. This is further evidence that disability is both a health- and an environment-driven phenomenon.

THE EMPLOYMENT EXPERIENCE OF THOSE WITH SPECIFIC PATHOLOGIES OR IMPAIRMENTS

In this section, we move to the outermost circle in Figure 3.1 and look at the work experience of men and women who report a specific pathology or impairment. Data limitations prevent us from capturing the entire population with pathologies or impairments, but we can demonstrate that this population is larger than that captured by the Nagi concept of work limitation.

It is not possible to contrast the different employment experiences of the impairment-based disability population with that of the population with work limitations using CPS data or with the SSDI–SSI applicant population using SIPP–SSA data. The CPS contains no questions on an individual's health conditions or impairments. Although it is theoretically possible

[6]Recall that CPS information on employment is based on the previous year.

to capture an impairment-based disability population with SIPP–SSA administrative records data, the samples are too small.

However, Houtenville (2002) compared an impairment-based disability population to a work limitation-based disability population using the NHIS, focusing on the employment of those with visual impairments. To do so, he used a representative subsample of NHIS respondents for the years 1983–1996 based on their responses to a set of questions about specific impairments. Although some in this impairment-based subsample had a work limitation and therefore would have been included in a work limitations-based subsample, others did not report a work limitation and therefore would not have been included in a work limitations-based subsample. This impairment-based disability subsample was most closely representative of the ADA population. Houtenville then compared a representative sample of persons reporting a particular impairment to a population drawn from those who first reported a work limitation or some other health-related indicator (e.g., sick days, doctor's visits) and then a particular impairment. This was a choice-based sample because it excluded those who had impairments who did not first report a work limitation or other health-related indicators. Houtenville found that the employment rates in the random sample were significantly larger than in the choice-based sample. This is an important finding because it is the first to demonstrate that choice-based samples such as those drawn from the CPS significantly underestimate the employment experience of the population most closely representative of the ADA-eligible population.

In the tables that follow, we expand on this insight by first showing the prevalence of several different pathologies or impairments in the working-age population and comparing them to the prevalence among those who report both those impairments and a work limitation. We find a dramatic difference in the employment rates of these two conceptually different populations, which for a given impairment can be considered the employment rates for the middle and outer circles of Figure 3.1. We use NHIS pathology or impairment categories and their names in the categories below.

Because the prevalence of specific impairments is very low in any given year, we must pool the NHIS data over a number of years to establish a sample size sufficient for analysis. Table 3.6 reports the prevalence for various pathologies or impairments among working-age men and women pooled over the years 1983 through 1996.

Column 1 of Table 3.6 shows the percentage of men who report having one of the impairments in the list. Column 2 shows the percentage of men who report having both an impairment and a work limitation.[7] The values

[7]Note that their work limitation need not be caused by the impairment.

in column 2 are always smaller than or equal to the values in column 1 because the numerators of column 2 values exclude persons with impairment who do not report a work limitation. Column 3 contains the ratio of column 2 to column 1. When the value in column 2 equals its counterpart in column 1, then every person reporting that impairment also reports being work limited, and the value in column 3 equals 1.00. The closer the values in column 3 are to 1.00, the greater the proportion of men reporting those impairments who also report a work limitation. Columns 4, 5, and 6 contain the same information for women.

Table 3.6 shows that the population within the outermost circle in Figure 3.1 is dramatically understated if we use a choice-based work limitation question or the choice-based sample in the NHIS to describe it.[8] In essence, a work limitation-based disability population ignores people with impairments who are sufficiently integrated into the workforce such that they do not report being work limited. The importance of this becomes clearer if we consider an impairment that might be expected to generate an overwhelmingly positive response to a work limitation question. For instance, only 35% (65%) of men who report being deaf (blind) in both ears (eyes) also report being unable to work or to be limited in the kind or amount of work they do. Although the severity of the impairment undoubtedly explains much of the variance in the ratios reported in columns 3 and 6, it does not explain all of it. This suggests that this ratio can be influenced by the work environment, rehabilitation opportunities, or the inner capacity of individuals to overcome both their pathologies and the barriers to work they face. There is no global question in the NHIS, SIPP, or CPS that attempts to capture all those who have impairments or, more broadly, who would be considered to have a disability under the ADA.

Table 3.7 shows the employment rates of those with impairments and those with both impairments and work limitations, as well as the ratio of these two values, for both men and women. Although the employment rate of men with work limitations in the entire population (47.7%) is close to that found in our CPS data in Table 3.3, the employment rate of the entire population with these impairments is far higher (81.5%). The employment rate of the middle circle of our Figure 3.1 conceptualization of disability is substantially lower than that of the largest circle.

Table 3.7 also provides information about specific impairment groups.

(text continues on p. 83)

[8] Trupin, Sebesta, Yelin, and LaPlante (1997) used NHIS over the period 1983 to 1994 to look at time trends in labor force participation rates of many different pathology or impairment categories, but they restricted their sample to those who first report activity limitations and then the primary pathology or impairment causing activity limitations. Thus, they ignored those with pathology or impairment who do not report activity limitations.

TABLE 3.6. Prevalence of Selected Impairments Among the Civilian Population Ages 25–61, by Gender, Pooled Over Survey Years 1983–1996[a]

	Men			Women		
Impairment[b]	All	With Work Limitations	Ratio[c]	All	With Work Limitations	Ratio[c]
One or more of the impairments below	23.4	5.8	0.25	17.7	5.3	0.30
Sensory impairments	15.0	3.2	0.21	8.2	2.5	0.30
Visual impairments	4.8	1.2	0.24	2.4	1.0	0.40
Blind in both eyes	0.2	0.1	0.65	0.2	0.1	0.75
Other visual impairments	4.7	1.1	0.23	2.2	0.8	0.37
Hearing impairments	10.8	2.3	0.22	5.9	1.7	0.28
Deaf in both ears	0.5	0.2	0.35	0.3	0.1	0.43
Other hearing impairments	10.2	2.1	0.21	5.7	1.6	0.28
Sensation impairments[d]	0.5	0.1	0.26	0.4	0.1	0.35
Speech impairments	1.0	0.5	0.47	0.5	0.3	0.52
Stammering and stuttering	0.6	0.2	0.32	0.3	0.1	0.41
Other speech impairments	0.4	0.3	0.69	0.2	0.1	0.64

(continues)

TABLE 3.6 *Continued.*

Impairment Subpopulation[b]	Men			Women		
	All	With Work Limitations	Ratio[c]	All	With Work Limitations	Ratio[c]
Paralysis	0.4	0.3	0.87	0.3	0.2	0.81
Paraplegia, hemiplegia, or quadriplegia	0.2	0.2	0.95	0.1	0.1	0.84
Paraparesis, hemiparesis	0.1	0.1	0.91	0.1	0.1	0.80
Cerebral palsy	0.1	0.1	0.68	0.1	0.1	0.79
Absence of one or both legs	0.1	0.1	0.77	—	—	—
Deformity/orthopedic impairments	10.0	3.0	0.30	10.6	3.1	0.30
Back /spine	8.7	2.5	0.29	9.8	2.8	0.29
Shoulder(s)	1.8	0.7	0.40	1.3	0.5	0.42
Mental retardation	0.5	0.4	0.88	0.4	0.3	0.87

Note. Authors' calculations using the National Health Interview Survey, survey years 1983–1996.

[a]Persons are considered to have a work limitation if they have any impairment or health problem that now keeps them from working at a job or business or that limits them in the kind or amount of work they can do. Only individuals who were directly asked about these impairments are included, which is approximately one sixth of the NHIS sample in each year. Cells with sample sizes of less than 30 respondents are reported.

[b]Category terms are based on the language of the survey.

[c]The ratio of column 2 (4) to column 1 (5). When these ratios were calculated, four decimal points were allowed in the components of the ratios.

[d]Sensation impairments include taste, smell, and loss or disturbance of sensation and numbness of any body part.

TABLE 3.7. Employment Rates of Civilians Ages 25–61 in Selected Impairment Subpopulations, by Gender and Work Limitation Status, Pooled Over Survey Years 1983–1996[a]

Impairment Subpopulation[b]	Men			Women		
	All	With Work Limitations	Ratio[c]	All	With Work Limitations	Ratio[c]
Total population with and without impairments	88.4	48.9	0.55	68.8	37.4	0.54
One or more of the impairments below	81.5	47.7	0.59	61.4	37.6	0.61
Sensory impairments	82.4	45.8	0.56	57.7	31.7	0.55
Visual impairments	81.2	43.5	0.54	53.0	27.3	0.52
Blind in both eyes	49.4	28.1	0.57	30.0	16.0	0.53
Other visual impairments	82.4	45.2	0.55	54.7	29.1	0.53
Hearing impairments	81.6	44.9	0.55	58.4	32.5	0.56
Deaf in both ears	75.4	49.1	0.65	50.3	26.5	0.53
Other hearing impairments	81.9	44.5	0.54	58.7	32.9	0.56
Sensation impairments[c]	79.9	50.5	0.63	60.9	44.4	0.73
Speech impairments	61.7	30.1	0.49	42.2	18.9	0.45
Stammering and stuttering	70.2	28.3	0.40	51.1	16.2	0.32
Other speech impairments	48.5	31.4	0.65	32.4	20.7	0.64

(*continues*)

TABLE 3.7 *Continued.*

Impairment Subpopulation[b]	Men			Women		
	All	With Work Limitations	Ratio	All	With Work Limitations	Ratio
Paralysis	32.2	26.4	0.82	25.5	15.6	0.61
Paraplegia, hemiplegia, or quadriplegia	22.3	21.8	0.98	17.7	5.1	0.29
Paraparesis, hemiparesis	25.3	23.7	0.94	29.0	18.8	0.65
Cerebral palsy	58.3	43.7	0.75	27.8	21.9	0.79
Absence of one or both legs	34.2	27.8	0.81	—	—	—
Deformity/orthopedic impairments	81.1	52.6	0.65	64.8	44.0	0.68
Back /spine	81.4	51.8	0.64	64.9	43.3	0.67
Shoulder(s)	76.4	52.6	0.69	64.2	48.1	0.75
Mental retardation	34.6	32.8	0.95	29.1	26.4	0.91

Note. Authors' calculations using the National Health Interview Survey, survey years 1983–1996.

[a]Persons are considered to have a work limitation if they have any impairment or health problem that now keeps them from working at a job or business or that limits them in the kind or amount of work they can do. Only individuals who were directly asked about these impairments are included, which is approximately one sixth of the NHIS sample in each year. Cells with sample sizes of less than 30 respondents are reported.

[b]Category terms are based on the language of the survey.

[c]Sensation impairments include taste, smell, and loss or disturbance of sensation and numbness of any body part.

Although the employment rate of men who are deaf (blind) in both ears (eyes) and report having a work limitation is 49.1% (28.1%), the overall employment rate of men who are deaf (blind) in both ears (eyes) is 75.4% (49.4%). These differences suggest that factors other than severity of the impairment influence the employment outcomes of people with disabilities.

Tables 3.8 and 3.9 show the prevalence rates of SSDI and SSI in an impairment-based disability population and a work limitation-based disability population. These tables show that the prevalence of public disability-based transfers is much greater in the latter than in the former. Men who report being deaf (blind) in both ears (eyes) and also report a work limitation are 2.76 (1.25) times as likely to be receiving SSDI benefits (Table 3.8) and 2.97 (1.47) times as likely to be receiving SSI benefits (Table 3.9) as men who only report being deaf (blind) in both ears (eyes). This increased prevalence of receiving public disability-based transfers varies in magnitude across impairments but is found to be greater than 1 for all impairments listed, with the exception of those with paraplegia, hemiplegia, or quadriplegia.

CONCLUSIONS

Figure 3.1 provides a useful framework for considering the employment experience of working-age people with disabilities gained from currently available data sets. The inner circle of Figure 3.1 contains men and women whose pathologies and impairments are so severe that they apply for SSDI or SSI benefits. Not surprisingly, Bound et al. (in press), using SIPP–SSA data, found that near the time of application, most people in this population were not working. But even among this population there was great variation in employment experience in the years prior to application—SSDI applicants have substantial work experience, whereas SSI applicants have almost none—and thereafter—those denied benefits increase their employment more than those who are accepted. These findings suggest that even in this population of SSDI and SSI applicants, differences in the severity of pathology and impairment do not fully explain the differences in employment between SSDI and SSI applicants and within these programs based on acceptance. But to focus on the employment experience of this population greatly underestimates the employment potential of broader populations with disabilities.

Those working-age men and women who report having a work limitation (an operationalized version of the Nagi definition of a work disability) have higher employment rates than those who also apply for SSDI or

(*text continues on p. 88*)

TABLE 3.8. Percentage Receiving SSDI Among Civilians Ages 25–61 in Selected Impairment Subpopulations, by Gender and Work Limitation Status, Pooled Over Survey Years 1990–1992, 1994–1995[a]

	Men			Women		
Impairment Subpopulation[b]	All	With Work Limitations	Ratio	All	With Work Limitations	Ratio
Total population with and without impairments	2.4	21.2	8.90	1.6	12.2	7.69
One or more of the impairments below	6.0	22.7	3.76	4.2	12.9	3.07
Sensory impairments	5.4	22.9	4.21	5.2	15.7	3.04
Visual impairments	7.4	26.6	3.59	9.9	23.6	2.40
Blind in both eyes	28.6	35.6	1.25	34.8	44.1	1.27
Other visual impairments	6.5	25.6	3.96	7.7	19.8	2.57
Hearing impairments	5.3	22.6	4.29	4.4	13.6	3.11
Deaf in both ears	13.0	35.9	2.76	19.5	—	—
Other hearing impairments	4.8	21.4	4.43	3.9	12.5	3.21
Sensation impairments[c]	6.2	—	—	3.9	12.4	3.14
Speech impairments	20.3	40.4	1.99	10.9	18.7	1.72
Stammering and stuttering	12.1	32.7	2.71	9.8	19.2	1.96
Other speech impairments	33.0	46.3	1.40	12.5	18.2	1.46

Paralysis	48.9	52.2	1.07	23.2	26.2	1.13
Paraplegia, hemiplegia, or quadriplegia	56.1	56.1	1.00	—	—	—
Paraparesis, hemiparesis	—	—	—	—	—	—
Cerebral palsy	—	—	—	—	—	—
Absence of one or both legs	—	—	—	—	—	—
Deformity/orthopedic impairments	5.3	17.0	3.19	2.4	7.3	3.04
Back /spine	5.6	18.5	3.33	2.3	7.2	3.20
Shoulder(s)	6.3	14.2	2.24	3.5	7.0	2.00
Mental retardation	34.3	36.2	1.06	33.2	38.4	1.15

Note. Authors' calculations using the National Health Interview Survey, survey years 1983–1996.

[a]Persons are considered to have a work limitation if they have any impairment or health problem that now keeps them from working at a job or business or that limits them in the kind or amount of work they can do. Only individuals who were directly asked about these impairments are included, which is approximately one sixth of the NHIS sample in each year. Cells with sample sizes of less than 30 respondents are reported.

[b]Category terms are based on the language of the survey.

[c]Sensation impairments include taste, smell, and loss or disturbance of sensation and numbness of any body part.

TABLE 3.9. Percentage Receiving SSI Among Civilians Ages 25–61 in Selected Impairment Subpopulations, by Gender and Work Limitation Status, Pooled Over Survey Years 1990–1992, 1994–1995[a]

	Men			Women		
Impairment Subpopulation[b]	All	With Work Limitations	Ratio	All	With Work Limitations	Ratio
Total population with and without impairments	1.2	9.8	8.17	1.8	12.5	6.98
One or more of the impairments below	3.0	10.7	3.60	4.9	14.2	2.88
Sensory impairments	2.2	8.8	4.03	5.5	15.9	2.87
Visual impairments	3.5	12.4	3.56	9.8	22.8	2.31
Blind in both eyes	18.3	26.9	1.47	22.4	28.4	1.27
Other visual impairments	2.8	10.4	3.72	8.8	21.8	2.48
Hearing impairments	1.9	7.6	4.04	4.8	13.8	2.88
Deaf in both ears	4.2	12.4	2.97	15.4	—	—
Other hearing impairments	1.8	7.2	4.09	4.5	13.2	2.97
Sensation impairments[c]	2.6	—	—	2.5	8.0	3.14
Speech impairments	12.7	24.2	1.91	16.7	31.5	1.89
Stammering and stuttering	7.8	22.2	2.86	13.9	28.3	2.04
Other speech impairments	20.2	25.8	1.28	20.8	35.0	1.68

Paralysis	26.7	28.4	1.07	32.0	39.4	1.23
Paraplegia, hemiplegia, or quadriplegia	25.5	25.5	1.00	—	—	—
Paraparesis, hemiparesis	—	—	—	—	—	—
Cerebral palsy	—	—	—	—	—	—
Absence of one or both legs	—	—	—	—	—	—
Deformity/orthopedic impairments	2.1	6.5	3.04	2.8	7.7	2.78
Back /spine	2.0	6.3	3.11	2.7	7.7	2.88
Shoulder(s)	2.9	6.0	2.10	3.3	6.8	2.08
Mental retardation	44.3	45.3	1.02	57.3	60.1	1.05

Note. Authors' calculations using the National Health Interview Survey, survey years 1983–1996.

[a]Persons are considered to have a work limitation if they have any impairment or health problem that now keeps them from working at a job or business or that limits them in the kind or amount of work they can do. Only individuals who were directly asked about these impairments are included, which is approximately one sixth of the NHIS sample in each year. Cells with sample sizes of less than 30 respondents are reported.

[b]Category terms are based on the language of the survey.

[c]Sensation impairments include taste, smell, and loss or disturbance of sensation and numbness of any body part.

SSI benefits. The employment rates of this middle circle of Figure 3.1 were captured by Burkhauser et al. (2002) over time and by Houtenville (2001b) across states. Using CPS data they found a dramatic difference in employment over time and states that is unlikely to be explained by the difference in the pattern of pathology or impairment. Most important, the dramatic drop in employment and the equally dramatic rise of disability transfer receipts of men who report work limitations in the 1990s is unlikely to be entirely or even substantially health driven.

But to focus on this self-reported population with work limitations is to miss an even broader population with disabilities that is closer in conceptualization to the ADA definition. This outer circle population contains people with pathologies and impairments who nevertheless work, through environmental accommodations, access to rehabilitation, or their own inner capacity to overcome both their pathologies and external barriers to work. Using data from the NHIS, we look within specific pathology or impairment categories of this population. We find it to be a population that is larger and more likely to be employed than that captured by a choice-based sample of people with both pathologies or impairments and work limitations. Even among those with impairments that appear to be synonymous with a work limitation (e.g., blind in both eyes, deaf in both ears), a substantial percentage do not report having a work limitation. More important, this broader population with disabilities reports far higher employment rates than are likely to be based solely on differences in severity of impairment.[9]

The employment experiences we report vary dramatically both across and within the three circles of disability conceptualized in Figure 3.1. To fully capture this diversity of experiences, it is necessary to look beyond the results from any one of the currently available data sets we review. But a single theme emerges from the data we explore. Our findings suggest that social-environmental forces are likely to play a large role in the employment outcomes of the various subpopulations with disabilities we identify. To improve policies that affect the employment of the working-age population with disabilities, it will be necessary to collect data that incorporate the

[9] Burkhauser et al. (2002) used data from the NHIS, CPS, and matched CPS to more systematically document our findings that the employment rate of the impaired working-age population is significantly higher than the employment rate of the work-limited working-age population. They also showed that the employment rate of the working-age population reporting a work limitation in a single year is significantly higher than the employment rate of the working-age population reporting a work limitation in 2 consecutive years. But more important, they showed that there is no significant difference in the employment rate trends in these three populations over the years 1983–1996. All three data sets show dramatic declines in the employment rate of people with disabilities in the 1990s.

strengths of each of the data sets we review to better measure the relative importance of health and social environment on employment outcomes.

REFERENCES

Age Discrimination in Employment Act Amendments of 1996, 29 U.S.C. § 621 *et seq.*

Americans with Disabilities Act of 1990, 42 U.S.C. § 12101 *et seq.*

Bound, J., Burkhauser, R., & Nichols, A. (in press). Tracking the household income of SSDI and SSI applicants. In S. W. Polachek (Ed.), *Research in labor economics*.

Burkhauser, R., Daly, M., Houtenville, A., & Nigras, N. (in press). *Relative outcomes of working-age people with disabilities over the business cycle* (Cornell Rehabilitation Research and Training Center Working Paper). Ithaca, NY: Research and Rehabilitation Training Center for Economic Research on Employment Policy for Persons with Disabilities, Cornell University.

Burkhauser, R., Daly, M., Houtenville, A., & Nigras, N. (2002). Self-reported work limitation data: What they can and cannot tell us. *Demography, 39*(3), 541–555.

Daly, M., & Burkhauser, R. (in press). The Supplemental Security Income Program. In R. Moffit (Ed.), *Means-tested transfer programs in the United States*. Chicago: University of Chicago Press.

Gordon, K., & Groves, C. (Eds.). (2000). ADA symposium issue [Special issue]. *Berkeley Journal of Employment and Labor Law, 21*(1).

Houtenville, A. (2000a). *Economics of disability research report #1: Estimates of the prevalence of disability in the United States by state, 1981 through 1999*. Ithaca, NY: Research and Rehabilitation Training Center for Economic Research on Employment Policy for Persons with Disabilities, Cornell University.

Houtenville, A. (2000b). *Economics of disability research report #2: Estimates of employment rates for persons with a disability in the United States by state, 1980 through 1998*. Ithaca, NY: Research and Rehabilitation Training Center for Economic Research on Employment Policy for Persons with Disabilities, Cornell University.

Houtenville, A. (2002). Employment and economic consequences of visual impairment. In P. Lennie & S. B. Van Hemel (Eds.), *Visual impairments determining eligibility for Social Security benefits*. Washington, DC: National Academy Press.

Kirchner, C., Schmeidler, E., & Todorov, A. (1999). *Looking at employment through a lifespan telescope: Age, health, and employment status of people with serious visual impairments*. New York: American Foundation for the Blind.

LaPlante, M. (1993). *State estimates of disability in America* (Disability Statistics Rep. No. 3). Washington, DC: National Institute of Disability and Rehabilitation Research.

Library of Congress. (1998). *Vocational factors in the Social Security disability decision process: A review of the literature*. Washington, DC: The Federal Research Division Library of Congress.

Loprest, P., & Maag, E. (2001). *Barriers to and supports for work among adults with disabilities: Results from the NHIS-D*. Washington, DC: Urban Institute.

Mashaw, J., & Reno, V. (1996). *Balancing security and opportunity: The challenge of disability income policy* (Report of the Disability Policy Panel). Washington, DC: National Academy of Social Insurance.

McCoy, J., & Weems, K. (1989). Disabled-worker beneficiaries and disabled SSI recipients: A profile of demographics and program characteristics. *Social Security Bulletin, 52*(5), 16–28.

Nagi, S. (1965). Some conceptual issues in disability and rehabilitation. In M. B. Sussman (Ed.), *Sociology and rehabilitation*. Washington, DC: American Sociological Association.

Nagi, S. (1969). *Disability and rehabilitation: Legal, clinical and self-concepts of measurement*. Columbus: Ohio State University Press.

Nagi, S. (1991). Disability concepts revisited: Implications to prevention. In A. M. Pope & A. R. Tarlove (Eds.), *Disability in America: Toward a national agenda for prevention*. Washington, DC: National Academy Press.

Trupin, L., Sebesta, D., Yelin, E., & LaPlante, M. (1997). *Trends in labor force participation among people with disabilities* (Disability Statistic Rep. No. 10). Washington, DC: National Institute for Disability and Rehabilitation Research.

Career Development Theories, Constructs, and Research: Implications for People with Disabilities

Edna Mora Szymanski, Mary S. Enright, David B. Hershenson, and Judith M. Ettinger

The study of career development advanced considerably during the last quarter of the 20th century. For example, developments in cognitive psychology influenced career theory (see, e.g., Bandura, 1977, 1982; Hackett & Betz, 1981; Lent & Hackett, 1994). Similarly, inclusion of contextual factors in career development (Fitzgerald & Betz, 1994; Vondracek & Fouad, 1994), including family influences (e.g., Young & Collin, 1992; Young & Friesen, 1992), increased. Finally, theory convergence was considered (see, e.g., Brown & Brooks, 1996; Osipow, 1990).

Counselors and educators must not only gain a working understanding of current theories and research, but they must also identify the special considerations for applying theories to people with disabilities. To this end, this chapter introduces readers to the broad topic of career development of people with disabilities through coverage of (a) history, (b) selected current theories, (c) an ecological model for vocational behavior, (d) considerations for diverse populations, (e) a framework for using current theories in practice, and (f) research on career development of people with disabilities.

HISTORY

The practice of career development, which formerly was termed *vocational guidance*, emerged in the United States near the turn of the 20th century in advance of career development theory. This practice, which responded to social, political, economic, and legislative conditions, influenced the later development of theory (Herr, 2001).

The first career development theory, for all practical purposes, dates back to the work of Frank Parsons (1909). Parsons proposed a three-step process for choosing a vocation, consisting of (a) gaining information about the person, (b) gaining information about the world of work, and (c) matching these two to arrive at an appropriate occupation for that person. This approach, which still provides (in updated form) the basis for much contemporary career counseling (see Chapter 8, this volume), is based on a conception of occupational choice as a one-time event that can best be handled by employing a linearly logical matching process.

Some 40 years later, Ginzberg, Ginsburg, Axelrod, and Herma (1951) proposed that occupational choice was a developmental process rather than a one-time event. Meanwhile, Donald Super's work led him to move the developmental conceptualization one step beyond Ginzberg et al.'s formulation, to the concept of career development as a complex, multi-event, lifelong process (see, e.g., Super, 1953, 1957). The current state of Super's and other theories is presented in the next section of this chapter.

Although the field of vocational rehabilitation dates back at least to 1920 in the United States (Jenkins, Patterson, & Szymanski, 1998; Rubin & Roessler, 1994; G. Wright, 1980), almost no systematic attention was paid to conceptualizing the career development of persons with disabilities until the middle 1960s. (To his great credit, almost a decade earlier, Super [1957] devoted 5 pages of his 322-page book, *The Psychology of Careers*, to the topic of the effects of disabilities on career development.) Osipow (1976) attributed this omission to the fact that persons with disabilities did not conform to many of the assumptions and did not have many of the experiences of the nondisabled population on whom most theories were based (usually middle-class White males). These included the premises that career development is systematic, continuously developmental, and not continuously stressful. The existing models of career choice and development also assumed that the total person was evolved in the process, that the person was multipotential regarding careers, and that the person had relatively free choice of options. These premises were often not true for persons with disabilities, whose experiences and options were frequently highly constricted and whose career development was typically chaotic, discontinuous, and stressful. Interestingly, as noted in the next section of this chapter, a number of the newer theories, including developmental contextualism, derive from similar realizations about the applicability of established theories to women and members of racial and ethnic minority groups.

Because the concepts of career development and career choice that existed in the literature were not considered applicable to persons with disabilities, theories of work adjustment began to be formulated to account for vocational behavior in terms that were applicable to persons with disabilities and to their vocational rehabilitation. These theories focused on how individuals coped with their work environments, a set of experiences equally applicable to persons with and without disabilities. As might be expected from what existed in the general career field, one model of work adjustment evolved that followed a job-specific, person–environment matching approach (Lofquist & Dawis, 1969), whereas another model of work adjustment evolved that followed a developmental approach (Hershenson, 1974, 1981). Both these theories received empirical support and have evolved further over time.

Meanwhile, the study of career development of the general population (i.e., people without disabilities) continued to advance. By 1990, there were multiple theories and numerous, interrelated constructs—a state of affairs partially attributed to the multidisciplinary nature of career studies along with its relatively early stage of development (Brown, 1990a; Schein, 1986).

The Career Convergence Project, which resulted in an edited text (Savickas & Lent, 1994a), addressed the possibility that the theories could be converged into a more encompassing model. The chapters of the text contributed comprehensive perspectives to the state of career development theories and their interrelations. It was suggested that convergence, revision, and revitalization are natural parts of theory development (Osipow, 1994). Although there was sentiment that theory convergence should not be forced (Osipow, 1994), some has occurred as a result of natural evolution (Osipow, 1994; Super, 1994). Nonetheless, differences among the theories remain. Career Convergence Project authors suggested that theories had different audiences (Holland, 1994) and addressed diverse aspects of vocational behavior (Dawis, 1994; Krumboltz, 1994). The editors concluded that "the theories need each other in order to comprehensively address the complexity of career development. Furthermore, the results of research studies acquire deeper meaning when they are viewed from the perspectives of two or more theories" (Savickas & Lent, 1994b, p. 2).

At the time of this revision, it appears that the convergence discussion has influenced subsequent theory and model development. Two theories covered in this chapter, Krumboltz's learning theory of career counseling (Mitchell & Krumboltz, 1996) and Lent, Brown, and Hackett's (1996) social cognitive career theory, have evolved as a result of the convergence discussion. Inasmuch as the convergence discussion focused attention on contextual, nonnormative, and cognitive aspects of career development, it is suspected that the affected theories will continue to evolve in ways that make them more applicable to people with disabilities.

Finally, in the first edition of this volume, somewhat influenced by both the convergence discussion and ecological theories, we proposed an ecological model of career development that drew on the constructs of existing theories. In 1998, we expanded this model with the addition of theoretical processes. Basically, the model posits that, due to the wide variation in the population of people with disabilities, no one theory can be either fully applicable or nonapplicable to the population. Rather, the constructs and processes of the various theories can help explain individual situations of people with and without disabilities (Szymanski & Hershenson, 1998). The model is explained and expanded later in this chapter.

The study of career development has continued and perhaps accelerated during the past decade. In the next section of this chapter, we review selected current theories.

SELECTED CURRENT THEORIES

Career theories inform both professional practice and research. Volumes have been written on the theories (see, e.g., Brown & Brooks, 1990, 1996; Holland, 1992; Osipow, 1983). Numerous authors also have discussed the potential limitations of the theories in application to people with disabilities (see, e.g., Conte, 1983; Curnow, 1989; Szymanski & Hershenson, 1998; Thomas & Parker, 1992), minorities (see, e.g., Bowman, 1993; Fouad, 1993; Leong, 1995), and women (Fitzgerald, Fassinger, & Betz, 1995). Even with their limitations, the theories offer important ways of understanding the vocational behavior of a wide range of individuals, including people with disabilities.

"Career development approaches encompass perspectives from multiple disciplines that provide windows into both the structure of and the longitudinal changes in career behavior" (Herr & Cramer, 1992, p. 197). The multiple disciplines studying career development (e.g., sociology, counseling, organizational and industrial psychology) present both a great richness and a source of confusion. According to Schein (1986), "Each academic discipline happily develops its own concepts but does not feel obligated to connect them to the concepts that flow from other disciplines" (pp. 315–316).

In this section, we attempt to illuminate some of the disciplinary approaches to career development through a summary of selected theories. The selection of theoretical approaches for inclusion is based on our judgment of their potential utility in application with people with disabilities. The following theories and approaches are discussed: (a) person–environment interaction theories, (b) Holland's theory, (c) Super's theory,

(d) selected additional counseling-related career theories (i.e., Krumboltz's theory, Hershenson's theory, social cognitive career theory, and developmental contextualism), and (e) theories in other fields (i.e., sociological and economic perspectives, organizational career theory).

Person–Environment Interaction Theories

Current person–environment interaction theories have evolved from early models of vocational counseling, dating back at least to the work of Frank Parsons in 1909 (Hackett & Lent, 1992). "Parsons advocated personal analysis, job analysis, and matching through scientific advising as the basis of occupational choice making" (Brown, 1990b, p. 14). Until recently, these theories had been referred to as trait and factor models (Hackett & Lent, 1992), a reference that described their common approach of matching individual traits with environmental factors.

The major criticism of early trait and factor theories seems to have been countered with recent theory development. Specifically, trait and factor approaches had been considered atheoretical. However, Rounds and Tracey (1990) have suggested that trait and factor approaches can be considered to be informed by the various developing person–environment fit theories, including those that account for the reciprocal interaction of people and their environments.

The Theory

Early trait and factor theory was based on the assumptions that (a) individuals have stable measurable traits, (b) occupations require specific groups of traits, and (c) it is possible to match individuals to jobs (Brown, 1990b). Current person–environment (PE) interaction models are based on the following assumptions:

1. Individuals seek out and create environments (used in a generic sense, e.g., occupations, jobs, situations, positions) that provide and/or allow for behavioral trait manifestation; for example, extroverts seek out and/or create stimulating environments, and dominant individuals may choose occupations that offer possibilities of leadership and managerial roles and may structure situations such that they are in charge.
2. Degree of fit between the person and environment is associated

with significant outcomes that can substantially affect the individual and environment—for example, performance, productivity, satisfaction, turnover, and stress. The better the PE fit, the better the outcomes.

3. The process of PE fit is reciprocal, involving the individual shaping the environmental context and the environmental context influencing the individual (Rounds & Tracey, 1990, p. 18).

The Minnesota theory of work adjustment (TWA) is a type of PE theory. Although it was initially developed in the 1960s, its authors have recently updated and extended it in a text, *Essentials of Person Environment Correspondence Counseling* (Lofquist & Dawis, 1991). A special issue of the *Journal of Vocational Behavior* was devoted to TWA (Tinsley, 1993). Articles in the issue provided empirical support for aspects of the theory and suggested further research (e.g., Bizot & Goldman, 1993; Breeden, 1993; Dawis, Dohm, & Jackson, 1993).

According to TWA, "individuals differ, environments differ, and each individual-environment interaction is unique" (Lofquist & Dawis, 1991, p. 2).

> Work adjustment is the dynamic process by which persons attain and preserve correspondence with their work environments. Stronger P-E correspondence leads to increased tenure, which is the chief outcome of work adjustment. More specifically, tenure depends on both individuals' satisfaction with the environment and their satisfactoriness in meeting environmental demands. (Hackett & Lent, 1992, p. 420)

Proponents of person–environment interaction theories, including TWA, use assessment instruments to help clients understand their interests and aptitudes. This information is matched to requirements obtained from job analyses (Brown, 1990b). Thus, sources of occupational information (e.g., the *Dictionary of Occupational Titles* [U.S. Department of Labor, 1991]) are vital to the trait and factor approach (see Chapter 7, this volume). Interestingly, many computerized career guidance systems are based on this approach (Brown, 1990b).

An underlying premise of PE theories is that good matches of traits and job requirements are predictive of job success and satisfaction (Brown, 1990b). A variety of traits have been tested in this approach and have proven predictive of work behaviors. These include personality, vocational interests, work values, and cognitive abilities (Rounds & Tracey, 1990). However, critics have contended that "trait measures cannot account for more than 36% of the variance associated with various criteria, and usually the proportion was less" (Brown, 1990b, pp. 18–19). However, because individual and situational factors not included in the research can have potent effects that decrease accounted variance, 36% is far from negligible. Thus, trait and factor models cannot be dismissed as a partial explanation of vocational behavior (Brown, 1990b; Rounds & Tracey, 1990).

Although the trait and factor and subsequent PE models have been heavily criticized, they are nonetheless among the "few counseling approaches that developed from the study of vocational behavior" (Rounds & Tracey, 1990, p. 5). Some critics (e.g., Herr & Cramer, 1992) have questioned the validity of the assumption that career choice is normally a conscious, cognitive approach. This point has been supported by the role played by chance in career development (Cabral & Salomone, 1990). Nonetheless, it would seem that individual traits and environmental factors cannot be discarded as important to career counseling. In addition, it is important to note that the evolved PE interaction theory provides a dynamic and workable approach to counseling (Chartrand, 1991).

Applications to People with Disabilities

Person–environment interaction approaches have been the foundation to much of vocational rehabilitation. The Minnesota theory of work adjustment addressed people with disabilities in its development. Earlier, matching approaches underlie the assessment and planning aspects of the rehabilitation process (see, e.g., Rubin & Roessler, 1994; G. Wright, 1980). The reciprocal interaction aspect of such theories is reflected in the systems approaches suggested by Cottone (1986) and Hershenson (1998) and the ecological approach to rehabilitation suggested by Szymanski and colleagues (Szymanski, Dunn, & Parker, 1989; Szymanski & Hershenson, 1998; Szymanski, Hershenson, Ettinger, & Enright, 1996; Szymanski, Hershenson, & Power, 1988; Szymanski & Parker, 1989).

Professionals applying PE theories to people with disabilities must exercise caution. These theories are excellent for the identification and generation of alternatives for consideration. However, they must not be used in isolation of considering the impact of the disability or job accommodation. In summary, we concur with the recommendations of Rounds and Tracey (1990), who advised that "counselors selectively use relevant aspects of . . . PE fit theories, tailoring them to the situation at hand" (p. 21).

Holland's Theory

Holland's theory is technically a PE fit theory, although it has some developmental aspects. However, its lengthy history and voluminous research require separate treatment.

John Holland's theoretical work has spanned more than 42 years and profoundly influenced the practice of career counseling. Many of the instruments used in career counseling have evolved from his theory (e.g., the *Self-Directed Search*, the *Vocational Preference Inventory*, *My Vocational Situation*, the *Career Attitudes and Strategies Inventory*), and his theory has been connected to another commonly used instrument, the *Strong–Campbell Interest Inventory* (Borgen, 1990). Thus, Holland's theory is vital to any consideration of career development.

The Theory

The foundation of Holland's theory is based on the following three propositions.

> First, we can characterize people by their resemblance to each of six personality types: Realistic, Investigative, Artistic, Social, Enterprising, and Conventional. The more closely a person resembles a particular type, the more likely he or she is to exhibit the personal traits and behaviors associated with that type. Second, the environments in which people live and work can be characterized by their resemblance to six model environments: Realistic, Investigative, Artistic, Social, Enterprising, and Conventional. Finally, the pairing of persons and environments leads to outcomes that we can predict and understand from our knowledge of the personality types and the environmental models. These outcomes include vocational choice, vocational stability and achievement, educational choice and achievement, personal competence, social behavior, and susceptibility to influence. (Holland, 1997, pp. 1–2)

Five secondary concepts moderate or qualify the major propositions. They are consistency, differentiation, identity, congruence, and calculus. Consistency refers to the relative similarity of different subtypes. Differentiation refers to the degree to which a person or environment is defined by one as opposed to many types. "Personal identity is defined as the possession of a clear and stable picture of one's goals, interests, and talents. Environmental identity is present when an environment or organization has clear, integrated goals, tasks, and rewards that are stable over long time intervals" (Holland, 1985a, p. 5). Congruence refers to the proposition that different personal types require different environmental types. Finally, calculus refers to the hypothesized hexagonal model that defines the relationships between types (Holland, 1985a).

Key instruments that operationalize aspects of Holland's theory are the *Self-Directed Search* (SDS; Holland, Fritzsche, & Powell, 1994), the *Vocational Preference Inventory* (VPI; Holland, 1985b), *My Vocational Situation* (MVS; Holland, Daiger, & Power, 1980), and the *Career Attitudes and Strategies Inventory* (CASI; Holland & Gottfredson, 1994). A hallmark of Holland's instruments is that they are self-administered and can be used to actively engage clients in career planning.

A review suggests that the congruence dimension of Holland's theory has been widely researched and, in many situations, supported. So, too, has the vocational identity proposition, which has been found to be related to career maturity and career decidedness (Hackett & Lent, 1992).

Holland's instruments, themselves, appear to have some effect on career planning. A review of research has suggested that the SDS has positive effects on career planning. In reporting on 22 studies of the SDS, Holland et al. (1994) noted that the most common findings were that the SDS "(a) increases the number of career options a person is considering, (b) increases satisfaction with a vocational aspiration, and (c) increases self-understanding" (p. 53). Although it is still early in its history, there have been anecdotal reports of effects of the CASI on career planning (G. Gottfredson, personal communication, June 29, 2001).

Like other approaches, Holland's theory has its critics and supporters. The theory has been criticized for being static, overly simplistic, and sexist. However, these criticisms have been countered with both theory and research (Holland, 1997; Weinrach & Srebalus, 1990). In addition, it is important to note that although variables such as ethnicity, gender, social class, and disability are "incorporated indirectly in the theory, . . . direct assessments of these variables are also required to secure more positive applications" (Holland, 1997, p. 13). Thus, although limitations may exist, as they do with any theory, Holland's theory remains a valuable tool for counselors.

Applications to People with Disabilities

Various instruments based on Holland's theory are quite applicable for people with disabilities. For example, the SDS, which has both normal and low reading level versions, is an excellent tool for actively involving clients in generating alternatives for consideration in career planning. Clients should be cautioned not to eliminate possibilities that appear limited by disability-related barriers because such barriers may be resolved by job modifications or accommodations. Similarly, MVS is a nice tool to involve clients in appraising their readiness for career planning. It has also been used as a measure of the success of interventions (see, e.g., Conyers & Szymanski, 1998; Farley, Bolton, & Parkerson, 1992; Merz & Szymanski, 1997; Wenkman, 1994). Finally, although it is still relatively new, it is suspected that the CASI could have some good clinical applications for people with acquired disabilities. Research on such applications is encouraged.

In summary, Holland's theory and instruments are important components of the tool kit that counselors can use to assist people with disabilities in career planning. In fact, the self-administered SDS and MVS can be used to promote active engagement in career planning (i.e., to promote consumer involvement). However, as with general PE theories, Holland's theory should be not be applied without full consideration of the impact of the disability and the potential of job accommodation.

Super's Theory

Donald Super's work, which spanned more than six decades, permeates much of current career counseling in the United States (Borgen, 1990; Super, Savickas, & Super, 1996) and has been extended internationally (Super, 1990). The September 1994 special issue of the *Career Development Quarterly* honored his memory and described the way in which his contributions stimulated a wide range of current theory, research, and practice (Savickas, 1994).

The Theory

Although Donald Super's theory is often classified as developmental, it contains many elements of the PE theories (Super, 1994). This fact is illustrated by Super's 14 propositions, which follow.

1. People differ in their abilities and personalities, needs, values, interests, traits, and self-concepts.
2. People are qualified, by virtue of these characteristics, each for a number of occupations.
3. Each occupation requires a characteristic pattern of ability and personality traits, with tolerances wide enough to allow some variety of occupations for each individual and some variety of individuals in each occupation.
4. Vocational preferences and competencies, the situations in which people live and work, and, hence their self-concepts change with

time and experience, although self concepts, as products of social learning, are increasingly stable from late adolescence until late maturity, providing some continuity in choice and adjustment.

5. This process of change may be summed up in a series of life stages (a "maxicycle") characterized as a sequence of growth, exploration, establishment, maintenance, and decline, and these stages may in turn be subdivided into (a) the fantasy, tentative, and realistic phases of the exploratory stage and (b) the trial and stable phases of the exploratory stage. A *small (mini) cycle takes place in transitions from one stage to the next or each time an individual is destabilized by a reduction in force, changes in type of manpower needs, illness or injury, or other socioeconomic or personal events. Such unstable or multiple-trial careers involve new growth, reexploration, and reestablishment (recycling)* [italics added].
6. The nature of the career pattern, that is, the occupational level attained and the sequence, frequency, and duration of trial and stable jobs is determined by the individual's parental socioeconomic level, mental ability, education, skills, personality characteristics (needs, values, interests, traits, and self-concepts), and career maturity and by the opportunities to which he or she is exposed.
7. Success in coping with the demands of the environment and of the organism in that context at any given life-career stage depends on the readiness of the individual to cope with these demands (that is, on his or her career maturity). Career maturity is a constellation of physical, psychological, and social characteristics; psychologically, it is both cognitive and affective. It includes the degree of success in coping with the demands of earlier stages and substages of career development, and especially with the most recent.
8. Career maturity is a hypothetical construct. Its operational definition is perhaps as difficult to formulate as that of intelligence, but its history is much briefer and its achievement even less definitive. . . . It does not increase monotonically, and it is not a unitary trait.
9. Development through the life stages can be guided, partly by facilitating the maturing of abilities and interests and partly by aiding in reality testing and in the development of self-concepts.
10. The process of career development is essentially that of developing and implementing occupational self-concepts. It is a synthesizing

and compromising process in which the self-concept is a product of the interaction of inherited aptitudes, physical makeup, opportunity to observe and play various roles, and evaluations of the extent to which the results of role playing meet with the approval of superiors and fellows (interactive learning).

11. The process of synthesis of or compromise between individual and social factors, between self-concepts and reality, is one of role playing and learning from feedback, whether the role is played in fantasy, in the counseling interview, or in such real-life activities as classes, clubs, part-time work, and entry jobs.
12. Work satisfactions and life satisfactions depend on the extent to which the individual finds adequate outlets for abilities, needs, values, interests, personality traits, and self-concepts. They depend on establishment in a type of work, a work situation, and a way of life in which one can play the kind of role that growth and exploratory experiences have led one to consider congenial and appropriate.
13. The degree of satisfaction people attain from work is proportional to the degree to which they have been able to implement self-concepts.
14. Work and occupation provide a focus for personality organization for most men and women, although for some persons this focus is peripheral, incidental, or even non-existent. The other foci, such as leisure activities and homemaking, may be central. (Social traditions, such as sex-role stereotyping and modeling, racial and ethnic biases, and the opportunity structure, as well as individual differences, are important determinants of preferences for such roles as worker, student, leisurite, homemaker, and citizen.) (Super, 1990, pp. 206–208)[1]

The combination of the propositions and instruments makes Super's theory useful, at least for majority populations. The 14 propositions indicate how Super's theory encompasses a wide range of important career development concepts, including PE considerations, multiple life roles, de-

[1]From "A Life-Span, Life-Space Approach to Career Development," by D. E. Super, in D. Brown and L. Brooks (Eds.), *Career Choice and Development: Applying Contemporary Theories to Practice* (2nd ed., pp. 197–261), 1990, San Francisco: Jossey-Bass. Copyright 1990 by Jossey-Bass. Reprinted with permission.

velopment through the life span, and the impact of gender, socioeconomic status, race, and ethnicity. Instruments include the *Career Development Inventory* (Super, Thompson, Lindeman, Jordan, & Myers, 1981), the *Adult Career Concerns Inventory* (Super, Thompson, Lindeman, Myers, & Jordan, 1986), the *Salience Inventory* (Super & Nevill, 1986a), and the *Values Scale* (Super & Nevill, 1986b).

Super's theory is generally supported by research, although much more research is needed and ongoing (Hackett & Lent, 1992; Super et al., 1996). Although it has been criticized for its complexity and loose integration, the theory is, nonetheless, quite useful to practitioners (Brown, 1990a). In addition, the utility of the theory is growing again with a recent multinational study (Super & Šverko, 1995) and research on role salience, which should be particularly important in application to diverse populations, possibly including people with disabilities.

The Achilles' heel of Super's theory appears to be its relative omission of cultural and contextual variables. A particular challenge is the "implicit assumption of European-American career developmental trends as the norm" (Leong & Serafica, 2001, p. 172). Contextual factors, such as socioeconomic status and opportunity structure, are also considered critical to understanding the career development of minorities (Leong & Serafica, 2001; Vondracek & Fouad, 1994) but are not adequately included in Super's theory.

Applications to People with Disabilities

Super's theory has many applications for people with disabilities. For example, the career maturity construct has been used in descriptive studies of people with disabilities (see, e.g., Biller, 1988) and in measuring the impact of interventions (see, e.g., Ericson & Riordan, 1993). The salience concept appears quite promising for research with people with disabilities and other minorities. In addition, the mini-cycles described in Proposition 5 are applicable in explaining acquired disabilities.

Cautions that apply to PE theories also apply to Super's theory. Instruments or theoretical constructs must be applied with an understanding of the limitations resulting from disability and the potential for accommodation. In addition, for persons with congenital disabilities, the impact of disability on development must be considered. Initial evidence suggests some relationship of disability with career decisiveness (Tseng, 1992) and career maturity (Biller, 1988). However, similar cautions to those suggested by Leong and Serafico (2001) in relation to ethnic minorities apply here as well.

Selected Additional Counseling-Related Career Theories

The first group of theories presented were major forces in the study of career development. Although the first group of theories could be considered classic, the next are more recently developed models that the authors consider important in application to people with disabilities.

Krumboltz's Theory

Krumboltz's social learning theory of career decision making (SLTCDM) represented one of the earlier applications of Bandura's (1977) social learning concepts to career development (Hackett & Lent, 1992). According to the theory, the following four categories of factors influence individual career decision making: (a) genetic endowment and special abilities, (b) environmental conditions and events, (c) learning experiences, and (d) task approach skills. The following outcomes result from learning experiences: self-observation generalizations, worldview generalizations, task approach skills, and actions (e.g., work habits, mental response sets; Mitchell & Krumboltz, 1990, 1996).

As a result of the convergence project described earlier in this chapter, Krumboltz and associates extended the theory to form Krumboltz's learning theory of career choice and counseling (LTCC). This is a two-part theory, with the first part being the SLTCDM described in the previous paragraph. The second part of the theory proposes the following trends as key to career counseling practice.

> 1. People need to expand their capabilities and interests, not base decisions on existing characteristics only. . . .
> 2. People need to prepare for changing work tasks, not assume that occupations will remain stable. . . .
> 3. People need to be empowered to take action, not merely be given a diagnosis. . . .
> 4. Career counselors need to play a major role in dealing with all career problems, not just occupational selection. (Mitchell & Krumboltz, 1996, pp. 250–252)

In 1999, Mitchell, Levin, and Krumboltz extended the theory into planned happenstance theory. Essentially, this adds a new proposition to the LTCC that counselors should help clients develop curiosity, persistence, flexibility, optimism, and risk taking to take advantage of chance in their career development.

The theory has some important potential applications for career counseling and research for people with and without disabilities, including ethnic minorities. Parts of the SLTCDM theory are well supported by research (Mitchell & Krumboltz, 1996), although there has been some contention that the results remain somewhat vague (Hackett & Lent, 1992). In addition, a major SLTCDM instrument, the *Career Beliefs Inventory* (Krumboltz, 1988), may have some operational difficulties in application to people with disabilities (Enright, 1996).

It is still too early to have empirical evidence in support of the LTCC. However, the four trends cited in this section certainly appear to resonate with both research and application in career counseling with people with disabilities and ethnic minorities (see, e.g., Conyers, Koch, & Szymanski, 1998; Leong, 1995, Leong & Serafica, 2001; Treviño & Szymanski, 1996).

Hershenson's Theory

Hershenson (1974, 1981, 1996) proposed a model of work adjustment in which the two principal elements are the person and the person's environment. Within the person, three domains develop sequentially, each in relation to a particular environment. The first domain to develop is the *work personality*, which is composed of two elements: the person's self-concept as a worker and the person's system of work motivation. Work personality is the focus of development during the preschool years, when the family is the principal environmental influence. Then, during the school years, the domain of *work competencies* is the focal area of development. This domain is composed of three elements: work habits, physical and mental skills that are applicable to jobs, and interpersonal skills in the work setting. Work competencies are largely shaped by the successes and failures experienced in meeting the physical, mental, and social demands of the school environment. The final domain to develop is appropriate, crystallized work goals. This domain becomes focal as the person prepares to move from school to work and is primarily influenced by the person's peer or reference group.

As each successive domain develops, it both is influenced by and influences the domain(s) that underwent focal development earlier. Each domain can only develop to a level that is supported by its predecessor, but subsequent domains can reciprocally influence their predecessors and thereby affect the limits of their own further development. Thus, one's successes and failures at school (competencies) will reciprocally affect one's self-concept as a worker, which initially was formed earlier in the preschool, family environment. Successes at school may lead to the improvement of an initially negative self-concept formed in a rejecting or overdemanding home environment, just as failures at school may bring about a downward revision of an unrealistically omnipotent self-concept formed in an overprotective home environment. This modified self-concept as a worker will, in turn, either facilitate or impede the further development of competencies. Similarly, as work goals develop, competencies that are not relevant to them may atrophy. The three domains continue to develop throughout the person's life, although not as rapidly or dramatically as during the developmental period in which that domain is focal. The domains establish a dynamic balance, so that changes in one domain precipitate changes in the other two domains, in order to restore a balance.

It may be noted that the three successive formative environments (home, school, and reference group) are not completely independent of each other, in that the family largely determines the school the child will attend and the school often provides the reference group. Nonetheless, the normal process of work development entails two major environmental transitions: (a) from home to school and (b) from school to work. For those who become disabled in the course of their career, a third and possibly a fourth major environmental transition must be integrated, involving rehabilitation and/or possibly a shift in the nature of their work. The experience of each transition, starting with home to school, shapes how successful its successor(s) will be.

As the three domains develop and function throughout the person's career, they interact with each other and with the environment. The product of this interaction is called *work adjustment* (Hershenson, 1981, 1996; Hershenson & Szymanski, 1992). Work adjustment has three components: (a) task performance (i.e., the quantity and quality of work output), (b) work-role behavior (i.e., behavior appropriate to the workplace, such as being neat, being prompt, taking responsibility, following directions, getting along with coworkers, accepting supervision), and (c) work satisfaction (i.e., the person's gratification from his or her work). Task performance is linked primarily to work competencies and secondarily to work personality. Work-role behavior is linked primarily to work personality and secondarily to the work habits component of work competencies. Work satisfaction is linked primarily to work goals and secondarily to work personality.

An important aspect of work adjustment theories, including Hershenson's, is that they were designed to be applicable to persons with and without disabilities. According to Hershenson's (1981) model, disability (by definition) has its initial impact on work competencies, but its impact rapidly spreads to the interconnected domains of work personality and work goals. The degree of spread depends on the level of development of the domains and the extent to which the disability disrupts the congruence between the individual and his or her current or desired occupation.

Social Cognitive Career Theory

Sociocognitive approaches to career theory are now coming into their own and can be quite useful in application to a wide range of individuals, including minorities and people with disabilities. Although this effort began more than a quarter century ago, it appears to be moving at full speed today.

During the 1970s and 1980s, a few theorists began to extend Bandura's (see, e.g., 1977, 1982) concepts of self-efficacy (SE) to career development. For example, Hackett and Betz "posited that SE influences the career decisions, achievements, and adjustment behaviors or both men and women, but they stressed SE theory's potential in explaining women's career development" (cited in Hackett & Lent, 1992, p. 433). During the same period, Moos (1986) similarly introduced cognitive elements into the relationship of individuals and work behavior. Specifically, he proposed that the personal system (e.g., demographic and personal factors, type of job and work role) was related to the environmental system (organizational and work context, nonwork stressors and resources) and that these systems were related to individual adaptation (i.e., work morale and performance, overall well-being and health). The relationship of the environmental and personal systems to individual adaptation is mediated by two factors: cognitive appraisal and coping responses.

More recently, in discussing the potential convergence of career development theories, Lent and Hackett (1994) proposed a model based on sociocognitive mechanisms of personal agency. This model, which included self-efficacy, incorporated the contextual factors that were often omitted in early career development theories. Specifically, Lent and Hackett's model proposed that performance outcomes were influenced by the interactive relationship of the following factors: personal inputs (i.e., predispositions, gender, race/ethnicity, disability, health status), background (i.e., context), learning experiences, self-efficacy, outcome expectations, interests, goals, choice actions, contextual influences proximal to choice behavior, and performance outcomes.

The approach continued to evolve in 1996 with a major chapter on social cognitive career theory (SCCT; Lent, Brown, & Hackett, 2000). Continuing to build on their earlier work, Lent et al. (2000) emphasized self-efficacy, outcome expectations, and personal goals as key variables in a scheme in which

> (1) personal attributes, such as internal cognitive and affective states, and physical attributes, (2) external environmental factors, and (3) overt behavior (as distinct from internal and physical qualities of the person)

> all operate as interlocking mechanisms that affect one another bidirectionally. (p. 379)

> Lent et al. (1996) describe their theory a bridging theory which (a) bring[s] together conceptually related constructs (e.g., self-concept, self-efficacy); more fully explain[s] outcomes that are common to a number of career theories (e.g., satisfaction, stability); and (c) account[s] for the relations among seemingly diverse constructs (e.g., self-efficacy, interests, abilities, needs). (p. 375)

Research support for various aspects of SCCT appears quite promising (Lent et al., 1996). Recently, the theory has been applied to the school-to-work transition (Lent, Hackett, & Brown, 1999) and to exploring contextual supports and barriers to career choice (Lent et al., 2000). These applications are extremely promising in increasing understanding of career development in general as well as the special circumstances of people with disabilities and ethnic minorities.

Developmental Contextualism

Developmental contextualism emerged during the 1980s as a new approach to career theory. In their landmark text, *Career Development: A Life-Span Developmental Approach*, Vondracek, Lerner, and Schulenberg (1986) "urged the inclusion of a developmental contextual perspective that recognizes the changing character of the individual's social, physical, and cultural milieus" (p. 5). In this ecological model, "both the individual and the context [are seen] as changing interdependently over time, which thus requires a *dynamic interactional* view of career development" (Vondracek et al., 1986, p. 8).

Developmental contextualism was intended to guide theory development and future research. It (a) added a transactional approach to career theory, (b) provided emphasis for the cultural context of career development, and (c) reaffirmed the place of career development in the human development domain (Vondracek & Fouad, 1994). In addition, the developmental contextualism approach has highlighted "the fact that stage models of career development (all current developmental theories in the field) cannot account for the ever-changing socioeconomic and cultural influences on career development" (Vondracek & Fouad, 1994, p. 211).

Two key and interrelated concepts have contributed to the developmental contextual approach. First, contextual factors were broadly constructed to include influences related to age (e.g., maturity, graduating from school), history (e.g., a war, the 1960s), and nonnormative events (e.g., winning the lottery, inheriting the family business; Vondracek &

Schulenberg, 1992). Second, a multilevel approach, termed *embeddedness*, was used to emphasize that

> key phenomena of human life exist at multiple levels of analysis (e.g., biological, individual-psychological, dyadic, organizational, social, societal, cultural, physical-ecological, historical). At any time, variables and processes from any and all of these multiple levels may contribute to human functioning. . . . These levels do not act independently; rather, each level reciprocally interacts with the others, resulting in *dynamic interaction*. (Vondracek & Fouad, 1994, p. 212)

The developmental contextual model is not a theory but rather an approach. It does suggest future approaches to research that include longitudinal, cohort-sequential research designs (Vondracek & Fouad, 1994). In addition, it may suggest alternative explanations for current research findings, especially when explained variance falls short of expectations. The importance of this approach is borne out by research and theory suggesting the importance of cultural and contextual factors in the development of career maturity (see, e.g., Hardin, Leong, & Osipow, 2001; Leong & Serafica, 2001).

Applications for Persons with Disabilities

The theories described in this section offer great promise for research and practice with people with disabilities. They extend consideration of the cognitive and contextual factors of career development and of the interaction among factors.

The constructs of task approach skills and self-observation generalizations of Krumboltz's theory may stimulate exploration of ways in which disability affects career development. In addition, self-efficacy and outcome expectations of SCCT are potent constructs that can inform research on the relationship of disability and career development and the effectiveness of rehabilitation interventions. The trends of Krumboltz's LTCC seem particularly important for rehabilitation counseling in light of the effects of the changing labor market.

The dynamic and contextual elements of developmental contextualism are particularly important for future research in career development of people with disabilities. Although dynamic models have previously been suggested in rehabilitation (see, e.g., Cottone, 1986; Szymanski et al., 1989), the Vondracek et al. (1986) model nonetheless adds important considerations. First, the contextual importance of culture is vital. It not only influences how career development and work are perceived but also affects how disability is viewed (see, e.g., Treviño & Szymanski, 1996).

Culture and context are critical aspects of rehabilitation planning (see, e.g., Szymanski, 1994; Szymanski et al., 1996).

Second, the effect of historical context is critical. It is probable that critical legislation (e.g., the Individuals with Disabilities Education Act of 1990; Sections 503 and 504 of the Rehabilitation Act of 1973; the Americans with Disabilities Act of 1990) and surrounding social changes (see Chapter 2, this volume) have had at least some effect on the career development of people with disabilities. For example, Ferguson, Ferguson, and Jones (1988) provided a compelling description of the impact of such contextual forces on the school-to-work transition of students with severe disabilities.

Theories in Other Fields

Career counseling and vocational psychology professionals do not have the corner on the career theory market. Sociologists, economists, and industrial psychologists have also been studying work for decades.

Sociological and Economic Perspectives

From a sociological perspective, work is the "activity performed by individuals to produce goods and services of value to others. It is typically performed in a socially structured context" (Hotchkiss & Borow, 1990, p. 262). There are a variety of sociological theories relating to work, including segmentation, reproduction, status attainment, human capital, labor market, race and gender, and assessment of new structuralism (Hotchkiss & Borow, 1996; Maranda & Comeau, 2000). Maranda and Comeau (2000, p. 38) organized theories along two axes: (a) structure (choices determined by constraints, norms, and sanctions)—voluntarism (individual autonomy and free will) and (b) adaptation (change people so that they can integrate into society)—transformation (change society in order to integrate people).

Two prevalent processes in sociological theories are (a) socialization, which is influenced by parental occupation, gender, social class, race, and ethnicity, and (b) allocation, a process in which gatekeepers (i.e., parents, teachers, vocational counselors, school administrators, and personnel directors) channel people in certain directions based on external criteria (Rothman, 1987). Topics in sociological theories tend to center on the following themes: (a) work and the person, (b) work and the wider society, (c) forms of work, (d) the politics of work and unemployment, and (e) the future of work (Erickson & Vallas, 1990).

Gottfredson's (1996) theory of circumscription and compromise brought some sociological and psychological approaches together. The theory, which has been evolving for 20 years, focuses on how people tend to circumscribe and compromise their options in a way that tends to replicate the inequities of earlier generations.

Career development is both influenced by and influences economic factors. In their report of a longitudinal study of American families, *Succeeding Generations: On the Effects of Investments in Children*, Haveman and Wolfe (1994) provided a detailed view of the way in which the economic and social situations of parents affect the future work status of their children.

Organizational Career Theory

Like other approaches, organizational career theory has evolved considerably in the past 20 years. Organizational career development is "a planned effort to link the individual's career needs with the organization's workforce requirements" (Gutteridge, Leibowitz, & Shore, 1993, p. 1). Lately, however, some approaches (e.g., Hall & Mirvis, 1996) have looked at how individuals manage careers across organizations in an era of fast-paced change.

There are two dimensions of the organizational approach to career development: *career planning*, which addresses individual needs, and *career management*, which addresses organizational factors. The following are descriptions of key elements of the organizational career approach. Career planning, which bears similarity to the person–environment models discussed in the previous section, is

> a deliberate process of (1) becoming aware of self, opportunities, constraints, choices, and consequences, (2) identifying career-related goals, and (3) programming work, education, and related developmental experiences to provide the direction, timing, and sequence of steps to attain a specific career goal. Career management is an ongoing process of preparing, implementing, and monitoring career plans undertaken by the individual alone or in concert with the organization's career systems. (Hall, 1986, p. 3)

Strategic human resource planning is "the process of linking the organization's strategy for managing human resources to its basic business goals and objectives" (p. 5).

Authors in Hall's (1986) volume emphasized that individual and organizational flexibility and planning would be keys to survival in the future (Gutteridge, 1986; London & Stumpf, 1986). In 1996, Hall and associates took the importance of flexibility to a new level in their provocative volume, *The Career Is Dead: Long Live the Career*.

Hall and Mirvis (1996) suggested that "the company's commitment to the employee extends only to the current need for that person's skills and performance" (p. 17). As a result, Hall's earlier concept of a protean approach to career has taken on increased relevance. In this free agent-like approach, "organizations provide a context, a medium in which individuals pursue their personal aspirations" (Hall & Mirvis, 1996, p. 21).

> The protean career is a process which the person, not the organization, is managing. It consists of all of the person's varied experiences in education, training, work in several organizations, changes in occupational field, etc. The protean person's own personal career choices and search for self-fulfillment are the unifying or integrative elements of his or her life. The criterion of success is internal (psychological success), not external. (Hall & Moss, 1998, p. 25)

Flexibility, autonomy, and continuous learning are the hallmarks of the protean model (Hall & Mirvis, 1996). Szymanski (1999) built on the protean approach to suggest a career resilience portfolio to help individuals with disabilities manage their protean careers and avoid detrimental effects of job stress.

Applications to People with Disabilities

Both the sociological and organizational approaches are of great importance to counselors and educators serving people with disabilities. Both approach employment from structural and individual perspectives, with lenses that are different from the prevailing theories in counseling.

Sociological theories focus on social and systemic structures relating to career development and employment. These approaches are important balances to the somewhat individually oriented approaches of counseling, rehabilitation, and special education. The sociological processes also address forces that are uncomfortable for counselors but necessary for understanding the lives of many people with disabilities and ethnic minorities. "People's employment situations are the result of both constraints due to the economic context and more or less strategic individual and collective behaviour" (Maranda & Comeau, 2000, p. 50). Failure to acknowledge the economic and societal aspects of career development will seriously limit the effectiveness of professional practice.

Similarly, organizational approaches help to frame understanding of the dynamic interplay of organizational and individual forces in a rapidly changing labor market. These approaches are particularly important in helping people with disabilities to prepare to adapt and thrive during times of constant change (Szymanski, 1999). Both organizational and sociological theories are quite helpful in understanding and planning strategies to address the glass ceiling experienced by people with disabilities (Braddock & Bachelder, 1994).

AN ECOLOGICAL MODEL FOR VOCATIONAL BEHAVIOR

Different theories are needed, but their number and interrelation present significant challenges to students, educators, and practitioners. We therefore began to develop an ecological model that could synthesize information from various theories and guide research and practice applications.

In the first edition of this book, we proposed the constructs of the model. In 1998, Szymanski and Hershenson added six processes to the model. In this chapter, we add a seventh process. The revised model is presented in Figure 4.1.

The model remains a work in progress, evolving as new applications reveal limitations. To this end, it is important to note that the "Model" section of the chapter is partially adapted from Szymanski and Hershenson (1998). Of course, the "Model" section in that chapter was partially adapted from the earlier edition of this chapter.

Constructs

Some definitions and examples are in order as we introduce this section. First, a "*construct* is a concept . . . [that has] been deliberately and consciously invented or adopted for a special scientific purpose" (Kerlinger, 1986, p. 27). "A *concept* expresses and abstraction formed by generalization from particulars" (p. 26). For example, *educational opportunity* is a concept that is formed from a generalization about the opportunities available to various individuals and groups and the significant evidence that some groups have had less access to high-quality education than other groups (see, e.g., Kozol, 1991). The concept of educational opportunity has been adopted as a construct to explain the career development of diverse populations (see, e.g., Fitzgerald & Betz, 1994).

Following the leads of Fitzgerald and Betz (1994), Lent and Hackett (1994), Osipow (1994), and Rounds and Hesketh (1994), we organized career development around common theoretical constructs, which fall into the following five interrelated groups: context, individual, mediating, work environment, and outcome. We have paid particular attention to constructs related to disability or other minority status. Then we added

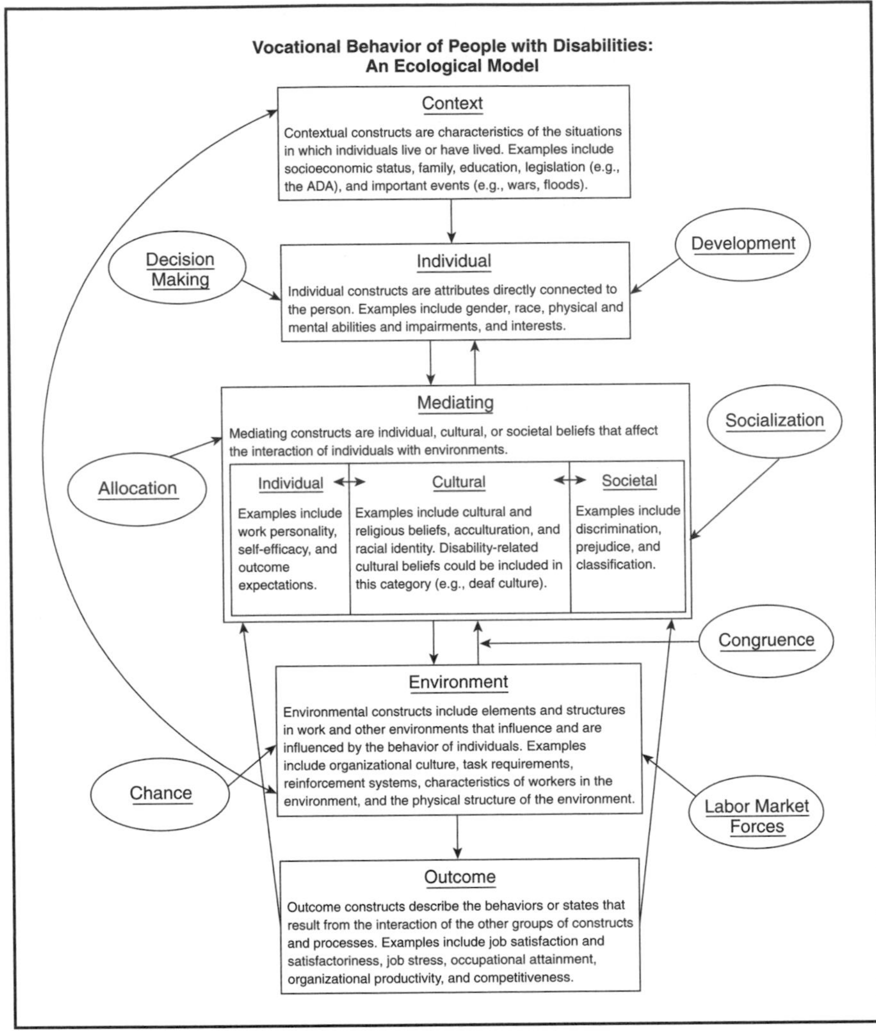

FIGURE 4.1. An ecological model of vocational behavior of people with disabilities.

processes that affect the interaction of the constructs. The organization of the constructs, processes, and their interrelation is described in Figure 4.1.

Individual

Individual constructs include physical and psychological attributes of the person. Examples are gender; race; physical and mental abilities, including work competencies; predispositions and limitations; interests; needs; and values. The aspect of disability that is an individual attribute (i.e., a physical or mental characteristic) rather than a social construction is, therefore, an individual construct. All theoretical approaches include individual constructs, although they are often constructed differently.

Context

Context constructs include those aspects of an individual's current or past situation that are external to the person. Examples include socioeconomic status, family, and educational and other opportunity structures. This group of constructs also includes nonnormative influences—for example, war, natural disasters, winning the lottery, and relevant legislation (e.g., the Americans with Disabilities Act of 1990).

Mediating

Mediating constructs are individual, cultural, and societal beliefs that affect the interaction of individuals with their environments. Individual mediating constructs are personal beliefs about abilities and characteristics, habits or behavior patterns, or potential outcomes. Examples include self-concept, work personality (Hershenson, 1981; Holland, 1985a), vocational identity (Holland, Daiger, & Power, 1980), self-efficacy (see, e.g., Bandura, 1982; Lent & Hackett, 1994), task approach skills, self-observation generalizations (Krumboltz, 1994), outcome expectations (Lent & Hackett, 1994), career maturity (Super, 1990), career decisiveness (Osipow, Carney, Winer, Yanico, & Koschier, 1976), and adjustment to disability (see, e.g., D. Cook, 1992; B. Wright, 1983).

Cultural mediating constructs are individual beliefs, which are grounded in a larger cultural structure, that affect how individuals perceive and act on their environments. Examples include worldview generalizations (Mitchell & Krumboltz, 1990), cultural and religious beliefs (see, e.g., Trueba, Rodriguez, Zou, & Cintron, 1993), acculturation (see, e.g., LaFramboise, Coleman, & Gerton, 1993), and racial identity (see, e.g., Rowe, Behrens, & Leach, 1995).

Societal mediating constructs are aspects of societal belief structures that affect individual–environment interaction. They include stereotypes, discrimination (see, e.g., James, 1994), castification (the way in which one group systematically marginalizes another group; Trueba et al., 1993), and attitudes toward persons with disabilities (Makas, 1985; Yuker & Block, 1986).

Environment

Environmental constructs describe various characteristics or conditions of work environments. This group of factors includes Holland's (1997) modal work environments, the environmental task requirements and reinforcement systems of the theory of work adjustment (Dawis, 1994; Lofquist & Dawis, 1991), organizational considerations (see, e.g., Burke & Nelson, 1998; Gutteridge et al., 1993; Hall & Mirvis, 1996), and disability-related access and accommodation (see Chapter 6, this volume).

Outcome

Outcome constructs are the behaviors or states that result from the interactions of groups of the other factors. This group includes persistence (Holland, 1985a); satisfaction, satisfactoriness, and tenure (Lofquist & Dawis, 1991); organizational productivity and competitiveness (Burke & Nelson, 1998; Hall, 1990; Hall & Mirvis, 1996); and job stress (Ross & Altmaier, 1994; Szymanski, 1999).

Processes

The constructs represent characteristics, beliefs, conditions, and states. The constructs interact with each other. For example, the context of individual lives influences the interaction of the individual, mediating, and environment constructs in relation to outcomes. Similarly, there are processes that affect the system. The first six of these processes (development, congruence, decision making, socialization, allocation, and chance) were added to the model in 1998.

> *Congruence* (Holland, 1985a), also described as correspondence (Lofquist & Dawis, 1991), is the process of relative match or mismatch of individuals with their environments. *Decision making*, for the purposes of this chapter, is the process by which individuals consider career-related alternatives and formulate decisions (D. Brown, 1990a). The *developmental* process involves systematic changes over time (Vondracek et al., 1986), which are interwoven with characteristics and perceptions of the individual (see, e.g., Super, 1990) and reciprocally influenced by the environment (Bronfenbrenner, 1977). *Socialization* is the process by which people learn work and life roles. It is influenced by parental occupation, gender, social class, race, and ethnicity (Rothman, 1987). *Allocation* is the process by which societal gatekeepers (i.e., parents, teachers, vocational counselors, school administrators, and personnel directors) use external

criteria to channel individuals into or exclude them from specific directions. *Chance* is the occurrence of unforeseen events or encounters (Cabral & Salomone, 1989). (Szymanski & Hershenson, 1998, p. 354)

At this time, we add a seventh process, *labor market forces*. These are the economic and business forces that affect individual and organizational opportunities. Examples include globalization, changing technologies (Storey, 2000), changing economics of business (Martin & Freeman, 1998), downsizing, changing corporate structures and practices (Burke & Nelson, 1998), and the general health of the economy.

We also make explicit the inclusion of disability role socialization under the socialization process. This is a very powerful and frequently overlooked process that affects the lives of many individuals with disabilities (Gove, 1976; Scott, 1969).

The first three of the processes—development, congruence, and decision making—represent the results of individual processes or actions, which may be influenced by or related to external factors. The other four processes are primarily external to the individual, although they interact with internal factors and processes.

Model Characteristics

The constructs and processes present a framework to understand career development, classify theories, and plan research, assessment, and interventions. According to this model, career development is determined by the dynamic interaction of individual, contextual, mediating, environment, and outcome constructs with the processes of congruence, decision making, development, socialization, allocation, chance, and labor market forces.

In looking at the model, it is important to note that most of the elements are highly interrelated. Constructs within each group are usually highly related with each other (e.g., the context constructs of socioeconomic status and education, the individual constructs of needs and values). Constructs and processes also are related to each other. Therefore, it is often difficult to classify interventions or phenomena according to one construct or process.

A constant iterative relationship exists between groups of constructs and processes. For example, interests are learned (Mitchell & Krumboltz, 1996) and relate, in part, to contextual and mediating constructs. Interests are not only affected by such factors but also affect how individuals choose to interact with their environments through the processes of congruence and decision making.

The interrelation among the constructs and processes must also be viewed in a developmental and historical perspective. The combination of states and interactions at any one time influences future interaction patterns.

Relationship of the Model to the Theories

As noted by a number of authors in their discussions of theory convergence, theories focus on different aspects of the complex phenomena of career-related behavior. These aspects, which are operationalized by the constructs and processes in Figure 4.1 might be compared to the facets of a prism. Theories can then be thought of as light approaching the prism from different angles.

For example, the theories normally considered in counseling have a strong individual focus with some extension to other constructs. Specifically, PE interaction theories, including Holland's typology and the Minnesota theory of work adjustment, have a relatively broad focus and usually address individual, environmental, and outcome constructs with some consideration of mediating constructs. On the other hand, developmental theories, such as Super's, concentrate on individual and mediating constructs with some extension to context and environmental constructs. Similarly, developmental contextual approaches emphasize the contextual, individual, and mediating constructs with some extension to environmental and outcome constructs. On the same line, sociocognitive approaches focus on mediating constructs with extension to individual and environmental constructs.

Theories from other fields often begin with an environmental focus that extends to individual considerations. For example, sociological theories address the social structure of the work environment into which individuals are socialized or allocated. Similarly, organizational theories address organizational and managerial concerns of the workplace in which individuals provide the human capital.

In addition, the theories vary in their relative emphases of the model's processes. Development is a major process in Super's theory, whereas congruence is a major force in Holland's typology. Socialization and allocation are hallmarks of sociological approaches, and labor market forces are especially important in both sociological and organizational theories.

Table 4.1 presents our interpretation of the relationship of the theories in this chapter to the constructs and processes of the ecological model. As with any prism, examination of only one or two facets yields an

TABLE 4.1. Relationship of the Ecological Model to the Constructs and Processes of Career Development Theories

	Theories									
Model Elements	Super's Theory	Holland's Typology	Trait–Factor	LTCC[a]	TWA[b]	HWAT[c]	SCCT[d]	DC[e]	S&E[f]	Org.[g]
Constructs										
Individual	X	X	X	X	X	X	X	X	X	X
Contextual	X			X			X	X	X	
Mediating	X			X		X	X	X	X	
Environment	X	X	X	X	X	X	X	X	X	X
Outcome	X	X	X	X	X	X	X	X	X	X
Processes										
Development	X			X		X	X	X		
Decision making				X					X	X
Congruence	X	X	X		X			X		
Socialization	X			X		X	X	X	X	
Allocation									X	
Chance				X		X	X	X	X	X
Labor market forces	X			X					X	X

Note. Adapted from "Career Development of People with Disabilities: An Ecological Model," by E. M. Szymanski and D. B. Hershenson, in R. M. Parker and E. M. Szymanski (Eds.), *Rehabilitation Counseling: Basics and Beyond* (3rd ed., p. 356), 1998. Austin, TX: PRO-ED. Copyright 1998 by PRO-ED. Adapted with permission.

[a]LTCC = Krumboltz's learning theory of career counseling.

[b]TWA = Minnesota theory of work adjustment.

[c]HWAT = Hershenson's work adjustment theory.

[d]SCCT = Social Cognitive Career Theory.

[e]DC = Developmental Contextualism.

[f]S&E = sociological and economic theories.

[g]Org. = organizational theories.

incomplete picture. So, too, current theories only illuminate parts of the complex picture of career behavior. However, as recommended by Savickas and Lent (1994c), concurrent examination of the phenomena or of research results from more than one angle produces substantially more illumination. Similarly, triangulation is an important tool for enhancing the validity of both quantitative (Cook & Campbell, 1979) and qualitative research (Maxwell, 1996; Strauss & Corbin, 1990).

Triangulation is just plain good science. The multiple theoretical approaches to career development afford a variety of angles to help illuminate the complex phenomena. Such multiple approaches can be particularly helpful as the application of theory to racial and ethnic minorities and people with disabilities is planned.

Application of the Model

The model has been used in application to ethnic minorities with disabilities (Szymanski et al., 1996), the school-to-work transition (Szymanski, 1997, 1998), disability and vocational behavior (Szymanski, 2000), people with developmental disabilities (Szymanski & Hanley-Maxwell, 1996), college students with congenital disabilities (Conyers et al., 1998), and people with psychiatric disabilities (Tschopp, Bishop, & Mulvihill, 2001).

CONSIDERATION FOR DIVERSE POPULATIONS

A common criticism of many prevailing theories has been that they are not directly applicable to racial and ethnic minorities (see, e.g., Brown, 1990a; Fitzgerald & Betz, 1994; Leong & Serafica, 2001; Osipow & Littlejohn, 1995; Pope-Davis & Hargrove, 2001; Vondracek et al., 1986) and to people with disabilities (see, e.g., Conte, 1983; Curnow, 1989; Hershenson & Szymanski, 1992). Rather than listing criticisms, we would like to take a different approach to the applicability of theories of career development to minority populations. To this end, the following topics are discussed: (a) heterogeneity of racial and ethnic minority populations, (b) heterogeneity of people with disabilities, and (c) the complex impact of gender.

Heterogeneity of Racial and Ethnic Minority Populations

During the past decades, a number of books and journal articles have addressed general issues related to counseling persons who are members of racial and ethnic minority groups (see, e.g., Cox, 1993; Lee & Richardson, 1991; Pederson, 1994; Sue & Sue, 1990). Similarly, a number of publications have addressed issues of diversity in relation to vocational behavior (see, e.g., Atkinson & Thompson, 1992; Bowman, 1993; Fouad, 1993; Hawks & Muha, 1991; Leong, 1995; Martin, 1991; Tinsley, 1994; Walsh, Bingham, Brown, & Ward, 2001). So, too, some authors have addressed concerns of racial and ethnic minorities with disabilities (see, e.g., Atkins, 1988; Marshall, Johnson, Martin, Saravanabhavan, & Bradford, 1992; Smart & Smart, 1991; Szymanski et al., 1996). The many works in counseling along with others in psychology (see, e.g., Wertsch, 1991), anthropology (see, e.g., Trueba et al., 1993), and other fields have highlighted the immense complexity and heterogeneity of the influences of race and ethnicity. Of particular concern are issues related to culture and context.

Culture, which is a system of concepts, beliefs, and principles that affect interpretation of events and behavior (Trueba et al., 1993), further mediates the complex, interactive effects of race and ethnicity with the factors of career behavior. Essentially, culture affects how we perceive and how we act (Wertsch, 1991). The cultural context of "career choice cannot be overemphasized" (Vondracek & Fouad, 1994, p. 209). For example, culture influences the relative acceptability of types of interventions (e.g., individual vs. family centered) and the value hierarchy of life roles (e.g., worker, homemaker, family member; see, e.g., Martin, 1991; Trueba, 1991). Acculturation, which reflects an individual's degree of affiliation with native and majority culture, mediates the impact of culture (LaFramboise et al., 1993).

Context includes such factors as socioeconomic status, opportunity structure, and education. These factors are considered critical to the career development of ethnic minorities, yet they are reflected in relatively little research and theory (Leong & Serafica, 2001).

The above brief tour of complexity due to ethnicity was designed to remind readers of the inherent heterogeneity of diverse populations. Career development is influenced not only by race and ethnicity but also by culture, acculturation, religious beliefs, immigration experiences, opportunity structure, and a host of other factors. Fitzgerald and Betz (1994) suggested that structural and cultural factors, which we have considered as context and social mediating constructs, "provide an overlay to, or a new perspective for, the consideration of career theories. It is not a theory itself, but rather a unifying perspective or context within which to examine and modify current theoretical formulations" (p. 113).

Heterogeneity of People with Disabilities

People with disabilities represent a very diverse population. There are many different types of disabilities (e.g., degenerative disk disease, cerebral palsy, multiple sclerosis, low vision, deafness, mental retardation, AIDS), all of which have substantial variation in possible degrees of severity and functional limitations. Even within specific disabilities, there is great variation in resultant functional limitations (see Chapter 6, this volume). Age of acquisition, work personality, work competencies, and work goals all affect the way that disability affects career development (Hershenson & Szymanski, 1992; Szymanski & Hershenson, 1998).

Like race, ethnicity, and culture, the impact of disability on career development cannot be simply explained. As noted in the discussion of Figure 4.1, context, individual, mediating, and environmental factors all include disability-related examples. Thus, like race and ethnicity, disability is multifaceted and cannot be examined in isolation to its impact on career development.

The Complex Impact of Gender

Gender has a potent impact on career development. The concept of gender-role socialization has been a frequent topic in the literature. The limitation of traditional theories and the limited predictive validity of PE interaction approaches have been discussed in the literature (see, e.g., Fitzgerald & Betz, 1994; Walsh & Osipow, 1994). Although differences in the interaction of career development factors have been observed (see, e.g., Rounds, 1990), there is still much to learn about how work and life roles interact and how this interaction differs between men and women (see, e.g., E. P. Cook, 1991, 1993).

FRAMEWORK FOR USING CURRENT THEORIES IN PRACTICE

The heterogeneity of people with disabilities and racial and ethnic minorities means that there can be no simple application or nonapplicability of any theory. Theories are useful in that they help to explain natural phenomena (Kerlinger, 1986). However, the predictive utility of theories depends, at least to some extent, on the degree to which the individuals comprising the populations of interest are relatively homogeneous with normal population distributions on the phenomena of interest. Mixture of population groups that have different distributions (i.e., different variance) threatens the validity of statistical conclusions for commonly used parametric procedures (Hays, 1988). Certainly, race, ethnicity, culture, and disability introduce sufficient variability to call into question blanket, normative applications of any theory.

Theories do, however, suggest lines of inquiry for clinical practice. The theories themselves can help counselors and their clients to focus information-gathering activities. Furthermore, the instruments that help to operationalize the various theories can be used effectively with people with disabilities, women, and racial and ethnic minorities as long as they are not used in a normative manner. However, as a prerequisite for using career development theories with diverse populations, counselors and educators should be sensitive to the impact of (a) level of ethnic identity and acculturation, (b) family influences, (c) gender-role socialization, (d) religious and spiritual influences, (e) immigration experiences (Lee, 1991), and (f) the complex medical, psychological, social, and environmental aspects of disability (see, e.g., Szymanski & Trueba, 1994; Chapter 6, this volume).

The ecological model in Figure 4.1 can be used to conceptualize career development practices, including use of theoretical conceptions and instruments with people with disabilities, members of racial and ethnic minority groups, and women. Counselors provide the compass to direct and integrate the information available from the diverse theoretical perspectives (Mastie, 1994). Thus, to facilitate this compass function, we provide assessment questions and interventions according to the constructs and processes of the ecological model in Table 4.2. Readers are referred to Szymanski and Hershenson (1998) for a more thorough discussion of applying the model to career planning and intervention with people with disabilities.

In summary, as we have previously noted, no theory is directly applicable or not applicable to a particular individual. Rather, theories provide counselors with keys to understanding and planning that must be chosen on the bases of individual circumstances. The framework presented in this section has been designed to assist counselors planning intervention. By using this framework, counselors can select from the many interventions suggested by different theories and apply them in ways that respect the unique situations of consumers. Research, the topic of the next section, furthers theory development and provides additional guides for application.

TABLE 4.2. Assessment Questions and Possible Interventions According to the Ecological Model of Career Development

Model Elements	Assessment Questions	Possible Interventions
Individual constructs	What are current abilities, interests, and limitations?	Active involvement in self-assessment
	What skills have been learned as a result of education or work experience?	Career portfolio
	What values are considered important to career planning by the consumer and by the family?	Career portfolio
	Has the consumer had sufficient and sufficiently recent experiences to foster broad and current interest development?	Volunteer and paid work experience, job enrichment, job or skill exploration
	How can individual abilities be enhanced?	Skills training, further education, job supports, remediation
	How can limitations be lessened?	Assistive technology, job accommodation
Contextual constructs	How have family background and neighborhood influenced perception of opportunities and responsibilities?	Work role models, mentors, chores, work experience, community empowerment
	How has education facilitated or impeded identification and realization of potential?	Remedial education
	What are the financial incentives or disincentives perceived by the individual and family as associated with work?	Inclusion of financial considerations in career planning
Mediating constructs	How does the consumer perceive his or her work-related abilities?	Career counseling, successful work experiences
	What outcomes does the consumer expect from employment preparation or rehabilitation?	Discussion of family and community work role models, additional appropriate role models, mentors
	What are the consumer's and family's cultural and religious beliefs that relate to education and work?	Culturally sensitive career planning and portfolios
	How have stereotypes and discrimination affected the consumer and her or his family?	Development of self-advocacy skills, advocacy

Environmental constructs	How physically accessible are various target environments and job tasks?	Barrier removal, assistive technology, job accommodation
	What is the organizational culture of the target work environment?	Job analysis
	How prone is the potential work environment to producing negative job stress? For example, how much control do workers have over work tasks and environment? How repetitive are tasks? How much pressure is there?	Job analysis
	How has the consumer gotten along in previous work or school environments? What types of environments or situations seem to cause difficulty?	Interviews with consumers, family, and teachers
	What are the reinforcements in the job and work environment?	Job analysis, planning for career advancement
Outcome constructs	How well do the consumer's skills and behaviors meet the requirements of possible work environments?	Additional training, on-the-job training, social skills training
	How well do the reinforcements of the work environment meet the consumer's needs?	Additional training for career advancement, possible job change
	Has the consumer experienced job-related stress? How well is the consumer equipped to cope with job-related stress?	Stress reduction techniques, wellness planning, encouragement to use social support, leisure and lifestyle planning, career resilience portfolio
Congruence processes	Is the consumer aware of potential job accommodations or assistive devices? Have these possibilities been considered?	Discussion and exploration of accommodation possibilities and assistive technology
	Have ability scores been artificially lowered due to disability-related construct validity problems (e.g., a person with limited vision tested without accommodation)?	Ecological or qualitative approaches to assessment
	Is social class or self-efficacy limiting the types of occupations considered?	Enrichment experiences, encouragement, role models

(*continues*)

TABLE 4.2. *Continued.*

Model Elements	Assessment Questions	Possible Interventions
Decision-making processes	What are the cultural practices of the consumer and her or his family relating to decision making and independence?	Incorporate the consumer's culture into interventions and goals, involve family members if appropriate
	What are the consumer's skills and experiences related to making choices or decisions?	Decision-making training, multiple trial work experiences
Developmental processes	Has disability limited developmental experiences?	Longitudinal approach to career planning, cautious approach to interpretation of interest measures
	Has social skill development been limited?	Social skills training
	Have work personality and work competency development been impeded?	Chores, supervised work experiences
Socialization processes	How have socialization processes affected the consumer's current role or consideration of future roles?	Enrichment experiences, role models, psychoeducational interventions
Allocation processes	Have opportunities been limited by gatekeeping functions in education, rehabilitation, or other service delivery systems?	Remedial education, mentoring, enrichment programs, special recruitment programs, job tryout experiences, instruction in self-advocacy, advocacy
	Do the requirements or processes of current service delivery programs restrict options, create dependency, or otherwise disempower?	Empowerment evaluation, capacity-building interventions
Chance processes	Is the consumer prepared to recognize and capitalize on chance opportunities?	Career planning workshops; career portfolio
Labor market force processes	Is the consumer prepared for the increasing competitiveness and decreasing stability of the current market?	Career portfolio, cross training
	Is the consumer prepared for possible sudden job loss due to an economic downturn?	Benefits and financial counseling, cross training

Note. Adapted from "Career Development of People with Disabilities: An Ecological Model," by E. M. Szymanski and D. B. Hershenson, in R. M. Parker and E. M. Szymanski (Eds.), *Rehabilitation Counseling: Basics and Beyond* (3rd ed., pp. 366–369), 1998. Austin, TX: PRO-ED. Copyright 1998 by PRO-ED. Adapted with permission.

RESEARCH ON CAREER DEVELOPMENT OF PEOPLE WITH DISABILITIES

Research on career development of people with disabilities presents some interesting problems of methodology, which obscure the value of some of the studies reported in the literature. In this section, we (a) discuss methodological problems of career research on people with disabilities, (b) summarize selected research, and (c) discuss considerations for future research.

Methodological Problems of Career Research on People with Disabilities

Several issues related to the conception, design, and implementation of career research on people with disabilities have diminished the direct application of findings to practice. In the 1996 edition of this book, we identified (a) low statistical power and mistaken acceptance of the null hypothesis, (b) the heterogeneity of the population, and (c) overreliance on hypothesis testing as key methodological issues. These issues remain problematic, and consequently, we discuss their relevance below. In addition, we describe several other design-related problems that have further curtailed the generalizability of career research on people with disabilities. These problems include (d) heterogeneity of constructs, (e) breadth of field, and (f) lack of consistent operational definitions.

Low Statistical Power and Mistaken Acceptance of the Null Hypothesis

Statistical conclusion validity refers to the degree to which one can draw valid conclusions from statistical tests. Two major threats to this type of validity, which can be seen in intervention research, are mistaken acceptance of the null hypothesis and low statistical power (Cook & Campbell, 1979).

Briefly, statistical power is the probability of finding relationships or differences that in fact exist in the population of interest. Among other things, it depends on the number of study participants and the effect size, that is, the size of differences between groups (Cohen, 1988). Power is known to be generally inadequate for rehabilitation research (Kosciulek & Szymanski, 1993) as well as for research in many behavioral sciences (Cohen, 1988).

The interrelated problem of the mistaken acceptance of the null hypothesis is related to the Fischerian model of hypothesis testing. This method relies on null hypotheses, which are logical alternatives to the hypothesis of interest. When these statements, which often suggest that the mean of the experimental group is not statistically different from the mean of the control group, are rejected at a given level of significance (e.g., alpha = .05), the rejection is taken as support for the alternative research hypothesis (e.g., that there are differences between the experimental and control groups). The problem is that the converse is not true. When no differences are found, researchers can only fail to reject the null hypothesis; they cannot accept it. Failure to find differences can result from low statistical power (Cohen, 1988).

The moral of the discussion in this section is that not much can be learned from studies with insignificant results. Studies with fewer than 300 participants may not have had adequate statistical power to find existing differences, especially with interventions known to have low effects (e.g., counselor-free interventions). Such studies, which do exist in the literature on career development of people with disabilities, should not be used to discourage use of interventions. At the time of this chapter revision, we note that small samples continue to be the norm.

Heterogeneity of the Population

As noted earlier in this chapter, people with disabilities are a heterogeneous population. Disabilities vary by type, age of onset, number and severity of functional limitations, degree of visibility, degree of stigma, perceived cause, progression (e.g., chronic, episodic, acute onset), prognosis, and treatment required, among other variables (Brodwin, Parker, & DeLaGarza, 1996; Livneh & Antonak, 1997; Smart, 2001). Each of these variables has been linked to psychosocial adjustment, career development, or job satisfaction (e.g., Brodwin et al., 1996; Smart, 2001; Szymanski & Hershenson, 1998), but further empirical research is warranted to document their influence, if any. For example, preliminary research has demonstrated that age of onset (e.g., Tseng, 1992) and type of disability (e.g., Anderson & Antonak, 1992) can influence career choice or job tenure, but the impact of variables such as disability progression and prognosis is even less understood. In an extensive review of research on psychosocial adaptation to disability, Livneh and Antonak (1997) offered valuable insights into methodological problems that contributed to disparate and conflicting findings in the adaptation literature. Among other conclusions, they discussed the tendency for researchers to focus on between-group differences (i.e., type of disability) and to employ cross-sectional designs. Livneh and Antonak advocated for studies that examine within-group differences and incorporate longitudinal designs. Given the diverse ways that disabilities can vary and the developmental nature of career, these recommendations are equally relevant to career research.

Overreliance on Hypothesis Testing

Null hypothesis testing practices have seriously limited research due to limitations in the logic of application (Cohen, 1994). In addition, hypothesis testing research requires that we know enough about the phenomena of interest to be able to construct hypotheses and choose measures (Cook & Campbell, 1979). Put simply, we have to know what we are looking for so that we will recognize it when we find it.

Although hypothesis testing research is the most common approach in studying career development and rehabilitation, there are other approaches. Commenting on the poor design of much career development research with special populations, Phillips, Strohmer, Berthaume, and O'Leary (1983) recommended an alternative approach that combines exploratory research with hypothesis testing, allowing theory to be generated from data.

Qualitative research is another means by which the career development of people with disabilities may be described. It provides for richer description of phenomena and can be used to generate and enrich theory (see, e.g., Strauss & Corbin, 1990). Such research has been used successfully in studying the transition of students with disabilities from school to work (see, e.g., Ferguson et al., 1988; Hanley-Maxwell, Whitney-Thomas, & Pogoloff, 1995) and the career development of people with disabilities (see, e.g., Conyers et al., 1998; Treviño & Szymanski, 1996).

Heterogeneity of Constructs and Terminology

Empirical research on career development and vocational behavior represents a vast body of literature that transcends multiple disciplines (Szymanski, 2000). One of the greatest challenges in synthesizing this research has been finding a common conceptual base among the multitude of interrelated constructs that authors have studied. A review of keywords and descriptors in the educational (ERIC) and psychological research databases revealed more than 30 relevant constructs, including career awareness, career choice, career development, career indecision, career maturity, career salience, career self-efficacy, job satisfaction, job placement, occupational choice, vocational behavior, vocational identity, vocational maturity, and work adjustment. The length of this list reflects, in part, the tendency of researchers from different disciplines to adopt their own terminology (Schein, 1986). As noted earlier in this chapter, the call for theory convergence related to career development (e.g., Savickas & Lent, 1994a) during the past 20 years has begun to bridge the conceptual gap involving career research originating from different branches of counseling, vocational psychology, rehabilitation psychology, and sociology. Despite a movement toward bridging theories (see, e.g., Lent et al., 1996), we suspect that the gap will not be closed in the near future. Thus, the problem of heterogeneous constructs will remain (Szymanski, 2000). Our ability to compare and extract meaningful results from different studies will consequently continue to be impeded.

Breadth of Field

Related to the issue of multiple constructs, career development is a complex process that exerts influence on virtually every stage of an individual's life (Savickas & Lent, 1994a; Super, 1990). Consequently, the scope of the field of career research is inherently large. When the presence and influence of a disability are considered, the scope of the field grows further. Szymanski (2000) noted the multidisciplinary nature of the study of disability and vocational behavior. The breadth of relevant research makes the call for the consistent use of terminology and constructs more urgent. It also underscores the point that empirical research on career processes and behavior will never be devoid of methodological challenges and issues.

Lack of Consistent Operational Definitions of Constructs

Compounding the challenges inherent in conceptualizing such a broad field, even when researchers have studied the same constructs, they have frequently used different operational definitions. For example, career indecision has been commonly been measured using the *Career Decision Scale* (Osipow et al., 1976) or *My Vocational Situation* (Holland et al., 1980). If researchers were to routinely use both instruments to measure career indecision, they would not only avoid mono-operational bias but would also link their results to a much larger number of studies. Finally, we note that the validity of many commonly used career-related assessment instruments may be compromised when used with people with disabilities. Many norm-referenced tests have not included a representative sample of people with disabilities in their normative samples (e.g., Enright, Conyers, & Szymanski, 1996). Furthermore, due to the learned nature of interests (Mitchell & Krumboltz, 1996), people with disabilities who have had limited life experiences may have flat profiles on commonly used interest inventories

(Szymanski & Hershenson, 1998). Finally, some career-related instruments (e.g., *Career Decision Scale*, *Career Salience Inventory*, and *My Vocational Situation*) contain language directed at college students, which suggests they should not be used with people with disabilities who are not in college, unless they are modified and the modifications are validated.

Summary of Selected Research and Career-Related Literature

The methodological issues associated with career research and people with disabilities have resulted in a fragmented body of research. Yet, despite their design problems, the results of virtually all intervention studies have supported the efficacy of a variety of career programs. Encouragingly, since the 1996 edition of this book, qualitative research on career development and disability has burgeoned and provided further support to the need and value of career- and work-based interventions for people with disabilities. The largely consistent findings across the studies suggest several possible conclusions. First, the complex nature of career development and related vocational behavior implies that measurable changes can occur in a wide variety of intrapersonal and environmental domains. Second, despite our proclivity to label these domains in different ways, they are real, interconnected phenomena that influence people's lives in tangible ways. In a sense, then, the concordant findings from such diverse studies can be thought of as a form of validity triangulation.

In this section, we describe research related to the career development and vocational behavior of people with disabilities. We have organized our discussion in relation to the constructs proposed in Figure 4.1. However, it should be noted that a multitude of interrelated factors and processes involved in career behavior implies that most studies can be categorized in multiple ways. Finally, our discussion of these studies is meant to suggest directions for future research and, accordingly, is designed to be illustrative, not comprehensive.

Context

Contextual research focuses on the contexts in which people live. Contexts in this sense are broadly defined, encompassing influences from the immediate role of family and significant others to socioeconomic status, neighborhood customs, the labor market to disability-related laws, cultural blueprints, and the impact of natural disasters and historic events (Bronfenbrenner, 1977). With regard to contextual constructs, literature focusing on the impact of the American with Disabilities Act of 1990 (e.g., Moore & Feist-Price, 1999) and the changing nature of the labor market (e.g., Ryan, 1995) have added to the rehabilitation literature during the past decade. In addition, the contextual factor of the economy has been shown to be a potent influence on the lives of people with disabilities (see, e.g., Yelin, 1992; Yelin & Cisternas, 1996), and research has suggested that the contextual factors of race and gender may have an additive impact on the career development of some individuals with disabilities (Conyers et al., 1998).

The influence of family on the career development of people with disabilities has continued to receive considerable attention over the years (see, e.g., Hanley-Maxwell, Pogoloff, & Whitney-Thomas, 1997; Hanley-Maxwell et al., 1995). Findings from a qualitative study of 10 Hispanics with disabilities supported the salience of contextual influences on career development. Using a grounded theory approach, Treviño and Szymanski (1996) found career development to be strongly influenced by context, particularly by family and cultural belief structures. For example, several individuals spoke to the significant role a family member played in the development of their work motivation and their perception of the meaning of work. From these in-depth interviews, Treviño and Szymanski posited an interactive relationship between socioeconomic status, self-efficacy, and work personality, a relationship that demonstrates the interconnected spheres of influence in career development.

Individual

Individual research focuses on personal characteristics. Perhaps the most compelling research on affecting individual constructs comes from a meta-analysis conducted by the Arkansas Rehabilitation Research and Training Center. Bolton and Akridge (1995) analyzed the data of 10 skill-based interventions serving 220 clients with disabilities. Their analysis produced an estimated true effect size of .93, suggesting that these skills programs can have a strong effect in changing individual attributes. Significant effects have also been reported from outcome studies of work hardening programs (for reviews, see Lechner, 1994; Neimeyer, Jacobs, Reynolds-Lynch, Bettencourt, & Lang, 1994).

Many other studies using people with disabilities have reported significant effects from work experience programs and various forms of career counseling. Examples of such studies include a summer work experience program for college students with disabilities (Wenkman, 1994), a career assessment and planning program for adolescent students in special education (Farley, Johnson, & Parkerson, 1999), a situational assessment for vocational rehabilitation clients (Scroggin, Kosciulek, Sweiven, & Enright, 1999), and resume counseling and vocational assessment feedback for veterans with disabilities (e.g., Krieshok, Hecox, Wettersten, & Ulven, 2000).

Mediating

As readers will recall from the model introduced earlier in this chapter, mediating constructs can be classified as individual, cultural, and societal. Again, this categorization is not mutually exclusive, and many studies tend to address more than one type of construct.

The individual mediating construct of self-efficacy has received much attention in the literature during the past decade (e.g., Becker & Schaller, 1995; Strauser, 1995; Szymanski & Hershenson, 1998). Interventions designed to improve self-efficacy have shown significant effects for persons with chronic low back pain (e.g., Altmaier, Russell, Kao, Lehmann, & Weinstein, 1993) and college students with physical disabilities (Conyers & Szymanski, 1998), among other groups.

The influence of locus of control has also been explored. For example, in a sample of 200 Israelis with work-related disabilities, Duvdevany and Rimmerman (1996) found that people with an internal locus of control have more favorable attitudes to work than people with an external locus of control.

Additional insights into the role of individual mediating factors can be gleaned from qualitative research into work and disability. Conyers et al. (1998) interviewed 9 employed college graduates with physical and sensory disabilities (ages 23–35 years) regarding their perspectives on work and disability. Their responses suggested three phases of career development: establishing an occupational self-concept, beginning a career, and advancing in a career. Interestingly, the mediating construct, perceived expectations of significant others, appeared as a significant theme in the career development of these individuals. In another study involving 12 persons with multiple sclerosis, the meaning of career and work surfaced as a recurring theme. As a theme, it encompassed a variety of cognitive mediating factors, including the importance of work, work values, and understanding of career (Salomone & O'Connell, 1998). These qualitative studies underscore how an individual's thoughts and perceptions can substantially influence the career development process. They also suggest the need for further research on constructs such as occupational self-concept, the meaning of work, and work values.

Cultural constructs that can mediate vocational behavior include racial identity, level of acculturation, religiosity, and religious and cultural beliefs. The role of cultural influences has received growing attention in the disability and rehabilitation literature (e.g., Fouad, 1993; Ingstad & Whyte 1995; Schaller, Parker, & Garcia, 1998; Smart & Smart, 1991;

Szymanski, Treviño, & Fernandez, 1996). Culture emerged as an important consideration in Treviño and Szymanski's (1996) qualitative research, described earlier in this section.

Data from some descriptive and correlational studies (e.g., Atkins & Wright, 1980; Dziekan & Okocha, 1993) have indicated that people with disabilities from minority backgrounds may be less likely to be accepted for vocational rehabilitation services than White applicants. However, other studies have found no significant differences in acceptance rates (e.g., Wheaton, 1995; Wilson, 1999).

Societal mediating constructs include prejudice and attitudes toward people with disabilities. The presence of prejudice and discrimination against people with disabilities in the workplace, both before and after the passage of the ADA, is well documented in the literature (see, e.g., Holzbauer & Berven, 1996; Smart, 2001; Yuker, 1988). The interplay of factors influencing the development of prejudice and discrimination against people with disabilities presents a challenge to interventions designed to change societal attitudes, yet research shows promise. In a series of studies, Catherine Fichten and her colleagues (e.g., Fichten & Bourdon, 1986; Fichten et al., 1996; Fichten, Tagalakis, & Amsel, 1989) have studied the efficacy of various interventions designed to change attitudes toward people with disabilities. Although limited to college students, their results suggest that interventions can improve attitudes, but they need to be carefully designed to avoid a negative impact. Similarly, in another study using college students, Erickson (1996) found that the attitudes of undergraduate psychology students toward people with serious mental illnesses could be changed both through coursework and field experiences. Such research suggests the possibility that employer and coworker attitudes toward people with disabilities can be changed, if properly designed and implemented.

Individual and Mediating

The largest number of intervention studies have addressed both individual and mediating constructs. During the 1990s, Szymanski and her colleagues at the Rehabilitation Research and Training Center on Career Development and Advancement at the University of Wisconsin–Madison conducted several career intervention studies. The studies assessed the efficacy of short-term, cognitively based career workshops using different populations of people with disabilities and employing a variety of research designs. Using an experimental design, Conyers and Szymanski (1998) found a statistically significant effect for a 10-hour career decision-making workshop for 49 college students, including 18 who had disabilities. Merz and Szymanski (1997) employed a pretest–posttest experimental design to study the effect of a career planning workshop. Their results produced an attribute-treatment interaction, wherein participants who began with high levels of career indecision and weak vocational identity benefited more from the program than participants with low levels of career indecision and strong vocational identity. In a similar study using a posttest-only experimental design, Enright (1997) investigated the effectiveness of a 3-week, 12-hour career development program for 38 underemployed or unemployed people with disabilities. No statistically significant effects emerged, though qualitative exit interview data supported the value of the program for the participants.

Other studies have assessed the effectiveness of psychosocial and vocational interventions. For example, Ericson and Riordan (1993) found a psychoeducational career workshop to be successful for young adults with end-stage renal disease. Ellis, McInerney, DiGiuseppe, and Yeager (1988) summarized research documenting the efficacy of rational–emotive therapy, a cognitively based therapy that incorporates a variety of skill development for people with alcohol or other drug addictions.

Environment

As noted earlier in this chapter, factors in the work environment can be strong determinants of career development of people with disabilities. Recent labor market dynamics and the rising costs of health care and worker compensation claims have propelled employers to develop or contract disability management programs (Habeck, Kress, Scully, & Kirchner, 1994). Habeck et al. (1994) concluded that companies can save 50% of their disability costs and 25% to 30% of their workers' compensation costs with the implementation of an effective disability management program (Habeck et al., 1994). Bruyère and Shrey (1991) reported on research indicating that both employers and injured workers benefit when the occupational bond is strengthened. This research suggests that work environment interventions are likely to increase.

The importance of work environment variables has been corroborated by qualitative studies. For example, in a study of 13 university students with disabilities and 9 university staff, Aune and Kroeger (1997) found work environment variables to be an important component of enhancing the career development of college students with disabilities. More specific support for the importance of work environment variables comes from a focus group study conducted by Fabian, Luecking, and Tilson (1995). Fabian et al. used a participatory action approach to assess employers' and rehabilitation personnel's perspectives on job placement. A major conclusion from their study involved how employers and rehabilitation personnel held different assumptions and perceptions regarding job development and job placement. Fabian et al. recommended that rehabilitation personnel should strive to have collaborative relationships with employers to bolster the employers' ability and confidence in hiring people with disabilities.

Individual and Environment

Interactions of individual and environmental constructs can influence career development. For example, Gates, Akabas, and Kantrowitz (1996) examined the role of supervisors in the job maintenance of people with disabilities. They obtained the input of 31 workers and 28 supervisors at one company's disability management program. Their data suggested a dynamic relationship between worker problems, accommodations, and performance evaluations. In particular, they found that workers whose disabilities were not adequately accommodated received lower performance evaluations and had lower levels of job satisfaction than workers whose disabilities were either adequately accommodated or who received accommodations they did not need. Other studies have challenged employers' reluctance to hire people with disabilities for fear of the expense of accommodations. Many accommodations do not cost anything, and the average cost ranges between $50 and $100 ("How to Hire and Evaluate Potential Employees with Disabilities," 2000).

Mentoring appears to be one method of improving individual–environment interactions. Its influence on vocational behavior was documented in a study conducted by Powers, Sowers, and Stevens (1995), although their sample was limited to adolescents with physical disabilities.

Outcome

The interaction of the constructs and processes of the model proposed in this chapter can produce a variety of outcomes. Examples of such outcomes are employment, disability and job stress, and job satisfaction.

Employment can be considered an outcome of the constructs and processes of the model. In a survey of 1,000 individuals with disabilities, Harris (1986) found that 66% of these individuals were unemployed, but two thirds of these expressed a desire to work. DeLoach (1989) examined the employment outcomes of 501 Illinois university alumni with disabilities. Of that group, 417 were employed. DeLoach's data revealed significant relationships of gender to marital status, college major, occupational category, part- or full-time work, and salary level.

Freedman and Fesko (1996) convened four focus groups designed "to identify key issues regarding the meaning of work for individuals with significant disabilities and their families" (p. 50). Their findings reinforced the notion that doing meaningful work is vital to job satisfaction.

Finally, disability itself can be a result of the interaction of the constructs and processes in Figure 4.1. Work by a number of authors, including Karašek and Theorell (1990), Fizgerald (1992), Keita and Hurrell (1994), and Sauter and Murphy (1995), has suggested that some interactions between individuals and their work environments can produce unhealthy job stress, which can produce physical and mental disabilities. It has been hypothesized that some people with disabilities may be at higher risk for negative job stress outcomes, which could exacerbate disabilities (Szymanski, 1999).

Considerations for Future Research

Research on the career development of people with disabilities presents interesting challenges. On one hand, it is important to study this special population because of its limited access to employment opportunities. On the other hand, it is important to note that there are inherent flaws in studying this or any population in isolation or in simple comparison with another group (e.g., people without disabilities; B. Wright, 1991). Not only do such studies distort understanding of the phenomena under consideration, but they also limit the extent to which the interaction of disability and the phenomena can be studied. With these considerations, the following considerations can be made for future research on career development of people with disabilities.

1. Career development is a complex phenomenon, and disability compounds the complexity. Organizing research into an integrated model of the relevant constructs and processes provides a framework for understanding links and considerations that may otherwise remain latent. The model in Figure 4.1 is a work in progress, which will continue to be shaped as new knowledge emerges. To that end, we recommend ongoing research into the constructs and processes of the model.
2. Our discussion of research was illustrative. Meta-analyses (where possible) and literature reviews for each of the constructs and processes would be timely and fruitful. It would be essential for any meta-analysis or literature review to incorporate research from a wide variety of fields, including counseling, educational

psychology, industrial and organizational psychology, health psychology, child psychology, rehabilitation psychology, sociology, special education, and the allied health fields.

3. Consider a variety of research methods. Qualitative research (see, e.g., Denzin & Lincoln, 1994; Ferguson, Ferguson, & Taylor, 1992; Maxwell, 1996; Strauss & Corbin, 1990; Young & Collin, 1992) should continue to help develop theory and offer insight into thoughts, perceptions, contexts, and processes that influence career behavior. Descriptive and exploratory approaches to research are also important. As recommended by Phillips et al. (1983), even quantitative research can be used to generate as well as test theory.

4. Include people with disabilities as well as people from racial and ethnic minority groups in larger scale research on career development of general populations (Fitzgerald & Betz, 1994). In this way, not only will career development of people with disabilities be understood in a broader context, but the general understanding of career development will also benefit. In addition, people with preexisting disabilities need to be included in large-scale job stress research. This strategy will not only help identify possible risk factors associated with disabilities but will also increase the utility of such large-scale stress research.

5. Be cautious about generalizations regarding study populations. The population of people with disabilities is too diverse to permit large-scale generalizations on the basis of disability. In addition, because many aspects of career development appear to be related to cognitive factors (Lent & Hackett, 1994), level and type of cognitive impairment must be controlled for either by selection or inclusion in the research design.

6. Quantitative researchers should strive for large samples and avoid small convenience samples. When planning hypothesis testing studies, researchers should do preanalysis power estimation to ensure a large enough sample size for adequate statistical power (Cohen, 1988). Similarly, in descriptive and ex post facto studies, researchers should carefully choose sampling strategies to ensure adequate representation of the target population.

7. When possible, try to use established instruments. This will allow the research to be tied to larger bases of study. However, the reliability of the instruments for the study populations must be established as part of the research (Pedhazur & Schmelkin, 1991). Similarly researchers will want to consider validity by asking how the impact of disability might affect the construct of interest.

SUMMARY AND RECOMMENDATIONS

Advances in career development theories have accelerated during recent years. Theories that currently inform counseling and education include person–environment interaction models, Super's theory, Holland's typology, Krumboltz's social learning theory, Hershenson's work adjustment model, social cognitive career theory, developmental contextualism, sociological and economic models, and organizational career theory. The interrelation of some of these theories was addressed by the convergence project. Although the project stimulated understanding of the field, it was suggested that different theories have different audiences, and their concurrent use to interpret research can further illuminate knowledge in the field. Nonetheless, the project appears to have affected the evolution of some of the theories.

Applicability of career development theories to people with disabilities remains a concern. In this chapter, we repeat the approach from our previous work. Essentially, we believe that theories are neither applicable nor nonapplicable. Rather, they provide conceptual frameworks that must be adjusted for use according to the circumstances of the individual. This approach is especially important when working with diverse populations (e.g., people with disabilities, members of racial and ethnic minority groups). Borrowing from Mastie (1994), we contend that the counselor is the compass for selectively using and interpreting the theories based on the individual client situation.

To assist counselors and researchers in interpreting theories and conceptualizing the career development of people with and without disabilities, we expanded our ecological model, first introduced in the last version of this chapter. The model consists of five groups of constructs and seven groups of processes. The constructs are context, individual, mediating, environmental, and outcome; the processes are development, decision making, congruence, socialization, allocation, chance, and labor market forces.

Research must further understanding of the nature of career development of people with and without disabilities. We have pointed to some of the methodological problems inherent in studying the career development of people with disabilities. We suggest that research on career development of people with disabilities should proceed cautiously on both qualitative and quantitative fronts.

REFERENCES

Altmaier, E. M., Russell, D. W., Kao, C. F., Lehmann, T. R., & Weinstein, J. N. (1993). Role of self-efficacy in rehabilitation outcome among chronic low back pain patients. *Journal of Counseling Psychology*, *40*, 335–339.

Americans with Disabilities Act of 1990, 42 U.S.C. § 12101 *et seq*.

Anderson, R. J., & Antonak, R. F. (1992). The influence of attitudes and contact on reactions to persons with physical and speech difficulties. *Rehabilitation Counseling Bulletin*, *35*, 240–247.

Atkins, B. (1988). An asset-oriented approach to cross-cultural issues: Blacks in rehabilitation. *Journal of Applied Rehabilitation Counseling, 19*(4), 45–49.

Atkins, B. J., & Wright, G. N. (1980). Three views of the vocational rehabilitation of Blacks: The statement. *Journal of Rehabilitation*, *46*(2), 40–46.

Atkinson, D. R., & Thompson, C. E. (1992). Racial, ethnic, and cultural variables in counseling. In S. D. Brown & R. W. Lent (Eds.), *Handbook of counseling psychology* (2nd ed., pp. 349–382). New York: Wiley.

Aune, B. P., & Kroeger, S. A. (1997). Career development of college students with disabilities: An interactional approach to defining the issues. *Journal of College Student Development*, *38*, 344–355.

Bandura, A. (1977). *Social learning theory*. Englewood Cliffs, NJ: Prentice Hall.

Bandura, A. (1982). Self-efficacy mechanism in human agency. *American Psychologist*, *37*, 122–147.

Becker, H., & Schaller, J. (1995). Perceived health and self-efficacy among adults with cerebral palsy. *Journal of Rehabilitation*, *61*(2), 36–42.

Biller, E. F. (1988). Career decision making attitudes of college students with learning disabilities. *Journal of Postsecondary Education and Disability*, *6*(4), 14–20.

Bizot, E. B., & Goldman, S. H. (1993). Prediction of satisfactoriness and satisfaction: An 8-year follow up. *Journal of Vocational Behavior*, *43*, 19–29.

Bolton, B., & Akridge, R. L. (1995). A meta-analysis of skills training programs for rehabilitation clients. *Rehabilitation Counseling Bulletin*, *38*, 262–273.

Borgen, F. H. (1990). Megatrends and milestones in vocational behavior: A 20-year counseling psychology retrospective. *Journal of Vocational Behavior*, *39*, 263–290.

Bowman, S. L. (1993). Career intervention strategies for ethnic minorities. *Career Development Quarterly*, *42*, 14–25.

Braddock, D., & Bachelder, L. (1994). *The glass ceiling and persons with disabilities* (Public Policy Monograph No. 56). Chicago: University of Illinois at Chicago, Institute on Disability and Human Development.

Breeden, S. A. (1993). Job and occupational change as a function of occupational correspondence and job satisfaction. *Journal of Vocational Behavior*, *43*, 30–45.

Brodwin, M., Parker, R. M., & DeLaGarza, D. (1996). Disability and accommodation.

In E. M. Szymanski & R. M. Parker (Eds.), *Work and disability: Issues and strategies in career development and job placement* (pp. 165–208). Austin, TX: PRO-ED.

Bronfenbrenner, U. (1977). Toward an experimental ecology of human development. *American Psychologist, 32*, 513–531.

Brown, D. (1990a). Summary, comparison, and critique of the major theories. In D. Brown & L. Brooks (Eds.), *Career choice and development: Applying contemporary theories to practice* (2nd ed., pp. 338–363). San Francisco: Jossey-Bass.

Brown, D. (1990b). Trait and factor theory. In D. Brown & L. Brooks (Eds.), *Career choice and development: Applying contemporary theories to practice* (2nd ed., pp. 13–36). San Francisco: Jossey-Bass.

Brown, D., & Brooks, L. (Eds.). (1990). *Career choice and development* (2nd ed.). San Francisco: Jossey-Bass.

Brown, D., & Brooks, L. (Eds.). (1996a). *Career choice and development* (3rd ed.). San Francisco: Jossey-Bass.

Brown, D., & Brooks, L. (1996b). Introduction to theories of career development and choice: Origins, evolution, and current approaches. In D. Brown & L. Brooks (Eds.), *Career choice and development* (3rd ed., pp. 1–13). San Francisco: Jossey-Bass.

Bruyère, S. M., & Shrey, D. E. (1991). Disability management in industry: A joint labor-management process. *Rehabilitation Counseling Bulletin, 34*, 227–242.

Burke, R. J., & Nelson, D. (1998). Mergers and acquisitions, downsizing, and privatization: A North American perspective. In M. K. Gowing, J. D. Kraft, & J. C. Quick (Eds.), *The new organizational reality: Downsizing, restructuring, and revitalization* (pp. 21–54). Washington, DC: American Psychological Association.

Cabral, A. C., & Salomone, P. R. (1990). Chance and careers: Normative versus contextual development. *The Career Development Quarterly, 39*, 5–17.

Chartrand, J. M. (1991). The evolution of trait-and-factor career counseling: A person × environment fit approach. *Journal of Counseling and Development, 69*, 518–524.

Cohen, J. (1988). *Statistical power analysis for the behavioral sciences* (2nd ed.). Hillsdale, NJ: Erlbaum.

Cohen, J. (1994). The earth is round ($p < .05$). *American Psychologist, 49*, 997–1003.

Conte, L. (1983). Vocational development theories and the disabled person: Oversight or deliberate omission. *Rehabilitation Counseling Bulletin, 26*, 316–328.

Conyers, L. M., Koch, L. C., & Szymanski, E. M. (1998). Life-span perspectives of disability and work: A qualitative study. *Rehabilitation Counseling Bulletin, 42*, 51–75.

Conyers, L., & Szymanski, E. M. (1998). The effectiveness of an integrated career intervention on college students with and without disabilities. *Journal of Postsecondary Education and Disability, 13*(1), 23–34.

Cook, D. (1992). Psychosocial impact of disability. In R. M. Parker & E. M. Szymanski (Eds.), *Rehabilitation counseling: Basics and beyond* (pp. 249–272). Austin, TX: PRO-ED.

Cook, E. P. (1991). Annual review: Practice and research in career counseling and development. *Career Development Quarterly, 40*, 99–131.

Cook, E. P. (1993). The gendered context of life: Implications for women's and men's career-life plans. *Career Development Quarterly*, *41*, 227–237.

Cook, T. D., & Campbell, D. T. (1979). *Quasi-experimentation: Design and analysis issues for field settings*. Boston: Houghton Mifflin.

Cottone, R. R. (1986). Toward a systemic theoretical framework for vocational rehabilitation. *Journal of Applied Rehabilitation Counseling, 17*(4), 4–7.

Cox, T. (1993). *Cultural diversity in organizations: Theory, research, and practice*. San Francisco: Berrett-Koehler.

Curnow, T. C. (1989). Vocational development of persons with disability. *Vocational Guidance Quarterly*, *37*, 269–278.

Dawis, R. V. (1994). The theory of work adjustment as convergent theory. In M. L. Savickas & R. W. Lent (Eds.), *Convergence in career development theories: Implications for science and practice* (pp. 33–43). Palo Alto, CA: Consulting Psychologists Press.

Dawis, R. V., Dohm, T. E., & Jackson, C. R. S. (1993). Describing work environments as reinforcer systems: Reinforcement schedules versus reinforcer classes. *Journal of Vocational Behavior*, *43*, 5–18.

DeLoach, C. P. (1989). Gender, career choice and occupational outcomes among college alumni with disabilities. *Journal of Applied Rehabilitation Counseling, 20*(4), 8–12.

Denzin, N. K., & Lincoln, Y. S. (Eds.). (1994). *Handbook of qualitative research*. Thousand Oaks, CA: Sage.

Duvdevany, I., & Rimmerman, A. (1996). Individuals with work-related disabilities: Locus of control, attitudes toward work, and cooperation with the rehabilitation worker. *Journal of Applied Rehabilitation Counseling, 27*(2), 30–35.

Dziekan, K. I., & Okocha, A. G. (1993). Accessibility of rehabilitation services: Comparison by racial-ethnic status. *Rehabilitation Counseling Bulletin*, *36*, 183–189.

Ellis, A., McInerney, J. F., DiGiuseppe, R., & Yeager, R. J. (1988). *Rational-emotive therapy with alcoholics and substance abusers*. Elmsford, NY: Pergamon.

Enright, M. S. (1996). The relationship between disability status, career beliefs, and career indecision. *Rehabilitation Counseling Bulletin*, *40*, 134–153.

Enright, M. S. (1997). The impact of a short-term career development program on people with disabilities. *Rehabilitation Counseling Bulletin*, *40*, 285–300.

Enright, M. S., Conyers, L. M., & Szymanski, E. M. (1996). Career and career-related educational concerns of college students with disabilities. *Journal of Counseling and Development*, *75*, 103–114.

Erickson, K. A. (1996). Effects of didactic and experiential education of conception of persons with serious mental illness. *Dissertation Abstracts International*, 56(8-B), 4568.

Ericson, G. D., & Riordan, R. J. (1993). Effects of a psychosocial and vocational intervention on the rehabilitation potential of young adults with end-stage renal disease. *Rehabilitation Counseling Bulletin*, *37*, 146–162.

Erikson, K., & Vallas, S. P. (Eds.). (1990). *The nature of work: Sociological perspectives*. New Haven, CT: Yale University Press.

Fabian, E. S., Luecking, R. G., & Tilson, G. P. (1995). Employer and rehabilitation personnel perspectives on hiring people with disabilities: Implications for job development. *Journal of Rehabilitation, 61*(1), 42–49.

Farley, R. C., Bolton, B., & Parkerson, S. (1992). Effects of client involvement in assessment on vocational development. *Rehabilitation Counseling Bulletin, 35*, 146–153.

Farley, R. C., Johnson, V., & Parkerson, S. S. (1999). Effects of a career assessment and planning intervention on the vocational development of secondary students with disabilities: A pilot study. *Vocational Evaluation and Work Adjustment Journal, 31*(1), 15–21.

Ferguson, P. M., Ferguson, D. L., & Jones, D. (1988). Generations of hope: Parental perspectives on the transitions of their children with severe disabilities from school to adult life. *Journal of the Association for Persons with Severe Handicaps, 13*, 177–187.

Ferguson, P. M., Ferguson, D. L., & Taylor, S. J. (Eds.). (1992). *Interpreting disability: A qualitative reader*. New York: Teachers College Press.

Fichten, C. S., & Bourdon, C. V. (1986). Social skill deficit or response inhibition: Interaction between disabled and nondisabled college students. *Journal of College Student Personnel, 27*, 326–333.

Fichten, C. S., Lennox, H., Robillard, K., Wright, J., Sabourin, S., & Amsel, R. (1996). Attentional focus and attitudes toward peers with disabilities: Self-focusing and a comparison of modeling and self-disclosure. *Journal of Applied Rehabilitation Counseling, 27*(4), 30–39.

Fichten, C. S., Tagalakis, V., & Amsel, R. (1989). Effects of cognitive modeling, affect, and previous contact on attitudes, thoughts, and feelings toward college students with physical disabilities. *Journal of the Multihandicapped Person, 2*(2), 119–137.

Fitzgerald, T. E. (1992). Psychological aspects of work-related musculoskeletal disability. In J. C. Quick, L. R. Murphy, & J. J. Hurrell, Jr. (Eds.), *Stress and well-being at work: Assessments and interventions for occupational mental health* (pp. 117–133). Washington, DC: American Psychological Association.

Fitzgerald, L. F., & Betz, N. E. (1994). Career development in cultural context: The role of gender, race, class, and sexual orientation. In M. L. Savickas & R. W. Lent (Eds.), *Convergence in career development theories: Implications for science and practice* (pp. 103–117). Palo Alto, CA: Consulting Psychologists Press.

Fitzgerald, L. F., Fassinger, R. E., & Betz, N. E. (1995). Theoretical advances in the study of women's career development. In W. B. Walsh & S. H. Osipow (Eds.), *Handbook of vocational psychology: Theory, research, and practice* (2nd ed., pp. 67–109). Mahwah, NJ: Erlbaum.

Fouad, N. A. (1993). Cross-cultural vocational assessment. *Career Development Quarterly, 42*, 4–13.

Freedman, R. I., & Fesko, S. L. (1996). The meaning of work in the lives of people with disabilities: Consumer and family perspectives. *Journal of Rehabilitation, 62*(3), 49–55.

Gates, L. B., Akabas, S. H., & Kantrowitz, W. (1996). Supervisors' role in successful job maintenance: A target for rehabilitation counselor efforts. *Journal of Applied Rehabilitation Counseling, 27*(3), 60–66.

Ginzberg, E., Ginsburg, S. W., Axelrod, S., & Herma, J. L. (1951). *Occupational choice: An approach to a general theory*. New York: Columbia University Press.

Gottfredson, L. S. (1996). Gottfredson's theory of circumscription and compromise. In D. Brown & L. Brooks (Eds.), *Career choice and development* (3rd ed., pp. 179–232). San Francisco: Jossey-Bass.

Gove, W. R. (1976). Social reaction theory and disability. In G. L. Albrecht (Ed.), *The sociology of physical disability and rehabilitation* (pp. 57–71). Pittsburgh, PA: University of Pittsburgh Press.

Gutteridge, T. G. (1986). Organizational career development systems: The state of the practice. In D. T. Hall (Ed.), *Career development in organizations* (pp. 50–94). San Francisco: Jossey-Bass.

Gutteridge, T. G., Leibowitz, Z. B., & Shore, J. E. (1993). *Organizational career development: Benchmarks for building a world-class workforce*. San Francisco: Jossey-Bass.

Habeck, R., Kress, M., Scully, S., & Kirchner, K. (1994). Determining the significance of the disability management movement for rehabilitation counselor education. *Rehabilitation Education*, *8*, 195–240.

Hackett, G., & Betz, N. E. (1981). A self-efficacy approach to the career development of women. *Journal of Vocational Behavior, 18*, 326–339.

Hackett, G., & Lent, R. W. (1992). Theoretical advances and current inquiry in career psychology. In S. D. Brown & R. W. Lent (Eds.), *Handbook of counseling psychology* (2nd ed., pp. 419–451). New York: Wiley.

Hall, D. T. (1986). Introduction: An overview of current career development theory, research, and practice. In D. T. Hall (Ed.), *Career development in organizations* (pp. 1–20). San Francisco: Jossey-Bass.

Hall, D. T. (1990). Career development theory in organizations. In D. Brown & L. Brooks (Eds.), *Career choice and development: Applying contemporary theories to practice* (pp. 422–454). San Francisco: Jossey-Bass.

Hall, D. T. (Ed.). (1996). *The career is dead: Long live the career*. San Francisco: Jossey-Bass.

Hall, D. T., & Mirvis, P. H. (1996). The new protean career: Psychological success and the path with a heart. In D. T. Hall (Ed.), *The career is dead: Long live the career* (pp. 15–45). San Francisco: Jossey-Bass.

Hall, D. T., & Moss, J. E. (1998). The new protean career contract: Helping organizations and employees adapt. *Organizational Dynamics*, *26*(3), 22–37.

Hanley-Maxwell, C., Pogoloff, S., & Whitney-Thomas, J. (1997). Family involvement. In F. R. Rusch & J. Chadsey-Rusch (Eds.), *Transition from school to work: New opportunities for adolescents* (pp. 234–264). Pacific Grove, CA: Brookes/Cole.

Hanley-Maxwell, C., Whitney-Thomas, J., & Pogoloff, S. (1995). The second shock: A qualitative study of parents' perspectives and needs during their child's transition from school to adult life. *Journal of the Association of Persons with Severe Handicaps*, *20*, 3–15.

Hardin, E. E., Leong, F. T. L., & Osipow, S. H. (2001). Cultural relativity in the conceptualization of career maturity. *Journal of Vocational Behavior*, *58*, 36–52.

Harris, L. (1986). *The ICD survey of disabled Americans: Bringing disabled Americans into the mainstream*. New York: Author.

Haveman, R., & Wolfe, B. (1994). *Succeeding generations: On the effects of investments in children*. New York: Russell Sage Foundation.

Hawks, B. K., & Muha, D. (1991). Facilitating the career development of minorities: Doing it differently this time. *Career Development Quarterly, 39*, 251–260.

Hays, W. L. (1988). *Statistics* (4th ed.). New York: Holt, Rinehart, & Winston.

Herr, E. L. (2001). Career development and its practice: A historical perspective. *Career Development Quarterly, 49*, 196–211.

Herr, E. L., & Cramer, S. H. (1992). *Career guidance and counseling through the lifespan: Systematic approaches* (4th ed.). New York: HarperCollins.

Hershenson, D. B. (1974). Vocational guidance and the handicapped. In E. Herr (Ed.), *Vocational guidance and human development* (pp. 478–501). Boston: Houghton Mifflin.

Hershenson, D. B. (1981). Work adjustment, disability, and the three r's of vocational rehabilitation: A conceptual model. *Rehabilitation Counseling Bulletin, 25*, 91–97.

Hershenson, D. B. (1996). Work adjustment: A neglected area in career counseling. *Journal of Counseling and Development, 74*, 442–448.

Hershenson, D. B. (1998). Systemic, ecological model for rehabilitation counseling. *Rehabilitation Counseling Bulletin, 42*, 40–50.

Hershenson, D. B., & Szymanski, E. M. (1992). Career development of people with disabilities. In R. M. Parker & E. M. Szymanski (Eds.), *Rehabilitation counseling: Basics and beyond* (2nd ed., pp. 273–303). Austin, TX: PRO-ED.

Holland, J. L. (1985a). *Making vocational choices: A theory of vocational personalities and work environments* (2nd ed.). Englewood Cliffs, NJ: Prentice Hall.

Holland, J. L. (1985b). *Vocational Preference Inventory*. Odessa, FL: Psychological Assessment Resources.

Holland, J. L. (1994). Separate but unequal is better. In M. L. Savickas & R. W. Lent (Eds.), *Convergence in career development theories: Implications for science and practice* (pp. 45–51). Palo Alto, CA: Consulting Psychologists Press.

Holland, J. L., Daiger, D. C., & Power, P. G. (1980). *Manual for My Vocational Situation*. Palo Alto, CA: Consulting Psychologists Press.

Holland, J. L., Fritzsche, B. A., & Powell, A. B. (1994). *The Self-Directed Search (SDS) technical manual*. Odessa, FL: Psychological Assessment Resources.

Holland, J. L., & Gottfredson, G. D. (1994). *The Career Attitudes and Strategies Inventory*. Odessa, FL: Psychological Assessment Resources.

Holzbauer, J. J., & Berven, N. L. (1996). Disability harassment: A new term for a longstanding problem. *Journal of Counseling and Development, 74*, 478–483.

Hotchkiss, L., & Borow, H. (1990). Sociological perspectives on work and career development. In D. Brown & L. Brooks (Eds.), *Career choice and development: Applying contemporary theories to practice* (2nd ed., pp. 262–307). San Francisco: Jossey-Bass.

Hotchkiss, L., & Borow, H. (1996). Sociological perspectives on work and career development. In D. Brown & L. Brooks (Eds.), *Career choice and development* (3rd ed., pp. 281–334). San Francisco: Jossey-Bass.

How to hire and evaluate potential employees with disabilities. (2000, January). *HR Focus*, 4.

Individuals with Disabilities Education Act of 1990, 20 U.S.C. § 1400 *et seq.*

Ingstad, B., & Whyte, S. R. (1995). *Disability and culture*. Berkeley: University of California Press.

James, K. (1994). Social identity, work stress, and minority workers' health. In G. P. Keita & J. J. Hurrell, Jr. (Eds.), *Job stress in a changing workforce: Investigating gender, diversity, and family issues* (pp. 127–145). Washington, DC: American Psychological Association.

Jenkins, W., Patterson, J. B., & Szymanski, E. M. (1998). Philosophical, historic, and legislative aspects of the rehabilitation counseling profession. In R. M. Parker & E. M. Szymanski (Eds.), *Rehabilitation counseling: Basics and beyond* (3rd ed., pp. 1–40). Austin, TX: PRO-ED.

Karasek, R., & Theorell, T. (1990). *Healthy work: Stress, productivity, and the reconstruction of working life*. New York: Basic Books.

Keita, G. P., & Hurrell, J. J., Jr. (Eds.). (1994). *Job stress in a changing workforce: Investigating gender, diversity, and family issues*. Washington, DC: American Psychological Association.

Kerlinger, F. N. (1986). *Foundations of behavioral research* (3rd ed.). New York: Holt, Rinehart, & Winston.

Kosciulek, J. F., & Szymanski, E. M. (1993). Statistical power analysis of rehabilitation counseling research. *Rehabilitation Counseling Bulletin, 36*, 212–219.

Krieshok, T. S., Hecox, J. L., Wettersten, K., & Ulven, J. C. (2000). Resume therapy and vocational test feedback: Tailoring interventions to self-efficacy outcomes. *Journal of Career Assessment, 8*, 267–281.

Krumboltz, J. D. (1988). *Career Beliefs Inventory*. Palo Alto, CA: Consulting Psychologists Press.

Krumboltz, J. D. (1994). Improving career development theory from a social learning perspective. In M. L. Savickas & R. W. Lent (Eds.), *Convergence in career development theories: Implications for science and practice* (pp. 9–31). Palo Alto, CA: Consulting Psychologists Press.

LaFromboise, T., Coleman, H. L. K., & Gerton, J. (1993). Psychological impact of biculturalism: Evidence and theory. *Psychological Bulletin, 114*, 395–412.

Lechner, D. E. (1994). Work hardening and work conditioning interventions: Do they affect disability? *Physical Therapy, 74*, 471–493.

Lee, C. C. (1991). Cultural dynamics: Their importance in multicultural counseling. In C. C. Lee & B. L. Richardson (Eds.), *Multicultural issues in counseling: New approaches to diversity* (pp. 11–17). Alexandria, VA: American Counseling Association.

Lee, C. C., & Richardson, B. R. (Eds.). (1991). *Multicultural issues in counseling: New approaches to diversity*. Alexandria, VA: American Counseling Association.

Lent, R. W., Brown, S. D., & Hackett, G. (1996). Career development from a social cognitive perspective. In D. Brown & L. Brooks (Eds.), *Career choice and development* (3rd ed., pp. 373–421). San Francisco: Jossey-Bass.

Lent, R. W., Brown, S. D., & Hackett, G. (2000). Contextual supports and barriers to career choice: A social cognitive analysis. *Journal of Counseling Psychology, 47,* 36–49.

Lent, R. W., & Hackett, G. (1994). Sociocognitive mechanisms of personal agency in career development: Pan theoretical prospects. In M. L. Savickas & R. W. Lent (Eds.), *Convergence in career development: Implications for science and practice* (pp. 77–101). Palo Alto, CA: Consulting Psychologists Press.

Lent, R. W., Hackett, G., & Brown, S. D. (1999). A social cognitive view of school-to-work transition. *Career Development Quarterly, 47,* 297–311.

Leong, F. T. L. (Ed.). (1995). *Career development and vocational behavior of racial and ethnic minorities.* Mahwah, NJ: Erlbaum.

Leong, F. T. L., & Serafica, F. C. (2001). Cross-cultural perspective on Super's career development theory: Career maturity and cultural accommodation. In F. T. L. Leong & A. Barak (Eds.), *Contemporary models in vocational psychology* (pp. 167–205). Mahwah, NJ: Erlbaum.

Livneh, H., & Antonak, R. (1997). *Psychosocial adaptation to chronic illness and disability.* Gaithersburg, MD: Aspen.

Lofquist, L. H., & Dawis, R. V. (1969). *Adjustment to work: A psychological view of man's problems in a work-oriented society.* New York: Appleton-Century-Crofts.

Lofquist, L. H., & Dawis, R. V. (1991). *Essentials of person environment correspondence counseling.* Minneapolis: University of Minnesota Press.

London, M., & Stumpf, S. A. (1986). Individual and organizational career development in changing times. In D. T. Hall (Ed.), *Career development in organizations* (pp. 21–49). San Francisco: Jossey-Bass.

Makas, E. (1985, August) *The measurement of attitudes toward disabled people: A new approach.* Paper presented at meeting of the American Psychological Association, Los Angeles.

Maranda, M. F., & Comeau, Y. (2000). Some contributions of sociology to the understanding of career. In A. Collin & R. A. Young (Eds.), *The future of career* (pp. 37–52). Cambridge, United Kingdom: Cambridge University Press.

Marshall, C., Johnson, M. J., Martin, W. E., Saravanabhavan, R. C., & Bradford, B. (1992). The rehabilitation needs of American Indians with disabilities in an urban setting. *Journal of Rehabilitation, 58*(2), 13–21.

Martin, R. E., & Freeman, S. J. (1998). The economic context of the new organizational reality. In M. K. Gowing, J. D. Kraft, & J. C. Quick (Eds.), *The new organizational reality: Downsizing, restructuring, and revitalization* (pp. 5–20). Washington, DC: American Psychological Association.

Martin, W. E. (1991). Career development and American Indians living on reservations: Cross cultural factors to consider. *Career Development Quarterly, 39,* 273–283.

Mastie, M. M. (1994). Using assessment instruments in career counseling: Career assessment as compass, credential, process and empowerment. In J. T. Kapes, M. M. Mastie,

& E. A. Whitfield (Eds.), *A counselor's guide to career assessment instruments* (3rd ed., pp. 31–40). Alexandria, VA: National Career Development Association.

Maxwell, J. A. (1996). *Qualitative research: An interactive approach.* Thousand Oaks, CA: Sage.

Merz, M. A., & Szymanski, E. M. (1997). The effects of a vocational rehabilitation based career workshop on commitment to career choice. *Rehabilitation Counseling Bulletin, 41,* 88–104.

Mitchell, K. E., Levin, A. S., & Krumboltz, J. D. (1999). Planned happenstance: Constructing unexpected career opportunities. *Journal of Counseling and Development, 77,* 115–124.

Mitchell, L. K., & Krumboltz, J. D. (1990). Social learning approach to career decision making: Krumboltz's theory. In D. Brown & L. Brooks (Eds.), *Career choice and development: Applying contemporary theories to practice* (2nd ed., pp. 145–196). San Francisco: Jossey-Bass.

Mitchell, L. K., & Krumboltz, J. D. (1996). Krumboltz's learning theory of career choice and counseling. In D. Brown & L. Brooks (Eds.), *Career choice and development* (3rd ed., pp. 233–280). San Francisco: Jossey-Bass.

Moore, C. L., & Feist-Price, S. (1999). Societal attitudes and the civil rights of persons with disabilities. *Journal of Applied Rehabilitation Counseling, 30*(2), 19–24.

Moos, R. H. (1986). Work as a human context. In M. S. Pallak & R. Perloff (Eds.), *Psychology and work: Productivity, change, and employment* (pp. 9–52). Washington, DC: American Psychological Association.

Neimeyer, L. O., Jacobs, K., Reynolds-Lynch, K., Bettencourt, C., & Lang, S. (1994). Work hardening: Past, present, and future—the work programs special interest section National Work-Hardening Outcome Study. *American Journal of Occupational Therapy, 48,* 327–339.

Osipow, S. H. (1976). Vocational development problems of the handicapped. In H. Rusalem & D. Malikin (Eds.), *Contemporary vocational rehabilitation* (pp. 51–60). New York: New York University Press.

Osipow, S. H. (1983). *Theories of career development* (3rd ed.). Englewood Cliffs, NJ: Prentice Hall.

Osipow, S. H. (1990). Convergence in theories of career choice and development: Review and prospect. *Journal of Vocational Behavior, 36,* 122–131.

Osipow, S. H. (1994). Moving career theory into the twenty-first century. In M. L. Savickas & R. W. Lent (Eds.), *Convergence in career development theories: Implications for science and practice* (pp. 217–224). Palo Alto, CA: Consulting Psychologists Press.

Osipow, S. H., Carney, C. G., Winer, J. L., Yanico, B., & Koschier, M. (1976). *The Career Decision Scale* (3rd ed.). Odessa, FL: Psychological Assessment Resources.

Osipow, S. H., & Littlejohn, E. M. (1995). Toward a multicultural theory of career development: Prospects and dilemmas. In F. T. L. Leong (Ed.), *Career development and vocational behavior of racial and ethnic minorities* (pp. 251–261). Mahwah, NJ: Erlbaum.

Parsons, F. (1909). *Choosing a vocation.* Boston: Houghton Mifflin.

Pederson, P. (1994). *A handbook for developing multicultural awareness* (2nd ed.). Alexandria, VA: American Counseling Association Press.

Pedhazur, E. J., & Schmelkin, L. P. (1991). *Measurement, design, and analysis: An integrated approach*. Hillsdale, NJ: Erlbaum.

Phillips, S. D., Strohmer, D. C., Berthaume, B. L. J., & O'Leary, J. C. (1983). Career development of special populations: A framework for research. *Journal of Vocational Behavior, 22*, 12–29.

Pope-Davis, D. B., & Hargrove, B. K. (2001). Future directions in career counseling theory, research, and practice with African Americans. In W. B. Walsh, R. P. Bingham, M. T. Brown, & C. M. Ward (Eds.), *Career counseling for African Americans* (pp. 177–192). Mahwah, NJ: Erlbaum.

Powers, L. E., Sowers, J., & Stevens, T. (1995). An exploratory, randomized study of the impact of mentoring on the self-efficacy and community-based knowledge of adolescents with severe physical challeges. *Journal of Rehabilitation, 61*(1), 33–41.

Rehabilitation Act of 1973, 29 U.S.C. § 701 *et seq.*

Ross, R. R., & Altmaier, E. M. (1994). *Intervention in occupational stress*. London: Sage.

Rothman, R. A. (1987). *Working: Sociological perspectives*. Englewood Cliffs, NJ: Prentice Hall.

Rounds, J. B. (1990). The comparative and combined utility of work value and interest data in career counseling with adults. *Journal of Vocational Behavior, 37*, 32–45.

Rounds, J., & Hesketh, B. (1994). The theory of work adjustment: Unifying principles and concepts. In M. L. Savickas & R. W. Lent (Eds.), *Convergence in career development theories: Implications for science and practice* (pp. 177–186). Palo Alto, CA: Consulting Psychologists Press.

Rounds, J. B., & Tracey, T. J. (1990). From trait-and-factor to person-environment fit counseling: Theory and process. In W. B. Walsh & S. H. Osipow (Eds.), *Career counseling: Contemporary topics in vocational psychology* (pp. 1–44). Hillsdale, NJ: Erlbaum.

Rowe, W., Behrens, J. T., & Leach, M. M. (1995). Racial/ethnic identity and racial consciousness: Looking back and looking forward. In J. G. Ponterotto, J. M. Casas, L. A. Suzuki, & C. M. Alexander (Eds.), *Handbook of multicultural counseling* (pp. 218–235). Thousand Oaks, CA: Sage.

Rubin, S. E., & Roessler, R. T. (1994). *Foundations of the vocational rehabilitation process* (4th ed.). Austin, TX: PRO-ED.

Ryan, C. P. (1995). Work isn't what it used to be: Implications, recommendations, and strategies for vocational rehabilitation. *Journal of Rehabilitation, 61*(4), 8–15.

Salomone, P. R., & O'Connell, K. R. (1998). The impact of disability on the career development of people with multiple sclerosis. *Journal of Career Development, 25*, 65–81.

Sauter, S. L., & Murphy, L. R. (Eds.). (1995). *Organizational risk factors for job stress*. Washington, DC: American Psychological Association.

Savickas, M. L., & Lent, R. W. (Eds.). (1994a). *Convergence in career development theories: Implications for science and practice*. Palo Alto, CA: Consulting Psychologists Press.

Savickas, M. L., & Lent, R. W. (1994b). Introduction: A convergence project for career psychology. In M. L. Savickas & R. W. Lent (Eds.), *Convergence in career development theories: Implications for science and practice* (pp. 1–6). Palo Alto, CA: Consulting Psychologists Press.

Savickas, M. L., & Lent, R. W. (1994c). Postscript: Is convergence a viable agenda for career psychology? In M. L. Savickas & R. W. Lent (Eds.), *Convergence in career development theories: Implications for science and practice* (pp. 259–271). Palo Alto, CA: Consulting Psychologists Press.

Schaller, J., Parker, R., & Garcia, S. (1998). Moving toward culturally competent rehabilitation counseling: Issues and practices. *Journal of Applied Rehabilitation Counseling, 29*(2), 40–48.

Schein, E. H. (1986). A critical look at current career development theory and research. In D. T. Hall (Ed.), *Career development in organizations* (pp. 310–331). San Francisco: Jossey-Bass.

Scott, R. A. (1969). *The making of blind men: A study of adult socialization*. New York: Russell Sage Foundation.

Scroggin, C., Kosciulek, J. F., Sweiven, K. A., & Enright, M. S. (1999). Impact of situational assessment on the career self-efficacy of people with disabilities. *Vocational Evaluation and Work Adjustment Bulletin, 32*(2), 97–107.

Smart, J. (2001). *Disability, society, and the individual*. Gaithersburg, MD: Aspen.

Smart, J. F., & Smart, D. W. (1991). Acceptance of disability and the Mexican American culture. *Rehabilitation Counseling Bulletin, 34*, 357–367.

Storey, J. A. (2000). 'Fracture lines' in the career environment. In A. Collin & R. A. Young (Eds.), *The future of career* (pp. 21–36). Cambridge, United Kingdom: Cambridge University Press.

Strauser, D. R. (1995). Applications of self-efficacy theory in rehabilitation counseling. *Journal of Rehabilitation, 61*(1), 7–11.

Strauss, A., & Corbin, J. (1990). *Basics of qualitative research: Grounded theory procedures and techniques*. Newbury Park, CA: Sage.

Sue, D. W., & Sue, D. (1990). *Counseling the culturally different: Theory and practice* (2nd ed.). New York: Wiley.

Super, D. E. (1953). A theory of vocational development. *American Psychologist, 8*, 185–190.

Super, D. E. (1957). *The psychology of careers*. New York: Harper & Row.

Super, D. E. (1990). A life-span, life-space approach to career development. In D. Brown & L. Brooks (Eds.), *Career choice and development: Applying contemporary theories to practice* (2nd ed., pp. 197–261). San Francisco: Jossey-Bass.

Super, D. E. (1994). A life span, life space perspective on convergence. In M. L. Savickas & R. W. Lent (Eds.), *Convergence in career development theories: Implications for science and practice* (pp. 63–74). Palo Alto, CA: Consulting Psychologists Press.

Super, D. E., & Nevill, D. D. (1986a). *The Salience Inventory*. Palo Alto, CA: Consulting Psychologists Press.

Super, D. E., & Nevill, D. D. (1986b). *The Values Scale*. Palo Alto, CA: Consulting Psychologists Press.

Super, D. E., Savickas, M. L., & Super, C. M. (1996). The life-span, life-space approach to careers. In D. Brown & L. Brooks (Eds.), *Career choice and development* (3rd ed., pp. 121–178). San Francisco: Jossey-Bass.

Super, D. E., & Šverko, B. (Eds.). (1995). *Life roles, values, and careers: International findings of the Work Importance Study*. San Francisco: Jossey-Bass.

Super, D. E., Thompson, A. S., Lindeman, R. H., Jordan, J. P., & Myers, R. A. (1981). *The Career Development Inventory, school and college forms*. Palo Alto, CA: Consulting Psychologists Press.

Super, D. E., Thompson, A. S., Lindeman, R. H., Myers, R. A., & Jordan, J. P. (1986). *Adult Career Concerns Inventory*. Palo Alto, CA: Consulting Psychologists Press.

Szymanski, E. M. (1994). Transition: Life-span, life-space considerations for empowerment. *Exceptional Children, 60,* 402–410.

Szymanski, E. M. (1997). School to work transition: Ecological considerations for career development. In W. E. Martin & J. L. Swartz (Eds.), *Applied ecological psychology for schools within communities: Assessment and intervention* (pp. 167–185). Hillsdale, NJ: Erlbaum.

Szymanski, E. M. (1998). Career development, school to work transition, and diversity: An ecological approach. In F. R. Rusch & J. Chadsey-Rusch (Eds.), *Beyond high school: Transition from school to work* (pp. 127–145). Belmont, CA: Wadsworth.

Szymanski, E. M. (1999). Disability, job stress, the changing nature of careers, and the career resilience portfolio. *Rehabilitation Counseling Bulletin, 42,* 279–289.

Szymanski, E. M. (2000). Disability and vocational behavior. In R. G. Frank & T. R. Elliott (Eds.), *Handbook of rehabilitation psychology* (pp. 499–517). Washington, DC: American Psychological Association.

Szymanski, E. M., Dunn, C., & Parker, R. M. (1989). Rehabilitation of persons with learning disabilities: An ecological framework. *Rehabilitation Counseling Bulletin, 33,* 38–53.

Szymanski, E. M., & Hanley-Maxwell, C. (1996). Career development of people with developmental disabilities: An ecological model. *Journal of Rehabilitation, 62*(1), 48–55.

Szymanski, E. M., & Hershenson, D. B. (1998). Career development of people with disabilities: An ecological model. In R. M. Parker & E. M. Szymanski (Eds.), *Rehabilitation counseling: Basics and beyond* (3rd ed., pp. 327–378). Austin, TX: PRO-ED.

Szymanski, E. M., Hershenson, D. B., Ettinger, J., & Enright, M. S. (1996). Career development interventions for people with disabilities. In E. M. Szymanski & R. M. Parker (Eds.), *Work and disability: Issues and strategies in career development and job placement* (pp. 255–276). Austin, TX: PRO-ED.

Szymanski, E. M., Hershenson, D. B., & Power, P. W. (1988). Enabling the family in supporting transition from school to work. In P. W. Power, A. Dell Orto, & M. B.

Gibbons (Eds.), *Family interventions throughout chronic illness and disability* (pp. 216–233). New York: Springer.

Szymanski, E. M., & Parker, R. M. (1989). Rehabilitation counseling in supported employment. *Journal of Applied Rehabilitation Counseling, 20*(3), 65–72.

Szymanski, E. M., Treviño, B., & Fernandez, D. (1996). Rehabilitation career planning with minorities. *Journal of Applied Rehabilitation Counseling, 27*(4), 45–49.

Szymanski, E. M., & Trueba, H. T. (1994). Castification of people with disabilities: Potential disempowering aspects of classification in disability services. *Journal of Rehabilitation, 60*(3), 12–20.

Thomas, K. T., & Parker, R. M. (1992). Applications of theory to rehabilitation counselling practice. In S. E. Robertson & R. I. Brown (Eds.), *Rehabilitation counselling: Approaches in the field of disability* (pp. 34–78). London: Chapman & Hall.

Tinsley, H. E. A. (Ed.). (1993). Special issue on the theory of work adjustment [Special issue]. *Journal of Vocational Behavior, 43*(1).

Tinsley, H. E. A. (Ed.). (1994). Racial identity and vocational behavior [Special issue]. *Journal of Vocational Behavior, 44*(2).

Treviño, B., & Szymanski, E. M. (1996). A qualitative study of the career development of Hispanics with disabilities. *Journal of Rehabilitation, 62*(3), 5–9.

Trueba, H. T. (1991). Linkages of macro-micro analytical levels. *Journal of Psychohistory, 18*, 457–468.

Trueba, H. T., Rodriguez, C., Zou, Y., & Cintron, J. (1993). *Healing multicultural America: Mexican immigrants rise to power in rural California*. London: Falmer.

Tschopp, M. K., Bishop, M., & Mulvihill, M. (2001). Career development of individuals with psychiatric disabilities: An ecological perspective on barriers and interventions. *Journal of Applied Rehabilitation Counseling, 32*(2), 25–30.

Tseng, C. C. (1992). A study of the relationship of disability status and life experience among college students (Doctoral dissertation, University of Wisconsin–Madison). *Dissertation Abstracts International, 53*, 1883A.

U.S. Department of Labor. (1991). *Dictionary of occupational titles* (4th ed., rev.). Washington, DC: U.S. Government Printing Office.

Vondracek, F. W., & Fouad, N. A. (1994). Developmental contextualism: An integrative framework for theory and practice. In M. L. Savickas & R. W. Lent (Eds.), *Convergence in career development: Implications for science and practice* (pp. 207–214). Palo Alto, CA: Consulting Psychologists Press.

Vondracek, F. W., Lerner, R. M., & Schulenberg, J. E. (1986). *Career development: A life-span developmental approach*. Hillsdale, NJ: Erlbaum.

Vondracek, F. W., & Schulenberg, J. (1992). Counseling for normative and nonnormative influences on career development. *Career Development Quarterly, 40*, 291–301.

Walsh, W. B., Bingham, R. P., Brown, M. T., & Ward, C. M. (2001). *Career counseling for African Americans*. Mahwah, NJ: Erlbaum.

Walsh, W., & Osipow, S. (1994). *Advances in vocational psychology: Career counseling for women*. Hillsdale, NJ: Erlbaum.

Weinrach, S. G., & Srebalus, D. J. (1990). Holland's theory of careers. In D. Brown & L. Brooks (Eds.), *Career choice and development: Applying contemporary theories to practice* (2nd ed., pp. 37–67). San Francisco: Jossey-Bass.

Wenkman, J. (1994). *The effect of work experience on career decisiveness of college students with disabilities*. Unpublished doctoral dissertation, University of Wisconsin–Madison.

Wertsch, J. V. (1991). *Voices of the mind: Sociocultural approaches to mediated action*. Cambridge, MA: Harvard University Press.

Wheaton, J. E. (1995). Vocational rehabilitation acceptance rate for European Americans and African Americans: Another look. *Rehabilitation Counseling Bulletin, 38*, 224–231.

Wilson, K. B. (1999). Vocational rehabilitation acceptance: A tale of two races in a large midwestern state. *Journal of Applied Rehabilitation Counseling, 30*(2), 25–31.

Wright, B. A. (1983). *Physical disability—A psychosocial approach*. Cambridge, MA: Harper & Row.

Wright, B. A. (1991). Labeling: The need for greater person-environment individuation. In C. R. Snyder & D. R. Forsyth (Eds.), *Handbook of social and clinical psychology: The health perspective* (pp. 469–487). New York: Pergamon.

Wright, G. N. (1980). *Total rehabilitation*. Boston: Little, Brown.

Yelin, E. H. (1992). *Disability and the displaced worker*. New Brunswick, NJ: Rutgers University Press.

Yelin, E. H., & Cisternas, M. (1996). The contemporary labor market and the employment prospects of persons with disabilities. In J. L. Mashaw, V. Reno, R. Burkhauser, & M. Berkowitz (Eds.), *Disability, work, and cash benefits* (pp. 33–58). Kalamazoo, MI: Upjohn Institute for Employment Research.

Young, R. A., & Collin, A. (Eds.). (1992). *Interpreting career: Hermeneutical studies of lives in context*. Westport, CT: Praeger.

Young, R. A., & Friesen, J. D. (1992). The intentions of parents in influencing the career development of their children. *Career Development Quarterly, 40*, 198–207.

Yuker, H. E. (Ed.). (1988). *Attitudes toward persons with disabilites*. New York: Springer.

Yuker, H. E., & Block, J. R. (1986). *Research with the Attitude Toward Disabled Persons Scales: 1960–1985*. Hempstead, NY: Hofstra University Center for the Study of Attitudes Toward Persons with Disabilities.

Vocational Assessment and Disability

Randall M. Parker and James L. Schaller

Assessment of people with disabilities has long been a focal area for both research and applied rehabilitation professionals. In fact, the advent of modern psychological testing occurred with Binet's commission in 1904 by the minister of public instruction in Paris, France, to study procedures for identifying children with severe developmental delays. His subsequent work led to the first modern intelligence test that formed the prototype for the numerous tests to be developed over the remainder of the century (Anastasi, 1993).

Binet's work on the measurement of intelligence was received with considerable excitement in the United States. Perhaps the best-known product of this excitement was the Stanford-Binet Intelligence Scale, developed by Lewis Terman at Stanford University (Terman, 1916). From Binet's work begun in the early 1900s to the present day, there have been scores of tests developed for measuring the intelligence and many other characteristics and traits of people with disabilities. These tests include instruments to assess (a) mental retardation (e.g., intelligence tests, adaptive behavior scales), (b) psychiatric disorders (e.g., objective and projective personality tests), (c) neurological disorders (e.g., neuropsychological instruments), and (d) instruments used in vocational counseling (e.g., aptitude, interest, value, vocational evaluation, work sample, and situational assessment scales). Given that much of modern psychological testing initially was developed for the assessment of people with disabilities, it is difficult to understand the current state of psychological assessment of individuals with disabilities, which might be described as one of considerable controversy.

The controversy appears to be the result of numerous disagreements on many technical and practical issues. For example, are tests developed on a "normal population" reliable and valid for people with disabilities? Are such tests reliable and valid for those who are culturally and linguistically diverse? Should general norms be used in scoring the results of a test given to a person with a disability, or are special norms of similar individuals preferred? May a professional change the administration procedures to accommodate the needs of a person with a disability without affecting the accuracy of the results? Which types of instruments are preferable in the vocational assessment of an individual with a disability: standardized psychological tests, work samples, or situational assessment ratings? These and myriad other questions pervade everyday rehabilitation practice and current rehabilitation research literature.

The questions surrounding the assessment process have given rise to a multitude of critics discouraged not only by disappointing research findings but also by the resultant vagaries of implementing research findings into practice. One early critic was E. L. Thorndike, who, after an extensive study of the relationship of vocational test scores to later vocational outcomes (Thorndike et al., 1934), exclaimed that vocational guidance resembled the randomness of the game of billiards (Austin & Villanova, 1992; Lorge, 1936).

Thorndike's comments refer to the typical use of objective, paper-and-pencil vocational instruments. These instruments are also referred to as standardized, norm-referenced, and quantitative measures. We will refer to this group of instruments as objective or traditional vocational inventories.

Although our approach in this chapter will be to present issues and problems, we will attempt to keep our criticism constructive. We will explore major issues concerning the vocational assessment of individuals with disabilities, particularly those from culturally and linguistically diverse backgrounds. The topics will be developed from theoretical, conceptual, and technical perspectives. The final section will present alternatives to traditional assessment.

SURVEY OF OBJECTIVE VOCATIONAL INSTRUMENTS

We begin this section with a caution to counselors to be circumspect when using objective vocational tests to identify potential job goals for consumers of rehabilitation services. Too often counselors are misled by the siren songs of test promoters.

Vocational assessment is big business. Walsh (1990) indicated that since 1971, the *Self-Directed Search* has been taken by 9 million people. In 1988 alone, 1.5 million people took the *Myers-Briggs Type Indicator*, and

1 million *Strong–Campbell Interest Inventory* answer sheets were scored. These instruments are generally highly regarded both for their technical qualities and usability. However, when economics come into play, both consumers and counselors are subjected to hyperbole, misinformation, and marginal services. An attitude of healthy skepticism and adherence to the admonition "caveat emptor" (let the buyer beware) is essential. Counselors must gain competence in critical test evaluation and employ that capability before using any psychometric instrument.

There are many resources to assist the counselor in this evaluative task—for example, *Handbook of Measurement and Evaluation in Rehabilitation* (Bolton, 2001), *Tests and Examinations: Measuring Abilities and Performance* (Aiken, 1998), *The Thirteenth Mental Measurements Yearbook* (Impara & Plake, 1998), *Test Critiques* (Keyser & Sweetland, 1984–1994), *A Counselor's Guide to Career Assessment Instruments* (Kapes & Whitfield, 2001), and *A Consumer's Guide to Tests in Print* (Hammill, Brown, & Bryant, 1992), to name a few.

Even with reputable instruments, consumers may be misled by inaccurate interpretation of the results. Several vocational instruments, such as the *Self-Directed Search* (Holland, 1985), were developed to require little professional interpretation despite the fact that they may yield complex information. Consumers would be well advised to participate only in vocational assessment as part of a vocational counseling relationship. Well-trained professionals, such as rehabilitation psychologists and rehabilitation counselors, are trained to assist the consumer in sorting through the information and developing a holistic plan of action. Professional knowledge and common sense are both essential. To emphasize this point, Walsh (1990) quotes an anonymous educator: "Education without common sense is a load of books on the back of an ass" (p. 262). Much the same can be said of the voluminous testing data gathered for an individual to use in vocational decision making.

Although this chapter critiques the use of traditional, objective vocational instruments with people with disabilities, especially women and people from minority backgrounds, the results of vocational assessment may be extremely helpful in career development counseling. Because of the many dangers of misusing such instruments, professionals must be proficient in evaluating tests and treating test results with healthy skepticism. In our opinion, test results are best used in combination with consumer-voiced aspirations, interests, aptitudes, values, personality factors, and other information concerning consumers and their total ecological situation. The consumer must have the primary role in reviewing, integrating, and interpreting these data. The counselor must act as a collaborative consultant, supplying information, providing encouragement, and acting as a resource. The sum total of this information should be presented in a manner that will stimulate discussions about how these data relate to various potential occupational goals.

We believe that encouraging individuals to (a) explore their vocational attributes and (b) gain information and experience in the world of work must be at the center of vocational counseling. It is essential that decision making be done by the consumer, even though agency policy may run counter to the consumer's decision. The counselor's role is supportive and consultative and may be most effective when the counselor assists the consumer in obtaining a conceptual integration of the information that has been gathered.

The appropriate use of vocational tests requires both common sense and expertise in collaborating with the consumer to (a) define desired goals and outcomes, (b) select appropriate assessment approaches and necessary accommodations, (c) carry out the assessment procedures and collect other relevant information, (d) interpret the resulting information, (e) plan actions based on the best available information, (f) carry out the plan in an organized fashion, and (g) evaluate intermediate outcomes and modify the plan accordingly to attain the desired goals.

Throughout this chapter, we reference various tests, some of which will not be included in this section. Figure 5.1 presents a sample of 23 major vocational tests representative of several categories. Following the lead of Isaacson and Brown (2000) and Kapes et al. (1994), the categories are aptitude batteries, and values, interest, personality, diagnostic, and multipurpose inventories.

THEORETICAL AND CONCEPTUAL ISSUES IN VOCATIONAL ASSESSMENT

The 23 objective vocational instruments described in Figure 5.1 are representative of instruments that have been widely used to assist consumers in identifying vocational goals. In this section, we focus on theoretical and conceptual issues that question the use of objective vocational measures with individuals with disabilities.

The theoretical basis of assessing individual traits and characteristics is of particular importance in understanding the controversial issues surrounding the use of assessment procedures with people with disabilities. According to Kerlinger (1986), theory development is the primary purpose of science. It is only through the development and testing of theories that we will arrive at an understanding of human behavior. Theories typically

(*text continues on p. 163*)

APTITUDE BATTERIES (3)

Differential Aptitude Tests (DAT)
Authors: G. Bennett, H. Seashore, and A. Wesman
Publication date: 1990
Publisher: The Psychological Corporation, 655 Academic Court, San Antonio, TX 78204
Norms group: Grades 7 through 12 and adults
Constructs measured: Verbal Reasoning, Numerical Reasoning, Abstract Reasoning, Perceptual Speed and Accuracy, Mechanical Reasoning, Space Relations, Spelling, Language Usage, and Scholastic Aptitude

Armed Services Vocational Aptitude Battery (ASVAB)
Authors: U.S. Department of Defense
Publication date: 1990
Publisher: U.S. Military Entrance Processing Command, 2500 Green Bay Road, North Chicago, IL 60064
Norms group: Grades 10 through 12 and postsecondary students
Constructs measured: General Science, Word Knowledge, Paragraph Comprehension, Electronics Information, Code Speed, Arithmetic Reasoning, Mathematics Knowledge, Mechanical Comprehension, Auto and Shop Information, Numerical Operations

General Aptitude Battery Test (GABT)
Authors: U.S. Employment Service
Publication date: 1982
Publisher: U.S. Employment Service, 200 Constitution Avenue, NW, Washington, DC 20210
Norms group: Grades 9 and 10 and adults
Constructs measured: General Learning Ability, Verbal Aptitude, Numerical Aptitude, Spatial Aptitude, Form Perception, Clerical Perception, Motor Coordination, Finger Dexterity, Manual Dexterity

VALUES INVENTORIES (4)

Minnesota Importance Questionnaire (MIQ)
Authors: D. Weiss, R. Davis, and L. Lofquist
Publication date: 1981
Publisher: Vocational Psychology Research, University of Minnesota, N620 Elliott Hall, 75 East River Road, Minneapolis, MN 55455
Norms group: Males and females ages 16 and older
Constructs measured: 20 needs scales (e.g., Ability Utilization) and 6 values scales (Achievement, Altruism, Autonomy, Comfort, Safety, and Status)

(*continues*)

FIGURE 5.1. Sample of 23 major vocational tests.

Values Scale (VS)
Authors: D. Super and D. Nevill
Publication date: 1986
Publisher: Consulting Psychologists Press, 577 College Ave., Palo Alto, CA 94306
Norms group: Grade 8 and up
Constructs measured: 21 values (e.g., Achievement, Advancement, Authority, Prestige)

Salience Inventory (SI)
Authors: D. Nevill and D. Super
Publication date: 1986
Publisher: Consulting Psychologists Press, 577 College Ave., Palo Alto, CA 94306
Norms group: Grade 9 and up
Constructs measured: 3 scales (Participation, Commitment, and Value Expectations) measure values across 5 roles (Study, Working, Community Service, Family, and Leisure Activities)

Life Values Inventory (LVI)
Authors: R. K. Crace and D. Brown
Publication date: 1996
Publisher: Live Values Resources, 620 Bayberry Dr., Chapel Hill, NC 27514
Norms group: Grade 9 and up
Constructs measured: 14 values (e.g., Belonging, Creativity, Prosperity, Dependability)

INTEREST INVENTORIES (7)

Career Occupational Preference System (COPS)
Authors: R. R. Knapp and L. Knapp
Publication date: 1990
Publisher: EdITS, P.O. 7234, San Diego, CA 92107
Norms group: Junior high through college students
Constructs measured: Interests in 8 career clusters (Science, Consumer Economics, Outdoor, Business, Clerical, Communications, Arts, Services)

Self-Directed Search (SDS)
Author: J. Holland
Publication date: 1994
Publisher: Psychological Assessment Resources, P.O. Box 998, Odessa, FL 33556
Norms group: Junior high students through adults
Constructs measured: Realistic, Investigative, Artistic, Social, Enterprising, Conventional

(*continues*)

FIGURE 5.1. *Continued.*

Career Decision-Making System (CDM)
Authors: T. Harrington and A. O'Shea
Publication date: 1993
Publisher: American Guidance Service, Publishers Building, Circle Pines, MN 55014
Norms group: Junior high students through adults
Constructs measured: Crafts, Scientific, Arts, Business, Clerical, and Social

Strong Interest Inventory (SII)
Authors: E. K. Strong, Jr., J. C. Hansen, and D. Campbell
Publication date: 1994
Publisher: Consulting Psychologists Press, 577 College Ave., Palo Alto, CA 94306
Norms group: Late adolescents and adults
Constructs measured: 23 basic interest scales, 6 general occupational themes (Realistic, Investigative, Artistic, Social, Enterprising, Conventional), and 207 occupational interest scales

Kuder Occupational Interest Survey Form DD (KOIS)
Author: G. F. Kuder
Publication date: 1991
Publisher: Science Research Association, 155 N. Wacker Dr., Chicago, IL 60606
Norms group: Grade 10 through adults
Constructs measured: 104 occupational scales, 39 college major scales, 10 vocational interest estimates, and 8 experimental scales

Reading-Free Vocational Interest Inventory–Revised (RFVII)
Author: R. L. Becker
Publication date: 1988
Publisher: Elbern Publications, P.O. Box 09497, Columbus OH 43209
Norms group: 13- to 60-year-old people with mental retardation and learning disabilities
Constructs measured: Automotive, Building Trades, Clerical, Animal Care, Food Service, Patient Care, Horticulture, Housekeeping, Personal Service, Laundry Service and Materials Handling

USES Interest Inventory (II)
Author: U.S. Employment Service
Publication date: 1982
Publisher: U.S. Employment Service, 200 Constitution Ave., NW, Washington, DC 20210
Norms group: Grade 9 through adults
Constructs measured: Artistic, Scientific, Plants and Animals, Protective, Mechanical, Industrial, Business Detail, Selling, Accommodating, Humanitarian, Leading–Influencing, and Physical–Performing

(*continues*)

FIGURE 5.1. *Continued.*

PERSONALITY INVENTORIES (2)

Myers-Briggs Type Indicator (MBTI)
Authors: I. Briggs Myers and K. Briggs
Publication date: 1998
Publisher: Consulting Psychologists Press, 577 College Ave., Palo Alto, CA 94306
Norms group: High school students through adults
Constructs measured: Extraversion–Introversion, Sensing–Intuition, Thinking–Feeling, Judging–Perceiving

Sixteen P. F. Personal Career Development Profile (16PFQ)
Author: V. Waller
Publication date: 1985
Publisher: Institute for Personality and Ability Testing, 1801 Woodfield Dr., Savoy, IL 61874
Norms group: High school students through adults
Constructs measured: 16 Personality Factor Scores and personality-based themes similar to Holland's RIASEC

DIAGNOSTIC INVENTORIES (4)

Career Decision Scale (CDS)
Author: S. Osipow
Publication date: 1987
Publisher: Psychological Assessment Resources, P.O. Box 998, Odessa, FL 33566
Norms group: High school students through adults
Constructs measured: Certainty and Indecision

My Vocational Situation
Authors: J. L. Holland, D. C. Daiger, and P. G. Power
Publication date: 1980
Publisher: Psychological Assessment Resources, P.O. Box 998, Odessa, FL 33566
Norms group: Grade 8 through college age
Constructs measured: Career Planning, Career Exploration, Decision Making, World of Work Information, Knowledge of Preferred Occupation Group, Career Development—Attitudes, Career Development—Knowledge of Skills, Career Orientation—Total

Career Beliefs Inventory
Author: J. D. Krumboltz
Publication date: 1988
Publisher: Consulting Psychologists Press, 577 College Ave., Palo Alto, CA 94306
Norms group: High school students through adults
Constructs measured: 25 scales organized under 5 headings: My Current Career Situation, What Seems Necessary for My Happiness, Factors That Influence My Decisions, Changes I Am Willing to Make, and Efforts I Am Willing to Initiate

(*continues*)

FIGURE 5.1. *Continued.*

MULTIPURPOSE INVENTORIES (3)

Occupational Aptitude Survey and Interest Schedule–Third Edition (OASIS–3)
Author: R. M. Parker
Publication date: 2002
Publisher: PRO-ED, 8700 Shoal Creek Blvd., Austin, TX 78757-6897
Norms group: Grades 8 through 12 and adults
Constructs measured: 6 Aptitude Factors (General Ability, Verbal Aptitude, Numerical Aptitude, Spatial Aptitude, Perceptual Aptitude, and Manual Dexterity) and 12 Interest Factors (Artistic, Scientific, Nature, Protective, Mechanical, Industrial, Business Detail, Selling, Accommodating, Humanitarian, Leading–Influencing, and Physical–Performing)

McCarron–Dial System (MDS)
Authors: L. T. McCarron and J. G. Dial
Publication Date: 1986
Publisher: McCarron–Dial Systems, P.O. Box 45628, Dallas, TX 75245
Norms group: Persons with learning disabilities, emotional disturbance, mental retardation, cerebral palsy, head injuries, or social disadvantage
Constructs measured: Verbal–Spatial–Cognitive, Sensory, Motor, Emotional, and Integration–Coping

Valpar 17–Pre-Vocational Readiness Battery (PVRB)
Author: Valpar International Corp.
Publication date: 1986
Publisher: Valpar, P.O. Box 5767, Tucson, AZ 85703
Norms group: High school students through adults
Constructs measured: Developmental Assessment, Workshop Evaluation, Interpersonal and Social Skills, Independent Living Skills

FIGURE 5.1. *Continued.*

propose lawful relationships between hypothetical constructs, and it is these hypothetical constructs that assessment procedures endeavor to measure.

Hypothetical constructs include *aptitudes*, *interests*, *values*, *intelligence*, and so on. For instance, the term *mechanical aptitude* refers to a hypothesized characteristic of people. It is both hypothetical and abstract; we cannot open a person's skull and directly observe an individual's mechanical aptitude. Mechanical aptitude may only be inferred from observable behavior (e.g., a person's facility in repairing a bicycle brake, designing a pulley system to lift a heavy object, or answering test items depicting relationships between mechanical parts).

In fact, the foregoing examples are samples of behavior that may allow us to measure a portion of the construct of mechanical aptitude. One would require a very large, perhaps an infinite, number of relevant behavioral samples to fully measure a hypothetical construct. Quite obviously, a small number of samples of behavior cannot adequately encompass any construct. Thus, we are left with a paradox that prevents us from dependably and accurately measuring a construct without obtaining a huge amount of data composed of different samples of theoretically relevant behavior. Not only are we constrained by the number of behavioral samples we can gather, but we are also faced with the problem of identifying theoretically relevant behavior.

Theories and Vocational Assessment

As just suggested, theories play an important role in vocational assessment because they not only identify the domain of relevant behavior but also specify the constructs that are related to vocational decision making (Fitzgerald & Betz, 1994a, 1994b; McFall, 1990). Surprisingly, few vocational tests are based explicitly on a particular theory. Among the few exceptions is the *Self-Directed Search* (SDS; Holland, 1985), which is based on Holland's theory of career development (Holland, 1966, 1973, 1992, 1997). Holland's theory specifies both the behavioral domain of interest (work-related behaviors) and the constructs that are important to assess (Realistic, Investigative, Artistic, Social, Enterprising, and Conventional work personality types). The same six types also describe work environments. The SDS provides self-report measures of these six personality types, which may be matched to the work environments.

Most instruments, however, are based on implicit, or unspecified, theoretical bases. The *Differential Aptitude Tests* (Bennett, Seashore, & Wesman, 1990) and the *Strong Interest Inventory* (Hansen & Campbell, 1985) are examples. Both of these highly respected vocational tests have a considerable research base underpinning their use but paradoxically lack a well-defined theoretical foundation. This atheoretical stance is common among instruments developed in the tradition of test development through empirical criterion keying, which involves creating a scoring key mechanically by identifying items that correlate with an external criterion (see Anastasi, 1988, pp. 524–525; Anastasi & Urbina, 1997). Items thus selected may or may not have an obvious connection in content to the construct underlying the scale. Theory-based test development usually involves selecting items whose content has a high relationship to the theoretical construct measured by the test.

Although the direct effect on the practical use of the instrument may be minor, the lack of an explicit theory poses technical difficulties. The technical adequacy of any psychometric instrument, including vocational assessment devices, is primarily determined by its construct validity. That is, (a) are the test's constructs meaningful within the context of a theory, model, paradigm, or integrated system of findings and speculations, and (b) does the test adequately measure the relevant constructs? The meaningfulness of constructs is determined largely by a theory, model, or paradigm that specifies the relationships between the constructs and between other variables detailed by the theory. Because constructs are hypothetical, it is important to be able to evaluate the constructs' adequacy through research into the theory's ability to describe, predict, and explain the domain of behavior it addresses (Anastasi, 1988; Anastasi & Urbina, 1997; Sechrest, 1993; Walsh & Betz, 1990). However, developing evidence of construct validity, which will be more fully addressed later in this chapter, is not the only hurdle faced by researchers and test developers. At a less abstract and less technical level, another barrier is the limitless variation of human individual differences combined with the innumerable facets of the work environment.

Conceptual Complexity of Career Development

Consider for a moment the tremendous diversity and variability of human characteristics. Each person has a unique set of experiences, traits, characteristics, and other qualities. Similarly, consider the diversity among work environments. There are more than 12,000 different job titles in our economy, each demanding different skills, knowledge, capabilities, and motivation (Farr, 1993; Herr & Cramer, 1992; Isaacson & Brown, 2000; Mayall, 1994). Finally, consider the practically innumerable combinations of individual differences in personal characteristics with enormous variability of contextual and environmental factors.

This complex melange of factors has been expressed as a relatively simple mathematical formula. Lewin (1935) originally suggested that behavior is a function of the person and the environment; one might also add the interaction between the person and the environment, as indicated in the following equation:

$$B = f(P, E, P \times E),$$

where B stands for behavior, f for function, P for person, E for environment, and $P \times E$ for the person-by-environment interaction.

A few examples of personal and work environment factors in career development are listed in Table 5.1. In addition, each of the personal factors may interact in multitudinous ways with the environmental factors. A worker's values, for example, may interact with, or reciprocally influence, an employer's attitudes toward the worker.

TABLE 5.1. Selected Personal and Work Environment Factors in Career Development

Personal Factors	Work Environment Factors
Gender	Gender role socialization
Cultural identity	Stereotypes/discrimination
Health	Environmental barriers
Goals	Community characteristics
Values	Economic conditions
Interests	Family variables
Aptitudes	Friends
Personality	Employer attitudes
Preferences	Rate of employment
Interpersonal skills	Availability of training
Aspirations	Availability of transportation

Clearly, a legion of other personal, contextual, and environmental factors, as well as the interactions among them, affect career choice (Fitzgerald & Betz, 1994a, 1994b). To complicate things further, individuals, jobs, and job environments are dynamic. Personal and environmental factors are constantly changing in response to numerous internal and external factors. The multiplicity of facets of human beings in combination with, and in interaction with, the tremendous variety of work environments is truly daunting. Ecological assessment, which is covered in more detail later in this chapter, attempts to take all salient facets of the *P*, *E*, and *P*×*E* factors into account (Parker, Szymanski, & Hanley-Maxwell, 1989).

Problems with Vocational Predictions for Individuals

The conceptual complexity of career development calls into question (a) simplistic theories, such as Holland's theory referred to above; (b) assessment driven by such simplistic theories; and (c) approaches to job matching that dominate current rehabilitation counseling practice. The erroneous notion that a professional can readily catalog a consumer's traits and characteristics and match them to a successful job outcome is both logical and appealing. In the real world, job-matching strategies are seriously deficient when it comes to making valid predictions for an individual. Even the impressive wizardry of computers cannot rescue the simplistic job-matching strategy from the company of astrology, tea leaf reading, and other pseudosciences when making predictions for individuals. In short, efforts at vocational prediction, including job matching and other strategies using information gained from vocational assessment instruments, are of questionable validity in making predictions about individuals with disabilities; this is especially true for women with disabilities and people from minority backgrounds with disabilities (Bowman, 1993; Conte, 1983; Fitzgerald & Betz, 1994a, 1994b; Hershenson & Szymanski, 1992; Smith, 1983).

Applicability of Career Development Theories and Instruments to Diverse Groups

To recap, we have just discussed the fact that many vocational assessment instruments are not theory based, resulting in a basic construct validity problem. Compounding this state of affairs is the circumstance that many theories of career development themselves are overly simplistic and fundamentally flawed. Additional criticisms of theories of career development and the instruments they have spawned include their lack of attention to cultural factors (e.g., values, beliefs, and attitudes) and structural factors (e.g., poverty, discrimination, and sexism; Fitzgerald & Betz, 1994a, 1994b) that unquestionably shape vocational behavior. Furthermore, these theories typically use constructs that may be irrelevant or meaningless for people with disabilities, women, and individuals from culturally diverse backgrounds (Hershenson & Szymanski, 1992; Smith, 1983). For example, the trait–factor approach, which attempts to match salient individual characteristics to job factors, fails to adequately describe female career patterns. Consider the widely held assumptions that (a) vocational choice is driven by a match between an individual's traits and the requirements of a job, and (b) the distribution of vocational traits (especially specific aptitudes and general abilities) is largely similar for men and women. Then the trait–factor approaches would predict that men and women would be found in roughly equal numbers across various occupations and occupational levels (Fitzgerald & Betz, 1994). This is obviously not the case. Equally obviously, disproportional representation across occupations may be primarily due to socially driven factors that affect career development of women and people from culturally diverse groups, including people with disabilities.

In addition, use of trait–factor theories may include the notion that the most important and relevant characteristics regarding career development behavior have been identified and reliably measured. However, Brown (1995) suggested that this is not the case for African Americans. Research that controls for variables such as skin tone, gender, geographic region, and socioeconomic status is sorely needed. Brown also suggested that more research is needed to investigate relationships between self-concept variables and career choice, in addition to research on the role of socioeconomic status and discrimination on the development of occupational and self-concepts.

In addition, trait–factor and job-matching approaches to predicting career development of people with disabilities typically do not account for societal factors, chance factors, or environmental variables that typically affect career development (Hershenson & Szymanski, 1992). These approaches clearly do not consider limited early experiences that affect consumers making informed choices about jobs or the possibility that adaptive devices or job modifications could augment functioning at work.

Smith (1983) noted that if career development is viewed as a process of implementing one's self-concept (e.g., see Super, 1990), jobs held by some individuals from culturally diverse backgrounds may actually constitute a challenge to their self-concept. These individuals, who may be underemployed, may have to separate their personal self-concept from their work self-concept to protect their feelings of self-worth. Also, implementation of one's self-concept through work may contradict collective value orientations that stress choosing occupations based on preservation of the family and culture of origin (Fitzgerald & Betz, 1994). Consequently, theory-based assessments of self-concept and other traits thought to be related to career development may be specious when applied to individuals, particularly individuals from experientially diverse groups.

We must quickly add, however, that trait–factor and job-matching procedures may be relatively valid, reliable, and efficient for the placement of large groups of people (e.g., assignment of large groups of military inductees to specific military jobs and training programs). In situations where one can tolerate prediction hit rates of, for example, 70%, vocational assessment and job matching or similar strategies may be useful and efficient for administrators wishing to make decisions for sizable groups. When it comes to counseling situations involving an individual's future, however, professionals must be wary of using any procedures that have the potential to do harm to consumers. Even error rates as low as 30% are likely to be unacceptable when making specific predictions that will affect an individual's career development.

TECHNICAL LIMITATIONS OF TRADITIONAL VOCATIONAL ASSESSMENT

Vocational assessment is used by rehabilitation and other counseling professionals to describe, explain, and predict consumers' psychological, social, and vocational behavior, as well as to identify specific vocational goals for the consumer. In rehabilitation settings, vocational assessment typically embraces the medical model, which prescribes a lock-step approach to rehabilitation, similar in many respects to job matching previously mentioned. The medical model consists of (a) diagnosing the problem; (b) developing a treatment plan; (c) administering the treatment; (d) evaluating the effectiveness of the treatment; (e) modifying the treatment, as necessary; and (f) when the patient has obtained maximum benefit, terminating the treatment. Unfortunately, the medical model typically does not fully address consumers' needs for a holistic and individualized approach (Parker et al., 1989; Szymanski, Dunn, & Parker, 1989).

Assessment for consumers, particularly those with severe disabilities and those who are culturally and linguistically diverse, presents problems because of the technical limitations in traditional vocational assessment. Such limitations include (a) instructions and test items that require reading and comprehension levels that exceed examinees' abilities, (b) general norms that are questionable for people with disabilities or from diverse backgrounds, (c) required test-taking skills and abilities (e.g., reading, understanding abstract language) that are often not related to the construct being predicted (e.g., work performance), and (d) vocational tests and work evaluation systems that typically possess inadequate reliability and validity for people with severe disabilities from diverse backgrounds (Bond & Dietzen, 1990; Halpern, 1981; Orelove & Sobsey, 1987).

Similarly, Menchetti and Rusch (1988) and Hagner and Dileo (1993) cited several other limitations; traditional vocational assessment (a) typically lacks predictive validity, (b) is based on the assumption that the criteria of successful employment are the same for all individuals, (c) fails to consider the interaction of training factors with performance outcomes, and (d) is based on correlations with other similar tests rather than with actual job performance.

Cultural and Gender Considerations

As a result, vocational testing for people with disabilities, especially women and people from culturally diverse backgrounds with disabilities, has generated considerable debate. Cultural and gender considerations for vocational assessment, particularly for vocational aptitude and interest testing, include performance motivation, response style, level of acculturation, inappropriate norms, and gender restrictiveness (Alston & McCowan, 1994; Fouad, 1993; Smart & Smart, 1992; Walsh & Betz, 1990).

Performance Motivation

Motivation to perform in a testing situation may vary for individuals from culturally diverse backgrounds with disabilities. Harry (1992), for example, suggested that parents with a child in special education may mistrust the testing and assessment process because this process has been used historically to establish and maintain discriminatory practices. Similarly, Fouad (1993) indicated that individuals from culturally diverse backgrounds may not trust the use of standardized tests for the same reasons.

Certain individuals may not be comfortable disclosing information, which may lead to missing chunks of information on a test. Smart and Smart (1992) stated that the process of vocational assessment that uses self-analysis and introspection may be unfamiliar and uncomfortable for some Hispanic Americans. Atkins (1988) indicated that negative attitudes and racism can constitute a powerful barrier in the rehabilitation process for African Americans with disabilities. If the consumer and rehabilitation agency staff have low expectations for success, the assessment process may be affected. Should poor performance occur, rehabilitation staff may interpret this as lack of ability or low motivation, rather than distrust and lack of faith in the rehabilitation system by the individual with a disability (Alston & McCowan, 1994). Rehabilitation professionals should find out what the individual's and family members' experiences with testing have been before introducing the possibility of vocational testing.

Response Style and Item Bias

Individuals from different cultures may approach testing with different styles (Lonner, 1990). For example, if an individual does not attempt a response when given a question or terminates a response before completing the question the person will likely obtain a low score (Alston & McCowan, 1994; Moore, 1986). Moore (1986) suggested that when African Americans perform poorly on a test, the performance may be due to an unwillingness to retrieve information and solve problems on demand, rather than a lack of accumulated knowledge or ability.

Test questions that are more familiar to one group than another may reflect item content bias. Stories or pictures of suburban, middle-class families with physical features of a single racial type and the portrayal of male doctors and business executives and female nurses and secretaries are examples of content bias (Walsh & Betz, 1990).

Level of Acculturation

The level of acculturation may also affect the assessment process (Dana, 1993; Fouad, 1993; Smart & Smart, 1992; Sue & Sue, 1990). Performance on language-based measures may be influenced by the level of acculturation of the test taker and test giver, and assessment may be loaded against an individual with limited proficiency in English. Not many tests have been translated into other languages and systematically validated. One of the few exceptions is the *Strong Interest Inventory* (Hansen & Campbell, 1985), which has been translated into Spanish and validated (Fouad, 1993). Walsh and Betz (1990) suggested that the use of tests that have not been validated in the population for which they are to be used is problematic and should be avoided. Finally, employing a vocational assessment process that (a) stresses rational, linear problem solving; (b) emphasizes long-range goals; (c) focuses solely on individual needs; and (d) has a nondirective approach to counseling may not adequately address the needs, values, and views of individuals from culturally diverse backgrounds (Fouad, 1993).

Assessing level of acculturation as a part of the assessment process may provide extremely valuable information. Smart and Smart (1992, 1993) suggested that a psychometrically sound instrument that assesses the level of acculturation would broaden the assessment process, increase the understanding of consumers, and promote rehabilitation counselors becoming more sensitive to cultural characteristics. Smart and Smart also indicated that knowing the acculturation level of consumers would facilitate the evaluation process through the use of a combination of evaluation procedures tailored to meet a consumer's needs.

Use of Inappropriate Norms

It is extremely important that a test's normative group be appropriate for the individual taking the test (Anastasi, 1988; Anastasi & Urbina, 1997; Fouad, 1993). A concern specific to gender is the use of combined sex norms when assessing the vocational interests of men and women (Walsh & Betz, 1990). Although the separate measurement of vocational interests for men and women has been largely eliminated, the use of combined sex normative scores may restrict women's choices by failing to suggest occupational alternatives that may be nontraditional. Combined sex norms use a standardization sample of both men and women. For example, items on the *Self-Directed Search* (Holland, 1985) and similar interest instruments may reflect the experiences of men and women (e.g., "I like to build things with wood" or "I like to take care of children"). When raw scores are summed, women frequently score higher on Social, Artistic, and Conventional themes, whereas men often score higher on Realistic, Investigative, and Enterprising themes (Walsh & Betz, 1990). Additional issues concerning test norms will be presented later in this chapter.

Gender Restrictiveness

The occupational suggestions resulting from the assessment process may tend to reinforce existing segregation of men and women into traditional male and female occupations. For example, women's lower scores on Realistic, Investigative, and Enterprising themes may result in less frequent identification of occupations defined as traditionally male, such as the skilled trades, management, and science.

Two approaches advocated for reducing gender restrictiveness of tests are same-sex norms and sex-balanced items (Walsh & Betz, 1990). Same-sex norms compare an individual's scores on dimensions of vocational interest to those of people of the same sex. The intent of same-sex norms is to identify vocational interests that have developed, despite the limiting effects of gender role socialization, by using a comparison sample whose background socialization experiences are similar to those of the individual taking the test.

Sex-balanced items include items that characterize male and female gender role socialization, with the desired result of both men and women obtaining similar raw scores. The intent of sex-balanced items is for men and women to have more equivalent score distributions across, for example, the six Holland themes (Realistic, Investigative, Artistic, Social, Enterprising, or Conventional). The use of same-sex norms and sex-balanced items may increase the probability that women interested in Realistic, Investigative, or Enterprising occupations will obtain interest inventory profiles that suggest those areas.

Worell and Remer (1992) suggested that the manuals accompanying vocational interest, aptitude, and other vocational tests should contain appropriate nonstereotyped (and quite possibly nontraditional) examples of the application of test results for both men and women. Counselors should be provided models or suggestions regarding how to use testing information to assist individuals in exploring a diversity of occupations.

Validity and Reliability Limitations of Vocational Instruments

Of the preceding limitations, perhaps the most perplexing are the relatively low validity and reliability of the instruments typically used in vocational rehabilitation counseling. Validity and reliability are particularly important because they are generally regarded as the two most important technical characteristics of vocational tests, psychological assessment tools, and work evaluation instruments. Whereas validity gauges the *accuracy* with which a test measures a construct (e.g., mechanical comprehension, verbal aptitude, interest in artistic work), reliability reflects an instrument's *consistency* of measurement (Anastasi, 1988; Anastasi & Urbina, 1997; Bond & Dietzen, 1990; Parker et al., 1989). Interestingly, some authorities make no distinction between validity and reliability. According to Sechrest (1993), Shavelson and Webb (1991), and Shavelson, Webb, and Rowley (1989), validity and reliability are not distinct technical qualities of tests. Both are concerned with the generalizability of test scores obtained in a measurement context to unobserved behaviors that occur outside the measurement context. The following descriptions of validity and reliability, however, rely on the more traditional viewpoint that they are distinct conceptual entities.

Validity

Validity is most frequently defined as a measure of the degree to which a test score actually measures the characteristic, trait, or construct that it was designed to measure (Anastasi, 1988; Anastasi & Urbina, 1997). Cronbach (1990), however, offered a unique definition: "Validation looks into the soundness and relevance of a proposed interpretation" (p. 150). Cronbach further stated that a test may be valid for one decision but be inaccurate for another. Consequently, speaking of "*the* validity of a specific test" conveys the misconception that one can make a general statement about the validity of a test. Actually, there is a separate validity for every possible decision and for each possible group for which a test score may be used (Thompson, 1994).

Validity is usually considered as composed of three major subtypes: *content-related, criterion-related,* and *construct-related* validity (Anastasi, 1988; Anastasi & Urbina, 1997; Steinberg, Thissen, & Wainer, 2000). Although validity is often considered to be composed of the above three major categories, Anastasi (1988) suggested that all forms of validity are, in fact, construct-related validity:

> Further consideration of these [validity] procedures, however, shows that content-, criterion-, and construct-related validation do not correspond to distinct or logically coordinate categories. On the contrary, construct-related validity is a comprehensive concept, which includes the other types. All the specific techniques for establishing content- and criterion-related validity . . . [may be considered] construct-related validity. The

> reader must keep the comprehensive nature of construct-related validity in mind as we describe each of the three subtypes. (p. 163)

Content-related validation is usually conceived of as a process of determining whether the test items are representative of the domain being measured. Frequently, test authors build content-related validity into their tests by writing items that are representative of the content domain or factor measured by the test.

Criterion-related validity is determined by the correlation between the scores on a test and a criterion of performance. If the test and the criterion measure are obtained at about the same time, their correlation constitutes *concurrent validity*. In contrast, when the test scores are gathered first and the criterion measures are obtained some time later, the validity index is referred to as a *predictive validity* coefficient. According to Cronbach (1990), the most difficult task in determining predictive validity is obtaining satisfactory criterion data. More about this topic will be presented later in the section on the criterion problem.

Finally, construct-related validity refers to the extent to which a test is consistent with theory and research. Research programs designed to determine whether behaviors operationally defined by test scores vary according to theoretical expectations are one way to estimate construct-related validity.

Reliability

Reliability is an index of *consistency* or *precision* of a test score and indicates whether the items of a test are answered similarly from one testing to a later testing, or from one part of the test to another. By subtracting a reliability coefficient from 1.0, an estimate of the error variance in a test score is obtained. Thus, reliability reflects the degree to which a test contains error of measurement or error variance. Error variance is reduced through careful development, standardization, and administration of vocational tests (Anastasi, 1988; Anastasi & Urbina, 1997; Cronbach, 1990; Helmstadter, 1964).

Four types of reliability are commonly employed in test development: (a) *alpha*, (b) *split-half*, (c) *alternate forms*, and (d) *test–retest reliability*. Alpha reliability provides an index of *interitem consistency*, that is, the homogeneity or unidimensionality of the items in a scale. A test composed of items that measure the same construct would be expected to have a high degree of alpha reliability (Anastasi, 1988).

A second type of reliability, split-half reliability, is determined by dividing test items into two equivalent parts and correlating the part scores. A procedure frequently used to split the test items into two equivalent parts is called the *odd–even technique*. This technique involves scoring odd-numbered and even-numbered items separately and correlating the two scores. Split–half reliability provides a measure of consistency regarding sampling of item content and is referred to as a coefficient of *internal consistency*. Because reliability is directly related to test length, the reliability based on split-halves is lower than the reliability of the complete test. The Spearman–Brown formula is usually used to estimate the reliability of the full test from the split-half correlation (Cronbach, 1990; Guilford & Fruchter, 1973).

In contrast, alternate-forms reliability requires an instrument to have two or more separate forms that are made up of very similar items measuring the same construct. One form of the test is administered to obtain alternate-forms reliability, and at some later time the second form of the test is administered to the same group. The resulting two test scores are then correlated to obtain the alternate-forms reliability coefficient, which provides a measure of *equivalence* or degree of similarity in content sampling of the two test forms. The last major type of reliability, test–retest reliability, is obtained by administering the same test to the same group at two different times, usually separated by 1 or 2 weeks, and correlating the resulting scores. Test–retest reliability measures *stability* of the test scores over time (Anastasi, 1988; Anastasi & Urbina, 1997).

Of particular importance is the standard error of measurement (*SEM*), which is a practical translation of a reliability coefficient into the amount of variation likely to occur in a test score due to the unreliability of a test. The *SEM* is calculated by multiplying the standard deviation of a test score by the square root of the quantity: one minus the reliability of the test score. Adding and subtracting one *SEM* from a person's score gives the range within which the score will vary 68% of the time upon retest. For example, consider an examinee who received an IQ of 115 for which the reliability coefficient is .84. Because the standard deviation of the test is, for example, 15, the *SEM* equals 15 times the square root of the error (1 – .84). This simplifies to 15 times .4 or 6.0. The person's true score, therefore, would fall in the 109 to 121 range (because 115 – 6 = 109 and 115 + 6 = 121). It can be stated that the person's true score falls within the range of 109 to 121 with 68% confidence. To reach the 96% level of confidence, two *SEMs*, or 12 IQ points, must be added and subtracted from a test score, yielding a range of 103 to 127.

Generalizability Theory

Generalizability theory (Brennan, 1983; Cronbach & Drenth, 1972) posits how error can be broken down into components, providing additional information about measurement error. Using generalizability theory, one can identify specific components of error, for example, error due to (a) observers, (b) situations, and (c) occasions. Instead of simply saying that a reliability coefficient of .70 reflects .30 (i.e., 1.0 − .70), or 30% error, generalizability theory allows one to determine that, for example, the 30% error is made up of 20% due to observers, 8% due to situations, and 2% due to occasions. The value of this approach is that it can assist in the refinement of the measurement process. In the above example, most of the unreliability is due to observer error. To improve the reliability of the instrument, one might focus on reducing the 20% error due to observers. For example, one could use only observers with relevant experience, give observers more training, or provide observers more time to make their observations. The interested reader may consult Shavelson and Webb (1991) for additional details.

Additional Validity and Reliability Considerations

As previously suggested, it is important to stress that the reliability and validity of a test or evaluation instrument may vary considerably depending on the specific group and specific decision for which the test results are used. A particular test does not have one reliability and one validity index. Each test must have separate reliability and validity information for each decision and each group for which it is intended. Thus, some tests may be reliable and valid for certain situations and neither reliable nor valid for others. The single most important technical quality of a test is its validity for a specific decision for a particular group (Anastasi, 1988; Anastasi & Urbina, 1997; Cronbach, 1990).

Another important consideration in the vocational assessment of persons with disabilities is that reliability and validity indices, as well as test norms, are based on *group* performance. In practice, however, counselors usually wish to use test data with *individuals*. Because individuals often possess relevant, unique traits that are not adequately represented in the validity, reliability, and normative groups, decisions based on test results are likely to be specious and misleading. This consideration becomes more important as the individuals evaluated depart from the cultural, linguistic, and experiential characteristics of the normative sample, as is the case with many consumers of rehabilitation services (Anastasi, 1988; Anastasi & Urbina, 1997; Power, 2000).

Additional Issues Concerning Test Norms

Shertzer and Linden (1979) described norms as "group-relevant reference data . . . used as the basis for evaluating the performance of a given examinee" (p. 545). Norms are usually expressed in a table that allows one to convert a raw score to a derived score. A derived score—for example, a percentile, IQ, or stanine score—compares an individual's performance with all individuals in the normative sample. Normative samples are selected to be representative of a population of interest, for example, all individuals in the United States, all 12th-grade students in the Midwest, or perhaps all productive employees in an electronics assembly job nationwide. Therefore, a rehabilitation professional would seek to use tests with norms made up of individuals who are not only similar to the consumer examinee but also functioning in a situation similar to the circumstance desired by the consumer.

Norms may be described as the most basic kind of interpretative aid at the descriptive level (Parker, 2001). They are restricted to describing the consumer's level of performance relative to a comparison group. Raw scores, usually taken as the number of items answered correctly, are meaningless in and of themselves. Knowing that a consumer answered 50 items correctly on a verbal ability test gives no information whatsoever about the relative level of performance. If, however, it had been established previously that a raw score of 50 on this particular test was equivalent to the average performance of college graduates, the score *might* then become meaningful, assuming the test is reliable and valid for the specific decision with similar persons.

To reiterate, tables of norms allow the conversion of raw scores to derived scores, such as percentiles. Although there are numerous derived scores (e.g., *z* scores, *T* scores, deviation IQ scores), percentiles are usually the most meaningful and easily understood derived score. A percentile score indicates the percentage of people in the normative group who obtained lower raw scores. Thus, a person who receives a percentile of 95 on a mechanical ability test based on a norm group of high school seniors performs at a higher level than 95% of this group.

Considerable judgment must be exercised in selecting the proper table of norms when several are available. One issue that is frequently faced by rehabilitation professionals concerns whether general or special norms should be used with individuals with disabilities, particularly if the consumers are culturally and linguistically diverse.

General Versus Special Norms

The frequent and troublesome question encountered by rehabilitation professionals is, "Should general norms be used with consumers with disabilities, or should special norms be developed that compare them only to those with similar disabilities and backgrounds?" On one side of this issue are those who proclaim that general norms should be used because consumers will have to compete with the general population in obtaining employment. Those on the other side, however, argue that the use of general norms discriminates unfairly against people with disabilities. This issue is most confusing until one carefully considers the purpose for the assessment. Specifically, was the assessment done to compare the individual's standing with another group (description) or to estimate the individual's future behavior or performance (prediction; Parker, 2001)?

Descriptive tools, such as norms, serve merely to locate the individual's performance within a reference group. One might find, for example, that a particular consumer scored at the 95th percentile in mechanical aptitude (i.e., he scored higher than 95% of the comparison group). If the norm group consisted of successful auto mechanics, one might predict that the individual would also be successful as an auto mechanic. However, this kind of prediction involves an inferential leap, given that there is no research demonstrating that a score at the 95th percentile ensures a high probability of success in auto mechanics. As addressed previously, many attributes determine success in a career beyond a measure of aptitude.

In any particular instance, the same test scores could be used both to describe and to make predictions about an individual's behavior. However, rehabilitation personnel frequently fail to make a conceptual separation between descriptions and predictions, and this is a major cause for the confusion surrounding the general versus the special norms controversy.

If all the relevant variables in auto mechanic performance had been identified and a prediction formula had been developed (e.g., a regression equation; see Hays, 1994), the individual's chances for success in auto mechanics could be directly determined with a specified degree of statistical certainty. This latter procedure would require little or no subjectivity in making the prediction. On the other hand, a vocational counselor might study the scores and, based on his or her experience, make a subjective prediction about the likelihood of success. The above two predicting modes are frequently referred to as clinical (or subjective) prediction and statistical (or actuarial) prediction.

For descriptive purposes, one may easily decide to use either or both special and general norms to describe an individual's standing within the selected norm group. A rehabilitation professional, for example, may wish to assess a consumer's fine motor performance compared to individuals with a similar disability. Assuming that such special norms exist, the decision to use special norms is obvious. On the other hand, if the professional wishes to compare the consumer's fine motor performance with the general adult population, he or she would use norms based on a representative sample of adult U.S. residents. Knowing that the consumer scored at the 34th percentile, for example, compared to the adult population, however, does *not* allow the professional to generalize beyond that description. This knowledge, for instance, would not allow the prediction that the consumer would have difficulty in a training program or in a job. Descriptive information derived from a table of norms, strictly speaking, is time bound, fixed at the time the norms were gathered, and is group specific, limited to the nature of the norm group. Such normative information is quite restricted; it does not allow one to make accurate predictions about how a consumer will perform at times much beyond the date the norms were gathered and to groups much different from the norm group (Parker, 2001).

The general versus special norms issue becomes most confused within the realm of prediction. Predictions based solely on scores derived from norms involve "armchair speculation," or what has been referred to as *clinical judgment*. A number of authors (e.g., Dawes, Faust, & Meehl, 1993; Meehl, 1954) have pointed out the precariousness of making clinical judgments. If possible, predictive devices (e.g., regression equations) should be used in making predictions; in this way, one can be aware of one's chances of making a correct prediction. The general versus special norms issue dissipates when prediction is the goal because the norms are descriptive, not predictive, in nature.

When one wishes to use norms in a descriptive fashion, there should be no difficulty in selecting either or both general and specific norms, assuming both are available. The professional may wish to compare a consumer's performance to a generally representative normative group or to a group similar to the consumer on important characteristics. In some situations, disability may not be as important a concern as gender or cultural factors. In selecting an appropriate normative group, the rehabilitation professional is faced typically with using general norms because disability-specific norms often are not available. The solution would be to develop local norms (Anastasi, 1988; Anastasi & Urbina, 1997), which are norms for a specific decision with a particular group of individuals usually in one locale. Such norms are readily developed when adequate numbers of consumers with specified characteristics are available to be tested. However, adequate numbers may not be accessible, particularly for individuals with low-incidence disabilities. Bootstrapping may provide a novel solution to address the small *N* quandary.

Bootstrapping

When faced with the dilemma of too few individuals to create local norms, the resourceful professional could consider some statistical "magic" called bootstrapping (Diaconis & Efron, 1983). Whereas developing stable, local norms using traditional methods might require several hundreds or thousands of individuals, bootstrapping might require as few as 15 individuals. Bootstrapping uses computer-intensive methods to create tens of thousands of subsamples of the original sample of scores; then the statistics needed for norm generation are calculated for all the subsamples and distributed. Typically, one would use bootstrap methods to estimate the population mean and standard deviation. Given the mean and standard deviation, and assuming that the population of scores is approximately normally distributed, it would be easy to create a table of norms. Alternatively, one could use the bootstrap to generate a simple frequency distribution if only percentiles were desired. The interested reader may consult Mooney and Duval (1993) for a general introduction to bootstrapping.

Clinical Versus Statistical Prediction

The history of science is replete with examples of human error in making predictions about human behavior. Meehl (1954) sought to determine the relative accuracy of clinical (subjective) judgment when compared to statistical (objective) prediction. In a review of the literature, Meehl located 19 relevant studies. Of the studies, 10 indicated no difference between the two methods of prediction, and 9 favored statistical prediction. In response to criticisms of Meehl's work by Gough (1962), Holt (1958), and others, Sawyer (1966) replicated and extended Meehl's earlier investigation. Sawyer reviewed 45 studies that compared the accuracy of clinical versus statistical prediction in both data collection and data integration. The results were supportive of Meehl's findings; statistical prediction was clearly equal or superior to clinical prediction, regardless of the mode of data utilization (Parker, 2001).

In the rehabilitation arena, Bolton, Butler, and Wright (1968) compared counselors' statistical and clinical assessments of the feasibility of providing services to rehabilitation consumers in a state rehabilitation program. As with previous studies, statistical predictions were usually more accurate than clinical predictions. Of 28 counselors who closed at least 35 cases, only 2 exceeded the statistical formula in predictive accuracy. No relationship was found between predictive accuracy and either education or experience of the counselor.

Although only a few selected studies relating to this issue have been reviewed here, other reviews (e.g., Dawes, Faust, & Meehl, 1989, 1993; Meehl, 1986; Nisbett & Ross, 1980) have led to the same conclusion—statistical predictions are, with few exceptions, equally as accurate as, or more accurate than, the judgment of professionals. These conclusions may place the rehabilitation professional in a quandary because predictive interpretive methods (i.e., statistical formulas for making specific predictions) are often unavailable. Consequently, professionals must continue to use their qualitative clinical skills in decision making but, in doing so, should be aware of the fallibility of their intuitive judgments (Parker, 2001).

Criterion Problem

One of the most vexing difficulties faced by test developers and test users alike is obtaining good criteria that may be employed in validating or evaluating tests. Indices of predictive validity, obviously, are useless unless the criterion employed itself is reliable, valid, and relevant. Because they are relatively easy to obtain, employer or supervisor ratings are frequently used as criteria. Such ratings, however, are troublesome because of their characteristic lack of reliability and validity. Other criterion measures frequently used include speed of work, quality of work, number of absences, safety record, and so forth (Austin & Villanova, 1992; Parker, 2001).

Some rehabilitation personnel tend to ignore the issue criterion problem because they believe state rehabilitation agencies have found that the "ultimate" criterion is case closure. It is unquestionably true that with this criterion, one can determine an individual's employment status with nearly perfect reliability. There is, however, a question regarding the validity of this measurement. Referring to earlier discussions in this chapter, validity attempts to determine whether a test score actually measures the characteristic, trait, or construct that it was designed to measure. A valid criterion for measuring the success of an individual's rehabilitation should provide a holistic, global assessment of his or her ability to function successfully. Certainly, success in a rehabilitation program cannot be measured solely by whether a person obtains and maintains employment. Undeniably, there are other more humanistic aspects involved in rehabilitation, for instance, a measure of the individual's level of psychological adjustment to his or her disability. It is the humanistic, as well as the economic, justification of the rehabilitation program that has engendered general support for the program. Suffice it to say, the criterion problem in rehabilitation will most likely remain a central issue for some time.

ALTERNATIVES TO TRADITIONAL ASSESSMENT

Surprisingly, few counselors make use of the many alternatives to traditional testing, which include self-ratings, criterion assessment, ecological assessment, and qualitative assessment. Each of these approaches provides avenues to readily glean rich information with consumer involvement.

Self-Ratings

Considerable disagreement exists over whether self-ratings of vocational aptitudes, interests, values, and so on provide as much information as psychometrically determined measures of the same constructs (Mabe & West, 1982; Parker & Schaller, 1994; Westbrook, Sanford, Gilleland, Fleenor, & Mervin, 1988). If, for instance, a self-rating on a single 5-point scale of mechanical interests correlates highly with a 40-item psychometric measure of the same construct, self-ratings would appear to be a viable substitute for the longer scale. Some research suggests that consumers waste time taking aptitude and interest tests because the same information could be obtained simply by asking them what their interests are or having them do simple ratings of their interests. Kline (1993), for example, indicated that although interest tests may help an individual discriminate among his or her interests in various occupations, some tests do no better than simply ask the individual about his or her interests in different occupations.

Parker and Schaller (1994) conducted a canonical correlation analysis between self-ratings of 6 aptitudes and 12 interests and vocational test scores on the same 6 aptitudes and 12 interests of 564 eighth-grade students in four middle schools. The analysis between self-ratings and test scores revealed 10 statistically significant canonical variates accounting for 97% of the common variance. Univariate correlations between each rating–score pair ranged from .10 to .36 for aptitudes and .38 to .56 for interests. All univariate correlations were statistically significant ($p \geq .05$). The results suggested that eighth graders, who are regarded as moving from the growth to the exploratory stage of vocational development (Super, 1990), are able to provide considerable information regarding their vocational interests and aptitudes through self-ratings.

In another study, Westbrook et al. (1988) reported that self-estimated scores on the *Differential Aptitude Tests* (DAT) correlated from .23 to .64 (median = .55) with measured DAT scores. Similarly, in a meta-analysis of 55 studies, Mabe and West (1982) found that correlations between self-evaluations of ability and measures of performance among college students and various workers averaged .29.

More recently, Westbrook, Buck, and Wynne (1994) found that the correlations between self-rated and measured abilities on the *Differential Aptitude Tests* (Bennett et al., 1990) ranged from the .30s to the .60s, with medians in the .50s. Complex differences across gender and ethnicity were also noted.

Clearly, self-ratings and scores on psychometrically determined aptitude, interest, and other similar constructs contain sizable common variance. These findings may be of considerable importance, considering the mandates of the 1992 amendments to the Rehabilitation Act, which emphasize consumer involvement in the rehabilitation process, including vocational assessment. Counselors may be able to avoid the expense of formal vocational testing by having consumers do simple self-ratings or by interviewing consumers to determine their interests, aptitudes, and other relevant career development factors. Either the self-rating or interview procedure appears to provide the consumer with more involvement and control over the assessment process than typically conferred during formal vocational testing or evaluation.

However, the low to moderate correlations between self-ratings and tested aptitude and interest scores suggest that substantial variance is unaccounted for. Even a correlation of .60 accounts for only 36% ($.60^2 \times 100$) of the variance in common between self-ratings and tested scores. Self-ratings and test scores measure somewhat different domains, and one score cannot be substituted for the other without a loss of information. Determining when self-ratings are acceptable, or when more in-depth psychometric measures are necessary, is an issue requiring more research. Consequently, rehabilitation professionals are taking a risk when they make decisions solely based on their, or their clients', ratings of abilities, interests, values, and so on.

Criterion Assessment

Unquestionably, the best predictor of a person's performance in a particular supported employment position is the person's actual performance in that job for an adequate period of time with appropriate support services (Callahan & Garner, 1997; Ford, 1995; Power, 2000; Wehman, 1981). Not only is a supervised job tryout more motivating and often less expensive than the typical regimen of psychological testing, work evaluation, and work adjustment training, it also provides better data from which to make decisions regarding the appropriateness of a specific placement and the types of support services required to enhance success (Gaylord-Ross, 1986; Moon, Goodall, Barcus, & Brooke, 1986; Pancsofar, 1986; Renzaglia & Hutchins, 1988; Smith, Belcher, & Juhrs, 1995).

Criterion-referenced assessments can be used to measure productivity rate, production accuracy, and the ability to check for and correct errors on the job as these three work skills can be the basis for reliable job performance across many positions (Smith et al., 1995). In addition, this type of assessment is useful for people with severe disabilities for a variety of reasons. Criterion assessments can be performed by individuals who are known to the person with a disability, such as a job coach or job trainer, and these assessments can be done in familiar surroundings, such as a supported employment agency or on the job. Familiarity with both the individual doing the assessment and the surroundings can create circumstances that optimize performance for the individual with a disability (Smith et al., 1995).

Criterion-referenced assessments are also useful for the ongoing assessment of work skills as the individual achieves and surpasses set criteria and for the assessment of both work skills and effectiveness of training procedures as the job changes through the addition of new responsibilities. Finally, criterion assessment is also useful for evaluating the generalization of learned skills across contexts, which can be important for workers with severe disabilities (Ford, 1995; Power, 2000; Smith et al., 1995).

Ecological Assessment

An ecological model may be the most appropriate form of vocational assessment for people with severe disabilities (Browder, 1991; Callahan & Garner, 1997; Everson, 1995). Ecological assessment includes comprehensive information about the individual, including current and potential environments; perceptions of parents, family, service providers, and employers; and interactions between an individual and the environment (Browder, 1991; Parker et al., 1989).

There are a variety of approaches to ecological assessment (e.g., Browder, 1991; Callahan & Garner, 1997; Everson, 1995; Power, 2000; Smith et al., 1995), and there are commonalties across approaches. There is not enough space here to present any one approach comprehensively; therefore, the following information is a compilation of commonalties across approaches, and the interested reader is referred to any or all of the authors cited for more information. Ecological assessment includes (a) information about an individual, (b) assessment of the environment, and (c) ongoing assessment of congruence between the individual and environments.

Information About an Individual

The following areas of vocational assessment include basic work skills, communication skills, behaviors, requisite skills, functional academic skills, learning style assessment, vocational preferences, and support needs.

Basic work skills such as grooming, toileting, attendance, and punctuality can make or break an individual getting and keeping a job, and the lack of these skills has been used to exclude persons with severe disabilities from the workforce (Smith et al., 1995). Stable supports that assist an individual to arrive on time and be appropriately groomed for a given work setting are critical for people with severe disabilities.

Communication skills need to be evaluated across a variety of community-inclusive environments and involve receptive, expressive, symbolic, and nonsymbolic skills (Everson, 1995). Receptive communication enables a person with severe disabilities to understand and react to messages from another person or source of information. Object cues, signs, and tactual signs can be used to communicate routines, activities, or requests in addition to written information and spoken language.

Expressive communication may use a variety of formats to convey information, including written and verbal communication, signs, or objects. Work-related communication, including expressing personal information such as name and address, asking for assistance when necessary, clarifying instructions, or requesting work materials, should be assessed.

Symbolic communication includes formally organized systems of words, signs, or objects to represent concepts, actions, objects, and people (Goodall & Everson, 1995). A symbolic communication system includes receptive and expressive communication that is effective only when both the communicator and receiver understand the system. Symbolic communication includes American Sign Language, visual and tactual cues, print on palm, Braille, spoken and written languages, and picture and symbolic systems, including Blissymbols and rebus pictures. An individual with severe disabilities may use multiple systems for communication, including speech for expressive communication and Braille or finger spelling for receptive communication (Everson, 1995).

Finally, nonsymbolic communication systems may be highly individualistic and include facial expressions, vocalizations, object manipulations, and behaviors. For example, gestures may be used to give and receive information and express wants or needs, boredom, desire for attention, or frustration or difficulty with an activity (Goodall & Everson, 1995). Service providers may need to assess patterns of communicative behaviors across contexts to reliably recognize the communicative intent of nonsymbolic behavior and provide reinforcement through symbolic and nonsymbolic communication. Development of a system of nonsymbolic communication that can be used across community-inclusive settings can be crucial for individuals with severe disabilities.

The behavior of individuals with severe disabilities such as mental retardation or autism may have a variety of issues for appropriate socialization (Callahan & Garner, 1997; Smith et al., 1995). These issues can range from inappropriate greeting of others, destructive behaviors, or aggression. In the workplace, it may become obvious which behaviors are job threatening and which are not; a behavior that is a problem in one environment may not be an issue in another (Callahan & Garner, 1997; Ford, 1995). For example, pacing in school may be a problem, but walking back and forth in a warehouse is a part of the job. A thorough assessment of behaviors across contexts should be done before decisions about level of support are made. Issues to consider include the nature of the behavior, number of behaviors, frequency, severity, duration, predictability, and an individual's ability to respond to redirection (Smith et al., 1995). Behaviors that require one-to-one supervision and intervention from a job coach should not be used as a reason to exclude an individual from community-based employment as these behaviors would require a high level of support whether the individual was in an institution, vocational center, or community-based employment. However, potential work sites and levels of support are extremely important considerations. There are many sources of information on behavior analysis, management, and nonaversive interventions, and the following references are provided for the interested reader (Ford, 1995; Lucyshyn, Olson, & Horner, 1999; Scotti & Meyer, 1999; Smith et al., 1995).

Requisite skills vary with each job, and it is important to assess whether an individual has the skills for a particular job or can learn them (Smith et al., 1995). Requisite skills include work rate and accuracy, gross and fine motor skills, mobility, attention to task, strength, and endurance. Although requisite skills are a part of every job description for existing jobs, Callahan and Garner (1997) suggested that for some individuals with severe disabilities, an individually negotiated job description assists individuals with severe disabilities to make contributions to an employer without having to perform all or some of the tasks of an existing job description.

Functional academic skills include an individual's ability to read, write, and do math. Even if an individual does not have high levels of academic skills, these skills may be taught specific to a work site with support from a job coach, or other skills (e.g., match-to-sample skills) could be used instead. For example, an individual who cannot read could work at the library, sorting books into bins by matching the letter codes on the spine of the book with the letters on the bins (Smith et al., 1995).

Learning style includes how an individual best learns a task or series of tasks. For example, does the person learn best with verbal instruction, physical prompts, modeling, or combinations of all three? In addition, other factors to consider include the number of steps of instruction a person comprehends, pacing and sequencing of instruction a person best responds to, and environmental conditions that may affect learning such as noise or people entering and leaving the work space.

Vocational preferences and work goals for people with severe disabilities may be difficult to determine, and perceptions of the family and individual may be the starting point for developing a plan. Hagner and Dileo (1993) have pointed out that the stated goal may not have an occupational name but may be a location in the community (downtown), a type of social context (very busy or quiet), or a type of setting (outdoors). What may be important for the individual is to work with certain types of equipment, wear certain clothes, or be close to an important person in the individual's life.

Hagner and Dileo (1993) also cautioned against dismissing stated vocational goals that sound unrealistic (e.g., a person with severe mental retardation wanting to be a firefighter or country music singer) because these goals may include important information about how individuals perceive and incorporate work into their lives. Several approaches to the constructive use of vocational goals that may initially appear unrealistic are suggested in Hagner and Dileo (1993, pp. 72–73).

By ascertaining which aspects of the vocational goal fundamentally attract or intrigue a person, it may be possible to determine what facets of the job are meaningful. If the social setting, uniform, equipment, or location is particularly meaningful, these aspects may be used to identify potential jobs and thus bring the individual closer to his or her vocational goal. If, for example, an individual indicates that he or she wants to be a country-and-western singer, what about that job is attractive? Are there other ways to work in the field of music—for example, at a recording studio, music store, or radio station—that incorporate the qualities that are attractive to the individual?

An additional approach is exploring the origin of a stated vocational goal. This activity may provide additional information about how a person came to select a particular goal and what about the goal is attractive. If a consumer wants to be a country music singer, how did he or she get the idea? If the individual admires someone who is a country music singer, are there other people he or she also admires? This information can lead individuals in different directions and may help them to identify other goals that may be more readily attainable.

What also may be important for the individual is to have a sense that service providers are making a best effort to achieve as much of what is important to the person as is possible. If a certain goal is not attainable, aspects of the goal may certainly be.

Although assessing an individual's level of need for support is embedded into an ecological assessment process in regard to transportation, communication, learning, behavior, and overall functioning in a job, the family also has a critical role (Power, 2000). Issues that may be particularly important for families include internal and external resources, financial disincentives or incentives, beliefs about disability and working, family roles and responsibilities for all members, an understanding of service delivery options and providers, and the roles and responsibilities of service providers and families throughout the rehabilitation process.

Assessment of the Environment

Assessment of potential work environments includes identification and initial analysis of potential jobs in the community (Browder, 1991; Callahan & Garner, 1997). Analysis of the local labor market provides a general idea of job availability. Analyses of potential jobs may also provide information on specific job skills needed, social characteristics of the workplace, task sequencing, work environment, rate of work, physical requirements of the job, naturally occurring cues and reinforcers, variation of tasks, and quality standards. This information may also identify one or several aspects of a job that can be created for an individual to make a contribution to the business. Determining employer perceptions on the level of involvement in training and supervision, training for coworkers and supervisors, and unacceptable behaviors in the workplace are also critical for a successful working relationship.

Ongoing Assessment of Congruence Between the Individual and Environment

Information from assessment of the individual and of potential work environments can assist in identifying and matching jobs with an individual. Steps in a matching process include (a) identification of potential individual job matches; (b) task analyses of specific job tasks based on the needs of a specific individual; (c) clarification of perceptions of job requirements by the employer, individual, service providers, and parents or significant others; (d) identification of discrepancies between work requirements and the individual's strengths, skills, and skill acquisition needs; and (e) resolutions to the discrepancies (Parker et al., 1989).

Resolutions to discrepancies between work environments and the individual's skills, strengths, and skill acquisition needs may be anything but straightforward. Piuma and Udvari-Solner (1993, p. 17) noted that discrepancies may fall into four categories: (a) instructional/student learning, (b) environmental, (c) physical/motor sensory, and (d) motivation/behavioral factors. By systematically selecting and varying instructional interventions, altering the environment, and modifying behavioral strategies and materials, service providers can identify strategies that maximize an individual's productivity and determine whether physical adaptations are needed. The interested reader may wish to consult Piuma and Udvari-

Solner for a more detailed discussion of discrepancy analysis. One powerful methodology that may be employed in nontraditional forms of assessment is qualitative assessment.

Qualitative Assessment

Let us focus specifically on how professionals can gather and process comprehensive data about a consumer, including test data, to most effectively assist the consumer. First, professional counselors require a philosophical and theoretical framework from which to operate. Vocational data on one individual often comprise hundreds, perhaps thousands, of pieces of information, including observed personal traits, social and historical information, and scores on test scales whose meanings may be obscure. The consumer may particularly regard the scores as cold numbers without personal reference or meaning. This impersonal quality of test scores derives, in part, from the scientific tradition on which modern measurement is based—the hypothetico-deductive, quantitative research tradition of the "hard sciences" (e.g., physics). Kelly (1955) and Pepinski and Pepinski (1954), among other counseling theorists, regarded the professional counselor as a scientist who follows the traditional, hard science approach to assisting consumers. These positions were derived from logical positivism, which is the philosophical foundation on which most physical sciences were based during the 19th and 20th centuries (Polkinghorne, 1983).

It is not hard science but the humanistic art of vocational counseling that brings comprehensive data, including test scores, to life, making them personally meaningful to the consumer. Making data meaningful in personal, human terms fits much better within the qualitative research paradigm than the quantitative approach. Imbuing data derived from human beings with subjective, human qualities is the quest of the avant-garde, antipositivist approach to research—the qualitative approach.

Qualitative research methodology sprang from postpositivist philosophies into a crucible of ideas at the University of Chicago in the 1920s. The likes of John Dewey, George Herbert Mead, and Robert Park, who had been a student of William James at Harvard, were a few of the seminal thinkers in the qualitative research movement. Much of the thinking about research was strongly influenced by the philosophy of pragmatism. If science studies problems of living, then it should provide solutions to those problems. Furthermore, pragmatists believed that experience is the beginning and end of knowledge; that is, we cannot know anything beyond our experience. This latter tenet will be recognized by students of counseling theories as originating with phenomenology. Finally, to be understood, humans must be viewed within the natural world, and rational human thought must be regarded as an essential source of knowledge (Hammersley, 1989).

Clearly, these ideas depart substantially from those brandished in the so-called quantitative, physical sciences. In fact, it is instructive to compare the characteristics of qualitative and quantitative research (see Table 5.2) and consider how qualitative methods may be applied to vocational assessment in counseling.

The reader may be curious about how this discourse on qualitative and quantitative research methodologies relates to vocational assessment. The fact is that much of vocational assessment is qualitative in nature. Data from interviews with a consumer, family, friends, and so on; observations of the consumer in a variety of settings; historical records (e.g., vocational, medical, educational, and military records); and similar information are essentially qualitative data. One could argue that all human data, by definition, are qualitative, even test scores or measures of physical characteristics. Such data have little meaning outside a human context. Clearly, reformation and reformulation of vocational assessment are required to achieve greater utility in the consumer–professional relationship.

Vocational assessment must be reformed to avoid fostering consumer dependency, encourage consumer self-assessment and assessment of consumer contexts, and emphasize not only consumer choice but implement-

TABLE 5.2. Comparison of Quantitative and Qualitative Methods

Quantitative	Qualitative
Reality is singular, tangible, and separate from the researcher	Reality is multiple, subjective, and influenced by the researcher
Focus is on quantity (how many, how much)	Focus is on quality (nature, essence)
Researcher attempts to be value free and unbiased	Researcher attempts to be value laden and biased
Researcher uses deductive logic	Researcher uses inductive logic
Causes and effects may be identified	All things are intertwined in a mutual simultaneous shaping so causes and effects are indiscernible
Design is formulated in advance	Design emerges during the study
Sample is large and representative	Sample is small and nonrandom
Researcher remains objective by using inanimate instruments, scales, tests, surveys, and so on	Researcher is the primary instrument—gathers data through observation and interviews
The results are precise, narrow, and reductionistic	The results are comprehensive, holistic, and expansive

Note. Adapted from Creswell (1994), Lincoln and Guba (1985), and Merriam (1988).

ing the choice. Healy (1990) called for such a reform of vocational assessment through the following actions:

> (1) Cast clients as collaborators and equip them for the role. . . .
> (2) Accentuate self assessments and stimulate clients to recall how accurate self assessment has helped them. . . .
> (3) Help clients to recognize that they become who they are through dynamic interaction with contexts by expanding the number and focus of assessments. . . .
> (4) Design appraisals so that they improve decision making and follow-through. (pp. 221–224)

These actions are consonant with the emphases of qualitative assessment. Goldman (1990) called counseling professionals to action in learning about and applying qualitative assessment methodologies. He cited six reasons why qualitative assessment was needed:

> (1) Qualitative methods tend to foster an active role for the client in the process of collecting and teasing meaning out of data, rather than the role of a passive responder who is being measured, predicted, placed, or diagnosed. . . .
> (2) Qualitative assessment emphasizes holistic study of the individual rather than the isolation and precise measurement of narrowly defined discrete elements of ability, interest, or personality. . . .
> (3) Qualitative assessment methods tend to emphasize the concept of learning about oneself and understanding oneself in a *developmental* framework. . . .
> (4) Qualitative assessment methods often *work well in groups* of clients and, in fact, are often at their best in a group setting, where each individual may learn something about individual differences as well as understanding him- or herself better, through the comparison with others in the group. . . .
> (5) Qualitative assessment reduces the distinction between assessment and counseling. . . .
> (6) At a time when professional psychology as a whole is called upon to relate more effectively to persons of different cultural and ethnic groups, socioeconomic levels, sexual identities, and to people with disabilities, the qualitative methods are especially valuable. (pp. 205–206)

One form of qualitative assessment already has been discussed, *ecological assessment*. This type of assessment has commonalties with personal futures planning (Mount & Zwernick, 1988) and developing a personal profile (Hagner & Dileo, 1993). All these approaches include people who are important to the consumer, with the consumer himself or herself at the center of a process of collecting information (assessment) and determining what kind of work would be satisfying. What is important is that the process assist individuals in identifying what is important to them, who the important people are in their lives, and what their career goals are.

Another approach to qualitative assessment sets the stage for the individual's active participation by exploring feelings, needs, fantasies, values, lifestyle alternatives, perceptions of opportunity, and fears as a part of the vocational counseling process (Dewey, 1977; Worell & Remer, 1992). The intent of this process is to assist the individual through his or her direct involvement in the generation of career information. One way to achieve active participation is by using the nonsexist vocational card sort (Dewey, 1977).

Dewey (1977) suggested that the insights into discriminations made by individuals concerning their interests, values, and feelings while taking a paper-and-pencil interest inventory, and how these discriminations relate to the resulting test profile, may be lost if there is not an opportunity for individuals to explore their discriminations. Using card sort procedures assists individuals in organizing their thinking and talking about themselves in relation to work and occupations.

The individual is told that key words, values, and themes will be recorded during the card-sorting process and discussed after the process is finished. The individual sorts cards into "Would Not Choose," "In Question," and "Might Choose" categories. After the initial sort, the individual is asked to identify cards in the "Would Not Choose" pile that he or she had similar or the same reasons for not choosing and to group these cards into piles. Each group is discussed in turn as to the reasons for the grouping. The cards in the "In Question" and "Might Choose" categories are discussed following the same procedure.

For the cards in the "Might Choose" category, the individual is asked to identify what influenced his or her choices and to rank order 8 to 10 occupations that are most preferred. Dewey (1977) suggested that the individual is ranking the importance of values and needs associated with each occupation as well. The notes on key words and themes taken during the session are also discussed, and the individual is asked if there are occupations of interest that were not included in the cards. It is also important for individuals to recognize that they have generated their own results through the card sort process. Individuals may also obtain further information about their preferred occupations by identifying short-term and long-term advantages to each. For the interested reader, Slaney, Moran, and Wade (1994) discussed a variety of vocational card sorts.

Although this approach has been presented as individually centered, it is important to remember that people fall on a continuum from individually to collectively oriented (Hofstede, 1991). If rehabilitation professionals use interactive methods of assessment and view vocational choice as an individual decision, individuals and families may view the vocational choice as a group or family decision. Professionals may feel they are fostering independence when the individual or family is concerned with interdependence. The professional must explore issues concerning whether an individual prefers family members present when vocational assessment occurs.

Ecological assessment (or personal futures planning) and the nonsexist vocational card sort are but two approaches to qualitative vocational assessment. Each approach includes aspects of qualitative assessment considered advantageous by Healy (1990) and Goldman (1990). By using an assessment process that reduces the distinction between assessment and counseling and emphasizes a holistic, interactive approach, vocational assessment will likely be more effective for all consumers.

Unfortunately, most counseling professionals are not trained in qualitative approaches to gather and analyze such data and information. This problem of lack of training is compounded by the fact that qualitative methodologies, particularly case study qualitative methodologies, have developed rapidly in recent years (Merriam, 1988; Sechrest & Figueredo, 1993; Yin, 1989). Consequently, we exhort counselor educators to become knowledgeable about qualitative research methods and develop ways to include these methods in counselor education curricula.

SUMMARY

In this chapter, we have presented a description of traditional, objective vocational instruments, theoretical and conceptual issues in vocational assessment, technical limitations of traditional vocational assessment, and alternatives to traditional assessment. In particular, we reminded readers of the relative lack of theory in vocational assessment, the group rather than individual orientation of traditional vocational tests, problems in applying occupational assessment instruments to people with disabilities and other individuals with diverse backgrounds, technical limitations of such tests, and alternatives to traditional assessment. In particular, we recommended that counseling professionals make greater use of consumer self-ratings, criterion assessment, ecological assessment, and qualitative assessment.

REFERENCES

Aiken, L. (1998). *Tests and examinations: Measuring abilities and performance*. New York: Wiley.

Alston, R., & McCowan, C. (1994). Aptitude assessment and African-American clients: The interplay between culture and psychometrics in rehabilitation. *Journal of Rehabilitation*, *60*(1), 41–46.

Anastasi, A. (1988). *Psychological testing* (6th ed.). New York: Macmillan.

Anastasi, A. (1993). A century of psychological testing: Origins, problems, and progress. In T. Fagan & G. VandenBos (Eds.), *Exploring applied psychology: Origins and critical analyses* (pp. 9–36). Washington, DC: American Psychological Association.

Anastasi, A. & Urbina, S. (1997). *Psychological testing* (7th ed.). Englewood Cliffs, NJ: Prentice Hall.

Atkins, B. (1988). An asset-oriented approach to cross-cultural issues: Blacks in rehabilitation. *Journal of Applied Rehabilitation Counseling, 19*(4), 45–49.

Austin, J., & Villanova, P. (1992). The criterion problem: 1917–1992. *Journal of Applied Psychology*, *77*, 836–874.

Bennett, G., Seashore, H., & Wesman, A. (1990). *Differential Aptitude Tests: Administrator's manual* (5th ed.). San Antonio, TX: Psychological Corporation.

Bolton, B. (1988). *Special education and rehabilitation testing: Practical applications and test reviews*. Austin, TX: PRO-ED.

Bolton, B. (Ed.). (2001). *Handbook of measurement and evaluation in rehabilitation* (3rd ed.). Austin, TX: PRO-ED.

Bolton, B., Butler, A., & Wright, G. (1968). *Clinical versus statistical prediction of client feasibility* (Wisconsin Studies in Vocational Rehabilitation, Monograph No. 7). Madison: University of Wisconsin, Regional Rehabilitation Institute.

Bond, G., & Dietzen, L. (1990). Predictive validity and vocational assessment: Reframing the question. In R. Gleuckauf, L. Sechrest, G. Bond, & E. McDonel (Eds.), *Improving assessment in rehabilitation and health* (pp. 61–86). Newbury Park, CA: Sage.

Bowman, S. (1993). Career intervention strategies for ethnic minorities. *Career Development Quarterly*, *42*, 14–25.

Brennan, R. (1983). *Elements of generalizability theory*. Iowa City, IA: ACT Publications.

Browder, D. (1991). *Assessment of individuals with severe disabilities: An applied behavior approach to life skills assessment* (2nd ed.). Baltimore: Brookes.

Brown, M. (1995). The career development of African Americans: Theoretical and empirical issues. In F. Leong (Ed.), *Career development and vocational behavior of racial and ethnic minorities* (pp. 8–36). Mahwah, NJ: Erlbaum.

Callahan, M., & Garner, J. (1997). *Keys to the workplace: Skills and supports for people with disabilities*. Baltimore: Brookes.

Conte, L. (1983). Vocational development theories and the disabled person: Oversight or deliberate omission? *Rehabilitation Counseling Bulletin*, *26*, 316–328.

Cresswell, J. (1994). *Research design: Qualitative and quantitative approaches*. Thousand Oaks, CA: Sage.

Cronbach, L. (1990). *Essentials of psychological testing* (5th ed.). New York: HarperCollins.

Cronbach, L., & Drenth, P. (Eds.). (1972). *Mental tests and cultural adaptation*. The Hague, Netherlands: Mouton.

Dana, R. (1993). *Multicultural assessment perspectives for professional psychology*. Boston: Allyn & Bacon.

Dawes, R. M., Faust, D., & Meehl, P. (1989). Clinical versus actuarial judgment. *Science, 243*, 1668–1674.

Dawes, R. M., Faust, D., & Meehl, P. (1993). Statistical prediction versus clinical prediction: Improving what works. In G. Keren & C. Lewis (Eds.), *A handbook for data analysis in the behavioral sciences: Methodological issues* (pp. 351–367). Hillsdale, NJ: Erlbaum.

Dewey, C. (1977). Vocational counseling with women: A nonsexist technique. In E. Rawlings & D. Carter (Eds.), *Psychotherapy for women: Treatment toward equality* (pp. 207–220). Springfield, IL: Thomas.

Diaconis, P., & Efron, B. (1983). Computer intensive methods in statistics. *Scientific American, 248*(5), 116–130.

Everson, J. (Ed.). (1995). *Supporting young adults who are deaf-blind in their communities: A transition planning guide for service providers, families, and friends*. Baltimore: Brookes.

Farr, J. M. (1993). *The complete guide for occupational exploration*. Indianapolis, IN: JIST.

Fitzgerald, L., & Betz, N. (1994a). Career development in cultural context: The role of gender, race, class, and sexual orientation. In M. Savickas & R. Lent (Eds.), *Convergence in career development theories: Implications for science and practice* (pp. 207–214). Palo Alto, CA: Consulting Psychologists Press.

Fitzgerald, L., & Betz, N. (1994b). Cultural development in context: The role of gender, race, class, and sexual orientation. In M. Savickas & R. Lent (Eds.), *Convergence in career development theories: Implications for science and practice* (pp. 103–115). Palo Alto, CA: Consulting Psychologists Press.

Ford, L. (1995). *Providing employment support for people with long-term mental illness*. Baltimore: Brookes.

Fouad, N. (1993). Cross-cultural vocational assessment. *Career Development Quarterly, 42*, 4–13.

Gaylord-Ross, R. (1986). The role of assessment in transitional, supported employment. *Career Development for Exceptional Individuals, 9*, 129–134.

Goldman, L. (1990). Qualitative assessment. *The Counseling Psychologist, 18*, 205–213.

Goodall, D., & Everson, J. (1995). Communication instruction and support strategies for young adults who are deaf-blind. In J. Everson (Ed.), *Supporting young adults who are deaf-blind in their communities: A transition planning guide for service providers, families, and friends* (pp. 203–225). Baltimore: Brookes.

Gough, H. (1962). Clinical vs. statistical prediction in psychology. In L. Postman (Ed.), *Psychology in the making* (pp. 526–584). New York: Knopf.

Guilford, J. P., & Fruchter, B. (1973). *Fundamental statistics in psychology and education* (5th ed.). New York: McGraw-Hill.

Hagner, D., & Dileo, D. (1993). *Working together: Workplace culture, supported employment, and persons with disabilities*. Cambridge, MA: Brookline.

Halpern, A. (1981). Mental retardation. In W. Stolov & M. Clowers (Eds.), *Handbook of severe disability* (pp. 265–277). Washington, DC: Government Printing Office.

Hammersley, M. (1989). *The qualitative method: Herbert Blumer and the Chicago tradition*. New York: Routledge Kegan Paul.

Hammill, D., Brown, L., & Bryant, B. (1992). *A consumer's guide to tests in print* (2nd ed.). Austin, TX: PRO-ED.

Hansen, J. C., & Campbell, D. P. (1985). *Manual for the Strong Interest Inventory* (4th ed.). Stanford, CA: Stanford University Press.

Harry, B. (1992). *Cultural diversity, families, and the special education system: Communication and empowerment*. New York: Teachers College Press.

Hays, W. (1994). *Statistics* (5th ed.). New York: Harcourt Brace.

Healy, C. C. (1990). Reforming career appraisal to meet the needs of clients in the 1990s. *The Counseling Psychologist*, *18*, 214–226.

Helmstadter, G. (1964). *Principles of psychological measurement*. New York: Appleton-Century-Crofts.

Herr, E., & Cramer, S. (1992). *Career guidance and counseling through the lifespan: Systematic approaches* (4th ed.). New York: HarperCollins.

Hershenson, D., & Szymanski, E. (1992). Career development of people with disabilities. In R. Parker & E. Szymanski (Eds.), *Rehabilitation counseling: Basics and beyond* (2nd ed, pp. 273–303). Austin, TX: PRO-ED.

Hofstede, G. (1991). *Cultures and organizations: Software of the mind*. London: McGraw-Hill.

Holland, J. (1966). *The psychology of vocational choice: A theory of personality types and model environments*. Waltham, MA: Blaisdell.

Holland, J. (1973). *Making vocational choices: A theory of careers*. Englewood Cliffs, NJ: Prentice Hall.

Holland, J. (1985). *The Self-Directed Search: Professional manual—1985 edition*. Odessa, FL: Psychological Assessment Resources.

Holland, J. (1992). *Making vocational choices: A theory of vocational personalities and work environments* (2nd ed.). Odessa, FL: Psychological Assessment Resources.

Holland, J. (1997). *Making vocational choices: A theory of vocational personalities and work environments* (3rd ed.). Odessa, FL: Psychological Assessment Resources.

Holt, R. (1958). Clinical and statistical prediction: A reformulation and some new data. *Journal of Abnormal and Social Psychology*, *56*, 1–12.

Impara, J., & Plake, B. (Eds.). (1998). *The thirteenth mental measurements yearbook*. Lincoln: University of Nebraska–Lincoln, Buros Institute of Mental Measurements.

Isaacson, L., & Brown, D. (2000). *Career information, career counseling, and career development* (7th ed.). Boston: Allyn & Bacon.

Kapes, J., & Whitfield, E. (2001). *A counselor's guide to career assessment instruments* (3rd ed.). Alexandria, VA: National Career Development Association.

Kelly, G. A. (1955). *The psychology of personal constructs: Vol. 2. Clinical diagnosis and psychotherapy*. New York: Norton.

Kerlinger, F. (1986). *Foundations of behavioral research* (3rd ed.). New York: Holt, Rinehart, & Winston.

Keyser, D. J., & Sweetland, R. C. (Eds.). (1984–1994). *Test critiques* (Vols. 1–10). Austin, TX: PRO-ED.

Kline, P. (1993). *The handbook of psychological testing*. London: Routledge Kegan Paul.

Lincoln, Y., & Guba, E. (1985). *Naturalistic inquiry*. Newburg Park, CA: Sage.

Lonner, W. (1990). An overview of cross-cultural testing and assessment. In R. Brislin (Ed.), *Applied cross-cultural psychology* (pp. 56–76). Newbury Park, CA: Sage.

Lorge, I. (1936). Criteria for guidance. *Occupations, 14*, 958–962.

Lucyshyn, J., Olson, D., & Horner, R. (1999). Building an ecology of support for a young woman with severe problem behaviors living in the community. In J. Scotti & L. Meyer (Eds.), *Behavioral intervention: Principles, models, and practices* (pp. 269 289). Baltimore: Brookes.

Mabe, P., & West, S. (1982). Validity of self-evaluation ability: A review and meta-analysis. *Journal of Applied Psychology, 67*, 280–296.

Mayall, D. (Ed.). (1994). *The worker traits data book*. Indianapolis, IN: JIST.

McFall, R. (1990). The essential role of theory in psychological assessment. In R. Gleuckauf, L. Sechrest, G. Bond, & E. McDonel (Eds.), *Improving assessment in rehabilitation and health* (pp. 11–32). Newbury Park, CA: Sage.

Meehl, P. (1954). *Clinical versus statistical prediction*. Minneapolis: University of Minnesota Press.

Meehl, P. (1986). Causes and effects of my disturbing little book. *Journal of Personality Assessment, 50*, 370–375.

Menchetti, B. M., & Rusch, F. R. (1988). Vocational evaluation and eligibility for rehabilitation services. In P. Wehman & M. S. Moon (Eds.), *Vocational rehabilitation and supported employment* (pp. 79–90). Baltimore: Brookes.

Merriam, S. (1988). *Case study research in education: A qualitative approach*. San Francisco: Jossey-Bass.

Moon, M. S., Goodall, P., Barcus, M., & Brookes, V. (1986). *The supported work model for citizens with severe handicaps: A guide for job trainers* (Rev. ed.). Richmond: Virginia Commonwealth University, Rehabilitation Research and Training Center.

Mooney, C., & Duval, R. (1993). *Bootstrapping: A nonparametric approach to statistical inference* (Quantitative Applications in the Social Sciences, Sage University Paper No. 95). Newbury Park, CA: Sage.

Moore, E. (1986). Family socialization and the IQ test performance of traditionally and transracially adopted Black children. *Developmental Psychology, 22*, 317–322.

Mount, B., & Zwernick, K. (1988). *It's never too early, it's never too late: A booklet about personal futures planning.* Minneapolis, MN: Metropolitan Council.

Nisbett, R. E., & Ross, L. (1980). *Human inferences: Strategies and shortcomings of human judgment.* Englewood Cliffs, NJ: Prentice Hall.

Orelove, F. P., & Sobsey, D. (1987). *Educating children with multiple disabilities: A transdisciplinary approach.* Baltimore: Brookes.

Pancsofar, E. L. (1986). Assessing work behavior. In F. R. Rusch (Ed.), *Competitive employment issues and strategies* (pp. 93–102). Baltimore: Brookes.

Parker, R. (2001). Aptitude testing. In B. Bolton (Ed.), *Handbook of measurement and evaluation in rehabilitation* (3rd ed., pp. 103–124). Gaithersburg, MD: Aspen.

Parker, R., & Schaller, J. (1994). Relationships among self-rated and psychometrically determined vocational aptitudes and interests. *Educational and Psychological Measurement, 54,* 155–159.

Parker, R., Szymanski, E., & Hanley-Maxwell, C. (1989). Ecological assessment in supported employment. *Journal of Applied Rehabilitation Counseling, 20*(3), 26–33.

Pepinski, H. B., & Pepinski, P. N. (1954). *Counseling theory and practice.* New York: Ronald.

Piuma, C., & Udvari-Solner, A. (1993). *Materials and process manual: Developing low cost vocational adaptations for individuals with severe disabilities.* Madison: University of Wisconsin–Madison, Madison Metropolitan School District.

Polkinghorne, D. (1983). *Methodology for the human sciences: Methods of inquiry.* Albany: State University of New York Press.

Power, P. (2000). *A guide to vocational assessment* (3rd ed.). Austin, TX: PRO-ED.

Rehabilitation Act Amendments of 1992, 29 U.S.C. § 701 *et seq.*

Renzaglia, A., & Hutchins, M. (1988). A community-referenced approach to preparing persons with disabilities for employment. In P. Wehman & M. S. Moon (Eds.), *Vocational rehabilitation and supported employment* (pp. 91–110). Baltimore: Brookes.

Sawyer, J. (1966). Measurement and prediction, clinical and statistical. *Psychological Bulletin, 66,* 178–200.

Scotti, J., & Meyer, L. (Eds.). (1999). *Behavioral intervention: Principles, models, and practices.* Baltimore: Brookes.

Sechrest, L. B. (1993). Measurement in rehabilitation: From the beginning to what end? In R. Gleuckauf, L. Sechrest, G. Bond, & E. McDonel (Eds.), *Improving assessment in rehabilitation and health* (pp. 253–273). Newbury Park, CA: Sage.

Sechrest, L. B., & Figueredo, A. J. (1993). Program evaluation. *Annual Review of Psychology, 44,* 645–674.

Shavelson, R., & Webb, N. (1991). *Generalizability theory: A primer.* Newbury Park, CA: Sage.

Shavelson, R., Webb, N., & Rowley, G. (1989). Generalizability theory. *American Psychologist, 44,* 922–932.

Shertzer, B., & Linden, J. (1979). *Fundamentals of individual appraisal*. Boston: Houghton Mifflin.

Slaney, R., Moran, W., & Wade, J. (1994). Vocational card sorts. In J. Kapes, M. Mastie, & E. Whitfield (Eds.), *A counselor's guide to career assessment instruments* (3rd ed., pp. 347–360). Alexandria, VA: National Career Development Association.

Smart, J., & Smart, D. (1992). Curriculum changes in multicultural rehabilitation. *Rehabilitation Education*, *6*, 105–122.

Smart, J., & Smart, D. (1993). Acculturation, biculturalism, and the rehabilitation of Mexican Americans. *Journal of Applied Rehabilitation Counseling*, *24*(2), 46–51.

Smith, E. (1983). Issues in racial minorities' career behavior. In W. Walsh & S. Osipow (Eds.), *Handbook of vocational psychology: Foundations* (Vol. 1, pp. 161–222). Hillsdale, NJ: Erlbaum.

Smith, M., Belcher, R., & Juhrs, P. (1995). *A guide to successful employment for individuals with autism*. London: Brookes.

Steinberg, L., Thissen, D., & Wainer, H. (2000). Validity. In H. Wainer (Ed.), *Computerized adaptive testing: A primer* (2nd ed., pp. 185–229). Hillsdale, NJ: Erlbaum.

Sue, D. W., & Sue, D. (1990). *Counseling the culturally different: Theory and practice* (2nd ed.). New York: Wiley.

Super, D. (1990). A life-span, life-space approach to career development. In D. Brown & L. Brooks (Eds.), *Career choice and development* (pp. 197–261). San Francisco: Jossey-Bass.

Szymanski, E., Dunn, C., & Parker, R. (1989). Rehabilitation counseling with people with learning disabilities: An ecological framework. *Rehabilitation Counseling Bulletin*, *33*, 38–53.

Terman, L. M. (1916). *The measurement of intelligence*. Boston: Houghton Mifflin.

Thompson, B. (1994). Guidelines for authors. *Educational and Psychological Measurement*, *54*, 837–847.

Thorndike, E. L., Bregman, E., Lorge, I., Metcalfe, Z., Robinson, E., & Woodward, E. (1934). *Prediction of vocational success*. New York: Commonwealth Fund.

Walsh, W. B. (1990). Putting assessment in context. *The Counseling Psychologist*, *18*, 262–265.

Walsh, W. B., & Betz, N. (1990). *Tests and assessment* (2nd ed.). Englewood Cliffs, NJ: Prentice Hall.

Wehman, P. (1981). *Competitive employment: New horizons for severely disabled individuals*. Baltimore: Brookes.

Westbrook, B., Buck, R., & Wynne, D. (1994). Career maturity in adolescence: Reliability and validity of self-ratings of abilities by gender and ethnicity. *Journal of Career Assessment*, *2*, 125–161.

Westbrook, B., Sanford, E., Gilleland, K., Fleenor, J., & Mervin, G. (1988). Career maturity in Grade 9: The relationship between accuracy of self-appraisal and ability to appraise the career-relevant capabilities of others. *Journal of Vocational Behavior*, *32*, 269–283.

Worell, J., & Remer, P. (1992). *Feminist perspectives in therapy: An empowerment model for women*. New York: Wiley.

Yin, R. K. (1989). *Case study research: Design and methods* (Rev. ed.). Newbury Park, CA: Sage.

Disability and Accommodation

Martin Brodwin, Randall M. Parker, and Denise DeLaGarza

The purpose of this chapter is to familiarize the reader with the major disabilities within the broad context of sociocultural theory, with the more specific dimension of accommodation, and with the rehabilitation goal of facilitating a successful return to work. We briefly review the major types of disabling conditions and their possible functional limitations. Our emphasis is on the functional limitations and the potential mediating impact (see Chapter 1, this volume) of accommodation in improving the individual's interaction with the work environment.

First, we review various conceptions of disability. Second, we discuss conceptions of disability in functional terms, including information on functional limitations, rehabilitation potential, psychosocial considerations, and cultural and psychosocial perspectives. In the third section, we discuss the incidence and prevalence of major categories of medical disabilities seen by rehabilitation professionals. Although many counselors specialize in providing rehabilitation services to specific populations, knowledge of the different disabilities allows them a broad base of information.

In the fourth section, we describe categories of functional limitations, establishing a conceptual framework for considering mediating factors related to these limitations. In the fifth section, we discuss accommodations in the workplace, and we present different definitions of reasonable accommodation. Next, we describe categories of accommodation with examples for each category. In the sixth section, we describe material on accommodating individuals with specific functional limitations in the workplace, computers in the workplace and we review in the seventh section. We conclude the chapter with information on preventing and managing disability in the workplace.

CONCEPTIONS OF DISABILITY

A review of the various definitions of disability is intended to help in developing an accurate concept of disability and disabling conditions. Disability may be defined and viewed from several perspectives. Although presently regarded as anachronistic, the definition that had been most commonly cited in the literature is by Hamilton (1950), who defined disability as "a condition of impairment, physical or mental, having an objective aspect" (p. 17). A handicap, as defined by Hamilton, "is the cumulative result of the obstacles which disability interposes between the individual and his (or her) maximum functional level" (p. 17). A modern definition that differs considerably from Hamilton's is put forth in the Americans with Disabilities Act (ADA) of 1990. According to the ADA definition, a person with a disability

> (1) has a physical or mental impairment that substantially limits one or more major life activities,
>
> (2) has a record of such an impairment, or
>
> (3) is regarded as having such impairment. (Americans with Disabilities Act, 1990)

This definition is unique in that it recognizes the serious consequences of labeling a person as having a disability. Labeling alone, without a disability actually being present, may cause vocational and social limitations.

Medical definitions, on the other hand, usually require that a medical condition be identified and a diagnostic label be given for a disability to be recognized. However, many definitions cited in medical texts emphasize limitations of function as essential to the meaning of disability. For example, Stolov (1981) stated that "disability is present . . . when a set of functions, either desired or required, exists, which cannot be independently performed when attempted in a specific environment" (p. 1).

Taber's Cyclopedic Medical Dictionary (1997) defines disability as "any physical or mental impairment that limits a major activity" (p. 551). *Stedman's Concise Medical Dictionary for the Health Professions* (1997) defines disability as "(1) any restriction or lack of ability to perform an activity in a manner or within the range considered normal for a human being, or (2) an impairment or defect of one or more organs or members" (p. 24). A third medical definition of disability is offered by *Mosby's Medical, Nurs-*

ing and Allied Health Dictionary (1998): "the loss, absence, or impairment of physical or mental fitness" (p. 496).

When we compare these definitions of disability to the definitions of handicap within these same dictionaries, we see that the term *handicap* is more negative and judgmental. *Taber's* (1997) definition of *handicap* refers to "a disadvantage for a given individual resulting from an impairment or disability that limits or prevents the fulfillment of a role that is normal, depending on age, sex, and social and cultural factors, for that individual" (p. 490). *Stedman's* (1997) definition of *handicap* is "(1) a physical, mental, or emotional condition that interferes with an individual's normal functioning, (2) reduction in a person's capacity to fulfill a social role as a consequence of an impairment, inadequate training for the role, or other circumstances" (p. 381). Last, *Mosby's* (1998) definition of *handicap* refers to a person who has "a congenital or acquired mental or physical defect that interferes with normal functioning of the body systems or the ability to be self-sufficient in modern society" (p. 728). One can readily see the negative evaluations inherent in these definitions of *handicap*.

In like manner, rehabilitation textbooks tend to emphasize functionally limiting aspects of disability. For instance, G. Wright (1980) defined *disability* as "any physical, mental, or emotional condition that is chronic or long-lasting (not acute or temporary), which is severe enough to limit the individual's functioning, and which results in, or threatens to be, a handicap to productive activity" (p. 9). Similarly, B. Wright (1983) defined *disability* as "a limitation of function that results directly from an impairment at the level of specific organ or body system" (p. 11).

CONCEPTION OF DISABILITY IN FUNCTIONAL TERMS

As we have just seen from the preceding review, a common focus in current definitions of disability is on functional limitations. Although medical professionals focus on objective functional limitations, the reader is urged to keep in mind the ADA definition of disability, which recognizes the psychosocial effects of disability labels, regardless of the actual existence of disability (Danek et al., 1996).

Functional Limitations

A functional limitation is the inability to perform an action or a set of actions, either physical or mental, because of a physical or emotional restriction (often referred to as a disability). A clearly specified limitation of function may help the counselor understand the actual limitation(s) of the consumer. Vocational implications of disability may be understood more clearly when medical conditions or disabilities are translated into functional limitations. The following examples assist in clarifying this idea.

1. An individual has a below-the-knee amputation of the left lower extremity. In functional terms, this particular person is limited to maximum ambulation of 1 hour during an 8-hour workday, no ambulation on rough or uneven surfaces, and no stair climbing.
2. A consumer has a lower back injury and difficulty with lifting and carrying. Functionally, the individual has limitations of lifting a maximum of 20 pounds on an occasional basis, with repetitive lifting and carrying not to exceed 10 pounds.
3. Another person has a psychiatric diagnosis involving moderate depression and anxiety. In functional terms, this individual needs a low-stress work setting with an understanding female supervisor (because of a problem with dominant male authority figures).
4. An individual has a diagnosis of schizophrenia, chronic undifferentiated type. In functional terms, this particular person needs work that involves simple, routine, and repetitive activity with minimal personal interaction and a structured work environment.

Medical conditions described in functional terms enable the counselor to readily understand the consumer's limitations. First, the rehabilitation professional evaluates the vocational (educational, social, psychological, etc.) history of the consumer. The second step is to review the consumer's medical file to ensure the limitations are understood in functional terms. The rehabilitation professional can then determine the consumer's potential for vocational rehabilitation. "Determining how characteristics of chronic illness and disability affect capability to function given specific situations is a key to successful rehabilitation" (Brodwin & Falvo, 1998, p. 26).

Rehabilitation Potential

Attaining one's rehabilitation potential requires three ingredients: (a) attaining increased functioning in the direction of maximizing physical and emotional growth, (b) having a sense of well-being, and (c) facilitating development of a personally satisfying level of independence. All three factors relate to work and employment, as well as to socioemotional adjustment. Other factors, such as psychosocial and cultural attitudes toward disability, may also affect rehabilitation potential.

Cultural and Psychosocial Perspectives

Negative attitudes and behaviors toward people with disabilities have existed in all cultures and nations from early times to the present. D. Cook (1998) noted that society determines whether a group of people will be regarded as different through selecting certain facets of their being and attaching to these facets negative labels and identifications.

Negative attitudes toward people with disabilities have been the rule, not the exception. Degrees of acceptance or rejection toward people with disabilities have generally varied according to the type of disability, with physical disabilities receiving more positive acceptance. The least debilitating disabilities usually are more accepted. Those disabilities that are regarded as self-imposed (e.g., substance abuse) are the least accepted. People are more accepting of disability when there is no perceived fault on the part of the person who has the disability. In some cultures, however, adults with disabilities have been protected and assigned specialized tasks, although with little latitude or public support and with isolation from normal everyday interaction in an established social network (Scheer & Groce, 1988). Because social isolation may occur, people with disabilities have problems with social adaptation, not to mention the functional limitations related to their disabilities. These social and functional factors tend to force them out of the mainstream and assign them to their own "minority" group.

Disability and Minority Issues

Statistically speaking, people with disabilities are the largest minority group in the United States (Fine & Asch, 1988; Russell, 1998). Yet, until recently, they have not been able to make the progress in obtaining equal rights and benefits attained by other minority groups. The minority-group model of disability embraces Dworkin and Dworkin's (1976) definition of a minority group and applies it to disability. The criteria for the definition include "identifiability, differential power, differential and pejorative treatment, and group awareness" (p. viii).

Throughout history, people with disabilities have been viewed as different. Beyond this, they have been classified as deviant from the majority and forced into an inferior social position with the negative evaluations often given ethnic minority groups (Fine & Asch, 1988; B. Wright, 1983). The primary limitations people with disabilities have, according to this model, are not the physical, mental, or emotional disabilities but the social and psychological reactions of the surrounding society and the sociopolitical structure of that society (Russell, 1998; Wendell, 1997).

A significant disadvantage for people with disabilities is that, as a group, they lack a minority-group consciousness. Most other minorities have been able to develop commonalities that give them strength as a group. However, people with disabilities have been geographically and socially dispersed and historically have shown little political activism. In recent years, however, a more formalized organizational structure has emerged with the disability rights movement of the 1980s. This has increased society's awareness of disability and also helped establish a group consciousness for persons with disabilities (Davis, 1997; Linton, 1998; Russell, 1998).

Given a changed sociopolitical structure, Fine and Asch (1988) suggested a different view of disability. How disabling would paraplegia be if all cities were barrier free? How disabling would deafness be if everyone learned a sign language as a required course in school?

The sociopolitical approach views disability as a product of interaction between the individual and the environment. Disability-related functional limitations are viewed as located in the environment, not within people with disabilities. A disabling environment (e.g., architectural and attitudinal barriers) is seen as causing functional limitations. To change this environment, people must change public policy (Hahn, 1982, 1988; Oliver, 1996; Russell, 1998).

According to Vargo (1989), dealing with disabilities in the context of interpersonal relationships and society at large means dealing with all social ills that affect ethnic minorities. "Double discrimination" occurs if a person with a disability belongs to a minority group, resulting in additional discrimination, possible poverty, and barriers to social and economic resources (Vargo, 1989). This double discrimination is an area that merits more research and the attention of policymakers. One may safely hypothesize a greatly magnified impact on individuals when ethnic or racial minority membership and disability are combined. When clients are female, elderly, recent immigrants, or gay/lesbian they face further discrimination (Harley, 2000).

To the extent that disabilities might result in discrimination and social barriers, ethnic minorities with disabilities are minorities within minorities, faced with multiple barriers to equality. In examining the issues faced by ethnic minorities with disabilities, there are two major questions to address: (a) How is that particular disability viewed by the mainstream culture and the minority culture? (b) How is that particular minority group viewed by the mainstream group?

The first question pertains to the ways various cultures perceive different disabilities. To address the issue of discrimination toward people with disabilities, one must examine the mainstream culture and the particular minority culture, instead of assuming that the presence or absence of social barriers or stigma in mainstream society holds true for every group. In working with ethnic minorities with disabilities, rehabilitation professionals and other service providers must be sensitive to the needs and feelings of individuals and their families in dealing with their own ethnic group as well as with the mainstream group (Brodwin, 1995; Mellott & Swartz, 1996).

The second question pertains to the status of minorities in mainstream U.S. society. Despite civil rights and equal opportunity legislation, attitudinal barriers to minorities, particularly in education and employment, have been slow to change. It is important for human service professionals to be fully aware of the many obstacles faced by minority consumers. To what extent is an employer genuinely willing to hire an ethnic minority person? To what extent are fellow employees interested in befriending and relating to him or her as an equal? To what extent are rehabilitation and counseling services available to minorities living in the inner cities or ethnic enclaves? Can institutions provide culturally sensitive services to these populations? Are bilingual services available to those who have not yet acquired sufficient English proficiency?

Counselors and other service providers must be careful not to focus on singular factors when assisting a consumer. For example, a consumer's disability may obscure ethnic or racial issues. Counselors can adequately serve the consumer only by maintaining a holistic perspective (Brodwin, 1995; Mellott & Swartz, 1996; Vargo, 1989). "Effective counseling is individualized and an emphasis should be on understanding what is useful or meaningful to the client as a person, rather than viewing the person only as a representative of a certain racial/ethnic/cultural group" (Stebnicki, Rubin, Rollins, & Turner, 1999, p. 3).

Disability and Gender Issues

Although statistically they are a majority group (51% of the U.S. population), socioculturally women are a minority group (Dworkin & Dworkin, 1976; Leal-Idrogo & Gonzalez-Calvo, 1996; Romero, 1997). In general, women in this culture have fewer resources, less power, and lower status (D. Cook, 1998; Lakoff, 1990; Rieker & Janowski, 1995); are identifiable as a group; and are subjected to negative treatment (Agonito, 1993; Amott & Matthaei, 1991; Romero, 1997). The word *gender* is often used to refer to the socially constructed characteristics and roles that differentiate men and women. One's gender, as well as race/ethnicity, disability status, and socioeconomic class, has considerable social, psychological, and vocational implications (E. Cook, 1993). The interconnected social processes regarding gender, race/ethnicity, disability status, and class determine much about an individual's opportunities, experiences, and roles in society (Amott & Matthaei, 1991). The disadvantage and discrimination experienced by people with disabilities generally are exacerbated for minority women with disabilities (Asch & Fine, 1988; Cottone & Cottone, 1992; Danek, 1992; Leal-Idrogo & Gonzalez-Calvo, 1996).

As discussed previously, women with disabilities from minority cultures may be considered "multiple minorities." This combination of devalued statuses is considered to be interactive (i.e., multiplicative) rather than simply additive (Hanna & Rogovsky, 1992; Leal-Idrogo & Gonzalez-Calvo, 1996). As previously noted, differential treatment is typically more extreme for the person from a multiple minority group compared to someone from a single minority group. In addition, the discrimination against the person may be from members of both majority and minority groups (Deegan & Brooks, 1985; Wendell, 1997). Women experience the devaluation and sex role stereotypes of the majority culture, as well as the devaluation and discrimination specific to their racial or ethnic group. In addition, they are likely to experience the negative attitudes of both the majority and minority culture toward disability.

Women's roles typically fall into two categories: caretaking roles, which traditionally have also been the vocational goals assigned to women, and sexual roles. The result of this multiplicity of devalued statuses may be stigma so severe that women with disabilities have been characterized as "role less" (Asch & Fine, 1997; Lonsdale, 1990). Fine and Asch (1985, 1988) used this term to describe women with disabilities who society views as inadequate to pursue occupational achievements and incapable of traditional nurturing roles typically ascribed to women (i.e., wife, mother, caretaker). Obviously, being perceived or perceiving oneself as having no valued role or purpose in life may negatively affect both the self-confidence and self-efficacy of an individual woman. The socially constructed definitions of "womanhood" involve having a body that meets standards of perfection. The socially imposed shame about having a less than perfect body is damaging to most women, particularly for women with disabilities (Asch & Fine, 1988; Driedger & Gray, 1992; Thomason, 1997; Wendell, 1996). Women with disabilities are often perceived as physically undesirable by men, as asexual, and as not needing information and resources about sexuality. Denial of a woman's sexuality is denial of her very humanness and may negatively affect her view of herself as well as her place in the world.

A human service professional working with women with disabilities must examine his or her own acculturation and resulting attitudes, ideas, and stereotypes toward women with disabilities. Women with disabilities are less frequently employed than men with disabilities, and their income is typically lower. An awareness of how the rehabilitation system can influence counselor behavior as well as client perceptions and outcomes may help a counselor provide equitable services (Cottone & Cottone, 1992; Mellott & Swartz, 1996; Robles, 1997).

Some women with disabilities feel that their status as a woman is more detrimental to their success than their status as a person with a disability (Driedger & Gray, 1992). However, each status for a person who is a "multiple minority" may have different implications in different contexts. The factors that influence a woman's view of herself and her place in the world are complex and not necessarily obvious. If attaining rehabilitation potential requires facilitating emotional growth and attention to a person's sense of well-being, a rehabilitation professional must consider how gender influences those personal factors. A person devalued by society both because of disability and gender may internalize low self-esteem and low expectations for success. Abuse, battery, rape, depression, fear, exploitation, eating disorders, childcare concerns, relationship problems, social isolation, and financial difficulties are all realities in the lives of many women with disabilities. Counselors working with women with disabilities, particularly minority women, should explore the implications of gender, disability, and race and consider how each of those factors may limit the attainment of goals.

PREVALENCE OF MAJOR CATEGORIES OF MEDICAL DISABILITIES

One may view prevalence of medical disabilities from a variety of perspectives. The ADA legislation stated that 43 million Americans had disabilities (West, 1991). This figure was obtained from the 1979 National Health Interview Survey and is "based on an estimated 43.8 million people with visual, hearing, orthopedic, and other anatomical impairments, regardless of whether the impairments caused them to be limited in activity" (LaPlante, 1992, p. 2). The ADA definition, however, includes only disabilities that "substantially limit one or more life activities." LaPlante (1992) estimated that, using this definition of disability, there are 33.8 million Americans who have disabilities, or 13.7% of the 246 million people in the United States (see Table 6.1). This excludes institutionalized individuals, which total 2.3 million. Including institutionalized people, LaPlante estimated there is a total of 36.1 (14.7%) million people with disabilities in the United States.

Another way of assessing the impact of various disabilities is by reviewing categories of functional limitations. Functional limitations are useful to the rehabilitation professional in that they suggest barriers that people with particular disabilities may face in the workplace. In Table 6.2, we present lists of functional limitations developed by G. Wright (1980) and Mueller (1990). From these lists, we developed a comprehensive list of 19 categories of functional limitations by adopting 14 of Mueller's categories, excluding limitation of speech, and by modifying and adding 5 of Wright's functional limitation categories. The 5 include cognitive limitations (Wright's mental limitation), emotional limitations (Wright's dysfunctional behavior), limitation due to disfigurement (Wright's atypical appearance), substance abuse (Wright's substance dependency), and pain limitations (unchanged). Each of the 19 functional limitations will be discussed later in this chapter regarding their relationship to employment and accommodation in the workplace.

TABLE 6.1. Prevalence of Impairments Causing Activity Limitation in the United States

Main Cause	Number of People (in 1000s)	% of People Limited in Activity
Orthopedic impairments	5,873	17.4
Arthritis	4,010	11.9
Heart disease	3,430	10.2
Intervertebral disk disorders	1,762	5.2
Asthma	1,710	5.1
Nervous disorders	1,560	4.6
Mental disorders	1,525	4.5
Visual impairments	1,347	4.0
Mental retardation	1,069	3.2
Diabetes	1,032	3.1
Hypertension	837	2.5
Cerebrovascular disease	679	2.0
Hearing impairments	649	1.9
Emphysema	560	1.7
Osteoporosis/bone disorders	322	1.0
All impairments	33,753	100.0

TABLE 6.2. Categories of Functional Limitations

G. Wright's (1980)[a] Functional Limitation Categories	
1. Mobility limitation	8. Mental limitation
2. Communication limitation	9. Substance dependency
3. Sensory limitation	10. Pain limitation
4. Dysfunctional behavior	11. Consciousness limitation
5. Atypical appearance	12. Uncertain prognosis
6. Invisible limitation	13. Debilitation limitation
7. Restricted environment	14. Motivity limitation

Mueller's (1990)[b] Functional Limitation Categories	
1. Difficulty in interpreting information	8. Limitation of head movement
2. Limitations of sight and total blindness	9. Limitation of sensation
3. Limitations of hearing and total deafness	10. Difficulty in lifting, reaching, and carrying
4. Limitation of speech	11. Difficulty in handling and fingering
5. Susceptibility to fainting, dizziness, and seizures	12. Inability to use the upper extremities
6. Incoordination	13. Difficulty in sitting
7. Limitation of stamina	14. Difficulty in using the lower extremities
	15. Poor balance

Revised and Expanded List of Functional Limitation Categories	
1. Difficulty in interpreting information	10. Difficulty in handling and fingering
2. Limitations of sight and total blindness	11. Inability to use the upper extremities
3. Limitations of hearing and total deafness	12. Difficulty in sitting
4. Susceptibility to fainting, dizziness, and seizures	13. Difficulty in using the lower extremities
5. Incoordination	14. Poor balance
6. Limitation of stamina	15. Cognitive limitation
7. Limitation of head movement	16. Emotional limitation
8. Limitation of sensation	17. Limitation due to disfigurement
9. Difficulty in lifting, reaching, and carrying	18. Substance abuse
	19. Pain limitation

[a] From *Total Rehabilitation*, by G. Wright, 1980, Boston: Little, Brown.

[b] From *The Workplace Workbook: An Illustrated Guide to Job Accommodation and Assistive Technology*, by J. Mueller, 1990, Washington, DC: Dole Foundation.

ACCOMMODATIONS IN THE WORKPLACE

Legal Definitions

Reasonable accommodation is defined by the U.S. Office of Personnel Management as a logical adjustment to a job and/or the work environment that enables a qualified person with a disability to perform the duties of that position (Berkeley Planning Associates, 1982). The ADA describes reasonable accommodation as including making existing facilities used by employees readily accessible to and usable by individuals with disabilities; job restructuring; part-time or modified work schedules; reassignment to vacant positions; acquisition or modification of equipment or devices; appropriate adjustment or modifications or examinations, training materials, or policies; provision of qualified readers or interpreters; and other similar accommodations. Application of reasonable accommodation is fact specific and varies depending on the particular situation (West, 1991). Simply stated, reasonable accommodation is a modification or adjustment to a job or work environment.

The term *qualified individual with a disability* is defined as "an individual with a disability who, with or without reasonable accommodation, can perform the essential functions of the employment position that such person holds or desires" (West, 1991, p. 35). The individual must be able, with or without reasonable accommodation, to perform the *essential functions* of the position. Essential functions are the fundamental or primary job duties of the position.

Employers need not provide accommodation if it will cause an *undue hardship* on the business. Undue hardship is defined by the ADA as when an action or accommodation requires significant difficulty or expense. This is determined on a case-by-case basis (West, 1991).

The rehabilitation professional must remember that "job accommodations should be done *with* an individual who has a disability, not *for* the individual" (Kutsch, 1990, p. 3). The employee, employer, and rehabilitation counselor must participate and share in the accommodation process. There are seven questions to consider in the accommodation process:

1. Was the employee actively part of the accommodation process through all of its phases?
2. Does special equipment take advantage of the employee's unique abilities?

3. Was a simple, minimal cost solution found?
4. Was the "right" problem solved?
5. Is the solution portable and appropriate for other assignments within the company?
6. Has an accessible career path been provided for the employee?
7. Were all accommodations that the employee requested truly "reasonable?" (Kutsch, 1990, p. 8)

Section 503 of the federal Rehabilitation Act of 1973 and the ADA of 1990 mandated reasonable accommodation (ADA, 1990, P.L. 101-336; Greenwood & Johnson, 1985; King & Backer, 1989; West, 1991). Employers now have an obligation to make reasonable accommodation for physical and mental limitations, unless the accommodation imposes an "undue hardship" on the employer. Undue hardship depends on several factors, including cost; financial resources of the company; overall size of the employer; employer's operation, including composition and structure of the workplace; and the nature and cost of the proposed accommodation.

The ADA states that modifications necessary under the "reasonable accommodation" provisions include

1. modifying the physical layout of a job facility to make it accessible to individuals who use wheelchairs or who have other impairments that make access difficult;
2. restructuring a job to enable the person with a disability to perform the essential functions of the job;
3. establishing a part-time or modified work schedule (e.g., accommodating people with disabilities who have medical treatment appointments or fatigue problems);
4. reassigning a person with a disability to a vacant job;
5. acquiring or modifying equipment or devices (e.g., buying a hearing telephone amplifier for a person with a hearing impairment);
6. adjusting or modifying exams, training materials, or policies (e.g., giving an application examination orally to a person with dyslexia or modifying a policy against dogs in the workplace for a person with a service dog);
7. providing qualified readers or interpreters for people with vision or hearing impairments. (West, 1991, p. 93)

Cost of Reasonable Accommodations

Reasonable accommodation rarely involves considerable cost. Berkeley Planning Associates (1982) conducted a study for the U.S. Department of Labor on accommodation in private-sector employment and noted the following results:

1. About 50% of the reasonable accommodations surveyed cost nothing.
2. Thirty percent cost between $50 and $500.
3. Ten percent cost between $500 and $2,000.
4. Ten percent cost in excess of $2,000.

The Department of Labor study concluded that, based on the above figures, reasonable accommodation is "no big deal." This study reported that the most expensive and extensive accommodations tended to be provided to individuals who are blind and to those persons who use wheelchairs. Usually, the reasonable accommodations that are expensive and extensive are provided by employers to current employees to maintain their ability to continue work. Some types of reasonable accomodation are presented in Table 6.3.

Roessler and Sumner (1997) found that most employers they surveyed considered $500 to $5,000 an acceptable cost for an accommodation. These figures exceed what was previously reported. Accommodations costing these amounts were considered both effective and acceptable and involved a wide variety of types of reasonable accommodation. The Job Accommodation Network (JAN)[1] reported that in more than 100,000 cases of reasonable accommodation, 20% of the accommodations cost nothing, 51% cost between $1 and $501, and only 25% cost more than this (Rubin & Roessler, 2001). Certainly, the atmosphere and practice of providing

[1]The Job Accommodation Network (JAN; 800/526-7234 [Voice & TT/TDD]; http://www.jan.wvu.edu/) is a resource available for additional information on employer accommodations. Telephone service is provided at no cost and allows counselors, employers, and consumers to access information on restructuring possibilities and costs. There are consultants available Monday through Friday.

Before calling this resource, it is necessary to have specific medical restrictions (functional limitations) regarding the consumer, job duties that are precluded as a result of the restrictions, and general information about the industry in which the job is located. The JAN consultant will provide information at the time of the telephone call; supplemental information may be mailed. JAN also provides referrals to companies that provide restructuring and accommodation materials for specific costs.

TABLE 6.3. Types of Reasonable Accommodation

- I. Physical access accommodation
  - A. A change or modification of the physical structure
  - B. Examples—Accessibility/ambulation solutions
    1. Situate job on first floor
    2. Situate job near employee parking lot
    3. Situate job near restroom
- II. Resource accessibility accommodation
  - A. Providing an assistive person to enable the individual to do the job duties
  - B. Examples
    1. Hearing impairment—Provide note taker or sign language interpreter
    2. Visual impairment—Provide reader or note taker
    3. Developmental disability (mental retardation)—provide a job coach
- III. Adaptive equipment accommodation
  - A. The provision of "low-tech" and "high-tech" assistive devices
  - B. Examples
    1. Person with arthritis or carpal tunnel syndrome—provide special pen/pencil holders
    2. Orthopedic problems
       - a. Provide desk or chair modifications
       - b. Provide speaker and earphone on telephone
    3. Reaching problems
       - a. Provide a turntable on a desk
       - b. Provide a special desk that has easy accessibility
    4. Neck problems—Provide a slant board on a desk
    5. Visual impairment—Provide a talking calculator or talking computer
    6. Hearing impairment
       - a. Provide a telephone amplifier
       - b. Provide a speaker telephone

(*continues*)

reasonable accommodation in business and industry have changed in a positive and productive way, both for employers and their workers who have disabling conditions.

The public perceives accommodation efforts as helping persons with disabilities become employed or remain successful on the job. There appears to be no significant relationship between accommodation and upward mobility, either in providing an advantage to a specific employee or in limiting job promotion. Highly skilled workers and professionals more often receive environmental adaptations of the workplace or special

TABLE 6.3. *Continued.*

7. Quadriplegia—Provide a computer with a specialized keyboard and an electronic wheelchair with assistive devices

IV. Job modification
   A. Modifying the performance of job duties while maintaining the same job duties
   B. Examples
      1. Energy or ambulation problems—Salesperson does more telephone sales with fewer field appointments
      2. Energy problem—Design drafter works part-time for less pay
      3. Orthopedic problems
         a. Parking lot attendant uses a chair for sitting instead of standing throughout the day
         b. Warehouse worker lifts and carries lesser weights by making more frequent trips with lighter weights
      4. Scheduling—secretary leaves early for physical therapy appointments by coming to work earlier

V. Job restructuring
   A. Changing some of the actual job duties performed (maintain, eliminate, or replace job duties)
   B. Examples
      1. Ambulation problem—rehabilitation counselor is assigned more office work (initial interviews, testing, labor market surveys, and job development) and less fieldwork activity (on-site job analyses, school visits, and employer visits)
      2. Emotional stress
         a. Social worker is assigned more case file analysis and paperwork and less interviewing and field visits
         b. Attorney does more research, case preparation, and legal briefs and spends less time litigating in court
      3. Lower extremity problems—Shipping and receiving clerk is assigned more clerical work (typing reports, bills of lading, and expediting) and less lifting, carrying, standing, walking, and forklift driving

equipment, whereas lower skilled workers receive job redesign, retraining, or selective placement.

Large firms are most likely to hire and accommodate persons with disabilities for the following reasons (Berkeley Planning Associates, 1982):

1. the existence of affirmative action mechanisms in larger firms
2. the likelihood of encountering persons with disabilities because of the sheer numbers of workers employed
3. the much greater diversity of job types in larger firms that lead to more possibilities of hiring and greater flexibility in job assignments

ACCOMMODATING INDIVIDUALS WITH FUNCTIONAL LIMITATIONS

The rehabilitation counselor seeks to maximize a person's potential in the world of work. One means of doing this is by finding ways to minimize a person's functional limitations through provision of accommodation. The 19 categories of functional limitations covered in Table 6.2 may be used when the counselor provides accommodations to improve an individual's interaction with the work environment. This includes persons currently employed who have had a recent injury or chronic illness resulting in permanent disability and those individuals with disabilities entering the workforce for the first time.

Title I of the ADA of 1990 (P.L. 101-336) prohibits discrimination by a public entity in providing public services to a qualified individual with a disability in the terms and conditions of employment. The ADA extends the prohibition of job-related discrimination against persons with disabilities to all firms employing 15 or more employees in both the public and private sectors.

WORKPLACE ACCOMMODATIONS FOR FUNCTIONAL LIMITATIONS

We now will review the 19 categories of functional limitation described in Table 6.2. For each category, we will provide information concerning disabilities falling in the category, their relationship to employment, and reasonable workplace accommodations for each limitation.

Difficulty in Interpreting Information

This limitation involves an impaired ability to read or understand written or spoken information. About 1 million workers in the United States report having a permanent problem with difficulty in interpreting information.

This limitation affects the areas of reading and understanding written or spoken information. Disabilities within this category include stroke, learning disabilities, traumatic brain injury, mental retardation, and some types of neurological deficits.

Persons with stroke may have intellectual deficits, verbal and written communication difficulties, and perceptual problems. Aphasia may involve the absence of or impairment in the ability to communicate through speech, reading, writing, or listening. Persons with learning disabilities may demonstrate deficits in social skills and appropriate communication with others. Besides deficits in social skills, some individuals have language-related learning disabilities. Receptive and expressive language problems, as well as reading and writing problems, occur (Little, 1993). Acquired traumatic brain injury may result in speech deficits. Dysarthria is weakness and slowing in the muscles related to speech; the person appears to slur words and has significant articulation problems. In addition, there may be memory and concentration problems; memory problems are considered to be the most significant for persons with brain injury (Falvo, 1999; Wulz, 1993).

Persons with mental retardation may have deficits in sensory–motor skills, communication skills, reasoning, judgment abilities, and socialization skills. Emotional abnormalities may further complicate communication (Halpern & Furher, 1984).

Cerebral palsy may result in functional limitations of intellect, emotion, and a variety of physical deficits. "Distorted physical appearance resulting from motor involvement and accompanying speech problems associated with many individuals with cerebral palsy encourages negative assumptions to be made regarding intellectual abilities" (Kopriva & Taylor, 1993, p. 531).

A wide variety of neurological conditions result in difficulty in interpreting information. There may be slight to gross problems with abilities to follow verbal commands and to speak. Receptive aphasia is a disturbance of comprehension in spoken and written language. The person may be unable to produce speech that is clear or write without gross errors (receptive aphasia). There also may be problems in the capability to form language and express oneself (expressive aphasia). A person who has difficulty reacting to spoken commands has a condition called conduction aphasia. Global aphasia results in deficits in both expression and comprehension of language, which causes major functional limitations (Falvo, 1999; Goldman, 1993).

Conditions such as stroke, other neurological illnesses, traumatic brain injury, and learning disabilities may lead to limitations in this area. The counselor can accommodate for persons with expressive communication deficits by suggesting the increased use of written material and computer-based communication within the workplace. In discussing learning disabilities, Little (1993) stated, "Deficits in communication result in inadequate development of personal relationships, social skills, and vocational competencies" (p. 502). Professionals often forget the crucial area of appropriate use of social skills in the communication with others. A common reason for being fired from a job is inappropriate communication with supervisors or fellow employees. The counselor should work with the person to identify and minimize deficits in the specific problem area and communicate with the individual's supervisor to explain the nature of the problem.

Persons with stroke or traumatic brain injuries may face similar difficulties. Employer understanding, enhanced through intervention of a rehabilitation professional, can help the worker maintain employment. Persons with mental retardation may have limitations in their ability to interpret certain types of information, especially material that is difficult to comprehend. The counselor who breaks down complex or detailed information into readily understandable units assists both employer and employee in ensuring improved worker productivity and continued success on the job. Workers may, in time, become ready for additional responsibilities and challenges; a method of determining this readiness on an ongoing basis can be instituted by the counselor.

Limitations of Sight and Total Blindness

Legal blindness is defined as a central visual acuity of 20/200 or worse in the better eye, with correction, or a residual field of vision of 20 degrees or less in the best eye, with best correction. This category of visual impairments also includes persons who do not meet the criteria for legal blindness but have visual problems that limit their ability to perform some typical life functions. For example, a person may have problems with near vision, resulting in limited access to printed materials, or distance vision, resulting in difficulties in reading road signs or chalkboards. An individual may have a field loss that does not meet the definition of legal blindness yet is limiting in terms of mobility (i.e., a loss that affects the lower half of the visual field). Individuals may have a loss in both acuity and field, which may severely limit functioning but not meet legal definitions for blindness.

Visual impairment is the major cause of disability for 558,000 people, of whom 189,000 report blindness in both eyes (LaPlante & Carlson, 1996). According to Mueller (1990), approximately 700,000 workers in the United States have limitations of sight; an additional 130,000 have total blindness, bringing the total to 830,000 workers who have limitations of sight or total blindness.

The functional limitations of an individual with a visual impairment depend on the physiology of the impairment (amount and type), the environmental conditions (e.g., lighting, contrast), an individual's motivation in a particular context, and how well the individual has learned to use remaining vision. The International Classification of Impairments, Disabilities, and Handicaps (Colenbrander, 1977) proposed five parameters to measure the effect of visual loss on daily life: (a) physical independence, (b) mobility, (c) economic independence, (d) employment, and (e) social integration. These parameters may be viewed as the functional limitations that visual disabilities cause. In considering the functional limitations caused by a visual loss, it is important to focus on the actual performance of a person in a given environment doing a specific task. Because of the variability and individuality in functioning, it should never be assumed that a person cannot do a particular task without *asking and observing behavior*. Functioning often may be improved by orientation and mobility (O & M) skills training and training in independent living skills, including social skills, technology, and development of specific vocational abilities (Espinola & Croft, 1992; Panek, 1993).

Diseases causing visual loss include glaucoma, periocular disease, cataracts, retinal diseases (senile macular degeneration, diabetic retinopathy, sickle cell retinopathy, AIDS-related cytomegalovirus [CMV] retinitis, retinitis pigmentosa), corneal diseases, and optic nerve and central nervous system diseases, among others. Some conditions result in vision that fluctuates or is progressive, eventually leading to total blindness; some eye conditions are painful or disfiguring. An individual's reaction to the unique aspects of his or her visual condition is a major determinant of functioning.

For workers with visual impairments who have residual vision, workplace accommodations may include adaptations in illumination, color and contrast, space and arrangement, and size and distance (Levack, 1991). Accommodations typically include low-vision devices, which may be optical or nonoptical. The most common optical devices are magnifiers and telescopes, which come in a variety of types and sizes. Typical nonoptical low-vision aids are closed-circuit televisions that enlarge print electronically and personal computers and peripherals with the capability of large-print magnification, speech output, and optical scanning.

For workers who are totally blind, accommodations often involve the use of other senses such as auditory and tactual input, as well as the use of memory and organizational skills to adapt the workplace. Adaptations may include using Braille or tactual labels for files or other information, using Braille translation programs and Braille printers, and organizing the workspace so that items are easily located and retrieved. Auditory adaptations may include talking calculators and clocks, as well as speech output devices on computers. Obtaining materials on audiotape, having a reader actually present to read information, or having a reader record often used information on audiotape are all ways a person who is totally blind can access written materials. The combination of a scanner, speech synthesizer, Braille printer, and regular print printer can give a person who is totally blind access to most information used in employment and allow the individual to produce work in a format accessible to everyone (Espinola & Croft, 1992).

An orientation and mobility specialist can teach a person with total blindness or low vision to safely and efficiently navigate a new work environment. For some individuals, it may be important to limit the variety of workstations involved in a particular job. By asking individuals what they need, observing the work environment, and working with an orientation and mobility specialist, simple environmental modifications can be made.

It is important to remember to ask the person who has a visual impairment what would be an effective adaptation in a specific environment. By describing work tasks specifically, the counselor and consumer can work together to develop an effective, nonintrusive accommodation. A person who is congenitally visually impaired has had a lifetime of experience making simple adaptations. A person with an adventitious visual disability may need more assistance in developing creative solutions; it may be helpful to consult a person with a similar visual impairment about adaptations. Through problem solving with the individual, assessing the work environment, and evaluating the person's functional vision as well as nonvisual competencies specific to that work environment, the counselor can greatly improve the employability of persons with visual disabilities (Espinola & Croft, 1992; Panek, 1993).

Many organizations and resources within the community can assist the rehabilitation counselor who is developing work environments for people with visual impairments. Braille foundations, Lions Clubs, centers for individuals with partial sight, university programs, and public school programs are typically aware of services and specialists available. Several national organizations serve as clearinghouses for information about blindness and visual impairment, including the American Foundation for the Blind and the American Printing House for the Blind.

Limitations of Hearing and Total Deafness

People in this category have difficulty in comprehending usable speech, with or without amplification. In the U.S. workforce, limitations of hearing affect 425,000 individuals.

Deafness may be defined as a hearing impairment that interferes with the ability to understand normal conversation. There are lesser degrees of impairment that are functionally limiting. Hearing losses are classified as (a) conductive, (b) sensorineural, and (c) mixed. Diminished hearing is due to congenital disease and disorders, presbycusis (hearing impairment due to aging), trauma, infection, tumors, Ménière's disease, and otosclerosis. Functional disabilities depend on the degree of impairment of auditory discrimination in the speech frequencies and age of onset. In general, the greater the loss of ability to distinguish single words and the earlier the onset, the more functional limitations that result. The communication loss may be manifested in both reception and expression (Danek & Seidman, 1993; Lerner & Hauck, 1999).

Section 504 of the Rehabilitation Act of 1973 provides for interpreter services as a reasonable accommodation for individuals with hearing impairments. The ADA requires telephone companies offering services to the public to provide 24-hour telephone relay services to persons with hearing loss. In the area of employment, examples of workplace accommodations include qualified interpreters, amplified telephones, telecommunication devices, audioloops, flashing lights and alarms, well-lighted areas, and vibrating pocket pagers.

Many employers, especially larger businesses, will have TDDs (telephone devices for the deaf). The rehabilitation professional may wish to discuss installation of a TDD for employers who do not have one already in place (Danek & Seidman, 1993). Employers may not understand hearing impairments and be unaware of the special technological advances available that improve communication ability for individuals with hearing impairments. Because some of these devices are costly, the counselor should help the employer and employee prioritize options. Hearing aids may greatly enhance the performance of some workers (Falvo, 1999). Before recommending more expensive and extensive workplace accommodations, the counselor may want to ensure that this alternative has been fully explored.

Mueller (1990) described the utility of modifications to seating, storage, and work areas. For seating, swivel-based chairs may be used to allow face-to-face communication. Storage areas should have clear and simple labels to minimize the need for verbal assistance. Recommendations for workstations involve providing adequate lighting, installing amplified telephones, minimizing ambient noise and vibrations, providing clear written instructions to minimize need for verbal assistance, and orienting the workstation for greater face-to-face communication.

Susceptibility to Fainting, Dizziness, and Seizures

This disability category involves persons who have spontaneous or inducible fainting, dizziness, or seizures. There are 7.2 million persons working in the United States affected by this limitation.

These limitations of function are found in individuals with such disabilities as epilepsy, cerebral palsy, brain injury, migraine/tension headaches, vertigo, certain cardiac conditions, and various neurological diseases. Functional limitations are based on severity and duration of symptoms, frequency of symptoms, whether loss of consciousness is partial or total, and whether there is a warning (aura) of the impending occurrence (Fraser, 1999).

Limitations at the workplace may involve prohibition from heights, dangerous equipment, moving machinery, and driving. Control of seizures is paramount in assessing the degree of vocational impairment that may occur; the counselor should be aware of the many stereotypes employers will have regarding employees with epilepsy and other seizure disorders. An employee may have excellent control of his or her seizures and need little or no accommodation, yet the employer may not have a clear understanding of the condition.

Certainly, some important aspects to consider in the workplace for this limitation are the presence of dangerous equipment, unprotected heights, moving machinery, and driving; accommodations may be a necessity under these circumstances. Type, severity, and frequency of seizures, dizziness, or fainting must be considered when evaluating potential for accommodation. Many persons with these limitations are on a regimen of medication to control symptoms; the rehabilitation counselor should make sure the consumer's symptoms are under optimal medical management, which is often not the case. The use of alcohol with other drugs may have a deleterious effect on the medical management of the person's symptoms. As stated by G. Wright (1980), "The most important task in epilepsy rehabilitation is to achieve maximum control of seizures" (p. 110). The counselor must make sure there are no stimuli in the workplace that may precipitate seizures.

Mueller (1990) outlined the following accommodations in the workplace for employees with this type of medical condition. Employees should avoid the need for frequent and rapid rising from a seated position. Storage area accommodations include providing a wheeled cart or other aide for carrying materials, using securely enclosed carts and other equipment for messy/hazardous materials, and providing protective gear (e.g., for handling hazardous/messy items). Mueller's suggestions for workstation accommodations include providing secure support (grab bars), avoiding slippery surfaces, minimizing isolated workstations, avoiding activities of bending down to lift, and maintaining a consistent daily level of physical exertion.

Incoordination

Individuals who have this limitation experience lack of control in placing or directing extremities or have spasticity. Three million U.S. workers have incoordination as a disability.

This classification includes symptoms of spasticity and lack of normal control of the extremities. Conditions causing incoordination include cerebral palsy and involuntary movements seen in certain types of paralysis. Limitations of function involve use of the extremities, eye–hand–foot coordination, manual dexterity, ambulation, strength, agility, speed, endurance, balance, perception, and spontaneous movement (G. Wright, 1980).

When working with people who have problems with coordination, activities such as manual dexterity, speed, and eye–hand–foot coordination may be affected. One also sees limitations in ambulation, lifting, and carrying. Accommodations include assistive devices to improve dexterity, computers to aid in minimizing writing, walking devices, motorized carts for mobility, and hoists to assist in lifting and carrying. Nonessential work tasks may be reassigned in exchange for other tasks.

Workstation modification may provide the assistance needed to allow the individual to successfully perform his or her job. These modifications involve providing weighted writing implements, raised desk edges to keep materials from falling, grab bars for support, "universal cuffs," gloves with gripping surfaces, and tool handles with grips or holders (Mueller, 1990).

Limitation of Stamina

Limitation of stamina may involve shortness of breath and/or abnormal elevation of blood pressure with mild exercise. Approximately 10.3 million workers in the United States have limitations involving stamina.

One sees this limitation in multiple sclerosis, pulmonary conditions, cardiac dysfunction, neurological conditions, AIDS, arthritis, stroke, sickle cell disease, uncontrolled hypertension, muscular dystrophy, diabetes mellitus, renal failure, endocrine disorders, and paralyses. Functional limitations may include dyspnea (shortness of breath) on exertion, fatigue, and weakness, which limit the individual to light or sedentary exertion, part-time work, or occasional time off work during illness or exacerbation of symptoms. Environmental conditions such as pollutants, dust, extremes of temperature, and rapid temperature changes are some limiting factors for these disabling conditions, especially those involving the pulmonary system (Brodwin, Tellez, & Brodwin, 2002).

Stamina limitations may involve certain activities or be present for a wide range of functions. For severe limitations, full-time work may not be possible, but the person may be able to consider part-time work. Because most employers will not have thought of this possibility, counselors are encouraged to discuss reducing working hours first with the worker and then with the employer, citing advantages of this possibility to both employer and employee. As discussed by Falvo (1999), accessibility of the workplace requires careful assessment for a worker who may need to use a wheelchair at work. "The availability of elevators as opposed to stairs, desk or workbench height, width of doorways, and size of bathrooms are all important environmental considerations" (p. 76).

If the worker has rotating work shifts, a regular shift may improve stamina and preserve energy for work activity. Job functions that are more physically demanding can be traded for less strenuous ones. Accommodation may involve modifying the exertional requirements of the job to the extent a job of medium exertion becomes light or sedentary. A motorized cart or power wheelchair will decrease the worker's walking and carrying on the job. One needs a thorough evaluation to determine which of these two devices will be most effective within the particular work environment. Movable nonpowered carts can diminish physical requirements of the work position. For some conditions, intermittent use of a wheelchair may help preserve the person's stamina and allow for work activity on a full-time basis.

In assessing the limitation of stamina, Mueller (1990) offered the following potential workplace accommodations: provide a foot stool or a step stool for shifting weight at standing stations; minimize frequent changes in work schedule or level of exertion; avoid smoke, dust, and extreme temperature changes; minimize job stress; and minimize bending, ambulation, reaching, lifting, and carrying.

Limitation of Head Movement

People with this limitation have difficulty in looking up, down, and/or to the sides due to limited ability to move the head. There are 7.6 million U.S. workers with this condition.

Persons with disabilities such as high-level quadriplegia, neck injuries not resulting in paralysis, arthritis, cerebral palsy, muscular dystrophy, Parkinson's disease, diseases involving spinal cord infection, acquired traumatic brain injury, stroke, degenerative changes in the neck, or amyotrophic lateral sclerosis, among other neurological diseases, may have functional limitations of head movement. These medical conditions may be temporary or permanent and may be stable or progressive. Certain neck injuries produce temporary or intermittent pain, especially with particular movements of the neck; the counselor must evaluate whether the consumer has acute or chronic pain. Progressive disabling diseases, in particular, will require periodic reevaluation (Brodwin et al., 2002; Eisenberg, Glueckauf, & Zaretsky, 1999).

Many conditions cause limitation of head movement. These may range from neck muscle pain to total paralysis from the neck down. Chronic pain in the neck region may limit a person's grip strength, dexterity, and rapid head movement; other potential limitations are activities that involve lifting and carrying. Often, neck pain leads to fatigue, especially with prolonged physical activities. Although it may precipitate pain symptoms, emotional stress may be difficult to control in the workplace. Paralyses of neck and shoulder muscles frequently require assistive orthotic devices to maintain neck and head stability. Computers at the work site may assist individuals with severe limitations of the neck and upper back.

Mueller (1990) suggested the following guidelines when accommodating the workplace for employees with limitation of head movement. Regarding seating, he recommended provision of a swivel-base chair with an adjustable recline feature. For storage areas, increasing the worker's field of vision with "fish-eye" window inserts and mirrors and minimizing the need for reaching behind or bending down will aid in adaptation. Workstation accommodation may include orienting the workstation to maximize face-to-face communication, minimizing the need to reach outside the field of vision (up, down, and behind), and clustering tools and materials within the visual field.

Limitation of Sensation

This involves an impairment of nerve reception (heat, touch, pain, or pressure) in various parts of the body. Of the working population in the United States, 3.2 million have this limitation.

This limitation involves impaired nerve sensation, including the sense of touch, pain, pressure, heat, and cold. Spinal cord injuries, strokes, polio, and other kinds of trauma may precipitate these limitations (Falvo, 1999).

Employees with limited touch, pain, pressure, heat, and cold sensations will have diverse degrees of impairment and functional limitations. The loss of sensation may be partial, intermittent, or total. Various conditions cause limitations of sensation, including spinal cord injury, neurological conditions, cerebral vascular accidents, acquired traumatic brain injuries, congenital anomalies, burns, diabetes, and certain severe lacerations.

Limitation of sensation in the lower extremities occurs with spinal cord injuries. Conditions such as diabetes and multiple sclerosis may diminish sensation in the feet. The worker with this limitation must be careful of foot injuries. Persons with a severe injury to the hands may have difficulty perceiving pain and other sensations; work injury may occur because of the individual's inability or decreased ability to immediately perceive damaging situations.

Accommodations at the workplace include protective clothing for the hands or feet to minimize the probability of injury. For workers with loss of sensation in the buttocks, Mueller (1990) recommended providing pressure-distributing seat cushions and scheduling regular breaks for posture changes to avoid sitting for long periods of time.

Difficulty in Lifting, Reaching, and Carrying

This limitation involves impaired mobility, range of motion, and/or strength in the upper extremities and the trunk. There are 4.6 million workers in the United States with permanent difficulties in this category.

Impaired mobility, range of motion deficits, and upper extremity/trunk limitations produce difficulty in using the hands and feet and may impair eye–hand coordination, manual dexterity, and strength required for lifting, carrying, pushing, and pulling. Spinal cord injury, congenital deformities, multiple sclerosis, cerebral palsy, partial or complete amputation, arthritis, other permanent injuries involving the extremities, and various neurological diseases cause physical limitations in lifting, reaching, and carrying (Eisenberg et al., 1999; Falvo, 1999).

There are numerous accommodations in the workplace for these frequently seen functional limitations. Heavy items often can be divided into more manageable, smaller, or lighter units. Equipment such as mechanical lifts may assist the worker; movable carts will decrease the distance items must be carried. A primary emphasis is to decrease the amounts lifted and carried. If weights cannot be decreased, it may be possible to eliminate the particular lifting and carrying activity in question. Other job duties may then be substituted for those being eliminated. Typically, one explores the possibility of replacing the physical activities with job functions of a more clerical nature.

As noted by Falvo (1999), when discussing functional limitations in respiratory conditions, "If the work demands lifting and carrying that increase dyspnea, alternate strategies may be devised so that the work can be performed with less exertion" (p. 308). Similar circumstances are true for workers with cardiovascular disease. Persons with AIDS typically have or will have energy restrictions; a primary manifestation of this disease is fatigue. Persons experience lowered energy that restricts daily activities; employed individuals often become exhausted and need rest periods while at work (Howard & Brodwin, 1993).

Certainly, when working with people who have paralysis in one or more extremities, there will be restrictions that need modification of workplace lifting and carrying. These conditions include quadriplegia and paraplegia, cerebral vascular accidents, acquired traumatic brain injuries, cerebral palsy, rheumatic diseases, and various neurological conditions. Persons who have had strokes, depending on lower extremity involvement, may be capable of lifting and carrying with one upper extremity; accommodations suggested will depend on careful task analysis of specific job functions.

Mueller (1990) recommended the following modifications to seating, storage, and workstations for workers with difficulty in lifting, reaching, and carrying (impaired mobility, range of motion, and strength in trunk or upper extremities). In the area of seating, an employer can locate adjustment controls as close as possible to the worker. For storage, one can store items within easy reach or on a "lazy Susan" carousel, provide desktop files/organizers, facilitate sliding of items instead of lifting and carrying, use wheeled carts for transport of items, and minimize the need for reaching up, reaching behind, or bending down (provide mechanical "reachers"). In the area of workstations, Mueller suggested use of mechanical reachers, a lazy susan work surface, and powered lift tables for positioning of heavy work.

Injuries to the back and neck that do not result in paralysis also may require temporary or permanent accommodations of lifting and carrying. These injuries are common occurrences in the workplace and one of the frequent areas needing the intervention of a rehabilitation counselor.

Difficulty in Handling and Fingering

These limitations include impairment of mobility, range of motion, dexterity, and/or strength in the hands. It is reported that 4.3 million in the U.S. workforce have this difficulty.

Disabilities relating to this functional limitation include permanent injury to the hands, quadriplegia, stroke, congenital deformities, arthritis, carpal tunnel syndrome, and certain neurological conditions (Brodwin et al., 2002; Falvo, 1999).

"Dexterity refers to skill and rapidity in physical activity, especially expertise in using the hands and fingers" (G. Wright, 1980, p. 114). A wide variety of disabling conditions give rise to functional limitations in this area. Because the vast majority of jobs require use of the hands and fingers, the counselor must be adept at providing accommodation for workers with dexterity problems. Adaptive devices improve function in many individuals. These devices are particularly useful with severe hand injuries and partial paralysis; a variety of prosthetic and orthotic devices are available. Prostheses are artificial devices used to replace a missing body part, and orthoses are specialized mechanical devices used to support or supplement weakened or abnormal joints or limbs.

Orthoses may be used to relieve pain (by limiting motion or weight bearing), for immobilization and protection, to reduce load, to correct deformities, and for improvement of function. Prostheses used for amputations may allow an employee some dexterity, grasp, and pinch. The use of upper extremity prostheses increases manual dexterity, bilateral dexterity, and eye–hand coordination; some upper extremity prostheses are able to restore function for tasks needed on the job (Clark, 1993). Careful work task analysis by the rehabilitation counselor, in consultation with a prosthetist or orthotist, may allow the worker to maintain current employment with the use of adaptive devices and equipment.

Many of the recommendations appearing in the "Difficulty in Lifting, Reaching, and Carrying" section also apply here. The counselor should assess the importance of providing easy accessibility to drawers, storage areas, files, cabinets, and similar work areas. Carpal tunnel syndrome complaints by a secretary or office clerk who does extensive typing or word processing may be decreased by provision of a foam bar to rest the hands and minimize unnecessary movements. Various assistive devices are available for persons who have carpal tunnel syndrome; most of these devices minimize movement in the wrist.

Inability To Use the Upper Extremities

Persons with this limitation experience complete paralysis, severe incoordination, or an absence of the upper extremities. There are 280,000 U.S. workers with this limitation.

This category includes quadriplegia, amputation, stroke, congenital anomalies, cerebral palsy, and arthritis. Some of these disabilities result in absence of one or both upper extremities, paralysis, or severe incoordination. Many industrial injuries involve the hands. Amputation or partial amputation of the fingers causes varying degrees of impairment depending on the extent of the injury, loss of function, and whether the injury is to the dominant or nondominant hand (Falvo, 1999; G. Wright, 1980).

There is a wide range of functional limitations involving use of the upper extremities and, hence, many potential accommodations. Desks and file cabinets may be arranged for easier accessibility. Prosthetic and orthotic devices, through custom design, will help maximize performance of particular essential job functions. A detailed job task analysis will enable the counselor to provide recommendations to a consulting prosthetist or orthotist. What is needed are insight and creativity on the part of the counselor and consumer working together, along with an understanding and involved employer.

With conditions such as advanced arthritis and quadriplegia, ability to grip, capacity to pinch objects, and capability to extend the joints through a normal range of motion all may require job accommodation. Orthotic devices, especially designed for the particular individual, may help improve function of the hands. Surgical joint replacement relieves pain and improves range of motion. Resumption of work activities may occur after joint replacement. If a worker chooses surgery to improve function, the employer needs an understanding of the disease and potential improvement following surgical intervention. Surgery should be aimed at improving function specifically for work activities; the rehabilitation counselor can be instrumental in identifying work tasks that will benefit from surgical intervention.

The following orthoses may improve a worker's upper extremity function: wrist–hand orthosis, wrist-driven wrist–hand orthosis, and shoulder–elbow orthosis. Upper limb orthoses may substitute for absent muscle power, assist or support weak segments of an upper extremity, or be used for the attachment of specialized assistive devices (Clark, 1993).

Difficulty in Sitting

Difficulty in sitting includes lack of strength, restricted range of motion, or limitations in control of the trunk in activities of bending, turning, or balancing. About 8 million U.S. workers have some difficulty in sitting.

This functional problem includes a wide range of limitations to the back, especially the low back. Pain that places limitations on the amount of time a person can sit in one place may change daily, with variations during any particular day. Paraplegia and quadriplegia, in which the person is unable to stand or walk, cause varying impairments involving occasional shifting of weight, trunk instability, and sitting in a wheelchair. Persons with back pain, especially with accompanying chronic pain, may need to alternatively sit and stand or walk to relieve pain (Falvo, 1999; Hu & Cressy, 1993).

One may provide special chairs for persons with limited sitting tolerance due to back pain. Accommodations on the job allowing a worker to sit and stand alternately can minimize back pain complaints in some individuals. Mueller (1990) recommended the following for employees with sitting limitations: avoid forward-leaning posture, add a cushion or backrest, provide pressure-distributing seat cushions, install an assist cushion or complete chair that rises, and add a seat belt and full backrest for added stability. For invisible disabilities, such as back pain, careful and appropriate intervention will help an employer understand the condition and allow the worker to alternate sitting and standing as needed.

Difficulty in Using the Lower Extremities

These limitations involve slowness of gait and impairment of ability to kneel, rise, walk, stand, and/or climb stairs. In the U.S. workforce, 1.3 million people have this condition.

Activities such as ambulation, carrying objects, walking on uneven surfaces, using stairs or ladders, kneeling, bending, and slowness or incoordination of gait will be affected to varying degrees. The ability to use a wheelchair effectively and efficiently partially will determine the effect of this functional inability. Disabling conditions, including spinal cord injury, amputation and other permanent injuries to the lower extremities, postpolio syndrome, arthritis, stroke, diabetes mellitus, cerebral palsy, multiple sclerosis, muscular dystrophy, congenital deformities, and various additional neurological diseases, may cause difficulties in using the lower extremities. Cardiovascular and pulmonary diseases may limit the amount of time and activities one can perform with the lower extremities (Brodwin et al., 2002).

Mueller (1990) recommended the following accommodations when working with employees with lower extremity involvement (weakness or paralysis): wheeled carts for carrying, shoulder bags/backpacks for transport of smaller items, powered carts or scooters for mobility, and minimizing the need for reaching up, reaching behind, bending down, or squatting. Providing a chair with wheels will assist the worker who needs to move about in close proximity to the workstation (such as from the desk to an adjacent file cabinet). Organizing the workstation so that file cabinets and supplies are contained in the workstation is another possible accommodation. For persons experiencing lower extremity limitations, a foot rest may be a helpful accommodation.

Orthotic devices may help individuals with weakness or paralysis in one or both legs to ambulate. Several types of lower extremity orthoses are available, including ankle–foot, knee–ankle–foot, and hip–knee–ankle–foot orthoses. These orthotic devices, when used properly, increase function, thereby improving work potential (Clark, 1993).

If the worker uses a wheelchair, desks or worktables may have to be raised to allow sufficient space for wheelchair access. Other accommodations include easy restroom accessibility and clear access throughout the work facility. For a worker who has undergone amputation of a lower extremity, the amount of standing and walking will need to be decreased; ambulation will require significantly greater energy consumption.

Poor Balance

This involves difficulty in maintaining one's balance. There are 4.5 million workers in the United States with this restriction.

Poor balance may occur when a person is stationary, moving about, or both. Activities such as rising, standing in one place, walking, and bending or stooping may cause difficulties. Conditions that give rise to this limitation are stroke, Ménière's disease, traumatic brain injury, amputation involving the lower extremities, infection or trauma of the inner ear, and various neurological diseases (Eisenberg et al., 1999; G. Wright, 1980).

For employees with medical conditions resulting in poor balance, several recommendations apply. The rehabilitation counselor first must consider whether the person is under appropriate medical care. If the person is seeing a general physician, referral to a specialist, such as a neurologist, may be beneficial. One also must be certain that the worker is taking medication in the prescribed manner. Often, if an individual does not have symptoms, there may be the incorrect belief that medication is no longer necessary.

In the workplace, hazardous situations, dangerous tools or equipment, unprotected heights, and the like must be eliminated to ensure that the person is not a danger to self or others. If a worker is prone to losing balance without warning, it is suggested that carts and similar devices be used to minimize carrying so that objects will not be dropped and become damaged. Seated jobs, with no extensive standing and walking, are ideal for workers having problems with balance. A motorized cart or power wheelchair may be used for ambulation; baskets or storage containers can be attached to the cart for transport of items. It is important to minimize the need for reaching up, reaching behind, and bending down.

It cannot be emphasized sufficiently that the counselor must make sure the person is under maximum medical care for the condition that is causing poor balance before making attempts at workplace accommodation. Referral for a second medical opinion may help in resolving symptoms previously under less than optimal control, without the necessity of providing reasonable accommodation at the workplace.

Cognitive Limitation

Limitations in intellectual functioning and learning deficiencies may involve deficits in many areas or in specific functioning, such as language or mathematics. Mental retardation is a restriction in cognitive functioning manifested by a slowness in making transitions in assigned tasks (G. Wright, 1980).

Ficke (1991) reported that 477,000 individuals between the ages of 15 and 64 had mental retardation as the cause of physical, activities of daily living (ADL), or instrumental activities of daily living (IADL) limitations. ADL refers to basic tasks required for independent functioning (i.e., functioning without the help of another person) and includes (a) bathing, (b) dressing, (c) toileting, (d) transferring (in and out of a bed or chair), (e) continence, and (f) eating. IADL, on the other hand, refers to (a) handling personal finances, (b) preparing meals, (c) shopping, (d) traveling, (e) doing housework, (f) using the telephone, and (g) taking medications (Ficke, 1991, pp. 8–9).

Although the statistic (477,000 individuals) reported above is lower than the total number of individuals with mental retardation, it provides an estimate that is tied to functional limitations. This figure is useful because it suggests the number of individuals who may need assistance in these areas regardless of work setting.

Learning disabilities refer to limitations in the areas of social competence, language, and mathematics, singly or in combination (Falvo, 1999; Little, 1993). Ficke (1991) noted that 223,000 individuals between the ages of 15 and 64 had learning disabilities as the reported cause of physical, ADL, or IADL limitations. In addition, acquired traumatic brain injury and stroke affect diverse cognitive functioning, as may occur with AIDS, longstanding substance abuse, emotional disorders, and a variety of other conditions.

"Cognition is the ability to think, understand, learn about, and be aware of the environment through the senses" (G. Wright, 1980, p. 96). With cognitive limitations, any of the following capacities may be affected: intelligence, memory, concentration, attention, thought processes, perception, organization, conceptualization, reasoning, problem solving, orientation, and psychomotor skills (Falvo, 1999; Wulz, 1993). One of the major mistakes made with workers with brain injury is returning them to work too soon. Healing, reorientation, and maximum return of function often take longer than expected. It is incumbent on the rehabilitation professional to ensure that the person with a brain injury is ready to return to work and also to adequately prepare the employer for possible unanticipated events. A caring and involved employer who consults with the counselor when problems arise will facilitate successful, long-term vocational rehabilitation.

Workers with residuals of head injury may be unable to do certain job tasks; other work tasks may need modification or elimination. In cases of severe head trauma, the person may have to begin with simple, repetitive work activities and gradually perform more detailed, complicated functions as success occurs. It should be remembered that memory problems pose the greatest obstacle for persons with brain injury when returning to work (Wulz, 1993). The counselor, working with both employer and employee, should assist the employer in understanding this and other limitations and develop effective plans for workplace accommodation.

In the case of brain trauma, injured employees are frequently returned to work too soon, before the worker is ready. As a result, the relationship between employee and employer is strained. Strub and Black (1988) suggested that individuals be put on gradually increasing work schedules and only when ready to return to work. Many will never be able to return to the prior level of skill. Yet, rehabilitation professionals must endeavor to maximize consumers' skills and abilities and plan for upward mobility and advancement.

Emotional Limitation

Mental illness is manifested in various limitations, ranging from mild conditions to severe dysfunction. These conditions include psychoses, neuroses, organic brain syndromes, personality disorders, posttraumatic stress disorders, and emotional dysfunctions due to substance abuse. According to the National Institute on Disability and Rehabilitation Research (NIDRR), 651,000 individuals ages 15–64 reported mental or emotional disorders as the cause of physical, ADL, or IADL limitations (Ficke, 1991).

Many individuals with disorders causing emotional limitations of function experience wide ranges of symptoms that affect both psychological and cognitive areas. Medications may control symptoms but not cure the disorder; they may also cause side effects. If the side effects are causing job-related problems, a change in dosage or type of medication by the treating physician may produce a decrease in the side effects interfering with successful work activities. Even with appropriate medical treatment, many residual symptoms, deficits, and impairments may occur along with periodic relapses with recurrence of symptomatology (Falvo, 1999). Job stress may exacerbate symptoms in a previously stabilized worker. Stress may result in deteriorating social behavior necessary for maintenance of employment. The counselor should assist both consumer and employer with careful evaluation on the job. For persons with severe mental illness, supported employment may provide successful reentry into the labor market.

The main components of supported employment include marketing and job development, job matching, job coaching, and follow-along services. Through careful analysis of essential job functions, a consumer can be matched with a job that is within his or her limitations. With the supported employment model, ongoing support is available through a job coach whenever problems occur at work. As seen by Bishop and Falvey (1993), "The rehabilitation potential for persons with psychiatric disabilities seems limited only by the systems, agencies, and individuals who provide support" (p. 160).

Employers tend to discriminate against people with mental illnesses more than those with other disabilities. Counselors should counter this discrimination and advocate for their consumers who have emotional limitations. Through education of employers, more opportunities will become available to these individuals in the future (Bishop & Falvey, 1993).

Limitation Due to Disfigurement

This impairment is due to society's negative reaction to atypical appearance, especially facial disfigurement (Kammerer-Quayle, 1993; G. Wright, 1980). Besides other people's reactions to the condition, one's positive self-image and self-esteem may neutralize the reaction of others to disfigurement. Statistics regarding the incidence or prevalence of this disorder are not readily available, perhaps due to the subjectivity in determining the severity of this condition.

There are no simple answers or perfect solutions for the complications surrounding a person with disfigurement. Macgregor (1979) believed the primary goal of rehabilitation is to prevent or minimize the potentially devastating social and psychological consequences. Plastic and reconstructive surgery may help minimize the actual damage and disfigurement. The consumer and the family, nonetheless, require emotional support; employers must be educated to dispel myths and misconceptions about the causes of facial anomalies and the notions linking disfigurement to negative character traits (Kammerer-Quayle, 1993).

Appearance enhancement techniques include grooming, appropriate diet, exercise, hairstyles, clothing, corrective cosmetics, and eye contact, among others. "To include these factors within the rehabilitation programs of persons with facial disfigurement and physical disability are essential for optimal results" (Kammerer-Quayle, 1993, p. 141). Issues for employment include coping with the public, communicating a positive image, and developing self-esteem.

Substance Abuse

This disorder involves abuse of substances such as alcohol, hallucinogenic drugs, marijuana, nicotine, opiates, sedatives, stimulants, and inhalants. It is estimated that 150,000 individuals ages 15–64 reported alcohol or drug problems as the cause of physical, ADL, or IADL limitations (Ficke, 1991). There are two types of substance abuse according to G. Wright (1980): habituation (psychological needs) and addiction (physical dependence).

"Besides detoxification, strengthening of the ego, increasing self-esteem, and developing a constructive support system, the recovering drug abuser needs to be able to return to living in a healthy environment" (Stude, 1993, p. 61). A job situation that reinforces nonenabling behavior will be most successful in helping the worker with a substance abuse disorder maintain employment. Employers discriminate against persons with substance abuse perhaps more so than with any other disability. Educating employers about this disability will help recovering persons become reemployed. The work environment must reinforce non–drug-abusing behavior.

Functional limitations of recovering substance abusers are usually psychosocial rather than physical. Impatience, inaccurate self-appraisal, unrealistic expectations, and an inability to handle work-related or personal stress are frequently more limiting than either physical or cognitive disabilities (Rogolsky & Little, 1993). Counselors will need special skills to help these individuals cope psychologically and socially with work, as well as to facilitate accommodation by employers in dealing with these personality dimensions.

Rehabilitation counselors, as well as employers, must realize that relapses are common. These workers will need an understanding employer who is able to accept occasional relapses and realizes that relapses are part of the recovery process and do not reflect a lack of motivation (Stude, 1993).

Pain Limitation

Pain sensation may be classified according to duration, origin, nature of disease, precipitating causes and onset, and resulting limitations in function and behavior (G. Wright, 1980). As stated by Pinsky (1993), pain is a subjective, personal, and perceptual experience that eludes a comprehensive definition. Because of its ubiquity, accurate prevalence statistics are not available for pain that leads to long-term functional limitations. Chronic pain causes a wide variety of functional limitations, from slight to severe. How an individual copes with pain will alleviate or intensify the accompanying limitations.

Causes of pain are legion. Chronic pain is optimally treated through a multimodal and interdisciplinary treatment approach. This approach involves physical modalities of treatment, psychological support, psychophysiological treatment, mediation management, and rehabilitation counseling. Early intervention may enhance the motivation of the employee in returning to work (Pinsky, 1993). Involvement of the employer in treatment planning may also ease a potential work return. Precipitating causes of pain should be identified; detailed job task analysis may identify precipitating factors that require modification. Side effects of medication may require changes in certain work duties; in some cases, a change in medication regimen may alleviate problematic side effects. Employers who understand chronic pain will be more willing to consider potential accommodation. Workplace accommodations for chronic pain will be as variable as chronic pain itself. Each type of chronic pain needs individualized case handling.

COMPUTERS AND THE WORKPLACE

Computers in business and industry have had the effect of increasing productivity of almost all workers who use them, especially employees who have disabilities. An employee with a disability with the right computer technology can function as effectively as a worker without limitations. "Technology removes limitations; what we as individuals with disabilities can do then depends strictly upon our abilities, training, and experience" (Bowe, 2000, p. vii).

Computers in business and industry allow for greater productivity and self-sufficiency. Computer applications include input and output devices (e.g., voice, Braille), alternate access aids (headsticks, light pointers, pointing aids, eye gaze, touch screens), interface devices, modified and alternate keyboards, trackballs, joysticks, switches, and special software that enable individuals with disabilities to access and use computers. Additional adaptive devices include touch pads, tongue switches, air cushion switches, arm slot controls, video cameras, and voice input. Specialized software includes voice recognition, scanners, and optical character recognition. Hands-free mouse adaptations allow someone to use an on-screen keyboard controlled by a head pointer or similar device. Eye-tracking technology permits the individual to activate and operate the computer with eye movement alone. Voice recognition technology recognizes a person's speech and types accordingly; it is both reliable and flexible (Lazzaro, 1991; Rubin & Roessler, 2001; Scherer, 2000).

Alternative output-talking work processors, large-print word processors, and computer magnification software assist employees with limited vision and blindness. Modifications range from low-tech to high-tech devices. The best means for working a computer depends on the functional limitations and residual abilities of the user (Rubin & Roessler, 2001). Workers with coordination, dexterity, strength, and visual impairments may need modification of the computer keyboard (the user interface). There is both hardware and software designed to help people with disabilities operate the keyboard. Enlarged keyboards, key guards, miniature keyboards, split keyboards, and Morse code data entry are examples. For those with visual impairments, examples include closed-circuit television magnifiers, refreshable Braille displays, Braille embossers, screen readers, speech synthesizers, and monitor additions (screen magnifiers, antiglare filters, and monitor mounts [to provide adjustment to monitor position]). According to Lazzaro (1991), "If a person has at least one functional, voluntary movement, for example, a finger, foot, eye blink, or such, an adaptation system can be configured to suit that individual" (p. 249).

Computer technology serves to enhance and improve a person's functional capabilities, enabling an individual with a disability to compete on an equal playing field with workers without disabilities through minimizing the impact of the particular disabilities.

In recommending and monitoring the use of computer technology within the workplace, Gates, Akabas, and Kantrowitz (1996) recommended the following to workers' supervisors, who should play active roles in the accommodation process:

1. Making an accurate assessment of when the disabling condition interferes with job performance.
2. Identifying problems caused by the condition.
3. Developing appropriate accommodations.
4. Monitoring accommodations to ensure their effectiveness.
5. Assessing sensitive communication between the worker with a disability and co-workers. (p. 64)

An issue to be considered is whether an employee who has been provided with a reasonable accommodation involving assistive technology at the work site will continue to use the technology. In a review of factors associated with assistive technology discontinuance among people with disabilities, Riemer-Reiss and Wacker (2000) pointed out that "relative advantage" is significantly associated with continuance/discontinuance (abandonment) of assistive technology. Relative advantage includes effectiveness, reliability, ease of use, comfort, and enhancement of the user's performance. A consumer-driven model, in which the person is involved in the selection process and has a sense of ownership and responsibility, leads to continued use of the equipment (Scherer, 2000).

PREVENTION AND MANAGEMENT OF DISABILITY

Before concluding this chapter on disability and accommodation, a few words should be stated about preventing disability from occurring at the workplace and appropriately managing the disabilities and chronic illnesses that do occur. In a study of business and industry, VanTol and Habeck (2000) found that employers with fewer lost workday cases, fewer total lost workdays, and lower workers' compensation claims had the following characteristics:

- Diligent and consistent emphasis on safety
- Accountability and active leadership support for these activities
- Timely and pertinent safety training
- Proactive and coordinated process for injury management and meaningful return to work

Furthermore, companies that were effective in preventing and managing disability had the following strategies in place:

- Used injury and disability data to identify their needs and guide solutions
- Made safety goals a priority and involved top-level management
- Held managers accountable and recognized good safety performance
- Responded immediately to accidents and identified risks
- Used ergonomics to design prevention into the work process

The above methods diminish disability within the workplace, increase productivity, and benefit employer and employee alike. Through proactive rehabilitation, rehabilitation counselors employed within business and industry can help prevent disability, minimize its consequences, and effectively implement policies and procedures to achieve successful return to work for those workers with injuries, disabilities, and chronic illnesses.

CONCLUSIONS

The major emphasis of this chapter on disability and accommodation has been to assist the rehabilitation professional in recognizing that disability has broad sociocultural implications that go beyond physical, mental, or emotional limitations. Also, central to this chapter are recommendations as to how the professional can best facilitate return to gainful employment through such means as reasonable accommodation and client advocacy.

Sociocultural considerations include discrimination by employers simply because an individual has a disability, regardless of the person's ability to meet all the requisite job requirements. Social and psychological reactions of employers and the sociopolitical structure of society have created a "disabling environment" resulting in significantly diminished job and career possibilities for people with disabilities. Recent legislation, particularly the Americans with Disabilities Act of 1990, attempts to overcome these discriminatory practices. It now appears that the ADA is having a positive impact on people with disabilities in the areas of employment, public accommodations, transportation, and telecommunications. Although employment is the main thrust of this chapter, other areas addressed by the ADA either directly or indirectly affect the opportunities of persons with disabilities who desire to maintain employment or become gainfully employed.

One of the most effective means that rehabilitation professionals have to assist people with disabilities in returning to work and maintaining employment is the provision of reasonable work site accommodations. To provide reasonable accommodations, one must first fully comprehend the person's disability in terms of functional limitations. A clearly specified limitation of functions may help the counselor understand the actual work limitations and, therefore, more successfully provide suggestions and recommendations to an employer for accommodating these limitations. This specificity allows all parties involved to view the consumer as someone who has limitations and strengths, rather than as a "disabled person."

In working with employers, rehabilitation practitioners must advocate for people with disabilities to dispel or diminish the stereotypical notions of society. The sociocultural approach (Hahn, 1982, 1988) views disability-related functional limitations as located within the environment, not in the person with a disability. Through knowledge of functional limitations, provision of cost-effective reasonable accommodation, use of computer technology, and consumer advocacy, rehabilitation professionals can expand job and career opportunities for people with disabilities and maximize their potential in the world of work. Prevention and management of disability are two components of minimizing disability and disabling conditions within the workplace. Through careful assessment of needs and awareness of the level of functioning and existing kinds of accommodations and assistive devices, rehabilitation practitioners can greatly improve the employability of persons with disabilities.

REFERENCES

Agonito, R. (1993). *No more "nice girl": Power, sexuality and success in the workplace*. Holbrook, MA: Adams.

Americans with Disabilities Act of 1990, 42 U.S.C. § 12101 *et seq*.

Amott, T., & Matthaei, J. (1991). *Race, gender, and work: A multicultural economic history of women in the United States*. Boston: South End.

Asch, A., & Fine, M. (1988). Introduction: Beyond pedestals. In M. Fine & A. Asch (Eds.), *Women with disabilities: Essays in psychology, culture, and politics* (pp. 1–37). Philadelphia: Temple University Press.

Asch, A., & Fine, M. (1997). Nurturance, sexuality, and women with disabilities. In L. Davis (Ed.), *The disability studies reader* (pp. 241–259). New York: Routledge Kegan Paul.

Berkeley Planning Associates. (1982). *A study of recommendations provided to handicapped employees by federal contractors* (Contract No. J-9-E-1-009). Berkeley, CA: Author.

Bishop, K. D., & Falvey, M. A. (1993). Psychiatric disabilities. In M. G. Brodwin, F. Tellez, & S. K. Brodwin (Eds.), *Medical, psychosocial and vocational aspects of disability* (pp. 151–164). Athens, GA: Elliott and Fitzpatrick.

Bowe, F. (2000). Preface. In M. J. Scherer (Ed.), *Living in a state of stuck: How assistive technology impacts the lives of people with disabilities* (3rd ed., pp. vii–x). Cambridge, MA: Brookline.

Brodwin, M. G. (Ed.). (1995). Cultural diversity [Special issue]. *National Association of Rehabilitation Professionals in the Private Sector Journal, 10*(2).

Brodwin, M. G., & Falvo, D. (1998). Medical aspects of disability, functional limitations, and employment. *National Association of Rehabilitation Professionals in the Private Sector Journal,* 6(6), 26–32.

Brodwin, M. G., Tellez, F., & Brodwin, S. K. (Eds.). (2002). *Medical, psychosocial and vocational aspects of disability* (2nd ed). Athens, GA: Elliott and Fitzpatrick.

Clark, D. R. (1993). Orthotics and prosthetics. In M. G. Brodwin, F. Tellez, & S. K. Brodwin (Eds.), *Medical, psychosocial and vocational aspects of disability* (pp. 407–420). Athens, GA: Elliott and Fitzpatrick.

Colenbrander, A. (1977). Dimensions of visual performance. *Transaction—American Academy of Ophthalmology and Otolaryngology, 83*, 332–337.

Cook, D. (1998). Psychosocial impact of disability. In R. M. Parker & E. M. Szymanski (Eds.), *Rehabilitation counseling: Basics and beyond* (3rd ed., pp. 303–326). Austin, TX: PRO-ED.

Cook, E. (1993). *Women, relationships, and power: Implications for counseling*. Alexandria, VA: American Counseling Association.

Cottone, L., & Cottone, R. (1992). Women with disabilities: On the paradox of empowerment and the need for a trans-systemic and feminist perspective. *Journal of Applied Rehabilitation Counseling, 23*(4), 20–25.

Danek, M. (1992). The status of women with disabilities revisited. *Journal of Applied Rehabilitation Counseling, 23*(4), 7–13.

Danek, M., Conyers, L., Enright, M., Munson, M., Hanley-Maxwell, C., & Gugerty, J. (1996). Legislation concerning career counseling and job placement for persons with disabilities. In E. M. Szymanski & R. Parker (Eds.), *Work and disability* (pp. 39–78). Austin, TX: PRO-ED.

Danek, M. M., & Seidman, M. D. (1993). Hearing disabilities. In M. G. Brodwin, F. Tellez, & S. K. Brodwin (Eds.), *Medical, psychosocial and vocational aspects of disability* (pp. 195–216). Athens, GA: Elliott and Fitzpatrick.

Davis, L. (1997). Constructing normalcy. In L. Davis (Ed.), *The disability studies reader* (pp. 9–28). New York: Routledge Kegan Paul.

Deegan, M., & Brooks, N. (1985). Introduction—Women with disabilities: The double handicap. In M. Deegan & N. Brooks (Eds.), *Women and disability: The double handicap* (pp. 1–5). New Brunswick, NJ: Transaction Books.

Driedger, D., & Gray, S. (1992). *Imprinting our image: An international anthology by women with disabilities*. Charlottetown, Winnipeg, Canada: Gynergy.

Dworkin, A., & Dworkin, R. (Eds.). (1976). *The minority report*. New York: Praeger.

Eisenberg, M. G., Glueckauf, R. L., & Zaretsky, H. H. (Eds.) (1999). *Medical aspects of disability: A handbook for the rehabilitation professional* (2nd ed.). New York: Springer.

Espinola, O., & Croft, D. (1992). *Solutions: Access technologies for people who are blind*. Boston: National Braille Press.

Falvo, D. R. (1999). *Medical and psychosocial aspects of chronic illness and disability* (2nd ed.). Gaithersburg, MD: Aspen.

Ficke, R. C. (1991). *Digest of data on persons with disabilities*. Washington, DC: National Institute on Disability and Rehabilitation Research (NIDRR).

Fine, M., & Asch, A. (1985). Disabled women: Sexism without the pedestal. In M. Deegan & N. Brooks (Eds.), *Women and disability: The double handicap* (pp. 6–22). New Brunswick, NJ: Transaction Books.

Fine, M., & Asch, A. (1988). Disability beyond stigma: Social interaction, discrimination, and activism. *Journal of Social Issues, 44*, 3–21.

Fraser, R. T. (1999). Epilepsy. In M. G. Eisenberg, R. L. Glueckauf, & H. H. Zaretsky (Eds.), *Medical aspects of disability: A handbook for the rehabilitation professional* (2nd ed., pp. 225–244). New York: Springer.

Gates, L., Akabas, S., & Kantrowitz, W. (1996). Supervisors' role in successful job maintenance: A target for rehabilitation counselor efforts. *Journal of Applied Rehabilitation Counseling, 27*(3), 60–66.

Goldman, J. (1993). Neurological conditions. In M. G. Brodwin, F. Tellez, & S. K. Brodwin (Eds.), *Medical, psychosocial and vocational aspects of disability* (pp. 421–437). Athens, GA: Elliott and Fitzpatrick.

Greenwood, R., & Johnson, V. A. (1985). *Employer concerns regarding workers with disabilities*. Hot Springs: Arkansas Research and Training Center in Vocational Rehabilitation.

Hahn, H. (1982). Disability and rehabilitation policy: Is paternalistic neglect really benign? *Public Administration Review, 43*, 385–389.

Hahn, H. (1988). The politics of physical differences: Disability and discrimination. *Journal of Social Issues, 44*, 39–47.

Halpern, A., & Furher, M. J. (1984). *Functional assessment in rehabilitation*. Baltimore: Brookes.

Hamilton, K. W. (1950). *Counseling the handicapped in the rehabilitation process*. New York: Ronald.

Hanna, W., & Rogovsky, E. (1992). On the situation of African-American women with physical disabilities. *Journal of Applied Rehabilitation Counseling, 23*(4), 39–45.

Harley, D. A. (Ed.). (2000). Cultural diversity [Special issue]. *Journal of Applied Rehabilitation Counseling, 31*(1).

Howard, J., & Brodwin, M. G. (1993). The acquired immunodeficiency syndrome: Implications for rehabilitation counselors. *National Association of Rehabilitation Professionals in the Private Sector Journal, 8*, 17–29.

Hu, S. S., & Cressy, J. M. (1993). Paraplegia and quadriplegia. In M. G. Brodwin, F. Tellez, & S. K. Brodwin (Eds.), *Medical, psychosocial and vocational aspects of disability* (pp. 369–391). Athens, GA: Elliott and Fitzpatrick.

Kammerer-Quayle, B. (1993). Image of people with visible disfigurement and disabilities. In M. G. Brodwin, F. Tellez, & S. K. Brodwin (Eds.), *Medical, psychosocial and vocational aspects of disability* (pp. 139–150). Athens, GA: Elliott and Fitzpatrick.

King, R. B., & Backer, T. E. (1989). *Overcoming challenges: A guide to selective job placement of workers with disabilities*. Los Angeles: National Medical Enterprises.

Kopriva, P., & Taylor, J. R. (1993). Cerebral palsy. In M. G. Brodwin, F. Tellez, & S. K. Brodwin (Eds.), *Medical, psychosocial and vocational aspects of disability* (pp. 519–536). Athens, GA: Elliott and Fitzpatrick.

Kutsch, J. A., Jr., (1990). The consumer's role in job accommodation. In R. Greenwood (Ed.), *Applying technology in the work environment* (pp. 3–9). Hot Springs: Arkansas Research and Training Center in Vocational Rehabilitation.

Lakoff, R. (1990). *Talking power: The politics of language*. New York: Basic Books.

LaPlante, M. P. (1992). How many Americans have a disability? *Disability Statistics Abstract, 5*. Washington, DC: U.S. Department of Education, National Institute of Disability and Rehabilitation Research.

LaPlante, M. P., & Carlson, D. (1996). *Disability in the United States: Prevalence and causes, 1992* (Disability Statistics Rep. No. 7). Washington, DC: U.S. Department of Education, National Institute on Disability and Rehabilitation Research.

Lazzaro, J. (1991). Opening doors for people with disabilities: Adaptive technology lets personal computer users lead more productive lives. *Rehabilitation Education, 5,* 245–252.

Leal-Idrogo, A., & Gonzalez-Calvo, J. (1996). Issues of multicultural women in health, disability, and rehabilitation. In A. Leal-Idrogo, J. Gonzalez-Calvo, & V. Krenz (Eds.), *Multicultural women* (pp. 1–22). Dubuque, IA: Kendall-Hunt.

Lerner, P. K., & Hauck, E. K. (1999). Speech, language, hearing, and swallowing disorders. In M. G. Eisenberg, R. L. Glueckauf, & H. H. Zaretsky (Eds.), *Medical aspects of disability: A handbook for the rehabilitation professional* (2nd ed., pp. 245–272). New York: Springer.

Levack, N. (1991). *Low vision: A resource guide with adaptations for students with visual impairments.* Austin: Texas School for the Blind and Visually Impaired.

Linton, S. (1998). *Claiming disability: Knowledge and identity.* New York: New York University Press.

Little, J. (1993). Learning disabilities. In M. G. Brodwin, F. Tellez, & S. K. Brodwin (Eds.), *Medical, psychosocial and vocational aspects of disability* (pp. 491–505). Athens, GA: Elliott and Fitzpatrick.

Lonsdale, S. (1990). *Women and disability: The experience of physical disability among women.* New York: St. Martin's.

Macgregor, F. C. (1979). *After plastic surgery: Adaptation and adjustment.* New York: Bergin.

Mellott, R., & Swartz, J. (1996). Multicultural women with disabilities: Integrating cultural and contextual factors into the rehabilitation process. In A. Leal-Idrogo, J. Gonzalez-Calvo, & V. Krenz (Eds.), *Multicultural women* (pp. 331–366). Dubuque, IA: Kendall-Hunt.

Mosby's medical, nursing and allied health dictionary (5th ed.). (1998). St. Louis, MO: Mosby.

Mueller, J. (1990). *The workplace workbook: An illustrated guide to job accommodation and assistive technology.* Washington, DC: Dole Foundation.

Oliver, M. (1996). *Understanding disability: From theory to practice.* New York: St. Martin's.

Panek, W. C. (1993). Visual disabilities. In M. G. Brodwin, F. Tellez, & S. K. Brodwin (Eds.), *Medical, psychosocial and vocational aspects of disability* (pp. 217–231). Athens, GA: Elliott and Fitzpatrick.

Pinsky, J. (1993). Chronic pain syndromes and their treatment. In M. G. Brodwin, F. Tellez, & S. K. Brodwin (Eds.), *Medical, psychosocial and vocational aspects of disability* (pp. 170–193). Athens, GA: Elliott and Fitzpatrick.

Rehabilitation Act of 1973, 29 U.S.C. § 701 *et seq.*

Rieker, P., & Janowski, M. (1995). Sexism and women's psychological status. In C. Willie, P. Rieker, B. Kramer, & B. Brown (Eds.), *Mental health, racism, and sexism* (pp. 27–50). Pittsburgh, PA: University of Pittsburgh Press.

Riemer-Reiss, M. L., & Wacker, R. R. (2000). Factors associated with assistive technology discontinuance among individuals with disabilities. *Journal of Rehabilitation, 66*(3), 44–50.

Robles, B. (1997). An economic profile of women in the United States. In E. Higginbotham & M. Romero (Eds.), *Women and work: Exploring race, ethnicity, and class* (pp. 5–27). Thousand Oaks, CA: Sage.

Roessler, R. T., & Sumner, G. (1997). Employer opinions about accommodating employees with chronic illness. *Journal of Applied Rehabilitation Counseling, 28*(3), 29–34.

Rogolsky, E. H., & Little, J. (1993). Alcoholism. In M. G. Brodwin, F. Tellez, & S. K. Brodwin (Eds.), *Medical, psychosocial and vocational aspects of disability* (pp. 67–78). Athens, GA: Elliott and Fitzpatrick.

Romero, M. (1997). Epilogue. In E. Higginbotham & M. Romero (Eds.), *Women and work: Exploring race, ethnicity, and class* (pp. 235–248). Thousand Oaks, CA: Sage.

Rubin, S. E., & Roessler, R. T. (2001). *Foundations of the vocational rehabilitation process* (5th ed.). Austin, TX: PRO-ED.

Russell, M. (1998). *Beyond ramps: Disability at the end of the social contract*. Monroe, MA: Common Courage Press.

Scheer, J., & Groce, N. (1988). Impairment as a human constant: Cross-cultural and historical perspectives. *Journal of Social Issues*, *44*, 23–37.

Scherer, M. J. (2000). *Living in the state of stuck: How technology impacts the lives of people with disabilities* (3rd ed.). Cambridge, MA: Brookline.

Stebnicki, M. A., Rubin, S. E., Rollins, C., & Turner, T. (1999). A holistic approach to multicultural rehabilitation. *Journal of Applied Rehabilitation Counseling, 30*(2), 3–6.

Stedman's concise medical dictionary for the health professions (3rd ed.). (1997). Baltimore: Williams & Wilkins.

Stolov, W. C. (1981). Comprehensive rehabilitation: Evaluation and treatment. In W. C. Stolov & M. R. Clowers (Eds.), *Handbook of severe disability* (pp. 1–11). Washington, DC: U.S. Department of Education, Rehabilitation Services Administration.

Strub, R. L., & Black, F. W. (1988). *Neurobehavioral disorders: A clinical approach*. Philadelphia: Davis.

Stude, E. W. (1993). Drug abuse. In M. G. Brodwin, F. Tellez, & S. K. Brodwin (Eds.), *Medical, psychosocial and vocational aspects of disability* (pp. 51–66). Athens, GA: Elliott and Fitzpatrick.

Taber's cyclopedic medical dictionary (18th ed.). (1997). Philadelphia: Davis.

Thomason, R. G. (1997). Feminist theory, the body, and the disabled figure. In L. Davis (Ed.), *The disability studies reader* (pp. 279–292). New York: Routledge Kegan Paul.

VanTol, B., & Habeck, R. V. (2000). How can disability be prevented and managed? *The Rehabilitation Professional*, *8*(1), 25.

Vargo, J. W. (1989). *In the house of my friend: Dealing with disability* (pp. 281–286). Toronto, Canada: Kluwer Academic, Faculty of Rehabilitation Medicine.

Wendell, S. (1996). *The rejected body: Feminist philosophical reflections on disability*. New York: Routledge Kegan Paul.

Wendell, S. (1997). Toward a feminist theory of disability. In L. Davis (Ed.), *The disability studies reader* (pp. 260–278). New York: Routledge Kegan Paul.

West, J. (Ed.). (1991). *The Americans with Disabilities Act: From policy to practice*. New York: Milbank Memorial Fund.

Wright, B. (1983). *Physical disability: A psychosocial approach*. New York: Harper & Row.

Wright, G. (1980). *Total rehabilitation*. Boston: Little, Brown.

Wulz, S. V. (1993). Acquired traumatic brain injury. In M. G. Brodwin, F. Tellez, & S. K. Brodwin (Eds.), *Medical, psychosocial and vocational aspects of disability* (pp. 473–489). Athens, GA: Elliott and Fitzpatrick.

Occupational and Labor Market Information: Resources and Applications

Jeanne Boland Patterson

Work is important to most people, including people with disabilities. One's career choice can affect one's lifestyle, earnings, job security, friends, leisure time, and residence (Rosenthal & Pilot, 1988). It contributes to our identity (Ettinger, 1991) and gives meaning to our lives (Lester & Warnat, 1992). As Hoppock (1976) noted, occupational choice influences "almost every other aspect of life" because it determines

> whether one will be employed or unemployed . . .
> success or failure . . .
> whether one will enjoy or detest his [or her] work . . .
> how a democratic society will utilize its labor force. (pp. 1–3)

Various definitions of occupational and labor market information have been set forth. Wright (1980) defined occupational information as "any and all kinds of information regarding any position, job, or occupation" (p. 345), whereas Isaacson (1986) more narrowly defined occupational information as "information that is directly concerned with duties, requirements for entrance, conditions of work, rewards, patterns of advancement, and worker supply and demand in various occupations" (p. 207). Labor market information, which is encompassed in the preceding definitions, specifically "indicates what jobs exist, estimates their frequency in the economy of any region, and forecasts their growth or decline in the future" (Vandergoot, Swirsky, & Rice, 1982, p. 94). In addition, it provides "information about occupational distribution and trends, ranging from the national to the local level" (Tolbert, 1980, p. 144).

This chapter provides an overview of the various types, sources, and classifications of occupational and labor market information. In addition, the chapter includes an introduction to job analysis, which is useful in determining the essential and marginal functions of particular jobs, identifying job accommodations and assistive technology for people with disabilities, and matching the individual and the job in those circumstances (e.g., supported employment) in which selective placement is required. The following topics are covered: (a) role of occupational information in career counseling and job development, (b) sources and evaluation of occupational and labor market information, (c) national classification systems and resources, (d) state and local resources, (e) computer-assisted resources, and (f) transferable skills assessment and job analysis, including their relationship to the Americans with Disabilities Act of 1990 and ethical issues.

ROLE OF OCCUPATIONAL AND LABOR MARKET INFORMATION

Only 3 out of 10 individuals with disabilities are working full- or part-time, and two thirds of individuals who are not working would like to be working (National Organization on Disability/Louis Harris & Associates, 2000). It is evident that unemployment and underemployment are significant problems for individuals with disabilities. Moreover, with more than 35,000 occupations in the United States (National Occupational Information Coordinating Committee [NOICC], 1986) and new occupations emerging every year, counselors face formidable challenges in their ability to stay abreast of occupational and labor market changes.

The Need for Occupational and Labor Market Information

Limited knowledge of occupations is often problematic for youth and for individuals who have engaged in satisfying careers but, as the result of disabilities, must change their vocation. Occupations that an individual considered at age 20 may not be viable at age 40, and the requirements and conditions for occupations change over time. Other individuals, because of the nature of their disabilities (e.g., some congenital disabilities), may have had limited opportunities for vocational exploration, which further reduces their knowledge of the world of work (Curnow, 1989). Finally, counselors may have had little experience with the world of work or very focused experiences related to a few occupations. Therefore, if counselors are to help individuals with disabilities explore career options and identify career goals, they must have an in-depth knowledge of occupational and labor market information and embrace the concept of lifelong learning as it relates to obtaining and maintaining an up-to-date knowledge of occupational information and future trends in the labor market.

Using Occupational Information in Career Counseling and Job Development

The goal of career counseling and job placement activities is for people with disabilities to obtain and maintain satisfying careers. By providing career counseling, counselors help consumers "integrate and apply an understanding of self and the environment to make the most appropriate career decisions and adjustments" (Sears, 1982, p. 139). Counselors facilitate informed choice in the selection of a career goal by helping consumers transform occupational and labor market data into information that can be used in career planning (Drier, 1980; Levine, 1997). The focus is on career, not just obtaining a job. According to Sharf (1993), "*Job* refers to work done for an employer for pay. *Occupation* refers to the type of work that an individual does. *Career* refers to a commitment to an occupation, or a series of related occupations, for a good portion of one's life" (p. 2).

Both the counselor and consumer enter the vocational counseling relationship with different values, experiences, traits, personalities, knowledge of the world of work, knowledge of self, and skills. However, the counselor should enter the career counseling relationship with a specialized knowledge of occupations, occupational resources, and labor market trends to assist consumers who lack knowledge of the world of work or of specific career opportunities or requirements. Through the process of career counseling, the consumer identifies strengths and weaknesses in self-knowledge and occupational knowledge, obtains information that addresses these gaps in knowledge, and learns and/or applies decision-making skills to arrive at a vocational goal.

SOURCES AND EVALUATION OF OCCUPATIONAL AND LABOR MARKET INFORMATION

By understanding the various types of occupational and labor market information and knowing key areas to assess in evaluating information, counselors can more effectively meet the needs of the consumer. Although many resources can be used jointly by the consumer and counselor (e.g., Bureau of Labor Statistics, 2002), others may be of primary benefit to the counselor; for example, a book such as *Workforce 2020* (Judy, D'Amico, & Geipel, 1997) analyzes labor market trends and provides important information on areas such as telecommuting, employee leasing, and industries and jobs affected by technological advancements. Occupational information is not limited to print materials; it also includes audiotapes and videotapes. Pryor and Pincham (1986) found that the preferred medium (e.g., career leaflets, memos, career compendiums/books, audiotapes, and videotapes) for career counselors, in terms of effectiveness and usefulness, depended on three factors: (a) target audience (counselors or consumers), (b) consumer characteristics, and (c) what occupational information is to be communicated.

Another source of occupational information is individuals who are employed in fields of interest to consumers (Zunker, 1990). Counselors may find it helpful to maintain a "resource-persons file," which includes contact information for individuals willing to serve as resource persons by engaging in personal interviews or providing work shadowing programs. Personal contact through work shadowing, which focuses on worker *roles* rather than work tasks, provides a number of benefits such as exposure to a wider range of occupations. It also consumes less time than work experience (Herr & Watts, 1988).

Ellis (1993) promoted volunteerism as another source of occupational information. In addition to providing firsthand information about one or more jobs with a particular employer, volunteering can provide the opportunity for individuals to acquire or demonstrate work behaviors, which may facilitate their job search process.

Rehabilitation counselors must critically evaluate occupational information and are cautioned not to view all occupational information as equal. Any information should be evaluated in terms of its credibility, comprehensiveness, timeliness, the reputation of the information developer (Rosenthal & Pilot, 1988), and the information needs of the consumer. Timeliness is especially important for quantitative information (e.g., earnings, job outlook), which quickly becomes obsolete. Although the rapid growth of the Internet has increased the availability of major, up-to-date occupational resources for both consumers and counselors (Patterson, 2000), which helps to address the problem of outdated resources, counselors should use similar standards in evaluating Web sites and occupational information obtained from the Internet—that is, "authenticity, applicability, authorship, bias, and usability" (Schrock, 2000, p. 1). Table 7.1 provides an overview of the various types of information needs that can be addressed by occupational resources.

TABLE 7.1. Types of Occupational Information Needs

Element	Use
Nature of work and working conditions	User can compare interests and abilities with job characteristics; user can determine disability-related restrictions and possible accommodations
Employment	Larger occupations tend to have more jobs; the availability of part-time work will be helpful to individuals who lack the stamina for full-time work; individuals interested in self-employment can compare the proportion of jobs in a particular occupation held by individuals who are self-employed
Training, other qualifications, and advancement	The types of training allow the user to compare requirements with aptitudes, as well as the availability of training in a local area; relationships between occupations and movement within or between occupations assist users in both short-term and long-range planning
Job outlook	User can identify factors that may influence job opportunities; if few jobs are available in a field, the user can balance this information with other factors of importance
Earnings	The variability of earnings within occupations makes earnings a factor that must be considered in terms of education, experience, mobility, and types of employers; the user can identify the potential income that may be available
Sources of information	Paper materials (books, pamphlets), videos, and films; computer guidance systems; personal contact

Note. Adapted from "Information Needs for Initial and Ongoing Work Transition," by N. H. Rosenthal and M. Pilot, 1988, *Journal of Career Development*, *15*(1), pp. 22–25. Adapted with permission.

NATIONAL CLASSIFICATION SYSTEMS AND RESOURCES

Multiple systems exist for classifying occupational information due to the large number of occupations and the various uses for occupational information. Sharf (1993) listed three reasons why it is important for counselors to be aware of various classification systems:

> First, occupational classification systems provide a way of grouping similar occupations into a manageable number of categories. This means that if you know how one occupation is classified, you can find similar ones that you didn't know existed. Second, occupational classification systems

> provide different views of occupations. . . . Third, occupational classification systems provide an indirect method of self-assessment. Selecting careers of interest within a category, or selection of occupations within a narrow group of careers, implies that the selection is based on a combination of one's interests, abilities, personality, and/or values. (p. 2)

Information is most frequently classified according to occupations or industries (NOICC, 1986). These have been defined as follows:

> *Occupation*. An occupation is a group of similar jobs found in various organizations; it is made up of the tasks people perform in the workplace. Examples of occupations within the industries are carpenter (in construction), assembler (in manufacturing), and airline pilot (in transportation). *Industry*. Industry categories classify work by the goods or services produced. Three examples of industries are construction, manufacturing, and transportation. (NOICC, 1986, p. 83)

Although many consumers will focus first on possible occupations, knowledge of industries can help consumers focus on local opportunities and increase their knowledge of other options.

National Classification Systems

Dictionary of Occupational Titles (DOT)

The DOT has long been the most commonly used resource by counselors. (Although the DOT is being replaced by the Occupational Information Network [O*NET], the DOT is still used in many rehabilitation settings. Therefore, overviews of both systems are provided.) The DOT uses a nine-digit occupational code to classify occupations. Each digit has a specific meaning: The first digit provides information on one of nine broad categories of occupations (i.e., 0/1, Professional, Technical, and Managerial; 2, Clerical and Sales; 3, Service; 4, Agricultural, Fishery, Forestry, and Related; 5, Processing; 6, Machine Trades; 7, Benchwork; 8, Structural Work; and 9, Miscellaneous). *Divisions* within each occupation are denoted by the first two digits, whereas the occupational groups are defined by the first three digits. For example, 07 refers to occupations in Medicine and Health and 076 refers to Therapists.

The middle three digits provide information on the *worker function ratings* for tasks performed in the occupation. The fourth digit refers to worker functions in relationship to *data*, the fifth digit refers to worker functions in relationship to *people*, and the sixth digit refers to worker functions in relationship to *things*. The numerical assignments for each of these relationships are as follows:

Data	People	Things
0 Synthesizing	0 Mentoring	0 Setting Up
1 Coordinating	1 Negotiating	1 Precision Working
2 Analyzing	2 Instructing	2 Operating–Controlling
3 Compiling	3 Supervising	3 Driving–Operating
4 Computing	4 Diverting	4 Manipulating
5 Copying	5 Persuading	5 Tending
6 Comparing	6 Speaking–Signaling	6 Feeding–Offbearing
	7 Serving	7 Handling
	8 Taking Instructions–Helping	

In reviewing these tasks and their related numbers, it is evident that functions requiring more responsibility and judgment generally have lower numbers, whereas less complex functions have higher numbers (e.g., comparing is a less complex function than coordinating). If an individual is able to perform "coordinating" functions, it is assumed the individual is also able to "compare."

The last three digits of the DOT code differentiate different occupations. Many occupations may have the same first six digits; however, the last three digits identify the specific occupation. The last three digits are in multiples of four (e.g., 010, 014, 018) and the occupations are listed alphabetically (e.g., 045.107-030 Psychologist, Industrial Organizational, precedes 045.107-034 Psychologist, School). In those cases where the first six digits refer to only one occupation, the last three digits are always 010. However, no two occupations have the same nine-digit code. For example, the occupational code for Recreation Aide is 195.367-030, whereas the occupational code for Social Services Aide is 195.367-034. The DOT is available online at http://www.oalj.dol.gov/libdot.htm.

*O*NET*

In contrast to the DOT, the O*NET is a database rather than a book. The newest database is O*NET 3.0, which replaced the original database referred to as O*NET 98. Although O*NET contains fewer occupations than the DOT (1,122 vs. 12,741), the DOT includes a number of obscure or obsolete occupations, as well as occupations that employ few individuals (Mariani, 1999). Another major difference between the DOT and the O*NET is that the DOT focuses on tasks and the O*NET focuses on skills.

Using 483 variables, O*NET is composed of six domains: worker characteristics, worker requirements, experience requirements, labor market characteristics, occupation requirements, and occupation-specific information (Mariani, 1999). Worker characteristics encompass 52 abilities (e.g., oral expression, written expression, spatial orientation), interests (i.e., six categories based on Holland's model of personality types and work environments), and 17 work values/styles (e.g., achievement, independence). Worker requirements include education, knowledge, basic skills (e.g., reading, writing, science), and transferable/cross-functional skills (e.g., social skills, technical skills, resource management skills).

Labor market characteristics include both wage data and national employment projections. Occupational requirements include (a) 42 generalized work activities (e.g., organizing, planning, and interacting with computers), based on their level, importance, and frequency; (b) work context, which includes 46 physical and social skills related to the nature of work, according to the level of skill required and importance (e.g., dealing with external customers, being responsible for others' health and safety); and (c) organizational context, which encompasses 51 organizational characteristics related to how people do their work. Experience requirements include training and experience (and, in the future, licensure requirements), with each occupation assigned to one of five zones, depending on the experience, education, and training needed to perform the job. Occupation-specific information currently focuses on occupational knowledge, occupational skills, tasks, and duties; however, in the future it will include machines, tools, and equipment (Mariani, 1999; National O*NET Consortium, 2001).

In contrast to the DOT's nine-digit classification system, the O*NET uses an eight-digit code. The first six digits are based on the Standard Occupational Classification (SOC). The last two digits are sequentially numbered beginning with "01" to identify unique O*NET occupations within the SOC system. O*NET information is available at http://www.doleta.gov/programs/onet. O*NET On-Line is available at http://online.onetcenter.org.

Standard Occupational Classification (SOC) Manual

The classification system used by all federal statistical agencies is the Standard Occupational Classification (SOC), which encompasses all occupations in which work is performed for pay. Therefore, occupations unique to volunteers are excluded. Revised in 1998, the SOC uses a four-level classification system consisting of 23 major groups (e.g., Management Occupations, Community and Social Service Occupations). The major groups encompass 96 minor groups, 449 broad occupations, and 822 detailed occupations. For example, 21-0000 Community and Social Services Occupations consists of two minor groups (i.e., 21-1000 Counselors, Social Workers, and Other Community and Social Service Specialists; 21-2000 Religious Workers). Within the minor category of Counselors, Social Workers, and Other Community and Social Service Specialists, there are three broad occupations (i.e., 21-1010 Counselors, 21-1020 Social Workers, 21-1090 Miscellaneous Community and Social Service Specialists). Within the Counselor occupation, there are six detailed occupations: Substance Abuse and Behavioral Disorder Counselors (21-1011); Educational, Vocational, and School Counselors (21-1012); Marriage and Family Therapists (21-1013); Mental Health Counselors (21-1014); Rehabilitation Counselors (21-1015); and Counselors, All Other (21-1019). Each of the digits has meaning; the first two digits represent the major group, the third digit represents the minor group, the fourth and fifth digits represent the broad occupation, and the final digit denotes the detailed occupation. According to the Bureau of Labor Statistics (2000), (a) the 2004–2005 edition of the *Occupational Outlook Handbook* will include occupational descriptions and data based solely on the SOC. The SOC is available online at http://www.bls.gov/soc/.

Standard Industrial Classification (SIC) System

The Standard Industrial Classification (SIC) System classifies industries/establishments by economic activity. (Although the SIC is being replaced by the North American Industrial Classification System [NAICS], both are described because some crosswalks [links from one database to another] have not yet incorporated the NAICS.) According to the SIC manual,

1. The classification is organized to reflect the structure of the U.S. economy. It does not follow any single principle, such as end use, nature of raw materials, product, or market structure.
2. The unit classified is the establishment. An establishment is an economic unit that produces goods or services—for example, a farm, mine, factory, or store. In most instances, the establishment is at a single physical location and is engaged in one, or predominantly one, type of economic activity. An establishment is not necessarily identical with a company or enterprise.
3. Each establishment is classified according to its primary activity. Primary activity is determined by identifying the predominant product or group of products produced or handled, or service rendered.
4. An industry (four-digit SIC) consists of a group of establishments primarily engaged in the same activity. To be recognized as an industry,

> such a group of establishments must meet certain criteria of economic significance. (Office of Management and Budget, 1987, p. 699)

The 1987 SIC includes 11 divisions (e.g., retail trade, public administration, services) that are subclassified into 80 major groups (e.g., food stores, real estate, membership organizations, water transportation). The SIC is available online at http://www.osha.gov/oshstats/sicser.html.

The North American Industrial Classification System (NAICS)

The North American Industrial Classification System (NAICS) is a collaborative effort of Mexico, Canada, and the U.S. Office of Management and Budget to facilitate (a) international comparability, (b) consistency (i.e., similar production processes are grouped together), (c) relevance (e.g., hundreds of new technological industries have been identified, and some industries have been reorganized into more meaningful sectors), and (d) adaptability (the NAICS will be reviewed every 5 years to maintain the currency of information; U.S. Census Bureau, 1998).

In contrast to the 11 SIC divisions, the NAICS has 20 sectors. The increased number primarily results from a reorganization of the service industries into more meaningful sectors (i.e., Information; Professional, Scientific, and Technical Services; Administrative Support–Waste Management Services; Educational Services; Health Care and Social Assistance; Arts, Entertainment, and Recreation; and Other Services, except Public Administration). Also, the coding system has changed; the four-digit SIC codes have been replaced by six-digit NAICS codes. The five-digit NAICS code is standard among the three countries; however, the sixth digit, when used, identifies subdivisions of NAICS industries that accommodate the needs of individual countries. The following is an example of the code and description of the six NAICS levels:

Sector	51	Information
Subsector	513	Broadcasting and telecommunications
Industry Group	5133	Telecommunications
Industry	51332	Wireless telecommunications carriers, except satellite
U.S. Industry	513321	Paging

The NAICS is available online at http://www.census.gov/epcd/www/naics.html.

Other National Resources

The following books are examples of resources that are based on information from the preceding classification systems.

Occupational Outlook Handbook (OOH)

Using the SOC structure, the OOH provides an overview of about 200 occupations, which are clustered into 19 broad occupational categories. Information contained in the OOH includes nature of the work, training and other qualifications, employment outlook, earnings and working conditions, and sources of additional information. In contrast to the job analyses, which provide the foundation for occupations noted in the DOT, the OOH information is obtained from trade associations, professional associations, educational institutions, and governmental agencies. Published every 2 years, the OOH is an excellent resource for counselors that can be used directly with consumers. The OOH is available online at http://stats.bls.gov/oco/.

A companion and quarterly update to the OOH is the *Occupational Outlook Quarterly* (OOQ), which provides easy-to-read articles that can be helpful to both counselors and consumers. The OOQ is available online at http://stats.bls.gov/opub/ooq/ooqhome.htm.

Career Guide to Industries (CGI)

The CGI, a publication of the Bureau of Labor Statistics, U.S. Department of Labor, is a companion guide to the OOH. It provides career information by industry. The 2000–2001 Edition contains information on 42 industries. For each industry, it provides a description of the industry, working conditions, employment, earnings, outlook, occupations in the industry, training and advancement, and sources of additional information. The CGI is available online at http://stats.bls.gov/oco/cg/.

Classification of Jobs 2000 (COJ)

The COJ 2000, the fifth edition of the *Classification of Jobs*, is designed to aid counselors and consumers in assessing transferable work skills, defined as the worker attributes used on one job that can be used (i.e., transferred) to another job and that take into account diminished capacities of a worker to perform work as a result of disability or illness. There are four sections to the COJ 2000: The first section contains information on codes and occupational classification systems, including the NAICS system, and illustrates how the user can address transferability of skills with both the 1991 DOT and the O*NET 98 database. The second section of the COJ 2000 includes the 72 worker traits of the 1991 DOT and crosswalks to the work field (WF) and the *Guide for Occupational Exploration* (GOE) codes, with links to the O*NET 98, U. S. Census, SIC, and NAICS codes. The third section provides a separate listing of all light and sedentary titles grouped according to (a) GOE, (b) census codes, (c) NAICS, and (d) work fields, with each listing cross-referenced to the DOT and O*NET 98 codes. The final section contains references, including definitions of traits and elements, contained in the DOT and O*NET 98 database (Field & Field, 1999).

The COJ 2000 is available from Elliott & Fitzpatrick, Inc., 1135 Cedar Shoals Drive, Athens, GA 30607; http://www.elliottfitzpatrick.com.

Work Fields

Because of the importance of the *work field* code in assessing transferrable skills, Field and Field (1993) abstracted the work fields from the *Revised Handbook for Analyzing Jobs* and have published it as a separate reference, called *Work Fields*. Each of the 100 work field clusters contains the following five major elements of jobs: method verb, machines, tools, equipment, and work aids. As Field and Field (1993) noted, "The professional has the complete information for a job both in terms of the capacities to perform a job (worker traits) and the skills required for the job (work field data)" (p. 1), when both the COJ and *Work Fields* are used. Work fields may be more important in assessing transferrable skills than worker traits because one may identify appropriate jobs on the basis of worker traits (interests, aptitudes, physical factors) that fail to consider whether the worker has had any experience with the machines, tools, equipment, and work aids used on the job. *Work Fields* is available from Elliott & Fitzpatrick, Inc., 1135 Cedar Shoals Drive, Athens, GA 30607 and online at http://www.elliottfitzpatrick.com.

There are other well-known resources, such as the *Complete Guide for Occupational Exploration* (GOE; Farr, 1993); however, the GOE is old and is based on the DOT. Corresponding to the Interest Check List published by the U.S. Employment Service in 1979, the GOE divides 12 interest areas (e.g., artistic, scientific, mechanical) into 66 work groups and 348 subgroups. Although the GOE includes more occupations, the *Enhanced Guide for Occupational Exploration* (Maze & Mayall, 1995) categorizes the 2,800 jobs the authors consider most important and includes information on academic requirements, work fields, materials used, aptitudes, temperaments, physical demands, work environment, salary, and outlook. Each GOE entry addresses five major questions: (a) What kind of work would you do? (b) What skills and abilities do you need for this kind of work? (c) How do you know if you would like or could learn to do this kind of work? (d) How can you prepare for and enter this kind of work? (e) What else should you consider about these jobs? The GOE and the *Enhanced Guide* are available from JIST Works, 720 North Park Avenue, Indianapolis, IN 46202-3431; http://www.jist.com.

STATE AND LOCAL RESOURCES

Although national sources of occupational and labor market information are very comprehensive and provide excellent *general* information (e.g., salary ranges for certain occupations), they typically lack the specificity of local information (e.g., the annual number of openings in a particular occupation in a specific community). Therefore, national resources should be supplemented with state and local information to provide the most assistance to consumers.

Historically, two major sources of state and local information are state departments of labor (DOLs), which include employment security offices, and State Occupational Information Coordinating Committees (SOICCs), which were part of the National Occupational Information Coordination Committee (NOICC) network. However, NOICC/SOICC ceased functioning in 2000, with the information systems functions transferred to the Employment and Training Administration at the U.S. Department of Labor and the career development functions transferred to the Office of Vocational and Adult Education at the U.S. Department of Education (Lester, 2000). Counselors can most easily stay abreast of state and local information from the DOL and SOICC (some of which have been renamed) by using the Internet. Links to each of the state SOICCs are available online at http://www.acinet.org/acinet/resource/states.htm#soiccs. Links to each state's department of labor and the division that publishes labor market information are available online at http://www.lmi-net.org/contactinfo/states.htm or http://stat.bls.gov/oco/oco20024.htm.

In urban areas, chambers of commerce are a major resource for counselors. Chambers of commerce frequently maintain listings of major employers in the community and the number of employees at each of the businesses/industries. Using a resource such as the SIC or NAICS, a counselor can identify local industries that employ individuals in different occupations.

Local labor market surveys provide another means of procuring local labor market information. Frequently used in workers' compensation rehabilitation, labor market surveys help the counselor and/or consumer identify current jobs that are available, their minimum hiring requirements, and wages and benefits. Although most labor market surveys are conducted via telephone, face-to-face contact with employers and/or personnel departments can help build relationships that will help the counselor in future placement activities.

COMPUTER-ASSISTED RESOURCES

Historically, computer-assisted career counseling resources have been grouped into two categories: (a) computer-assisted career guidance systems and (b) computer-based career information systems (Harris-Bowlsbey, 1992; Mariani, 1995). Past (2000) added a third category, career information on the Internet (e.g., America's Career Infonet), which encompasses information not included in the first two categories. Nonetheless, overlap does exist among these three categories.

Computer-Assisted Career Guidance (CACG) Systems

Computer-assisted career guidance (CACG) systems, such SIGI PLUS, DISCOVER, or CHOICES, typically consist of six components: (a) assessment of user needs; (b) assessment of psychological and labor market constructs; (c) generation of occupational, educational, financial aid, and employment options; (d) delivery of occupational, educational, financial aid, and employment information; (e) instruction in career, educational, and employment decision making; and (f) development of an action plan to implement career choice (Sampson, 1997). CACG systems must be purchased, are typically installed on individual personal computers in career guidance offices or laboratories, and are only available to individuals receiving services from the agency or organization (Past, 2000). Sampson et al. (1998) conducted an extensive analysis of the features and costs of 17 CACG systems in the areas of (a) content (e.g., assessment, identifying and obtaining occupational alternatives, identifying and obtaining educational information, coping with adult transitions, decision making, employment planning, local data option), (b) user-friendly features (e.g., password protection, data collection for accountability and research, video clips), (c) support materials and services, (d) costs, and (e) availability of state-specific occupational information. As Sampson and Reardon (1990) noted, there is no one "best" system; the features and costs vary with consumer populations. The online addresses for major CACG systems are as follows:

DISCOVER	http://www.act.org/discover
SIGI PLUS	http://www.ets.org/sigi
Career Information System (CIS)	http://oregoncis.uoregon.edu
Career and College Quest	http://www.petersons.com
Career Visions	http://www.cew.wisc.edu
Career Futures, Choices, Choices CT	http://www.careerware.com
Career View	http://www.collegeview.com
FOCUS II	http://www.focuscareer.com
Guidance Information System (GIS 3.0)	http://www.riverpub.com

Career Information Delivery Systems (CIDS)

Career information delivery systems (CIDS), which are operated by SOICCs, state agencies, or universities, are the most common systems to provide state-based career information. Most states use computer-based systems that provide information on occupations and related education and training opportunities (Lester & Ollis, 1988). Although the CIDS vary by state, most systems contain descriptions of 300 to 500 occupations, including information on duties, working conditions, worker requirements, employment outlook, wage and salary levels, and educational and training requirements. Some of the CIDS include financial aid, major state employers, job openings that have been listed with the state employment security agency, and information related to postsecondary institutions, such as admission requirements (Ettinger, 1991). Many of the CACG systems have been designated by the state SOICC as a computer-based CIDS. For example, the designated CIDS for Maryland is VISIONS Plus, the Career Information System is the designated system for Alaska and Georgia, and Choices and Choices CT are the designated CIDS for Florida, Vermont, and Utah (Sampson et al., 1998). Some states, such as Michigan and Kentucky, have developed state-specific CIDS. CIDS typically include print and video, as well as computer resources. Links to each state's CIDS are available online at http://www.acinet.org/acinet/library.htm?category=1.6#1.6s.

Career Information on the Internet

The Internet has greatly facilitated access to occupational and labor market information for both counselors and consumers. Also, some Internet sites have features that are similar to CACG systems/CIDS. For example, the bottom of the O*NET Career Exploration page provides links to America's Job Bank, America's Learning Exchange, CareerInfoNet, the

Occupational Outlook Handbook, and the NOICC. America's CareerInfoNet includes links to (a) career resources; (b) state information; (c) career tools; (d) jobs, wages, and trends; and (e) financial aid. The link to state information includes a state map, demographic information, links to the largest employers, state resources, licensing information, and search capabilities that allow individuals to identify the fastest growing occupations or occupations with the most openings overall or by a worker's educational level. Also, it provides an employer locator. The user first selects an industry division (e.g., mining), then a state, and then a major industry. Using the example of mining, one would select the type of mining (i.e., coal mining; metallic mining; nonmetallic minerals, except fuels; or oil and gas extraction) and then select one geographic region within a state. The name and address of any employers are then provided.

The Career Resource Library, which is part of America's CareerInfoNet, includes brief descriptions of direct links in the following categories: career assessment, employment trends and projections, general career sites, performance reviews, salary and wage surveys, search engine career pages, and work / life issues. America's CareerInfoNet is available online at http://www.acinet.org/acinet. Table 7.2 contains a list of the Web sites that have been noted in this chapter, as well as other career counseling, occupational, and labor market resources that may be useful to counselors and consumers.

APPLYING OCCUPATIONAL INFORMATION IN TRANSFERABLE SKILLS ASSESSMENT AND JOB ANALYSIS

Many of the resources previously described are used in analyzing transferable skills or provide the direction for securing more detailed job information. By analyzing the skills that an individual has used on one job, the counselor and consumer can identify jobs that require similar skills. However, most occupational resources identify generic skills. For some consumers, it is essential for the counselor to analyze a job with a particular employer to determine the essential functions of the job or to identify activities required for the job by a particular employer.

Transferable Skills Analysis

When individuals have knowledge and/or skills used on one job that can be used on another job, they are said to have "transferable skills." To

TABLE 7.2. Sample Internet Resources for Occupational and Labor Market Information and Career Counseling

Occupational Employment Statistics, 1998 State Occupational and Wage Estimates	http://stats.bls.gov/oes/1998/oessrcst.htm
Center on Occupational Research and Development Library of the Workplace	http://cord.org/workplacelibrary/indices/jobs.html
New York Career Zone	http://www.nycareerzone.org
Monthly Labor Review	http://stats.bls.gov/opub/mlr/mlrhome.htm
School to Work	http://www.stw.ed.gov
Office of Vocational and Adult Education Career Clusters	http://www.ed.gov/offices/OVAE/clusters/index.html
National Centers for Career and Technical Education	http://www.nccte.com
National Crosswalk Service Center	http://www.state.ia.us/ncdc
Military Career Guide Online	http://www.militarycareers.com
General Career Planning	http://f.about.com/2/js/spr04.htm
JobWeb	http://www.jobweb.com
State Jobs	http://www.statejobs.com/
Career Development Manual	http://www.cdm.uwaterloo.ca
America's Labor Market Information System	http://www.lmi-net.org/
International Career Development Library	http://icdl.uncg.edu/
Job Futures 2000 — Canada	http://jobfutures.ca/doc/jf/index.shtml
Career Magazine	http://www.careermag.com/
Career Resource Center	http://www.careers.org/
Job Hunter's Bible Supplement to *What Color Is Your Parachute?*	http://www.jobhuntersbible.com/
The Riley Guide	http://www.rileyguide.com/
Career Planner	http://www.careerplanner.com/
Lycos Careers	http://careers.lycos.com/
Salary Wizard	http://www.salary.com
Quintessential Careers	http://www.quintcareers.com/index.html
Brass Ring	http://www.brassring.com
Researching Companies Online	http://home.sprintmail.com/~debflanagan/index.html
Job Star	http://jobsmart.org

(*continues*)

TABLE 7.2. *Continued.*

Job Seeking Skills for Persons with Disabilities	http://www.csun.edu/~sp20558/dis/shcontents.html
U.S. Census Bureau	http://www.census.gov/
Monster	http://www.monster.com/
Federal Jobs	http://www.usajobs.opm.gov/ http://www.fedworld.gov/jobs/jobsearch.html
Big Eye Job	http://www.bigeye.com/jobs.htm
U.S. News Online Career	http://www.usnews.com/usnews/work/wohome.htm
Cynthia Good's College and Career Planning Home Page	http://www.bridge-rayn.org/CGood.html

determine an individual's transferable work skills, one first lists the primary jobs previously held by an individual. After the DOT or O*NET code has been identified for each of these jobs, a worker trait profile is developed for each job. The worker trait profile includes Specific Vocational Preparation (SVP), General Educational Development (GED), aptitudes, physical demands, environmental conditions, and temperaments. Applicable worker field, data–people–things, GOE, and/or MPSMS (materials, products, subject matter, and services) codes are also included. An Unadjusted Vocational Profile is created by listing the highest level of demonstrated functioning for each of the worker traits. For example, if an individual has held jobs requiring both medium and heavy lifting, heavy lifting would be noted. A Residual Functional Capacity Profile (RFCP) is then calculated, which takes into consideration any reduction in an individual's capacity due to illness or injury. For example, a worker may have previously held positions that required lifting 20 to 50 pounds occasionally (medium) and climbing, but the worker is now restricted to sedentary work (10 pounds occasionally) and prohibited from climbing. To find similar or related jobs, the counselor would (a) maintain the same occupational area by looking for positions with the same first digit of the DOT; (b) maintain the same work field (MSPSM); and (c) identify jobs that do not exceed the worker trait requirements in the RFCP (Havranek, Field, & Grimes, 2001). The jobs that are identified through this process are then evaluated in terms of the local labor market.

Because changes in physical capacities frequently result from industrial injuries (i.e., individuals served by workers' compensation programs), the COJ 2000 and *Work Fields* manuals are helpful resources in conducting transferable work skills analyses. However, two limitations to the transferable work skills approach to placement should be noted. First, the approach is targeted to individuals who have a work history. Second, the transferable skills approach does not take into consideration assistive devices and accommodations that may expand the range of jobs under consideration. For example, if vision has been a requirement of previous jobs but the worker has lost his or her vision, the RFC profile would eliminate all positions that require vision. It is important to keep in mind that the worker may be able to perform some of the jobs requiring vision if the appropriate assistive devices are provided.

O*NET Online provides a computerized assessment of transferable skills, which results in a list of alternative occupations the consumer may consider. To some extent, O*NET Online addresses the limitation related to accommodations and assistive devices with the following statement: "If your search identifies skills or abilities that may be difficult to perform because of a health problem or disability, please consider *job accommodations*. Accommodations may involve a change in the work environment, the way a specific job is performed, or the use of special equipment." O*NET provides direct links to the Job Accommodation Network (JAN) and JAN's Searchable Online Accommodation Resource (SOAR). (JAN is available online at http://janweb.icdi.wvu.edu.)

Job Analysis

All of the occupational resources previously described rely to varying degrees on generic descriptions of occupations and jobs. In many instances, counselors need more specificity or detailed information (e.g., information from a local company about a specific position) to better match a consumer's skills, abilities, and interests with a particular job. Or the counselor may need to know what kinds of accommodations (McCray, 1987) may be possible. For example, standing may be included as a requirement of an occupation. Without evaluating the specific job/position, the counselor would be unable to determine whether, in fact, standing *was* a requirement or whether there were various types of accommodations that could eliminate the need for standing. Similarly, a physician may have placed restrictions on the amount of weight a consumer can lift or a particular type of activity (bending/stooping). When this level of specificity is required about a particular job or position, a counselor may wish to perform a job analysis. Job analysis has been defined as

> the gathering, evaluating, and recording of accurate, objective, and complete job data . . . [it] identifies and describes, in a systematic and comprehensive but succinct manner:
>
> - *What* the worker does in terms of activities or functions.

- *How* the work is done—the methods, techniques, or processes involved, and the work devices used.
- *Results* of the work—the goods produced, services rendered, or materials used.
- *Worker Characteristics*—the skills, knowledge, abilities, and adaptabilities needed to accomplish the tasks involved.
- *Context* of the work in terms of environmental and organizational factors, and the nature of the worker's discretion, responsibility, or accountability. (Materials Development Center [MDC], 1982, p. 5)

These factors constitute two major types of information: work performed (i.e., worker functions, work fields, and MPSMS) and worker characteristics (i.e., general educational development, specific vocational preparation, aptitudes, temperaments, interest areas, physical demands, and environmental conditions; U.S. Department of Labor, 1991).

Three definitions are critical to understanding job analysis and are dictated by the purpose of the job analysis:

1. Job: A single position or group of positions at one establishment, whose major work activities and objectives are similar in terms of worker actions, methodologies, materials, products, and/or worker characteristics; and whose array of work activities differs significantly from other positions.
2. Task: A grouping of elements and work activities of a job that have a common purpose, and are closely related in terms of methodologies, materials, products, services, and types and sequences of worker actions.
3. Element: The smallest step into which it is practicable to subdivide a work activity for purposes of a job description. It is the component of a task, but more comprehensive than individual motions of the worker. (MDC, 1982, pp. 5–6)

It is important to remember that "elements, task, and job are relative concepts; that is, an activity that is an element in one job, could be a task in another job, and could be a job in and of itself" (U.S. Department of Labor, 1991, pp. 1–2). The nature of the disability and functional limitations/accommodations dictate the degree to which tasks, elements, or the job remain the primary focus of the counselor, as well as the specificity of the job analysis. For example, a great deal of specificity and focus on the components of each task may be necessary in developing a supported employment site for an individual with severe mental retardation. In contrast, the physical elements of a job may be less critical for an individual with persistent mental illness. In this case, the counselor will focus the job analysis primarily on the stress level of the job, worker emotional supports, and the emotional work environment. Lastly, an analysis of elements and tasks can be critical for the counselor who is working with a rehabilitation engineer to devise accommodations for an individual with physical limitations (e.g., spinal cord injury or amputation).

Job analyses are typically conducted for one of two purposes—to learn more about particular jobs for future consumers or to critically analyze a job with a particular consumer in mind. Both of these situations require the counselor to proceed through a series of steps, which culminate in the written job analysis.

Steps in Job Analysis

The first step in the job analysis sequence is to conduct background research on the industry and occupation. Some of the occupational resources previously cited will assist the counselor in acquiring an understanding of the terminology, materials, and equipment that are used at an employment site.

The second step is to select a business or industry. The following six factors determine which business or industry is selected: "purpose of the job study, type of product or service, number of employees, number of representative industry jobs likely to be found in the establishment, location of the establishment, and policy or history of the establishment in allowing studies of various kinds" (MDC, 1982, p. 20). For example, a counselor may select a business or industry because it is the largest local employer (i.e., number of employees), or the counselor may select a business or industry because it is located close to the bus line, which would facilitate transportation for a particular consumer.

The third step is to actually contact the establishment. Although some job analyses may be arranged through personnel offices, it is frequently more efficient to send a letter or call the CEO, a top administrator, or the manager.

The fourth step is to hold an initial meeting with the company representative. Although the purpose may have been discussed in the initial letter or telephone call, it is important to explain the purpose and scope of the proposed analysis, obtain permission, and gather preliminary information, such as job descriptions (if available), union contracts, and other information on the company that was not part of the counselor's initial research. It is important during the initial meeting to stress that a draft of the job analysis will be submitted to the company's designated individual to review for accuracy and completeness and that any confidentiality requested by the company will be maintained. It is frequently helpful to learn at the initial meeting whether the counselor will have certain time limits or whether certain attire is necessary. Some of the ground rules that companies may establish for purposes of "safety, security, and minimal disruption to workers" include "observe workers from a distance, avoid entering restricted areas, adhere to rules covering confidentiality of forms and documents, wear safety equipment, and keep designated personnel informed of whereabouts" (MDC, 1982, p. 22).

The fifth step is to take a tour of the plant or facility. A tour may follow the initial meeting or may be arranged for a later date. Even if a counselor is only interested in one position, a tour provides an overview of the total operation and may suggest possible future job analyses.

The sixth step is to conduct the job analysis or analyses, depending on the number of jobs that will be studied. Various methods of job analysis include questionnaires, work diaries/logs, worker task inventories, interviews, observations, and observation interviews. The latter method is preferred because it (a) "involves firsthand observation, (b) provides an opportunity to evaluate interview data and to sift essential from nonessential facts in terms of that observation, and (c) permits the workers to demonstrate as well as describe job functions" (MDC, 1982, p. 26).

Job Analysis and Rehabilitation Service Delivery Systems

In the state–federal rehabilitation program, the extent of counselor involvement ranges from direct intervention with employers (e.g., selective placement) to little or no direct intervention with employers. Job analysis is generally an essential component of selective placement and rarely used in client-centered placement.

In most state workers' compensation programs, job analysis is an important part of the vocational rehabilitation placement process (Weed, Taylor, & Blackwell, 1991). Seyler and Chauvin (1989) found that 78% of workers' compensation clients who were successfully rehabilitated had had job analyses performed, compared to 58% in the sample as a whole. Weed et al. (1991) also noted that California requires a job analysis prior to direct placement for individuals receiving workers' compensation. In addition to the uses of a job analysis that have been previously noted, another application of the job analysis in private-sector rehabilitation is educating the client's physician "about the details of a client's potential job and provid[ing] a formal method for review and approval/modification" (Weed et al., 1991, p. 154). When the job analysis is used for this purpose, pictures and/or a video of the job being performed can be very helpful in supplementing the written record of worker characteristics and work performed.

Relationship of Job Analysis and ADA

Under Title I of the Americans with Disabilities Act of 1990 (ADA; P.L. 101-336), employers with 15 or more employees "shall not discriminate against a qualified individual with a disability because of the disability of such individual in regard to job application procedures, the hiring, advancement, or discharge of employees, employee compensation, job training and other terms, conditions, and privileges of employment" (Sec. 102[a]). In considering the relationship of ADA and job analysis to placement, it is important to consider the following definitions:

1. *Qualified individual with a disability*. An individual with a disability who, with or without reasonable accommodation, can perform the essential functions of the employment position that such individual holds or desires. For the purposes of this title, consideration shall be given to the employer's judgment as to what functions of a job are essential, and if an employer has prepared a written description before advertising or interviewing applicants for the job, this description shall be considered evidence of the essential functions of a job. (Sec. 101[8])
2. *Reasonable accommodation*. May include (a) making existing facilities used by employees readily accessible to and usable by individuals with disabilities; and (b) job restructuring, part-time or modified work schedules, reassignment to a vacant position, acquisition or modification of equipment or devices, appropriate adjustment or modifications of examinations, training materials or policies, the provision of qualified readers or disabilities. (Sec. 101[9])
3. *Undue hardship*. An action requiring significant difficulty or expense, when considered in light of the [following] factors . . . (a) the nature and cost of the accommodation needed under this Act; (b) the overall financial resources of the facility or facilities involved in the provision of the reasonable accommodation; the number of persons employed at such facility; the effect on expenses and resources, or the impact otherwise of such accommodation upon the operation of the facility; (c) the overall financial resources of the covered entity;

the overall size of the business of a covered entity with respect to the number of its employees; the number, type, and location of its facilities; and (d) the type of operation or operations of the covered entity, including the composition, structure, and functions of the workforce of such entity; the geographic separateness, administrative, or fiscal relationship of the facility or facilities in question to the covered entity. (Sec. 101[10] A, B)

4. *Direct threat.* Means a significant risk to the health or safety of others that cannot be eliminated by reasonable accommodation. (Sec. 101[3])

Job analyses are the primary means of determining the fundamental job duties (i.e., essential functions of a job). Most jobs consist of both essential functions and marginal functions.

A job function may be considered essential for any of several reasons, including but not limited to the following: (a) the reason the position exists is to perform the function, (b) there are a limited number of employees available among whom the performance of that job function can be distributed, and/or (c) the function may be highly specialized so that the incumbent in the position is hired for his or her expertise or ability to perform the particular function. Some of the factors that may be considered in determining whether a job function is essential include the amount of time spent performing the function and the consequences of not requiring an individual to perform the function (*Federal Register*, 1991).

Rehabilitation professionals may be called on to conduct job analyses for employers. A job analysis may be fairly simple (e.g., listing the major work duties) or quite complex (e.g., examining individual motions), depending on "the purpose of the job analysis and the level of repetitiveness of the job being studied" (McQuistion, 1992, p. 77). Although the employer, not the rehabilitation counselor, ultimately determines which job functions are essential, it is important for the rehabilitation counselor to delineate the major tasks of the job and list them by (a) the sequence in which they are performed or (b) priority from most important to least important. The criticality of each job function must also be addressed by asking two questions: "Would the flow of principal work be stopped without this task?" and "Would the main mission be disrupted if this task were not done?" (Blackwell, Conrad, & Weed, 1992, p. 15). If the answer to either of these questions is yes, then the job analyst would indicate that the job function is essential. The job analyst should also indicate the percentage of time the worker spends performing each of the tasks, so that the total of all tasks is 100% (Blackwell et al., 1992). Although the percentage of time a worker spends performing a task may be small, it may be an essential function. An example would be the airline pilot who uses emergency procedures rarely. The percentage of time for this task may be extremely small, but the pilot's ability to perform this task is critical and essential. Finally, in evaluating aptitudes, temperaments, environmental conditions, and physical demands, the analyst should indicate (a) which job function the item is related to and (b) whether it is critical (Blackwell et al., 1992). Figure 7.1 contains a sample job analysis for a scaleperson.

Occupational Information and Job Analysis: Ethical Implications

Knowledge and skills in using occupational and labor market information and conducting job analyses are critical for rehabilitation professionals who assist individuals with disabilities to enter or return to the workforce. There are, however, numerous ethical implications related to using occupational and labor market information and conducting job analyses. First, rehabilitation counselors must keep in mind three ethical principles: beneficence (doing good/being helpful), nonmaleficence (not causing harm), and autonomy (making one's own decisions). Identifying a vocational goal or providing training for an area in which there is little or no likelihood that a consumer will secure employment can cause harm to the consumer. Therefore, vocational goals and related training programs should be based on occupational and labor market information that is *current* and *accurate*. In presenting occupational and labor market information, the counselor should remember that it is the consumer, not the counselor, who makes decisions based on the information.

Job analyses must be carefully conducted to ensure that consumers do not aggravate existing conditions. Noting that "even the most innocent assumption about a job must be confirmed with objective, accurate data, [because] . . . the client can be made to suffer as a result of an analysis performed in a slipshod manner," Weed et al. (1991, p. 157) provided the example of a railroad engineer with a below-knee amputation and back injury who was restricted from lifting more than 25 pounds. Although it initially appeared that the engineer could return to his duties, further discussions with the engineer and a job analysis revealed that occasionally the engineer had to carry 50-pound bags of sand, which, when loaded into a sander, were dropped onto the tracks when the train went up hills.

There are also ethical issues related to labor market surveys, which have been used to facilitate the settlement of cases between clients and insurance companies (Weed & Taylor, 1990). Sometimes labor market surveys focus exclusively on the physical demands associated with jobs and the consumer's physical limitations and "specifically leave out significant placeability factors, including interests and personality factors as criteria

(text continues on p. 276)

Position:	Scaleperson
DOT#:	920.685-090
Date of Job Analysis:	3/6/92
Location:	Union Camp Paper Mill Franklin, Virginia

People Present

Roger Weed, PhD, CRC; Howard Soucek (personnel department); Carrol Story (union representative and coworker); Jimmy Carr (shift supervisor); Jeff Jacobs (day supervisor); Sue Riddick, RN; Caryn George, rehabilitation counselor, Learning Services Corporation.

General Job Description

(*Source*: Union Camp Paper Mill)
The scaleperson has two primary functions: (a) to properly identify all first-quality, offgrade, reject, and downgrade rolls coming from the paper machine winder; to generate and apply proper core tags and bar codes for rolls produced and to enter the required information into the computer; and (b) to move these rolls from the scale table onto the roll handling system and operate that portion of the roll handling system that serves the scale table. Additionally, the scaleperson is responsible for maintaining a neat and orderly scale table.

Communication and cooperation with other mill employees are required to facilitate the filling of orders. The scaleperson is responsible for informing the supervisor of potential backlogs or problems to prevent winder shutdown. When necessary, the scaleperson directs the activities of the scaleperson helper.

Salary and Benefits

As of the date of this report, the scaleperson position paid $15.27 per hour (approximately $32,000 for 2,080 hours of work). Occasionally, income can vary with increased duties. Overtime opportunities are often available.

In addition to wages, comprehensive benefits are included. Employees receive 2 weeks of vacation after 3 years, 3 weeks after 8 years, 4 weeks after 12 years, 5 weeks after 18 years, and 6 weeks after 25 years.

Work Hours and Schedule

Shifts are not routine. A general schedule is as follows:

11:00 P.M. to 7:00 A.M., 7 straight days with 2 days off
3:00 P.M. to 11:00 P.M., 7 straight days with 1 day off
7:00 A.M. to 3:00 P.M., 7 straight days with 5 days off

(*continues*)

FIGURE 7.1. Job analysis narrative report. From *Job Analysis and the ADA: A Step by Step Guide* (pp. 119–122) by T. L. Blackwell, D. A. Conrad, and R. O. Weed, 1992, Athens, GA: Elliott and Fitzpatrick. Copyright 1992 by Elliott and Fitzpatrick. Reprinted with permission.

Essential Functions

1. Measure diameter of new set and enter into computer with order information previously entered.
2. Stencil ends of rolls as required.
3. Print proper core tags and bar codes and apply them to corresponding rolls.
4. Move rolls from scale table to roll handling system.
5. Operate portion of roll handling system serving scaleperson's table.
6. Communicate with mill personnel to find out about offgrade, reject, and downgrade rolls and reasons. Enter order numbers and reason codes in computer system.
7. Keep work area (scale table) clean and orderly.

This scope of work is not an all-inclusive listing of the duties for this position. Nonroutine duties are not included in the list of essential functions; additional duties may be assigned as circumstances dictate.

Qualifications

The position requires a high school diploma or General Equivalency Diploma. As computerized equipment is added to the paper mill, more cognitive skills and increased judgment are required; however, the computerized equipment is not considered complex. No specific certifications or licenses are required. The employee learns on-the-job and works up the ladder and through various job stations as he or she is competent to do so and as positions become available. A check-off system conducted by supervisors will certify the work capabilities of the employer.

General Educational Development

No specific math level requirements were identified. However, the employer reports that math requirements have become increasingly more important. Presently, skill to perform the four basic mathematical functions (add, subtract, multiply, divide) is adequate.

Practical communication language is required. Hand signals, due to the noisy environment, are often used. Listening and understanding what is being said and being able to follow written directions are required. Although computers are likely to compile reports, occasionally written communication for reports is required. Little writing is required as the computer compiles the information and the employee enters the data via computer screen and keyboard. Paperwork consists of orders for rolls and sets of paper.

(*continues*)

FIGURE 7.1. *Continued.*

Aptitudes

When working at the scale, rapid decision making and stress are not critical. However, operating the paper machine requires rapid decision making and good judgment when paper breaks occur.

No general testing was conducted. No job description in the *Dictionary of Occupational Titles* precisely fits the job observed. The closest title, Roll Finisher (920.685-090), appears to generally fit the requirements of the position.

Aptitude	Explanation
Intelligence	Below Average
Verbal	Below Average
Numerical	Negligible
Spatial	Below Average
Form Perception	Below Average
Clerical Perception	Below Average
Motor Coordination	Below Average
Finger Dexterity	Below Average
Manual Dexterity	Average
Eye/Hand/Foot	Negligible
Color	Negligible

Temperaments

This position involves frequent repetitive work. When working at the scale, rapid decision making and stress are not critical; however, the paper machine can be dangerous and requires rapid decision making and good judgment when paper breaks. Although not normally a job task, the scaleperson helps others with paper breaks.

Reportedly no specific production quotas are required, and the amount of stress one feels is reported to be dependent upon the individual's perception. The employer reports there is "generally a fair amount of pressure."

The scaleperson works on his or her own but not alone. Other people with different responsibilities are in the immediate area. Communication and cooperation with other mill employees (including supervision, other scalepersons, quality control staff, planning personnel, and office clerk) are required. When necessary, the scaleperson directs the activities of the scaleperson helper.

Environmental Conditions

The scaleperson works at the end of a line where paper is made, processed, rolled, and cut. The job is performed entirely indoors and, therefore, is not subject to extremes of temperature. The environment is that of a large warehouse that is generally noisy and requires ear protection. Occasionally, periods of loud or shrill noises are accented by a variety of bells, whistles, horns, and other alerting mechanisms.

(*continues*)

FIGURE 7.1. *Continued.*

No significant fumes or odors were noted. The employer reports that TRS gasses pass through the area once per month, when vented from the pulp mill. Normally, no health or medical problems result from this brief exposure.

Operating the paper machine can be dangerous due to high speed rollers and cramped location. Water and other apparent nontoxic chemicals were in the area. Contact with toxic chemicals is rare.

No exposure to electrical shock, unprotected heights, radiation, explosives.

The worker must wear safety shoes, helmet, ear protection, and eye protection. No uniforms are worn.

Exertional Physical Demands

The employer states that *standing* varies depending on the duties and the size of the rolls of paper. Larger rolls of paper allow more rest and *sitting*, although sitting is allowed less than 30 minutes per shift. Smaller rolls require *standing* and moving around. On average, approximately two thirds of the time during a work day involves standing. *Walking* is described as a minor part of the job. General walking involves an approximately 30-foot square area with occasional walking to the paper machine to help clean up a paper break. Walking to the work site from the parking lot, estimated to be one fourth mile, is the most significant walking requirement.

According to the employer, the maximum amount of *lifting* is generally 10 to 15 pounds. Occasionally, rolls of paper weighing 2,000 pounds or more may need to be *pushed* with the aid of a pry bar. The work area observed during this job analysis rarely required pushing of rolls due to the angle of incline on the floor. There is overhead *pulling* of 20 to 30 feet of wrapper paper off an overhead spool 20 to 30 times per month. There is also above-the-head pulling of a cord that controls a conveyor belt.

Nonexertional Physical Demands

No significant *climbing* was observed, although stairs to and from the work site and climbing into and around the paper machine are required. *Stooping* and/or *bending* is not a significant part of the job. The worker must be able to bend over to place plugs into the center of a roll of paper and to apply stenciling and bar code labels. General body functioning is required; however, excellent physical conditioning is not necessary. *Crawling* is not a significant part of the job.

The position requires data entry into a computer and *handling* bar code labels (peeling them from paper and placing them on the plugs of a set of paper). A control panel with dials ranging from .5 to 2 inches in diameter is used. Fine *finger dexterity* is not generally required. The worker must use hands and arms to *reach* and *handle* the plugs for the rolls of paper, apply stenciled lettering and numbers, and utilize wood mallets and pry bars. Use of both hands appears to be important. Accommodation may be possible.

(*continues*)

FIGURE 7.1. *Continued.*

The scaleperson must be able to answer a telephone several times each day in a *noisy* environment to receive and pass along instructions.

Near *vision* is required to the extent that the scaleperson needs to be able to read a computer screen, bar codes, and small numbers associated with bar codes. This task is required 20 to 30 times per day for a period of about 5 minutes each time. Depth perception and far vision are not a significant part of the position. Field of vision is not generally significant, although the loss of one may pose safety problems due to moving machinery and rolls of paper.

Balancing, kneeling, crouching, feeling, and smelling are not generally required in the position.

FIGURE 7.1. *Continued.*

in job selection in order to de-emphasize the human element, or so-called subjective factors" (Weed et al., 1991, p. 154).

In addition to possessing the requisite knowledge and skills in the area of occupational and labor market information, job analyses, and labor market surveys, rehabilitation professionals must "use the knowledge and skills in an ethical manner" (Patterson, 1998, p. 207) because "ethical and professional behaviors are every bit as much a relevant index of a professional's competence as are levels of knowledge, skill, and experience" (Pharis & Hill, 1983, p. 183).

SUMMARY

Knowledge of occupational and labor market information and skills in acquiring and using the information are essential for counselors who assist individuals with disabilities in career exploration, career decision making, and job placement. Awareness of the various classification systems and major references (O*NET, SOC, NAICS, OOH, OOQ, GOE) can help the counselor (and consumer) expand the range of career options under consideration. Similarly, labor market surveys and job analyses are excellent tools to help counselors stay abreast of local labor market conditions, which can help consumers make more informed decisions.

A primary goal of career/vocational counseling is to help individuals match their needs, interests, values, and aptitudes with the world of work. To achieve this goal, counselors must have up-to-date, accurate, and appropriate occupational and labor market information. Competence in using the Internet can greatly facilitate counselors' access to requisite information.

REFERENCES

Americans with Disabilities Act of 1990, 42 U.S.C. § 12101 *et seq*.

Blackwell, T., Conrad, A., & Weed, R. (1992). *Job analysis: A step by step guide*. Athens, GA: Elliott and Fitzpatrick.

Bureau of Labor Statistics. (2000). *Standard Occupational Classification (SOC) system*. Retrieved from http://www.bls.gov/soc/

Bureau of Labor Statistics. (2002). *Occupational outlook handbook, 2002–03 edition*. Retrieved from http://www.bls.gov/oco/

Curnow, T. C. (1989). Vocational development of persons with disability. *Career Development Quarterly, 37*, 269–278.

Drier, H. N. (1980). Career information for youth in transition: The need, systems, and models. *Vocational Guidance Quarterly, 32*, 277–282.

Ellis, J. R. (1993). Volunteerism as an enhancement to career development. *Journal of Employment Counseling, 30*, 127–132.

Ettinger, J. M. (Ed.). (1991). *Improving career decision making in a changing world: Training manual*. Garrett Park, MD: Garrett Park.

Farr, M. (1993). *The complete guide for occupational exploration*. Indianapolis, IN: JIST.

Federal Register. (26 July, 1991). 29 CFR Part 1630, 56(144), 35726–35756.

Field, J., & Field, T. (1993). *Work fields*. Athens, GA: Elliott and Fitzpatrick.

Field, J., & Field, T. (1999). *Classification of jobs 2000*. Athens, GA: Elliott and Fitzpatrick.

Harris-Bowlsbey, J. (1992). Systematic career guidance and computer-based systems. In Z. B. Leibowitz & H. D. Lea (Eds.), *Adult career development: Concepts and practices* (2nd ed., pp. 102–114). Alexandria, VA: American Association for Counseling and Development.

Havranek, J., Field, T., & Grimes, J. (2001). *Vocational assessment: Evaluating employment potential*. Athens, GA: Elliott and Fitzpatrick.

Herr, E. L., & Watts, A. G. (1988). Work shadowing and work-related learning. *Career Development Quarterly, 37*, 78–86.

Hoppock, R. (1976). *Occupational information* (4th ed.). New York: McGraw-Hill.

Judy, R. W., D'Amico, C., & Geipel, G. L. (1997). *Workforce 2020*. Indianapolis, IN: Hudson Institute.

Isaacson, L. E. (1986). *Career information in counseling and career development* (4th ed.). Boston: Allyn & Bacon.

Lester, J. (2000). The NOICC/SOICC network: In transition. Retrieved from http://icdl.uncg.edu/ft/061900-01.html

Lester, J. N., & Ollis, H. T. (1988). Future challenges to career information providers: A NOICC perspective. *Journal of Career Development, 14*, 205–215.

Lester, J. N., & Warnat, W. I. (1992). From promising experiment to widespread practice.

In J. Lester (Ed.), *From pilot to practice: Strengthening career development programs* (pp. 1–8). Washington, DC: National Occupational Information Coordinating Committee, U.S. Department of Education.

Levine, L. (1997). *Labor market information: An overview*. Washington, DC: Congressional Research Service, Library of Congress. Retrieved from http://wdr.doleta.gov/research/rlib_doc.asp?docn=5808

Mariani, M. (1995). Computers and career guidance: Ride the rising tide. *Occupational Outlook Quarterly, 39*(4), 16–27.

Mariani, M. (1999). Replace with a database: O*NET replaces the *Dictionary of Occupational Titles*. *Occupational Outlook Quarterly, 43*(1), 3–9.

Materials Development Center (MDC). (1982). *Guide to job analysis*. Menomonie: University of Wisconsin, Stout Vocational Rehabilitation Institute.

Maze, M., & Mayall, D. (1995). *The enhanced guide for occupational exploration* (2nd ed.). Indianapolis, IN: JIST.

McCray, P. M. (1987). *The job accommodation handbook*. Verndale, MN: RPM.

McQuistion, L. (1992). Job accommodation. In J. K. O'Brien (Ed.), *National short-term training program: Americans with Disabilities Act* (pp. 68–95). Carbondale, IL: Region V Rehabilitation Continuing Education Program.

National Occupational Information Coordinating Committee (NOICC). (1986). *Using labor market information in career exploration and decision making: A resource guide*. Garrett Park, MD: Garrett Park.

National O*NET Consortium. (2001). *Career exploration*. Retrieved from http://www.onetcenter.org/usingOnet.html

National Organization on Disability/Louis Harris & Associates. (2000). *The 2000 N.O.D./Harris Survey of Americans with Disabilities*. Washington, DC: Author. (Executive summary available from http://www.nod.org/hs2000.html)

Office of Management and Budget (OMB). (1987). *Standard Industrial Classification manual*. Springfield, VA: National Technical Information Service.

Past, T. (2000). *The status of computer-assisted resources for career counseling in the 21st century: An Internet-referenced guide*. Retrieved from http://pages.prodigy.net/tpast1/homepage/Computer-assist.htm

Patterson, J. B. (1998). Ethics and ethical decision making in rehabilitation counseling. In R. M. Parker & E. M. Szymanski (Eds.), *Rehabilitation counseling: Basics and beyond* (3rd ed., pp. 181–223). Austin, TX: PRO-ED.

Patterson, J. B. (2000). Using the Internet to facilitate the rehabilitation process. *Journal of Rehabilitation, 61*(1), 4–10.

Pharis, M., & Hill, K. (1983). Training for responsible professional behavior in psychology and social work. *Clinical Social Work Journal, 11*, 178–183.

Pryor, R. G., & Pincham, S. (1986, December). Counselors' views of occupational information media. *Journal of Employment* Counseling, pp. 178–187.

Rosenthal, N. H., & Pilot, M. (1988). Information needs for initial and ongoing work transition. *Journal of Career Development, 15*(1), 20–29.

Sampson, J. P. (1997). *Helping clients get the most from computer-assisted career guidance systems*. Retrieved from http://www.career.fsu.edu/techcenter/Councda1.html

Sampson, J. P., & Reardon, R. C. (1990). Evaluating computer-assisted career guidance systems: Synthesis and implications. *Journal of Career Development, 17*, 143–149.

Sampson, J. P., Reardon, R. C., Reed, C., Rudd, E., Lumsden, J., Epstein, S., et al. (1998). *A differential feature-cost analysis of seventeen computer-assisted career guidance systems* (Technical Rep. No. 10). Tallahassee: Florida State University Center for the Study of Technology in Counseling and Career Development. Available from http://www.career.fsu.edu/techcenter/tr10.html

Schrock, K. (2000). *Kathy Shrock's guide for educators*. Retrieved from http://school.discovery.com/schrockguide/eval.html

Sears, S. (1982). A definition of career guidance terms: A National Vocational Association perspective. *Vocational Guidance Quarterly, 31*, 137–143.

Seyler, C., & Chauvin, J. (1989). Placement technique variables and subject variables associated with successful rehabilitation outcome. *Journal of Private Sector Rehabilitation, 4*(1), 3–7.

Sharf, R. D. (1993). *Occupational information overview*. Pacific Grove, CA: Brooks/Cole.

Tolbert, E. L. (1980). *Counseling for career development* (2nd ed.). Boston: Houghton Mifflin.

U.S. Census Bureau. (1998). *Why is NAICS better?* Retrieved from http://www.census.gov/epcd/www/naicsben.htm

U.S. Department of Labor. (1991). *The revised handbook for analyzing jobs*. Washington, DC: Government Printing Office.

Vandergoot, D., Swirsky, J., & Rice, K. (1982). Using occupational information in rehabilitation counseling. *Rehabilitation Counseling Bulletin, 26*, 94–100.

Weed, R., & Taylor, C. (1990). Labor market surveys: The backbone of the rehabilitation plan. *NARPPS Journal and News, 5*(4), 27–32.

Weed, R., Taylor, C., & Blackwell, T. (1991). Job analysis for the private sector. *NARPPS Journal and News, 6*, 153–158.

Wright, G. N. (1980). *Total rehabilitation*. Boston: Little, Brown.

Zunker, V. G. (1990). *Career counseling: Applied concepts of life planning*. Pacific Grove, CA: Brooks/Cole.

Career Counseling with Diverse Populations: Models, Interventions, and Applications

David B. Hershenson and James J. Liesener

Chapter 4 examined career development theory, whereas this chapter will focus on career counseling, with special reference to persons with disabilities and members of other diverse groups. The distinction between career development theory and career counseling is illustrated by the following two quotations: "In essence, career theory primarily elaborates the targets for intervention rather than provides a theory of intervention itself" (Herr, 1996, p. 17), whereas a model of career counseling "is a descriptive guide, often for change, and is judged by pragmatic outcomes" (Chartrand, 1996, p. 121). The relationship between career development and career counseling truly exemplifies the aphorism that life imitates art. In 1594, Shakespeare wrote *A Midsummer Night's Dream* (Wright, 1936), a play in which two principal characters, Helena and Lysander, each in love with someone else, wander through an enchanted forest, occasionally catching a fleeting glimpse of each other (although in the end, they are fated to marry). Similarly, career development, enamored of personality theory, and career counseling, enamored of empirical counseling practice, pass by each other in pursuit of their true loves, barely acknowledging each other's existence, although in the end, they too are destined to come together.

HISTORY

Probably one major source of this star-crossed relationship is to be found in the fact that career counseling has its own history that is largely separate from that of career development theory (Herr, 2001). A brief review of the evolution of career counseling was provided by Hershenson (1995). The first scientific approach to career counseling is credited to Frank Parsons, who in 1908 founded the first documented career counseling program, the Vocation Bureau in Boston, Massachusetts. The stated purpose of the bureau was

> to aid young people in choosing an occupation, preparing themselves for it, finding an opening in it, and building up a career of efficiency and success. And to help any, young and old, who seek counsel as to opportunities and resources for the betterment of their condition and the means of increasing their economic efficiency. (Parsons's statement in *The Arena*, July 1908, quoted in Davis, 1969, pp. 113–114)

This statement of purpose was amazingly prophetic of the direction that the field would take for the next 90 years, in that it both incorporated the words *career* and *counsel* and sought to be inclusive as to those the field should serve. In Parsons's (1909) posthumously published book, *Choosing a Vocation*, he outlined the factors involved in the choice of a vocation as

> (1) a clear understanding of yourself, your aptitudes, abilities, interests, ambitions, resources, limitations, and their causes; (2) a knowledge of the requirements and conditions of success, advantages and disadvantages, compensation, opportunities, and prospects in different lines of work; (3) true reasoning on the relations of these two groups of facts. (p. 5)

For the next 40 years, career counseling focused on developing objective measures by which a person could gain that "clear understanding of [themselves and their] aptitudes, abilities, interests, ambitions, resources, limitations" and on administering and interpreting these measures to clients.

Just before World War II, influenced by European psychiatrists and child psychologists who emigrated to America to escape Nazi persecution, the field of counseling assumed a strong orientation toward human development. This orientation found its way into the career field primarily through the work of Super, who in 1953 published "A Theory of Vocational Development." Thus as alternative paradigm was introduced, shifting from Parsons's focus on the single event of choosing a vocation to a new conception of vocational *development* as an ongoing, lifelong process. This shift also manifested itself in the evolution of alternative approaches to career counseling that emphasized examining career issues as life span issues of personal growth and development rather than as a single, time-limited issue of vocational choice.

Discussing the then-current state of career counseling (and providing insight into how greatly the developmental approach had influenced the field in just 15 years), O'Hara (1968) stated, " There has been such a concentration on affective elements that a researched understanding of cognitive approaches has been neglected" (p. 637). Thus, a third major approach that focused on cognitive processes and information processing arose, with support from two sources. One source was the need to deal with the increasing availability and complexity of occupational information in career counseling, and the other source was the developing fields of cognitive psychology and computer modeling, with their interest in how people take in, store, and use information to make decisions. Because occupational choice generally involves deciding on something that one has never before fully experienced, information about possible options and how that information is processed are extremely important. The application of this approach to career counseling is best exemplified by the social learning model of Krumboltz (1979) and the cognitive information-processing model of Peterson, Sampson, and Reardon (1991). In these models, career counseling focuses on assisting clients to develop their information-seeking, information-processing, and decision-making skills and to apply these skills to resolving their career issues. Since the late 1980s, attempts have been made in the literature to define a general process of career counseling that incorporates insights from all three major approaches.

We shall next review some of the models of career counseling that represent this evolution. Then, we shall discuss a variety of interventions that are used across a number of career counseling models. Finally, we shall consider the application of these models and interventions to diverse populations, with special emphasis on persons with disabilities, and conclude by presenting a new, inclusive framework to guide the career counseling process.

MODELS OF CAREER COUNSELING

Before presenting some of the most prevalent models in the literature, it might be helpful to provide several definitions of career counseling that illustrate the scope of the concept. In a 1991 position paper, the National Career Development Association (NCDA) stated,

> Career counseling is defined as counseling individuals or groups of individuals about occupations, careers, life/career roles and responsibilities, career decision making, career planning, leisure planning, career pathing, and other career development activities (e.g., resume preparation, interviewing and job search techniques), together with the issues or conflicts that individuals confront regarding their careers. (p. 1)

This definition emphasizes the first word of the term *career counseling*. Another definition, which instead emphasizes the second word of the term, was proposed by Brooks and Brown (1986): " Career counseling is an interpersonal process designed to assist individuals with career development problems. . . . Career problems include, but are not limited to, career indecision and undecidedness, work performance, stress and adjustment, incongruence of the person and work environment, and inadequate or unsatisfactory integration of life roles with other life roles (e.g., parent, friend, citizen)" (p. 98).

As noted earlier, the first model of career counseling was developed by Frank Parsons (1909). Parsons's model employed a strategy of matching personal traits with occupational factors. This simple three-stage model of career counseling laid the foundation on which most other models were built. Underlying this and most subsequent models of career counseling are three basic assumptions:

1. People seek out and create environments that provide and/or allow for behavioral trait manifestations.
2. Degree of fit between the person and environment is associated with significant outcomes that can substantially affect the individual and environment; for example, performance, productivity, satisfaction, turnover, and stress. The better the person-environment fit, the better the outcomes.
3. The process of person-environment fit is reciprocal, involving the individual shaping the environment and the environmental context influencing the individual (Rounds & Tracey, 1990, p. 18).

Nevertheless, some contemporary career counselors have seen shortcomings in this model and have developed their own models of career counseling to address their concerns (e.g., Brown & Brooks, 1991; Cochran, 1997; Fouad & Bingham, 1995; Gysbers, Heppner, & Johnston, 1998; Mitchell & Krumboltz, 1996; Nathan & Hill, 1992; Salomone, 1996; Spokane, 1991; Yost & Corbishley, 1987). These models typically add stages to either end of Parsons's (1909) model or shift the primary focus to the relationship between the counselor and the client or to the client's cognitive processes. These models also reflect various theoretical orientations. However, if one looks closely, or sometimes even not so closely, one can see Parsons's model of career counseling and the assumptions of trait and factor/matching theory at the core of many of these models. Some of the more recent models of career counseling that have expanded Parson's original ideas are presented below.

Parsonian Models

Nathan and Hill

Nathan and Hill's (1992) model of career counseling closely resembles Parsons's in form but incorporates the assumptions of current person–environment interaction and person-centered theories. Within this model, greater emphasis is placed on the relationship and the effect of the individual's feelings and beliefs as potential barriers or supports. In addition, this model extends the career counseling process beyond occupational choice and includes support throughout the placement process and beyond.

Nathan and Hill's (1992) model of career counseling consists of three stages: (a) screening, contracting, and exploring; (b) enabling clients' understanding; and (c) action and endings. During the screening, contracting, and exploring stage, the individual's readiness for and the appropriateness of career counseling are assessed, presenting concerns and influences on career and educational choices are explored, expectations of career counseling are established, and a contract is established. During the enabling clients' understanding stage, the client explores the following questions: Who am I? Where am I? What do I want? Where do I want to be? In addition, self-understanding is facilitated through the use of assessments, and occupational information is explored by the client. Finally, in the action and endings stage, possible career options are explored, and the client chooses between options in developing an action plan that is subsequently put into action. Fears of change are addressed, and the need for continued support are evaluated, and progress made toward objectives during career counseling is assessed.

Krumboltz

Krumboltz's (1979; Mitchell & Krumboltz, 1996) social learning theory of career decision making incorporates principles from behavioral and cognitive theories of development into the process of career counseling. According to Krumboltz (1979), four factors influence decision making: genetic endowment and special abilities, environmental conditions and events, learning experiences, and task approach skills. Interactions among these factors produce self-observation generalizations (e.g., self-evaluations of strengths and weaknesses, interests, values), task approach skills (e.g., career decision-making skills, such as information seeking, goal setting, and planning), and subsequent actions (e.g., job-seeking and job entry behaviors). Thus, the individual's learning experiences and task approach skills were added to Parsons's original conceptualization of the factors influencing career decision making. Within Krumboltz's model of career counseling, much attention is paid to the effect of experiences on the individual's learning and beliefs about one's self and one's abilities through the process of social learning (Bandura, 1986).

On the basis of this formulation, Krumboltz and Hamel (1977) evolved a seven-step model of career decision making, the first letter of each step spelling out the acronym "DECIDES." These steps are as follows:

1. Define the problem
2. Establish an action plan
3. Clarify values
4. Identify alternatives
5. Discover probable outcomes
6. Eliminate alternatives systematically
7. Start action

In 1996, Mitchell and Krumboltz expanded this theory to include a learning theory of career choice and counseling (LTCC) that was intended "to provide a guide to practicing career counselors who want to know what they can do now to help people troubled with a variety of career-related concerns" (p. 250). As discussed in Chapter 4, this volume, LTCC is based on the needs of people choosing careers at this time in history to learn how to (a) expand the range of their interests and capabilities, (b) cope with changing work roles and tasks, and (c) be able to locate and process relevant career and personal information, make decisions based on that information, and act on those decisions. According to LTCC, career counselors must promote their clients' learning how to cope with the full range of career issues, from occupational choice to job hunting to work adjustment to retirement planning, including unanticipated and unplanned events (Mitchell, Levin, & Krumboltz, 1999). Client assessment is to be used to create new learning on the part of the client, rather than to provide the counselor with diagnostic information. Interventions used in career counseling include (a) developmental and preventive interventions (e.g., career education, job clubs, occupational information, simulations) and (b) tailored and remedial interventions (e.g., cognitive restructuring, behavioral interventions such as desensitization and role-playing). New criteria for evaluating interventions are also called for by LTCC, including how well a particular intervention stimulates new client learning and improves client coping with the world of work.

Yost and Corbishley

Like Krumboltz, Yost and Corbishley (1987) incorporated principles from cognitive theories into their model of career counseling. However, rather than focusing on the effects of social learning on decision making, Yost and Corbishley focused on the effects of cognitive constraints, in the form of the clients' self-thoughts, on the career development process. Within this model of career counseling, "cognitive constraints must be dealt with if the process is to be successful" (Isaacson & Brown, 1997, p. 376). On the basis of these ideas, Yost and Corbishley developed an eight-stage model of career counseling consisting of (a) providing an initial assessment, (b) gaining self-understanding, (c) making sense of self-understanding, (d) generating alternatives, (e) gathering occupational information, (f) making the choice, (g) making plans, and (h) implementing plans. In 1991, Yost and Corbishley outlined a four-step interview process for conducting the first stage of their model, initial assessment. This process consists of (a) analyzing the client's work history, (b) examining work-related preferences, (c) investigating the client's lifestyle context, and (d) summarizing the accumulated information.

Spokane

Spokane (1991) also developed a model of career counseling based on cognitive theories of career development. Within this model, the counselor explores any irrational beliefs that the client may hold that are inhibiting his or her motivation. In addition, within this model, much emphasis is placed on the counselor–client relationship, especially in the first stage. Spokane's model of career counseling consists of three stages and eight substages: (a) beginning: opening, aspiring, and loosening; (b) activation: assessment, inquiry, and commitment; and (c) completion: execution and follow-through.

Salomone

Salomone's (1996) model of career counseling incorporates principles from client-centered theories with Parsons's (1909) matching model of career counseling. The primary objectives of this model are to facilitate the development of client independence and responsibility. In addition, Salomone sees career as developing across the life span and including midlife changes as development occurs. Therefore, the role of the counselor in this model moves away from that of expert and toward that of teacher and supporter who imparts the capacity to deal with these career transitions. The five stages of Salomone's model of career counseling are (a) helping the client to understand the self, (b) helping the client to understand the environment, (c) helping the client to understand decision making, (d) implementing career and educational decisions, and (e) adjusting, adapting, and advancing.

Gysbers, Heppner, and Johnston

The last model of career counseling that fits Parsons's (1909) three-stage model was developed by Gysbers, Heppner, and Johnston (1998). Gysbers et al. sought to develop a model of career counseling that would take into consideration issues of gender, culture, and ethnicity and be applicable to women and minorities, a documented shortcoming of other models (Arbona, 1996; Conte, 1983; Curnow, 1989; Gysbers et al., 1998; Leong, 1996; Szymanski, Hershenson, Enright, & Ettinger, 1996). In creating this model, Gysbers et al. incorporated principles from client-centered, cognitive, and multicultural theories of counseling and career development. The model consists of two stages, each containing three substages.

The first stage, client goal or problem identification, clarification, and specification, consists of the following substages: opening, gathering client information, and understanding and hypothesizing behavior. During opening, the counselor forms a working alliance with the client by identifying initial client-presented goals or problems; listening for internal thoughts, feelings, and underlying dynamics; and defining and clarifying the client – counselor relationship and responsibilities. During the gathering client information substage, the counselor uses the interview, quantitative instruments, and qualitative procedures to clarify and specify the presenting goals or problems for the purpose of exploring clients' views of themselves, others, and their worlds; exploring clients' ways of making sense of their life roles, settings, and events; exploring possible personal and environmental barriers or constraints; and exploring clients' decision-making styles. Finally, during the understanding and hypothesizing client behavior substage, the counselor applies the language and knowledge from career, counseling, and personality theories as well as the multicultural and gender literature to understand and interpret client information and behavior in light of the clients' presenting goals or problems by forming hypotheses, focusing on cultural or gender-specific variables, and listening for and responding to possible client resistance.

The second stage of Gysbers et al.'s model, client goal or problem resolution, consists of the following substages: taking action, developing career goals and plans of action, and evaluating results and closing relationships. During the taking action substage, the counselor uses counseling techniques, quantitative and qualitative assessments, and information to assist clients in achieving their goals or respond to their problems in the context of the working alliance. This substage typically involves the client seeking information about the world of work and various occupational alternatives. During the developing career goals and plans of action substage, the counselor and the client collaborate to establish career goals and plans of actions to achieve these goals, as well as to resolve problems and overcome environmental and bias barriers when and where present. Finally, the evaluating results and closing relationships substage occurs when the client's goals are achieved or problems that are blocking career development are resolved.

As can be seen in Table 8.1, although most personality and career development theories have had an influence on career counseling, the framework for the process of career counseling is based primarily on person–environment interaction theories, particularly Parsons's (1909) tripartite model. At their core, all of these approaches involve assessing the individual, assessing the available occupational options, and matching the two based on a logical approach. Nevertheless, career counseling has advanced dramatically since 1909, and various lenses for understanding the individual, the impact of the environment, the interaction between the two, and the varied processes of decision making have been incorporated into these more recent models. In addition, the concept of career has been expanded to include the various roles that people play (i.e., work, family, religion, culture, and leisure) and their development across the life span. This change in the conceptualization of career is also evident in the current models of career counseling.

Alternative Models

Another phenomenon in career counseling that has occurred in the past two decades is the recognition that most career theories and models of career counseling were developed around White, male norms and may not be applicable to women and minorities (Arbona, 1996; Conte, 1983; Curnow, 1989; Gysbers et al., 1998; Leong, 1996; Szymanski et al., 1996). This recognition has resulted in an abundance of information about differences in the identity development of women and minorities (Gilligan, 1982; Helms, 1995), the effects of various cultural values on career development and decision making (Brown, 1996; Gysbers et al., 1998; Ponterotto, Casa, Suzuki, & Alexander, 1995), and the impact of bias and discrimination on career development and decision making (Betz & Hackett, 1981; Gysbers et al., 1998; Ponterotto et al., 1995; Subich, 1996). We will discuss this topic in more detail later in this chapter, but at this point it must be noted that the emergence of multicultural career theories has resulted in the development of models of career counseling that are purposefully designed to be applicable to women and minorities.

TABLE 8.1. Comparison of Current Career Counseling Models with Parsons's Model

Parsons (1909)[a]	Nathan and Hill (1992)[b]	Krumboltz (1979)[c]	Yost and Corbishley (1991)[d]	Spokane (1991)[e]	Salomone (1996)[f]	Gysbers, Heppner, and Johnston (1998)[g]
1. Understand one's self	1. Screening, contracting, and exploring 2. Enabling client's understanding (self)	1. Define the problem 2. Establish an action plan 3. Clarify values	1. Initial assessment 2. Self-understanding 3. Making sense of self-understanding	1. Beginning a. Opening b. Aspiring c. Loosening 2. Activation a. Assessment	1. Helping the client understand self	1. Client goal or problem identification, clarification, and specification a. Opening b. Gathering client information c. Understanding and hypothesizing client behavior
2. Understand the requirements of available jobs	3. Enabling client's understanding (occupational)	4. Identify alternatives 5. Discover probable outcomes	4. Generating alternatives 5. Gathering occupational information	b. Inquiry	2. Helping the client understand the environment	2. Client goal or problem resolution a. Taking action
3. Choose using true reasoning	4. Action and endings	6. Eliminate alternatives systematically 7. Start action	6. Making the choice 7. Making plans 8. Implementing plans	c. Commitment 3. Completion a. Execution b. Follow-through	3. Helping the client understand decision making 4. Implementing career and educational decisions 5. Adjustment, adaptation, and advancement	b. Developing career goals and plans of action c. Evaluating results and closing relationship

[a] *Choosing a Vocation*, by F. Parsons, 1909, Boston: Houghton Mifflin.
[b] *Career Counseling*, by R. Nathan and L. Hill, 1992, London: Sage.
[c] "A Social Learning Theory of Career Decision Making," by J. D. Krumboltz, in *Social Learning and Career Decision Making*, by A. M. Mitchell, G. B. Jones, and J. D. Krumboltz (Eds.), 1979, Cranston, RI: Carroll Press.
[d] "A Pschological Interview Process for Career Assessment," by E. B. Yost and M. A. Corbishley, 1991, *Journal of Business and Psychology*, 5, pp. 513–523.
[e] *Career Intervention*, by A. R. Spokane, 1991, Englewood Cliffs, NJ: Prentice Hall.
[f] "Career Counseling and Job Placement," by J. Salomone, in *Work and Disability: Issues and Strategies in Career Development and Job Placement*, by E. M. Szymanski and R. M. Parker (Eds.), 1996, Austin, TX: PRO-ED.
[g] *Career Counseling: Process, Issues, and Techniques*, by N. C. Gysbers, M. J. Heppner, and J. A. Johnston, 1998, Boston: Allyn & Bacon.

Fouad and Bingham

Fouad and Bingham (1995) have created a model of career counseling based on multicultural career theory that diverges from Parsons's (1909) model in both focus and structure. This model was developed to address the issues raised by Helms (1995) and Meyers, Haggins, and Speight (1994) that racial factors have not been included in the initial theoretical conceptualizations of major theories and that these theories generally reflect only one worldview. In addressing these concerns, Fouad and Bingham developed a seven-stage model of career counseling that consists of the following: (a) establish rapport/culturally appropriate relationship, (b) identify the career issue, (c) assess the impact of cultural variables, (d) set counseling goals, (e) make culturally appropriate counseling interventions, (f) make a decision, and (g) implement and follow up.

According to this model, various racial, ethnic, and cultural worldviews; identity formation and acculturation; and the interaction between worldview and the environment are important considerations throughout the process. This model differs from Parsons's (1909) in that the focus is on development and implementation, rather than assessment and choice. In addition, this model requires counselors to move out of the traditional dyadic role and consider such approaches as conducting group interventions, providing interpreters, and involving family members and/or community members (Bingham & Ward, 1996).

Brown and Brooks

Finally, another model of career counseling that differs from Parsons's (1909) framework has been created by Brown and Brooks (1991). Brown and Brooks's model adds an additional beginning stage, of assessing the client's cognitive clarity and motivation for career counseling, to the traditional career counseling process. On the basis of this assessment, the counselor will engage in one of three options. If the client possesses cognitive clarity and the motivation for career counseling is based on informational deficits or stereotypical views, then the counselor will engage in career counseling, following Parsons's model. If the client does not possess cognitive clarity but rather is assessed as having mild mental health problems (e.g., faulty decision-making style, low self-esteem, or illogical thinking) or severe mental health problems (e.g., psychosis or substance abuse), then the counselor will enlist other interventions, such as a referral for services, before engaging in career counseling. Finally, if the client possesses cognitive clarity but is motivated by external forces, such as a temporary crisis or stress, then the counselor is advised to engage in personal counseling with the client before career counseling. Brown and Brooks's model of career counseling is based on the assumptions that individuals must have previously dealt with personal problems to have attained the cognitive clarity necessary for successful career counseling and that career counseling is distinct in both process and focus from personal counseling. However, both of these assumptions are arguable (see Gysbers et al., 1998).

Having reviewed this representative sample of current career counseling approaches, we now turn to a consideration of major types of career interventions that are employed across a number of approaches.

CAREER COUNSELING INTERVENTIONS

Career counseling models, be they matching (e.g., Parsons, 1909), developmental (e.g., Gysbers et al., 1998), cognitive (e.g., Peterson et al., 1991), or integrative (e.g., Yost & Corbishley, 1987), provide a way of conceptualizing a client, his or her career problem, and how that problem can best be addressed. At the same time, in career counseling practice, a number of interventions can be applied within the framework of almost any model. Although the rationale for applying them may differ from model to model, the intervention will be essentially the same across models. Szymanski, Hershenson, Ettinger, and Enright (1996) proposed some general principles that underlie the choice of interventions. These include the following: The intervention chosen (a) is consistent with applicable codes of ethics, (b) ensures that the client learns a process that can be applied to similar career issues that may arise in the future, (c) assists the client in acquiring skills needed to cope with an unpredictable labor market and to plan for career changes in the future, and (d) is not unduly intrusive or aberrant in the work setting. Moreover, as Blustein (1992) indicated, the intervention should enhance the client's sense of control, competence in self- and environmental exploration, and range of options.

In the earlier edition of this book, Szymanski, Hershenson, Ettinger, and Enright (1996) reviewed a number of interventions that were applicable to persons both with and without disabilities. These included (a) individual career counseling, (b) career planning systems, (c) career decision-making strategies, (d) experiential interventions, and (e) the use of career portfolios. We shall now summarize, update, and expand on each of these categories.

Individual and Group Career Counseling

Herr and Cramer (1996) defined individual career counseling as "(1) a largely verbal process in which (2) a counselor and counselee(s) are in dynamic interaction and in which (3) the counselor employs a repertoire of diverse behaviors (4) to help bring about self-understanding and action in the form of 'good' decision making in the counselee, who has responsibility for his or her own actions" (p. 592). Whiston (2000) has recently summarized the research related to effective individual career counseling. Furthermore, Pope (1999) has discussed the benefits of using group career counseling for career exploration, using visual imagery, developing locally relevant occupational information, teaching career decision making, and teaching job interview skills.

A recently introduced individual approach, based on a constructionist perspective, is the narrative approach to career counseling. In Cochran's (1997) view, "We make decisions on courses of action that correspond to an implicit narrative plot that we seek to enact, rejecting those courses that violate the narrative in significant ways. . . . [A] career decision is a dramatization of one's course of life in work" (p. 11). Consequently, the aim of career counseling is to locate problems or gaps within one's career script, decide how to deal with them (e.g., fill in the gap, revise the script), and take action. In working with the client to elicit, examine, and resolve the problem, "a career counselor has a repertoire of episodes that can be selected, flexibly ordered, and coordinated"; the episodes include the following:

Elaborating a career problem
Composing a life history
Founding a future narrative
Constructing reality
Changing a life structure
Enacting a role
Crystallizing a decision (Cochran, 1997, p. 42)

Career Planning Systems

As defined by Szymanski, Hershenson, Ettinger, and Enright (1996), "Career planning systems (CPSs) are materials and processes that involve the integration of information. They address at least two of the following functions: (a) discovery of career-related information about self (e.g., interests, values), (b) provision of information about occupational alternatives, (c) relation of self-information to occupational information, (d) assistance with decision-making strategies, and (e) consideration of next steps in career planning" (pp. 259–260). Among the categories of CPSs reviewed were (a) interest inventories with accompanying planning programs, (b) career planning books, (c) general computer-assisted career information delivery systems, and (d) classes and workshops. We have removed Szymanski et al.'s fifth category, transferability of skills analysis, from this list as we believe that it merits presentation as a separate type of intervention in its own right. We have, however, added one item to the list of CPSs, career genograms.

Interest Inventories with Accompanying Planning Activities

As Szymanski, Hershenson, Ettinger, and Enright (1996) noted, a number of interest inventories have been integrated with career planning activities. For example, Holland's (1985) *Self-Directed Search* has been supplemented by a variety of information resources—for example, *The College Majors Finder* (Rosen, Holmberg, & Holland, 1994), *The Dictionary of Holland Occupational Codes* (Gottfredson & Holland, 1989), and *You and Your Career* (Holland, 1994). Other examples include the *California Occupational System*, *Ohio Vocational Interest Survey*, *Personal Career Development Profile*, and *World of Work Inventory* (Szymanski, Hershenson, Ettinger, & Enright, 1996).

Career Planning Books

The best known career planning book, *What Color Is Your Parachute?* (Bolles, 2001), which has been in print for 30 years and has been revised annually since 1975, "contains client self-assessment activities, facilitates linkages with occupational information, assists in integration of such information, and provides sources of further information or assistance. Major sections include putting things in perspective; job hunting; choosing or changing a career; [and] securing and conducting an interview successfully" (Szymanski, Hershenson, Ettinger, & Enright, 1996, p. 260). Szymanski, Hershenson, Ettinger, and Enright (1996) noted that books such as this, as well as Witt's (1992) *Job Strategies for People with Disabilities*, can help clients (in the latter case, specifically those with disabilities) make more effective use of counseling resources.

General Computer-Assisted Career Information Delivery Systems

This category of CPS was thoroughly addressed in Chapter 7.

Career Classes and Workshops

Various types of career classes and workshops (e.g., full-semester courses, brief workshops, intensive Job Club–type programs; Azrin, Besalel, Wisotzek, McMorrow, & Bechtel, 1982) have been found to be effective in improving career maturity, self-exploration, career exploration, career planning, job-hunting behaviors, job-interviewing skills, and social skills needed for job retention. These classes and workshops have been used with high school students, college students, and adults both with and without disabilities (Halasz & Kempton, 2000).

Career Genograms

A number of career counselors (e.g., Brown & Brooks, 1991; Gysbers et al., 1998; Heppner, O'Brien, Hinkelman, & Humphrey, 1994; Moon, Coleman, McCollum, Nelson, & Jensen-Scott, 1993; Okiishi, 1987; Okocha, 1998) have advocated for the use of genograms in career counseling. A career genogram is a visual representation of the occupations present in one's family history, created by the client and processed with the counselor. Genograms can be useful in clarifying family trends or expectations that have consciously or unconsciously affected one's perception and selection of occupations as appropriate for oneself. The genogram can also highlight generational shifts in occupations chosen by family members that can help clients expand their range of options or resist family pressures as to what occupational choices are deemed acceptable.

Transferable Skills Analysis

As Szymanski, Hershenson, Ettinger, and Enright (1996) noted, "An important career intervention in rehabilitation is transferability of skills analysis. This procedure uses a systematic examination of individuals' work histories, their functional limitations and capacities, and occupational and labor market information to generate potential alternatives" (p. 262). This intervention is also widely used with persons without disabilities (e.g., Bolles, 2001). Recent applications of transferable skills analysis have ranged from training medical students in information retrieval and analysis (McLachlan, 2000) to evaluating persons with traumatic brain injury for return to work (Fraser, 1997).

Career Decision-Making Interventions

Implicit in Parsons's (1909) third factor in choosing a vocation, "true reasoning" about the relations between one's self-understanding and one's knowledge about the world of work, is the process of decision making. Savickas (2000) has reviewed various measures of career decision making and concluded that each assesses different variables in the career decision-making process. These variables are difficulties in making a career choice (the *Career Decision Scale;* Osipow, Carney, Winer, Yanico, & Koschier, 1987), adaptability for mastering career development tasks (the *Career Development Inventory;* Super, Thompson, Lindeman, Jordaan, & Myers, 1981), and dispositions for vocational decision making (the *Career Maturity Inventory;* Crites, 1978). Clearly, career decision making is a complex phenomenon. Working on developing clients' decision-making skills has remained a widely used technique in career counseling from the early work of Tiedeman (1967–1969) on the Harvard–NEEDS–Newton Information System for Vocational Decisions to the present. Two of the most thoroughly elucidated approaches in current use are Krumboltz's (1979; Krumboltz & Hamel, 1977) behavioral approach to career decision making, discussed earlier under models of career counseling, and Peterson et al.'s (1991) cognitive information-processing model.

Peterson et al. (1991) posited a five-stage cycle of cognitive information-processing skills used in career decision making, to which they applied the acronym CASVE, based on the first letter of each of five sequentially employed skills. The first skill is the *communication* of signals from some external or internal problem, which identifies a gap or discontinuity between an existing state and an ideal state. This calls for *analysis* of the problem by breaking it into its causal components and their interrelationships. The next stage is *synthesis*, which involves extracting and restructuring information to create alternative ways to eliminate the gap. These alternatives are evaluated as to their likelihood of being effective and their cost–benefit ratio and, on these bases, are prioritized during the *valuing* stage. Then, during the *execution* stage, a plan to implement the alternative selected is developed and carried out. Finally, the results of carrying out that plan are evaluated by returning to the *communication* stage, where it is determined whether the initial gap has been reduced or eliminated.

In addition, over the past 30 years, several decision-making models that are driven by the person's value system have been proposed (Brown, 1996; Katz, 1966). Furthermore, Lee and Johnston (2001) have argued for the inclusion of "chance, luck, or happenstance" (p. 181) in career decision making. Finally, Gati, Fassa, and Houminer (1995) proposed a nine-step sequential elimination approach to decision making in career counseling:

1. Define and structure the decision problem
2. Identify relevant aspects
3. Rank aspects by importance
4. Identify optimal and acceptable levels
5. Eliminate occupations incompatible with preferences
6. Test sensitivity to changes in preferences
7. Collect additional information
8. Rank alternatives by overall desirability
9. Outline steps to actualize the most preferred alternative (p. 220)

This approach clearly presupposes that the process is a rational one.

Herr and Cramer (1996) indicated that in their opinion, Bergland's (1974) synthesis of the career decision-making literature is still valid. Bergland concluded that problem solving is the basic strategy for decision making and so should follow an eight-stage sequence:

1. Defining the problem
2. Generating alternatives
3. Gathering information
4. Developing information seeking skills
5. Providing useful sources of information
6. Processing information
7. Making plans and selecting goals
8. Implementing and evaluating plan (p. 352)

Another consideration in career decision-making interventions is the individual's decision-making style. Arroba (1977) proposed a taxonomy of six styles: (a) logical (objective and rational), (b) no thought (impulsive), (c) hesitant (postpone or unable to make a decision), (d) emotional (based on subjective desires), (e) compliant (based on perceived expectations of others), and (f) intuitive (based solely on a personal feeling that the alternative is right or inevitable). Several years later, Harren (1979) proposed a taxonomy of three career decision-making styles: (a) rational, (b) intuitive (emotional), and (c) dependent (denial of responsibility). Recognition of the fact that persons use different decision-making styles clearly casts doubt on the premise that career decision making is a totally rational process.

Perhaps the most sobering appraisal of the career decision-making literature is provided by Krieshok (1998), who reviewed the research on career decision making over the past 50 years and concluded that the literature substantially supports 10 propositions:

> 1. Counselors can assess decidedness, career decision-making skills, [and] career decision-making self-efficacy . . .
> 2. Individuals vary in degree of decidedness.
> 3. Career decidedness develops over time.
> 4. Gender, . . . socioeconomic status, educational attainment, and ethnicity . . . affect career decisions.
> 5. Individuals having the most difficulty with decision making often have many other difficulties.
> 6. Indecision does not always disappear once a decision is made.
> 7. Interventions increase decidedness.
> 8. The decision-making process is complex . . .
> 9. As information processors, humans err.
> 10. [People cannot accurately articulate the constructs they used in making decisions.] (pp. 211–216)

Krieshok (1998) therefore concluded that because so large a component of decision making is neither conscious nor rational, many forms of occupational information, client self-reports, and reflecting on the client's decision-making process are of questionable value in career counseling.

Perhaps the most balanced conclusion is provided by Herr and Cramer (1996):

> Although formal decision theory conceives of decision-making as (1) a process, (2) having an essentially rational base, and (3) involving the selection of a single alternative at a particular point in time (Costello & Zalkind, 1963), the influence of individual subjectivity in interpreting information about onself and about various options gives substantial credence to Hansen's (1964–1965) position that decisions are frequently more psychological than logical. Every counselor must keep the possibility of personally introduced bias in information constantly in mind, as

> clients are assisted to determine what sorts of information they need and what the acquired information means. Rather than assuming that the client will process information rationally and comprehend its full implications instead of filtering it through a personal set of incomplete or stereotyped images, the counselor must be directly involved in insuring that the client considers pertinent information with as much objectivity as is possible. (p. 197)

Experiential Interventions

Experiential interventions involve direct contact between the client and the world of work. Some examples of experiential interventions are informational interviews, job shadowing, volunteering, internships and apprenticeships, trial work experience (e.g., Blankertz & Robinson, 1996), and supported employment. These interventions encompass a large range in the degree of contact and effort required, but they all require great commitment and active involvement by the client.

Experiential interventions can be beneficial to career counseling throughout the process, to assist the client in gaining information about himself or herself and the world of work and providing opportunities to engage in decision making in a protected environment. Participating in experiential interventions provides clients with the opportunity to identify their values and interests in relation to their satisfaction with the experience, to assess their skills and abilities within the environment in which they will be applied, and to acquire new skills or hone existing ones. In addition, client successes during these interventions serve to boost clients' self-efficacy. Experiential interventions also provide clients with important information about occupations and work environments that could not be gained through passive information sources (e.g., books and Internet databases). Finally, choosing occupations and sites for these experiences provides clients with the opportunity to engage in decision making without the pressure and risk of having to choose a career.

Experiential interventions can be especially beneficial when working with clients from diverse populations. The literature suggests that individuals belonging to minority populations and persons with disabilities may have limited career-related experiences, lower than average self-efficacy or self-concept, and limited decision-making experiences (Betz & Hackett, 1981; Conte, 1983; Curnow, 1989; Hershenson & Szymanski, 1992). For persons with disabilities, experiential interventions can be used to identify and test any job accommodations that may be needed.

An example of a career intervention that combines multiple experiential components is the Youth Leadership Forum for Students with

Disabilities (YLF), sponsored by the President's Committee for the Employment of Persons with Disabilities. The YLF is a 4-day program for high school juniors and seniors that was developed by the California Governor's Committee for Employment of Disabled Persons in 1992 and is currently active in 22 states. During the program, students engage in activities that facilitate self-knowledge, efficacy, leadership skills, and decision-making skills. Through programs such as the YLF, deficits in early career exploration and decision-making opportunities that youth with disabilities typically face (Conte, 1983; Curnow, 1989) can be ameliorated to facilitate clients' career development.

Career Portfolios as Interventions

Career portfolios offer the client a technique to document, integrate, and analyze his or her entire career history and the information gathered during the career counseling process. Through creating a portfolio, clients take charge in the process of finding meaning in the information gathered, connecting learning and training to future successes, and using this information in making choices (McDivitt, 1994). Career portfolios typically include information organized in the following sections:

> (a) self-knowledge, which is fundamental to any decision making because of each individual's unique blend of interests, aptitudes, traits, backgrounds, and personal styles; (b) life roles, which highlight the cultural and social influences that have a strong impact on people's lives; (c) career development, which encourages clients to both understand their own learning needs and progress and assume responsibility for planning future experiences; and (d) career exploration planning, which explores how choices of various occupations can influence other facets of one's life. (Szymanski, Hershenson, Ettinger, & Enright, 1996, p. 264)

Information that could go into the client's career portfolio includes but is not limited to the following: assessment outcomes, career autobiographies, career genograms, academic transcripts, resumes, projects from previous jobs, career journals, job and occupational information, performance reviews, and lists of career goals. Such items provide evidence of the client's knowledge about career interests and values, training, vocational skills, work experiences, career planning resources, decision-making and planning competencies, knowledge about the labor market, job-seeking skills, and job retention and advancement skills (Koch & Johnston-Rodriguez, 1997).

Szymanski (1999) has further proposed that counselors can assist clients in developing career resilience portfolios. Career resilience portfolios differ from traditional career portfolios in that they focus specifically on helping clients organize an approach to deal with currently existing or potential job distress. Szymanski noted that the career resilience portfolio may be especially beneficial for individuals with disabilities, as disability can serve as a risk factor for job distress in the following ways: (a) People with disabilities tend to be employed in high-turnover and dead-end jobs, which are both sources of job distress; (b) negative societal attitudes and communication barriers can block social support that could mediate the negative effects of job stress for persons with disabilities; (c) the progression of functional limitations that occurs with certain disabilities can be a source of job distress; (d) job stress can compromise the immune system and cause distress for persons with disabilities; and (e) persons with certain disabilities need to expend a disproportionate amount of energy on tasks of daily living (e.g., dressing, hygiene, and transportation) that can increase job distress. As a primary intervention to mediate the potential negative effects of job distress, career resilience portfolios should include sections on (a) current work-related knowledge and skills; (b) future job goals and the knowledge, skills, and experience required for them; (c) a plan for acquiring the needed knowledge, skills, and experience; and (d) stress analysis and strain prevention.

When using a career portfolio or a career resilience portfolio, the counselor should introduce its purposes, provide instructions for creating it, and facilitate the integration of the information, but should allow the client to decide what information to include and what this information means to him or her. In addition to providing a process for clients to integrate all of the information gathered in the career counseling process, portfolios also foster personal responsibility, enhance self-esteem, assist in goal setting, allow opportunities for collaboration, and foster the development of personal qualities (McDivitt, 1994). The career portfolio should reveal information about the client's "journey through the career development process and information showing the client's progress toward reaching his or her goals" (McDivitt, 1994, p. 363). Based on information within the portfolio, the client and counselor can work together to develop plans to reach the identified career goals. Thus, portfolios increase the client's responsibility in the career counseling process, provide means for integrating all of the information gathered, and assist in developing career plans.

Having looked at a number of career counseling models and interventions, we shall next examine how these models and interventions apply to diverse populations, with particular emphasis on persons with disabilities.

APPLICATION OF CAREER COUNSELING TO DIVERSE POPULATIONS

As mentioned earlier, models of career counseling have been criticized for not being applicable to ethnic and/or racial minorities, women, persons of diverse sexual orientations, and individuals with disabilities (Arbona, 1996; Conte, 1983; Curnow, 1989; Gysbers et al., 1998; Leong, 1996; Pope, 1995; Szymanski, Hershenson, Enright, & Ettinger, 1996). According to Gysbers et al. (1998), the major models of career counseling, excluding those based on multicultural theory, are based on five tenets from White culture. These five tenets are "(a) individualism and autonomy, (b) affluence, (c) structure and opportunity open to all, (d) the centrality of work, and (e) the linearity, progressiveness, and rationality of the career development process" (Gysbers et al., 1998, pp. 33–34). These values and assumptions do not all hold true for those from cultures with different values or who have been denied access to opportunities due to systematic bias. Consequently, the potential for inadequate career counseling exists when using these five tenets in working with persons from diverse populations. The tenet of individualism and autonomy disregards the valuing of communalism, interdependency, and duty to family that exists in many non-Western cultures (e.g., Asian, African, Hispanic, and Native American cultures). As a result, the valuing of deference of choice to family members, elders, or societal good in many non-Western cultures has been pathologized in career counseling.

The tenet of affluence assumes that all individuals have the economic means to pursue whatever career they choose (Gysbers et al., 1998). This assumption of affluence is at the core of all career counseling and decision-making models that are based on matching theory. However, within the United States, more than 13% of the population lives below the poverty line, with racial and ethnic minorities, single women, and individuals with disabilities all disproportionately represented (U.S. Census Bureau, 2001). For many individuals, if not the majority, career choice based on self-actualization is a luxury that they cannot afford. Instead, more basic needs guide and limit their career paths. Likewise, in the United States, the tenet of structure and opportunity open to all is hardly applicable to the majority of the population. All of the nonmajority groups are faced with bias and discrimination in their career development (Arbona, 1996; Conte, 1983; Curnow, 1989; Gysbers et al., 1998; Leong, 1996; Szymanski, Hershenson, Enright, & Ettinger, 1996). Even within the majority White group, few enjoy the affluence that enhances one's career opportunities.

The tenet of the centrality of work is based on the Western, Protestant work ethic that is not shared by many cultural groups. In addition, research by Gilligan (1982) on the moral development of women has suggested that women's morality and decision-making process are heavily based on relationships and connectedness with others. Thus, for many women, family takes precedence over career (Lips, 1992). For many individuals with disabilities, health care needs take priority and may result in disrupting career development when the individual is faced with the possibility of losing health insurance by going to work.

Finally, the tenet of the linearity, progressiveness, and rationality of the career development process is also arguable. In fact, a whole theory of career development exists that is based on the premise that the process is neither linear, progressive, nor rational (i.e., accident theory; Cabral & Salomone, 1990). In applying his theory of work adjustment to individuals with acquired disabilities, Hershenson (1981) noted the nonlinearity of the development of work competencies, work personality, and work goals for many of these individuals. Regarding the rationality of career development, multiple authors have discussed the prevalence of intuition and other nonrational components of the career decision-making process (Cabral & Salomone, 1990; Liptak, 2001).

In addition, in our discussion of models of career counseling, we suggested that most of the current models follow the basic structure developed by Parsons (1909). Although on its surface this structure appears comprehensive and universally applicable, with its focus on the person, the workplace, and the choice process, it has been argued that this formulation is blind to the social realities and cultural values of nonmajority group members, as well as many majority group members (Arbona, 1996; Gysbers et al., 1998; Leong, 1996; Szymanski, Hershenson, Enright, & Ettinger, 1996). Furthermore, within these models of career counseling, "clients are often still cast in a dependent role, contextual factors often are still deemphasized, and the focus during the process often remains on choice to the exclusion of implementation issues" (Subich, 1996, p. 278).

One major risk of adhering to the values and assumptions underlying these matching-based models is that career counseling may contribute to the castification of nonmajority group members. The process of castification is defined as the relegating of individuals to a lesser status based on minority group membership (Szymanski & Trueba, 1994). This occurs in career counseling when group membership is used to prescribe interventions and to explain failures (Szymanski & Trueba, 1994). Examples of castification include focusing primarily on traditionally female careers with women or matching functional limitations with career options when working with individuals with disabilities. One difficult aspect of castification is that it can easily occur at a subconscious level and not be apparent to either the counselor or the client. According to Szymanski and Trueba (1994), "At least some of the difficulties faced by persons with disabilities are not the result of functional impairments related to the disability, but rather are the result of a castification process embedded in societal institutions for rehabilitation and education and enforced by well-meaning professionals" (p. 12). This is undoubtedly true for many minority group members who seek career counseling as well.

Extensive information regarding the career counseling of ethnic and racial minorities, women, and persons with diverse sexual orientation has been provided by Gysbers et al. (1998), Ponterotto et al. (1995), Pope (1995), and Savickas and Walsh (1996). In the remainder of this chapter, we shall focus on those aspects of the career counseling of persons with disabilities that are not taken into account by the models of career counseling presented earlier. We will then propose a framework for career counseling designed to be applicable to individuals from diverse backgrounds, with special attention given to persons with disabilities.

Career Counseling of Persons with Disabilities

From 1920 to 1973, federal legislation authorizing programs for the rehabilitation of persons with disabilities preceded the word *rehabilitation* with the modifier *vocational*; even today, return to work has remained the principal goal of the state–federal rehabilitation program. Moreover, return to work has always been the designated goal of insurance rehabilitation and of disability management programs in industry. Thus, the goal of both career counseling and vocational rehabilitation has been to help the client (in the former case, school leavers, immigrants, or able-bodied unemployed or disemployed persons; in the latter case, persons with disabilities) to choose and obtain an appropriate line of work (Hershenson, 1995).

Therefore, theoretically, career counseling for persons with disabilities in the rehabilitation process should not materially differ from career counseling for any other client. As Thomas and Berven (1984) observed, (a) there is greater diversity among persons with disabilities than between them and persons without disabilities, and (b) the heterogeneity of persons with disabilities precludes the possibility of a single theory common to them all. Moreover, most of the career counseling models and interventions used with nondisabled persons have been used effectively with some persons with disabilities as well. In practice, however, this premise is less than totally true, primarily because the person with a disability has undergone experiences that were not faced by the nondisabled population on whom career counseling approaches were developed. According to both Conte (1983) and Curnow (1989), these experiences include (a) limitations in early career exploratory experiences, (b) limited opportunity to develop decision-making abilities, and (c) negative self-concept resulting from societal attitudes toward persons with disabilities. It is, therefore, not surprising that many misconceptions and negative attitudes about persons with disabilities exist among professionals providing career counseling to persons with disabilities (Cook, Kunce, & Getsinger, 1976; Huitt & Elston, 1991; Schofield & Getsinger, 1971). Therefore, when engaging in career counseling with persons with disabilities, certain factors unique to this group must be taken into consideration. For example, Luzzo, Hitchings, Retish, and Shoemaker (1999) found significantly lower career decision-making self-efficacy and a more pessimistic attributional style for career decision making in college students with disabilities than in their peers without disabilities. At the same time, one must be cautious not take these considerations as a given and, in doing so, contribute to the castification process.

Earlier in this chapter, we noted how the relationship between career development and career counseling followed that of the principal characters in *A Midsummer Night's Dream*. Life further imitates art in that *A Midsummer Night's Dream* contains a play within a play. Unbeknownst to the principal characters (Demetrius, Hermia, Lysander, and Helena), a troupe of actors (Quince, Snug, Flute, Snout, etc.) is also to be found in the same enchanted forest, busily engaged in preparing a revel to celebrate the impending marriage of the principals. Similarly, the field of rehabilitation counseling, with its mandated focus on vocational rehabilitation, has developed a substantial and growing literature on the vocational behavior of persons with disabilities that is often disregarded by the principal characters in the career development drama. Thus, for example, Osipow and Fitzgerald's (1996) *Theories of Career Development* completely omits the topic of career development of persons with disabilities, although it contains chapters on the career development of women and minorities. Similarly, Savickas and Walsh's (1996) 459-page *Handbook of Career Counseling Theory and Practice* contains several chapters that focus on multicultural and gender considerations but has only three references to persons with disabilities, two of which merely acknowledge the existence of these persons as one category in a list of special populations whose needs career counseling should begin to think about addressing (as though nobody had addressed this issue in the past). Even in the enchanted career forest, it is surprising that works can lay claim to being comprehensive reviews of the career literature while failing to notice that a PsychINFO search of "career and disability" yields 139 citations. Given this omission, the field of career counseling of persons with disabilities gains less than one would hope for from the literature on career counseling of persons without disabilities.

In considering the career development of persons with disabilities, one can identify three distinct subgroups that undergo different career development processes: those with precareer onset disabilities (e.g., cerebral palsy or congenital deafness or blindness), those with midcareer onset disabilities (e.g., spinal cord injury, amputation, or adventitious deafness or blindness), and those with progressive or episodic disabilities (e.g., multiple sclerosis or bipolar disorder; Beveridge, Heller Craddock, Liesener, Stapleton, & Hershenson, 2002). The distinction among these groups relates more to the timing of the onset of the disability than the characteristics of the disability itself. Depending on the age of initial onset or diagnosis, the effects of progressive or episodic disabilities can be similar to those of precareer or midcareer disabilities. An important difference is that each significant functional change in an individual's disability has the potential to have an effect similar to that of acquiring a midcareer disability, as well as a potential cumulative effect. It is necessary to understand the effect of each episode or change in functional abilities on the individual's attitudes about both work and disability and their interaction. In addition, the counselor and the client must be particularly aware of the potential for the development of learned helplessness (Maier & Seligman, 1976). What can cause the career development of persons with disabilities to be so idiosyncratic is that career development typically follows a fairly predictable course across an individual's life (e.g., Super's [1957] five career stages), but disabilities and their progression occur much more randomly.

The INCOME Framework

The heterogeneity of people with disabilities and racial and ethnic minorities means that there can be no simple statement as to the applicability of any theory to this population (Szymanski, Hershenson, Enright, & Ettinger, 1996). Despite the theoretical and methodological problems discussed throughout this chapter, there is still a need for a conceptual framework to guide career and rehabilitation counselors in tracking and facilitating the career development of ethnic and racial minorities, women, persons with differing sexual orientation, and persons with disabilities, as well as White males. To address that need, we propose the following framework, consisting of six statuses that form the acronym INCOME: *i*magining, *in*forming, *c*hoosing, *o*btaining, *m*aintaining, and *e*xiting (Beveridge et al., 2002). INCOME is intended as neither a theory of career development nor a model of career counseling, but rather as an inclusive framework to assist career counselors in responding systematically to the great heterogeneity among those with whom they work.

The INCOME framework addresses this heterogeneity with statuses, not stages. Kohlberg (1968) defined *stages* as having the following characteristics: They unfold in an invariant sequence, describe qualitatively different patterns, refer to general properties of thought, represent hierarchical integration, and are culturally universal. This framework, instead, uses Helms's (1995) concept of statuses, which she arrived at in her study of racial identity development. In this concept, there is no necessary implication that one must achieve each status before moving on to the next one. One can skip or revisit statuses, and they may recur in any order. Moreover, a person can be in more than one status at the same time, for example, choosing a different occupation while maintaining a job in one occupation. Logically, however, the first time the individual enters each of the statuses, he or she must have gone through all of the preceding ones at least once. For example, one cannot maintain a job until one has obtained it. One may, however, have obtained several jobs before maintaining one of them.

This framework draws particularly on the work of those theorists who sought to make their models applicable to individuals from diverse groups. These include Super (1957, 1990), who, to his great credit, included a chapter titled "Disabilities in Vocational Development" in his 1957 book; Danley and Anthony's (1987) "choose–get–keep" model for psychiatric rehabilitation; and the work adjustment models of Lofquist and Dawis (1969; Dawis & Lofquist, 1984) and Hershenson (1996). Other theories intended to be applicable to diverse groups, and so drawn upon, include Maslow's (1987) hierarchy of needs, Bandura's (1986, 1997) social cognitive theory, and the career development theories based on social cognitive theory (Hackett & Betz, 1981; Krumboltz, 1979; Lent, Brown, & Hackett, 1994).

We now turn to the task of defining the six statuses of the INCOME framework.

Imagining

Imagining is the status in which the individual comes to the realization that there are occupations; that work, jobs, or careers exist; or that jobs one was formerly unaware of exist. This status has three substatuses: awareness, fantasy, and reality-based imagining. In early childhood, the immediate family has the most impact. Then children begin to learn about the world of work through the media and through school. Using the mechanism of social learning, children observe the reactions of those in their environment, and they begin to form attitudes about work and occupations. During this status, children, or adults who are revisiting this status, begin to give meaning and develop (or reassess) values about the concept of work and career.

Informing

Informing is the status in which the individual acquires information about one's self, the world of work, the opportunities that exist, and one's cultural context. This status includes both the individual's development of work competencies and the acquisition of information about the self, the world of work, and the cultural supports and barriers to connecting the two. The interaction of these learnings with the messages obtained from the environment results in the individual's career-related self-efficacy and outcome expectations.

Choosing

Choosing is the status in which the individual integrates the information from the previous statuses and selects from among the known occupations. Occupational choice reflects the interaction of the information possessed by the individual, the fit between personality and environment type, the fit between the individual's needs and the job's benefits, the individual's decision-making style, and chance. The individual's career self-efficacy and outcome expectations also influence career choice by filtering the information that the individual has incorporated about himself or herself and the world of work. According to Maslow (1987), a needs hierarchy shapes the direction of an individual's motivation. At the bottom are basic needs, such as food and shelter. Until these needs are satisfied, the individual is not motivated to seek satisfaction of higher needs.

Obtaining

In the obtaining status, the client implements his or her career decision and obtains a job in the occupation of his or her choice. The environment plays a major role in determining outcomes during this status. The economy strongly influences the availability of jobs in the current labor market for all people. The person's family, culture, and society can also be considered as environmental influences during the obtaining status.

Maintaining

The maintaining status of career development is the process of adapting to, performing, and sustaining a career. To maintain a job, the individual must adjust to the work, and the work environment must be affected by the individual. Work adjustment involves "work competencies, which consist of work habits, physical and mental skills applicable in work, and interpersonal skills applicable in the work setting" (Hershenson, 1996, p. 442).

Exiting

Exiting, defined as the process of leaving one's current vocational situation, is the sixth status of the INCOME model. Exiting encompasses not only getting fired or retiring but also voluntary departure from one's present position to enter new work settings or nonwork experiences. New work settings include those resulting from promotion as well as from job change, whereas nonwork experiences may include volunteerism. Several factors influence an individual's desire or decision to exit, including worker needs, satisfaction, and goals and conditions in the workplace. These factors, which are subject to change throughout a person's career, are influenced by environmental, psychological, and social forces.

The INCOME framework was designed to suggest career counseling interventions appropriate to each of the statuses that an individual may be in. Examples of these interventions, most of which were discussed in the second section of this chapter, are given in Table 8.2. Thus, a client in the imagining status may benefit from guided imagery, a narrative approach to individual career counseling, or career awareness training (traditionally used with elementary school students). A client in the informing status may benefit from occupational information, formal and informal training and trial work experiences, construction of a career genogram, or formal and informal assessment of abilities, interests, values, and labor market conditions. A client in the choosing status may benefit from transferable skills analysis, decision-making training, and assistance in dealing with family or peer pressures. A client in the obtaining status may benefit from job-hunting skills training, selective placement, networking, or the construction and use of a career portfolio. A client in maintaining status may benefit from follow-on support, career pathing, or performance review. A client in exiting status, depending on whether the goal is a job change or retirement, may benefit from job change or preretirement counseling and, in both cases, from retraining. A client in more than one status at the same time may benefit from a combination of interventions that address each of these statuses concurrently. This framework may be applied within any of the career counseling models reviewed earlier in this chapter. As our society enters a time of increasing diversity, it is only appropriate that career counseling intentionally develop inclusive approaches. It is our hope that using the INCOME framework will make the career counseling process more applicable to women, members of minority groups, people of diverse sexual orientation, and individuals with disabilities (be they precareer, midcareer, or episodic or progressive), as well as White males.

TABLE 8.2. Example of Interventions Applicable to Each INCOME Status

Status	Examples of Applicable Interventions	
Imagining	Career awareness training	
	Guided imagery	
	Narrative approaches	
	Mass media	
Informing	Tests and assessments	Courses
	Occupational information, including local labor market	Career genogram
	Computer programs (e.g., SIGI, DISCOVER)	Trial employment
	Informational interviews	Internships
	Volunteer experiences	Shadowing
Choosing	Decision-making models	Classes, clubs
	Transferable skills analysis	Mentoring
	Vocational training	Addressing peer pressure
	Reactions to others' careers	
Obtaining	Job search skills	Opportunity structure
	Placement	Assessing bias factors
	Advocacy	Probationary employment
	Job fairs	Skills training
	Networking	Career portfolio
Maintaining	Follow-on support	Using new skills
	Continuing education	Career pathing
	Consultation to employer	Performance review
	Job coaching	
Exiting	Job change counseling	
	Preretirement counseling	
	Retraining	

REFERENCES

Arbona, C. (1996). Career theory and practice in a multicultural context. In M. L. Savikas & W. B. Walsh (Eds.), *Handbook of careeer counseling theory and practice* (pp. 45–54). Palo Alto, CA: Davies-Black.

Arroba, T. (1977). Styles of decision-making and their use: An empirical study. *British Journal of Guidance and Counseling, 5*, 149–158.

Azrin, N. H., Besalel, V. A., Wisotzek, I., McMorrow, M., & Bechtel, R. (1982). Behavioral supervision versus informational counseling of job seeking in the Job Club. *Rehabilitation Counseling Bulletin, 25*, 212–218.

Bandura, A. (1986). *Social foundations of thought and action: A social-cognitive theory*. Englewood Cliffs, NJ: Prentice Hall.

Bandura, A. (1997). *Self-efficacy: The exercise of control*. New York: Freeman.

Bergland, B. W. (1974). Career planning: The use of sequential evaluated experience. In E. L. Herr (Ed.), *Vocational guidance and human development* (pp. 350–380). Boston: Houghton Mifflin.

Betz, N., & Hackett, G. (1981). The relationship of career-related self-efficacy expectations to perceived career options in college men and women. *Journal of Counseling Psychology, 27*, 44–62.

Beveridge, S., Heller Craddock, S., Liesener, J., Stapleton, M., & Hershenson, D. (2002). INCOME: A framework for conceptualizing the career development of persons with disabilities. *Rehabilitation Counseling Bulletin, 45*, 195–206.

Bingham, R. P., & Ward, C. M. (1996). Practical applications of career counseling with ethnic minority women. In M. L. Savikas & W. B. Walsh (Eds.), *Handbook of career counseling theory and practice* (pp. 291–313). Palo Alto, CA: Davies-Black.

Blankertz, L., & Robinson, S. (1996). Adding a vocational focus to mental health rehabilitation. *Psychiatric Services, 47*, 1216–1222.

Blustein, D. L. (1992). Applying current theory and research in career exploration to practice. *Career Development Quarterly, 41*, 174–184.

Bolles, R. N. (2001). *What color is your parachute? A practical manual for job-hunters and career-changers*. Berkeley, CA. Ten Speed Press.

Brooks, L., & Brown, D. (1986). Career counseling for adults: Implications for mental health counselors. In A. J. Palmo & W. J. Weikel (Eds.), *Foundations of mental health counseling* (pp. 95–114). Springfield, IL: Thomas.

Brown, D. (1996). Brown's values-based, holistic model of career and life-role choices and satisfaction. In D. Brown & L. Brooks (Eds.), *Career choice and development* (3rd ed., pp. 337–372). San Francisco: Jossey-Bass.

Brown, D., & Brooks, L. (1991). *Career counseling techniques*. Needham Heights, MA: Allyn & Bacon.

Cabral, A. C., & Salomone, P. R. (1990). Chance and careers: Normative versus contextual development. *Career Development Quarterly, 39*, 5–17.

Chartrand, J. M. (1996). Linking theory to practice: A sociocognitive interactional model of career counseling. In M. L. Savickas & W. B. Walsh (Eds.), *Handbook of career counseling theory and practice* (pp. 121–134). Palo Alto, CA: Davies-Black.

Cochran, L. (1997). *Career counseling: A narrative approach*. Thousand Oaks, CA: Sage.

Conte, L. E. (1983). Vocational development theories and the disabled person: Oversight or deliberate omission? *Rehabilitation Counseling Bulletin, 26*, 316–328.

Cook, D., Kunce, J., & Getsinger, S. (1976). Perceptions of the disabled and counseling effectiveness. *Rehabilitation Counseling Bulletin, 19*, 470–475.

Crites, J. O. (1978). *Career Maturity Inventory*. Boulder, CO: Crites Career Consultants.

Curnow, T. C. (1989). Vocational development of persons with disability. *Career Development Quarterly*, *37*, 269–278.

Danley, K. S., & Anthony, W. A. (1987). The choose-get-keep model: Serving severely psychiatrically disabled people. *American Rehabilitation*, *13*(4), 6–9, 27–29.

Davis, H. V. (1969). *Frank Parsons: Prophet, innovator, counselor*. Carbondale: Southern Illinois University Press.

Dawis, R. V., & Lofquist, L. H. (1984). *A psychological theory of work adjustment: An individual-differences model and its application*. Minneapolis: University of Minnesota Press.

Fouad, N. A., & Bingham, R. P. (1995). Career counseling with racial/ethnic minorities. In W. B. Walsh & S. H. Osipow (Eds.), *Handbook of vocational psychology: Theory, research, and practice* (2nd ed., pp. 331–366). Mahwah, NJ: Erlbaum.

Fraser, R. T. (1997). Vocational evaluation of clients with traumatic brain injury. *The Hatherleigh guide to vocational and career counseling: Hatherleigh Guide Service* (Vol. 9, pp. 141–159). New York: Hatherleigh.

Gati, I., Fassa, N., & Houminer, D. (1995). Applying decision theory to career counseling practice: The sequential elimination approach. *Career Development Quarterly*, *43*, 211–220.

Gilligan, C. (1982). *In a different voice*. Cambridge, MA: Harvard University Press.

Gottfredson, G. D., & Holland, J. L. (1989). *The dictionary of Holland occupational codes* (Rev. ed.). Odessa, FL: Psychological Assessment Resources.

Gysbers, N. C., Heppner, M. J., & Johnston, J. A. (1998). *Career counseling: Process, issues, and techniques*. Boston: Allyn & Bacon.

Hackett, G., & Betz, N. E. (1981). A self-efficacy approach to the career development of women. *Journal of Vocation Behavior*, *18*, 326–339.

Halasz, T. J., & Kempton, C. B. (2000). Career planning workshops and courses. In D. A. Luzzo (Ed.), *Career counseling of college students* (pp. 157–170). Washington, DC: American Psychological Association.

Harren, V. (1979). A model of career decision-making for college students. *Journal of Vocational Behavior*, *14*, 119–133.

Helms, J. E. (1995). An update of Helm's White and people of color racial identity models. In J. G. Ponterotto, J. M. Casas, L. A. Suzuki, & C. M. Alexander (Eds.), *Handbook of multicultural counseling* (pp. 181–198). Thousand Oaks, CA: Sage.

Heppner, M. J., O'Brien, K. M., Hinkelman, J. M., & Humphrey, C. F. (1994). Shifting the paradigm: The use of creativity in career counseling. *Journal of Career Development*, *21*, 77–86.

Herr, E. L. (1996). Toward a convergence of career theory and practice: Mythology, issues, and possibilities. In M. L. Savickas & W. B. Walsh (Eds.), *Handbook of career counseling theory and practice* (pp. 13–35). Palo Alto, CA: Davies-Black.

Herr, E. L. (2001). Career development and its practice: A historical perspective. *Career Development Quarterly*, *49*, 196–211.

Herr, E. L., & Cramer, S. H. (1996). *Career guidance and counseling through the life span: Systematic approaches* (5th ed.). New York: HarperCollins.

Hershenson, D. B. (1981). Work adjustment, disability, and the three r's of vocational rehabilitation: A conceptual model. *Rehabilitation Counseling Bulletin, 25,* 91–97.

Hershenson, D. B. (1995). Career counseling. In A. E. Dell Orto & R. P. Marinelli (Eds.), *Encyclopedia of disability and rehabilitation* (pp. 140–146). New York: Macmillan.

Hershenson, D. B. (1996). Work adjustment: A neglected area in career counseling. *Journal of Counseling and Development, 74,* 442–446.

Hershenson, D. B., & Szymanski, E. M. (1992). Career development of people with disabilities. In R. M. Parker & E. M. Szymanski (Eds.), *Rehabilitation counseling: Basics and beyond* (2nd ed., pp. 273–303). Austin, TX: PRO-ED.

Holland, J. L. (1985). *The Self-Directed Search professional manual.* Odessa, FL: Psychological Assessment Resources.

Holland, J. L. (1994). *You and your career.* Odessa, FL: Psychological Assessment Resources.

Huitt, K., & Elston, R. (1991). Attitudes toward persons with disabilities expressed by professional counselors. *Journal of Applied Rehabilitation Counseling, 23,* 18–22.

Issacson, L. E., & Brown, D. (1997). *Career information, career counseling, and career development* (6th ed.). Boston: Allyn & Bacon.

Katz, M. R. (1966). A model of guidance for career decision making. *Vocational Guidance Quarterly, 15,* 2–10.

Koch, L., & Johnston-Rodriguez, S. (1997). The career portfolio: A vocational rehabilitation tool for assessment, planning, and placement. *Journal of Job Placement, 13,* 19–22.

Kohlberg, L. (1968). Early education: A cognitive-developmental approach. *Child Development, 39,* 1013–1062.

Krieshok, T. S. (1998). An anti-introspectivist view of career decision making. *Career Development Quarterly, 46,* 210–229.

Krumboltz, J. D. (1979). A social learning theory of career decision making. In A. M. Mitchell, G. B. Jones, & J. D. Krumboltz (Eds.), *Social learning and career decision making* (pp. 19–49). Cranston, RI: Carroll Press.

Krumboltz, J. D., & Hamel, S. A. (1977). *Guide to career decision-making skills.* Princeton, NJ: College Entrance Examination Board.

Lee, F. K., & Johnston, J. A. (2001). Innovations in career counseling. *Journal of Career Development, 27,* 177–185.

Lent, R. W., Brown, S. D., & Hackett, G. (1994). Toward a unifying social cognitive theory of career and academic interest, choice, and performance [Monograph]. *Journal of Vocational Behavior, 45,* 79–122.

Leong, F. T. L. (1996). Challenges to career counseling: Boundaries, cultures, and complexity. In M. L. Savikas & W. B. Walsh (Eds.), *Handbook of careeer counseling theory and practice* (pp. 333–346). Palo Alto, CA: Davies-Black.

Lips, H. M. (1992). Gender and science-related attitudes as predictors of college students academic choices. *Journal of Vocational Behavior, 40,* 62–81.

Liptak, J. J. (2001). *Treatment planning in career counseling.* Stamford, CT: Brooks/Cole.

Lofquist, L. H., & Dawis, R. V. (1969). *Adjustment to work: A psychological view of man's problems in a work oriented society.* East Norwalk, CT: Appleton-Century-Crofts.

Luzzo, D. A., Hitchings, W. E., Retish, P., & Shoemaker, A. (1999). Evaluating differences in college students' career decision making on the basis of disability status. *Career Development Quarterly, 48,* 142–156.

Maier, S. F., & Seligman, M. E. (1976). Learned helplessness: Theory and evidence. *Journal of Experimental Psychology, 105,* 3–46.

Maslow, A. H. (1987). *Motivation and personality* (3rd ed.). New York: Harper & Row.

McDivitt, P. J. (1994). Using portfolios for career assessment. In J. T. Kapes & M. M. Mastie (Eds.), *A counselor's guide to career assessment instruments* (3rd ed., pp. 361–371). Alexandria, VA: National Career Development Association.

McLachlan, J. C. (2000). Case study 4: Criterion-based assessment of transferable skills—information retrieval and analysis. *Medical Education, 34,* 73–74.

Meyers, L. J., Haggins, K. L., & Speight, S. (1994). Optimal theory and career assessment: Toward an inclusive, global perspective. *Journal of Career Assessment, 2,* 289–303.

Mitchell, L. K., & Krumboltz, J. D. (1996). In Krumboltz's learning theory of career choice and counseling. In D. Brown & L. Brooks (Eds.), *Career choice and development* (3rd ed., pp. 233–280). San Fransisco: Jossey-Bass.

Mitchell, L. K., Levin, A. S., & Krumboltz, J. D. (1999). Planned happenstance: Constructing unexpected career opportunities. *Journal of Counseling and Development, 77,* 115–124.

Moon, S. M., Coleman, V. D., McCollum, E. E., Nelson, T. S., & Jensen-Scott, R. L. (1993). Using the genogram to facilitate career decisions: A case study. *Journal of Family Psychotherapy, 4,* 45–56.

Nathan, R., & Hill, L. (1992). *Career counseling.* London: Sage.

National Career Development Association (NCDA). (1991). *Position paper approved by the board of directors, Jan. 11, 1991.* Alexandria, VA: Author.

O'Hara, R. P. (1968). A theoretical foundation for the use of occupational information in guidance. *Personnel and Guidance Journal, 46,* 636–640.

Okiishi, R. W. (1987). The genogram as a tool in career counseling. *Journal of Counseling and Development, 66,* 139–143.

Okocha, A. G. (1998). Using qualitative appraisal strategies in career counseling. *Journal of Employment Counseling, 35,* 151–159.

Osipow, S. H., Carney, C. G., Winer, J., Yanico, B., & Koschier, M. (1987). *Career Decision Scale* (3rd ed.). Odessa, FL: Psychological Assessment Resources.

Osipow, S. H., & Fitzgerald, L. F. (1996). *Theories of career development* (4th ed.). Boston: Allyn & Bacon.

Parsons, F. (1909). *Choosing a vocation*. Boston: Houghton Mifflin.

Peterson, G. W., Sampson, J. P., Jr., & Reardon, R. C. (1991). *Career development and services: A cognitive approach*. Pacific Grove, CA: Brooks/Cole.

Ponterotto, J. G., Casas, J. M., Suzuki, L. A., & Alexander, C. M. (Eds.). (1995). *Handbook of multicultural counseling*. Thousand Oaks, CA: Sage.

Pope, M. (1995). Career interventions for gay and lesbian clients: A synopsis of practice knowledge and research needs. *Career Development Quarterly, 44*, 191–203.

Pope, M. (1999). Applications of group career counseling techniques in Asian cultures. *Journal of Multicultural Counseling and Development, 27*, 18–31.

Rosen, D., Holmberg, K., & Holland, J. L. (1994). *The college majors finder*. Odessa, FL: Psychological Assessment Resources.

Rounds, J. B., & Tracey, T. J. (1990). From trait-and-factor to person-environment fit counseling: Theory and process. In W. B. Walsh & S. H. Osipow (Eds.), *Career counseling: Contemporary topics in vocational psychology* (pp. 1–44). Hillsdale, NJ: Erlbaum.

Salomone, J. (1996). Career counseling and job placement: Theory and practice. In E. M. Syzmanksi & R. M. Parker (Eds.), *Work and disability: Issues and strategies in career development and job placement* (pp. 365–414). Austin, TX: PRO-ED.

Savickas, M. L. (2000). Assessing career decision making. In C. E. Watkins, Jr. & V. L. Campbell (Eds.), *Testing and assessment in counseling practice* (2nd ed., pp. 429–477). Mahwah, NJ: Erlbaum.

Savickas, M. L., & Walsh, W. B. (Eds.). (1996). *Handbook of career counseling theory and practice*. Palo Alto, CA: Davies-Black.

Schofield, L., & Getsinger, S. (1971). Client disability and counselor behavior. *Rehabilitation Counseling Bulletin, 14*, 158–165.

Spokane, A. R. (1991). *Career intervention*. Englewood Cliffs, NJ: Prentice Hall.

Subich, L. M. (1996). Addressing diversity in the process of career assessment. In M. L. Savikas & W. B. Walsh (Eds.), *Handbook of careeer counseling theory and practice* (pp. 277–289). Palo Alto, CA: Davies-Black.

Super, D. E. (1953). A theory of vocational development. *American Psychologist, 8*, 185–190.

Super, D. E. (1957). *The psychology of careers: An introduction to vocational development*. New York: Harper & Bros.

Super, D. E. (1990). A life-span, life-space approach to career development. In D. Brown & L. Brooks (Eds.), *Career choice and development: Applying contemporary theories to practice* (2nd ed., pp. 197–261). San Francisco: Jossey-Bass.

Super, D. E., Thompson, A. S., Lindeman, R. H., Jordaan, J. P., & Myers, R. A. (1981). *Career Development Inventory*. Palo Alto, CA: Consulting Psychologists Press.

Szymanski, E. M. (1999). Disability, job stress, the changing nature of careers, and the career resilience portfolio. *Rehabilitation Counseling Bulletin, 42*, 279–289.

Szymanski, E. M., Hershenson, D. B., Enright, M. S., & Ettinger, J. M. (1996). Career development theories, constructs, and research: Implications for people with disabilities. In E. M. Szymanski & R. M. Parker (Eds.), *Work and disability: Issues and strategies in career development and job placement* (pp. 79–126). Austin, TX: PRO-ED.

Szymanski, E. M., Hershenson, D. B., Ettinger, J. M., & Enright, M. S. (1996). Career development interventions for people with disabilities. In E. M. Szymanski & R. M. Parker (Eds.), *Work and disability: Issues and strategies in career development and job placement* (pp. 255–276). Austin, TX: PRO-ED.

Szymanski, E. M., & Trueba, H. (1994). Castification of people with disabilities: Potential disempowering aspects of castification in disability services. *Journal of Rehabilitation, 60,* 12–20.

Thomas, K. R., & Berven, N. L. (1984). Providing career counseling for individuals with handicapping conditions. In N. C. Gysbers (Ed.), *Designing careers: Counseling to enhance education, work and leisure* (pp. 403–432). San Francisco: Jossey-Bass.

Tiedeman, D. V. (Ed.). (1967–1969). *First and second annual and third reports, Harvard-NEEDS-Newton Information System for Vocational Decision.* Cambridge, MA: Harvard Graduate School of Education.

U.S. Census Bureau. (2001). *1990 census information.* Retrieved from www.census.gov/dmd/www/2khome

Whiston, S. C. (2000). Individual career counseling. In D. A. Luzzo (Ed.), *Career counseling of college students: An empirical guide to strategies that work* (pp. 137–156). Washington, DC: American Psychological Association.

Witt, M. A. (1992). *Job strategies for people with disabilities.* Princeton, NJ: Peterson's Guides.

Wright, W. A. (Ed.). (1936). *The complete works of William Shakespeare.* Garden City, NY: Garden City Publishing.

Yost, E. B., & Corbishley, M. A. (1987). *Career counseling: A psychological approach.* San Francisco: Jossey-Bass.

Yost, E. B., & Corbishley, M. A. (1991). A psychological interview process for career assessment. *Journal of Business and Psychology, 5,* 513–523.

The Business Perspective on Employers, Disability, and Vocational Rehabilitation

Michael J. Millington, David J. Miller, Kimberly K. Asner-Self, and Donald Linkowski

The vocational rehabilitation (VR) profession has a legislative mandate to serve society by removing the employment barriers that workers with disabilities face. Despite the best efforts of dedicated professionals, as employment statistics have consistently demonstrated, these barriers have remained in place with staggering consequences for these potential workers. In a 1999 briefing paper, the American Civil Liberties Union characterized this group as "the poorest, least employed, and least educated minority in America" (American Civil Liberties Union, 1999, p. 1). And despite the fact that a Harris poll indicated that 79% of Americans with disabilities wanted to work, less than a third of those between the ages of 16 and 64 were employed (Harris & Associates, 1994).

Complex problems have complex solutions, which is why the profession was brought into being in the first place. Clearly, no simple answer to this problem is likely to emerge. Today, practitioners and researchers alike are forced to wrestle with the disturbing possibility that the models they have embraced are oversimplified, failing to adequately address the complexity of these problems. There is a pressing need for greater comprehension, for more complex and creative solutions to the problems of VR theory and craft. Practitioners begin by examining and questioning their time-honored practices and structures. They must be open to the very real possibility that these practices and structures have concealed barriers that required their attention and may have even created barriers where none need have existed.

In this chapter, we will take up what we consider to be one such blind spot: the conception of "the employer" traditionally understood in terms of an individual, whether a CEO, a department head, a supervisor, and so on. It is a conception that has garnered explicit attention and critique in the literature (Bissonnette, 1994; Gilbride & Stensrud, 1992; Habeck, Kress, Scully, & Kirchner, 1994; Millington, Butterworth, Fesko, & McCarthy, 1998). But we propose to go further here, arguing for a conception of "the employer" in terms of a structural heuristic, a dynamic interrelation of what we will call "management functions"—functions guided by and expressing the overarching motivation of business in a market economy: maximize profit, minimize cost. Our heuristic complicates, even confounds, traditional conceptions of the employer, and this, in turn, complicates and confounds traditional conceptions of VR. But it is our position that beyond the critical self-examination lie new possibilities for VR, new opportunities for success in its mission.

It is our intention to reaffirm placement as the fundamental value, the sine qua non of the VR profession, which perhaps seems oddly conservative. However, we wish to do so with the caveat that placement—being in the proper place—is essential to continued success in the work career of the individual and that the continued success of the individual contributes to the continuing success of the business. It is a relationship in which profiting from one another has the potential of supplanting a relationship in which one profits at the expense of the other. To view placement in this way, we must abandon the notion that employment is an event—the event of being hired or of returning to work—marking the point at which the task of the VR practitioner has run its course. We may see employment instead as an ongoing interplay of individual and organization that begins before selection takes place and continues through the entire career. Within this ongoing interplay, the role of the VR practitioner is recast as a facilitator of relations rather than of individuals, serving the process of employment on the part of both parties (Millington et al., 1998). Here success is built on a solid investment in relationships and evaluated in terms of long-term gains for business and workers alike rather than on quick returns.

Yet the mutual understanding that underlies such a cooperative relationship is confused when VR practitioners fail to consider the fundamental motivations of business within a market economy. Effectiveness of practitioners is, we posit, diminished when they do not access the various management functions that express those motivations within the context of business. In what follows, we will sketch out the beginnings of a structural heuristic of management functions as they relate to human resources. We point toward these functions as the medium of business partnership and innovation, as well as the locations of hidden barriers.

MOTIVATION AND THE MARKETPLACE

Maximizing profit and minimizing cost, two sides of the same coin, constitute the fundamental motivation of business venture in a market economy (Drucker, 1982; Williams, 1959). Businesses profit, amassing wealth, by acquiring and exploiting commodities (McConnell, 1981). This is accomplished by purchasing materials, equipment, and labor power at their lowest market cost (Braverman, 1982); using these commodities to create a product by the most efficient means manageable; and selling the product at the highest market price.

Simply put, the highest market price is determined in a given market niche by demand, supply, and competition, which keep the price of a given product in flux. A market niche consists of *consumers*, a group of persons or organizations with the motivation and means to purchase a particular product. *Demand* is the perceived need for the product within a market niche. The more intense the perceived product need is, the more consumers will pay for it, proportionally increasing the profit margin. *Supply*, the relative abundance or scarcity of the product in the market niche, moderates profit margin, as does competition. High demand and low supply are profit optimal for business. But any lucrative market niche will invariably attract competitors. Market share and profit margins shrink as competitors multiply. In addition, forces further beyond the control of business complicate matters and profit, as in so-called "acts of God," the shifting winds of politics, and the capricious whims of consumers.

When taken altogether, an atmosphere of economic unpredictability is created within a given market niche and the marketplace as a whole. Business operates in this world of happenstance, surviving by fending off competition, attracting customers, and coping with change. Business investment in the marketplace is a calculated risk in which profit is the prize, bankruptcy the punishment. Often only vaguely aware, if aware of it at all, it is into this chaotic economic world that the worker enters when entering the labor force.

Business Values

In pursuing its own ends, business, in turn, serves a variety of social needs such as responding to consumer demands for products and services, providing employment opportunities for members of the community, and, in the case of many businesses, giving to charities. However, the imperative to maximize profit while minimizing cost is not a moral imperative. The profit motive offers no inherent guidelines for socially responsible practices. Good corporate citizenship may be self-imposed when it reflects the values of the business leadership, but only law and consumer demand prescribe business behavior in the profit-taking game.

Perhaps the first thing the VR practitioner needs to realize about employers is that they do not necessarily share the VR profession values regarding disability. For business, cost and profit determine the relative market value of disability. Although it may be repugnant to some, the bottom line nevertheless remains the bottom line: The worker with a disability is a seller of labor competing with all other workers. Business will seek the best worker for the least expense. In the business's storefront, citizens with disabilities are seen by business as potential consumers of goods who, like all other consumers, may inhabit a number of market niches and, like no other consumers, have a market niche uniquely their own.

Disability, Labels, and the Bottom Line

There is always profit to be extracted from workers, disability not withstanding. But communicating the value of workers with disabilities to employers is often difficult. Much of the difficulty lies in the fact that the meaning of the term *disability* is context bound, understood in a technical sense by VR practitioners but in a very different sense by business. Strictly speaking, VR practitioners cannot point to any successful client placed in competitive employment and identify him or her as a "worker with a disability." Properly accommodated, successful workers are, by definition, simply workers. Unfortunately, there has been a certain laxness in the use of the language of disability. The politically correct label ". . . with a disability" follows the person into the workplace, and he or she becomes a worker with a disability, understood by VR practitioners as shorthand for "a worker with an impairment that is a potential work disability but who, if properly accommodated, is only a worker." Although this laxness may or may not cause difficulties within the context of the VR profession, it certainly causes difficulties when contexts are crossed.

The greatest obstacle when the label crosses into the workplace is the perceived expectation of unnecessary cost associated with disability. Herein lies one of the greatest dangers of the term *disability* itself. Within the business context, the term *disability* applied to a worker refers to an ongoing event, not a characteristic. "Work disability" plays out as a "work disruption" that denotes job performance limitations and connotes decreased productivity and increased cost (Thomason, Burton, & Hyatt, 1998).

Disability as Cost

As early as 1992, work-related injury costs were estimated at $16 billion (Baldwin & Johnson, 1998), today averaging $9,992 dollars per employee in health and productivity costs (Sarkis, 2000). Muscular–skeletal problems account for the greatest percentage of work disabilities. Back pain, the most expensive, costs businesses at least 38% more on the average than other work injuries (Baldwin & Johnson, 1998). Compensation claims for work-related distress and depression have been gradually rising (Druss, Rosenheck, & Sledge, 2000), up from 10% to 25% of all claims between 1982 and 1993. Businesses contend with increasing mental health costs both directly through compensation claims and indirectly through absenteeism, decreased productivity, and potential increase in waste and accidents.

The term *disability* also conjures up business fear of litigation. It is perhaps surprising to learn that of the 595 cases filed against employers under the American with Disabilities Act (ADA, 1990) between 1992 and 1997, only 2.7% of the cases resulted in findings of discrimination on the part of the employer. In the balance of the cases, 48% found no discrimination, with the remaining cases being settled out of court. This may speak less to the issue of discrimination than to who is using the law (the majority of cases have been filed by people who were already employed and who acquired disabilities in midlife) and the way in which the law is being used. Nevertheless, the cost to employers in these cases (excluding legal expenses incurred) was in the neighborhood of $150.5 million, with $1.659 million being the largest single ADA settlement awarded (Aronson, 2000). The myth of disability litigation can be fearsome indeed.

Profit from Disability?

The most obvious connection between disability and profit is the customer with a disability. As consumers with an estimated $175 billion in discretionary income at their disposal (Heid, 2000), the disability community has begun to command the attention of many businesses (Jones, 2000), a market niche too lucrative to ignore. Far from being accommodations mandated by law, "talking" ATM machines (Ammenheuser, 2000), "accessible" photocopiers (Polk, 2000), and "electronic curb cuts" on Web sites (Zielinski, 2000) represent a new phenomenon in mainstream business. They are not accommodations in the customary sense; they are product innovations designed to make inroads into a new market niche (Cantwell, 2000; Weinstein, 2000). Civil rights are not only won in the courts; they are also won in the marketplace, where discretionary income is the measure of a niche's economic power and potential influence. Profit knows no stigma.

The relationship between disability and profit from the worker perspective is more obscure. Successful placement professionals are inclined to promote the functional capabilities of workers with disabilities and to avoid labeling whenever possible. Job applicants are instructed to disclose information concerning disability only when necessary and to do so in ways that proactively neutralize employment concerns in selection decisions. Marketing asset rather than disability is good strategy, but before we leave the issue of disability and profit, we must ask, Is there any direct employment value to the phenomenon of disability? Are there conditions under which workers may be more desirable because they have a disability? Even if we disallow tax breaks as an artificial enticement, the answer is, potentially, yes.

For businesses (and agencies) providing products to consumers with disabilities, it is possible that the consumers themselves may prefer their business contact to be a person with a disability (cf. Brearly, 1980; Nosek, Fuhrer, & Hughes, 1991). Any business seeking the consumer-with-a-disability niche may find value in the insights of workers and managers who share the disability experience. Who better to hire in product development, marketing, and sales?

Disability has added value from the perspective of social responsibility. As we have pointed out, business serves society and is often motivated to be seen as a good corporate citizen. Promoting the employment of workers with disabilities is good public relations, and it makes disability-friendly values explicit in the workplace. For instance, disability management strategies advocate these values via aggressive return-to-work programs. They communicate a positive message to all workers that, no matter where or how you acquired a disability, you remain a valued employee. The value of a positive social response to disability in the workplace is its potential for raising group morale by reducing the stigma of disability and the threat of disenfranchisement.

MANAGEMENT IN THE MARKETPLACE

Management fills the decision-making role that allows business to pursue profit through changing market conditions. Businesses trade in commodities and gather resources—managers put those resources to work making profit. There is a management role for each resource whether financial, physical, or human, regardless of the size and complexity of the organization. Each applies the same set of management functions to staff, plan, organize, control, and direct (Drucker, 1982) their resources to most efficient use. Human resource management is responsible for workforce productivity. Among the human resource responsibilities are the issues of disability in the workplace (Pransky, 2000; Schair, 2000). Thus human resource management is the organizational interface for VR professionals.

Staffing

Staffing is unique to the management of human resources. Staffing is the management of worker movement into and within the company, facilitated through selection, training and development, and support processes (Smith, 1983). This is the function most closely associated with what has become known in the VR literature as the *employer,* more correctly defined as the *employer role*. This is an important distinction that requires further explanation. The employer is not a person, per se, but a function of management. The employer is a representative of the business to whom the authority and responsibility of making employment decisions has been delegated. The employer is the CEO, owner–operator, department head, or supervisor. Each is a manager engaged in various aspects of selecting, training, and supporting workers. VR professionals may interface with any of these and call them the employer, though each has a different role to play in the management of human resources.

Employee Selection

Employers recruit, screen, and hire new workers to fill present or anticipated labor needs through the process of employee selection. Recruitment attracts a pool of potential applicants from which to choose. Recruiting strategies use various combinations of internal posting, external advertising, public events, professional recruiters, and informal word of mouth depending on the job and the target market of workers (Arthur, 1991; DeWolff, 1989). Good recruitment reaches its target market and provides enough job information to help applicants self-select (Wanous, 1980). Screening removes undesirable workers by assessing applicants in terms of negatively weighted criteria (Barron & Bishop, 1985; Granovetter, 1984) such as insufficient experience or credentials, job hopping, absenteeism, tardiness, gaps in employment history, reasons for leaving past employment, and past wage rates (Bills, 1990). Hiring ranks the remaining applicants on positively weighted criteria. Negotiating compensation concludes the hiring process.

Screening and hiring processes use interviews (Roberston, Gratton, &

Rout, 1990), biographical data review (Rothstein, Schmidt, Erwin, Owens, & Sparks, 1990), employment tests, personality assessments (Day & Silverman, 1989), and work samples (Hattrup & Schmitt, 1990) to gather decision-making information. Methods of assessment must be unbiased to be legal and must have predictive validity to be useful. Organizational research into selection methods has advanced the "point-to-point" validation theory (Asher & Sciarrino, 1974) as a unifying framework for criterion validation across selection methods (Smith & George, 1994). Literature suggests that all selection methods, properly administrated and designed, have the potential of providing predictive validity to the selection process (Smith & George, 1994).

However, researchers confront a disturbing discrepancy between academic findings and actual practice (Dakin & Armstrong, 1989). More often than not, untrained employers hire on the basis of a casual, unstructured interview. Personality tests and work samples are purchased and used with no defensible correlation with the job. Unscientific, unprofessional selection practice is devoid of real utility, needlessly expensive, and potentially litigious (Cascio & Morris, 1990; Raju, Burke, & Normand, 1990), yet they prevail.

Employee Orientation, Training, and Development

Management is responsible for the formal socialization of new workers, as well as improving their productivity and exploiting their talents in new job assignments. Orientation facilitates the new workers' arrival. The purpose of orientation is to reduce unnecessary cost (start-up, turnover, amount of supervision) and to provide a smooth transition by reducing employee anxiety and suppressing hazing activities (Bedian, 1989). Formal programs are used when large groups of employees are hired at the same time. They may include a welcome by top management, a presentation of the company's philosophy and history, a tour of the plant, and introductions to the job, supervisors, and peers.

Training develops an employee's knowledge skills and abilities for the purpose of improving present and future work performance (Bedian, 1989). Training improves productivity, increases quality, reduces waste, and minimizes accidents. Basic skills training teaches remedial language, math, and problem-solving skills as a foundation for advanced job-specific skills (Szabo, 1990). Job-specific skills are taught through on-the-job training, job rotation (Bedian, 1989), coaching (Knippen & Green, 1990), mentoring, and apprenticeship (Hanley-Maxwell & Millington, 1992). A growing disparity between the skill demands of existing jobs and the academic preparedness of new workers has increased the management investment in training (Haas, 1993).

Development links career development to the organization's plans for future HR needs by identifying, grooming, and exploiting in-house talent (Sartain & Baker, 1978). Employee self-assessment tools available through in-house career planning workshops, workbooks, or software help the motivated employee to self-select into development efforts. Employees may also seek help from contracted career counselors or begin career discussions directly with human resource management staff. Management may also employ assessment centers to select from internal recruits and maintain internal labor market information exchanges and job-matching systems through job posting, skills audits or inventories, and replacement or succession planning (Gutteridge, 1986).

Employee Support

Pressures, demands, and conflicts within the workplace (Davis, 1991) as well as problems outside the workplace can affect worker productivity. For many employers, the costs of employee selection, training, and development are high enough to make employee attrition (literally through leaving the company or figuratively through poor job performance) a serious economic concern. Support services prevent or correct employee barriers to optimal production.

Employment assistance programs (EAPs) are advanced components of human resource management systems (Roman, 1988). EAPs traditionally deal with issues of alcohol abuse but have subsumed the gamut of behavior–medical problems that cause work disruption (Roman, 1988), including psychiatric problems, family issues, and drug dependence. EAP goals include reducing absenteeism, turnover, and related costs (including morale); increasing productivity; removing management involvement in counseling; and providing due process for problematic employees. Services are usually coordinated in-house with referrals to appropriate professionals in the community.

Wellness programs were created to curb health costs (Blanchard & Tager, 1985), and they succeed where less integrated health promotion programs have failed. Wellness programs create awareness of pertinent health issues through health risk assessments of personnel and family members. Counseling, in-service, and educational materials are used to inform employees of health risks and how to avoid them. Programs are designed based on need and may include topics of physical fitness, nutritional counseling, stress management, smoking cessation, weight loss, cardiovascular fitness, blood pressure screening, prenatal care, and injury prevention.

Disability and Staffing

Staffing is the employer's gatekeeping function, and this overview reveals that there are many gates to be kept. Recruitment, screening, and hiring are the job acquisition gates. Orientation and training are the job-keeping gates. Development is the career advancement gate. Workers with disabilities may find barriers at each.

VR services must ensure that job seekers receive recruitment information that alerts them to job openings and allows them to select into applicant pools. Screening needs to be disability sensitive so as not to remove candidates with disabilities as "false positives" when accommodation removes the barrier. The full value of the accommodated worker must be expressed in hiring so employers can fairly rank the applicant.

Orientation is an opportunity for the employer not only to socialize the new worker but also to raise disability awareness among coworkers and orient them to a new experience. We ignore coworkers at the peril of the new employee, for they also have say in who is ultimately selected for the job (Channon, 1992; Schein, 1992). Inclusion in training is a prerequisite for tenure, but for workers with disabilities, inclusion alone may be insufficient (Smith, Povall, & Floyd, 1991). Where current training methods do not facilitate improved performance for workers with disabilities, alternative methods must be developed. Because of the unique challenges of disability in the workplace, managers may need to be proactive about the career development of such workers (Smith et al., 1991). Steps may need to be taken to ensure that workers with disabilities are aware of opportunities for advancement and are encouraged to compete. Gatekeeping is not a capricious activity; management is looking for added value. If workers with disabilities are not well employed in business, it may be that management lacks the vision to see the value or may lack the skill to harness it. These are organizational disabilities that the VR profession must also accommodate.

Support services deal directly with issues of work disability. Management efforts in cost containment include the prevention, accommodation, and compensation (Thomason et al., 1998) of work disability. The movement in business is toward an integrated approach to cost containment called disability management (DM). DM illustrates a dramatic change in the business approach to employee support:

> In DM, the problem of work-related injuries does not begin or end with the residual loss of function experienced by the injured worker. DM problems are systemic, defined by 'work disruptions' within the organization rather than disabilities within the individual. Work dis-

> ruptions . . . are perceived by managers as human resource problems related to the productivity of the workforce, the cost of production, and ultimately the economic health of the business. (Millington & Strauser, 1998, p. 262)

DM is an employer-directed alternative to ineffective insurance-based models. It uses interdisciplinary teams of internal (human resource) and external professionals, coordinated by a case manager, to provide proactive interventions at individual and environmental levels (Shrey & Lacerte, 1995). The VR profession contributes to the interdisciplinary team in case management, counseling, and placement activities (Berkowitz & Dean, 1998). Indeed, VR professionals sometimes fill their support role as employees of the business.

Staffing is the most critical management function to VR practitioners. If human resource management is the interface between VR services and business, then staffing defines the points of intervention. To fully appreciate the employer role (which is essential to the strategic delivery of VR services), the practitioner must understand that staffing is but one function in an indivisible system of management functions. Employers also plan, organize, control, and lead the human resource they manage.

Planning

Two considerations in this management function need to be differentiated: planning and the plan. Planning precedes all intentional activities of business, including the other management functions (Bedian, 1989). Any attempt to adapt or improve the processes or structures of business includes some level of formal planning that involves "the explicit evaluation of alternative courses of action, selection of one of the alternatives for execution, and formal communication of the decision to interested persons throughout the organization" (Emery, 1969, p. 108).

Planning starts from the top down. The goals of planning become more specific and concrete as they are operationalized through a hierarchy of subgoals. High-level planning tends to be global in its expected outcomes, more long term, and strategic (Child, 1972; Mintzberg, 1988) in implementation. These global outcomes are the synthesis of the subgoals of the next level of management down, which pertain to more specific, tactical, and time-limited goals. These goals, in turn, are further subdivided into increasingly specific goals until the planning process reaches the workers who produce and the consumers who buy the business product.

Planning may be accomplished in a variety of ways, depending on who has the authority to make plans (Vroom & Yetton, 1973), how information is used (Koopman & Pool, 1994), and how formalized and complex the planning process is (Hickson, Butler, Cray, Mallory, & Wilson, 1986). Planning can vary in terms of the centralization of planning authority, the amount and type of information gathered and used, and the level of formalization. Any combination of these qualities can describe a planning process, from the high-centralization, high-information, and high-formality approach of bureaucracies to planning as "organized chaos" (Koopman & Pool, 1994). It also is possible that one might find different planning approaches at work at different levels in the planning hierarchy.

Plans are the output of the planning process. The purpose of a formal plan is to bring about the instrumental behaviors that will lead to one or more predetermined outcomes. Each set of subgoals requires a plan to achieve them. Thus, any one plan in an organization should describe actions to be taken, quantify expected outcomes, and allow for communication and coordination across a network of plans that constitute the global strategy of the business (Emery, 1969). Standing plans dictate the day-to-day activities of an organization and are formalized in the policies, rules, regulations, and so on of the work unit. This allows management to dictate behavior to lower level management and workers economically in routine or high-volume activities. Single-use plans are implemented in nonroutine situations or when insufficient information exists to create a standing plan. A plan may be specific in its procedural instructions, leaving little room for the discretion of the worker, or it may be a simple declaration of a desired outcome, leaving the means of achieving it up to the worker.

Organizing

Managers structure and coordinate their resources to expedite plans. Managers group workers in meaningful patterns, specify worker responsibilities and authorities, and establish formal lines of communication between groups and individuals (Sartain & Baker, 1978) based on the dictates of the strategic plan of the organization (Chandler, 1981). Form attempts to follow function in organizing endeavors (Hrebiniak & Joyce, 1985). Productive efficiency is the goal, but approaches to efficient organization differ.

We may first think of organization at the unit level. There are three approaches (Jelinek, Litterer, & Miles, 1981). The hierarchical approach to organizing breaks down large tasks into smaller and smaller component parts based on similarities. The work flow approach organizes units on the basis of where they fit in the production cycle rather than similarities of jobs. Autonomous work groups create units based on the interdependency of workers needed to complete a large task. Each approach has a different logic and results in a different structure overall. The degree of hierarchical control diminishes and intrinsic motivation increases as each approach is considered in turn.

Values of the business are reflected in organizing as well. Businesses that emphasize "human relations" will create structure that builds cohesion and morale among workers. Where organizational growth is key, business will stress innovation and opportunistic readiness in a flexible organizational structure. Productivity is a basic business value incorporated into structure by planning and goal setting. Businesses that value predictability and stability tend to emphasize information management and communication (Bedian, 1994). These approaches are thematic, not mutually exclusive. Good organizing often requires a blending of values.

Organizing at its most specific is job design. There are three basic approaches to job design: specialization, time and motion, and job enrichment. Specialization breaks large and complex tasks into increasingly smaller components, creating simpler jobs with fewer tasks repeated with greater frequency. Time and motion studies increase the efficiency of task procedures and develop objective standards for performance appraisal. Together, these approaches allow management to centralize authority over planning and control functions, increase productivity efficiency and thus profitability, and create a more equitable means to compensate workers based on output (Taylor, 1911). These "scientific" management methods have been vastly popular in business, if problematic. Their approach tends to disregard the human element of productivity, and they have unintended social (e.g., worker alienation), psychological (e.g., worker dissatisfaction), and physical (e.g., repetitive motion injury) costs that threaten long-run profitability (Walker & Guest, 1952). The overspecialization of work and loss of autonomy have created monotonous jobs with little intrinsic reward. Time and motion studies have created, rather than abated, alienation of workers from management. Job enlargement and job rotation are sometimes considered as alternatives but have little impact on the basic problems of specialization. Job enrichment reverses the trends of work specialization and time–motion study by enlarging the job around a natural work cycle, increasing worker control over process, and providing new lines of communication (i.e., feedback) between employers and workers as well as workers and consumers (Bedian, 1989; Hackman & Oldham, 1976). The objective of all job design is economic efficiency in production (Jelinek et al., 1981). The challenge for business is to find balance between the science and the human in organizing.

Controlling

The control function of management serves the plan by (a) tracking and evaluating planned behavior against process and product standards (Sartain & Baker, 1978) and (b) providing the means to correct unsatisfactory behavior and reward satisfactory behavior at the group or individual level. The unit goals defined in the plan provide the basis for evaluation at each level. Goals are interpreted in terms of one or more performance indicators, and the actual unit performance is compared against these benchmarks. Control is exercised at the individual level through the use of performance appraisals. Performance appraisals are generally provided by the employee's supervisor (Drucker, 1982) and are used to make staffing decisions concerning salary, promotion, training, reassignment, retention, termination, layoffs, disciplinary actions, and so forth (Donaldson & Scannell, 1987; Hubbell, 1974).

There are five potential types of objective measures included in performance appraisals (Fisher, Schoenfeldt, & Shaw, 1999). Production measures compare quantity of output directly. This measure is most appropriate when production is repetitive, an average can be computed, and external factors do not impede the employee's ability to produce. A measure of dollar sales is most appropriate for sales jobs, of course. When comparing one salesperson to another, care must be taken to make an adjustment for the quality of the territories (e.g., rural vs. urban). Personnel data (e.g., absenteeism, reprimands, and accidents) may figure into evaluation as long as a clear relationship between personnel data and job effectiveness is identified. Performance tests using work samples or simulations are used when procedures are tightly prescribed (e.g., fighter pilots, telephone sales representatives). Managers are evaluated on business unit performance indicators such as return on equity, profit margin, and market share. When comparing manager performance, evaluations should make allowance for economic factors (Fisher et al., 1999).

Performance appraisal is subject to the same legal standards that protect workers from discrimination in employment selection. A good and safe performance appraisal is based on a job analysis and should be able to demonstrate that the content is job related, comprehensive, and free of extraneous variables. The criterion should be as objective and concise as possible. The scoring and rating processes should be standardized, universally applied, and based on direct observation.

Directing

It is not enough for a worker to have the skills to do the job if the worker is not properly motivated to be productive. The underachieving worker is a hidden cost potentially more harmful than absenteeism (Harnett, 2000) because the lack of commitment to production has a negative impact on individual and group performance. Management is challenged with shaping or directing employee behavior through motivational methods.

Business's preferred means of motivating individuals is incentive pay. Business understands its workforce as a meritocracy managed by the human resource department. Here, individuals in the workforce are compensated relative to their ranking based on performance appraisal outcomes. This is an effective way to increase motivation to an extent, but incentive pay is reduced in its effectiveness by individual differences (not all workers are motivated by money), characteristics of the organization, how workers perceive the management of incentive pay (fairness), and the human resource department's actual proficiency at implementing an incentive pay scheme.

Worker motivation has many roots. Individual differences, such as personal values, interests, and cognitive choice (Deci, 1975; Deci & Ryan, 1980), are largely beyond the direct influence of management. So employers tend to deal with "proximal" factors (Kanfer, 1994) that are more closely associated with the work behavior. Employees respond positively to fair and equitable treatment, including participation in decision making and being informed of the reasons for policy decisions (Adams, 1965; Greenberg, 1982; Kanfer, Sawyer, Earley, & Lind, 1987). Goal setting, properly matched to the situation, facilitates greater productivity (Locke, 1968; Ross, 1985; Umstot, Bell, & Mitchell, 1973). Specific (Bryan & Locke, 1967) and appropriately challenging (Campbell & Ilgen, 1976) goals direct worker attention, initiate and sustain on-task behaviors, and engage the worker in strategic development (Locke, Shaw, Saari, & Latham, 1981). Feedback sustains motivation and has the ability to increase productivity and decrease absenteeism when linked with self-management (Latham & Frayne, 1989).

Leadership is the most ephemeral of management responsibilities. It is clear that supervisor behavior has a profound impact on worker performance and satisfaction, but there is no unifying theory of leadership to explain what is obviously a very complex dynamic. Instead, a loose confederation of theories has generated a patchwork of findings that view leadership from a variety of perspectives (Fiedler & House, 1994).

Attribution theory illustrates how labels can change workers' evaluations of their supervisors (Foti, Fraser, & Lord, 1982; Mitchell, Green, &

Wood, 1981). Cognitive resource theory (Fiedler, 1986) suggests that intelligent leaders are not always the best leaders. The contingency model (Fiedler & Garcia, 1987) suggests that a match between the supervisor and types of group motivation (task motivation vs. relationship motivation) is important. Charismatic and transformational theories suggest that leaders who communicate vision and sense of mission to subordinates can positively influence worker performance and satisfaction. Path goal theory suggests that effective leaders make the personal goals of the worker contingent on productivity goals (House, 1971). Personality theories suggest that a healthy need for social power is beneficial, but a self-serving need for personal power is counterproductive (McClelland & Burnham, 1979). All of these theories have developed some level of validity and utility over time, but when considered as a group they suggest that leadership is as much art as science.

Disability and the "Other" Management Functions

The placement of workers with disabilities is based on making a match between worker abilities (with or without accommodations) and essential functions of the job. This is a necessary but incomplete conceptualization of employment. Millington et al. (1998) defined *placement* as "any professional intervention that facilitates or supplements the naturally occurring employment selection process" (p. 379) to illustrate, in part, that placement takes place in a management context and that the management (employer) role must be considered in achieving a quality match that will persist over time. VR interventions directly serve the staffing function, but the employer is also described by planning, organizing, controlling, and directing behaviors aimed at workers.

Disability may be addressed directly and indirectly in a number of locations in the standing plan. Nondiscrimination hiring policies, job descriptions based on essential job functions, and evacuation procedures for people in wheelchairs are examples of issues in need of policy. There is likely to be a wide range in the number, quality, and degree of implementation of disability-directed policies across different businesses. VR practitioners with experience in ADA compliance can be of assistance to employers in policy review.

When job accommodations are required to make a placement, the worker has engaged the organizing function of management. It is interesting to note that employers have long been concerned with the effect of job design and productivity and have been willing to rearrange jobs and job functions in a variety of ways. We begin to realize that everyone is accommodated in their jobs and that accommodation is a natural extension of an existing management function.

Performance appraisals are the employer's control mechanism. Because they are used to make employment decisions, it is imperative that workers with disabilities have access to regularly scheduled performance appraisals and that the administration and interpretation of the performance appraisals be valid for workers with disabilities. It is also through the worker's performance appraisals that the quality of VR services may be evaluated. In establishing a working relationship with employers, the use of program evaluations may be helpful for improving services and accountability to the employer.

Leadership is a matter of personal style. The best leaders foster acceptance in the workplace for workers with disabilities. There are different ways this can be accomplished at different levels of leadership. Supervisors lead for production. They set achievable goals and help create an environment where goals can be met. They lead by equitable treatment and the value of the team. Upper management can lead by making employment of workers with disabilities part of the strategic plan and the values of the organization. Among their peers in the business community, business leaders can lead by example. Having implemented plans to hire large numbers of workers with disabilities, they share their success and values with others. Having influence on their own vendors, business leaders can leverage others to do the same.

MARKETING AND MANAGEMENT

To this point, we have discussed the market context and the management structures of business. In this section, we will discuss marketing as the process that brings market and business together. Broadly speaking, marketing may be defined as any activity in the marketplace taken by an individual or organization that is instrumental to creating an exchange relationship with another individual or organization (Holloway & Hancock, 1968). Buying and selling is the exchange—maximum profitability is the goal. Marketing defines the relationship between buyers and sellers and the meaning of maximum profitability.

The idea of marketing evolved as markets became more diverse and competitive. Until the 1950s, marketing was product oriented; the function was to stimulate consumer demand for existing products. The emphases were on advertising and sales. Marketing plans favored sales campaigns. The goal of business was increased sales volume. Marketing was limited in scope and relatively separate from the other business functions.

Marketing took on new meaning in the postwar years, when markets, and babies, boomed. Businesses began shifting the focus of marketing from the product to the consumer. The emphases of marketing broadened to include research and development, engineering, and production. The goal of business became profitability through marketing. Marketing became a strategy for marshalling resources across business functions, rather than a function itself. It became a philosophy of business rather than an adjunct of sales (Webster, 1994). Marketing and innovation thus became part of the strategic plan (Drucker, 1982). Through marketing (Sandhusen, 1987), management (a) gathers, analyzes, and disseminates market-based information concerning current product status and future trends in the market, as well as an accounting of internal strengths and weaknesses that mediate the business's abilities to capitalize on those market trends; (b) identifies opportunities for the expansion of market share and threats against the stability of current market share; (c) strategically plans for the proactive and reactive exploitation of market opportunities and defense against market threats through changes in the target markets, product offers, and structure of business; and (d) administers a system of controls to measure and report the effect of marketing efforts on the established organizational goals and to adjust strategy accordingly.

The Role of Innovation

As part of the strategic business plan, marketing is change management. It demands innovation as a response to customer feedback. Innovation is any change in business designed to, at least, maintain market share and, ideally, expand it. Innovation may mean a change in target markets. Business can expand market share by increasing the market penetration of current target market, adding new target markets, or shifting marketing efforts from one target market to another.

Marketing innovations can change the "offer" the business makes to its target markets. There are four components to the offer (Sandhusen, 1987): product, product price, product place, and product promotion. Management can manipulate these qualities to improve the desirability of the offer. Product innovations create new products and improve existing ones. Price innovations change the nature of purchase by adjusting price or by creating new financing arrangements. Place innovations change the where, when, and how of product delivery to customers. Indirect and direct promotion innovations change communication strategies for attracting customers. Indirect promotion is aimed at the market niche in a general way, as in public relations events and most advertising. Direct promotion is sales aimed at a specific consumer and involves changes in the way a sale is initiated, negotiated, and closed, as well as maintaining customer satisfaction (Sandhusen, 1987). Growth strategies are based on innovations in the target markets, the offer, or both (Webster, 1994).

Marketing has spurred innovation at a structural level in management. A marketing philosophy of business asserts that "structure follows strategy" (Webster, 1994): As markets and products change based on consumer value, so should the organization pursue continuous improvement of internal structures, processes, and resources (Walton, 1988). Marketing drives business planning and organizing by altering how decisions are made. There are three types of management decisions. Operational decisions dictate the allocation of resources within the organization. Administrative decisions dictate the process and physical structure of the organization. Strategic decisions are focused on the relationship between the business and the marketplace (i.e., what products to sell and what markets to enter). Businesses without a strong marketing foundation traditionally address problems of profitability operationally by changing the allocation of resources within the organization. If this fails, they implement administrative change by altering business process and structure. As a matter of last resort, they turn to strategic methods that consult consumers in their search for profit. Market-driven management reverses the order of decision making by anchoring plans in consumer research. Administrative and operational decisions follow. Thus, the structure and processes of production are subject to change to meet the needs of consumers.

Deming (1982) was the first major proponent of a market-driven approach to management. He developed a method of strategic internal innovation built on the idea of scientific management by introducing small sample statistics to quality control. His method of continuous quality improvement was customer driven and controlled by a mutual commitment of workers and management. The Deming approach linked the structures of business to market innovation. This new market-driven management thinking has spawned other models that view systematic change as a natural organizational function, such as total quality management (George & Weimerskirch, 1994) and the concept of a learning organization (Senge, 1990).

Marketing Implications for Vocational Rehabilitation

Marketing as a concept has influenced VR practice (Corthell & Boone, 1982; Fabian, Luecking, & Tilson, 1994; Gilbride, Stensrud, & Johnson, 1994) for years, but it remains to be fully integrated into the fabric of management. This is to be expected in a bureaucratic model exemplified by state–federal VR programs. Conceiving and implementing marketing beyond a sales approach is a foreign concept to an organization that is one step removed from the profit motive. Changes in target markets for state VR services have resulted from legislation that expanded the disability niche, not from an organizational drive to expand market share. The bureaucratic offer is slow to change because there is little incentive other than new legislation and budget cuts to do so. Management structures in bureaucracies are even more resistant to change simply because they are bureaucracies.

But change is coming because the profit motive cannot be denied. There is a bottom line for VR practice. The mandate has shifted from employability to employment outcomes. This change in mandate is more than a recommitment to employment on the part of the profession; it is a call from the public for results. Society expects outcomes. The VR profession can lay claim to moderate success over the years (Berkowitz, 1988), but the overall intransigence of employment statistics feeds an atmosphere of dissatisfaction. Eventually, agencies will have to prove their worth through expanded labor market share for workers with disabilities or be replaced by new structures.

Marketing philosophy is gaining inroads into VR service and management. VR has begun to recognize the employer as a target market. The antithetical "beg–place–pray" approach to placement (Fabian et al., 1994) is dying a natural market death. Agencies are using more "employer accounts" approaches that build business relationships with VR professionals. More service innovations are possible. Consider the skills and knowledge required of the placement professional: (a) awareness of employment trends in the local market; (b) knowledge of local business, job seekers, and the law; (c) management of a caseload of job seekers and a portfolio of employers; (d) assessment of jobs, employers, organizational cultures, and job seekers; (e) training abilities in job getting and keeping behaviors; (f) motivational skills with both employers and job seekers; and (g) ability to act as a referral source for employers and job seekers. The value of these skills to employers is unquestionable, but these are raw resources yet to be put to good use in the employer context. VR management structure must be willing to reinvent itself and its offer to employers before real best practices can take hold. In short, innovation is the key to meeting the employment outcome directives of the VR profession, and market-driven management is the best means to innovation.

REFERENCES

Adams, J. S. (1965). Inequity in social exchange. In L. Berkowitz (Ed.), *Advances in experimental social psychology* (Vol. 2, pp. 267–296). New York: Academic Press.

American Civil Liberties Union. (1999, March). *Disability rights* (Briefing Paper No. 21). New York: Author.

Americans with Disabilities Act of 1990, 42 U.S.C. § 12101 *et seq.*

Ammenheuser, M. (2000). Bank sued by advice groups for the blind. *Bank Systems and Technology, 37*(8), 12.

Aronson, P. (2000). Disability settlement sets record. *National Law Journal, 23*(1), B1, B4.

Arthur, D. (1991) *Recruiting, interviewing, selecting, and orienting new employees* (2nd ed.). New York: AMACOM.

Asher, J. J., & Sciarrino, J. A. (1974). Realistic work samples: A review. *Personnel Psychology, 27*, 519–534.

Baldwin, M. L., & Johnson, W. G. (1998). Dispelling the myths about work disability. In T. Thomason & D. E. Hyatt (Eds.), *New approaches to disability in the workplace* (pp. 39–61). Ithaca, NY: ILR Press.

Barron, J., & Bishop, J. (1985). Extensive search, intensive search, hiring costs: New evidence on employer hiring activity. *Economic Inquiry, 23*, 363–382.

Bedian, A. G. (1989). *Management* (2nd ed.). New York: Dryden.

Bedian, A. G. (1994). Organization theory: Current controversies, issues, and directions. In C. L. Cooper & I. T. Robertson (Eds.), *Key reviews in managerial psychology: Concepts and research for practice* (pp. 321–353). New York: Wiley.

Berkowitz, E. (1988). The cost-benefit tradition in vocational rehabilitation. In M. Berkowitz (Ed.), *Measuring the efficiency of public programs: Costs and benefits in vocational rehabilitation* (pp. 10–28). Philadelphia: Temple University Press.

Berkowitz, M., & Dean, D. (1998). Facilitating employment through vocational rehabilitation. In T. Thomason & D. E. Hyatt (Eds.), *New approaches to disability in the workplace* (pp. 183–203). Ithaca, NY: ILR Press.

Bills, D. (1990). Employers' use of job history data for making hiring decisions: A fuller specification of job assignment and status attainment. *Sociological Quarterly, 31*, 23–35.

Bissonnette, D. (1994). *Beyond traditional job development: The art of creating opportunity*. Chatsworth, CA: Wright and Associates.

Blanchard, M., & Tager, M. J. (1985). *Working well: Managing for health and high performance*. New York: Simon & Schuster.

Brearly, G. (1980). The need for disabled counselors. *Sexuality and Disability, 3*, 212–214.

Bryan, J., & Locke, E. (1967). Goal setting as a means of increasing motivation. *Journal of Applied Psychology, 51*, 274–277.

Campbell, D., & Ilgen, D. (1976). Additive effects of task difficulty and goal setting on subsequent task performance. *Journal of Applied Psychology, 61*, 319–324.

Cantwell, J. (2000). GM will market mobility program. *Automative News, 74*(5884), 27.

Cascio, W. F., & Morris, J. R. (1990). A critical analysis of Hunter, Schmidt, and Coggin's (1988) "Problems and pitfalls in using budgeting and financial accounting techniques in assessing the utility of personnel programs." *Journal of Applied Psychology, 75*, 410–417.

Chandler A. D., Jr. (1981). Strategy and structure. In M. Jelinek, J. A. Litterer, & R. E. Miles (Eds.), *Organization by design: Theory and practice* (pp. 23–46). Plano, TX: Business Publications.

Channon, J. (1992). Creating esprit de corps. In J. Renesch (Ed.), *New traditions in business* (pp. 53–66). San Francisco: Berett-Koehler.

Child, J. (1972). Organizational structure, environment, and performance: The role of strategic choice. *Sociology*, *6*, 1–22.

Corthell, D., & Boone, L. (1982). *Marketing: An approach to placement*. Menomonie, WI: Research and Training Center, Stout Vocational Rehabilitation Institute.

Dakin, S., & Armstrong, J. S. (1989). Predicting job performance: A comparison of expert opinion and research findings. *International Journal of Forecasting*, *5*, 187–194.

Davis, T. (1991). Using psychotherapy to deal with mental health problems in organizations. *Business Horizons*, *34*, 56–67.

Day, D. V., & Silverman, S. B. (1989). Personality and job performance: Evidence of incremental validity. *Personnel Psychology*, *42*, 25–36.

Deci, E. L. (1975). *Intrinsic motivation*. New York: Plenum.

Deci, E. L., & Ryan, R. M. (1980). The empirical exploration of intrinsic motivational processes. In L. Berkowitz (Ed.), *Advances in experimental social psychology* (pp. 39–80). New York: Academic Press.

Deming, W. (1982). *Out of crisis*. Cambridge, MA: MIT Press.

DeWolff, C. (1989). The changing role of psychologists in selection. In P. Herriot (Ed.), *Assessment and selection in organizations: Methods and practice for recruitment and appraisal* (pp. 81–92). New York: Wiley.

Donaldson, L., & Scannell, E. (1987). *Human resource development: The new trainer's guide* (2nd ed.). Reading, MA: Addison-Wesley.

Drucker, P. (1982). *The practice of management*. New York: Harper & Row.

Druss, B. G., Rosenheck, R. A., & Sledge, W. H. (2000). Health and disability costs of depressive illness in a major U.S. corporation. *American Journal of Psychiatry*, *157*, 1274–1278.

Emery, J. C. (1969). *Organizational planning and control systems: Theory and technology*. London: Collier-Macmillan.

Fabian, E., Luecking, R., & Tilson, G. (1994). *A working relationship: The job development specialist's guide to successful partnerships with business*. Baltimore: Brookes.

Fiedler, F. (1986). The contribution of cognitive resources and behavior to organizational performance. *Journal of Applied Social Psychology*, *16*(6), 532–548.

Fiedler, F., & Garcia, J. E. (1987). *New approaches to effective leadership: Cognitive resources and organizational performance*. New York: Wiley.

Fiedler, F., & House, R. J. (1994). Leadership theory and research: A report of progress. In C. L. Cooper & I. T. Robertson (Eds.), *Key reviews in managerial psychology: Concepts and research for practice* (pp. 97–116). New York: Wiley.

Fisher, C. D., Schoenfeldt, L. F., & Shaw, J. B. (1999). *Human resource management* (4th ed.). New York: Houghton Mifflin.

Foti, R. J., Fraser, S. L., & Lord, R. G. (1982). Effects of leadership labels and prototypes on perceptions of political leaders. *Journal of Applied Psychology*, *67*, 326–333.

George, S., & Weimerskirch, A. (1994). *Total quality management: Strategies and techniques proven at today's most successful companies*. New York: Wiley.

Gilbride, D., & Stensrud, R. (1992). Demand-side job development: A model for the 1990s. *Journal of Rehabilitation*, *51*, 34–39.

Gilbride, D., Stensrud, R., & Johnson, M. (1994). Current models of job placement and employer development: Research, competencies, and educational considerations. *Rehabilitation Education*, *7*, 215–239.

Granovetter, M. (1984). Placement as brokerage: Information problems in the labor market for rehabilitation workers. In D. Vandergoot & J. Worral (Eds.), *Placement in rehabilitation* (pp. 83–101). Austin, TX: PRO-ED.

Greenberg, J. (1982). Approaching equity and avoiding inequity in groups and organizations. In J. Greenberg & R. L. Cohen (Eds.), *Equity and justice in social behavior* (pp. 389–436). New York: Academic Press.

Gutteridge, T. (1986). Organizational career development systems: The state of the practice. In D. T. Hall (Ed.), *Career development in organizations* (pp. 50–94). San Francisco: Jossey-Bass.

Haas, R. (1993). The corporation without boundaries. In M. Ray & A. Rinzler (Eds.), *The new paradigm in business: Emerging strategies for leadership and organizational change* (pp. 101–106). New York: Putnam.

Habeck, R., Kress, M., Scully, S., & Kirchner, K. (1994). Determining the significance of the disability management movement for rehabilitation counselor education. *Rehabilitation Education*, 8(3), 195–240.

Hackman, J. R., & Oldham, G. (1976). Motivation through the design of work: Test of a theory. *Organizational Behavior and Human Performance*, *16*, 250–279.

Hanley-Maxwell, C., & Millington, M. (1992). Enhancing independence in supported employment. *Journal of Vocational Rehabilitation*, *2*(4), 51–58.

Harnett, C. A. (2000). Disability: Learning from the other guy's mistakes. *Business and Health*, *18*(9), 25–27.

Harris, L., & Associates (1994). *N.O.D./Harris survey on employment of Americans with disabilities*. New York: Author.

Hattrup, K., & Schmitt, N. (1990). Prediction of trades apprentices' performance on job sample criteria. *Personnel Psychology*, *43*, 453–466.

Heid, J. (2000). Create a barrier-free Web site. *MacWorld*, *17*(8), 109–111.

Hickson, D. J., Butler, R. J., Cray, D., Mallory, G. R., & Wilson, D. C. (1986). *Top decisions: Strategic decision-making in organizations*. Oxford, United Kingdom: Basil Blackwell.

Holloway, R. J., & Hancock, R. S. (1968). *Marketing in a changing environment*. New York: Wiley.

House, R. J. (1971). Path-goal theory of leader effectiveness. *Administrative Science Quarterly*, *16*, 321–338.

Hrebiniak, L. G., & Joyce, W. F. (1985). Organizational adaptation: Strategic choice and environmental determinism. *Administrative Science Quarterly, 30,* 336–349.

Hubbell, R. (1974). Making a top-level performer out of your merit increase program. *Administrative Management, 35,* 45–48.

Jelinek, M., Litterer, A., & Miles, R. E. (1981). Designing jobs and organizational units. In M. Jelinek, J. A. Litterer, & R. E. Miles (Eds.), *Organization by design: Theory and practice* (pp. 325–331). Plano, TX: Business Publications.

Jones, J. (2000). Users with disabilities push high-tech limits. *InfoWorld, 22*(36), 37.

Kanfer, R. (1994). Work motivation: New directions in theory and research. In C. L. Cooper & I. T. Robertson (Eds.), *Key reviews in managerial psychology: Concepts and research for practice* (pp. 1–53). New York: Wiley.

Kanfer, R., Sawyer, J., Earley, P. C., & Lind, E. A. (1987). Fairness and participation in evaluation procedures: Effects on task attitudes and performances. *Social Justice Research, 1,* 235–249.

Knippen, J., & Green, T. (1990). Coaching. *Management Accounting, 71,* 36–38.

Koopman, P. L., & Pool, J. (1994). Decision making in organizations. In C. L. Cooper & I. T. Robertson (Eds.), *Key reviews in managerial psychology: Concepts and research for practice* (pp. 189–236). New York: Wiley.

Latham, G. P., & Frayne, C. A. (1989). Self-management for increasing job attendance: A follow-up and replication. *Journal of Applied Psychology, 74,* 411–416.

Locke, E. A. (1968). Toward a theory of task motivation and incentives. *Organizational Behavior and Human Performance, 3,* 157–189.

Locke, E. A., Shaw, K. N., Saari, L. M., & Latham, G. P. (1981). Goal setting and task performance: 1969–1980. *Psychological Bulletin,* 90, 125–152.

McClelland, D., & Burnham, D. (1979). Power is the great motivator. In *Harvard Business Review: On human relations* (pp. 341–358). New York: Harper & Row.

McConnell, C. (1981). *Economics: Principles, problems, and policies* (8th ed.). New York: McGraw-Hill.

Millington, M. J., Butterworth, J., Fesko, S. L., & McCarthy, H. (1998). The constructs and practices of job placement. In R. M. Parker & E. M. Szymanski (Eds.), *Rehabilitation counseling: Basics and beyond* (pp. 379–409). Austin, TX: PRO-ED.

Millington, M. J., & Strauser, D. R. (1998). Planning strategies in disability management. *Work, 10,* 261–270.

Mintzberg, H. (1988). Opening up the definition of strategy. In J. B. Quinn, H. Mintzberg, & R. M. James (Eds.), *The strategy process: Concepts, contexts, and cases* (pp. 13–20). London: Prentice Hall.

Mitchell, T. R., Green, S. G., & Wood, R. E. (1981). An attributional model of leadership and the poor-performing subordinate: Development and validation. In B. Shaw & L. Cummings (Eds.), *Research in organizational behavior* (p. 3). Greenwich, CT: JAI Press.

Nosek, M. A., Fuhrer, M. J., & Hughes, S. O. (1991). Perceived counselor credibility by persons with physical disability: Influence of counselor disability status, professional status, and counseling content. *Rehabilitation Psychology, 36,* 153–161.

Polk, C. (2000). Office machines everyone can use. *Government Executive, 32*(9), 85–86.

Pransky, G. (2000). Disability: From research to reality. *Human Resource Professional, 13*(4), 21–23.

Raju, N. S., Burke, M. J., & Normand, J. (1990). A new approach for utility analysis. *Journal of Applied Psychology, 75*, 3–12.

Robertson, I. T., Gratton, L., & Rout, U. (1990). The validity of situational interviews for administrative jobs. *Journal of Organisational Behavior, 11*, 69–76.

Roman, R. (1988). From employer alcoholism to employee assistance. In F. Dickman, B. Challenger, W. Emener, & W. Hutchinson (Eds.), *Employee assistance programs: A basic text* (pp. 54–84). Springfield, IL: Thomas.

Ross, C. (1985). Supervision theory: A prescription for practice. In T. Riggar & J. Lorenz (Eds.), *Readings in rehabilitation administration* (pp. 78–88). Albany: State University of New York Press.

Rothstein, H. R., Schmidt, F. L., Erwin, F. W., Owens, W. A., & Sparks, C. P. (1990). Biographical data in employment selection: Can validities be generalizable? *Journal of Applied Psychology, 75*, 175–184.

Sandhusen, R. (1987). *Marketing* (2nd ed.). Hauppauge, NY: Barrons's Educational Series.

Sarkis, K. (2000). Survey figures total health productivity costs per employees. *Occupational Hazards, 62*(6), 26.

Sartain, A., & Baker, A. (1978). *The supervisor and the job* (3rd ed.). New York: McGraw-Hill.

Schair, S. (2000). Navigating the ADA and disability maze. *HR Focus, 77*(7), 10–11.

Schein, E. (1992). *Organizational culture and leadership*. San Francisco: Jossey-Bass.

Senge, P. (1990). *The fifth discipline: The art and practice of the learning organization*. New York: Doubleday/Currency.

Shrey, D. E., & Lacerte, M. (1995). *Principles and practices of disability management in industry*. Winter Park, FL: GR Press.

Smith, B., Povall, M., & Floyd, M. (1991). *Managing disability at work: Improving practice in organizations*. London: Jessica Kingsley Publishers and the Rehabilitation Resource Centre, City University.

Smith, M., & George, D. (1994). Selection methods. In C. L. Cooper & I. T. Robertson (Eds.), *Key reviews in managerial psychology: Concepts and research for practice* (pp. 54–96). New York: Wiley.

Smith, R. (1983). The development of human resources: HRD as a growing field. *Caps Capsule, 4*, 2–5.

Szabo, J. (1990). Learning at work. *Nation's Business, 78*, 27–38.

Taylor, F. W. (1911). *The principles of scientific management*. New York: Harper.

Thomason, T., Burton, J. F., & Hyatt, D. E. (1998). Disability in the workplace. In T. Thomason & D. E. Hyatt (Eds.), *New approaches to disability in the workplace* (pp. 1–37). Ithaca, NY: ILR Press.

Umstot, D., Bell, D., & Mitchell, T. (1973). Effects of job enrichment and task goals on satisfaction and productivity: Implications for the job design. *Journal of Applied Psychology, 57*, 379–394.

Vroom, V. H., & Yetton, P. W. (1973). *Leadership and decision-making*. Pittsburgh: University of Pittsburgh Press.

Walker, C. R., & Guest, R. H. (1952). *Man on the assembly line*. Cambridge, MA: Harvard University Press.

Walton, M. (1988). *The Deming method*. New York: Putnam.

Wanous, J. P. (1980). *Organizational entry: Recruitment, selection, and socialization of newcomers*. Reading, MA: Addison-Wesley.

Webster, F. E., Jr. (1994). *Market-driven management: Using the new marketing concept to create a customer-oriented company*. New York: Wiley.

Weinstein, E. (2000). Missing captions reduced ad audience. *Wall Street Journal, 235*(113), B18.

Williams, R. (1959). *American society*. New York: Knopf.

Zielinski, D. (2000). The age of access: How technology is opening the stage to people with disabilities. *Presentations, 14*(9), 40–51.

Job Development and Job Search Assistance

David Hagner

Job development and job search assistance are at the heart of the vocational rehabilitation process. Whether carried out by rehabilitation counselors, by community rehabilitation program staff, or by individuals with disabilities or their families and friends, it is through the establishment of satisfactory employment relationships for individuals with disabilities that vocational rehabilitation fulfills its promise and draws its meaning.

This chapter will review the current state of research and theoretical work on job development and employer decision making and apply this information in assisting job seekers with disabilities to find satisfactory employment. I will briefly set the stage with an outline of the context in which labor market decisions take place. Next I will summarize recent research regarding the relationship between disability and employer hiring practices. On the basis of this foundation, I will review and critique job development methods in current use, then outline some of the elements of a sound approach to job development. Finally, issues involved in advancement beyond entry-level employment will be discussed.

LABOR MARKETS AND HIRING DECISIONS

Individuals with and without disabilities and their prospective employers attempt to match labor availability with labor needs and negotiate employment arrangements within an arena known as the labor market

(Reynolds, 1987). Employers with a need for human resources to produce goods and services constitute the demand side of the market, and workers seeking to use their skills to earn a living constitute the supply side. For each of these groups, two distinct tasks are involved: (a) scanning the environment for suitable exchange partners and then (b) deliberating about or assessing the quality of potential partnerships to arrive at a satisfactory employment arrangement. The environmental scanning and decision-making tasks of job seekers and employers are illustrated in Table 10.1.

Environmental scanning on the part of an employer might include such activities as talking with other managers about potential in-house applicants, announcing openings through want ads or job search Web sites, and hosting a booth at a job fair. Environmental scanning on the part of a prospective applicant might include checking want ads, sending letters of inquiry to employers in one's desired field, checking the college placement service bulletin board, and asking acquaintances if they know of any job leads. Once potential exchange partners are located, each party attempts to determine whether an individual opportunity is a good match of the employer's requirements with the job seeker's skills and of the workplace culture with the job seeker's social style and preferences (Wanous, 1992). Employer decision-making processes might involve reviewing resumes, interviewing, and checking references. Applicant decision-making processes might include checking the company literature or Web site, interviewing, and talking with former employees. Each party attempts to select the option that it expects will maximize benefits over costs in relation to any available alternatives.

Hiring has been called an investment in uncertainty (Bailey & Waldinger, 1991) because environmental scanning and decision making are generally based on incomplete information (Wright, 1997). Employers must predict future productivity and return on their investment in wages, benefits, orientation, training, and supervision based on a small sample of information about each applicant. Job seekers are faced with a similar difficult decision in trying to estimate in advance whether a company is a good fit and a good investment of their time and effort.

TABLE 10.1. Job Search Tasks

	Job Seeker	Employer
Environmental scanning	Job search—identifying potential employers	Recruitment—identifying potential employees
Decision making	Employer negotiation—selecting and accepting an offer from the right employer	Selection—selecting and negotiating an offer with the right employee

Neither party has the time or resources to collect all the information needed or the luxury to put off the decision until enough information is available. In addition, some of the factors themselves, such as whether a person and a job will have the right "chemistry" and make a good social fit, are extremely difficult to predict. Applicant perceptions of the culture of an organization, for example, are often highly inaccurate (Cable, Aiman-Smith, Mulvey, & Edwards, 2000).

Information is a scarce commodity, and a cost is incurred each time a new piece of information is collected. And mistakes are expensive. There is a period of orientation and socialization for a new employee (Wanous, 1992) in which the investment in a new employee exceeds the return. For example, a national sample of employers reported that it takes an average of 20 weeks for a new employee to become fully productive (Barron, Berger, & Black, 1997). The employer experiences a loss if the job does not work out. Undoing a bad hiring decision also involves the expense of the termination process itself, the cost of rehiring, and the productivity loss of the vacant position. Pfeffer (1998) has estimated the difference in costs between a firm of 5,000 employees with a 3% turnover and a firm of equal size with a 20% turnover at $50 million per year. Unsuccessful work attempts are costly for job seekers as well, in terms of lost income, reduced self-esteem, and work history gaps that can create problems in the next job search.

Looking at labor market decisions for a moment from the employer perspective, to adequately interview, test, and check references on every potential employee would be astronomically expensive. And letting a position remain unfilled would sacrifice productivity and lose income. Employers must make recruitment and selection decisions within a reasonable time frame and within manageable cost constraints. They do this by means of three labor-saving mechanisms. These mechanisms are far from perfect, but they provide the "minimum misallocation" of the labor market in the long run, given the time and resources available (Gottfries & McCormick, 1995).

Estimating from Samples and Signals

Employers use a variety of screening factors to reduce their recruitment and selection costs (Reynolds, 1987). Screening involves looking for pieces of information that serve as positive or negative signals or proxy indicators of future productivity and fit with the organization (Gottfries & McCormick, 1995; Wright, 1997). Each signal has two components: the information content (what is indicated) and the quality or reliability of the information (its source). Inferences are then drawn from these signals.

Evidence of educational attainment, for example, is valued by many employers, even when the education itself does not have much direct relevance to the job (Reynolds, 1987). Educational attainment is taken as a signal of commitment to reaching a goal and following through on a project to completion. Thus, education is an example of a signaling factor that can help "screen people in." Good eye contact and a firm handshake in the job interview are similarly important not for themselves but because they signal self-confidence and good interpersonal skills to the employer. Negative signals "screen out" applicants. For example, gaps in work history might signal problem performance or only casual commitment to labor force participation, and misspellings on a resume might signal sloppiness or verbal deficits. Employer screening based on signals or proxy indicators seems to be especially important in three types of hiring situations. First, when only a small amount of information is available about an applicant, what little there is must be combed more thoroughly for clues. Second, when there is an urgent need to fill a position, signals assume a larger importance because signals can be read quickly. Third, when a large number of applicants are interested in a position, rough "cuts" based on screening indicators reduce to a manageable number the applicants to be considered carefully.

Estimation from signals is a notoriously imperfect process. For example, many managers are not particularly skilled at employment interviewing, and a number of idiosyncratic factors are known to creep into employment decisions based on interviews. Two interviewers of the same applicant for the same position may differ (a) in their skills at eliciting information in an interview, (b) in their subjective mental "pictures" of the ideal applicant, (c) in their ability to recall and process information, and (d) in their bias toward or away from the applicant based on similarity characteristics to themselves, even when the characteristics are irrelevant to the job (Graves & Karren, 1996). Employers are aware that perfection in recruitment and selection is unattainable. A signal may be a false indicator. Someone may be a great job interviewer, for example, but display poor social skills once on the job. The aim of employers is to keep the level of error within acceptable margins at an acceptable cost.

Labor Market Intermediaries

The second help to employers are organizations and social structures that serve as labor market intermediaries (Bailey & Waldinger, 1991; Rangan, 2000). Intermediaries distill and channel information to each party. By increasing the amount of relevant information and decreasing the volume of irrelevant information each party has to sift through, they increase the chance of identifying a suitable employer–employee match. Labor market intermediaries include job training programs, vocational education systems, job services, union hiring halls, trade associations, temporary employment agencies, and others. Within large companies, human resource departments or training and development programs internal to the organization sometimes fill the same function as an intermediary.

The value of an intermediary in helping employers sort through a large quantity of information of unknown or dubious quality lies with the confidence the employer has that the intermediary service is reliable and fair. For example, employers know that resumes may exaggerate qualifications (Bachle, 1995), that a lackluster work history can be made to seem impressive by an extraordinary interview performance, and so on. The intermediary inserts into the equation its own reputation and job-matching skill. An employer might judge information filtered through the intermediary to be more reliable because of prior positive experiences or because the employer is aware of the high cost the intermediary would incur if information provided turned out to be misleading.

Personal Networking

One of the most important strategies for getting relatively accurate information in a relatively cost-effective manner is networking (Rangan, 2000). Social networks are a low-cost source of information about potential exchange partners because network connections expand from person to person in a geometrical progression and the information comes from currently successful relationships.

Consider first the employer task of scanning the environment for potential job applicants. As a simplistic example, if an employer asks each of 30 people he or she knows if they know of someone interested in a job, and each of those individuals also knows and asks 30 people, 30 times 30 or 900 people have been canvassed. At the next higher level, 900 times 30 people have been accessed. As a result, networks enable us to "be there without being there" (Rangan, 2000, p. 823). In addition, one can network at relatively little expense because social relationships are maintained in the natural course of events for other purposes.

Consider next the task of decision making about potential applicants. If we recall that information must be evaluated in relation to its reliability, the information an employer receives from a network contact tends to be regarded as more reliable than information that comes in "cold." This is because through a history of interactions, each of us has built a level of trust in our social ties with family, friends, acquaintances, school buddies, team members, and so on. That trust extends at least to some degree to trusting the referrals they might make to us (Rangan, 2000).

Networking is to a large extent responsible for the phenomenon of the "hidden job market" (Jackson, 1991) of unadvertised jobs. When a job opening can be filled quickly and reliably through word-of-mouth contacts, an employer saves considerable cost and time.

The same considerations apply to job seekers. Applicants who canvass their social networks for potential employers find that they can quickly scan a particular geographical area or career field at low cost. Networking also has a better chance of getting the applicant's "foot in the door" when a job lead is uncovered because the applicant borrows, so to speak, some of the good will and social capital accumulated between the employer and the network contact (Hoff, Gandolfo, Gold, & Jordan, 2000).

It should also be mentioned that employers differ widely in their approach to the labor market and thus in the seriousness with which they engage in employee recruitment and selection. Some industries are too volatile or their profits are too small to make much of an investment in selecting the right person, providing training, and so on. Other companies simply choose not to invest much in employees or not to value their development. For example, some firms reduce the skill level of jobs as far as possible to reduce employee replacement costs and accept and plan for a high level of employee turnover. This difference in employer orientation toward labor is largely responsible for what is sometimes called the segmentation of the labor market into a primary and a secondary sector (Hagner, 2000; Reynolds, 1987; Waddoups & Assane, 1997). We will consider this situation more fully later in connection with career advancement.

EMPLOYMENT AND DISABILITY

The employment rate for individuals with disabilities remains distressingly low, despite (a) documentation of comparable job performance for individuals with and without disabilities, (b) the efforts of the rehabilitation system, and (c) the expansive protections of federal law. For example, it has been estimated that about 70% of adults with severe disabilities are unemployed (Hale, Hayghe, & McNeil, 1998). This percentage, upsetting enough as it is, jumps far higher if one adds those who are employed not in the general labor force but in sheltered facilities.

Research suggests that the relationship between disability and hiring decisions is more complex than was once thought. It is well established that employers, in evaluating applicants, tend to hold stereotypical and usually negative attitudes toward individuals with disabilities (Nordstrom, Huffaker, & Williams, 1998). For example, in one classic study, Bordieri, Drehmer, and Comninel (1988) asked human resource personnel to rate applicants based on a review of resumes and cover letters and found that applicants with disabilities were rated more negatively than those without disabilities, even when their qualifications were identical. This same pattern continues on the job. Boyle (1997) found that successfully employed individuals with severe disabilities reported having to make serious efforts to overcome negative stereotypical assessment of their abilities, and 53% of college graduates with disabilities reported employment discrimination (Hallock, Hendricks, & Broadbent, 1998). Clearly, it is primarily the disability label and not the reality that causes most of the difficulty (Scheid, 1999).

It is also well established that employers react differently to different disabilities. Employers tend to view applicants with physical disabilities less negatively (Callahan, 1994) and those with psychiatric disabilities more negatively (Stone & Sawatzki, 1980). Employers also view disability less negatively the more it is attributed to an external cause and more negatively if it is viewed as the employee's own responsibility (Bordieri & Drehmer, 1988).

What is less clear are the explanatory mechanisms that account for these findings. One obvious interpretation, based on our brief analysis of labor market decisions, is that disability is sometimes used by employers as a negative signal, indicating a potential performance problem. Employers report that they sometimes anticipate high accommodation costs, difficulty in supervising and communicating with the employee, problem behavior or attitudes, and difficulty with coworker acceptance (Blessing & Jamieson, 1999; Lee & Newman, 1995).

Additional hypotheses have also been advanced to explain the role of stereotyping in employer decision making. According to one hypothesis, disability serves as an unusual or novel stimulus that distracts the attention of the employer away from more job-relevant features of an applicant, resulting in idiosyncratic decision making. Disability does not directly affect assessment of qualifications, on this explanation, but it causes the more relevant job-related information to be given less weight or less careful consideration. Bordieri, Drehmer, and Taricone (1990) hypothesized in their "master status" theory that disability, once noticed or disclosed, is so prominent a characteristic that it tends to dominate one's perception of an individual. A study by Wright (1997) found support for this hypothesis. Employers' ratings of applicants who simulated poor, average, and excellent job interviews varied less across applicants when the applicants had disabilities than when they did not. That is, differences in qualifications among applicants were detected readily when applicants did not have a disability but were less well attended to or given less weight when applicants had a disability.

Two other hypothesized explanatory mechanisms have been advanced to help explain the impact of disability on employer decisions. One is that disability introduces an additional level of uncertainty into the decision-making process. We have seen that employers try to predict future performance and job fit based on a sample of information about an applicant. The level of uncertainty in this process may be greater when the applicant has a disability because the employer has less experience with and feels less competent in factoring the implications of impairments and accommodations into the prediction. Decision makers tend, other things being nearly equal, to avoid a less certain alternative (Wright, 1997).

A final explanatory hypothesis is that employers seek to avoid personal discomfort and to protect themselves and other employees from (imagined or predicted) discomfort. Interviewers report more discomfort when an interviewee has a disability (Wright, 1997), and they might project this discomfort into the future when making an overall assessment of an applicant's fit with the organization. Nordstrom et al. (1998) found that greater interviewer comfort in the job interview was associated with higher applicant ratings.

It is important to recognize that these explanatory hypotheses are not mutually exclusive; they may all operate simultaneously to some degree in individual circumstances and combine with or feed on one another in such a way that the "whole discrimination" is greater than the sum of its parts. Disability also may affect the job seeker's ability to conduct an adequate job search. For example, limited flexibility in transportation or communication differences may affect the ability to conduct a job interview. Job seekers with disabilities may also need some flexibility in job methodology (Boyle, 1997) and can be disadvantaged when employers prepackage, as it were, their labor needs into job openings with a predetermined list of essential functions.

Although discrimination detrimental to applicants with disabilities is all too familiar, a few studies have suggested that under certain conditions, employers evidence a bias *in favor of* applicants with disabilities. Although limited in scope and by no means conclusive, these studies have an important bearing on job development because they may offer clues as to how to maximize these favorable conditions.

Godfrey (1995) asked employers to review applicant resumes and videotaped job interviews. Applicant resumes and interview scripts were identical, but one employer group viewed an interview in which the interviewee had an observable physical disability. The applicant with a disability received significantly higher ratings of employability. The interviewers were also asked to provide the rationale for their ratings, and it was clear that the applicant with a disability was preferred for job-related reasons rather than out of sympathy or an effort to provide a "politically correct" response.

Nordstrom et al. (1998) asked interviewers to review resumes, letters of recommendation, and videotaped interviews. The interviewers then rated the extent to which applicants were qualified for a specific job and made a salary recommendation. Applicants with disabilities whose interview responses were average or above average received higher ratings than applicants without disabilities with the same interview responses and received higher salary recommendations. As with the Godfrey (1995) study, social desirability did not appear to play a role.

Lee (1998) studied the effect of accommodation requests on the hiring decisions and salary recommendations of 133 MBA students who viewed a videotaped interview and application materials. Disability and accommodation status were varied in the videotapes. The surprising finding was that the applicant who had a disability and requested an accommodation was preferred over and given a higher salary recommendation than the applicant without a disability.

Godfrey (1995), Nordstrom et al. (1998), and Lee (1998) reached similar conclusions in their analysis of their respective study findings. Godfrey hypothesized that an "augmentation principle" was at work, in which accomplishments of an interviewee were given more weight if the interviewer believed that the interviewee had overcome significant obstacles to achieve them. Nordstrom et al. felt that the level of self-sufficiency demonstrated by the average and above-average candidates with disabilities was viewed as more impressive by the interviewers than the same level as demonstrated by the applicant with no disability. Lee also posited an "admiration factor" that led raters to give the applicant "extra points" for achievements attained in the context of living with a disability. This admiration factor apparently functioned as a positive signal.

Just as employers differ in their orientation toward their employees in general, they also differ markedly in their response to disability. Cook, Razzano, Straiton, and Ross (1994) believed that employers who have experience with disability evidence less bias. Blessing and Jamieson (1999) compared employers with and without prior experience in employing individuals with disabilities and found that employers with experience reported less concern about possible negative work behaviors. But in a study of interviewer responses to interviewees with and without disabilities, Nordstrom et al. (1998) found no significant difference between those with and without prior experience. In addition, Godfrey (1995) found that employers with a family member with a disability rated applicants with disabilities no higher than employers without this personal experience. It may be that "experience" is not fine-grained enough to serve as a discriminating variable. Future research may need to look at the type, duration, and quality of employer prior experience.

There is some evidence that larger employers are more amenable to making accommodations for disability (Callahan, 1994). Employers who make more efforts in general to invest in human resources and establish a workplace that is supportive for all employees have been noted as being more accommodating for employees with disabilities (Akabas, 1994; Scheid, 1999). Finally, in one study (Callahan, 1994), women managers were found to be more receptive than men to making reasonable accommodations for employees with disabilities.

CURRENT JOB DEVELOPMENT MODELS

Using our analysis of the labor market and employer decision making as a backdrop, we are now in a position to look at the process of job development and job search assistance for individuals with disabilities. There have been numerous approaches to understanding job development in terms of a typology of approaches or models. The simplest and earliest division of job development approaches is into *selective placement* and *client-centered placement* (Salomone, 1996). In selective placement, one or more rehabilitation agency staff members functioning as job developers (not respective of job title or whether the individual also has other duties) canvasses the labor market and solicits employers who are receptive to hiring. Job leads are then matched to consumer abilities and interests. Employer contacts may be on behalf of a particular job seeker, on behalf of consumers of an organization as a whole, or both.

In client-centered placement, job developers guide consumers through the conduct of their own job search. Job development is specific to the individual and follows logically from a career planning or career counseling process. Job search assistance seldom involves direct employer contact. Rather, it usually centers on such things as helping prepare resumes and other job search tools, assisting with the logistics of planning employer contacts and visits, preparing for interviews, and so on (Salomone, 1996).

This division of job development into two approaches has a number of inadequacies. Traditional selective placement has been criticized as disempowering to consumers by removing them to an unnecessary degree from the job development process (Dwyre & Trach, 1996). Potentially, at least, selective placement risks establishing the primary relationship not between the employer and the employee but between the employer and the placement agency. Another weakness is that some of the appeals and promises made by selective placement job developers may send negative signals to employers. For example, an employer may interpret a typical job developer statement, such as "We are a nonprofit agency providing prevocational and vocational training to people with disabilities," as a signal that an applicant's future productivity may be problematic. Once a signal has been received, it is not easily taken back.

Selective placement has also been partly blamed for steering many consumers into the most menial jobs in the economy. For example, most supported employment jobs have been developed based on selective placement, and Shafer, Banks, and Kregel (1991) found that about 87% of supported employees in a national sample worked in only two occupational fields: food service and custodial. It may be that for the business community, the placement agency comes to be associated with supplying workers for a narrow segment of the labor market.

Traditional client-centered job development has also been criticized as overly narrow but for a different reason. The client-centered approach seems to require a level of independence and skill that not all job seekers with disabilities possess. Client-centered job developers, to be sure, do not expect consumers to be totally independent in conducting a job search. But the assistance provided, such as holding frequent meetings (Salomone, 1996), is limited in scope. Not all consumers can benefit from meetings or even get to them. As a result, this approach inevitably leaves those with the most severe disabilities unemployed.

Gilbride, Stensrud, and Johnson (1994) offered a more sophisticated categorization of job development approaches. They analyzed existing job development approaches into the following types: *vocational rehabilitation counseling*, *specialized professional placement*, *contracted services*, *supported employment*, *marketing*, *team networking*, and *mentoring*. In addition, they noted that these approaches share a common emphasis on the supply side of the labor market. They offered as an alternative a new perspective they called *demand-side* job development.

There have also been empirically based attempts to understand job development approaches. Hagner and Daning (1993) conducted qualitative interviews with 49 job developers about their efforts in relation to each of 167 successful job placements over a 6-month period. They found that employer contacts leading to successful employment could be categorized into three types: (a) *agency-centered* contacts, in which the focus was on the employment agency and its services; (b) *employee-centered* contacts, in which the focus was on an individual applicant's qualifications and interest; and (c) *company-centered* contacts, in which the primary focus was on learning about the employer's business and labor needs. All three perspectives came into play at some point, but only one was primary.

Fesko and Temelini (1997) surveyed a large national sample of 369 placement professionals and 191 consumers regarding the use of 95 placement practices identified in a survey of the literature. Factor analysis of successful placements uncovered five recurring patterns of job search activity. The *generic* job development approach centered on reviewing want ads and making cold calls to employers. The *agency marketing* approach involved practices to make the agency more widely known and visible to the business community. The *individually focused* approach placed the greatest emphasis on working with a business to design and accommodate a job for a specific identified individual. The *networking* approach involved identifying businesses to contact based on canvassing the personal social networks of the staff and/or consumer. Finally, the *traditional* approach highlighted the incentives and services the agency offered to make hiring more attractive to employers.

TOWARD AN EFFECTIVE APPROACH TO JOB DEVELOPMENT

Many job development approaches work for some people some of the time, in the sense that a positive employment outcome will sometimes occur following the use of the approach. In addition, many job developers are self-taught or learn their craft on-the-job from another practicing job developer, seldom referencing research-based literature or studying the functional characteristics of the labor market. These are ideal conditions for the emergence of what we might call "superstitious" job development practices—the routine and unquestioned use of methods associated with employment success once in a while, or once upon a time, but for which no validity can be ascribed. Such practices may come to be "the way we do things here," inflexible and immune from revision.

A sophisticated job development approach certainly leaves room for factors such as the unique characteristics of the community within which the job developer is working and individual job development styles and preferences. However, given the fact that current practices are not producing as substantial a positive impact as desired on the rate of employment of individuals with disabilities, it may be important to rethink current practices and redouble our efforts to base job development on a solid foundation of theory and research.

Granovetter (1979) first pointed out that job developers and vocational rehabilitation organizations function as labor market intermediaries, or brokers. Job development connects employers and job seekers with one another. Because the primary need in the job selection process is for information—job seekers need information about employers and employers need information about job seekers—job developers are information brokers. They provide information to one or both parties that is relevant to increasing the probability of making the right employment decision. This brokerage perspective has extremely important implications for understanding job development.

As an alternative approach to prescribing one or another job development "model," it may be more productive to analyze job development strategies from the perspective of their utility in brokering the tasks of environmental scanning and decision making as they apply to job seekers and employers. From this perspective, every job development strategy either assists job seekers in scanning the environment for employers and influencing potential employer decision making, or it assists employers in scanning the environment to recruit employees and selecting the right candidate (Rangan, 2000). Table 10.2 presents some sample job development activities associated with the two parties to the exchange and the two types of tasks each faces. As is usually the case with brokerage services, the same activity often serves both parties, and so with perhaps minor change in wording, the same activity can often be placed in either the job seeker or the employer column.

Because the task in environmental scanning is to uncover as many leads as possible, the use of as many strategies as possible by as many people as possible for as much time as possible will cast the widest net. The task of decision making is different, and our review of employer hiring theory and research can generate some fairly clear implications for the types of job development strategies that will have the most impact. This information can allow us to assess individual strategies and even to develop new strategies. As one example, we have seen that employers view labor market intermediaries as trusted sources of information. One strategy implication of this is that job developers might find out who the existing trusted intermediaries are for a group of employers and enlist those intermediaries in relaying information to those employers about the services rehabilitation can offer. A survey of employers in relation to the marketing of supported employment services (Owens-Johnson & Hanley-Maxwell, 1999) reported that the information source employers most preferred to receive information from was indeed an intermediary: their trade associations. This finding is readily understandable given that employers tend to have established productive relationships with their trade associations and information from that source is viewed as reliable. We can have a fairly high degree of confidence that approaching trade associations is a sound job development strategy.

In applying research and theory to job development practice, five overall themes can be used to guide a sound approach. These themes are not job development models but rather functional elements that can be used to varying degrees and in combination across a variety of job development contexts. These themes include maximum involvement of the job seeker; attention to service identity and stigma; networking; assistance to

TABLE 10.2. Sample Job Development Services by Brokerage Customer and Job Search Task

	Job Seeker		Employer	
	Tasks	Brokerage Services	Tasks	Brokerage Services
Environmental scanning	Job search	• Assist to identify personal network connections and make contacts • Provide training and support on job search methods • Establish business contacts and a businesslike reputation within the	Recruitment	• Assess skills and interests of a pool of potential applicants • Learn employer labor needs through job analysis • Arrange informational interviews with interested individuals
Decision making	Employer negotiation	• Teach job interview skills to applicants • Analyze workplace cultures to make recommendations about social fit • Develop long-term relationships with businesses and advise applicants about good matches • Make job creation proposals that use job seeker skills and make business sense for the employer	Selection	• Arrange on-the-job evaluations to obtain accurate information about ability to perform a job • Assist in arranging and conducting job interviews • Offer consultation on employee training and support

employers in designing, carving, and creating jobs; and an empowering use of incentives and services. Individual job development strategies particularly well suited to each theme will be noted.

Maximum Involvement of the Job Seeker

A common complaint of consumers has been that service providers have exerted too much control over the employment process (Boyle, 1997). Job seekers with disabilities have been urged to increase their participation in and "ownership" of their own job development (Lavin & Everett, 1995).

Job development research supports this recommendation. We have seen that demonstrated self-sufficiency and personal accomplishment tend to be viewed favorably by employers as signals of future productivity (Godfrey, 1995; Lee, 1998; Nordstrom et al., 1998). Job developer appeals to employers on behalf of a job seeker, but without the involvement of the job seeker, are not likely to signal self-sufficiency to the employer. The individual himself or herself is in the best position to send that signal. In addition, we have seen that the more information employers have about a prospective job match, the less uncertainty they experience and the less they need to rely on signals. Job seeker participation in the job search—for example, an in-person meeting between the employer and the employee in which the employee communicates his or her assets and qualifications—helps communicate accurate and relevant information.

Normative job search practices and tools such as developing resumes, conducting informational interviews, offering letters of recommendation, and sending thank-you notes signal professionalism, competence, and accomplishment to potential employers. Consumer participation in these practices and use of these tools as the foundation for a supported job search seem highly advisable. Ryan (2000) has adapted many job search techniques for use by individuals with a range of disabilities, and numerous models and methods of job-seeking skills training (e.g., Farley & Hinman, 1988) are available. In addition to skill acquisition, job-seeking skills training and job clubs help "innoculate" trainees against setbacks and provide social support during the process (VanRyn & Vinocur, 1992).

A wide range of options are available for job seeker/job developer partnerships in each phase of the job search. For example, when an applicant is not able to conduct a sterling job interview on his or her own, interview assistance possibilities include any or all of the following: (a) detailed preinterview preparation with the interviewee, (b) preinterview preparation of the employer, (c) postinterview debriefing with the employer, (d) job developer "on-call" availability during the interview, (e) an interview with the job developer and job seeker together, or (f) an adapted job interview, such as a shorter or less formal version. In some cases, it might be determined that a job seeker would not be able to productively participate at all in a job interview. Even in these situations, the job seeker can be involved in other job search tasks, such as developing and photocopying resumes, developing a script and placing phone calls to employers, reviewing Web-based position announcements, and tracking job leads. Developing job search partnerships that suit the needs of each individual turns job seeking from something that is done to or for an individual into something that is done with an individual. Hagner, McGahie, and Cloutier (2001) provided several examples of supported job search partnerships.

Attention to Service Identity and Stigma

Attention must be paid to the spoken and unspoken signals being communicated to employers by job developers and their host organizations, which is a clear implication that job development is a brokerage service or labor market intermediary. Any business will benefit from attention to its image in the eyes of its customer base. To foster productive relationships with a job developer's business customers, a businesslike approach and presentation are critical to a positive image (Callahan & Garner, 1997). We have seen that the benefits of brokerage depend on a perception of the broker's reliability and fairness, so developing and maintaining a reputation for quality service is an important ongoing task. It is this function that agency-centered and marketing approaches emphasize.

All aspects of an organization's presence in the community should reflect a businesslike approach. Part of an organization's image, for example, is embodied in its name. Representatives of an organization customarily begin any contact with a potential new customer by stating who they are and where they are from. If an organization's name identifies it with disability or dependency, negative signals that are connected with disability labels (Nordstrom et al., 1998; Scheid, 1999) will be sent instantly to every employer with every contact. Job developers will be in the unwelcome and essentially unfair position of having to overcome these massive negative signals. Rehabilitation organizations with a name or community image that overtly references disability have tended to adopt one of three approaches. Some change their name, create a "doing business as" identity, or use an acronym alone as their name. Other organizations expand their service mission to other consumer groups. For example, some community employment organizations have begun to include a welfare-to-work component. This strategy, sometimes called "reverse mainstreaming," identifies the organization more broadly in the eyes of employers as an employment and training resource that serves a wide range of individuals. For an organization taking this approach, the common characteristic across consumers seeking employment is not disability but wanting employment assistance.

In the third approach, some disability organizations create strategic alliances with other community organizations such as community colleges, "one-stop" employment services, community centers, adult education programs, or other generic and nonstigmatizing affiliations. The alliances are structured in such a way that job development efforts are combined or shared. Hagner et al. (2001) reported on a successful employment project carried out in conjunction with two community colleges. Because project staff became adjunct instructors, when contacting employers, they referenced their affiliation as career workshop instructors at the college, a message that sent a positive signal.

The name of an organization is only one of numerous factors that can be subjected to a thorough analysis in relation to developing the community image of a job development service as an effective labor market intermediary. Ongoing feedback from the business community, such as through an employer advisory board (Hagner, Fesko, Cadigan, Kiernan, & Butterworth, 1996) or employer consortium (Balser, Hagner, & Hornby, 2000), is a valuable resource in this effort.

Networking

Rangan (2000) noted that networking is an ideal strategy in situations such as a job search, where the maximum amount of reliable information needs to be made available with limited resources. Research has shown that networking is the source of most job leads (Silliker, 1993). Of the five job development approaches identified by Fesko and Temelini (1997), the networking approach was associated with the least amount of time spent in the job search.

The primary advantage of networking for job applicants is that employers obtain initial information about them from a trusted source and thus are more likely to trust the information. This is the power of the hidden job market (Jackson, 1991).

Network-based contacts are particularly advantageous to job seekers with disabilities. They are more likely to reach employers who are not stressed by the need to fill an immediate opening or to quickly screen large numbers of competing candidates. Employers are able to learn about an individual's skills and interests and have that individual in mind as job opportunities arise. Meetings can also be personal, relaxed, and comfortable, variables that are associated with higher ratings of applicants with disabilities (Nordstrom et al., 1998).

Networking tasks include both becoming aware of one's network of social contacts and approaching network members appropriately to make a request. Job developers can offer assistance with each of these tasks. A consumer may have social ties with members of the community but need assistance in reviewing various life domains and contexts to identify them. Network analysis or network mapping can assist the consumer in becoming aware of these ties. A consumer may also benefit from assistance in initiating networking contacts. A good discussion of the networking approach to job development is available in Hoff et al. (2000).

Informational interviewing, meeting with employers to research occupations and obtain advice (Callahan & Garner, 1997; Jackson, 1991; Ryan, 2000), is a particularly powerful job development strategy because it accomplishes two objectives simultaneously. Informational interviews provide job seekers with reliable and locally relevant occupational information, and they develop network contacts with individuals who are likely to hear of job opportunities.

Because the staff and other individuals associated with a rehabilitation service are part of the individual's network, these services can play a direct role in the networking process (Hoff et al., 2000). At the individual level, creative ideas for directly accessing the personal networks of staff and affiliates of a rehabilitation service include placing a brief profile of an individual looking for a job in employee pay envelopes, offering a small prize such as a gift certificate to a local restaurant for providing a job lead, and hosting "brown bag lunches" where staff brainstorm possible employment contacts for consumers. An agency can also engage in direct networking at the organizational level. For example, an organization can become a member of local business organizations and can approach its contractors and suppliers to promote making job opportunities available to consumers.

Assisting Employers To Design, Carve, and Create Jobs

A successful employment relationship involves a good match between employer and employee. Although employers may have substantial expertise in producing and supplying their product or service, their expertise does not always extend to the specialized function of analyzing job requirements (Rothwell & Kazanas, 1994) to make the best match of candidates to positions. Thus, job analysis and job matching have been mainstay services to employers since the earliest days of vocational rehabilitation.

Performing job analyses at a company provides a job developer with accurate information about jobs that can then be used to recommend candidates when a job opportunity arises (Callahan & Garner, 1997). Thus, it increases the amount and the timeliness of accurate information available to both the applicant and the employer, reducing the expense involved in making the correct match.

But job developers can take this process further than matching an applicant to an employer's predesigned job positions. Often a job applicant is able to perform a job well, provided the employer can overcome or suspend the assumption that there is only one way to do the job (Boyle, 1997). Thus, job developers have more potential for negotiating successful job matches if they are able to consult on the design of job positions and redesign or restructure jobs when needed (Cook et al., 1994). Recombining one or more individual tasks to form a new position is sometimes known as "job-carving." Griffin (1996) offers a good discussion of job-carving strategies.

Job developers in their role as brokers can also sometimes help an employer uncover areas of labor need where creating a new position makes economic sense for the business. Opportunities to create jobs are not as rare as it might seem. In Hagner and Daning's (1993) study of job development, 27% of jobs for individuals with developmental disabilities were created; that is, there was no position open at the time of hire.

The level of depth and trust in a relationship in which an employer is open to a job creation proposal usually develops over time and as a result of repeated demonstrations of competence and value by the job developer and his or her organization (Fabian, Luecking, & Tilson, 1994). Long-term relationships also serve to develop positive employer experiences in employing individuals with disabilities. Developing positive employer experiences is a demand-side intervention because it increases the employer's willingness to seek out or be receptive to future proposals related to employing individuals with disabilities.

Empowering Use of Incentives and Services

When a rehabilitation organization is able to offer incentives or services to an employer, the timing and focus of these incentives and services require careful attention. Cook et al. (1994) recommended that job developers make a variety of incentives available to employers as part of the hiring package. Such incentives as the Work Opportunities and Disabled Access Tax Credits, on-the-job training funds, and employer recognition and human service awards are commonly used. A sample of employers surveyed by Blessing and Jamieson (1999) expressed an interest in the availability of such incentives. The potential positive impact of incentives stems from the fact that they reduce the cost or increase the benefits of hiring by the employer and thus could make a positive decision more likely.

But a study by Culver, Spencer, and Gliner (1990) found that neither wage subsidies nor tax credits contributed to job development outcomes. This finding may be for two related reasons. First, we have noted that the most significant factor to an employer is not the cost of employing a worker—workers who contribute to the organization help the employer make more money than they cost—but the cost of making a hiring mistake. Incentives are not designed to replace this cost. Second, an offer of incentives backfires if the offer sends a negative signal to an employer. An employer might become suspicious about why a proposal to hire someone qualified and able to contribute to the organization has to be accompanied by extra inducements.

Hoff et al. (2000) adopted a helpful distinction between inherent selling points and "sweeteners." They recommended that job developers should always emphasize inherent selling points, such as the experience and skills of the applicant and the reputation of the job development organization, in initial employer contacts. Then, in an appropriate context, the decision might be made to offer a particular incentive as a "sweetener" to close the deal if and when it becomes clear that there is a particular job match issue that the incentive will address.

This same reasoning applies to agency service promises, such as the promise many supported employment job developers make that "our job coach will do the training" if the employer will hire an individual. On first glance, subsidized training may appear to be a valuable service because it reduces the employer's investment. But this service promise may send a negative signal that overwhelms the intended positive impact. It may signal, for example, that the training needs of the employee are far more complex and extensive than the employer can handle or that the job developer has no awareness of the difficulty involved in an outsider fully learning the job in order to correctly teach it. Of course, it may also be an unnecessary promise, disempowering the employer from bringing internal training resources to the table and reducing the quality of the employment experience for both parties (see Chapter 11, this volume). Assistance with training is an excellent service to offer employers. The issue is the timing and scope of the offer.

This same reasoning applies to other promises, such as "we will guarantee that your production standards are met." Too heavy a blanket of promises can be self-defeating. Hagner and Daning (1993) found that the most experienced job developers offered very few services in their initial employer contacts, preferring to wait until the time was right for a discussion of the individual accommodations a particular employee under consideration might need.

In addition to offering services, job developers may also request accommodations from employers (see Chapter 6, this volume). Because employers seek to make reliable predictions and remove as much uncertainty as possible from the hiring process, it is important to provide information about accommodations to the employer that are as clear and specific as possible. Young (2000) noted that when vague references to a reasonable accommodation are made, the employer's imagination tends to run wild with speculations about costs and complications. Young recommended that when significant accommodation costs are involved, such as in providing assistive technology, job developers should consider making cost-sharing arrangements and loans available.

A service particularly valuable for helping employers and job seekers obtain accurate information about one another is the arrangement of on-the-job assessments or job tryouts. Assessments can range from a day or two to several weeks, and a wide variety of arrangements is possible (Abrams, DonAroma, & Karan, 1994). The detailed job-related information collected through an on-the-job assessment or tryout helps counter the tendency of disability to assume a "master status" and interfere with an accurate perception of consumer strengths and weaknesses. Job assessments and tryouts significantly reduce the risk to the employer and the employee of making an unwise decision without special promises. An offer to subsidize the wages of an individual during an on-the-job assessment sends a more businesslike signal to the employer than an offer of incentives.

Employers view open communication with an employment agency able to respond to concerns and offer assistance as very important (Blessing & Jamieson, 1999). This availability of consultative support can help alleviate some of the supervisor's reluctance and concerns about communication with the employee, as noted by Lee and Newman (1995), and can help increase the level of comfort on the part of an employer in interacting with employees with disabilities.

Unger (1999) noted that many employers have the resources and the willingness to provide workplace supports to their employees with disabilities, including those with significant disabilities. However, employment service staff have an indispensable role to play in helping employers identify and, in some cases, modify what is generally available so that it suits an employee's individual needs. A consulting stance empowers employers to maximize the supports they are able to offer while bringing human service expertise and supplemental supports into the picture as needed. For example, Balser, Hagner, and Hornby (2000) outlined a collaborative consulting process to assist businesses in providing job support for individuals with serious mental illness.

Approaches that build employer competence in providing employment support affect the demand side of the labor market because increasing levels of employer comfort are associated with higher estimates of applicant employability for new applicants (Nordstrom et al., 1998). But there may be an important distinction between building employer capacity through consultation on specific accommodations and a general focus on "educating employers" (Cook et al., 1994). Employer education did not contribute to placement outcomes in Culver et al.'s (1990) study. It may not be education per se but specific types of information and skill provided "just in time" to the right individuals in the workplace that are most effective.

CAREER ADVANCEMENT ISSUES

Obtaining our first job is not an end point for most of us but the beginning of a series of job experiences, job searches, and career moves. Continual fluctuations and developments in the labor market partly stimulate these changes. In addition, our interests are also constantly changing and our skills are constantly growing.

By necessity, initial jobs tend to reflect the entry positions in the world of work. For example, Walls and Fullmer (1997) found that five occupations—janitor, chef/cook, attendant, porter/cleaner, and kitchen worker—accounted for more than 20% of all competitively employed consumers at the point of closure from the state–federal vocational rehabilitation system across all disability types during a 1-year period. The authors noted that these five occupations require relatively low training and skill levels characteristic of entry-level jobs. We have also noted that about 87% of supported employees in a national survey were working in only two occupational fields: food service and custodial (Shafer et al., 1991).

Rumrill and Roessler (1999) emphasized the need to address issues of career development for individuals with disabilities beyond initial jobs and warned that if these issues are not addressed, individuals risk becoming stuck in the secondary sector of the labor market. Scheid (1999) noted several disadvantages of long-term tenure in this sector for individuals with disabilities. First, secondary sector jobs by definition pay low wages, provide few benefits, and offer poor working conditions. Second, they may result in lower self-esteem for individuals who have the capacity for growth and development but find themselves relegated to entry-level positions. Third, people who may need substantial job supports wind up with precisely those employers who demonstrate the least interest in investing in human resources and provide the fewest supports for their employees.

As careers unfold in stages over time, employees tend to seek jobs with more personal meaning, with better wages, benefits, and working conditions and with a workplace culture more suited to individual preferences. Jobs in the secondary sector have value in the early stage of a career, but after a consumer has received the benefits that these jobs provide, continued tenure in an entry-level job can restrict career development (Waddoups & Assane, 1997).

Stages of career growth unfold in the context of active ongoing participation in the labor market. Some individuals with disabilities have the skills and motivation necessary to analyze vocational experiences and institute new job searches as needed, and thus they can independently engage in this developmental process. Others have strong family or other social network ties that provide support, encouragement, and connections. Still others obtain entry jobs with larger companies or with more progressive companies, and these companies assist their employees to work their way up the career ladder and develop vocational potential. But other individuals with disabilities have none of these things and, in the absence of specific career development assistance, may eventually experience "malemployment" (Romoser, 2000) in jobs beneath their abilities.

Historically, the rehabilitation system has paid little attention to job development and job search assistance beyond stabilization in an initial job (Pumpian, Fisher, Certo, & Smalley, 1997; Rumrill & Roessler, 1999), and the currently available options for funding such assistance have serious inadequacies. Some assistance is available in the form of postemployment services or reapplication for services. Ongoing supported employment services are provided to some individuals, usually through a state-funded mental health or developmental disability service. Those eligible for Supplemental Security Income (SSI) also may be able to direct a small amount of finances to career advancement purposes under the Plan for Achieving Self-Support, a work incentive that allows individuals receiving SSI to retain benefit amounts that would normally be reduced as a result of earned income by using these funds to increase their self-sufficiency. Within the confines of this admittedly inadequate and patchwork system, every effort should be made to make available a range of career advancement services to those who need them. These services include periodic career planning, social network maintenance, further job-seeking skills and tools, promotion and job enlargement assistance, and continuing exploration and contacts.

Periodic Career Planning

Consumers may need assistance with periodically reassessing their skills, interests, and goals in relation to the changing labor market. Initial jobs may be taken for very practical reasons (Wial, 1991). For example, they may be easily available because of high turnover. The wealth of in vivo information an individual collects during the course of such a job experience can lay the foundation for a more satisfying experience in the next job. A job that is satisfying for 6 months may not be as satisfying for 6 years. Making periodic career planning assistance available to a consumer will help ensure that this aspect of career growth is not neglected.

Social Network Maintenance

Maintaining a rich network of social ties serves to enhance the quality of our lives in general, and it also has a direct impact on our career development. Through network connections, most of us have ongoing access to information about and leads to a variety of occupations to assist in our career growth (Lin & Dumin, 1986).

Employees may require ongoing or periodic assistance in developing "networking competency" (Silliker, 1993) to maintain or expand their social support network. For example, maintaining social ties sometimes requires such skills as learning people's names, remembering their birthdays, and returning favors. Similarly, adding new members to one's network takes skill. For example, a purely work-related relationship with a coworker may have the potential to turn into a work friendship. But an employee might need encouragement or guidance in such relationship-building tasks as mentioning outside interests to the coworker, inviting the individual to have lunch, and so on. Employment follow-along services that include attention to network maintenance facilitate career development.

Further Job-Seeking Skills and Tools

Paradoxically, job search skills become more important once one has a job. Initial jobs seldom require sophisticated resume preparation or job interview skills. These skills become increasingly critical as one advances out of the secondary sector into the primary sector of the labor market (Romoser, 2000).

Retention of job search skills over time cannot be assumed. Rehabilitation consumers may receive initial job-seeking skills training, but job search skills, like any infrequently used skills, may need to be refreshed and updated. Expertise in making employer contacts, interviewing, following up, and so on will improve with practice in the context of real job searches (Hagner et al., 2001). As is the case during initial job development, rehabilitation professionals can also add any necessary assistance and support during the process. It is a good practice, whether or not one is contemplating a job change, to periodically review and update resume information. Once a job lead arises, there may not be time to focus carefully on these issues.

Promotion and Job Enlargement Assistance

Initially, an entry-level job may emphasize routine operations requiring little judgment and allowing little individuality. But once a job is stable, there may be opportunities to negotiate an enlargement or enrichment of job functions. For example, an element of judgment or flexibility or a closer connection with an employee's career aspirations can be added (Hagner, 2000). Sometimes this type of job enlargement is considered a "lateral promotion." A job with an added degree of autonomy and problem solving can become a stepping-stone to a more responsible job.

Follow-along consultation with an employee can include assisting the employee in identifying and recording noteworthy work accomplishments and communicating to the supervisor a desire for more responsibility or an interest in learning new things. Follow-along consultation with an employer can include a discussion of training and employee development opportunities. Performance review by a supervisor can also be an important growth opportunity. Rehabilitation staff may need to go over a performance review with an individual to make sure the individual has a clear picture of his or her personal assets or consult with supervisors on giving regular and clear feedback to an employee (Callahan & Garner, 1997).

Continuing Exploration and Contacts

Individuals can often combine working with volunteering, joining a club or organization, pursuing a personal hobby that is connected with a career interest, exploring career options, or pursuing training toward another more meaningful career goal. This "sideline" activity can take place while an individual is employed and can form the foundation for contacts and skills that lead at some point to a job change. For example, one participant in a project reported by Hagner et al. (2001) worked as a supermarket bagger, where she picked up some Spanish words and had begun speaking in Spanish to some of the Spanish-speaking customers. Project staff helped the consumer enroll in a Spanish class, networked with a colleague to establish an e-mail "pen pal" at the University of Puerto Rico, and set up informational interviews for the consumer to explore other jobs such as community center receptionist that had a bilingual focus. Exploratory activities of all kinds increase the probability of finding out about new career opportunities (Mitchell, Levin, & Krumboltz, 1999).

For consumers receiving ongoing supported employment services, career advancement assistance provided as an added dimension to follow up for job maintenance purposes can be an efficient use of ongoing employment support staff and resources. When a job change is called for, a successfully employed applicant will generally impress a prospective employer more than an unemployed individual, facilitating job development efforts. Career advancement tends to move employees into richer workplace cultures and into companies with a greater emphasis on investing in human resources, thus introducing more possibilities for replacing staff support with workplace support (Unger, 1999). Employees whose jobs relate more closely to their personal goals and interests are also more motivated to keep their jobs and improve performance.

CONCLUSION

Assisting individuals with disabilities to access and negotiate their way through the labor market is work of extraordinary importance. The impact of this work, one way or the other, on consumer quality of life and on the effectiveness of vocational rehabilitation programs in reaching the "bottom line" cannot be overstated.

Job development is not a matter of intuition, anecdotal experience, or "just getting out there" and learning by doing. All of these sources of information are valuable, but as supplements to and enhancements of a comprehensive approach grounded in research and a solid theoretical foundation. We have taken a look at some of this research, outlined a theoretical perspective on labor market factors and hiring practices as they affect job seekers with disabilities, and noted some of the most important elements of a sound approach.

Employers follow a fairly predictable and understandable process in making employment decisions, and job seekers with disabilities have substantial contributions to make in the labor market. Thus, a brokerage service has abundant opportunities to improve the chances that individuals with disabilities are hired. A great deal more can be learned about the hiring process and the relationship between specific practices and employment outcomes, and thus job development should remain a major ongoing theme in rehabilitation research.

But the more significant issue is that many of the services and practices in popular use ignore well-understood and well-established information about employer decision making. They work, but not well. They relegate far too many people to unemployment, underemployment, and malemployment. In some cases, they function not as services at all but as additional barriers to quality outcomes for individuals with disabilities. The elements we have outlined of a sound approach to job search assistance—maximum involvement of the job seeker; attention to service identity and stigma; networking; assistance to employers in designing, carving, and creating jobs; and an empowering use of incentives and services—are underdeveloped or missing altogether from the repertoires of many job development organizations.

A thorough and ongoing reexamination of current practices must be a continuous project of any organization providing job development or job search assistance. For some, this may require organizational change efforts of gargantuan proportions. But fulfilling the promise of bringing individuals with disabilities closer to realizing their proper and rightful place in the world of work is important enough to deserve those efforts.

REFERENCES

Abrams, K., DonAroma, P., & Karan, O. (1994). Person-centered situational assessment: A new direction for vocational rehabilitation services. *Journal for Vocational Special Needs Education*, *3*, 27–32.

Akabas, S. (1994). Workplace responsiveness: Key employer characteristics in support of job maintenance for people with mental illness. *Psychosocial Rehabilitation Journal*, *17*(3), 91–101.

Bachle, C. (1995). Resume fraud: Lies, omissions, and exaggerations. *Personnel Journal*, *74*(6), 51–60.

Bailey, T., & Waldinger, R. (1991). Primary, secondary, and enclave labor markets: A training systems approach. *American Sociological Review*, *56*, 432–445.

Balser, R., Hagner, D., & Hornby, H. (2000). Partnership with business community: The Mental Health Employer Consortium. *Journal of Applied Rehabilitation Counseling*, *31*(4), 47–53.

Barron, J., Berger, M., & Black, D. (1997). *On the job training*. Kalamazoo, MI: Upjohn Institute for Employment Research.

Blessing, L., & Jamieson, J. (1999). Employing persons with a developmental disability: Effects of previous experience. *Canadian Journal of Rehabilitation*, *12*(4), 211–221.

Bordieri, J., & Drehmer, D. (1988). Causal attribution and hiring recommendations for disabled job applicants. *Rehabilitation Psychology*, *33*(4), 239–247.

Bordieri, J., Drehmer, D., & Comninel, M. (1988). Attribution of responsibility and hiring recommendations for job applicants with low back pain. *Rehabilitation Counseling Bulletin, 32,* 140–149.

Bordieri, J., Drehmer, D., & Taricone, P. (1990). Personnel selection bias for job applicants with cancer. *Journal of Applied Social Psychology, 20*(3), 244–253.

Boyle, M. (1997). Social barriers to successful reentry into mainstream organizational culture: Perceptions of people with disabilities. *Human Resource Development Quarterly,* 8(3), 259–268.

Cable, D., Aiman-Smith, L., Mulvey, P., & Edwards, J. (2000). The sources and accuracy of job applicants' beliefs about organizational culture. *Academy of Management Journal, 43*(6), 1076–1085.

Callahan, M., & Garner, B. (1997). *Keys to the workplace.* Baltimore: Brookes.

Callahan, T. (1994). Managers' beliefs about and attitudes toward the Americans with Disabilities Act of 1990. *Applied Human Resource Management Research, 5*(1), 28–43.

Cook, J., Razzano, L., Straiton, D., & Ross, Y. (1994). Cultivation and maintenance of relationships with employers of people with psychiatric disabilities. *Psychosocial Rehabilitation Journal, 17*(3), 103–115.

Culver, J., Spencer, K., & Gliner, J. (1990). Prediction of supported employment placements by job developers. *Education and Training in Mental Retardation, 25,* 237–242.

Dwyre, A., & Trach, J. (1996). Consumer choice for people with cognitive disabilities: Who makes the choices in the job search process? *Journal of Applied Rehabilitation Counseling, 27,* 42–47.

Fabian, E., Luecking, R., & Tilson, G. (1994). *A working relationship: The job development specialist guide to successful partnerships with business.* Baltimore: Brookes.

Farley, R., & Hinman, S. (1988). Teaching rehabilitation clients effective job interview skills. *Vocational Evaluation and Work Adjustment Bulletin, 12,* 157–160.

Fesko, S., & Temelini, D. (1997). What consumers and staff tell us about effective job search strategies. In W. Kiernan & R. Schalock (Eds.), *Integrated employment* (pp. 67–81). Washington, DC: American Association on Mental Retardation.

Gilbride, D., Stensrud, R., & Johnson, M. (1994). Current models of job placement and employer development: Research, competencies and educational considerations. *Rehabilitation Education, 7,* 215–239.

Godfrey, K. (1995). *An examination of the bias for applicants with a physical disability in personnel decision-making.* Unpublished doctoral dissertation, Washington State University, Pullman.

Gottfries, N., & McCormick, B. (1995). Discrimination and open unemployment in a segmented labour market. *European Economic Review, 39,* 1–15.

Granovetter, M. (1979). Placement as brokerage. In D. Vandergoot & J. Worrall (Eds.), *Placement in rehabilitation: A career development perspective* (pp. 84–101). Baltimore: University Park Press.

Graves, L., & Karren, R. (1996). The employee selection interview: A fresh look at an old problem. *Human Resource Management, 35*(2), 163–180.

Griffin, C. (1996). Job carving as a job development strategy. In D. DiLeo & D. Langton (Eds.), *Facing the future: Best practices in supported employment* (pp. 32–36). St. Augustine, FL: TRN Press.

Hagner, D. (2000). Primary and secondary labor markets: Implications for vocational rehabilitation. *Rehabilitation Counseling Bulletin, 44*(1), 22–29.

Hagner, D., & Daning, R. (1993). Opening lines: How job developers talk to employers. *Career Development for Exceptional Individuals, 16*, 123–134.

Hagner, D., Fesko, S., Cadigan, M., Kiernan, W., & Butterworth, J. (1996). Securing employment: Jobs search and employer negotiation strategies in rehabilitation. In E. Szymanski & R. Parker (Eds.), *Work and disability: Issues and strategies in career development and job placement* (pp. 309–340). Austin, TX: PRO-ED.

Hagner, D., McGahie, K., & Cloutier, H. (2001). A model career assistance process for individuals with severe disabilities. *Journal of Employment Counseling, 38*, 197–206.

Hale, T., Hayghe, H., & McNeil, J. (1998). Persons with disabilities: Labor market activity, 1994. *Monthly Labor Review, 121*(9), 3–12.

Hallock, K., Hendricks, W., & Broadbent, E. (1998). Discrimination by gender and disability status: Do worker perceptions match statistical measures? *Southern Economic Journal, 65*(2), 245–263.

Hoff, D., Gandolfo, C., Gold, M., & Jordan, M. (2000). *Demystifying job development: Field-based approaches to job development for people with disabilities*. St. Augustine, FL: TRN Press.

Jackson, T. (1991). *Guerilla tactics in the new job market*. New York: Doubleday.

Lavin, D., & Everett, A. (1995). *Working on the dream: A guide to career planning and job success*. Spring Lake Park, MN: Rise.

Lee, B., & Newman, K. (1995). Employer responses to disability: Preliminary evidence and a research agenda. *Employee Responsibilities and Rights Journal, 8*(3), 209–229.

Lee, H. (1998). *Non disabled employees' attitudes toward the Americans with Disabilities Act requirement to reasonably accommodate co-workers with disabilities*. Unpublished doctoral dissertation, North Carolina State University, Raleigh.

Lin, N., & Dumin, M. (1986). Access to occupations through social ties. *Social Networks, 8*, 365–385.

Mitchell, K., Levin, A., & Krumboltz, J. (1999). Planned happenstance: Constructing unexpected career opportunities. *Journal of Counseling and Development, 77*, 115–124.

Nordstrom, C., Huffaker, B., & Williams, K. (1998). When physical disabilities are not liabilities: The role of applicant and interviewer characteristics on employment interview outcomes. *Journal of Applied Social Psychology, 28*(4), 283–306.

Owens-Johnson, L., & Hanley-Maxwell, C. (1999). Employer views on job development strategies for marketing supported employment. *Journal of Vocational Rehabilitation, 12*, 113–123.

Pfeffer, J. (1998). *The human equation: Building profits by putting people first*. Cambridge, MA: Harvard Business School Press.

Pumpian, I., Fisher, D., Certo, N., & Smalley, K. (1997). Changing jobs: An essential part of career development. *Mental Retardation, 35*, 39–48.

Rangan, S. (2000). The problem of search and deliberation in economic action: When social networks really matter. *Academy of Management Review, 25*(4), 813–828.

Reynolds, L. (1987). *Labor economics*. Englewood Cliffs, NJ: Prentice Hall.

Romoser, M. (2000). Malemployment in autism. *Focus on Autism and Other Developmental Disabilities, 14*(4), 246–247.

Rothwell, W., & Kazanas, H. (1994). *Improving on-the-job training*. San Francisco: Jossey-Bass.

Rumrill, P., & Roessler, R. (1999). New directions in vocational rehabilitation: A "career development" perspective on "closure." *Journal of Rehabilitation, 65*, 26–30.

Ryan, D. (2000). *Job search handbook for people with disabilities*. Indianapolis, IN: JIST.

Salomone, P. (1996). Career counseling and job placement: Theory and practice. In E. Szymanski & R. Parker (Eds.), *Work and disability: Issues and strategies in career development and job placement* (pp. 365–420). Austin, TX: PRO-ED.

Scheid, T. (1999) Employment of individuals with mental disabilities: Business response to the ADA's challenge. *Behavioral Sciences and the Law, 17*, 73–91.

Shafer, M., Banks, D., & Kregel, J. (1991). Employment retention and career movement among individuals with mental retardation working in supported employment. *Mental Retardation, 29*, 103–110.

Silliker, A. (1993). The role of social contacts in the successful job search. *Journal of Employment Counseling, 30*, 25–34.

Stone, C., & Sawatzki, B. (1980). Hiring bias and the disabled interviewee: Effects of manipulating work history and disability information of the disabled job applicant. *Journal of Vocational Behavior, 16*, 96–104.

Unger, D. (1999). Workplace supports: A view from employers who have hired supported employees. *Focus on Autism and Other Developmental Disabilities, 14*(3), 167–179.

VanRyn, M., & Vinocur, A. (1992). How did it work? An examination of the mechanisms through which an intervention for the unemployed promoted job search behavior. *American Journal of Community Psychology, 20*, 577–597.

Waddoups, J., & Assane, D. (1997). Duration and mobility of young male workers in a segmented labor market. *Applied Economics Letters, 4*, 173–176.

Walls, R., & Fullmer, S. (1997). Competitive employment: Occupations after vocational rehabilitation. *Rehabilitation Counseling Bulletin, 41*, 15–25.

Wanous, J. (1992). *Organizational entry: Selection, orientation, and socialization of newcomers*. Reading, MA: Addison-Wesley.

Wial, H. (1991). Getting a good job: Mobility in a segmented labor market. *Industrial Relations, 30*(3), 396–416.

Wright, K. (1997). *Uncertainty, attentiveness to performance-related information, and social affect in hiring decisions involving persons with disabilities*. Unpublished doctoral dissertation, Colorado State University, Fort Collins.

Young, C. (2000). The value of specifying what reasonable accommodations are expected from employers. *Journal of Visual Impairment and Blindness, 94*(1), 46–47.

Supported Employment

Cheryl Hanley-Maxwell, Laura Owens-Johnson, and Ellen Fabian

Supported employment was born in the mid-1970s (Rusch & Hughes, 1990) and came of age during the 1980s. Today we know it as an effective, cost-efficient way to enable people with severe disabilities to obtain and maintain employment in their local communities.

At its inception, supported employment services were developed to focus on improving employment-related outcomes for individuals with moderate, severe, or profound mental retardation. It was intended to answer questions related to whether people with severe disabilities could work in real jobs outside of the sheltered environment. Accordingly, it was founded on the beliefs that today are articulated as the following:

1. Competitive employment allows workers to earn wages and receive benefits. These enable greater independence and access to the community.
2. Engaging in productive work that has meaning in the community enhances the self-esteem and dignity of the individual.
3. Employment facilitates the development of new friendships and community social supports.
4. Employment enhances the ability of the individual to be independent of government subsidies. (Wehman, Revell, & Kregel, 1998)

The creation and refinement of supported employment have been influenced by many pieces of supporting legislation. Early work programs such as the work study programs for students with mental retardation in the 1950s laid some of the groundwork for the thinking behind supported employment. Legislation of the 1970s and early 1980s (e.g., Sections 503 and 504 of the Rehabilitation Act of 1973, the Education for All Handicapped Children Act of 1975, the Target Jobs Tax Credit, the Comprehensive Employment Training Act [CETA] of 1973, the Job Training Partnership Act [JTPA] of 1983) formed some of the philosophical and practical groundwork from which supported employment could emerge as an official rehabilitation program (Rusch & Hughes, 1990). Finally, in 1984, supported employment became part of the federal law in the Developmental Disabilities Assistance and Bill of Rights Act of 1984 (Rusch & Hughes, 1990; Wehman, 1996). It received its first public funding (Wehman et al., 1998) and became part of the federal–state vocational rehabilitation program (Unger, Parent, Gibson, Kane-Johnston, & Kregel, 1988) through the Rehabilitation Act Amendments of 1986. Subsequent legislation in the areas of civil rights (the Americans with Disabilities Act [ADA] of 1990), education (the Individuals with Disabilities Education Act [IDEA] of 1990; IDEA Amendments of 1997), labor (the Workforce Investment Act of 1998; the Ticket to Work and Work Incentives Improvement Act [TWWIIA] of 1999), and rehabilitation (the Rehabilitation Act Amendments of 1992, 1998) have supported and refined supported employment programs and practices.

Today, more than 3,600 agencies (Kregel, 1997) provide supported employment services to more than 140,000 supported employees who have a variety of disabilities (Wehman et al., 1998). These workers earn approximately $768 million annually. Thus, supported employment is an important part of any discussion of work and disability. The purpose of this chapter is to introduce the reader to supported employment through defining supported employment and its core features, discussing its efficacy, describing common models of supported employment, and describing its services.

DEFINING SUPPORTED EMPLOYMENT AND ITS CORE FEATURES

The current definition of supported employment is found in the 1992 Amendments to the Rehabilitation Act (P.L. 102-569). Supported employment is

> competitive work in integrated work settings for individuals with the most severe disabilities (i)(I) for whom competitive employment has not traditionally occurred; or (II) for whom competitive employment has

> been interrupted or intermittent as a result of a severe disability; and (ii) who, because of the nature and severity of their disability, need intensive supported employment services. . . . Such term includes transitional employment for persons who are individuals with the most severe disabilities due to mental illness. . . . (34) The term 'supported employment services' meanings ongoing support services and other appropriate services needed to support and maintain an individual with the most severe disability in supported employment, that—(a) are provided singly or in combination and are organized and made available in such a way as to assist an eligible individual in entering or maintaining integrated, competitive employment; (b) are based on a determination of the needs of an eligible individual, as specified in an individualized written rehabilitation program.

Over the years, supported employment has been operationalized in a variety of ways and within the context of several models. However, all variations of supported employment must adhere to specific core features. As described in the August 14, 1987, *Federal Register* (Hanley-Maxwell, Szymanski, & Owens-Johnson, 1998), supported employment has four core features: (a) competitive employment, (b) integrated settings, (c) workers with severe disabilities, and (d) ongoing support. As seen in the 1992 definition, these core features are still relevant today.

Competitive Employment

The first core feature is competitive employment. Competitive employment refers to working in jobs found in local communities. What makes these jobs competitive is that potential employees must compete with each other to fill any vacancies. Employees in these jobs are paid wages typical for that type of job in the particular community. They also receive any associated benefits (Wehman & Kregel, 1992).

Integrated Settings

Within the context of supported employment, the second core feature, integration, occurs when workers with the disabilities work alongside other workers without disabilities (Wehman & Kregel, 1992). This is referred to as physical integration. However, integration in supported employment must also include social aspects (Rusch, Chadsey-Rusch, & Johnson, 1991). Thus, the worker must not only be physically present in the work setting but must also have contact and relationships with nondisabled individuals who are not paid caregivers (i.e., social integration; Wehman & Kregel, 1992; Wehman & Moon, 1987).

Workers with Severe Disabilities

Workers with severe disabilities have come from many disability categories. These categories include persons with mental retardation (Buckley, Mank, & Cioffi, 1988), deafness and hearing impairments (Danek, Seay, & Collier, 1989), blindness and visual impairments (Hanley-Maxwell, Griffin, Szymanski, & Godley, 1990), chronic mental illness (McDonald-Wilson, Mancuso, Danley, & Anthony, 1989), traumatic brain injury (Kreutzer & Morton, 1988), or cerebral palsy (Wehman et al., 1990). However, for the most part, the disability label is largely irrelevant. The essential aspect of this feature is that without support services, these individuals are unable to obtain and maintain competitive employment. Furthermore, the 1992 amendments to the Rehabilitation Act require that those persons served in supported employment must be considered individuals with the most severe disabilities. Unfortunately, although federal law requires supported employment programs to serve persons with the most severe disabilities, current trends suggest that implementation has focused on other individuals. Specifically, examination of demographic data for supported employment participation reveals that 51.9% of these individuals have a primary disability label of mild mental retardation (Wehman et al., 1998).

Ongoing Support

The last feature, ongoing support, makes supported employment different from all other rehabilitation services (Wehman, 1988). In supported employment, ongoing support is not time limited because of the nature and severity of the disabilities of the supported workers. Ongoing support services are provided to the individual and the environments that support his or her work. These services are intended to increase the potential for job retention by assisting the individual and his or her coworkers, supervisors, or work environment to interact successfully (Szymanski & Parker, 1988; Szymanski, Hanley-Maxwell, & Parker, 1987). In addition, individuals with mental illness are entitled to receive off-site job coaching (Danley & Mellen, 1987).

EFFICACY OF SUPPORTED EMPLOYMENT

Supported employment has grown dramatically. This growth is in part due to economic changes and resulting labor needs that have occurred since its inception (Harper, 1993; Kiernan, Butterworth, Schalock, & Sailor, 1993). These changes include growth in available jobs and subsequent drops in unemployment. As unemployment rates have dropped, the composition of the workforce also has changed. It has gone from being primarily young, White, and male (Mank, 1996) to including more women, immigrants, people of color, workers, and, later, people with disabilities (Fabian, Luecking, & Tilson, 1994; Harper, 1993; Johnson & Packer, 1987; Swaboda, 1990). In fact, people of color, women, and immigrants account for 85% of the net growth of the workforce in America (Johnson & Packer, 1987). As the need for labor continues to grow, employers are finding they must access alternative labor sources (Fabian et al., 1994; Levinson, 1993; State of Wisconsin, Department of Workforce Development, 1996). Supported employees are one of those sources.

Supported employment not only meets employer labor needs; it is also a cost-effective service that provides benefits to taxpayers through more efficient use of taxpayer dollars (Cimera, 1998, 2000; Hill & Wehman, 1983; Wehman et al., 1985). When support is provided in a cost-effective manner, the average annual cost of supported employment is often less than other alternatives. Thus, taxpayers save money in foregone operating costs. Furthermore, supported employees are tax-paying citizens. Even if they receive full refunds at the end of the tax year, the taxpayer benefits from the interest accrued on the tax dollars paid across the course of the fiscal year (Cimera, 1998, 2000). Finally, there are savings in area of income subsidies. Early data suggested that once employed, most supported employees, but not all (Rusch, Conley, & McCaughrin, 1993), earned too much to access government subsidies (Baer, Simmons, Flexer, & Smith, 1995; Hill & Wehman, 1983; Lewis, Johnson, Bruininks, Kallsen, & Guillery, 1992; Tines, Rusch, McCaughrin, & Conley, 1990). However, more recent analyses suggest a more conservative benefit to taxpayers. Supported employment appears to result in *reduced reliance* on government subsidies, specifically Supplemental Security Income (SSI) and Social Security Disability Income (SSDI), as a primary source of financial support. It does not eliminate the need for some level of subsidy (Wehman et al., 1998).

Supported employment also benefits the workers. These benefits include better wages than they would have gotten in alternative placements, enhanced probability of getting fringe benefits, and work that is integrated within local communities (Kregel, 1997). In fact, when compared with all other alternatives for potential supported workers, supported employment increases the average annual earnings by 500% (Kregel, Wehman, & Banks, as cited in Kregel 1997; Thompson, Powers, & Houchard, as cited in Kregel, 1997). Furthermore, supported workers are satisfied with their employment situations, both in terms of actual jobs and the interpersonal relationships on the job (Kregel, 1997).

Issues related to the efficacy of supported employment for workers with severe mental illness are more complicated. These workers have diverse and fluid needs that are different from those of other supported employees (Noble, Honberg, Hall, & Flynn, 1997). For example, although many developmental disabilities, such as mental retardation, are stable conditions, many mental health disorders, such as schizophrenia, are more fluctuating conditions. These fluctuations can be seen both in the sometimes cyclic presentation of the symptoms of the illness, as well as in the dramatic changes that can occur over the course of the illness. Although the supported employment approach seemed uniquely suited to the needs of these consumers, early studies examining the efficacy of this approach were not particularly encouraging (Trotter, Minkoff, Harrison, & Hoops, 1988). A recent review of empirical studies in supported employment conducted by Gary Bond and his colleagues (Bond, Drake, Mueser, & Becker, 1997) found dropout rates of more than 40% common in supported employment programs for individuals with mental illness, with some studies reporting retention after 6 months at only 35%. Another troubling issue raised in the literature is the weak correspondence between supported employment success and quality-of-life indicators (Drake, McHugo, Becker, Anthony, & Clark, 1996; Fabian, 1992) for this population, a factor that needs to be taken into account in vocational planning. However, recent supported employment research for consumers with severe mental illness has identified model components that appear to be associated with successful outcomes. These components will be discussed in later sections.

SUPPORTED EMPLOYMENT MODELS

Support employment models are typically classified as group or individual (Moon & Griffin, 1988; Rhodes & Valenta, 1985). Within these models, supports are provided directly by an employment specialist who acts as a job coach or by using the existing support systems found within the place of employment. The most frequently used model for providing support is the individual placement model (Wehman et al., 1998). However, because supported employment is an "individualized service" (Kregel, 1997) and each individual, employment situation, and community is different, other types and sources of supports should be considered when attempting to meet the needs of the supported employee (Hanley-Maxwell et al., 1997). Regardless of support system used, any variation must retain the essential core elements (Bellamy, Rhodes, Mank, & Albin, 1988). Furthermore, regardless of support model used, any model must be maximally under the control of the supported worker and must enhance the independence of that individual.

This section describes the group and individual models of supported employment and discusses the most common support structures within the context of each model. Because supported employment for individuals with mental illness has taken on slightly different characteristics, this section concludes with a discussion of employment models for these persons.

Group Models

In supported employment group models, one job coach or employment specialist supports a group of supported workers who work at the same job site. Federal standards define what may constitute a group in these models; a "group" must not exceed eight individuals with disabilities (Hanley-Maxwell et al., 1997). The configuration of the groups varies as a result of the type of work the supported employees are performing, where the work is performed, availability and type of integration, and the wages earned and benefits received (Wolfe, 1992).

Group models are typically used for people for who have been judged as not appropriate for an individual placement. These models reflect low expectations for the abilities of the individuals they serve and for the individuals' potential for independence. In fact, these workers are thought to need intense, daily support that never fades (Johnson & Rusch, 1990). Furthermore, group models are more restrictive than the individual placement models, limiting the potential for integration of the supported workers with nondisabled workers (Hanley-Maxwell et al., 1997). Because the potential for integration is so limited, supported employment providers must seek other ways to ensure integration during breaks, lunches, and (preferably) working hours (Bellamy, Rhodes, & Albin, 1986; President's Committee on Employment of People with Disabilities [PCEPD], 1987; Szymanski et al., 1987).

Group models are the targets of severe criticism due to their inherent limits on integration. In addition, they have been accused of highlighting the deviance of the supported employment workers. Furthermore, group models appear to limit the benefits of working by providing fewer work hours per week and lower pay when compared with individual models (Hanley-Maxwell et al., 1997). Consequently, group placement models are not considered best practice in supported employment. As a result, fewer supported workers are being served within these models. However, they continue to serve 22.6% of all supported workers nationwide (Wehman et al., 1998). Thus, it is important to discuss the two most common examples of group placements: the enclave and the mobile work crew.

Enclave

An enclave is a group of individuals who collectively accomplish a set of work tasks at a specific place of employment. In keeping with federal regulations, the enclave employs no more than eight individuals and they share no fewer than two employee slots/vacancies (Hanley-Maxwell et al., 1997). The enclave model is described as being appropriate for individuals who have more severe disabilities and more behavior challenges than other supported employees (Mank, Rhodes, & Bellamy, 1986; Moon & Griffin, 1988; Rhodes & Valenta, 1985).

Enclaves take two forms: congregated and dispersed. In the congregated enclave, all employees with disabilities work in the same area (Rhodes & Valenta, 1985). When the enclave is dispersed, the supported employees are located within the same building or employment site, but they are dispersed throughout the available work areas (Udvari-Solner, 1990).

Enclave employees are paid one of two ways. First, they may be paid by the supported employment service provider. When the supported employment agency is the employer, work is contracted from the business and enclave employees are paid both wages and associated benefits from the supporting agency. Second, the enclave employees may be paid by the employer. In this case, the work is not contracted by the supported employment agency. Instead, the employees fill existing job vacancies; the number of vacancies filled is negotiated by the supported employment provider. The work required by these employee positions is distributed among the workers with disabilities (Mank et al., 1986; PCEPD, 1987; Szymanski et al., 1987). In all cases, an on-site job coach provides support and all work is done on the premises of the business. Integration with nondisabled workers is limited; the vast majority of workers who surround an enclave employee are workers with disabilities (Michigan, as cited in Wolfe, 1992). Thus, supported employment providers are encouraged to integrate the enclave workers throughout the employer's workspaces (Hanley-Maxwell et al., 1997).

Mobile Crew

A mobile crew moves from business to business performing a contractual service (e.g., janitorial service, lawn maintenance). Each crew includes a job coach who provides the needed training and ongoing supported services. The mobile crew is the most restrictive supported employment model in that it offers the fewest chances for integration with nondisabled workers (Kregel, Wehman, & Banks, 1989, as cited in Wolfe, 1992). Thus, it is critical to consider ways to enhance integration. One way to do this would be to employ coworkers without disabilities within each group. These nondisabled employees would not supervise. Instead, they would work alongside employees with disabilities. Another way would be to schedule mobile work crew hours during typical work hours (8:00 A.M. to 5:00 P.M.). This would enhance the potential for contact with nondisabled workers (Hanley-Maxwell et al., 1997).

Individual Models

Individual placement models of supported employment adhere more closely to the foundational values of supported employment because they support workers in integrated jobs (Hanley-Maxwell et al., 1997). They are considered the least restrictive models and are the most prevalently used approach to supported employment (77.4% of all supported employees; Wehman et al., 1998). In the past, there has been only one individual model, the employment specialist as primary service provider. However, with the advent of greater attention to the identification and use of typically available supports and services, an additional model has emerged. That model is the employment specialist as service facilitator or coordinator. Each of these models is discussed below.

Primary Service Provider

When the employment specialist is the primary service provider, he or she assists the supported worker in securing a job and trains the supported worker and the coworkers and supervisors working with the supported employee. When training is complete, the employment specialist decreases the support she or he provides at the employment site but continues to provide support as needed (Rogan, Banks, & Howard, 2000). Specifically, the employment specialist is primarily responsible for assessment, job development, placement, training, and ongoing support (Unger et al., 1998).

In this model, physical integration of the supported employee is ensured. However, the employment specialist must ensure social integration occurs as well. In fact, research has suggested that the presence of the service provider while job coaching may negatively influence social integration (Fabian & Luecking, 1991; Hagner, 1992; Hagner, Rogan, & Murphy, 1992). So care must be taken to reduce this impact. One way to do this would be to use the supports and services that are typically available to other employees (sometimes called natural supports). Use of these supports facilitates social integration by identifying and holding to the workplace norms and practices (Rogan et al., 2000). In fact, 85% of supported employment agencies report using natural supports usually during training and ongoing support but rarely in assessment, job development, or placement (West, Kregel, Hernandez, & Hock, 1997, as cited in Unger et al., 1998). If the supported worker is socially connected at work, an "ally" usually develops. This ally functions as a protector and advocate (Rogan et al., 2000).

Facilitator/Consultant

When the employment specialist works as a facilitator/consultant, she or he uses the natural supports available to all workers. Even though natural supports were specifically identified as an extended service option in the Rehabilitation Act Amendments of 1992 (Mank, Cioffi, & Yovanoff, 2000), the exact definition has varied from author to author. One of the more current and accepted definitions of natural supports defines them as

> any assistance, relationships, or interactions that allow a person with disabilities to secure, maintain, and advance in a community job of his or her choosing in a way that corresponds to the typical work routines and social interactions of other employees and that enhance that individual's social relationships. (Test & Wood, 1996, p. 155)

Using natural supports shifts the role of the employment specialist from direct service to problem-solving facilitation and consultation (Butterworth, Whitney-Thomas, & Shaw, as cited in Unger et al., 1998). More specifically, the employment specialists work as a facilitators when they identify and arrange potential supports. These supports may include coworkers, supervisors, and community organizations/services such as the one-stop job centers created in the Workforce Investment Act of 1998 (Callahan, 1999) and adult literacy programs (Unger et al., 1998). They fill their consultant role by sharing information and resources and functioning as a support consultant to employers (Hanley-Maxwell et al., 1997). As a consultant to the employer, the employment specialist completes job analyses, engineers the social and physical environments, and trains coworkers to behave differently in such areas as giving directions, providing feedback, and social interactions (Hagner et al., 1992; Nisbet & Hagner, 1988). Thus, the employment specialist must be knowledgeable about variety of support options, be able to develop and secure supports, and work collaboratively with all others.

The use of natural supports is not an alternative to job coaching. Instead, it is part of each stage of service delivery in supported employment. The employment specialist continues to provide any needed or supplementary supports and uses assistive technology, compensatory strategies, job modification, or any other support strategy when needed (Unger et al., 1998). In addition, she or he also continues to provide training to coworkers and supervisors as well as the individual.

Unger et al. (1998) proposed a model for identifying and organizing any needed supports at each stage of the job process for a supported employee. This model includes the following steps:

1. Determine individual needs and preferences.
2. Brainstorm potential options.
3. Assess job and community supports.
4. Identify individual choices
5. Develop strategies for accessing supports.
6. Evaluate support effectiveness.
7. Arrange provision for ongoing monitoring. (Unger et al., 1998, p. 28)

Regardless of what supports are used, naturally available in the environment or provided by the employment specialist, the most important aspect is the effectiveness or success of the supports. Finally, the employment specialist must remember that support is a customer service that is provided in an individualized style, varying from one individual and one setting to another (Inge & Tilson, 1997).

Employment Models for Individuals with Mental Illness

Among the first approaches to assisting consumers with mental illness to get and keep employment was the clubhouse model, pioneered at Fountain House in New York City (Beard, Propst, & Malamud, 1982). This approach was the first to use the word *members* as opposed to *clients* to emphasize the egalitarian nature of the program and to stress its difference from traditional patient-oriented approaches associated with medical and psychiatric care. Fountain House also developed the concept of "transitional employment programs"—namely, temporary, part-time jobs in the community secured by program staff. Consumers or members within Fountain House could participate in these jobs consistent with their preferences as well as their tolerance for work. Although similar to supported employment (and specifically noted in the 1986 Rehabilitation Act Amendments as a supported employment program), transitional employment differs in that the jobs are controlled by the program, not the individual employee. These jobs are meant to be temporary placements through which individual consumers rotate. Many psychosocial rehabilitation programs are an outgrowth of the Fountain House model (Pratt, Gill, Barrett, & Roberts, 1999). Generally, these programs include transitional or supported employment within an array of programmatic services offered to consumers with severe mental illness. The job coach model is the most prevalent supported employment approach in psychosocial rehabilitation programs, with funding generally obtained through the state departments of vocational rehabilitation (Pratt et al., 1999).

Somewhat distinct from the program-based approach to supported employment are rehabilitation services provided in natural settings. For example, the assertive community treatment model (Stein & Test, 1980) emphasizes a community-integrated multidisciplinary team approach to meeting consumer needs across multiple life domains, including work. Typically, the treatment team, including a vocational staff member, provides wraparound services to the consumer as they assist him or her in identifying and attaining specific rehabilitation goals.

One of the more recent supported employment alternatives for individuals with severe mental illness is the Individual Placement and Support approach (Drake, 1998). This approach emphasizes the traditional features of supported employment within a program setting that integrates mental health and vocational services through multidisciplinary teams. Thus, one of the distinguishing features of the Individual Placement and Support model is the wraparound provision of clinical and vocational services, as opposed to a mental health agency referring consumers to employment agencies for supported employment services. Empirical studies comparing this approach to other vocational models appear to demonstrate that it shows promise in alleviating some of the problems associated with other methods, such as job retention (Bond et al., 1997).

Finally, an underlying framework common to many of these approaches has emerged from the work of Anthony and his colleagues at Boston University. The "choose–get–keep" (Danley & Anthony, 1987) approach describes the fundamental processes necessary for successfully matching individuals to jobs that are consistent with their choices, skills, and work values. A distinguishing feature of this approach is its emphasis on career planning, or at least job choice, as a necessary step in any supported employment program.

SERVICE DELIVERY

Supported employment services consist of five overlapping phases: assessment, job development and marketing, job acquisition (placement), job learning and adaptation, and ongoing support (Parker, Szymanski, & Hanley-Maxwell, 1989). Service providers can combine these phases in different ways to create individualized service models. For example, the choose–get–keep model of supported employment for people with mental illness (McDonald-Wilson et al., 1989) combines these five phases into three phases. In this model, as with all models of supported employment service, the specific activities within each phase vary to meet the needs of the person served and the job or career. However, the essential structure remains the same. One caveat is important to note throughout all phases: The more a supported employee is like a typical employee in job acquisition, training, and support, the better the outcomes (wages, integration, benefits) will be for him or her (Mank, Cioffi, & Yovanoff, 1997). Because most service providers begin with assessment and job development and proceed through the remaining phases, this discussion follows that sequence. It concludes with a discussion of the supported employment components that are most effective for people with severe mental illness.

Assessment

Assessment occurs throughout all other supported employment phases. For assessment to be most effective, it should be ecological. This means that assessment should include evaluation of the job and the individual supported employee (Szymanski, 1994).

Assessment of the Job

Assessment of the job, usually referred to as job analysis, is a traditional part of rehabilitation services. However, in an effort to highlight the individualities of the job and the setting (Hanley-Maxwell, 1986), supported employment service providers add unique aspects to the content and application of job analyses. Supported employment providers extend the content to include the examination of social survival skills as well as job-related skills (Rusch, Schutz, & Agran, 1982). They extend the methodology used by moving from traditional sources of information (e.g., systematic observations of coworkers performing the job or highly similar jobs) to including seeking validating information from prospective employees, coworkers, and supervisors (Rusch, Menchetti, & Schutz, 1980).

Job analysis in supported employment identifies the duties and responsibilities directly (i.e., job description) and indirectly (e.g., wearing a clean uniform) related to the position. It also identifies the abilities, skills, and experiences needed by the jobholder (i.e., job specifications) and includes many related skills (e.g., bus taking, conversing with coworkers).

Furthermore, job analysis examines and describes the physical environment (e.g., light, temperature) and the psychosocial environment (e.g., amount of control over job demands, interaction with the public, style of supervision used). Finally, job analysis identifies supports that exist or could be developed in the areas of training, doing the job, and dealing with work-related issues (Unger et al., 1998). The type of supports available and the process for developing supports depend on the workplace culture and climate (Rogan et al., 2000). However, when employers assessed their own workplace regarding potential supports, they indicated that they provide supports in four areas: employee training, employee benefits, career advancement, and work culture (Unger, 1999).

The supported employment job analysis is the basis for matching an individual with a job, developing training plans, identifying potentially problematic areas to target for additional training or problem circumvention efforts, and matching or developing support services that meet the individual supported employee's needs. Problem circumvention includes accommodation, job restructuring, and the use of assistive devices and technology (Hanley-Maxwell & Bordieri, 1989). When potentially problematic areas are identified, the job analysis is supplemented with a task analysis of the problematic area (Hanley-Maxwell et al., 1997). The task analysis breaks each job element into its component steps and logically orders these steps. The task analysis is then used as the basis for focused training (Parker et al., 1989).

Individual Assessment

Ecological assessment also includes assessment of the individual supported employee. This assessment is not used to determine eligibility or readiness (Parker et al., 1989). Instead, it focuses on identifying the supported employee's strengths, limitations, existing support systems, and potential support systems (Pancsofar, 1986). Getting to know the supported employee, developing a general profile of the individual, and developing a more specific description in relation to potential jobs do this.

Getting to know the supported employee is often referred to as intake. This is a crucial step in identifying and planning for successful support systems. It is also the first step in developing the general profile of the individual. When developing a general profile of the supported employee, data are gathered from a variety of sources, including school-related information for students who are participating in IDEA-required transition planning. Specific types of data collected include, but are not limited to, psychological tests, work samples, behavioral observation, historical data, and vocational evaluation. Vocational evaluations often include assessment of aptitudes, abilities, skills, interests, work attitude, and knowledge about work (Hanley-Maxwell, Bordieri, & Merz, 1996). These data are used to build an understanding of the supported employee by learning about his or her interests, skills, and needs (Hanley-Maxwell et al., 1997). This profile is supplemented with information obtained from assessment that focuses on potential jobs, assessing the supported employee within the context of a targeted job.

Individual assessment should be ongoing process. It should also maximize the control that the individual supported employee has over the entire supported employment process (Hanley-Maxwell et al., 1997). In fact, Pancsofar, Steere, and Wood (1993) stated, "The art of assessment is the process of providing someone with a compass from which to chart their own course of action rather than laying out a detailed map from which they dare not deviate" (p. 1). Keeping this in mind, it is clear that all individual assessment in supported employment should be person centered and designed to uncover an individual's abilities and skills, past learning history, future goals and aspirations, interests, and likes and dislikes. Although it should acknowledge the limitations of the person, it also should not focus on deficiencies (Hanley-Maxwell et al., 1997). Effectively assessing an individual means that the assessor must spend time with the individual supported employee to determine if an appropriate job match exists and to identify the type and degree of supports needed by that person to do the targeted job (Hanley-Maxwell & Bordieri, 1989). Unfortunately, the amount of time that can be spent in these steps and the extent of the information gathered are influenced by external pressures, which include funding agency requirements (Rogan et al., 2000).

Job Development and Marketing

Job development and marketing are processes that occur throughout all phases of supported employment. They are essential to the success and expansion of supported employment (Mank, Buckley, & Rhodes, 1991). These processes identify potential jobs, refine available job options (Szymanski, Buckley, Parent, Parker, & Westbrook, 1988), and expand the number and type of jobs available to the supported employee (Hanley-Maxwell et al., 1997; Owens-Johnson & Hanley-Maxwell, 1999). As a result, supported employees are afforded opportunities for job mobility, development of their experiential histories, and access to increasingly better jobs (Patterson & Curl, 1990). Job development opens specific job sites and targets certain jobs. The more recent addition of marketing allows supported employment providers to establish a broader base from which to develop specific jobs.

Job development in supported employment is the process of identifying and making potential jobs available to supported employees. A comprehensive employment specialist or a specifically designated job developer does most job development. This individual usually uses a person-first approach to job development. In this approach, the skills and interests of the supported employee drive the job search. Occasionally, the job developer will develop a pool of jobs and then recruit individual supported employees to fill these job vacancies. This approach is known as the jobs-first approach (Rogan et al., 2000). Regardless of approach, most models of job development fall within two distinct paradigms: traditional and business responsive. In all models, job developers are encouraged to actively involve individual job seekers in their own job search (Rogan at al., 2000). Unger et al. (1998) found that although most supported employees indicate they need help in finding a job (usually from an employment specialist), they see themselves as active participants in the process.

Traditional Models

The beginnings of job development in supported employment are often described as "beg, place, and pray" (Fabian et al., 1994) or "hire the handicapped" (McLoughlin, Garner, & Callahan, 1987) approaches. Individuals with the disabilities were the only customers, and the primary reason employers should hire them was to meet the employment needs of the supported employee (Owens-Johnson & Hanley-Maxwell, 1999). In these approaches, the job developer had three functions: "(1) to lend competence to individuals with disabilities until the employee learned the job, (2) to be accountable for facilitating job opportunities, and (3) to target jobs which individuals with disabilities may not otherwise have knowledge or access" (Owens-Johnson & Hanley-Maxwell, 1999, p. 114). Thus, the job developer obtained many jobs for supported employees by appealing to a company's good will and charity (McLoughlin et al., 1987).

Traditional job development involves several steps. The first step is to identify potential jobs based on the information obtained from the assessment of the supported employee. The job developer pays particular attention to the individual's interests and goals. In addition, job development takes into account the ongoing support model that will be used with this supported employee (i.e., group models vs. individual placement models). This is because the model will affect the activities that occur when developing a job (Hanley-Maxwell et al., 1997). For example, when support is going to be provided via group models (i.e., mobile work crew, enclave), job development efforts must focus on identifying employment sites that can physically accommodate small groups of employees. In addition, these sites must be able to accept the structural and ideological changes (e.g., job sharing) that occur when small groups of individuals with disabilities work at the job site (Szymanski et al., 1987).

When developing a job for an individual supported employee, it is essential to remember that the targeted job is just a step in a career, not the individual supported employee's only job (Hanley-Maxwell et al., 1997). Thus, focusing on jobs that allow for career advancement (Cimera, 2000) or ensuring that each job builds on previous jobs is essential. In fact, most supported employees report that they do not expect to stay with current jobs permanently. Instead, they hope to move on to other more desirable jobs (Kregel, 1997).

Business-Responsive Models

Currently recommended job development and marketing techniques reflect the belief that supported employment providers must no longer ask employers to act as good corporate citizens by hiring individuals with disabilities. Instead, supported employment providers must become responsive to employer needs, shifting from a social services perspective to a business perspective (Cimera, 2000; Nietupski, Verstagen, & Hamre-Nietupski, 1992).

Supported employment providers who behave more like businesses and less like social services are more effective in helping supported employees. These providers are more successful in obtaining a wider selection of potential jobs for their supported employees, thereby enhancing the chances for good employee-job match (Owens-Johnson & Hanley-Maxwell, 1999). In turn, this match helps to reduce supported employee job turnover and the associated costs (Cimera, 2000).

Job development in supported employment today must reflect the reality that supported employment professionals actually work in two systems: business and human services. Thus, job development activities must include creation of rehabilitation-business relationships that reflect a mutual understanding of how job development fits within the business community (Owens-Johnson & Hanley-Maxwell, 1999).

Business-responsive models build on traditional job development activities and continue to focus on the individual job seeker. However, they also expand this focus to include the needs and desires of the business and the community at large (Owens-Johnson & Hanley-Maxwell, 1999). Attention to these aspects is critical. Supported employees not only need and want good jobs, but employers also need to diversify the workforce. Thus, supported employment providers are given the opportunity to create new employer–provider relationships (Mank, 1996).

Although becoming business responsive requires supported employment providers to develop an awareness of employer needs and desires, current practice has not yet achieved these goals (Owens-Johnson & Hanley-Maxwell, 1999). This was evident when Fabian et al. (1994) brought together focus groups of Maryland employers and job placement specialists who were asked, "How can you achieve greater success in job placements?" Employers and job placement specialists responded very differently. More than half of the placement professionals indicated they needed more time, available jobs, or employer understanding. None responded by saying they needed more information from employers. Employer responses clustered around the provision of good customer service, with the employer being the customer. They wanted placement personnel who responded to their needs and who could help them identify reasonable accommodations. It is critical that job development and placement personnel begin to see the employer's perspective. Without the change to a business-responsive model, job development will continue to use approaches that are narrow in scope and limit the view of the potential job market (Bissonnette, 1994). These old approaches will perpetuate problems and practices that contribute to failure for individuals with disabilities, employers, and developers (Owens-Johnson & Hanley-Maxwell, 1999).

A business-responsive model merges business marketing and sales techniques with traditional job development. In this model, job development professionals view employers as experts in their businesses who can share their knowledge in efficiency, motivation, economics, negotiation, and customer service. However, employers are not experts in assistive technology, job analysis, training, hiring, and job accommodation. This is the knowledge that the job development professional can contribute to the partnership (Fabian et al., 1994).

Marketing is an important and sometimes forgotten part of job development. Marketing in supported employment is the same as marketing in the larger business world. It promotes the business and seeks to ensure that the customers (employers) use the supported employment agency's services (Levinson, 1993). Although marketing includes selling the agency and its services to prospective employers, selling is only one part of marketing. The other components include analyzing the needs of potential employers and communities, designing services to meet those needs, connecting employers with these services, and ensuring use of the services (Kiernan, Carter, & Bronstein, 1989; Levinson, 1993; Sandhusen, 1993). Marketing also includes reconsideration of everything about the business or, in this case, the supported employment agency, from the name of the agency to how to follow up on contacts with employers.

The current economy, given recent trends in unemployment and other indicators, is prepared to receive the marketing from supported employment agencies. Businesses are beginning to acknowledge the potential of workers with disabilities. Evidence of this acknowledgment can be found in a recent U.S. Department of Labor study. This study quotes an equal employment opportunity manager of IBM as saying, "Disabled persons are a great untapped resource for American business" (Hudson Institute, 1988, as cited in Fabian et al., 1994, p. 6). Supported employment providers can make sure that employers see hiring from this untapped source makes good business sense. Furthermore, supported employment providers have the skills and knowledge to help employers meet ADA requirements. Thus, it is clear that the business climate will facilitate the shift in job development strategies from the traditional approaches of making placements to a marketing approach involving the development of employer relationships. However, it must be remembered that marketing-supported employment is a step in developing jobs for individuals with disabilities. It does not replace individualized job development.

Placement

The end goal of placement is to obtain the optimal job position for a person that is consistent with his or her existing abilities and interests (Geist & Calzaretta, 1982). However, it is important to remember that a specific job or position should be considered a step in each individual supported employee's career life.

Gilbride and Stensrud (1992) stated that rehabilitation services typically use one of three placement models. These models vary in who does the job placement: (a) placement done by rehabilitation counselors, (b) placement done by placement specialists, and (c) placement done by individual contractors (e.g., Projects with Industry, a federally funded placement program). They further stated that placement in supported employment is a distinct and additional model.

Regardless of who facilitates the securing of the job, the process of placement follows the same general steps. Once the individual and potential jobs have been assessed, the person responsible for placement begins the matching. The intent of the matching is to find a job that is compatible with the needs, desires, and assets of the job seeker (Powell et al., 1991). Attention to detail during matching is highly correlated with successful placements (Martin, 1986).

Supported employment placement is a fairly rapid process because it is not delayed due to preplacement training or skill requirements. This rapid entry into the job seems to be uniquely suited to the needs of persons with severe mental illness, for whom lengthy prevocational preparation has been shown to be negatively associated with job acquisition (Bond, Dietzen, McGrew, & Miller, 1995).

Supported employment services raise some unique issues in the placement process. Because ongoing support is provided to supported workers, coworkers, and employers, some reluctant employers can be encouraged to take a chance on hiring persons they might not typically consider for employment. However, because of the continued presence of the employment specialist in the provision of ongoing support services, the competency of the supported worker may be always in question. In addition, the employment specialist may become an intermediary between the employer and the supported worker, thus reducing employer commitment to that employee. In fact, when the employment specialist is physically present at the job site, the ongoing presence sometimes creates physical accommodation problems (Nisbet & Hagner, 1988). Thus, it is critical to develop and use natural supports whenever possible.

Training

Training is learning to do the job by acquiring, maintaining, and generalizing the necessary skills (Berg, Wacker, & Flynn, 1990). Training can be accomplished by using the existing resources of the employer or by having the employment specialist train the new employee. Funding for training has come from a variety of sources, although vocational rehabilitation is often the primary source (Wehman et al., 1998). Vocational rehabilitation provides initial funding for no more than 18 months unless there are unique circumstances that warrant extension of the time so that rehabilitation objectives in the Individualized Written Rehabilitation Plan (IWRP) can be met. Both the individual and the rehabilitation counselor must agree to the extension (Rehabilitation Act Amendments, 1994).

The activities typically included in this period are training or job stabilization. Other sources of funding include CETA/JTPA for disadvantaged youth and adults (Parent & Hill, 1990). For students still in special education, state–federal IDEA funding sometimes pays for the job training that occurs prior to graduating or leaving school (Wehman et al., 1998). For adults with disabilities, funding sources include mental health programs, mental retardation/developmental disabilities programs, developmental disabilities planning councils, home- and community-based Medicaid waivers (Wehman et al., 1998), and vouchers obtained through TWWIIA (King & Collins, 2000).

Training is planned as an individualized service, the content of which is the result of synthesizing and comparing the information obtained from individual and job assessments (Hanley-Maxwell, 1986). Training plans include consideration of the development and implementation of any adaptations needed to accommodate skill deficits that cannot be remediated through training. Adaptations should include assistive devices and technology, from the simplest to the most complex (Wehman et al., 1998). Considering adaptations at the beginning of training may produce more efficient training and enhanced independence of the supported worker.

Training methods should reflect the short- and long-term skill needs of the supported worker. Whether the employment specialist is the sole or supplemental source of training, he or she typically uses preplanned and systematic behaviorally based training methods. These methods include (but are not limited to) working from behavioral objectives, using individualized consequences (e.g., reinforcement, natural consequences), using levels of assistance and error correction procedures, and focusing on skill maintenance and generalization (Hanley-Maxwell et al., 1990, 1997; McLoughlin et al., 1987). However, supported employment service providers must remember that if supported employees follow the training and support processes used by typical employees, the integration, wage, and benefit outcomes are better (Mank et al., 1997). Thus, it is important to consider using coworkers and supervisors as the primary source of training and consider accessing employer-provided training opportunities. Use of coworkers and supervisors in training and support is not new but is an essential consideration (Unger et al., 1998).

Unger et al. (1998) provided an example of how natural supports and employment specialist services can be combined to effectively serve supported workers. They examined the support needs of 36 supported employees being served in a program that accessed natural or typically available support services in addition to those services provided by the employment specialist. They found that support needs were identified in six areas, including learning to do the job, doing the job, and dealing with work-related issues. A variety of supports met these needs. The employment specialist had primary responsibility for arranging the supports needed to continue to perform the job and to deal with work-related issues (the most prevalent need). In addition, the employment specialist also assisted in identifying and providing additional supports. However, in most cases, workplace personnel (not the employment specialist) arranged supports needed by the supported employee to learn to do the job.

Employers can help supported workers learn to do their jobs by providing training through coworkers or supervisors or using training and maintenance programs that are accessible to all their employees. Frequently available employer-provided training includes basic skills training, coaching, mentoring, and apprenticeship (Hanley-Maxwell et al., 1996). Each of these is described next.

Basic Skills Training

Basic skills training refers to on-the-job site education programs that teach reading, language skills, arithmetic, and problem solving. The education provided is related to job needs (Szabo, 1990). Although relatively new to business and industry (Hanley-Maxwell et al., 1996), initial results suggest that these programs are related to higher rates of employee retention and attendance, greater productivity, and reduced production errors (Szabo, 1990).

Coaching

Like coaching provided by employment specialists, coaching in business and industry is on-the-job training designed to assist an employee. However, unlike coaching in supported employment, this type of coaching is designed to correct relatively simple skill-related problems (Knippen & Green, 1990). Typically, the manager or supervisor is the coach. In this role, she or he provides training. The supervisor or manager typically sets learning goals and success criteria and then teaches by explaining the tasks, modeling or demonstrating the skills, requiring that the worker practice the new skills, and providing periodic feedback to the worker. This approach results in benefits for both the manager and the worker. The worker benefits from skill acquisition and gains greater productivity, morale, and loyalty to the company. Through coaching, the manager or supervisor develops improved communication and ways to deal with change. Finally, coaching results in improved relationships between manager and worker (Hanley-Maxwell et al., 1996).

Mentoring

In mentoring, a senior employee is matched with a new or inexperienced employee with the intention that the senior employee will provide formal or informal training. Mentoring is frequently used to address the problems of low productivity, high turnover, job-related changes, and organizational communication (Zey, 1988).

Apprenticeship

Apprenticeship is a very old model of employee training that has been used historically in the skilled trades (Hanley-Maxwell et al., 1996). Hanley-Maxwell and Millington (1992) described it as "a formal, long term training process (7 years is often required) that begins with full employment under the direction of one or more journey-workers and relies heavily on hands-on acquisition of skills through demonstration, modeling, and practice" (p. 55). Frequently, classroom or in-service training accompanies the on-the-job experience. Such training may be required to move onto journeyman status (Hanley-Maxwell & Millington, 1992).

Ongoing Support

Ongoing support is the most unique facet of supported employment services. Ongoing support in supported employment is the provision of any services needed to support and maintain an individual with severe handicaps on his or her job. These supports

> must include continuous or periodic job skill training services provided at least twice monthly at the worksite throughout the term of employment. . . . The term also includes other support services provided at or away from the work site . . . if skill training services are also needed by, and provided to, that individual at the work site. (*Federal Register*, 1987)

Federal law also requires that supported employees must be earning at least minimum wage at the time of transfer from time-limited to extended or ongoing support services (Wehman et al., 1998). Although ongoing support requirements apply to all supported employees, they are slightly amended for supported employees with mental illness in that the minimum support services schedule is not specified. It is important to remember that regardless of the support service schedule, the employment specialist should use typical or natural supports whenever possible.

Ongoing support services, sometimes called follow-up, are intended to enhance the long-term maintenance of skills that are directly or indirectly critical to the job and to enhance the flexibility of the supported employee in adapting to changes. Ongoing support also continually reassesses the appropriateness of the match between the person and the job. To ensure they meet these goals, providers work with employers to identify potential problems and intervene early by providing on-the-job intervention or coordinating intervention by others. They also establish and adjust follow-up schedules to meet the needs of the supported employee (Rusch, 1986). Support services are provided to many people (e.g., supported employees, employer, coworkers, residential service provider, parent/guardian). However, the end goal is to support the worker in her or his job. Unfortunately, most of the research studies examining employment and consumers with severe mental illness consistently report findings regarding the difficulty these persons have in job tenure (Bond et al., 1997), a factor that many thought could be addressed through the provision of unlimited support in and out of the workplace.

Prior to ending vocational rehabilitation funding, federal law requires that the source for funding ongoing support must be in place. These supports vary from state to state but are usually provided by another service agency (e.g., mental retardation or developmental disabilities agencies, mental health agencies; Hanley-Maxwell et al., 1997), Medicaid home- and community-based waivers (West, Johnson, Cone, Hernandez, & Revell, 1998), or, more recently, TWWIIA (King & Collins, 2000).

Unfortunately, funding for ongoing support is often limited. The result is that many individuals are on waiting lists, and other alternatives must be found. One alternative frequently considered is PASS (Plan to Achieve Self-Sufficiency), a Social Security work incentive program. This program allows individuals who receive SSI to set aside income or resources to pay for their own support services. The PASS must be individualized, written, and have a specified work goal and time frame. Typically, the time frame is for 18 months. However, the time can be extended up to 4 years. One major benefit of this alternative is that the individual supported employee controls who provides the support and what types of support he or she receives (Hanley-Maxwell et al., 1997). The more recent program, TWWIIA, began its four-year phase-in in January 2001 in 13 states. In 2002, 20 additional states and the District of Columbia began the program, with the remaining 17 states and 5 territories joining the program in 2003. Under this program, individuals receiving SSDI or SSI are eligible to obtain vouchers, or tickets to work, for vocational rehabilitation, employment services, and other supports needed to obtain and maintain employment (King & Collins, 2000). These supports include helping the ticket holder reach employment goals through the design of an individual employment plan. Furthermore, TWWIIA service providers work with eligible individuals to identify and use appropriate work incentives, including obtaining and retaining health care coverage. In fact, starting in 2000, individuals with disabilities can retain Medicare coverage for longer periods and for greater earnings following the end of their trial work period.

Components Most Effective for People with Severe Mental Illness

Supported employment, whether provided as a job coach or individual placement and support approach, seems to be more effective than other vocational rehabilitation methods for assisting people with severe mental illness to secure and maintain competitive jobs. Even though supported employment outcomes for people with severe mental illness continue to lag behind other disability groups (Bond et al., 1997; Trotter et al., 1988), ongoing research has moved the field forward in terms of identifying those elements that seem to be more closely associated with successful job tenure. The following programmatic components appear to be associated with supported employment success for these consumers:

1. Securing agency-wide endorsement of the value and meaning of employment. This means that work is incorporated in the agency's mission, and consumers are exposed early and often to employment opportunities (Pratt et al., 1999).
2. Using accelerated entry or reentry into competitive employment (Bond et al., 1997). Frequently, the careers of consumers with severe mental illness may reflect a pattern of jobs held for short lengths of time, or "serial employment" (Fabian, 1999). Reducing the downtime between jobs facilitates reentry while maximizing learning experiences.
3. Integrating mental health and vocational services through multidisciplinary teams (Drake, 1998). The coordination between clinical and rehabilitation services is critical in supporting employment efforts (Bond et al., 1997).
4. Providing unlimited job support on a flexible "as-needed" basis, with the assumption that support services may abate and peak across the span of the job, rather than following a pattern of gradual tapering off (Bond et al., 1997).
5. Assisting consumers in coping with potential job losses and job failures in a positive manner, rather than "pathologizing" (Baron & Salzer, 2000) them to avoid further comprising outcome expectations regarding work.
6. Making efforts to vary job opportunities in a manner consistent with consumer skills and interests. Some individuals with severe mental illness may have acquired considerable education and job skills prior to first experiencing symptoms of the illness. Thus, they challenge supported employment programs to offer a wide exposure to jobs consistent with more advanced backgrounds and skills (Baron & Salzer, 2000).
7. Promoting the concept of recovery from mental illness as a viable alternative to the concept of chronicity. This alternative view is a way to increase efficacy beliefs of consumers and promote positive outcome expectations of staff (Baron & Salzer, 2000).

SUMMARY, CONCLUSION, AND FUTURE SPECULATION

Supported employment brought people with severe disabilities from no employment or low-paying sheltered employment into community jobs. In the approximately two decades that have spanned its existence, supported employment has grown from a small handful of programs serving a small number of supported workers to over 3,600 providers serving more than 140,000 supported employees (Kregel, 1997). The success of these programs can be measured in the satisfaction of the supported workers and their employers and the benefits to the taxpayers (Cimera, 2000; Kregel, 1997).

Supported employees earn approximately $768 million annually. These wages are significantly better than they would have earned in alternative placements. In addition, supported employees report that they are satisfied with their jobs and with those people with whom they work (Kregel, 1997).

Employers report that they are satisfied with the reliability, dependability, loyalty, and attitudes of supported employees. They are also beginning to recognize that it makes good business sense to hire supported employees (Kregel, 1997).

Benefits to taxpayers can be measured in the taxes supported employees pay. They can also be seen in the reduced dependence of supported employees on subsidies (e.g., SSI) and the reduction in the cost of services that would have been incurred if supported employees were not participating in supported employment (Cimera, 2000; Kregel, 1997).

The growth in and the success of these programs are even more impressive when put within the context of the fact that supported workers are almost all individuals who would never have been thought to be able to work in community employment settings. This growth has been supported by legislation (e.g., ADA, IDEA, Workforce Investment Act), the demand for new labor, and a changing social climate that has resulted in more acceptance of people with disabilities. Although supported employment has grown and succeeded, it continues to face many challenges.

Challenges faced by supported employment programs today include ensuring that they serve individuals with severe disabilities. Despite the fact that supported employment was originally targeted as a service for these people, only 10.3% of supported employees with mental retardation are considered severely or profoundly retarded (Wehman et al., 1998). Rogan et al. (2000) postulated that this is because of inadequate funding for ongoing support. In fact, current funding patterns continue to more fully support facility-based programs (Kregel, 1997). Furthermore, Rogan et al.

suggested that providers lack adequate knowledge about assistive technology and employment options. It also appears that professionals and employers continue to have low expectations for these individuals (Kregel, 1997).

Persons with mental illness continue to struggle in employment programs. Although they are represented in supported employment, their outcomes are not as good as those of other supported employees (Noble et al., 1997). New models, more comprehensive services, and improved beliefs about these supported employees hold promise for their futures.

Supported employment programs also have to reconsider how they approach the provision of supports (e.g., who provides them, what supports are accessed) to ensure that they are as natural or typical as possible in each employment setting. The research of Mank et al. (1997) is clear: The more typical the job-getting, learning, and support process, the more successful the supported employee. This has implications for how the supported worker is involved in the process from job search to doing the job on an ongoing basis. Current research and thinking urge providers to maximally involve the supported employee in every stage of the process. In addition, they suggest that supported employees have greater control over the selection and implementation of supports (Unger et al., 1998). Furthermore, if supported employees are going to move out of the secondary labor market sectors, service providers need to attend to the career growth and development needs of these workers.

Finally, supported employment agencies are challenged to shed the social services image that they have used for many years. Instead of using the "hire the handicapped" approach (McLoughlin et al., 1987), they are encouraged to develop a more businesslike posture (Owens-Johnson & Hanley-Maxwell, 1999). The intended result is the development of agency–employer partnerships that benefit the supported employees and the businesses. Businesses become one more customer in the process.

Each of these challenges must be faced head-on if supported employment is to fulfill its promises. This chapter has presented foundational information on supported employment; it has also presented potential solutions to some of the challenges listed above. It is up to the agencies and their funders to meet these challenges and learn new ways of doing business.

REFERENCES

Americans with Disabilities Act of 1990, 42 U.S.C. § 12101 *et seq*.

Baer, R., Simmons, T., Flexer, R., & Smith, C. (1995). A study of the costs and benefits of supported employees with severe physical and multiple disabilities. *Journal of Rehabilitation Administration, 18*(1), 46–57.

Baron, R. C., & Salzer, M. S. (2000). The career patterns of persons with serious mental illness: Generating a new vision of a lifetime for those in recovery. *Psychiatric Rehabilitation Skills, 4*(1), 136–156.

Beard, J. H., Propst, R. N., & Malamud, T. J. (1982). The Fountain House model of psychiatric rehabilitation. *Psychosocial Rehabilitation Journal, 5*, 47–53.

Bellamy, G. T., Rhodes, L. E., & Albin, J. M. (1986). Supported employment. In W. E. Kiernan & J. A. Stark (Eds.), *Pathways to employment for adults with developmental disabilities* (pp. 129–138). Baltimore: Brookes.

Bellamy, G. T., Rhodes, L. E., Mank, D. M., & Albin, J. M. (1988). *Supported employment: A community integration guide*. Baltimore: Brookes.

Berg, W. K., Wacker, D. P., & Flynn, T. H. (1990). Teaching generalization and maintenance of work behavior. In F. R. Rusch (Ed.), *Supported employment: Models, methods, and issues* (pp. 145–160). Sycamore, IL: Sycamore.

Bissonnette, D. (1994). *Beyond traditional job development: The art of creating opportunity*. Chatworth, CA: Wright & Associates.

Bond, G. R., Dietzen, L. L., McGrew, J. H., & Miller, L. D. (1995). Accelerating entry into supported employment for persons with severe psychiatric disabilities. *Rehabilitation Psychology, 40*(2), 75–94.

Bond, G. R., Drake, R. E., Mueser, K. T., & Becker, D. R. (1997). An update on supported employment for people with severe mental illness. *Psychiatric Services, 48*, 335–346.

Buckley, J., Mank, D. M., & Cioffi, A. R. (1988). Supported employment for individuals with "other" disabilities. In C. Hanley-Maxwell & D. Harley (Eds.), *Special report: An examination of the impact of supported employment on our nation's citizens with severe disabilities* (pp. 25–33). Washington, DC: President's Committee for Employment of People with Disabilities.

Callahan, M. (1999). The promise and pitfalls of the Workforce Investment Act. *TASH Newsletter, 25*(5/6), 15–18.

Cimera, R. E. (1998). Are individuals with severe or multiple disabilities cost-efficient to serve via supported employment? *Mental Retardation, 36*, 280–292.

Cimera, R. E. (2000). Improving the cost efficiency of supported employment programs. *Journal of Disability Policy Studies, 11*, 145–151.

Comprehensive Employment Training Act of 1973, 29 U.S.C. § 1501 *et seq*.

Danek, M. M., Seay, P. C., & Collier, M. (1989). Supported employment and deaf people: Current practices and emerging issues. *Journal of Applied Rehabilitation Counseling, 20*(3), 34–43.

Danley, K., & Anthony, W. A. (1987). The choose-get-keep model: Serving severely psychiatrically disabled people. *American Rehabilitation, 13*(4), 27–29.

Danley, K. S., & Mellen, V. (1987). Training and personnel issues for supported employment programs which serve persons who are severely mentally ill. *Psychosocial Rehabilitation Journal, 11*(2), 87–102.

Developmental Disabilities Assistance and Bill of Right Act of 1984, 42 U.S.C. § 6000 *et seq*.

Drake, R. E. (1998). A brief history of the Individual Placement and Support Model. *Psychiatric Rehabilitation Journal, 22*(1), 3–7.

Drake, R. E., McHugo, G. J., Becker, D. R., Anthony, W. A., & Clark, R. I. (1996). The New Hampshire study of supported employment for people with severe mental illness. *Journal of Consulting and Clinical Psychology, 64*, 391–399.

Education for All Handicapped Children Act of 1975, 20 U.S.C. § 1400 *et seq.*

Fabian, E. S. (1992). Longitudinal outcomes in supported employment: A survival analysis. *Rehabilitation Psychology, 37*, 23–36.

Fabian, E. S. (1999). Rethinking work: The example of consumers with serious mental health disorders. *Rehabilitation Counseling Bulletin, 42*, 302–316.

Fabian, E. S., & Luecking, R. (1991). Doing it the company way: Using internal company supports in the workplace. *Journal of Applied Rehabilitation Counseling, 22*(2), 32–35.

Fabian, E. S., Luecking, R. G., & Tilson, G. P. (1994). *A working relationship: The job development guide to successful partnerships with business*. Baltimore: Brookes.

Federal Register. (1987, August 14). Rehabilitation Act Amendments of 1986: The State Supported Employment Services Program; final regulations (34 CFR Part 363), *52*(157), 30546–30552.

Geist, C., & Calzaretta, W. (1982). *Placement handbook for counseling disabled persons*. Springfield, IL: Thomas.

Gilbride, D. D., & Stensrud, R. (1992). Demand-side job development: A model for the 1990s. *Journal of Rehabilitation, 58*(4), 34–39.

Hagner, D. C. (1992). The social interactions and job supports of supported employees. In J. Nisbet (Ed.), *Natural supports in school, at work, and in the community for people with severe disabilities* (pp. 217–239). Baltimore: Brookes.

Hagner, D., Rogan, P., & Murphy, S. T. (1992). Facilitating natural supports in the work place: Strategies for support consultants. *Journal of Rehabilitation, 58*, 29–34.

Hanley-Maxwell, C. (1986). Curriculum development. In F. R. Rusch (Ed.), *Competitive employment: Issues and strategies* (pp. 187–198). Baltimore: Brookes.

Hanley-Maxwell, C., & Bordieri, J. E. (1989). Purchasing supported employment: Evaluating the service. *Journal of Applied Rehabilitation Counseling, 20*(3), 4–11.

Hanley-Maxwell, C., Bordieri, J., & Merz, M. A. (1996). Supporting placement. In E. M. Szymanski & R. M. Parker (Eds.), *Work and disability: Issues in career counseling and job placement* (pp. 341–364). Austin, TX: PRO-ED.

Hanley-Maxwell, C., Griffin, S. L., Szymanski, E. M., & Godley, S. H. (1990, April). Supported and time-limited transitional employment services. *Journal of Visual Impairment and Blindness, 84*(4), 160–166.

Hanley-Maxwell, C., & Millington, M. (1992). Enhancing independence in supported employment: Natural supports in business and industry. *Journal of Vocational Rehabilitation, 2*(4), 51–58.

Hanley-Maxwell, C., Szymanski, E. M., & Owens-Johnson, L. (1997). School-to-work transition and supported employment. In R. Parker & E. M. Szymanski (Eds.),

Rehabilitation counseling: Basics and beyond (2nd ed., pp. 143–179). Austin, TX: PRO-ED.

Harper, J. (1993). Securing a role for people with disabilities in the workforce. *Journal of Vocational Rehabilitation*, *3*, 70–73.

Hill, M., & Wehman, P. (1983). Cost benefit analysis of placing moderately and severely handicapped individuals into competitive employment. *Journal of the Association of Persons with Severe Handicaps*, *8*, 30–39.

Individuals with Disabilities Education Act of 1990, 20 U.S.C. § 1400 *et seq*.

Individuals with Disabilities Education Act Amendments of 1997, 20 U.S.C. § 1400 *et seq*.

Inge, K., & Tilson, G. P. (1997). Ensuring support systems that work: Getting beyond the natural supports versus job coach controversy. *Journal of Vocational Rehabilitation*, *9*(2), 133–142.

Job Training Partnership Act of 1983, 29 U.S.C. § 1501 *et seq*.

Johnson, J. R., & Rusch, F. R. (1990). Analysis of hours of direct training provided by employment specialists to supported employees. *American Journal of Mental Retardation*, *94*, 674–682.

Johnson, W., & Packer, A. (1987). *Workforce 2000: Work and workers for the twenty-first century*. Indianapolis, IN: Hudson Institute.

Kiernan, W. E., Butterworth, J., Schalock, R. L., & Sailor, W. (1993). *Enhancing the use of natural supports for people with severe disabilities*. Boston: Training and Research Institute for People with Disabilities.

Kiernan, W. E., Carter, A., & Bronstein, E. (1989). Marketing and marketing management in rehabilitation. In W. E. Kiernan & R. L. Schalock (Eds.), *Economics, industry, and disability: A look ahead* (pp. 49–56). Baltimore: Brookes.

King, M., & Collins, S. (2000). So you want to go back to work? *Inside MS*, *18*(2), 40–41.

Knippen, J. T., & Green, T. B. (1990). Coaching. *Management Accounting*, *71*, 36–38.

Kregel, J. (1997). Supported employment. *Remedial and Special Education*, *18*, 194–196.

Kreutzer, J. S., & Morton, M. V. (1988). Traumatic brain injury: Supported employment and compensatory strategies for enhancing vocational outcomes. In P. Wehman & M. S. Moon (Eds.), *Vocational rehabilitation and supported employment* (pp. 291–312). Baltimore: Brookes.

Levinson, J. C. (1993). *Guerrilla marketing: Secrets for making big profits from your small business*. New York: Houghton Mifflin.

Lewis, D. R., Johnson, D. R., Bruininks, R. H., Kallsen, L. A., & Guillery, R. P. (1992). Is supported employment cost-effective in Minnesota? *Journal of Disability Policy Studies*, *3*, 67–92.

Mank, D. (1996). Evolving roles for employers and support personnel in the employment of people with disabilities. *Journal of Vocational Rehabilitation*, *6*, 83–88.

Mank, D., Buckley, J., & Rhodes, L. (1991). Systems change to supported employment: An analysis of states' technical assistance needs. *Journal of Vocational Rehabilitation*, *1*, 19–24.

Mank, D., Cioffi, A., & Yovanoff, P. (1997). Analysis of the typicalness of supported jobs, natural supports, wages and integration outcomes. *Mental Retardation*, *35*, 185–197.

Mank, D., Cioffi, A., & Yovanoff, P. (2000). Direct supported employment and its relation to job typicalness, coworker involvement, and employment outcomes. *Mental Retardation, 38,* 506–516.

Mank, D. M., Rhodes, L. E., & Bellamy, G. T. (1986). Four supported employment alternatives. In W. E. Kiernan & J. A. Stark (Eds.), *Pathways to employment for adults with developmental disabilities* (pp. 139–154). Baltimore: Brookes.

Martin, J. E. (1986). Identifying potential jobs. In F. R. Rusch (Ed.), *Competitive employment: Issues and strategies* (pp. 165–186). Baltimore: Brookes.

McCaughrin, W. B., Rusch, F. R., Conley, R. W., & Tines, J. (1992). A benefit-cost analysis of supported employment in Illinois: The first two years. *Journal of Developmental and Physical Disabilities, 3,* 129–145.

McDonald-Wilson, K. L., Mancuso, L. L., Danley, K. S., & Anthony, W. A. (1989). Supported employment for people with psychiatric disability. *Journal of Applied Rehabilitation Counseling, 20,* 50–57.

McLoughlin, C. S., Garner, J. B., & Callahan, M. (1987). *Getting employed, staying employed.* Baltimore: Brookes.

Moon, S., & Griffin, S. (1988). Supported employment service delivery models. In P. Wehman & S. Moon (Eds.), *Vocational rehabilitation and supported employment* (pp. 17–30). Baltimore: Brookes.

Nietupski, J., Verstagen, D., & Hamre-Nietupski, S. (1992). Incorporating sales and business practices into job development in supported employment. *Education and Training in Mental Retardation, 27,* 207–218.

Nisbet, J., & Hagner, D. (1988). Natural supports in the workplace: A reexamination of supported employment. *Journal of the Association for Persons with Severe Handicaps, 13,* 260–267.

Noble, J., Honberg, R., Hall, L. L., & Flynn, L. M. (1997). *A legacy of failure: The inability of the federal-state vocational rehabilitation system to serve people with severe mental illness.* Washington, DC: National Alliance for the Mentally Ill.

Owens-Johnson, L., & Hanley-Maxwell, C. (1999). Employer views on job development strategies for marketing supported employment. *Vocational Rehabilitation, 12,* 113–123.

Pancsofar, E. L. (1986). Assessing work behavior. In F. R. Rusch (Ed.), *Competitive employment: Issues and strategies* (pp. 93–102). Baltimore: Brookes.

Pancsofar, E. L., Steere, D., & Wood, R. (1993). Consumer assessment: Ten important considerations. *The Advance, 4*(3), 1–3.

Parent, W. S., & Hill, M. I. (1990). Converting segregated sheltered employment to supported employment. In F. R. Rusch (Ed.), *Supported employment: Models, methods, and issues* (pp. 317–336). Sycamore, IL: Sycamore.

Parker, R. M., Szymanski, E. M., & Hanley-Maxwell, C. (1989). Ecological assessment in supported employment. *Journal of Applied Rehabilitation Counseling, 20,* 26–33.

Patterson, J. B., & Curl, R. M. (1990). Ethics education in supported employment preparation. *Rehabilitation Education, 4,* 247–260.

Powell, T., Pancsofar, E., Steere, D., Butterworth, J., Itzkowitz, J., & Rainforth, B. (1991).

Supported employment: Providing integrated employment opportunities for persons with disabilities. White Plains, NY: Longman.

Pratt, C. W., Gill, K. J., Barrett, N. M., & Roberts, M. M. (1999). *Psychiatric rehabilitation*. New York: Academic Press.

President's Committee on Employment of People with Disabilities (PCEPD). (1987). *Fact sheet on supported employment*. Washington, DC: Author.

Rehabilitation Act of 1973, 29 U.S.C. § 701 *et seq*.

Rehabilitation Act Amendments of 1986, 29 U.S.C. § 701 *et seq*.

Rehabilitation Act Amendments of 1992, 29 U.S.C. § 701 *et seq*.

Rehabilitation Act Amendments of 1994, 29 U.S.C. § 701 *et seq*.

Rehabilitation Act Amendments of 1998, 29 U.S.C. § 701 *et seq*.

Rhodes, L. E., & Valenta, L. (1985). Industry-based supported employment: An enclave approach. *Journal of the Association for Persons with Severe Handicapps, 10*, 12–20.

Rogan, P., Banks, B., & Howard, M. (2000). Workplace supports in practice: As little as possible, as much as necessary. *Focus on Autism and Other Developmental Disabilities, 15*(1), 2–11.

Rusch, F. R. (1986). Developing a long-term follow-up program. In F. R. Rusch (Ed.), *Competitive employment: Issues and strategies* (pp. 225–232). Baltimore: Brookes.

Rusch, F. R., Chadsey-Rusch, J., & Johnson, R. R. (1991). Supported employment: Emerging opportunities for employment integration. In L. H. Meyer, C.A. Peck, & L. Brown (Eds.), *Critical issues in the lives of people with severe disabilities* (pp. 145–169). Baltimore: Brookes.

Rusch, F. R., Conley, R. W., & McCaughrin, W. B. (1993). Benefit-cost analysis of supported employment in Illinois. *Journal of Rehabilitation, 59*, 31–36.

Rusch, F. R., & Hughes, C. A. (1990). Historical overview of supported employment. In F. R. Rusch (Ed.), *Supported employment: Models, methods, and issues* (pp. 5–14). Sycamore, IL: Sycamore.

Rusch, F. R., Rusch, J. C., Menchetti, B. M., & Schutz, R. P. (1980). *Survey-train-place: Developing a school-aged vocational curriculum for the severely handicapped student*. Unpublished manuscript, University of Illinois, Department of Special Education, Urbana.

Rusch, F. R., Schutz, R. P., & Agran, M. (1982). Validating entry-level survival skills for service occupations: Implications for curriculum development. *Journal of the Association for the Severely Handicapped, 7*, 32–41.

Sandhusen, R. L. (1993). *Marketing* (3rd ed.). Hauppauge, NY: Barrons Business Review Series.

State of Wisconsin, Department of Workforce Development. (1996). *A labor shortage you say? Tell me something I don't know! A Wisconsin employers' guide for recruitment and retention survival in the late 20th and early 21st century*. Madison, WI: Author.

Stein, L. I., & Test, M. A. (1980). Alternatives to mental hospital treatment: I. Conceptual model, treatment program, and clinical evaluation. *Archives of General Psychiatry, 37*, 392–397.

Swaboda, F. (1990, July 20). The future has arrived. *Washington Post*, pp. F1, F4.

Szabo, J. C. (1990). Learning at work. *Nation's Business*, *78*, 27–28.

Szymanski, E. M. (1994). Transition: Life-span, life-space considerations for empowerment. *Exceptional Children*, *60*, 402–410.

Szymanski, E. M., Buckley, J., Parent, W. S., Parker, R. M., & Westbrook, J. D. (1988). Rehabilitation counseling in supported employment: A conceptual model for service delivery and personnel preparation. In S. E. Rubin & N. M. Rubin (Eds.), *Contemporary challenges to the rehabilitation counseling profession* (pp. 111–133). Baltimore: Brookes.

Szymanski, E. M., Hanley-Maxwell, C., & Parker, R. M. (1987). *Supported employment and time-limited transitional employment service delivery: An introductory guide for rehabilitation professionals*. Austin: University of Texas at Austin, Special Education Department.

Szymanski, E. M., & Parker, R. M. (1988). Suppported employment and time-limited transitional employment training: Options for rehabilitation counselors. *Journal of Applied Rehabilitation Counseling*, *19*(2), 11–15.

Targeted Jobs Tax Credit, 26 U.S.C. § 1201 *et seq.*

Test, D., & Wood, W. (1996). Natural supports in the workplace: The jury is still out. *Journal of the Association for Persons with Severe Handicaps*, *21*(4), 155–173.

Ticket to Work and Work Incentives Improvement Act of 1999, 42 U.S.C. § 1320 *et seq.*

Tines, J., Rusch, F. R., McCaughrin, W. B., & Conley, R. W. (1990). Benefit-cost analysis of supported employment in Illinois: A statewide evaluation. *American Journal of Mental Retardation*, *95*, 44–54.

Trotter, S., Minkoff, K., Harrison, K., & Hoops, J. (1988). Supported work: An innovative approach to the vocational rehabilitation of persons who are psychiatrically disabled. *Rehabilitation Psychology*, *33*, 27–36.

Udvari-Solner, A. (1990). *Variables associated with the integration of individuals with intellectual disabilities in supported employment settings*. Unpublished doctoral dissertation, University of Wisconsin, Madison.

Unger, D. D. (1999). Workplace supports: A view from employers who have hired supported employees. *Focus on Autism and Other Developmental Disabilities*, *14*(3), 167–179.

Unger, D., Parent, W., Gibson, K., Kane-Johnston, K., & Kregel, J. (1998). An analysis of the activities of employment specialists in natural support approach to supported employment. *Focus on Autism and Other Developmental Disabilities*, *13*(1), 27–38.

Wehman, P. (1988). Supported employment: Toward zero exclusion of persons with severe disabilities. In P. Wehman & S. Moon (Eds.), *Vocational rehabilitation and supported employment* (pp. 3–16). Baltimore: Brookes.

Wehman, P. (1996). Editorial. *Journal of Vocational Rehabilitation*, *5*, 169–171.

Wehman, P., Hill, M., Hill, J., Brooke, V., Pendelton, P., & Britt, C. (1985). Competitive employment for persons with mental retardation: A follow-up six years later. *Mental Retardation*, *23*, 274–281.

Wehman, P., & Kregel, J. (1992). Supported employment: Growth and impact. In P. Wehman, P. Sale, & W. Parent (Eds.), *Supported employment: Strategies for integration of workers with disabilities* (pp. 3–28). Stoneham, MA: Butterworth-Heinemann.

Wehman, P., & Moon, M. S. (1987). Critical values in employment programs for persons with developmental disabilities: A position paper. *Journal of Applied Rehabilitation Counseling, 18*(1), 12–16.

Wehman, P., Revell, G., & Kregel, J. (1998). Supported employment: A decade of rapid growth and impact. *American Rehabilitation, 24*(1), 31–44.

Wehman, P., Revell, W. G., Kregel, J., Kreutzer, J., Callahan, M., & Banks, P. D. (1990). Supported employment: An alternative model for vocational rehabilitation of persons with severe neurologic, psychiatric, or physical disability. In J. Kregel, P. Wehman, & M. S. Shafer (Eds.), *Supported employment for persons with severe disabilities: From research to practice* (Vol. 3, pp. 101–114). Richmond: Rehabilitation Center on Supported Employment, Virginia Commonwealth University.

West, M., Johnson, A., Cone, A., Hernandez, A., & Revell, G. (1998). Extended employment support: Analysis of implementation and funding issues. *Education and Training in Mental Retardation and Developmental Disabilities, 33*, 357–366.

Wolfe, P. S. (1992). Supported employment: A review of group models. In P. Wehman, P. Sale, & W. Parent (Eds.), *Supported employment: Strategies for integration of workers with disabilities* (pp. 3–28). Stoneham, MA: Butterworth-Heinemann.

Workforce Investment Act of 1998, 29 U.S.C. § 2801 *et seq*.

Zey, M. G. (1988, January). A mentor for all. *Personnel Journal*, pp. 46–51.

Job Placement and Employer Consulting: Services and Strategies

Dennis Gilbride and Robert Stensrud

For more than 80 years, rehabilitation professionals have been committed to assisting people with disabilities in finding and retaining employment. From its inception, placement has been recognized as an essential function of rehabilitation counseling in public and private rehabilitation (Berven, 1979; Collignon, Barker, & Vencill, 1992; Gilbride, 1993; Lynch & Martin, 1982; Muthard & Salomone, 1969; Parker & Szymanski, 1992; Rubin, et al., 1984; Sink & Porter, 1978). As we enter the 21st century, rehabilitation professionals confront many new challenges in assisting people with disabilities to succeed vocationally. Changes in the expectations of consumers, public policy, and the world of work make this an exciting but demanding time for the field of rehabilitation.

In this chapter, we will provide a broad overview of placement and the manner in which rehabilitation organizations are structured to assist consumers in obtaining employment. We will begin with a short discussion of the history of placement services. The specific activities in which rehabilitation counselors engage as they provide placement services have changed several times since the beginning of the 20th century. The changes have often been due to legislation, employment opportunities, the knowledge and skills of rehabilitation professionals, and, most recently, consumer expectations. In the first section, we will review how each of these factors has influenced delivery of placement services.

In the second section, we will describe and discuss current service delivery models. A number of methods have been developed to provide placement services. In this section, we will review the major models and discuss who generally provides placement services.

In the third section, we will discuss basic placement strategies. Over the past 80 years, many strategies have been developed to assist people with disabilities in finding, obtaining, and retaining employment. These are services provided directly to or for people with disabilities to assist them in becoming employed. We will also discuss the use of the Internet in job search and placement services for people from specific populations such as consumers with psychiatric disorders.

In the fourth section, we will discuss employer-centered services. Although somewhat less traditional than direct placement services, many rehabilitation practitioners have provided services directly to employers in an attempt to enhance employment outcomes for consumers. In this section, we will outline current models of employer-focused services and discuss how they are designed to bridge the gap between rehabilitation agencies and the labor market.

In the fifth section, we will discuss two new initiatives that may have a significant effect on rehabilitation placement: the Ticket to Work and Work Incentives Improvement Act of 1999 (TWWIIA) and the Workforce Investment Act of 1998 (WIA). We will describe these new public policies and the implications they have for delivery of placement services.

We will conclude with a discussion of the need for rehabilitation organizations to modify their management approach in response to these new challenges. Just as most other sectors of our economy have had to undergo significant retooling to meet contemporary challenges, rehabilitation organizations, practitioners, and educators similarly need to change.

HISTORICAL OVERVIEW OF PLACEMENT SERVICES

Placement services have evolved in response to a number of factors, including legislation, the labor market, the expertise of rehabilitation providers, and consumer expectations. In this section, will discuss how placement services were delivered during different eras.

Early Rehabilitation Services

Beginning during World War I, the vocational rehabilitation of injured soldiers was viewed as a federal responsibility, and the rehabilitation of civilians with disabilities was viewed as a state responsibility (James, 1987; Obermann, 1967). Consequently, initial federal legislation provided a great deal of support for veterans with disabilities and only minimal support for civilians. Veterans were provided a range of vocational training and support services, but the civilian program was initially quite small and limited.

The labor market from the beginning of the 20th century through the 1940s provided jobs but little opportunity for advancement. Galbraith (1998) stated that this "Victorian" economy consisted of a few owners and many workers, which dramatically restricted employment options for people with no property or access to capital. Most people tended to get agricultural or industrial jobs and keep them as long as they were in the workforce. During the Great Depression, many people with disabilities who had obtained employment lost their jobs. The labor market took years to improve, and Obermann (1967) concluded that placement strategies were often not adequate to meet this challenge.

During these early years, vocational rehabilitation counselors were typically paraprofessionals with little autonomy. This lack of skills seriously limited the types of placement services that could be offered. These limited services were often provided in a paternalistic fashion that allowed little consumer participation or decision making.

Placement Between 1950 and 1973

During this period, federal legislation focused on expanding the scope of services provided to people with disabilities along with extending services to people with different disabilities. Placement continued to be recognized as a critical aspect of vocational rehabilitation services, but attention was diverted to expanding understanding of medical restoration and other rehabilitation issues (Cull & Hardy, 1972).

The labor market was also expanding during this period, resulting in many new vocational opportunities. Despite this, unemployment of people with disabilities remained high relative to the overall employment rate (President's Committee on Employment of the Handicapped, n.d.). The role of the rehabilitation counselor expanded to "selling" to employers the idea of employing people with disabilities (McGowan & Porter, 1967). Placement services became more sophisticated with many new strategies such as employer development, job-seeking skills training, job analysis, job engineering, selected placement, and client-centered placement (McGowan & Porter, 1967).

Placement Between 1973 and 1990

The expanding expertise of vocational rehabilitation (VR) counselors and other related medical professions, paired with the emergence of the disability civil rights movement, resulted in a serious critique of the VR system (Shapiro, 1994). Along with other political factors, this led in 1973 to a major rewriting of the Rehabilitation Act (P.L. 93-112). Although placement was still essential to the act, it became less central to actual practice (President's Committee on Employment of the Handicapped, n.d.). Rehabilitation counselors became more responsive to the procedural requirements of the legislation and less flexible in responding to the employment concerns of consumers.

At the same time, the labor market began experiencing severe restructuring. Major layoffs occurred for the first time in many businesses. Blue-collar workers especially faced difficult times as the United States adjusted to a global marketplace in which the price of commodities such as oil rose dramatically and the cost of produced goods declined due to international competition. Employers responded to this by seeking more white-collar managers who were expected to bring efficiency to their business, and they laid off production workers to reduce costs (Gharajedaghi, 1999). More than ever before, people with disabilities had to pursue higher education if they wanted quality employment.

Rehabilitation in the 1990s

In the 1990s, consumers stated with more clarity that a central goal of VR was employment (Shapiro, 1994). The legislation of the early 1990s—the Americans with Disabilities Act (ADA) of 1990 and the Rehabilitation Act Amendments of 1992—were increasingly designed to respond to consumers' expectations.

Although rehabilitation counselors were more professional and more well trained than ever before, they were expected to operate in a distinctly different manner. This new approach seemed to address the employment-related expectations of consumers (Stensrud, 2000). Furthermore, research in supported employment had demonstrated that even consumers with the most severe disabilities could work if provided appropriate supports. Placement meant more than getting a job. It also meant having the supports necessary to keep the job and maintain independence with the salary and benefits the job provided. The rehabilitation counselor of the 1990s had to address such consumer issues as transportation, childcare, housing, access to health care, on-the-job support, career advancement, and ongoing postemployment training.

As never before, the labor market played a dramatic role in placement options (Rifkin, 1995). Jobs that offered quality employment opportunities became centralized in metropolitan areas, creating a barrier to consumers who wished to live in rural areas. Furthermore, although unemployment rates reached historical lows by the late 1990s, many people with disabilities were still unemployed. New laws such TWWIIA and WIA were designed to reduce barriers to employment and improve placement services.

It is clear from this short historical review that legislation, labor markets, placement expertise, and, more recently, consumer empowerment have played important roles in the manner and type of placement services provided to people with disabilities. In the next section, we will review current service delivery models.

SERVICE DELIVERY MODELS

Almost all current placement and job development services are provided within one of the following four delivery systems: general rehabilitation counselor, specialized placement professional, contracted service, and supported employment (Gilbride, Stensrud, & Johnson, 1994). These service delivery models are not mutually exclusive. Most VR agencies use a combination of service providers to provide placement services, and similar placement techniques are generally used by professionals across delivery models (Gilbride, 2000). It is useful to delineate these approaches, however, because the manner in which an agency organizes its placement efforts reflects that agency's values concerning the centrality of placement to its mission. Furthermore, such delineation may facilitate future research and help determine the relative effectiveness of these models.

The model that has been used most consistently in the state VR system is placement provided by the *vocational rehabilitation counselor*. In this model, placement is viewed as the end state of the vocational rehabilitation counselor–consumer relationship (Vandergoot, 1987; Wright, 1980). In this model, rehabilitation counselors are often evaluated based on the number of consumers they place and close as rehabilitated (Status Code 26). Much research has focused on the skills rehabilitation counselors require to successfully place consumers and the specific services, techniques, and time required to attain placements (Vandergoot, 1987; Zadny & James, 1976, 1977; these techniques will be addressed in detail below).

In a recent study, Gilbride (2000) found that just over half of all placement services are still provided by rehabilitation counselors. He found that over the next 3 to 5 years, VR administrators anticipate that counselors will continue to provide this level of placement. Although this study suggested that counselors will continue to have a great deal of responsibility for placement, very significant interagency differences were found. Some agencies used rehabilitation counselors for all their placement, and others only required minimal placement activity by their counselors. State agencies across the country are clearly using a variety of placement staffing approaches.

At present, no research is available to help determine if these differences in staffing lead to differences in consumer employment outcomes. The decision to require rehabilitation counselors to provide placement services is often a result of the specific focus and belief system of the state administrator. Gilbride (2000) found that although a majority of state VR administrators have a strong commitment to placement, separation of the placement function may unintentionally limit rehabilitation counselors' knowledge of the labor market.

The second delivery system entails the use of *specialized professionals*. In a somewhat dated but comprehensive analysis of VR personnel needs, Cohen and Pelavin (1992) found that approximately 265 full-time equivalents nationwide in the public system were identified as placement specialists (in comparison to 6,827 counselors). Melia (1984) stated that the specialized professional model emerged during the mid-1970s. He indicated that a number of factors contributed to the development of this model, including the focus of the Rehabilitation Act of 1973 on people with the most severe disabilities and service delivery advances such as job clubs (Azrin, Flores, & Kaplan, 1975; Vandergoot, 1987). Gilbride (2000) found that currently 20% of all placement is provided by specialized placement personnel, and the use of specialists is expected to increase over the next 3 to 5 years to 28%.

Some research has focused on how specialized placement services should be structured to enhance client outcomes (McLoughlin, Garner, & Callahan, 1987; Molinaro, 1977). The use of placement specialists to provide job-seeking skills, job club, employer development, and other technical services have been widely discussed, but the cost-effectiveness of this approach remains uncertain (Vandergoot, 1987).

The third delivery system is *contracted services*. Many public agencies use not-for-profit organizations, called community rehabilitation programs, to provide placement services (Hayward, Reisner, & Choisser, 1986; Wehman & Melia, 1985). Cohen and Pelavin (1992) found 3,503 positions budgeted in the private sector for placement services.

Gilbride (2000) found that 28% of placement is currently contracted out, generally to community rehabilitation programs, and that VR administrators anticipate 30% will be contracted within the next 3 to 5 years. However, Gilbride again found very large interagency differences, with some agencies not using contractors and others contracting up to 80% of their placement services. Clearly, contracting is a significant and growing part of the placement service delivery system, even though its efficacy has not been empirically established.

Another related approach to contracted services is the federally funded program called Projects with Industry (PWI). In many states, VR contracts with a PWI provider for placement services. PWI was nationally funded during the 2000 fiscal year at $22,071,000, making it a relatively small program but potentially significant in the local communities in which it is available.

The central idea of PWI is to move the placement function closer to the employer. In PWI, placement specialists collaborate with business through the use of employer councils (Baumann, 1986; Kaplan & Hammond, 1982). PWI uses placement specialists as in the second model but also emphasizes the development of cooperative relationships between rehabilitation providers and employers. Kaplan and Hammond (1982) indicated that PWI is necessary because rehabilitation counselors often are not trained in job placement and do not know how to market people with disabilities effectively to employers. However, little research has been conducted on the effect of PWI on consumer employment outcomes.

The fourth delivery system, *supported employment,* is discussed in greater depth in Chapter 11, this volume. Supported employment represents a dramatic shift from the prior three service delivery systems. Supported employment de-emphasizes preplacement services but focuses instead on postplacement training, integration, and ongoing support. Supported employment represents a conceptual and public policy change from all previous rehabilitation services. This model was designed to work with people with severe disabilities who previously may not have been considered feasible for traditional rehabilitation services (Bellamy et al., 1984). There is a large literature on supported employment (Bellamy, Rhodes, Mank, & Albin, 1988; Hanley-Maxwell, Szymanski, Parent, & Schriner, 1990; Rusch, 1990; Shafer, Revell, Kregel, Wehman, & West, 1991; Wehman, 1988; Wehman & Moon 1988), and a comprehensive discussion of supported employment is beyond the scope of this chapter.

Gilbride (2000) found that supported employment comprised 11.5% of VR placement activity, with a range from .5% to 50%. He found that 69% of administrators anticipated that supported employment would increase over the next 3 to 5 years. Most supported employment was handled through contractors (74.8%, SD = 37.8).

Gilbride (2000) found significant differences between general/combined agencies and departments for persons who are blind in the extent and manner in which they used supported employment. He found that general/combined agency administrators classified 14.2% (SD = 11.4) of their placement services as supported employment services, whereas administrators of departments for persons who are blind reported 5.2% (SD = 3.5, $p < .005$). General and combined administrators contracted out 81.3% (SD = 34.6) of their supported employment, whereas administrators of departments for persons who are blind contracted out 59.9% ($SD = 41.9$, $p < .067$). Supported employment was clearly a more significant placement strategy for general/combined agencies. Similar to the data on staffing trends, there are significant interagency differences.

BASIC PLACEMENT STRATEGIES

In this section, we will discuss the specific types of placement services that rehabilitation professionals tend to provide. Gilbride and Stensrud (1992) differentiated between *supply-side* and *demand-side* job development approaches. Supply-side approaches include all those services designed to support and assist the consumer in seeking and applying for employment (i.e., providing a *supply* of applicants to employers). As indicated above, these services may be provided by rehabilitation counselors, specialized personnel, or contractors. This section will only include supply-side services; services provided to employers (demand side) will be discussed later. Research has consistently found that a core set of placement services increases the employment outcomes of people with disabilities (Gilbride et al., 1994; Vandergoot, 1987). In one of the most important and complete reviews of the empirical data on placement, Vandergoot (1987) found that job-seeking skills, job-finding clubs, and interviewing skills were the key services linked to successful placement. In this section, we will discuss these services along with the use of the Internet and other supportive services such as transportation, childcare and psychological support, and specialized services for specific populations.

Job-Seeking Skills Training

Job-seeking skills training includes a range of services designed to assist the person with a disability in developing the skills necessary to find potential jobs, apply for open positions, and effectively interview with employers. Although placement issues should be considered during all aspects of the rehabilitation process, job-seeking skills training generally occurs after a vocational goal is developed and the consumer is ready to seek employment.

Although a number of job-seeking skills training activities occur during the same general time frame, an initial activity is development of a *resume*. There are a number of approaches to resume development and many excellent resources to assist consumers and placement personnel in writing a resume.

No specific type of resume is appropriate for all consumers or even for a specific consumer in all situations. The consumer and placement professional need to consider how to best tell the consumer's "story" to an employer. The resume needs to be both accurate and relevant for the position being sought. The resume needs to highlight the consumer's relevant skills, education, and qualifications while still providing a coherent narrative concerning the person's work history. Employers are sensitive to unexplained gaps in work history or a work history with many brief unrelated positions.

Working with consumers to find a way to honestly and clearly describe their work histories is often challenging. For consumers with limited work histories or numerous employment gaps, a resume that focuses on related skills, rather than a chronological listing of positions, is generally more effective. In these situations, extra care needs to be taken with the cover letter. The *cover letter* is an opportunity for consumers to frame their abilities in a manner consistent with employers' needs. Given the ease with which word-processing documents can be edited and printed, many consumers should have designated versions of their resume designed to highlight their qualifications for positions with different requirements. Furthermore, all cover letters should be individualized, and demonstrate knowledge about and interest in the specific position for which the consumer is applying.

Once a resume has been developed and consumers are clear about their qualifications, employment opportunities need to be identified and pursued. Bolles (2000) identified a number of *job search strategies*. We will briefly list and discuss 10 of his job-seeking tips as they relate to best practices in rehabilitation.

1. *Treat the job hunt as a full-time job*. This is often a key issue for consumers who have been out of the labor market for extended periods of time or for consumers with no work history. Looking for a job is a job. It requires discipline, effort, and follow-through. Looking for a job is hard work. It is often frustrating, intimidating, and frightening. However, to succeed, the consumer needs to persist, even in the face of multiple failures.

2. *Find a support group*. One of the most effective support groups is a job club (see "Job Club" section in this chapter). If a job club is not available, the placement professional needs to assist the consumer in finding an alternative support group. Although the support provided by the placement professional himself or herself is significant and vital, it often is insufficient to meet the consumer's daily needs.

3. *Enlist contacts*. Research has consistently found that most openings are filled by personal contacts rather than formal job announce-

ments (Jones & Azrin, 1973; Vandergoot, 1987). The placement professional needs to use both his or her own contacts and assist consumers in using their contacts.

4. *Expand contacts*. Many people with disabilities have limited social networks. Consumers can increase their contacts by participating in job fairs, volunteering, and becoming more active in community events or religious organizations. Helping consumers to expand their social connections is useful for both the job search and other rehabilitation goals such as community integration.
5. *Seek employers of interest, not just those with current openings*. Consumers can be encouraged to conduct labor market research and identify employers with positions that match their interests and qualifications. Consumers can conduct informational interviews with these employers either in person or by phone. Even if these contacts do not result in a job, other related opportunities may be identified, and the consumer is gaining valuable labor market information and skill in interacting with employers (Gilbride & Burr, 1993).
6. *Focus on smaller employers*. Although it is clear that this is good strategy for people without disabilities, focusing on small employers is a more mixed technique for placement of people with disabilities, particularly if substantial accommodations are required. (See the section "Comfort Enhancement" in this chapter for a more detailed discussion of employer size and its relation to opportunities for people with disabilities.)
7. *Visit at least two employers each weekday, face-to-face*. It is vital that the consumer begin engaging with employers. For many consumers, this will be a challenging assignment. At least initially, placement professionals may need to accompany the consumer on visits to employers. One strategy to increase consumers' contact with employers in a minimally threatening manner is to assign them the task of collecting business cards from employers (D. Vandergoot, personal communication, December 10, 2000). This strategy often helps consumers to gain both confidence and labor market information without becoming overwhelmed.
8. *When all else fails, canvass by telephone*. Consumers need to be supported in using all available tools to find jobs. Helping them develop telephone skills is important both in identifying potential openings and later in discussing a position or setting up interviews.
9. *Be flexible about type of job*. If consumers have limited work histo-

ries or are trying to enter a new vocational field, they may need to take an entry-level job inconsistent with their long-term goals or desires. This is a very delicate issue because too often people with disabilities are relegated to undesirable jobs that do not enhance their career development potential. Placement professionals need to carefully balance the need for the consumer to quickly enter the labor market, with the impact of the specific placement on that consumer's long-term goals.

10. *Don't give up*. Salomone (1971) asserted that placement personnel should demonstrate "unrealistic optimism." He stated that a key role for rehabilitation professionals is their attitude of optimism. Looking for work is often hard and discouraging. Rehabilitation professionals know that success is possible and, if approached effectively, probable. Communicating this hopefulness to consumers can make a difference.

The third major component of job-seeking skills training is *interviewing skills*. A great deal has been written in the rehabilitation and business literature on interviewing (Bolles, 2000; McLoughlin et al., 1987). Rehabilitation professionals and consumers need to consider three key aspects of interviewing: appearance, attitude, and behavior.

Much has been written on the need for applicants to have an appropriate *appearance*. McLoughlin et al. (1987) asserted that dress is a symbolic method to communicate with and connect to employers. Consumers need to recognize that their clothes and grooming must meet the expectations and culture of the employer. To meet employers' expectations, both the rehabilitation professional and the consumer must have accurate information about the employer, and the consumer must be willing to comply with employer norms.

The *attitude* of the consumer will also have a significant effect on the success of the interview. Consumers need to demonstrate confidence in their ability to perform the essential functions of the job without appearing cocky or condescending toward the employer or the type of work they would be expected to perform. Consumers need to indicate interest in the employer and demonstrate an understanding of the employer's needs and expectations. Employers are generally looking for someone with a positive attitude toward work and an ability to get along with supervisors and peers. Assisting consumers to recognize potential limitations in their self-presentation and helping them to improve are an important responsibility for rehabilitation professionals.

Along with appearance and attitude, consumers also need to demonstrate appropriate *behavior* during the interview. There are many good lists of dos and don'ts during an interview; consequently, only a few key issues will be discussed here. First, the consumer must be on time to the interview. Employers are extremely concerned about basic work behaviors such as timeliness and consistency. Being late to the interview will be a major red flag for an employer and is likely to negate considerations of qualification and skill. Other key behaviors to avoid include not smoking or chewing gum during the interview, not discussing salary or benefits early in an interview, and not making derogatory statements about previous employers. On the positive side, consumers need to demonstrate an ability to listen to the employer and answer questions clearly and accurately. Rehabilitation professionals need to assist consumers to anticipate employer questions and practice answering them so they can be delivered in an effective manner.

The most difficult questions for consumers to answer will often concern disability-related gaps in employment and *accommodation* needs. Although not every consumer will require an accommodation, those who do should be provided instruction on how to raise and discuss their needs. It is vital that the consumer have an understanding of the essential functions of the position for which they are applying and a clear ability to describe how they can perform those job duties. The ability of consumers to provide the employer with a straightforward accommodation plan can greatly enhance their ability to get a job offer. Rehabilitation professionals need to help consumers identify their accommodation needs and then assist the consumer to develop a plan that the consumer can present to an employer. If the employer views the consumer as a "problem," the likelihood of employment is greatly reduced. It is also important for the rehabilitation professional to assist the consumer in accessing other community resources for accommodation needs such as computer technology for a person with a visual disability.

In general, interviewing is a complex process that is often the central determinate in employment decisions. Increasing consumers' ability to successfully interview will greatly enhance their employability.

Job Club

A *job club* is defined as an intensive behavioral counseling program that includes development of interpersonal and job-seeking skills, the use of a social informational network, and motivational strategies (Azrin & Philips, 1979). The standard job club procedure includes between 4 and 12 job seekers who meet for 2½ hours per day. Job searchers are assigned a partner (for direct support) and provided support by all members of the group. Professionals monitor and help coach job seekers during telephone calls and in preparation for interviews. The professional also conducts structured lessons each day on various aspects of the job-seeking process. The content of the daily lesson plans includes many of the components of job-seeking skills training as outlined above (Azrin & Philips, 1979; Jones & Azrin, 1973).

Azrin and Philips (1979) found that the job club method dramatically increased placement of people with disabilities, reduced the time it took consumers to be placed, and resulted in higher starting salaries. The job club method has been widely used in rehabilitation, and a majority of state agencies have indicated that they use this technique (Gilbride, 2000).

Although a majority of agencies indicate support for the job club strategy, it is often difficult for a specific office to maintain. Rehabilitation offices in more rural areas, or those that serve consumers from a broad geographic area, often find they cannot maintain a job club. To be effective, a job club must have an ongoing set of job seekers both to provide mutual support and to justify agency resources. Consequently, a job club is generally more practical for larger offices.

Use of the Internet in Job Search

It has been widely noted that the Internet has dramatically affected many aspects of our culture and economy. The potential transformative effect of the Internet on job seeking and placement is also clear (Patterson, 2000). Although the use of the Internet is evolving rapidly, significant innovations have already occurred in career planning, finding potential jobs, and applying for open positions. Our intent here is not to provide an exhaustive review of Internet Web sites but rather to provide a sample of the types of resources currently available to support placement of people with disabilities.

The Internet has already become one of the most effective methods to find current information about the world of work (Kirk, 2000). Many of the fundamental tools for vocational exploration are already online such as the *Occupational Outlook Handbook* (http://stats.bls.gov/ocohome.htm), O*NET (http://online.onetcenter.org/), and the U.S. Department of Labor (http://www.dol.gov/). Placement professionals and consumers can use these resources to find current information about jobs and careers. There are also numerous Web sites designed to assist job seekers with many of the job-seeking skills, already outlined, such as resume development and interviewing skills.

There are also many Web sites that list job openings. Excellent sources of online job openings include local newspapers and specific employers. If consumers are interested in working for a specific employer, they can often find current openings on that employer's Web site. There are also national databases such as Monster (http://www.monster.com/) or Careerbuilder (http://www.careerbuilder.com).

A third and growing use of the Internet concerns applying for positions online and posting resumes. Many employers already have procedures that allow applicants to submit their resumes directly online. Applying online has significant implications for rehabilitation consumers. Those implications include cover letter and resume design, along with ensuring that consumers have adequate access to the Internet. Increasingly, employers expect applicants to have e-mail accounts and be able to effectively communicate online.

Undoubtedly, the Internet will continue to have a growing effect on the job-seeking process. Gilbride (2000) found that state agencies seem to understand the importance of this tool, as every state agency indicated that it currently uses or anticipates using the Internet to support placement services.

Supportive Services

Along with the technical services listed above, most state agencies also provide a range of supportive services designed to reduce barriers to employment. Gilbride (2000) found that the two most common services involved assisting consumers to solve their transportation and childcare needs. Transportation has been one the most persistent barriers for people with disabilities. Despite improvements resulting from the ADA, many people with disabilities still do not have access to effective public transportation. Rehabilitation providers often advocate in their local communities for improvements in public transportation and help consumers access public systems that are available. However, in many communities, transportation remains a significant barrier.

Helping consumers to find and access childcare is also a significant barrier for many woman (and some men) with disabilities. Fortunately, many communities have low-cost or subsidized childcare. The role of the rehabilitation professional is to help the consumer find childcare and organize care in a manner that allows that consumer to seek, obtain, and retain employment.

Special Populations

Gilbride (2000) found that a majority of state agencies have specialized placement personnel working with people with specific disabilities or from distinct populations. Agencies overwhelmingly have transition specialists, and most have placement personnel specifically trained to work with consumers with mental illness and head injuries. A majority of agencies also have specialists in the areas of mental retardation, spinal cord injury, and substance abuse. Most administrators plan to retain specialized placement personnel, and a few of the agencies currently without specialists anticipate having them in the next 3 to 5 years. This is particularly the case in the areas of head injury and substance abuse.

There has also been a great deal of attention paid to the needs of consumers from traditionally underrepresented groups. Most of the major rehabilitation counseling journals had special editions dedicated to this issue during the 1990s. However, few specific placement strategies have been developed for these groups other than in the area of mental illness.

People with psychiatric disabilities are a group in which specialized services are among the most well developed. The clubhouse model advanced by Fountain House included a number of innovative vocational strategies, including *transitional employment* (Beard, Propst, & Malamud, 1982). Unlike other techniques, transitional employment is not designed to be a final job placement. In this model, a number of jobs are developed by the agency. The consumer can then try out these various jobs, but the jobs "belong" to the clubhouse. The purpose is not to place the consumer in one of those jobs but rather to assist him or her to gain work experience that can then be applied to another non–transitional employment position (Bilby, 1992). Nationwide, many clubhouses use this model. Little empirical research is available on the effectiveness of transitional employment, but the broader clubhouse model has been found to be very helpful and effective for people with psychiatric disabilities (Bond, 1992).

EMPLOYER-CENTERED SERVICES

In this section, we will focus on employers. The basic placement competencies outlined in the previous section are examples of supply-side techniques. Demand-side techniques are services provided to *employers* that make the workplace more user-friendly for people with disabilities and assist employers in meeting their personnel needs by "pulling in" (i.e., creating *demand* for) people with disabilities. Working within this model, rehabilitation professionals act as consultants to employers. They provide services to employers traditionally purchased from other consultants by larger employers and often unavailable to smaller employers.

Many placement researchers have suggested that both the consumer and employer need to be viewed as rehabilitation customers (Garvin, 1983; McDonald, 1974; Millington, Asner, Linkowski, & Der-Stepanian, 1996; Young, Rosati, & Vandergoot, 1986). Critics (Salomone, 1996) are concerned that attention to employer needs distracts rehabilitation counselors from their central mission of serving consumers and results in "selling people as products."

Despite the controversy over providing services directly to employers, as early as 1970, Michigan, along with other state VR agencies, attempted to improve consumer employment outcomes by providing services to employers. Molinaro (1977) described the "Michigan model" of the early 1970s that included an employer services unit. The employer services unit provided worker compensation assistance, disability awareness training, maintenance services, and troubled employee assistance directly to employers.

Gilbride (2000) found a great deal of support for employer-centered services in his recent survey of state VR agencies. He found that 83% of administrators indicated that they provided consulting services to employers, whereas 85% anticipated committing more resources to employer development over the next 3 to 5 years. None of the administrators anticipated decreasing resources.

Prior to looking at the specific competencies rehabilitation professionals need to develop to be effective employer consultants, we will review data from employers. This information can help in understanding the type of services employers say that they would like from the disability community.

Employer Needs and Concerns

In a recent comprehensive review of the literature, Hernanadez, Keys, and Balcazar (2000) concluded that employers expressed a willingness to hire people with disabilities, but in practice little hiring was actually accomplished. This conclusion is consistent with other research that has found a gap between the employment needs of people with disabilities and employers' statements concerning willingness to hire. Harris and Associates (1994) for example, found that many people with disabilities were unemployed or underemployed, with a majority of people stating they wanted to work but were unable to secure jobs. Gilbride and Stensrud (1993), however, found that employers were willing to hire people with disabilities but were unable to recruit them. This apparent contradiction has led to some confusion regarding why unemployment among people with disabilities has remained high.

In a recent study, Stensrud (1999) interviewed employers to determine why they did not hire more people with disabilities. He found that employers did not know how to tap the public and private agencies that served people with disabilities. Many were unaware of the existence of such agencies, and others knew of no method by which to request referrals. In other cases, employers mistrusted these agencies because they failed in the past to be helpful after placement.

Second, many employers were uncertain how to conduct the job selection process. Smaller employers were especially uncertain of their requirements under the ADA, were uncomfortable about talking about disabilities, and had little idea how to provide accommodations. Given these uncertainties, many preferred to avoid potential problems by not hiring people they knew to have disabilities.

Third, employers wanted a degree of comfort that there would be postemployment problem-solving assistance if they hired a person with a disability and confronted disability-related dilemmas. These problems could involve coworker conflicts, work performance issues, or accommodation concerns. In any case, the knowledge that someone could assist in their resolution would increase employers' comfort.

These findings suggest that both rehabilitation consumers and employers are correct. People with disabilities are unemployed at disproportionate rates, and employers are trying to tap people with disabilities as an employment resource. The problem is that disability service agencies (including both state VR and community rehabilitation programs) have not been effective at bringing these two groups together. Employers want VR to address four distinct issues: recruiting assistance, comfort enhancement, early employment assistance, and long-term employment assistance.

Recruitment Assistance

Many employers do not have the capacity to recruit from a targeted population. Either they announce openings through media such as want ads, or they target openings by approaching specific individuals with the skills they desire. Placement activities that assist employers in identifying, targeting, and reaching specific audiences would be valuable.

Comfort Enhancement

Many small employers are still uncertain about the impact the ADA could have on their selection processes. Employers would appreciate specific information on the requirements of the ADA, where they are in and out of compliance, and how to address accommodation and accessibility issues. Informally, many employers would like to learn about "disability etiquette." They do not know how to inquire about disabilities or how to be comfortable around people with some disabilities. These concerns hold true only for smaller employers. Larger employers, especially those with corporate objectives related to employing people with disabilities, are comfortable with all these issues. These larger employers also are willing to assist smaller employers and need only to be asked. This may be an area in which VR can expand its employer development activities.

Early Employment Assistance

Early employment assistance pertains to the first 90 days a person is on the job. During that time, employers look for specific work behaviors to determine whether an employee will be retained. Interestingly, employers are more concerned during this time with an employee's motivation, enthusiasm, tardiness, absenteeism, interpersonal relations, and ability to handle feedback than they are about his or her work skills. Employers believe work skills were assessed as part of the selection process, so they are less concerned about them. Employers are most interested in determining whether the employee seems motivated and cooperative with coworkers and supervisors. This has implications for any job-keeping skills training VR may develop. Behaving as though one is motivated improves relations with coworkers and supervisors, thus better ensuring one's continued employment. If an employee does not seem motivated because of social reluctance or any other reason, that person will be evaluated as though he or she is not. Also during this phase, employers expect rehabilitation personnel to be available to help resolve any problems. If they do not feel rehabilitation personnel are responsive to their needs, they will not trust their recommendations in the future.

Long-Term Employment Assistance

During the fourth phase, long-term employment assistance, employers continue to expect assistance if any problems arise. During this phase, which may last for many years, employers look for employees who have appropriate job skills, good communication with coworkers and supervisors, and an apparent willingness to advance in their position. They are clear that by offering a job to a person, they have made a long-term commitment to him or her. Employers expect that rehabilitation personnel should do the same for them. If VR counselors or contracted placement personnel do not provide long-term follow-up and problem resolution assistance, employers will not rely on them in the future as placement resources.

Given these employer concerns, we will now return to a discussion of the types of services that rehabilitation agencies may be in a position to provide to employers. We will begin with a discussion of the demand-side model proposed by Gilbride and Stensrud (1992, 1999). We will then discuss other employer consulting issues, and finally we will evaluate the "fit" between rehabilitation services and employer needs.

Essential Functions of a Demand-Side Placement Specialist

We have divided the essential functions of a demand-side specialist into four clusters: developing consulting relationships with employers, providing consulting services to employers, providing labor market consulting services to rehabilitation counselors and agencies, and using Internet technology to enhance employment solutions (see Table 12.1 for a list of the specific competencies). In this section we will discuss each of these four clusters of competencies.

Developing Consulting Relationships with Employers

The central purpose of this cluster of competencies is to develop and maintain relationships with employers. A number of researchers have discussed the importance of understanding employer needs and developing effective relationships with employers (Fry, 1997; Millington et al., 1996). The first step in instituting the demand-side model is determining which employers to contact and then developing ongoing consultative relationships with those companies.

Identifying the "right" employers to contact is a key aspect of this set of competencies; this is particularly significant because many consumers are placed into less desirable positions. Hagner (2000) has advanced an important theory concerning labor market access for people with disabilities. He asserted that the U.S. economy is divided into a primary and secondary labor market. The primary labor market includes those jobs with relatively high wages, fringe benefits, and worker-friendly workplace policies. The secondary labor market is marked by low wages, few benefits, and limited worker autonomy. He referred to these positions as being "food and filth" jobs. Hagner stated that the transition from the secondary to primary labor market is very difficult, and workers in the secondary market often become stuck. The need to assist rehabilitation consumers to access the primary, rather than secondary, labor market is an important function for the demand-side placement professional. Too often, consumers are placed into the secondary market and, according to Hagner, lose their ability for promotion or career development. Consequently, placement specialists need to be thoughtful about which employers they target.

Once appropriate employers have been identified, the demand-side

TABLE 12.1. Essential Functions of a Demand-Side Placement Specialist

A. Developing consulting relationships with employers
- Ability to identify employers with greatest employment opportunities
- Ability to develop effective consulting relationships with employers
- Ability to work with employers to identify both long- and short-term personnel needs
- Ability to identify and determine potential accommodations for hard-to-fill, growth, or easily accommodated jobs

B. Providing consulting services to employers

Ability to provide the following consulting services to employers:
- On-site job analyses to determine essential functions
- Job description development
- Cost-effective accessibility plans
- Ergonomic evaluations
- Identification and implementation of accommodations using rehabilitation engineering
- Assistance in recruiting and hiring people with disabilities
- Provision of training on disability-related topics
- Technical assistance in complying with the ADA and other state and federal laws
- Disability management and occupational safety programs
- Assistance to employer to support career development of all employees with disabilities (job saves)

C. Providing labor market consulting services to rehabilitation counselors and agencies
- Coordinating rehabilitation services for employers
- Developing employer–agency partnerships for training and economic development
- Developing relationships with other employment service agencies in the community
- Developing networks of smaller employers to develop disability-related training consortiums
- Accessing and analyzing labor market data from local, state, and national resources
- Educating rehabilitation counselors and other professionals in the entire community about employer's current and long-term personnel needs
- Assisting rehabilitation professionals to use labor market information in the development of rehabilitation plans for specific consumers

D. Using Internet technology to enhance employment solutions
- Using Internet resources to solve rehabilitation and employment problems
- Training and assisting employers to use Internet-based resources to increase employer's ability to hire and accommodate people with disabilities

specialist then needs to develop working relationships with those employers. The central focus in developing an effective relationship with an employer is a clear and authentic interest in that employer's personnel needs. The fundamental basis of the demand-side model involves assisting employers to reach out to people with disabilities to solve their company's personnel needs. As indicated above, many employers, particularly smaller businesses, would welcome such assistance. We can develop an effective relationship with employers to the extent that we can convince them we are interested in their business and that we are useful in helping them solve both their short- and long-term personnel needs. To be successful, the rehabilitation professional must demonstrate a business (in contrast to a social services) perspective. Sustainable placement strategies require rehabilitation professionals to understand that employers hire people to get work done, not because hiring them is the right thing to do.

Providing Consulting Services to Employers

Rehabilitation professionals have a great deal of expertise that can be used to help employers hire and accommodate employees with disabilities. An effective method to build a relationship with an employer is to provide a service that the employer views as useful and helpful. As indicated in Table 12.1, these services include many traditional rehabilitation competencies such as conducting job analyses to help determine essential functions, providing assistance in identifying and instituting reasonable accommodations, conducting ergonomic evaluations of work areas, and other services that make it easier for employers to hire, supervise, and benefit from employees with disabilities.

The central difference between the demand-side and traditional approach is that these services are provided generically to employers rather than merely conducted to support the placement of a specific consumer. A second difference is the demand-side specialist's interest in helping employers find and recruit people with disabilities rather than being only interested in the placement of agency caseload consumers.

Providing Labor Market Consulting Services to Rehabilitation Counselors and Agencies

Quality employment opportunities are enhanced for people with disabilities to the extent that labor market information is available and used during rehabilitation planning. Vandergoot (1987) found that rehabilitation professionals' familiarity with the world of work and their level of labor market contact increased the employment outcomes of their consumers.

An important component of this cluster of competencies is the educational responsibility of placement specialists.

A new challenge for the demand-side specialist is in developing effective consulting relationships both within his or her own agency and the broader disability community. Real consumer choice occurs when the individual has accurate and useful labor market information. This information needs to be available to rehabilitation professionals and consumers during all stages of the rehabilitation process. The quality of placement can be enhanced if employers are supported in making workplaces accessible (in a broad rather than narrow sense of that word), and consumers understand labor market trends and the skills they will require to succeed.

Once rehabilitation professionals are viewed by employers as resources, they are in positions to better inform rehabilitation agencies about current and long-term placement opportunities. Demand-side placement professionals can then act as consultants to rehabilitation counselors, providing accurate and timely labor market information that those counselors can use to inform and improve individual rehabilitation (employment) plans. This saves money for agencies that find themselves paying for training only to learn consumers are prepared for jobs that do not exist. Furthermore, consumers benefit by being empowered to make decisions on career goals informed by current, valid labor market information.

Developing relationships with other agencies in the community is a vital aspect of this model. Once a relationship is developed with an employer, as indicated above, that employer will look to that rehabilitation professional for continued assistance in personnel recruitment and support. If an employer contacts that rehabilitation professional with a job opening but no appropriate applicants are available in that professional's agency, the rehabilitation professional needs to reach out to other agencies in the community to try and find appropriate applicants. The goal of demand-side job development is for employers to view the disability community as a consistent source of appropriate applicants.

Using Internet Technology To Enhance Employment Solutions

As indicated previously, the Internet is an important new tool in the economy. Along with helping consumers, Internet resources can also help employers more readily hire and accommodate employees with disabilities. There are a number of ways rehabilitation professionals can assist employers to use this tool. The Internet can be used to increase communication between employers and the rehabilitation community, to assist employers in finding and using accommodation information, and to help employers to learn more about specific disabilities.

Thoughtful Web site development by rehabilitation agencies has the potential to communicate the resources of the agency that are available to employers as they struggle with disability-related issues. E-mail, job boards, and resume databases can readily and simply connect consumers with employer openings. Thoughtful use of technology can also be used to connect employers to the vast amount of disability information already available online. Assisting employers to access resources such as the Job Accommodation Network (JAN), ADA technical assistance centers, or other public and private resources can reduce employers' apprehension in hiring people with disabilities.

Disability-related resources are expanding and improving rapidly. Connecting employers to these resources is an important part of the educational role of rehabilitation professionals.

Horizontal Expansion of the Role of Rehabilitation Counselors

Jenkins and Strauser (1999) discussed the need for rehabilitation counselors to "horizontally expand" their current roles to include services directed toward employers. Along with the demand-side competencies already discussed, they asserted that rehabilitation professionals need to extend their competencies to assist employers in staff development and job and work design.

As indicated by Jenkins and Strauser (1999), this focus and attention will have a significant impact on the practice of rehabilitation counseling. Rehabilitation counselors will have to enhance their ability to provide employer-focused consulting services. In addition, they will need to develop additional knowledge and skills about employers and the world of work (Martin & Vieceli, 1988) and learn to balance the needs of both consumers and employers.

Such an approach is different from traditional placement strategies in that it offers a *systems* intervention in a labor market area. It should increase openness to diversity among employers, thus reducing the amount of time spent "selling" one consumer at a time. The goal of this approach is gainful, competitive, satisfying employment options in which labor market intermediaries (rehabilitation professionals) match consumers with *careers*, offering growth potential in settings that welcome diversity. This horizontal expansion is not designed to replace traditional models but rather to complement them by adding a new dimension to our service delivery system.

Providing consulting services to employers represents a potential new practice area for rehabilitation professionals. This area of research indicates that most effective rehabilitation counselors will not only have strong counseling and case management ability but will also be skilled as systems-based mediators, as described by Chubon (1992). Learning to negotiate the demands of multiple public and private systems will become more vital as placement becomes more complex and multidimensional.

The Fit Between VR Placement Services and Employers

Although many of these issues apply to all the providers working to improve employment outcomes for people with disabilities, our discussion will focus primarily on VR. As indicated above, many state agencies are willing to provide services to employers. These services may improve the productivity of current employees with disabilities, assist in supervision of those employees, save the jobs of existing employees, or improve the capacity of the employer to hire and accommodate new employees. This type of ongoing support speaks directly to employers' long-term concerns. Over time, employers encounter many disability-related issues. Those issues may concern a former VR consumer or may be related to an employee who develops a disability. Employers want to have a professional, responsive resource they can contact to assist them with these issues. In many states, VR wants to be that resource. The challenge comes in trying to mesh these two systems.

The current structure of VR services often makes it difficult for VR to be responsive to employer needs. The need to open a file and make an employee eligible before VR can provide services may be viewed as bureaucratic red tape by the employer. Furthermore, developing and maintaining employer relationships is resource intensive. In states under an order of selection, diverting resources to assist employers may be questioned. It is clear that many VR administrators want to provide services to employers (Gilbride, 2000), and many employers would welcome ongoing support, but barriers to this connection still exist.

These points pose significant implications for the plans of rehabilitation agencies. Employers view placement as a long-term process in which they receive assistance during all four of the phases outlined earlier. They will be more open to placement-related contacts if they know long-term follow-up will be provided. If they doubt rehabilitation personnel will be there later, they will be reluctant to use them for recruitment and placement.

In summary, working with employers represents an important challenge to the field of rehabilitation. This research has implications for rehabilitation practice, education, and certification. Rehabilitation professionals need to expand their expertise to include these new employer-focused competencies. Both pre- and in-service educational programs need to review their curriculum to ensure that they are assisting practitioners in developing these skills. Furthermore, certification boards such as CRCC and CORE need to consider expanding their criteria to include this important practice area. The need for expanding our scope of practice is further underscored by changes in public policy, the topic of the next section.

NEW INITIATIVES

The two most important new laws affecting placement of people with disabilities are the Ticket to Work and Work Incentives Improvement Act (P.L. 106-170) and the Workforce Investment Act (P.L. 105-220). The Ticket to Work Act pertains to people receiving SSDI and SSI. For these recipients, the Social Security Administration has provided a vehicle to reduce the disincentives for gaining employment. The primary disincentives that were addressed were cuts in payments and cuts in Medicaid based on earned income. Furthermore, for people who want to work, this act allows new consumer choice, as they can choose a provider to assist them with training and placement. Their "ticket" or voucher could be used to pay that provider for statutorily defined rehabilitation services.

The Ticket to Work initiative has just begun in selected pilot states. As a result of the voucher provisions of this program, which introduces competition to public rehabilitation, it has the potential to have significant implications for consumer choice, opportunity, and new methods of service delivery.

The second law, WIA, is already having a significant effect because it mandates a one-stop model of service delivery. The central idea behind the one-stop model is to combine all workforce development programs into one central service and/or location. The WIA combined most federally funded programs into one funding mechanism to be administered at a central location. Although VR services and funds were not merged into the one-stop funding stream, VR is a mandatory partner. The result has been a number of initiatives at both the federal and state levels to combine or at least colocate VR with other workforce development services.

Gilbride (2000) found that 19.6% (*SD* = 27) of VR offices were colocated with other workforce development agencies, and an additional 42.9% (*SD* = 41.8) of agencies had VR staff assigned to workforce offices on a regular schedule. He found that 40 (78%) VR administrators anticipated that colocating or staff assignment with workforce development offices would increase over the next 3 to 5 years. None of the administrators surveyed anticipated a decrease.

Clearly, the one-stop model has already had a significant impact on *where* VR services are being provided. Furthermore, this trend is likely to continue. The effect of this trend on *how* services are delivered will require serious attention in the next few years. Gilbride's (2000) results indicate that VR agencies are working to increase collaboration with other agencies, finding ways to merge "funding streams" and, in at least one case, contracting out most placement services to the one-stop shop.

There are a number of potential advantages and disadvantages for employers and people with disabilities within the one-stop shopping model. During the first two employment phases, recruitment and hiring, the one-stop model has the possibility of being of great benefit to employers and applicants with disabilities. Employers only need to make one call (or contact) to be provided with a number of potential applicants, and people with disabilities are more likely to be included in that initial pool. If employers are successful in recruiting and hiring from one-stop agencies, that agency will become a more important part of the employer's personnel development strategy. This, in turn, should increase access to employment for people with disabilities.

A key challenge for people with disabilities in this model is ensuring that their unique needs are met. State workforce development offices have often focused on low-skill, high-turnover jobs, whereas VR has focused on improving skills through training. Will one-stop staff be trained in career development or disability etiquette? Will the one-stop agency remove procedural barriers and develop the ability to see itself as a delivery system rather than a physical location?

The third and fourth employer issues concerning postplacement assistance are problematic for one-stop agencies. Most workforce development systems do not have a tradition or infrastructure to support long-term follow-up of placed workers. As indicated above, employers want and expect assistance when a disability-related issue arises in the workplace. How would the one-stop shop respond to an employer request for help with an employee placed 2 or 3 years earlier?

ORGANIZATIONAL ISSUES

Rehabilitation providers are facing significant challenges from these new public policy initiates, along with other trends such as increased demands for inclusion and participation by consumers and the changing labor market. We will conclude this section by exploring the manner in which organizations are attempting to manage for placement in this demanding new environment. We will describe the challenges that the state–federal partnership faces as it attempts to manage rehabilitation counselors to achieve the agency's targeted employment outcomes. We will also discuss some of the issues organizations need to address if they redesign themselves to better reward and support rehabilitation counselors for providing placement services. We will begin with a brief description of management theory.

Organizations develop management systems to ensure they attain the outcomes they desire through the methods they consider appropriate (Drucker, 1995). These management systems are designed to address the needs and expectations of the various stakeholders whose satisfaction is critical to the organization (Gharajedaghi, 1999). For the state–federal partnership, the stakeholders have remained the same since the early 1900s—primarily people with disabilities, legislators, employers, partnering agencies, and the voting public. Although the relative importance of each group has changed over time, these continue to be the people whose satisfaction provides the support to keep the state–federal partnership operating.

Gilbride et al. (1994) defined *traditional placement services* as those managerial and counselor activities that address the expectations of the 1970s and 1980s. During the time these management techniques were most used, administrators stressed effective case management, accurate case reporting, documented consumer involvement, and compliance with procedural controls. The management system defined the role of the rehabilitation counselor, whose responsibility was to work in accordance with the parameters of that system.

The employer-focused and collaborative placement competencies outlined in this chapter clearly require a different management system. As rehabilitation counselors find themselves working with consumers, employers, and collaborating agencies, more of the counselors' work will involve negotiation with these partners. Under such circumstances, the management system developed to meet the needs of the 1970s is obsolete and may be dysfunctional (Gharajedaghi, 1999). Gilbride and Stensrud (1999) examined how the existing management systems interfere with a newer model of placement. Their findings parallel those of other researchers (Ackoff, 1974; Ackoff & Emery, 1972; Gharajedaghi, 1999). They found that management systems were more concerned with directing and controlling the behavior of rehabilitation counselors than finding methods to creatively improve employment outcomes. Although these systems kept rehabilitation counselors from behaving in ways inconsistent with the intent of federal legislation, they also limited the flexibility of rehabilitation counselors as they sought to provide the best services to consumers.

The professional literature contains little information on how any rehabilitation agency—public, for-profit, or not-for-profit—has successfully addressed this issue. Gilbride and Stensrud (1999) found that local supervisors tended to use their positions to "buffer" counselors so they could be more flexible in providing placement services to consumers and employers. The more autonomy these rehabilitation counselors gain, however, the more able they are to become "free agents" and gain employment with partnering agencies or businesses. The most skilled rehabilitation counselors had the most career autonomy, making their satisfaction a critical management objective.

The management system of tightly controlling behavior through detailed reporting requirements and simple outcomes was effective after the Rehabilitation Act of 1973 but is not appropriate for the type of organization that must comply with the WIA. The dilemma created by federal legislation since 1990 is that substantial change must occur in management systems if rehabilitation counselors are to perform the duties related to effective placement. Rehabilitation counselors will be expected to operate more as autonomous agents to address the multidimensional needs of consumers. If the state–federal partnership does not develop a management structure to support this, rehabilitation counselors will find it difficult to perform the duties expected of them. The same holds true for other rehabilitation agencies. Those agencies that can design the most effective structure to support effective rehabilitation counseling and placement will offer the most enticing workplaces. We will conclude this chapter with a list of the specific factors that rehabilitation professionals will need to address as we move into this new century.

CONCLUSIONS

This chapter has demonstrated that the placement services provided by rehabilitation practitioners have evolved over the past century. Although placement has continued to be a cornerstone of the rehabilitation process, changes in consumer expectations, legislation, and labor markets have dramatically reshaped how placement is provided. In the era of the WIA, vouchers, and information technology, placement will require a new set of competencies. Rehabilitation counselors will be expected to demonstrate these competencies as they continue to serve people with disabilities. We recommend that administrators, practitioners, educators, and graduate students in rehabilitation counseling become aware of the following:

1. *Placement is a systems issue*. To address the placement needs of consumers, rehabilitation counselors must consider the systems that people with disabilities must negotiate and the barriers they will confront as they pursue their chosen goals. Thinking about and

working with systems will be critical for the rehabilitation counselor of the future.

2. *Placement occurs in the field.* Rehabilitation counselors will increasingly be expected to do their jobs away from the office. Supervisors and administrators need to understand the importance of this and provide the type of supervision and support necessary for rehabilitation counselors to function more autonomously.
3. *Collaborative leadership will be necessary.* For local communities to work together so quality employment opportunities are provided for people with disabilities, someone will have to exert collaborative leadership. This is a role many rehabilitation counselors will be expected to fulfill.
4. *Consumer choice is here to stay.* Many governmental agencies find it difficult to discard paternalistic practices and view service recipients as customers. Rehabilitation counselors and the agencies in which they work will be expected to find improved ways to ensure consumer choice. The type of agencies in which they work and the types of roles they play will change as organizations increase their responsiveness to consumers.
5. *Many rehabilitation counselors will do more consulting than counseling.* There is a need for disability consultants in public agencies, not-for-profit agencies, and businesses. Rehabilitation counselors have the expertise to assume these roles and bring needed expertise to those organizations. However, the role will need to be taught in our training programs and supported in practice settings.
6. *Finally, rehabilitation counselors need to recognize that they are part of a profession.* As such, their identity derives from association with their peers. Many agencies and companies seek to define what the profession of rehabilitation counseling is or should be. The professional identity of rehabilitation professionals must be decided by members of the profession, including educators, and entering graduate students. Our accrediting and certification bodies need to be responsive to these new trends in service delivery and support advancements in education and practice.

In sum, placement remains at the core of the rehabilitation profession. Over the past 80 years, we have developed many effective strategies to assist people with disabilities to actualize their vocational potential and dreams. However, the field must continue to grow, develop, and persist until strategies are developed and implemented that can effectively assist every consumer who wants to work to find and keep meaningful and rewarding employment.

REFERENCES

Ackoff, R. (1974). *Redesigning the future*. New York: Wiley.

Ackoff, R., & Emery, F. (1972). *On purposeful systems*. Chicago: Aldine-Atherton.

Americans with Disabilities Act of 1990, 42 U.S.C. § 12101 *et seq*.

Azrin, N., Flores, T., & Kaplan, S. (1975). Job finding club: A group-assisted program of obtaining employment. *Behavioral Research and Therapy, 13*, 17–27.

Azrin, N., & Philips, R. (1979). Job club method for the job handicapped: A comparative outcome study. *Rehabilitation Counseling Bulletin, 3*(2), 144–155.

Baumann, N. (1986). Keeping business advisory councils active and involved: The aging in America model. *Journal of Job Placement, 2*(2), 16–17.

Beard, J., Propst, R., & Malamud, T. (1982). The Fountain House model of psychiatric rehabilitation. *Psychosocial Rehabilitation Journal, 5*(1), 47–53.

Bellamy, G., Rhodes, L., Wilcox, B., Albin, J., Mank, D., Boles, S., Horner, R., Collins, M., & Turner, J. (1984). Quality and equality in employment services for adults with severe disabilities. *Journal of the Association for Persons with Severe Handicaps, 9*, 270–277.

Bellamy, G. T., Rhodes, L., Mank, D., & Albin, J. (Eds.). (1988). *Supported employment*. Baltimore: Brookes.

Berven, N. (1979). The roles and functions of the rehabilitation counselor revisited. *Rehabilitation Counseling Bulletin, 23*, 84–88.

Bilby, R. (1992). A response to the criticism of transitional employment. *Psychosocial Rehabilitation Journal, 16*(2), 69–82.

Bolles, R. (2000). *What color is your parachute?* Berkeley, CA: Ten Speed Press.

Bond, G. (1992). Vocational rehabilitation. In R. Liberman (Ed.), *Handbook of psychiatric rehabilitation* (pp. 244–275). New York: Macmillan.

Chubon, R. (1992). Defining rehabilitation from a systems perspective: Critical implications. *Journal of Applied Rehabilitation Counseling, 23*(1), 27–32.

Cohen, J., & Pelavin, D. (1992). *1992 survey of personnel shortages and training needs in vocational rehabilitation*. Washington, DC: Pelavin Associates.

Collignon, F., Barker, L., & Vencill, M. (1992). The growth and structure of the proprietary rehabilitation sector. *American Rehabilitation, 18*(4), 7–10, 43.

Cull, J., & Hardy, R. (1972). *Vocational rehabilitation: Profession and process*. Springfield, IL: Thomas.

Drucker, P. (1995). *Managing in times of great change*. New York: Dutton.

Fry, R. (Ed.). (1997). *Developing effective partnerships with employers as a service delivery mechanism*. Menomonie, WI: Stout Vocational Rehabilitation Institute.

Galbraith, J. (1998). *Created unequal: The crisis in American pay*. New York: Free Press.

Garvin, R. (1983). Industrial relations: A service-oriented approach to job development. *Journal of Applied Rehabilitation Counseling, 14*, 44–50.

Gharajedaghi, J. (1999). *Systems thinking: Managing chaos and complexity*. Boston: Butterworth-Heinemann.

Gilbride, D. (1993). Rehabilitation education in the private sector. In L. Perlman & C. Hansen (Eds.), *Private sector rehabilitation insurance: Trends and issues for the 21st century* (pp. 22–26). Alexandria, VA: National Rehabilitation Association.

Gilbride, D. (2000). Going to work: Placement trends in public rehabilitation. *Journal of Vocational Rehabilitation, 14*, 89–94.

Gilbride, D., & Burr, F. (1993). Self-directed labor market survey: An empowering approach. *Journal of Job Placement, 9*(2), 13–17.

Gilbride, D., & Stensrud, R. (1992). Demand-side job development: A model for the 1990s. *Journal of Rehabilitation, 58*(4), 34–39.

Gilbride, D., & Stensrud, R. (1993). Challenges and opportunities for rehabilitation counselors in the Americans with Disabilities Act era. *NARPPS Journal, 8*, 67–74.

Gilbride, D., & Stensrud, R. (1999). Demand-side job development and system change. *Rehabilitation Counseling Bulletin, 42*, 329–342.

Gilbride, D., Stensrud, R., & Johnson, M. (1994). Current models of job placement and employer development: Research, competencies and educational considerations. *Rehabilitation Education, 7*, 215–239.

Hagner, D. (2000). Primary and secondary labor markets: Implications for vocational rehabilitation. *Rehabilitation Counseling Bulletin, 44*(1), 22–29.

Hanley-Maxwell, C., Szymanski, E., Parent, W., & Schriner, K. (1990). Supported employment: Revolution, passing fad, or a remake of an old song? *Rehabilitation Education, 4*(4), 233–246.

Harris, L., & Associates. (1994). *N.O.D./Harris survey of Americans with disabilities*. New York: Author.

Hayward, B., Reisner, E., & Choisser, S. (1986). Evaluation of projects with industry: Findings and recommendations. *American Rehabilitation, 12*(3), 22–26.

Hernandez, B., Keys, C., & Balcazar, F. (2000). Employer attitudes toward workers with disabilities and their ADA employment rights: A literature review. *Journal of Rehabilitation, 66*(4), 4–16.

James, D. (1987, September). Seventy years of US veterans' vocational rehabilitation (1917–1987): History and commentary. *VR&C Professional Review*, pp. 4–9.

Jenkins, W., & Strauser, D. (1999). Horizontal expansion of the role of the rehabiliation counselor. *Journal of Rehabilitation, 65*(1), 4–9.

Jones, R., & Azrin, N. (1973). An experimental application of a social reinforcement approach to the problem of job-finding. *Journal of Applied Behavioral Analysis, 6*, 345–353.

Kaplan, I., & Hammond, N. (1982). Projects with industry: The concept and the realization. *American Rehabilitation, 8*(2), 3–7.

Kirk, J. (2000). Web-assisted career counseling. *Journal of Employment Counseling, 37*, 146–159.

Lynch, R., & Martin, T. (1982). Rehabilitation counseling: A training needs survey. *Journal of Rehabilitation, 48*, 51–52, 73.

Martin, T., & Vieceli, L. (1988). The business of rehabilitation placement. *Journal of Rehabilitation, 54*(4), 49–55.

McDonald, D. (1974). The rehabilitation counselor: A resource person to industry; a revitalized approach to selective placement. *Journal of Applied Rehabilitation Counseling, 5*(1), 3–7.

McGowan, J., & Porter, T. (1967). *An introduction to the vocational rehabilitation process*. Washington, DC: U.S. Department of Health, Education, and Welfare.

McLoughlin, C., Garner, J., & Callahan, M. (1987). *Getting employed, staying employed*. Baltimore: Brookes.

Melia, R. (1984). Job development and placement research. *American Rehabilitation, 10*(1), 23–26.

Millington, M., Asner, K., Linkowski, D., & Der-Stepanian, J. (1996). Employers and job development: The business perspective. In R. Parker & E. Szymanski (Eds.), *Rehabilitation counseling: Basics and beyond* (pp. 277–308). Austin, TX: PRO-ED.

Molinaro, D. (1977). A placement system develops and settles: The Michigan model. *Rehabilitation Counseling Bulletin, 21*(2), 121–130.

Muthard, J., & Salomone, P. (1969). Roles and functions of the rehabilitation counselor. *Rehabilitation Counseling Bulletin, 13* (I–SP).

Obermann, C. (1967). *A history of VR in America*. Minneapolis, MN: Denison.

Parker, R., & Szymanski, E. (1992). *Rehabilitation counseling: Basics and beyond* (2nd ed.). Austin, TX: PRO-ED.

Patterson, J. B. (2000). Using the Internet to facilitate the rehabilitation process. *Journal of Rehabilitation*, 66(1), 4–10.

President's Committee on Employment of the Handicapped. (n.d.). *Louis P. Ortale memorial lectures on placement: The first 10 years 1970–1980*. Washington, DC: Author.

Rehabilitation Act of 1973, 29 U.S.C. § 701 *et seq*.

Rehabilitation Act Amendments of 1992, 29 U.S.C. § 701 *et seq*.

Rifkin, J. (1995). *The end of work: The decline of the global labor force and the dawn of the post-market era*. New York: Tarcher/Putnam.

Rubin, S., Matkin, R., Ashley, J., Beardsley, M., May, V., Ontott, K., et al. (1984). Roles and functions of certified rehabilitation counselors. *Rehabilitation Counseling Bulletin, 27*, 199–224, 238–245.

Salomone, P. (1971). A client centered approach to job placement. *Vocational Guidance Quarterly, 14*, 266–270.

Salomone, P. (1996). Career counseling and job placement: Theory and practice. In E. Szymanski & R. Parker (Eds.), *Work and disability* (pp. 365–420). Austin, TX: PRO-ED.

Shafer, M., Revell, R., Kregel, J., Wehman, P., & West, M. (1991). Systems change efforts and supported employment: National strategies and outcomes. *Journal of Disability Policy Studies, 2*(1), 75–95.

Shapiro, J. (1994). *No pity: People with disabilities forging a new civil rights movement*. New York: Times Books.

Sink, J., & Porter, T. (1978). Convergence and divergence in rehabilitation counseling and vocational evaluation. *Rehabilitation Counseling Bulletin, 9*, 5–20.

Stensrud, R. (1999). *Reasons for success and failure of supported employment placements*. Retrieved September 23, 2002, from http://soe.drake.edu/nri/evaluation/employers.html

Stensrud, R. (2000). *Iowa Path systems change project: Barrier report 2—focus group results*. Retrieved September 23, 2002, from http://soe.drake.edu/nri/evaluation/barrierreport2.html

Ticket to Work and Work Incentives Improvement Act of 1999, 42 U.S.C. § 1320 *et seq*.

Vandergoot, D. (1987). Review of placement research literature: Implications for research and practice. *Rehabilitation Counseling Bulletin, 31*, 243–272.

Wehman, P. (1988). Supported employment: Toward equal employment opportunity for persons with severe disabilities. *Mental Retardation, 26*, 357–361.

Wehman, P., & Melia, R. (1985). The job coach: Function in transitional and supported employment. *American Rehabilitation, 11*(2), 4–7.

Wehman, P., & Moon, M. (Eds.). (1988). *Vocational rehabilitation and supported employment*. Baltimore: Brookes.

Workforce Investment Act of 1998, 29 U.S.C. § 2801 *et seq*.

Wright, G. (1980). *Total rehabilitation*. Boston: Little, Brown.

Young, J., Rosati, R., & Vandergoot, D. (1986). Initiating a marketing strategy by assessing employer needs for rehabilitation services. *Journal of Rehabilitation, 52*(2), 37–41.

Zadny, J., & James, L. (1976). *Another view on placement: State of the art 1976*. Portland, OR: Regional Rehabilitation Institute.

Zadny, J., & James, L. (1977). Time spent on placement. *Rehabilitation Counseling Bulletin, 21*(1), 31–38.

Author Index

Subject Index

About the Editors

Edna Mora Szymanski is professor and dean of the College of Education at University of Maryland, College Park. Previously, she served in a variety of capacities at University of Wisconsin–Madison, including professor in the Department of Rehabilitation Psychology and Special Education, department chair, associate dean, director of the Rehabilitation Research and Training Center on Career Development and Advancement, and chair of the Campus Committees on Retirement and Disability. Her major areas of scholarship have focused on disability and career development, rehabilitation counselor education and its relationship to rehabilitation client outcome, and research instruction. Dr. Szymanski has authored or coauthored more than 85 refereed articles and book chapters and received several national awards for her research, including three from the American Counseling Association, three from the American Rehabilitation Counseling Association, one from the American Association of Counselor Education and Supervision, and one from the National Council on Rehabilitation Education. She is a past coeditor of the *Rehabilitation Counseling Bulletin* and is a past president of the American Rehabilitation Counseling Association.

Randall M. Parker is the Melissa Elizabeth Stuart Centennial Professor of Education, a professor of special education, and the director of rehabilitation counselor education at the University of Texas at Austin. He is a fellow of the American Psychological Association, Division 22, Rehabilitation Psychology, and Division 17, Counseling Psychology. He is a past coeditor of the *Rehabilitation Counseling Bulletin* and is a past president of the American Rehabilitation Counseling Association and the Texas

Psychological Association. In addition, he received the 1998 School of Education Alumni Achievement Award, University of Wisconsin–Madison; the 1998 College of Education Outstanding Faculty Award from the College of Education, the University of Texas at Austin; and the 1996 James F. Garrett Award for Career Research from the American Rehabilitation Counseling Association.